LLB

TORT
Textbook

8th edition

E D Pitchfork

BSc, PhD, Barrister

HLT Publications

HLT PUBLICATIONS
200 Greyhound Road, London W14 9RY

First published 1987
8th edition 1994

© The HLT Group Ltd 1994

ISBN 0 7510 0257 7

British Library Cataloguing-in-Publication.
A CIP Catalogue record for this book is available from the British Library.

Acknowledgement
The publishers and author would like to thank the Incorporated Council of Law Reporting for England and Wales for kind permission to reproduce extracts from the Weekly Law Reports.

Printed and bound in Great Britain

Contents

Preface *vii*

Table of Cases *ix*

Table of Statutes *xxxv*

1 **Introduction** *1*

Introduction – Current difficulties in the law of tort – The interests protected – Tort and other legal subjects

2 **Parties to an Action in Tort** *10*

Introduction – Liability – Immunity

3 **Joint and Several Tortfeasors** *16*

Introduction – Independent liability – Several liability – Joint liability – Contribution between tortfeasors

4 **Vicarious Liability** *22*

Introduction – The rationale of vicarious liability – Who is an employee? – The employee must commit a tort – Course of employment – The master's indemnity – Principal and agent – Partnership

5 **Liability for Independent Contractors** *39*

Introduction and the general rule – Exceptions to the general rule – Conclusion

6 **Negligence: The Duty of Care – Some General Considerations** *43*

Introduction – The emergence of a general principle – The development of the general principle – Resiling from the general principle – A general principle or reasoning by analogy? – The incremental approach – Factors inhibiting the imposition of a duty of care – The distinction between misfeasance and non-feasance – The role of Parliament – The availability of an alternative remedy – No undermining of established principles of the common law or equity – No duty recognised before – The cost and availability of insurance? – Conclusion

7 **The Duty of Care and 'Protected Interests'** *69*

Introduction – Economic loss: introduction – Economic loss: a definition – Economic loss: the problem – Consequential economic loss – Negligent misstatement – Defective product economic loss – *Hedley Byrne* re-examined – '*Ross* v *Caunters* economic loss' – *Ministry of Housing and Local Government* v *Sharp* – *Morrison Steamship Co Ltd* v *Greystone Castle (Cargo Owners)* – Economic loss: conclusion – Psychiatric injury or 'nervous shock'

8 **The Duty of Care and 'Protected Parties'** *103*

Introduction – The character of the plaintiff – Judges and legal representatives – Police – Negligence in the exercise of a statutory power

9 Negligence: Breach of the Duty   *117*

Introduction – The reasonable man – Foreseeability – Magnitude of the risk – Utility of the defendant's activity – The practicality of precautions – Common practice – Children – Sport – Emergencies – Professionals – Proof of the breach – Res ipsa loquitur

10 Negligence: Causation   *133*

Introduction – But for test – Pre-existing condition – Omissions – Multiple causes – Proof of causation – Successive causes

11 Negligence: Remoteness of Damage   *143*

Introduction – *Polemis* and the directness test – *Wagon Mound* and foreseeability – Damage to the person – Damage to property – *Polemis* and *Wagon Mound* contrasted – Cases where the reasonable foresight test does not apply – Intervening acts (novus actus interveniens)

12 Contributory Negligence   *159*

Introduction – The position at common law – The 1945 Act - the general rule – Fault – The standard of care – Children – Workmen – Rescuers – Emergencies – Causation – Apportionment

13 Volenti Non Fit Injuria   *170*

Introduction – The intentional infliction of harm – The negligent infliction of harm – Voluntariness – Agreement – Knowledge – Volenti and exclusion clauses – Volenti and the standard of care

14 Breach of Statutory Duty   *179*

Introduction – Does the breach confer a right of action in tort? – The remedy provided in the Act – Statutes for the benefit of a class – Public rights and special damage – Ambit of the statute – Defences

15 Employers' Liability   *187*

Introduction – Competent staff – Proper plant and equipment – Safe place of work – Safe system of work – The economic welfare of employees – Defences

16 Product Liability   *196*

Introduction – Historical development – Defects in the common law – The Consumer Protection Act 1987

17 Occupiers' Liability   *205*

Introduction – The scope of the 1957 Act – Who is an occupier? – Visitors – Premises – The common duty of care – Children – Common calling – Warning of danger – Independent contractors – Volenti – Contributory negligence – Contractors – Damage to property – Trespassers – Exclusion of the occupier's duty – Liability of independent contractors who are not occupiers – Liability of vendors and lessors – Liability of builders

18 Private Nuisance   *232*

Introduction – The interests protected – Conduct amounting to a private nuisance – The duration of the nuisance – Abnormal sensitivity – Character of the neighbourhood – Utility of the defendant's conduct – Malice – Fault? – Who can be sued in nuisance? – Types of harm – Defences – Remedies – The future of the nuisance action

19 Public Nuisance   *255*

Introduction – The elements of the tort of public nuisance – Public nuisance and the highway

20 The Rule in *Rylands* v *Fletcher*   *261*

Introduction – The rule – Accumulation – Non-natural user – Dangerous things? – Escape – Occupation – 'His own purposes' – Foreseeability of damage – Protected interests – Defences

21 Fire   *272*

Introduction – Liability at common law – Defences at common law – The Fires Prevention (Metropolis) Act 1774 – The railway statutes

22 Animals   *276*

Introduction – Liability at common law – Dangerous animals – Non-dangerous animals – Defences – Straying livestock – Straying on to the highway – Protection of livestock against dogs

23 Defamation   *285*

Introduction – The distinction between libel and slander – Who may be defamed? – What is defamatory? – Refers to the plaintiff – Publication – Defences – Consent – Justification or truth – Absolute privilege – Qualified privilege – Fair comment – Apology and amends – Remedies – Conclusion

24 Trespass to the Person   *311*

Introduction – Battery – Assault – False imprisonment – The rule in *Wilkinson* v *Downton* – Conclusion

25 Trespass to Land   *324*

Introduction – Possession – Interference with possession – Nature of the interference – Defences – Remedies

26 Deceit   *334*

Introduction – False statement of fact – Knowledge of the falsity of the statement – Intention that the statement be acted upon – The plaintiff must act on the statement – Damage to the plaintiff

27 Malicious Falsehood   *341*

Introduction – Falsehood – Malice – Damage

28 Passing Off   *345*

Introduction – Methods of passing off – Made by a trader in the course of a trade – Remedies

29 The Economic Torts   *350*

Introduction – The ground rules – Conspiracy – Inducing breach of contract – Intimidation – Economic duress? – Interference with trade by unlawful means – The statutory immunities – Conclusion

30 Remedies *370*

Introduction – Types of damages – The protection of the reliance interest – Pecuniary loss – Loss of earnings: actual and prospective – The lost years – Loss of earning capacity – Loss of pension rights – Loss of housekeeping capacity – Medical expenses – Deductions – Other pecuniary losses – Non-pecuniary loss – Pain and suffering – Loss of amenity – Loss of expectation of life – The injury itself – Interest – Death in relation to tort – Damage to property – The commitment to the protection of the reliance interest – Tort and the expectation interest – Injunctions – Self-help

31 Miscellaneous Defences and Limitation *397*

Introduction – Mistake – Illegality – Necessity – Limitation

32 Torts to Chattels *402*

Introduction – Common law ingredients of the chattel torts – Trespass – Conversion – Detinue – The reversionary action – Redistribution of tort liability by statute – Title to sue – Pleading jus tertii – Double liability – Improvement to goods – Forms of judgment – Effect of judgment on title to goods – Title to lost goods

33 Malicious Prosecution *417*

Introduction – Prosecution – Prosecution ended in the plaintiff's favour – Without reasonable and probable cause – Malice – Damage

Index *421*

Preface

HLT Textbooks are written specifically for students. Whatever their course, they will find our books clear and concise, providing comprehensive and up-to-date coverage. Written by specialists in their field, our textbooks are reviewed and updated on an annual basis.

The Tort Textbook is designed for use by any undergraduates who have Tort Law within their syllabus. It will be equally useful for all CPE students who must study Tort Law as one of their 'core' subjects.

The last year has seen some interesting developments in the law of tort: a number of cases involving breach of statutory duty have come before the courts – see, for example, *West Wiltshire District Council* v *Pugh* [1993] NLJ 546 and the child care cases of *X* v *Bedfordshire County Council* [1993] NLJ 1783, *M* v *Newham London Borough Council* [1994] NLJ 357 and *T* v *Surrey County Council* [1994] NLJ 319. The Court of Appeal also appears to have retreated from the wider approach to the topic of nervous shock adopted by the House of Lords in *Alcock* in its judgment in *McFarlane* v *Caledonia Ltd* [1993] NLJ 1367. However, the most important tort case in the past year must be *Cambridge Water Co* v *Eastern Counties Leather plc* [1994] 2 WLR 53 where the House of Lords totally changed the basis of liability in *Rylands* v *Fletcher* and also considered the vexed question of natural user of land in this context.

The law is stated on the basis of the materials available to me at 15 April 1994.

Table of Cases

AB v South West Water Services Ltd [1993] 2 WLR 507   *257, 373, 374*

AMF International Ltd v Magnet Bowling Ltd [1968] 1 WLR 1028   *208, 217*

Abbott v Refuge Assurance Co Ltd [1962] 1 QB 432   *419*

Acrow v Rex Chainbelt Inc [1971] 1 WLR 1676   *365, 367*

Adams v Southern Electricity Board (1993) The Times 21 October   *164*

Adams v Ursell [1913] 1 Ch 269   *245–246, 249*

Addie (Robert) and Sons (Collieries) Ltd v Dumbreck [1929] AC 358   *221, 222, 225*

Addis v Crocker [1961] 1 QB 11   *299*

Admiralty Commissioners v SS Volute [1922] 1 AC 129   *160*

Alcock v Chief Constable of South Yorkshire [1992] 1 AC 310   *52, 94, 96, 98, 99, 100, 101, 102*

Alcock v Wraith (1992) 59 Build LR 16   *41*

Aldred's Case (1610) 9 Co 57b   *276*

Alexander v North Eastern Railway Co (1865) 6 B & S 340   *297*

Alexandrou v Oxford [1993] 4 All ER 328   *112*

Alicia Hosiery v Brown Shipley & Co Ltd [1970] 1 QB 195   *406*

Aliakmon, The; see Leigh and Sillivan v Aliakmon Shipping Co Ltd

Al-Kandari v J R Brown & Co [1988] QB 665; [1988] 1 All ER 833   *108*

Al Saudi Banque v Clarke Pixley (A Firm) [1990] 2 WLR 344   *80*

Allan v Liverpool Overseers (1874) LR 9 QB 180   *325*

Allen v Bloomsbury Health Authority [1993] 1 All ER 651   *105*

Allen v Flood [1898] AC 1   *352, 353, 365*

Allen v Gulf Oil Refining Ltd [1981] AC 1001   *246, 247, 251*

American Cyanamid Co v Ethicon Ltd [1975] AC 396   *396*

Anchor Brewhouse Developments Ltd v Berkley House (Docklands Developments) Ltd [1987] 2 EGLR 173   *327, 331–332*

Anderson v Gorrie [1895] 1 QB 668   *14*

Andrews v Hopkinson [1957] 1 QB 229   *197, 198*

Andrews v King (1991) The Times 5 July   *25*

Andrews v Mockford [1896] 1 QB 372   *338, 339*

Andrews v Schooling [1991] 1 WLR 783   *230*

Angus v Clifford [1891] 2 Ch 449   *337*

Angus v Glasgow Corporation 1977 SLT 206   *32*

Anns v Merton London Borough Council [1978] AC 728   *1, 2, 47, 48, 51, 53, 54, 59, 62, 65, 71, 72, 87, 113, 114, 228, 229, 230*

Antonelli *v* Wade Gery Farr (1993) The Times 29 December   *106*
Arbuthnot *v* Feltrin (1993) The Times 20 October   *62*
Archer *v* Brown [1985] QB 401   *340, 372*
Arenson *v* Casson Beckman Rutley & Co [1977] AC 405   *14*
Armagas *v* Mundogas SA, The Ocean Frost [1986] AC 717   *36*
Armory *v* Delamirie (1721) 1 Stra 505   *414*
Ashdown *v* Samuel Williams & Sons Ltd [1957] 1 QB 409   *225*
Ashton *v* Turner [1981] QB 137   *104, 174, 398*
Associated British Ports *v* Transport and General Workers Union [1989] 1 WLR
    939   *366*
Associated Newspapers Group plc *v* Insert Media Ltd [1988] 1 WLR 509   *350*
Aswan Engineering Establishment Co *v* Lupdine Ltd [1987] 1 All ER 135   *84, 87,*
    88, 198
Atkinson *v* Fitzwalter [1987] 1 All ER 483   *298*
Atkinson *v* Newcastle Waterworks Co (1877) 2 Ex D 441   *181, 182*
Attia *v* British Gas plc [1988] QB 304   *94, 99*
Attorney General *v* PYA Quarries [1957] 2 QB 169   *256*
Atwood *v* Small (1838) 6 Cl & Fin 232   *339*
Auty *v* National Coal Board [1985] 1 All ER 930   *381*

Baker *v* Willoughby [1970] AC 467   *16, 140, 141, 142*
Balden *v* Shorter [1933] Ch 247   *344*
Balfour *v* Barty-King [1957] 1 QB 496   *41*
Bamford *v* Turnley (1860) 3 B & S 62   *236*
Banister *v* Banister (1583) 4 Co Rep 17a   *341*
Banque Keyser Ullman SA *v* Skandia (UK) Insurance Co Ltd [1990] 1 QB 655;
    [1989] 3 WLR 25   *63*
Barber *v* Penley [1893] 2 Ch 447   *258*
Barkway *v* South Wales Transport Co Ltd [1950] 1 All ER 392   *131*
Barnes *v* Nayer (1986) The Times 19 December   *313, 316*
Barnett *v* Chelsea and Kensington Hospital Management Committee [1969] 1 QB
    428   *134*
Barretts & Baird (Wholesale) Ltd *v* Institution of Professional Civil Servants [1987]
    IRLR 3   *368*
Barton *v* Armstrong [1976] AC 104   *365*
Bartonshill Coal Co *v* Reid (1858) 3 Macq 266 (HL)   *187*
Barwick *v* English Joint Stock Bank (1867) LR 2 Ex 259   *36*
Basebe *v* Matthews (1867) LR 2 CP 684   *418*
Batty *v* Metropolitan Realisations Ltd [1978] QB 554   *228*
Bayley *v* Manchester, Sheffield and Lincolnshire Railway Co (1873) LR 8 CP 148
    29
Beauharnais *v* Illinois 343 US 250 (1952)   *294*
Beaulieu *v* Finglam (1401) YB Pasch 2 Hen 4 f 18 pl 6   *272*

Behrens *v* Bertram Mills Circus Ltd [1957] 2 QB 1   *278*
Bellew *v* Cement Co [1948] Ir R 61   *238*
Belmont Finance Corpn *v* Williams Furniture Ltd (No 2) [1980] 1 All ER 393
    354
Benham *v* Gambling [1941] AC 157   *380, 389*
Benjamin *v* Storr (1874) LR 9 CP 400   *184*
Benning *v* Wong (1969) 122 CLR 249   *266, 269*
Bernadin et Cie *v* Pavilion Properties Ltd [1967] RPC 581   *348*
Bernstein (Lord) of Leigh *v* Skyviews & General Ltd [1978] QB 479   *327, 328*
Berriello *v* Felixstowe Dock & Railway Co [1989] 1 WLR 695   *386*
Berry *v* British Transport Commission [1961] 1 QB 149   *420*
Bhoomidas *v* Port of Singapore [1978] 1 All ER 956   *27*
Biddle *v* Bond (1865) 6 B & S 225   *411*
Billings (AC) and Sons Ltd *v* Riden [1958] AC 240   *227*
Bird *v* Jones (1845) 7 QB 742   *319*
Bird *v* King Line [1970] 1 Lloyds Rep 349   *216*
Bishop *v* Commissioner of Police of the Metropolis (1989) The Times 30 November
    420
Bisset *v* Wilkinson [1927] AC 177   *336*
Blake *v* Barnard (1840) 9 C & P 626   *318*
Blennerhassett *v* Novelty Sales Services Ltd (1933) 175 LT 393   *292*
Bliss *v* Stafford (1573) Owen 37   *341*
Bloodworth *v* Gray (1844) 7 Man & G 334   *288*
Blyth *v* Birmingham Waterworks Co (1856) 11 Ex 781   *117*
Boardman *v* Sanderson [1964] 1 WLR 1317   *96*
Bolam *v* Friern Hospital Management Committee [1957] 1 WLR 582   *127, 128,*
    129
Bollinger (J) *v* Costa Brava Wine Co Ltd [1960] Ch 262   *347*
Bolton *v* Stone [1951] AC 850 (HL); [1950] 1 KB 201; [1949] 1 All ER 237 (QBD)
    120, 121, 236, 240
Bone *v* Seale [1975] 1 All ER 787   *253*
Bostik Ltd *v* Sellotape GB Ltd (1993) The Times 11 January   *346*
Bottomley *v* Bannister [1932] 1 KB 458   *228, 229*
Bottomley *v* Woolworth & Co (1932) 48 TLR 521   *296*
Boulting *v* Association of Cinematograph, Television and Allied Technicians [1963]
    2 QB 606   *357*
Bourhill *v* Young [1943] AC 92   *51, 95*
Bowater *v* Rowley Regis Corporation [1944] KB 476   *171*
Bower *v* Peate (1876) 1 QBD 321   *241*
Bradburn *v* Great Western Railway (1874) LR 10 Ex 1   *384*
Bradford *v* Robinson Rentals [1967] 1 WLR 337   *147*
Bradford Corporation *v* Pickles [1895] AC 587   *65, 66, 239*
Brice *v* Brown [1984] 1 All ER 997   *94*

Bridges v Hawkesworth (1851) 21 LJQB 75   *415*
Bridlington Relay Ltd v Yorkshire Electricity Board [1965] Ch 436   *235*
Brimelow v Casson [1924] 1 Ch 302   *362*
British Celanese v A H Hunt Ltd [1969] 1 WLR 959   *237, 253, 262, 265*
British Columbia Electric Railway v Loach [1916] 1 AC 719   *160*
British Railways Board v Herrington [1972] AC 877   *31, 222, 223, 225, 226, 227, 243*
British Road Services v Arthur Crutchley [1967] 1 WLR 835   *41*
British Road Services v Slater [1964] 1 WLR 498   *259*
British Transport Commission v Gourley [1956] AC 185   *376*
British Vacuum Cleaner Co Ltd v New Vacuum Cleaner Co Ltd [1907] 2 Ch 312   *348*
Brooke v Bool [1928] 2 KB 578   *17*
Brown v Cotterill (1934) 51 TLR 21   *197*
Brown v Raphael [1958] Ch 636   *336*
Brown v Rolls Royce Ltd [1960] 1 WLR 210   *123*
Browne v Stradling (1836) 5 LJPC 295   *418*
Browne v DC Thompson 1912 SC 359   *294*
Brunsden v Humphrey (1884) 14 QBD 141   *378*
Bryanston Finance Ltd v De Vries [1975] QB 703   *302*
Bryanston Leasings v Principality Finance [1977] RTR 45   *406, 412*
Buckland v Guildford Gas Light and Coke Co [1949] 1 KB 410   *227*
Burmah Oil Co v Lord Advocate [1965] AC 75   *399*
Buron v Denman (1848) 2 Exch 167   *14*
Burton v Islington Health Authority [1993] QB 204   *10, 61, 104*
Burton v Winters [1993] 1 WLR 1077   *332, 396*
Business Computers International Ltd v Registrar of Companies [1988] Ch 229; [1987] 3 All ER 465   *107*
Bute, Marquess of v Barclays Bank [1955] 1 QB 202   *409*
Butler v The Egg Board (1966) 114 CLR 185   *412*
Butterfield v Forrester (1809) 11 East 60   *160*
Bux v Slough Metals Ltd [1974] 1 All ER 262   *165, 195*
Byrne v Boadle (1863) 2 H & C 722   *130*
Byrne v Deane [1937] 1 KB 818   *290*
Byrne v Hoare [1965] Qd R 135 (FC)   *415*
Byron (Lord) v Johnson (1816) 2 Mer 29   *346*

CBS Songs Ltd v Amstrad Consumer Electronics plc [1988] AC 1013; [1988] Ch 61   *59, 180*
Cadbury-Schweppes Pty Ltd v Pub Squash Co Pty Ltd [1981] 1 WLR 193   *346*
Calgarth, The [1927] P 93   *211*
Caltex Oil (Australia) Pty Ltd v The Dredge 'Willemstad' (1976) 11 ALR 227   *91*
Calveley v Chief Constable of Merseyside Police [1989] AC 1228   *110*

Cambridge Water Company *v* Eastern Counties Leather plc [1994] 2 WLR 53; (1992) The Times 29 December *61, 262–263, 264, 265, 267, 268*

Campbell *v* Paddington Corporation [1911] 1 KB 869 *12*

Campbell *v* Spottiswoode (1863) 3 B & S 769 *305*

Canadian National Railway Co *v* Norsk Pacific Steamship Co Ltd (1992) 91 DLR (4th) 289 *74*

Candler *v* Crane Christmas & Co [1951] 2 KB 164 *46, 76*

Candlewood Navigation Corpn Ltd *v* Mitsui OSK Lines Ltd, The Mineral Transporter [1986] AC 1 *91, 407*

Caparo Industries Ltd plc *v* Dickman [1990] 2 AC 605; [1990] 2 WLR 358 *49, 50, 51, 70, 77, 78, 79, 80, 81, 93*

Capital & Counties Bank Ltd *v* Henty & Son (1882) 7 App Cas 741 *292*

Capps *v* Miller [1989] 2 All ER 333 *167, 169*

Carmarthenshire County Council *v* Lewis [1955] AC 549 *58*

Carslogie Steamship Co *v* Royal Norwegian Government [1952] AC 292 *155*

Cartledge *v* E Jopling & Sons Ltd [1963] AC 758 *400*

Cassell *v* Broome [1972] AC 1027 *2, 306, 371, 372, 373, 374*

Cassidy *v* Daily Mirror Newspapers Ltd [1929] 2 KB 331 *291, 293*

Caswell *v* Powell Duffryn Associated Collieries Ltd [1940] AC 152 *165*

Cattle *v* Stockton Waterworks Co (1875) LR 10 QB 453 *64, 73*

Cavalier *v* Pope [1906] AC 428 *207, 228*

Century Insurance Co *v* Northern Ireland Road Transport Board [1942] AC 509 *29, 35*

Chadwick *v* British Transport Commission [1967] 1 WLR 912 *97, 172*

Chapman *v* Honig [1963] 2 QB 502 *366, 367*

Chapman *v* Lord Ellesmere [1932] 2 KB 431 *296*

Charleston *v* News Group Newspapers (1994) The Times 12 January *290*

Charlton *v* EMAP plc (1993) The Times 11 June *308*

Chatterton *v* Gerson [1981] QB 432 *315*

Chatterton *v* Secretary of State for India [1895] 2 QB 189 *299*

Chaudry *v* Prabhakar [1989] 1 WLR 29 *82*

Cheshire *v* Bailey [1905] 1 KB 237 *35*

Chic Fashions (West Wales) Ltd *v* Jones [1968] 2 QB 299 *328*

China and South Sea Bank Ltd *v* Tan [1990] 2 WLR 56 *63*

Christie *v* Davey [1893] 1 Ch 316 *238*

Church of Scientology of California *v* Johnson-Smith [1972] 1 QB 522 *298*

Cinnamond *v* British Airports Authority [1980] 2 All ER 368 *329*

Clark *v* Chambers (1878) 3 QBD 327 *259*

Clark *v* MacLennan [1983] 1 All ER 416 *128*

Clarke *v* Bruce Lance & Co (a firm) [1988] 1 All ER 364 *91, 108*

Clough *v* Bussan (West Yorkshire Police Authority, third party) [1990] 1 All ER 431 *111*

Cocks *v* Thanet District Council [1983] 2 AC 286 *181*

Cole *v* Turner (1704) 6 Mod 149 *314, 315*

Colledge v Bass Mitchells & Butlers Ltd [1988] 1 All ER 536   *385*
Collier v Anglian Water Authority (1983) The Times 26 March   *208*
Collins v Wilcock [1984] 3 All ER 374   *316, 323*
Coltman v Bibby Tankers Ltd [1988] AC 276   *190*
Colvilles Ltd v Devine [1969] 1 WLR 475   *131*
Commercial Banking Co of Sydney v RH Brown & Co [1972] 2 Lloyd's Rep 360
    339
Commissioner for Railways v Quinlan [1964] AC 1054   *221*
Condon v Basi [1985] 2 All ER 453   *126*
Constantine v Imperial Hotels Ltd [1944] KB 693   *371*
Control Risks Ltd v New English Library Ltd [1990] 1 WLR 183   *303*
Conway v George Wimpey & Co Ltd [1951] 2 KB 266   *30, 329*
Cook v Lewis [1952] 1 DLR 1   *136*
Cook v Square D Ltd [1992] ICR 262   *192*
Cookson v Knowles [1979] AC 556   *377, 389*
Coote v Stone [1971] 1 WLR 279   *183*
Cork v Kirby MacLean Ltd [1952] 2 All ER 402   *133*
Corporation of Manchester v Farnworth [1930] AC 171   *247*
Cory Lighterage Ltd v TGWU [1973] ICR 339   *364*
Cox v Moulsey (1848) 5 CB 533   *327*
Cresswell v Eaton [1991] 1 All ER 484   *391*
Cresswell v Sirl [1948] 1 KB 241   *284*
Crofter Hand Woven Harris Tweed Co Ltd v Veitch [1942] AC 435   *356*
Croke v Wiseman [1981] 3 All ER 852   *380*
Cummings v Grainger [1977] QB 397   *281, 282*
Cunard v Antifyre [1933] 1 KB 551   *228*
Cunningham v Harrison [1973] QB 942   *382, 383, 384*
Cunningham v Reading Football Club (1991) The Independent 20 March   *214*
Cunningham v Whelan (1917) 52 Ir LT 67   *276*
Curran v Northern Ireland Co-ownership Housing Association Ltd [1987] AC 718
    48, 54, 55, 60
Curtis v Betts [1990] 1 All ER 769   *279, 280*
Cutler v McPhail [1962] 2 QB 292   *18, 295*
Cutler v United Dairies [1933] 2 KB 297   *172*
Cutler v Vauxhall Motors Ltd [1971] 1 QB 418   *134*
Cutler v Wandsworth Stadium Ltd [1949] AC 398   *180, 184*

D & F Estates Ltd v The Church Commissioners for England [1989] AC 177   *2,
    39, 60, 73, 74, 77, 84, 85, 87, 89, 90, 94, 228, 229–230*
Daborn v Bath Tramways [1946] 2 All ER 333   *122*
Daily Mirror Newspapers Ltd v Gardiner [1968] 2 QB 762   *365*
Dakhyl v Labouchere [1908] 2 KB 325   *304*
Dalgety Spillers Foods Ltd v Food Brokers Ltd (1993) The Times 2 December   *349*

Daly *v* General Steam Navigation Co Ltd [1980] 3 All ER 696   *381–382*

Daniels *v* R White & Sons Ltd [1938] 4 All ER 258   *199*

Dann *v* Hamilton [1939] 1 KB 509   *174, 175, 176, 177*

Darbishire *v* Warran [1963] 1 WLR 1067   *394*

Darley Main Colliery Co *v* Mitchell (1886) 11 App Cas 127   *378*

Davey *v* Harrow Corporation [1958] 1 QB 60   *245*

Davidson *v* Chief Constable of North Wales Police (1993) The Times 26 April   *322*

Davie *v* New Merton Board Mills Ltd [1959] AC 604   *189*

Davies *v* Mann (1842) 10 M & W 546   *160*

Davies *v* Swan Motor Co [1949] 2 KB 291   *162*

Dawkins *v* Lord Paulet (1865) LR 5 QB 94   *300*

De Beers Products *v* Electric Co of New York [1975] 1 WLR 972   *343*

De Franco *v* Commissioner of Police of the Metropolis (1987) The Times 8 May
    411

De L'Isle (Viscount) *v* Times Newspapers [1987] 3 All ER 499   *298*

Deaton's Property Ltd *v* Flew (1949) 79 CLR 370   *35*

Dennis *v* London Passenger Transport Board [1949] 1 All ER 779   *384*

Department of Transport *v* Williams (1993) The Times 7 December   *366*

Derbyshire County Council *v* Times Newspapers Ltd [1992] QB 770   *289, 310*

Derry *v* Peek (1889) 14 App Cas 337   *337, 338*

Devon Lumber Co Ltd *v* MacNeill (1988) 45 DLR (4th) 300   *234, 253*

Dews *v* National Coal Board [1988] AC 1   *381*

Deyong *v* Shenburn [1946] KB 227   *194*

Dimbleby & Sons Ltd *v* National Union of Journalists [1984] 1 WLR 427   *361*

Dimmock *v* Hallett (1866) LR 2 Ch App 21   *336*

Dodd Properties Ltd *v* Canterbury City Council [1980] 1 WLR 433   *393*

Doe d Bishop of Rochester *v* Bridges (1831) 1 B & Ad 847   *180*

Doleman *v* Deakin (1990) The Times 30 January   *389*

Donnelly *v* Joyce [1974] QB 454   *385*

Donoghue *v* Stevenson [1932] AC 562   *44, 45, 46, 50, 54, 59, 67, 69, 71, 74, 82,*
    85, 87, 144, 163, 196, 206, 222, 227, 229

Dooley *v* Cammell Laird & Co Ltd [1951] 1 Lloyd's Rep 271   *99*

Doughty *v* Turner Manufacturing Co [1964] 1 QB 518   *148*

Downsview Nominees Ltd *v* First City Corporation Ltd [1993] AC 295   *64*

Doyle *v* Olby (Ironmongers) Ltd [1969] 2 QB 158   *153, 340*

Drane *v* Evangelou [1978] 1 WLR 455   *331*

Draper *v* Hodder [1972] 2 QB 556   *277*

Dulieu *v* White [1901] 2 KB 669   *95, 99, 146*

Dunlop *v* Macedo (1891) 8 TLR 43   *325*

Dutton *v* Bognor Regis UDC [1972] 1 QB 373   *228, 229*

Dymond *v* Pearce [1972] 1 QB 497   *258, 259*

EETPU *v* Times Newspapers Ltd [1980] QB 585   *13*

Easson *v* LNE Railway [1944] 2 KB 421   *130*

East *v* Maurer [1991] 1 WLR 461   *340*

East Suffolk Rivers Catchment Board *v* Kent [1941] AC 74; [1940] 1 KB 319   *113*

Edgington *v* Fitzmaurice (1885) 29 Ch D 459   *336, 339*

Edward Wong Finance *v* Johnson, Stokes & Master [1984] AC 296   *127*

Edwards *v* Lee (1991) 141 NLJ 1517   *109*

Edwards *v* Railway Executive [1952] AC 737   *210*

Edwards *v* West Herts Group Hospital Management Committee [1957] 1 WLR 415
     194

Eglantine Inn Ltd *v* Smith [1948] NI 29   *294*

Electrical, Electronic, Telecommunication & Plumbing Union v Times Newspapers
     Ltd [1980] QB 585   *289*

Elias *v* Pasmore [1934] 2 KB 164   *328*

Ellis *v* Loftus Iron Co (1874) LR 10 CP 10   *283*

Ellis *v* Sheffield Gas Consumers Co (1853) 2 E & B 767   *40*

Elvin & Powell Ltd *v* Plummer Roddis Ltd (1933) 50 TLR 158   *405*

Emanuel (HN) Ltd *v* GLC [1971] 2 All ER 835   *273–274*

Emeh *v* Kensington and Chelsea and Westminster AHA [1985] QB 1012; [1984] 3
     All ER 1044   *104, 105*

Emerald Construction Co Ltd *v* Lowthian [1966] 1 WLR 691   *359*

Ephraim *v* Newham London Borough Council (1992) The Times 24 January   *66*

Erven Warnink BV *v* J Townend & Sons (Hull) Ltd [1979] AC 731   *345, 347, 348*

Esso Petroleum Co Ltd *v* Mardon [1976] 1 QB 801   *79*

Euro-Diam *v* Bathurst [1988] 2 All ER 23   *398*

Evans *v* London Hospital Medical College [1981] 1 All ER 715; [1981] 1 WLR 184
     14, 418

Evans *v* Triplex Safety Glass Co Ltd [1936] 1 All ER 283   *198, 199*

Everitt *v* Martin [1953] NZLR 298   *404*

F (mental patient: sterilisation), re [1990] 2 AC 1   *314, 404*

F *v* West Berkshire Health Authority [1990] 2 AC 1; [1989] 2 All ER 545   *316*

Farrer *v* Nelson (1885) 15 QBD 258   *264*

Fay *v* Prentice (1845) 1 CB 828   *252*

Fayed *v* Al-Tajir [1987] 2 All ER 396   *300*

Femis-Bank (Anguilla) Ltd *v* Lazar [1991] 3 WLR 80   *308*

Ferguson *v* Welsh [1987] 3 All ER 777   *212, 213, 218, 219*

Fetter *v* Beale (1701) 1 Ld Raym 339   *378*

Fields *v* Davis [1955] CLY 1543   *290*

Filliter *v* Phippard (1847) 11 QB 347   *274*

Fitzgerald *v* Cooke Bourne (Farms) Ltd [1964] 1 QB 249   *280*

Fitzgerald *v* Lane [1989] AC 328; [1987] QB 781   *138, 168*

Flint *v* Lovell [1935] 1 KB 354   *389*

Fontin *v* Katapodis (1962) 108 CLR 177   *316*

Forrester *v* Tyrell (1893) 9 TLR 257   *287*

Foster *v* Tyne and Wear CC [1986] 1 All ER 567   *381*

Fouldes *v* Willoughby (1841) 8 M & W 540   *403*

Fowler *v* Lanning [1959] 1 QB 426   *313*

Fraser-Armstrong *v* Haddow (1994) The Times 21 January   *302*

Froom *v* Butcher [1975] 3 WLR 379   *163, 167, 169*

Galoo *v* Bright Grahame Murray (1994) The Times 14 January   *136*

Gammell *v* Wilson [1982] AC 27, 78   *380*

Gandy *v* Jubber (1865) 9 B & S 15   *244*

Garnham, Harris & Elton *v* Ellis [1967] 2 All ER 940   *405*

Gee *v* Metropolitan Railway (1873) LR 8 QB 161   *130*

General Cleaning Contractors *v* Christmas [1953] AC 180   *191*

General Engineering Services *v* Kingston and St Andrew Corp [1989] 1 WLR 69   *34*

Gilbert *v* Stone (1647) Style 72   *329*

Giles *v* Walker (1890) 24 QBD 656   *263*

Gillette UK Ltd *v* Edenwest Ltd (1994) The Times 9 March   *346*

Gillingham Borough Council *v* Medway (Chatham) Dock Co Ltd [1993] QB 343   *256*

Gitsham *v* C H Pearce & Sons plc (1991) The Times 11 February   *191*

Glasgow Corporation *v* Muir [1943] 2 AC 448   *118, 243*

Glasgow Corporation *v* Taylor [1922] 1 AC 44   *215*

Glinski *v* McIver [1962] AC 726   *419*

Goddard *v* Smith (1704) 1 Salk 21   *418*

Gold *v* Haringey Health Authority [1988] QB 481; [1987] 2 All ER 888; [1987] 1 FLR 125   *129*

Goldman *v* Hargrave [1967] 1 AC 645   *242, 273, 274*

Goldsmith *v* Sperrings Ltd [1977] 1 WLR 478   *295–296*

Goodman *v* Boycott (1862) 2 B & S 1   *406*

Gordon *v* Harper (1796) 7 Term Rep 9   *409*

Gorris *v* Scott (1874) LR 9 Exch 125   *185*

Gough *v* Thorne [1966] 1 WLR 1387   *164*

Gould *v* McAuliffe [1941] 2 All ER 527   *211*

Graham *v* Peat (1861) 1 East 244   *325*

Granada Group Ltd *v* Ford Motor Co Ltd [1972] FSR 103   *349*

Gran Gelato Ltd *v* Richcliff (Group) Ltd [1992] Ch 560   *109*

Grant *v* Australian Knitting Mills Ltd [1936] AC 85   *197*

Greater Nottingham Co-operative Society Ltd *v* Cementation Piling and Foundations Ltd [1989] QB 71   *84, 86*

Green *v* Chelsea Waterworks (1894) 70 LT 547   *271*

Greenhalgh *v* British Railways Board [1969] 2 QB 286   *210*

Greenock Corporation *v* Caledonian Railway Co [1917] AC 556   *270*

Greenwood *v* Bennett [1973] QB 195   *413*

Greers Ltd v Pearman & Corder Ltd (1922) 39 RPC 406   *343*
Gregory v Piper (1829) 9 B & C 591   *325–326*
Griffiths v Arch Engineering Co [1968] 3 All ER 217   *198*
Griffiths v Liverpool Corporation [1967] 1 QB 374   *260*
Groves v Lord Wimborne [1898] 2 QB 402   *181, 182, 183*
Gulf Oil (GB) Ltd v Page [1987] Ch 327   *308*

H v Home Office (1992) The Independent 5 May   *320*
Hadmor Productions v Hamilton [1982] 2 WLR 322   *366*
Hale v Jennings Bros [1938] 1 All ER 579   *265, 268*
Haley v London Electricity Board [1965] AC 778   *121*
Halsey v Esso Petroleum Co Ltd [1961] 1 WLR 683   *245, 268, 269*
Hambrook v Stokes Bros [1925] 1 KB 141   *95*
Hannah v Peel [1945] KB 509   *416*
Harris v Birkenhead Corporation [1976] 1 WLR 279   *208, 222, 223*
Harris v Empress Motors Ltd [1983] 3 All ER 561   *380*
Harris v James (1876) 45 LJQB 545   *244*
Harris v Lombard (New Zealand) Ltd [1974] 2 NZLR 161   *410*
Harrison v British Railways Board [1981] 3 All ER 679   *166*
Harrison v Duke of Rutland [1893] 1 QB 142   *326*
Harrison v Southwark and Vauxhall Water Co [1891] 2 Ch 409   *236*
Harrison v Surrey County Council (1994) The Times 27 January   *82*
Hartt v Newspaper Publishing plc (1989) The Times 7 November   *290*
Haseldine v Daw [1941] 2 KB 343   *197, 218*
Hasselblad (GB) Ltd v Orbinson [1985] 1 All ER 173   *299*
Hay v Hughes [1975] QB 790   *392*
Hayden v Hayden [1992] 4 All ER 681   *391, 392*
Haynes v Harwood [1935] 1 KB 146   *58, 172*
Hayward v Thompson [1982] QB 47   *294*
Heasmans v Clarity Cleaning Co Ltd [1987] IRLR 286   *34*
Heath v Mayor of Brighton (1908) 98 LT 718   *237*
Heaven v Pender (1883) 11 QBD 503   *44, 67*
Hedley Byrne & Co Ltd v Heller & Partners Ltd [1964] AC 465   *46, 47, 69, 75, 76, 77, 80, 83, 86, 89, 90, 91, 93, 194*
Hellwig v Mitchell [1910] 1 KB 609   *288*
Hemmens v Wilson Browne [1993] 4 All ER 826   *92*
Hemmings v Stoke Poges Golf Club [1920] 1 KB 720   *332*
Henderson v Henry E Jenkins & Sons [1970] AC 282   *131*
Henderson v Radio Corporation Pty Ltd [1960] NSWR 576   *349*
Herd v Wearsdale Steel, Coal and Coke Ltd [1915] AC 67   *321*
Herniman v Smith [1938] AC 305   *419*
Herring v Boyle (1834) 1 Cr M & R 377   *318, 319*
Hevican v Ruane [1991] 3 All ER 65   *101*

Heydon *v* Kent County Council [1978] QB 343 *260*

Hickman *v* Maisey [1900] 1 QB 752 *326*

Hicks *v* Chief Constable of the South Yorkshire Police [1992] 2 All ER 65 *387*

Highland Leasing *v* Paul Field [1985] CLY 3224 *413*

Hilder *v* Associated Portland Cement Manufacturers Ltd [1961] 1 WLR 1434 *121*

Hill *v* Chief Constable of West Yorkshire [1989] AC 53 *51– 52, 53, 111, 112*

Hill *v* James Crowe (Cases) Ltd [1978] 1 All ER 812 *199*

Hill *v* Tupper (1863) 2 H & C 121 *325*

Hill (Edwin) & Partners *v* First National Finance Corporation [1989] 1 WLR 225 *362*

Hillesden Securities *v* Ryjack [1983] 1 WLR 959 *414*

Hiort *v* Bott (1874) LR 9 Ex 86 *405*

Hobbs (E) (Farms) Ltd *v* The Baxenden Chemical Co Ltd [1992] 1 Lloyd's Rep 54 *271*

Hoare and Co *v* McAlpine [1923] 1 Ch 167 *245*

Hodgson *v* Trapp [1989] AC 807 *377, 385, 386*

Holden *v* Chief Constable of Lancashire [1987] QB 380 *374*

Holden *v* White [1982] 2 WLR 1030 *210*

Hole *v* Barlow (1858) 4 CBNS 334 *236*

Holliday *v* National Telephone Co [1899] 2 QB 392 *41*

Hollywood Silver Fox Farm Ltd *v* Emmett [1936] 2 KB 468 *238*

Holmes *v* Wilson (1839) 10 Ad & El 503 *326*

Home Brewery plc *v* William Davis & Co (Loughborough) Ltd [1987] QB 339 *239, 243, 244*

Home Office *v* Dorset Yacht Co [1970] AC 1004 *46, 47, 49, 56, 58, 65, 111, 112, 113, 157, 214*

Honeywill and Stein Ltd *v* Larkin Brothers Ltd [1934] 1 KB 191 *41*

Horrocks *v* Lowe [1975] AC 135 *300*

Horsfall *v* Thomas (1862) 1 H & C 90 *339*

Hotson *v* East Berkshire AHA [1987] AC 50 *139*

Houghland *v* RR Low (Luxury Coaches) Ltd [1962] 1 QB 694 *406*

Housecroft *v* Burnett [1986] 1 All ER 332 *382, 383*

Howard Marine and Dredging Co *v* A Ogden and Sons (Excavations) Ltd [1978] QB 574 *79*

Hubbard *v* Pitt [1976] QB 142 *258*

Hudson *v* Ridge Manufacturing Co Ltd [1957] 2 QB 348 *189*

Hughes *v* Lord Advocate [1963] AC 837 *148, 149, 151*

Hughes *v* National Union of Mineworkers [1991] 4 All ER 278 *110*

Hulton *v* Jones [1910] AC 20 *292, 293*

Hunt *v* Severs [1993] 3 WLR 558 *383*

Hunt *v* Wallis (1991) The Times 10 May *280*

Hunter *v* Chief Constable of West Midlands [1982] AC 529 *105*

Huntley *v* Thornton [1957] 1 WLR 321 *356*

Hurley v Dyke [1979] RTR 265   *197*
Hurst v Picture Theatres Ltd [1915] 1 KB 1   *330*
Hussain v New Taplow Paper Mills Ltd [1988] 2 WLR 266; [1988] AC 514   *384,
    385, 386*
Hutchins v Maughan [1947] VLR 131   *403*
Huth v Huth [1915] 3 KB 32   *295*

Imperial Chemical Industries Ltd v Shatwell [1965] AC 656   *24, 28, 172, 174, 186*
International Factors v Rodriguez [1979] 1 QB 351   *410*
Island Records, ex p [1978] Ch 122   *367*
Irene's Success, The [1982] QB 481   *64, 65*
Irving v The Post Office [1987] IRLR 289   *34*

JEB Fasteners Ltd v Marks, Bloom and Co [1983] 1 All ER 583; [1981] 3 All ER
    289   *339*
Jaensch v Coffey (1984) 54 ALR 417   *101*
Janvier v Sweeney [1919] 2 KB 316   *322*
Jarvis v Williams [1955] 1 WLR 71   *410*
Jayes v IMI (Kynoch) Ltd [1985] ICR 155   *165*
Jefford v Gee [1970] 2 QB 130   *389*
Jerome v Bentley [1952] 2 All ER 114   *405*
Jobling v Associated Dairies [1982] AC 794   *141, 142, 376*
Joel v Morrison (1834) 6 C & P 501   *32*
Johnson v Coventry Churchill International Ltd [1992] 3 All ER 14   *27, 192, 193*
Jones v Boyce (1816) 1 Stark 493   *126, 166*
Jones v Department of Employment [1989] QB 1; [1988] 1 All ER 725   *62–63,
    115*
Jones v Ffestiniog Railway Co (1868) LR 3 QB 733   *275*
Jones v Gwyn (1712) 10 Mod 148   *418*
Jones v Jones [1916] 2 AC 481   *288*
Jones v Jones [1985] QB 704   *387*
Jones v Livox Quarries Ltd [1952] 2 QB 608   *163, 167*
Jones v Llanrwst UDC [1911] 1 Ch 393   *325*
Jones v Northampton Borough Council (1990) The Independent 25 May   *12*
Joyce v Motor Surveys Ltd [1948] Ch 252   *343*
Joyce v Sengupta [1993] 1 WLR 337   *63, 309, 342 344*
Junior Books Ltd v The Veitchi Co Ltd [1983] 1 AC 520   *2, 9, 62, 63, 72, 74, 84,
    85, 86, 90, 91, 199, 394*

K v P [1992] 3 WLR 1015   *19*
Kay v Ayrshire and Arran Health Board [1987] 2 All ER 417   *139*
Kaye v Robertson [1991] FSR 62   *309*
Kelsen v Imperial Tobacco Co Ltd [1957] 2 QB 334   *327*
Kemsley v Foot [1952] AC 345   *305*

Kennaway *v* Thompson [1981] QB 88   *250, 251*
Kerr *v* Kennedy [1942] 1 KB 409   *288*
Kerr *v* Shedden (1831) 4 C & P 528   *341*
Khorasandjian *v* Bush [1993] NLJ 329   *234, 235, 246*
Kiddle *v* City Business Premises Ltd [1942] 2 All ER 216   *270*
King *v* Liverpool City Council [1986] 3 All ER 544   *57*
King *v* Phillips [1953] 1 QB 429   *96*
Kingshott *v* Associated Kent Newspapers Ltd [1990] 3 WLR 675   *301*
Kirk *v* Gregory (1876) 1 Ex D 55   *404*
Kirkham *v* Chief Constable of Greater Manchester Police [1990] 2 QB 283; [1990] 2
    WLR 987; [1990] 3 All ER 246   *66, 110, 172, 398*
Kite *v* Napp (1982) The Times 1 June   *280*
Knight *v* Home Office [1990] 3 All ER 237   *124*
Knightley *v* Johns [1982] 1 WLR 349   *110, 156*
Knowles *v* Liverpool City Council [1993] 4 All ER 321   *190*
Knupffer *v* London Express Newspapers Ltd [1944] AC 116   *294*
Konskier *v* Goodman Ltd [1928] 1 KB 421   *326*
Koursk, The [1924] P 140   *17*
Kowal *v* Ellis (1977) 76 DLR (3d) 546   *415*
Kralj *v* McGrath [1986] 1 All ER 54   *372, 387*
Kubach *v* Hollands [1937] 3 All ER 907   *198*

Lady Gwendolen, The [1965] P 294   *119*
Lamb *v* Camden London Borough Council [1981] QB 625   *57, 67, 157*
Lancashire & Cheshire Association of Baptist Churches *v* Howard & Seddon
    Partnership [1993] 3 All ER 467   *74*
Lancashire & Yorkshire Railway *v* MacNicoll (1919) 88 LJKB 601   *404*
Lane *v* Holloway [1968] 1 QB 379   *316*
Langbrook Properties Ltd *v* Surrey County Council [1969] 1 WLR 167   *65*
Latham *v* R Johnson and Nephew Ltd [1913] 1 KB 398   *215*
Latimer *v* AEC Ltd [1953] AC 643   *122–123, 191*
Law Debenture Trust Corporation *v* Ural Caspian Oil Corporation Ltd (1994) The
    Independent 10 March; [1993] 1 WLR 138   *360*
Laws *v* Florinplace Ltd [1981] 1 All ER 659   *246*
Le Fanu *v* Malcolmson (1848) 1 HL Cas 637   *293*
League Against Cruel Sports Ltd *v* Scott [1985] 2 All ER 489   *329*
Leakey *v* National Trust [1980] QB 485   *223, 240, 242, 243, 244, 245, 263*
Leeman *v* Montagu [1936] 2 All ER 1677   *276*
Leigh and Sillivan Ltd *v* Aliakmon Shipping Co Ltd, The Aliakmon [1986] AC 785;
    [1986] 2 All ER 145; [1985] 1 QB 350 (CA)   *48, 53, 64, 65, 66, 91, 410*
Leitch & Co *v* Leydon 1931 SC (HL) 1   *404*
Lemon *v* Webb [1895] AC 1   *245, 252*
Lennard's Carrying Co *v* Asiatic Petroleum Co Ltd [1915] AC 705   *11*

Letang v Cooper [1965] 1 QB 232   *312, 313, 329, 404*
Lewis v Daily Telegraph Ltd [1964] AC 234   *291*
Liddle v Yorks (North Riding) CC [1934] 2 KB 101   *215*
Liesbosch Dredger v SS Edison [1933] AC 449   *145, 393*
Lim Poh Choo v Camden and Islington AHA [1980] AC 174   *376, 377, 379, 388*
Limpus v London General Ombibus Co (1862) 1 H & C 526   *30*
Lincoln v Hayman [1982] 1 WLR 488   *384*
Lister v Romford Ice and Cold Storage Co [1957] AC 555   *36*
Lister (RA) Ltd v Thomson (Shipping) Ltd [1987] 1 WLR 1614   *19*
Littler v Liverpool Corporation [1968] 2 All ER 343   *260*
Lloyd v Grace, Smith & Co [1912] AC 716   *36*
Lloyd Cheyham & Co Ltd v Littlejohn & Co QBD (1985) 30 September Unrep
    124
Lloyd's Bank Ltd v EB Savoury & Co [1933] AC 201   *123*
London Artists Ltd v Littler [1969] 2 QB 375   *303, 305*
London Corporation, The [1935] P 70   *393*
London Passenger Transport Board v Upson [1949] AC 155   *183*
Lonrho plc v Fayed [1992] 1 AC 448 (HL); [1990] 2 QB 479 (CA)   *355, 366*
Lonrho plc v Fayed (No 5) [1993] 1 WLR 1489   *356*
Lonrho Ltd v Shell Petroleum Co Ltd (No 2) [1982] AC 173   *180, 184, 185, 353
    366, 368*
Lonhro plc v Tebbitt [1991] 4 All ER 973   *115*
Lowery v Walker [1911] AC 10   *209, 210, 221*
Lucas-Box v News Group Newspapers Ltd [1986] 1 WLR 147   *297–298*
Lumley v Gye (1853) 2 El & Bl 216   *357, 361*
Luxmoore-May v Messenger May Baverstock [1990] 1 All ER 1067   *124*
Lyne v Nichols (1906) 23 TLR 86   *342*
Lyon v Daily Telegraph Ltd [1943] KB 746   *306*
Lyons v Gulliver [1914] 1 Ch 631   *258*

M v Newham London Borough Council [1994] NLJ 357   *61, 184*
McAuley v Bristol City Council [1992] 1 QB 134   *229*
McC v Mullan [1984] 3 All ER 908   *14*
McCall v Abelesz [1976] QB 585   *183*
McCamley v Cammell-Laird Shipbuilders Ltd [1990] 1 All ER 854   *386*
McCarey v Associated Newspapers Ltd [1964] 1 WLR 855   *307*
McCullagh v Lane Fox & Partners (1994) The Times 25 January   *82*
McCullough v May [1947] 2 All ER 845   *349*
McDermid v Nash Dredging and Reclamation Co Ltd [1987] AC 906   *42, 191,
    192, 193*
McFarlane v Caledonia Ltd [1993] NLJ 1367   *98*
McGhee v National Coal Board [1973] 1 WLR 1   *136, 137, 138, 139, 140*
McHale v Watson [1966] ALR 513   *125*

McKay *v* Essex Area Health Authority [1982] QB 1166 *10, 104*

McKew *v* Holland & Hannen & Cubbitts (Scotland) Ltd [1969] 3 All ER 1621 *154, 168*

McKinnell *v* White 1971 SLT (Notes) 61 *164*

McLoughlin *v* O'Brian [1983] 1 AC 410 *53, 60, 96, 98, 99, 100, 101*

McNaughten (James) Paper Group plc *v* Hicks Anderson & Co (a firm) [1991] 1 All ER 134 *78, 80*

McNerny *v* London Borough of Lambeth (1988) 21 HLR 188 *61, 228*

McWilliams *v* Sir William Arrol & Co Ltd [1962] 1 WLR 295 *135, 186*

Mahon *v* Osborne [1939] 2 KB 14 *130*

Malone *v* Laskey [1907] 2 KB 141 *233, 234, 235*

Malz *v* Rosen [1966] 1 WLR 1008 *418*

Manders *v* Williams (1849) 4 Ex 339 *409*

Marc Rich *v* Bishop Rock Marine (1994) The Times 23 February *62*

Mariola Marine Corporation *v* Lloyd's Register of Shipping, The Morning Watch (1990) The Times 21 February; [1990] 1 Lloyd's Rep 547 *70, 81*

Market Investigations Ltd *v* Minister of Social Security [1969] 2 QB 173 *25*

Marshall *v* Osmond [1983] QB 1034 *109*

Martin *v* Owen (1992) The Times 21 May *391*

Martin *v* Watson [1994] 2 WLR 500 *418*

Martindale *v* Duncan [1973] 1 WLR 574 *393*

Martine *v* South East Kent Health Authority (1993) The Times 8 March *115*

Mason *v* Levy Auto Parts of England Ltd [1967] 2 QB 530 *264, 272, 273*

Mason *v* Williams & Williams Ltd [1955] 1 WLR 549 *199*

Massey *v* Crown Life Insurance [1978] 1 WLR 676 *25*

Matania *v* National Provincial Bank Ltd [1936] 2 All ER 633 *246*

Matthews *v* Wicks (1987) The Times 25 May *283*

Mattocks *v* Mann (1992) The Times 19 June *145*

Maxim's Ltd *v* Dye [1977] 1 WLR 1155 *348*

Maynard *v* West Midlands Health Authority [1984] 1 WLR 634 *124, 128*

Maynegrain Pty Ltd *v* Campafina Bank [1984] 1 NSWLR 258 *404, 406, 410*

Meah *v* McCreamer [1985] 1 All ER 367 *387*

Mears *v* LSW Ry (1862) 11 CB (NS) 850 *406*

Meering *v* Graham-White Aviation Co (1919) 122 LT 44 *319*

Merivale *v* Carson (1887) 20 QBD 275 *305*

Merkur Island Shipping Corp *v* Laughton [1983] 2 AC 570 *359, 361, 365, 366*

Merricks *v* Nott-Bower [1965] 1 QB 57 *300*

Merryweather *v* Nixon (1799) 8 TR 186 *18*

Mersey Docks and Harbour Board *v* Coggins and Griffith (Liverpool) Ltd [1947] AC 1 *26, 193*

Metall und Rohstoff AG *v* Donaldson Lufkin & Jenrette Inc [1990] 1 QB 391; (1988) The Times 14 April *355, 356*

Metropolitan Properties Ltd *v* Jones [1939] 2 All ER 202 *234*

Metropolitan Saloon Omnibus Co v Hawkins (1859) 4 H & N 87   *289*

Middlebrook MushroomsLtd v Transport and General Workers Union (1993) The
    Times 18 January   *361*

Middleweek v Chief Constable of Merseyside [1992] 1 AC 179   *320*

Midland Bank Trust Co Ltd v Green (No 3) [1982] Ch 529   *354*

Midwood v Manchester Corporation [1905] 2 KB 597   *237*

Miller v Hancock [1893] 2 QB 177   *208*

Miller v Jackson [1977] QB 966   *248, 250, 252, 313*

Mills v Winchester Diocesan Board of Finance [1989] Ch 428   *63*

Ministry of Housing and Local Government v Sharp [1970] 2 QB 223   *69, 93*

Mint v Good [1951] 1 KB 517   *260*

Minter v Priest [1930] AC 558   *299*

Mitchell v Book Sales Ltd (1994) The Independent 25 March   *290*

Moeliker v A Reyrolle Ltd [1977] 1 All ER 9   *381*

Moffatt v Kazana [1969] 2 WLR 71   *414*

Mogul Steamship Co Ltd v McGregor Gow & Co [1892] AC 25   *351, 352, 353*

Moloney v Lambeth LBC (1968) 198 EG 895   *215*

Monk v Warbey [1935] 1 KB 175   *37, 183*

Monson v Tussauds Ltd [1894] 1 QB 671   *286*

Moore (DW) & Co v Ferrier [1988] 1 All ER 400   *401*

Moorgate Mercantile Co v Finch [1962] 1 QB 701   *405*

Moorgate Mercantile Co v Twitchings [1977] AC 890   *405*

Morales v Eccleston [1991] RTR 151   *164*

More v Weaver [1928] 2 KB 520   *299*

Morgan v Fry [1968] 2 QB 710   *364*

Morgan v Incorporated Central Council of the Girls Friendly Society [1936] 1 All
    ER 404   *39*

Morgan v Odhams Press Ltd [1971] 1 WLR 1239   *293*

Morgan Crucible v Hill Samuel Bank Ltd [1991] 1 All ER 148; [1990] 3 All ER 330
    80, 81

Morgans v Launchbury [1973] AC 127   *37*

Morrell v International Thomson Publishing Ltd [1989] 3 All ER 733   *309*

Morris v Breaveglen Ltd (1992) The Times 29 December   *27, 192, 193*

Morris v CW Martin & Sons Ltd [1966] 1 QB 716   *35, 41*

Morris v Murray [1991] 2 WLR 195   *173, 175*

Morris v Pugh (1761) 4 Burr 1241   *407*

Morris v Redland Bricks Ltd [1970] AC 652   *395*

Morrison Steamship Co Ltd v Greystone Castle (Cargo Owners) [1947] AC 265
    69, 93

Morriss v Marsden [1952] 1 All ER 925   *13*

Mortin v Shoppee (1828) 3 C & P 373   *317*

Mothercare UK Ltd v Penguin Books Ltd (1987) The Times 8 July   *348*

Motherwell v Motherwell (1976) 73 DLR (3d) 62   *234, 235*

Moukataff v BOAC [1967] 1 Lloyd's Rep 396   *407*

Muirhead v Industrial Tank Specialities Ltd [1986] QB 507; [1985] 3 All ER 705
    84, 85, 151

Mulcahy v R (1868) LR 3 HL 306; 317   *354*

Mulholland v Baker [1939] 3 All ER 166   *274*

Munro v Willmott [1949] 1 KB 295   *413*

Murphy v Bradford Metropolitan Council (1991) The Times 11 February   *214*

Murphy v Brentwood District Council [1990] 3 WLR 414   *2, 49, 60, 70, 72, 77,
    84, 87, 88, 89, 90, 91, 93, 94, 113, 114, 228, 230*

Murphy v Culhane [1977] QB 94   *316*

Murray v Ministry of Defence [1988] 2 All ER 521   *319*

Musgrove v Pandelis [1919] 2 KB 43   *273, 274, 275*

Mutual Life and Citizens Assurance Co v Evatt [1971] AC 793   *78, 79*

Nabi v British Leyland (UK) Ltd [1980] 1 All ER 667   *384*

Nance v British Columbia Electric Railway Co Ltd [1951] AC 601   *162*

National Coal Board v England [1954] AC 403   *398*

National Coal Board v Evans [1951] 2 KB 861   *312, 404*

Nettleship v Weston [1971] 2 QB 691   *119, 174, 262*

Newstead v London Express Newspapers Ltd [1940] 1 KB 377   *293*

Newton v Edgerley [1959] 1 WLR 1031   *13*

Ng Chun Pui v Lee Chuen Tat [1988] RTR 298   *126, 132*

Nichols v Marsland (1876) 2 Ex D 1   *269, 270*

Nitrigin Eireann Teoranta v Inco Alloys Ltd [1992] 1 All ER 854   *90*

Noble v Harrison [1926] 2 KB 332   *248*

Nocton v Lord Ashburton [1914] AC 932   *76*

Nor-Video Services Ltd v Ontario Hydro (1978) 84 DLR (3d) 221   *235*

North Western Utilities v London Guarantee and Accident Co [1936] AC 108
    271

Nottingham Health Authority v The City of Nottingham [1988] 1 WLR 903   *20*

Notts Patent Brick and Tile Co v Butler (1886) 16 QBD 778   *335*

O'Connell v Jackson [1972] 1 QB 270   *167*

O'Grady v Westminster Scaffolding [1962] 2 Lloyds Rep 238   *393*

O'Kelly v Trusthouse Forte plc [1983] ICR 728   *26*

Oakley v Lyster [1931] 1 KB 148   *405*

Ocean Estates Ltd v Pinder [1969] 2 AC 19   *325*

Ogwo v Taylor [1988] AC 431; [1987] 2 WLR 988; [1987] 3 All ER 961   *207, 216,
    273*

Oliver v Ashman [1962] 2 QB 210   *380*

Oliver v Birmingham and Midland Omnibus Co [1933] 1 KB 35   *164*

Ormrod v Crossville Motor Services [1953] 1 WLR 1120   *37*

Oropesa, The [1943] P 32   *155*

Osborne *v* Boulter [1930] 2 KB 226   *302*

Osman *v* Ferguson [1993] 4 All ER 344   *112*

Overseas Tankship (UK) Ltd *v* Miller Steamship Co Pty Ltd, The Wagon Mound (No 2) [1967] 1 AC 617   *150, 151, 152, 153, 239, 240, 253*

Overseas Tankship (UK) *v* Morts Dock & Engineering Co (The Wagon Mound (No 1)) [1961] AC 388   *143, 144, 145, 146, 150, 151, 152, 153, 340*

Owens *v* Brimmell [1977] QB 859   *167*

Padbury *v* Holliday and Greenwood (1912) 28 TLR 492   *42*

Palacath Ltd *v* Flanagan [1985] 2 All ER 161   *14*

Palmer *v* Durnford Ford (a firm) [1992] 1 QB 483   *14*

Pannett *v* McGuinness [1972] 2 QB 599   *222*

Paris *v* Stepney Borough Council [1951] AC 367   *121, 191*

Parker *v* British Airways Board [1982] 1 QB 1004   *408, 409, 415, 416*

Parker-Knoll Ltd *v* Knoll International Ltd [1962] RPC 265   *348*

Parmiter *v* Coupland and Another (1840) 6 M & W 105   *289*

Parry *v* Cleaver [1970] AC 1   *384, 385*

Parsons (H) (Livestock) Ltd *v* Uttley, Ingham & Co Ltd [1978] QB 791   *149*

Partington *v* Wandsworth London Borough Council (1989) The Independent 8 November   *58*

Pasley *v* Freeman (1789) 3 TR 51   *334*

Pau On *v* Lau Yiu Long [1980] AC 614   *365*

Payne *v* Rogers (1794) 2 H Bl 350   *244*

Peabody Donation Fund (Governors of) *v* Sir Lindsay Parkinson & Co Ltd [1985] AC 210   *47, 52, 59*

Peek *v* Gurney (1873) LR 6 HL 377   *338*

Penfolds Wines Pty Ltd *v* Elliott (1946) 74 CLR 204   *403, 404, 409*

Performance Cars *v* Abraham [1962] 1 QB 33   *134*

Perl (P) (Exporters) Ltd *v* Camden London Borough Council [1984] QB 342   *57, 157*

Perry *v* Kendrick Transport Ltd [1956] 1 WLR 85   *265, 269, 271*

Perry *v* Sidney Phillips & Son [1982] 1 WLR 1297   *145*

Perry, Howard E Ltd *v* British Railways Board [1980] 1 WLR 1375   *403, 405, 406, 407*

Petch *v* Commissioners of Customs and Excise (1993) The Times 4 March   *63, 81*

Phillips *v* Britannia Hygienic Laundry Co Ltd [1923] 2 KB 832   *182, 183*

Phillips Products Ltd *v* Hyland [1987] 2 All ER 620   *27, 28*

Phipps *v* Rochester Corporation [1955] 1 QB 450   *215*

Photo Production Ltd *v* Securicor Transport Ltd [1980] AC 827   *360–361*

Pickering *v* Rudd (1815) 4 Camp 219   *327*

Pickett *v* British Railways Engineering Ltd [1980] AC 136   *380*

Pidduck *v* Eastern Scottish Omnibuses Ltd [1990] 2 All ER 69   *392*

Pinn *v* Rew (1916) 32 TLR 451   *40*

Pirelli General Cable Works Ltd *v* Oscar Faber & Partners [1983] 2 AC 1   *90,*
   400–401
Pitts *v* Hunt [1991] 1 QB 24; [1990] 3 WLR 542; (1990) The Times 13 April;
   [1989] 3 WLR 795   *165, 168, 175, 398*
Plumb *v* Cobden Flour Mills Co [1914] AC 62, 67   *29*
Poland *v* John Parr and Sons [1927] 1 KB 236   *29, 35*
Polemis and Furness, Withy & Co, Re [1921] 3 KB 560   *143, 144, 145, 146, 152, 153*
Polhill *v* Walter (1832) 3 B & Ad 114   *338*
Pontardawe RDC *v* Moore-Gwyn [1929] 1 Ch 656   *263*
Ponting *v* Noakes [1894] 2 QB 281   *270*
Port Swettenham Authority *v* T W Wu [1979] AC 580   *35*
Portsea Island Mutual Co-operative Society Ltd *v* Michael Brashier Associates
   (1990) 6 Professional Negligence 43   *89*
Prager *v* Times Newspapers Ltd [1988] 1 All ER 300   *297*
Preston *v* Torfaen Borough Council (1993) The Times 21 July   *74*
Pride of Derby *v* British Celanese Ltd [1953] Ch 149   *250*
Pritchard *v* JH Cobden Ltd [1988] Fam 22   *387*
Punjab National Bank *v* De Boinville [1992] 1 WLR 1138   *82*

Quinn *v* Leatham [1901] AC 495   *153, 352, 353, 356*

R *v* Barnard (1837) 7 C & P 784   *335*
R *v* Billinghurst [1978] Crim LR 553   *315*
R *v* Callender [1993] QB 303   *26, 42*
R *v* Commissioner of Police of the Metropolis, ex parte Blackburn [1968] 2 QB 118
   111
R *v* Darlington Borough Council, ex parte The Association of Darlington Taxi
   Owners (1994) The Independent 13 January   *12*
R *v* Deputy Governor of Parkhurst Prison, ex parte Hague [1992] 1 AC 58   *32,*
   180, 183–184
R *v* McDonnell [1966] 1 QB 233   *354*
R *v* Manchester City Magistrates' Court, ex parte Davies [1989] 1 All ER 90   *14*
R *v* Meade and Belt (1823) 1 Lew CC 184   *317*
R *v* Self [1992] 1 WLR 657   *321*
R *v* Shorrock [1993] 3 WLR 698   *240, 256*
R *v* Smith and Jones [1976] 1 WLR 672   *211*
R *v* St George (1840) 9 C & P 483   *318*
R *v* Wilson [1955] 1 WLR 493   *317*
RCA *v* Pollard [1982] 3 WLR 1007   *367*
Racz *v* Home Office [1994] 2 WLR 23   *32*
Rainham Chemical Works *v* Belvedere Fish Guano Co [1921] 2 AC 465   *266, 267*
Rance *v* Mid-Downs Health Authority [1991] 2 WLR 159   *105*
Rantzen *v* Mirror Group Newspapers [1993] 3 WLR 953   *307, 310*

Ratcliffe *v* Evans [1892] 2 QB 524   *341, 344*

Ratnasingam *v* Kow Ah Dek [1983] 1 WLR 1235   *376*

Ravenscroft *v* Rederiaktiebolaget Transatlantic [1991] 3 All ER 73   *101*

Read *v* Coker (1853) 13 CB 850   *318*

Read *v* Croydon Corporation [1938] 4 All ER 631   *181*

Read *v* Lyons Ltd [1947] AC 156   *265, 266, 268, 269*

Reading *v* Attorney-General [1951] AC 507   *4*

Ready Mixed Concrete (South East) Ltd *v* Minister of Pensions [1968] 2 QB 497   *25*

Reddaway *v* Banham [1896] AC 199   *347*

Redgrave *v* Hurd (1881) 20 Ch D 1   *339*

Redler Grain Silos Ltd *v* BICC Ltd [1982] 1 Lloyd's Rep 435   *406*

Reid *v* Rush & Tompkins Group plc [1990] 1 WLR 212   *61, 63, 70, 188, 194*

Reynolds *v* Kennedy (1784) 1 Wils 232   *418*

Rickards *v* Lothian [1913] AC 263   *264, 271*

Rigby *v* Chief Constable of Northamptonshire [1985] 1 WLR 1242; [1985] 2 All ER 985   *110, 331*

Rimmer *v* Liverpool City Council [1984] 1 All ER 930   *228*

Roandale *v* Metropolitan Police Commissioner [1979] Crim LR 254 CA   *403*

Roberts *v* Johnstone [1987] QB 878   *382, 383*

Roberts *v* Ramsbottom [1980] 1 All ER 7   *119*

Roberts *v* Roberts (1864) 5 B & S 384   *287*

Robertson *v* Ridley [1989] 2 All ER 474   *12*

Robinson *v* Balmain Ferry Co Ltd [1910] AC 295   *320, 321*

Robinson *v* Kilvert (1889) 41 Ch D 88   *237*

Robinson *v* Post Office [1974] 1 WLR 1176   *147*

Robson *v* Hallett [1967] 2 QB 393   *209, 326, 330*

Roe *v* Minister of Health [1954] 2 QB 66   *120*

Roles *v* Nathan [1963] 1 WLR 1117   *216, 217*

Rondel *v* Worsley [1969] 1 AC 191   *106, 107, 108*

Rookes *v* Barnard [1964] AC 1129   *355, 362, 363, 364, 373*

Rose *v* Miles (1815) 4 M & S 101   *257*

Rose *v* Plenty [1976] 1 WLR 141   *31, 34*

Roshmer *v* Polsue and Alfieri Ltd [1906] 1 Ch 234   *237*

Ross *v* Caunters [1980] Ch 297   *2, 9, 63, 69, 71, 74, 91, 92, 108, 109, 394*

Rouse *v* Squires [1973] QB 889   *156*

Rowling *v* Takaro Properties [1988] AC 473   *114, 115, 116*

Royal Aquarium and Summer and Winter Garden Society *v* Parkinson [1892] 1 QB 431   *299*

Royal Bank Trust Co (Trinidad) Ltd *v* Pampellonne [1987] 1 Lloyd's Rep 218   *83*

Ryeford Homes *v* Sevenoaks District Council (1989) 16 Con LR 75   *253, 269*

Rylands *v* Fletcher (1868) LR 3 HL 330; affirming (1866) 1 LR 1 Ex 265   *40, 153, 161, 261–271, 272, 273, 275*

SCM (United Kingdom) Ltd v WJ Whittall and Son Ltd [1970] 1 QB 137; [1970] 1 WLR 1017 *237*

Saif Ali v Sydney Mitchell & Co Ltd [1980] AC 198 *106*

St Anne's Well Brewery Co v Roberts (1928) 140 LT 1 *245*

St Helens Smelting Co v Tipping (1865) 11 HL 642 *235, 237*

Salmon v Seafarer Restaurants Ltd [1983] 3 All ER 729 *216*

Salsbury v Woodland [1970] 1 QB 324 *41*

Saunders v Edwards [1987] 1 WLR 1186 *398*

Savile v Roberts (1698) 1 Ld Raym 374 *419*

Sawyer v H and G Simonds Ltd (1966) 197 EG 877 *214*

Sayers v Harlow UDC [1958] 1 WLR 623 *166*

Scala Ballroom (Wolverhampton) Ltd v Ratcliffe [1958] 1 WLR 1057 *357*

Schloendorff v Society of New York Hospital (1914) 211 NY 125 *314*

Schneider v Eisovitch [1960] 2 QB 430 *96*

Scott v London and St Katherine Docks Co (1865) 3 H & C 596 *130, 132*

Scott v Shepherd (1733) 2 Wm Bl 892 *155, 312*

Secretary of State for Defence v Guardian Newspapers [1985] AC 339; [1984] Ch 156 *403*

Sedleigh-Denfield v O'Callaghan [1940] AC 880 *241, 242, 245*

Selvanayagam v University of the West Indies [1983] 1 All ER 824 *394*

Sharpe v ET Sweeting & Sons [1963] 1 WLR 665 *197*

Shelfer v City of London Electric Lighting Co Ltd [1895] 1 Ch 287 *250, 254*

Sheppard v Glossop Corporation [1921] 3 KB 132 *112*

Shiffman v Order of St John [1936] 1 All ER 557 *269*

Sidaway v Bethlem Royal Hospital Governors [1985] AC 871 *128, 129, 315*

Sim v Stretch [1936] 2 All ER 1237 *289*

Simaan General Contracting Co v Pilkington Glass Ltd (No 2) [1988] QB 758; [1988] 2 WLR 761 *62, 84, 86*

Simkiss v Rhondda Borough Council (1983) 81 LGR 460 *215*

Simms v Leigh Rugby FC [1969] 2 All ER 923 *219*

Sirros v Moore [1975] QB 118 *14*

Six Carpenters' Case, The (1610) 8 Co Rep 146a *328*

Slim v Daily Telegraph Ltd [1968] 2 QB 157 *292, 305*

Slipper v British Broadcasting Corporation [1990] 3 WLR 967 *295*

Smith v Austin Lifts Ltd [1959] 1 WLR 100 *177*

Smith v Baker [1891] AC 325 *171, 189, 194*

Smith v Chadwick (1884) 9 App Cas 187 *339*

Smith v Crossley Brothers Ltd (1951) 95 Sol Jo 655 *189*

Smith v Eric S Bush (a firm) [1990] 1 AC 831; [1989] 2 WLR 790 *61, 66, 79, 80, 81, 82, 90, 93*

Smith v Jenkins (1970) 119 CLR 397 *398*

Smith v Kenrick (1849) 7 CB 515 *263*

Smith v Land and House Property Corporation (1884) 28 Ch D 7 *336*

Smith *v* Leech, Brain and Co [1962] 2 QB 405   *147*

Smith *v* Littlewoods Organisation Ltd [1987] AC 241   *56, 57, 58, 60, 157*

Smith *v* Stages [1989] AC 928; [1989] 2 WLR 529   *33*

Smith *v* Stone (1647) Style 65   *329*

Smithies *v* National Association of Operative Plasterers [1909] 1 KB 310   *362*

Smith Kline & French Laboratories Ltd *v* Long [1989] 1 WLR 1   *340*

Smoker *v* London Fire and Civil Defence Authority [1991] 2 All ER 449   *384*

Sochacki *v* Sas [1947] 1 All ER 344   *275*

Somasundaram *v* M Julius Melchior & Co [1989] 1 All ER 129   *106*

Sorrell *v* Smith [1925] AC 700   *355*

South Hetton Coal Co Ltd *v* North-Eastern News Association Ltd [1894] 1 QB 133
    303

Southern Portland Cement Ltd *v* Cooper [1974] AC 623   *222*

Southport Corporation *v* Esso Petroleum Co [1954] QB 182; [1953] 3 WLR 773
    240

South Staffordshire Water Co *v* Sharman [1896] 2 QB 44   *415*

South Wales Miners' Federation *v* Glamorgan Coal Co [1905] AC 239   *362*

Southwark LBC *v* Williams [1971] Ch 734   *399*

Spartan Steel and Alloys Ltd *v* Martin & Co (Contractors) Ltd [1973] QB 27   *53,
    66, 75*

Spicer *v* Smee [1946] 1 All ER 489   *273*

Spittle *v* Bunney [1988] 3 All ER 1031   *391*

Spring *v* Guardian Assurance plc [1993] 2 All ER 273   *63, 81, 300, 343*

Square Grip Reinforcement Co Ltd *v* MacDonald 1968 SLT 65   *357*

Stanley *v* Powell [1891] 1 QB 86   *312*

Stanley *v* Saddique [1991] 2 WLR 459   *392*

Stansbie *v* Troman [1948] 2 KB 48   *57*

Stapley *v* Gypsum Mines Ltd [1953] AC 663   *167*

Stephen, Harold Ltd *v* Post Office [1977] 1 WLR 1172   *403*

Stephens *v* Anglian Water Authority [1988] 2 WLR 333; [1987] 1 WLR 1381   *65,
    66*

Stephens *v* Myers (1830) 4 C & P 349   *318*

Stevens *v* Brodribb Sawmilling Co Pty Ltd (1986) 160 CLR 16   *41, 42*

Stevenson, Jordan and Harrison Ltd *v* MacDonald [1952] 1 TLR 101   *25*

Stone *v* Taffe [1974] 1 WLR 1575   *211, 220*

Stovin *v* Wise (1994) The Times 8 March   *260*

Storey *v* Ashton (1869) LR 4 QB 476   *32, 33*

Stratford (JT) & Sons Ltd *v* Lindley [1965] AC 269   *358, 359, 364, 365*

Stubbings *v* Webb [1993] 2 WLR 120   *400*

Stuart *v* Bell [1891] 2 QB 341   *302*

Sturges *v* Bridgman (1879) 11 Ch D 852   *237, 246, 248*

Summers (John) & Sons Ltd *v* Frost [1955] AC 740   *185*

Sun Life Assurance Co of Canada *v* WH Smith & Son Ltd (1934) 150 LT 211   *295*

Sunbolf v Alford (1838) 3 M & W 248   *321*

Sutcliffe v Pressdram [1990] 1 All ER 269   *307, 308*

Sutcliffe v Thackrah [1974] AC 727   *14*

Sutherland Shire Council v Heyman (1985) 60 ALR 1   *49, 50, 72*

Swordheath Properties Ltd v Tabet [1979] 1 All ER 240   *332*

Szalantnay-Stacho v Fink [1946] 1 All ER 303   *200*

T v Surrey County Council [1994] NLJ 319   *184*

Taff Vale Railway Co v Amalgamated Society of Railway Servants [1901] AC 426
    13

Taittinger v Albev Ltd (1993) The Times 26 June   *347*

Targett v Torfaen Borough Council [1992] 3 All ER 27   *228*

Tarry v Ashton (1876) 1 QBD 314   *41, 88, 259*

Tate & Lyle Industries Ltd v Greater London Council [1983] 1 All ER 1159   *84*

Taylor v O'Connor [1971] AC 115   *376, 377*

Telnikoff v Matusevitch [1992] 2 AC 343   *304, 305*

Tennant v Earl of Glasgow (1864) 2 M (HL) 22   *269*

Tetley v Chitty [1986] 1 All ER 663   *244*

Thackwell v Barclays Bank plc [1986] 3 All ER 676; [1986] 1 All ER 676   *398, 408*

Thake v Maurice [1986] QB 669; [1984] 2 All ER 513   *105*

Theaker v Richardson [1962] 1 WLR 151   *294*

Thomas v Bradbury Agnew [1906] 2 KB 627   *306*

Thomas v British Railways Board [1976] QB 912   *211*

Thomas v NUM (S Wales Area) [1985] 2 All ER 1   *258*

Thomas v Sorrell (1672) Vaughan 330   *330*

Thompson v Clive Alexander & Partners (1992) 28 Con LR 49   *230*

Thompson v Smiths Shiprepairers (North Shields) Ltd [1984] 1 All ER 881   *191*

Thompson v T Lohan (Plant Hire) Ltd [1987] 2 All ER 631   *27*

Thomson v Cremin [1956] 1 WLR 103   *217*

Thomson (DC) & Co Ltd v Deakin [1952] Ch 646   *357, 358, 361*

Thornton v Kirklees Metropolitan Borough Council [1979] QB 626   *181*

Thurston v Todd [1965] NSWLR 1158   *377, 379*

Tillet v Ward (1882) 10 QBD 17   *283*

Tinsley v Dudley [1951] 2 KB 18   *221*

Tinsley v Milligan [1993] 3 WLR 126; [1992] Ch 310   *399*

Titchener v British Railways Board [1983] 1 WLR 1427   *176*

Tobin v R (1864) 16 CBNS 310   *11*

Tolley v JS Fry & Sons Ltd [1931] AC 333   *291, 292*

Topp v London County Bus (South West) Ltd [1993] 3 All ER 448   *58*

Torquay Hotels Co Ltd v Cousins [1969] 2 Ch 106   *360, 361, 365*

Tremain v Pike [1969] 1 WLR 1556   *149*

Tremayne v Hill [1987] RTR 131   *162*

'Truth' (NZ) Ltd v Holloway [1960] 1 WLR 997   *296*

Tuberville v Savage (1669) 1 Mod Rep 3   *317, 318*
Twine v Bean's Express Ltd [1946] 1 All ER 202; (1946) 62 TLR 458   *28, 31*

Udale v Bloomsbury AHA [1983] 1 WLR 1098   *105*
Union Transport Finance v British Car Auctions Ltd [1978] 2 All ER 385   *410*
Universe Tankships of Monrovia v International Transport Workers Federation
    [1983] 1 AC 366   *364*

Vacwell Engineering v BDH Chemicals Ltd [1971] 1 QB 88   *150*
Vaughan v Taff Vale Railway Co (1860) 5 H & N 679   *275*
Victorian Railway Commissioners v Coultas (1888) 13 App Cas 222   *95*
Videan v British Transport Commission [1963] 2 QB 650   *221*
Vizetelly v Mudie's Select Library Ltd [1900] 2 QB 170   *296*

W v Meah and D v Meah [1986] 1 All ER 935   *372*
Wagon Mound (No 1), The; see Overseas Tankship (UK) v Morts Dock
    Engineering Co
Wagon Mound (No 2), The; see Overseas Tankship (UK) Ltd v Miller Steamship
    Co Pty Ltd
Wales v Wadham [1977] 1 WLR 199   *335*
Walker v Baird [1892] AC 491   *14*
Wallace v Newton [1982] 1 WLR 375   *280*
Walpole v Partridge & Wilson [1993] 3 WLR 1093   *106*
Walters v W H Smith Ltd [1914] 1 KB 595   *321*
Ward v London County Council [1938] 2 All ER 341   *122*
Ward v Tesco Stores Ltd [1976] 1 WLR 810   *131*
Warren v Henley's Ltd [1948] 2 All ER 935   *29, 35*
Watkins v Lee (1830) 5 M & W 270   *418*
Watson v Wilmott [1990] 3 WLR 1103   *393*
Watt v Hertfordshire County Council [1954] 1 WLR 835   *122*
Watt v Longsden [1930] 1 KB 130   *302*
Watts v Aldington (1993) The Times 16 December   *18*
Watts v Lowcur Ltd QBD 11 February 1988   *192, 193*
Wauchope v Mordecai [1970] 1 WLR 317   *129*
Wear Breeze, The [1969] 1 QB 219   *64*
Webb v Times Publishing Co [1960] 2 QB 535   *301*
Weldon v Home Office [1990] 3 WLR 465   *320*
Weller & Co v Foot and Mouth Disease Research Institute [1966] 1 QB 569   *269*
Welsh v Chief Constable of the Merseyside Police [1993] 1 All ER 692   *11, 107*
Wenman v Ash (1853) 13 CB 836   *294*
Wennhak v Morgan (1888) 20 QBD 635   *294*
Wentworth v Wiltshire County Council [1993] 2 WLR 175   *182, 260*
West v Bristol Tramways Co [1908] 2 KB 14   *267*

West (H) & Son Ltd *v* Shepherd [1964] AC 326   *388*
West London Commercial Bank Ltd *v* Kitson (1884) 13 QBD 360   *337*
West Wiltshire District Council *v* Pugh [1993] NLJ 546   *61, 184*
Westripp *v* Baldock [1938] 2 All ER 799   *325*
Westwood *v* Post Office [1974] AC 1   *186*
Whatman *v* Pearson (1868) LR 3 CP 422   *32*
Wheat *v* E Lacon & Co Ltd [1966] AC 552   *207, 208*
Wheeler *v* Copas [1981] 3 All ER 405   *213*
White *v* Blackmore [1972] 2 QB 651   *225, 226*
White *v* Holbrook Precision Castings Ltd [1985] IRLR 215   *194*
White *v* Jones [1993] 3 WLR 730   *63, 91, 92*
White *v* Mellin [1895] AC 154   *342*
White *v* St Albans City and District Council (1990) The Times 12 March   *223*
White Hudson & Co Ltd *v* Asian Organisation Ltd [1964] 1 WLR 1466   *346*
Whitehouse *v* Jordan [1981] 1 WLR 246 (HL); [1980] 1 All ER 650 (CA)   *127*
Wieland *v* Cyril Lord Carpets [1969] 3 All ER 1006   *154*
Wigg *v* British Railways Board (1986) The Times 4 February   *99*
Wilkinson *v* Downton [1897] 2 QB 57   *311, 322*
Wilks *v* Cheltenham Cycle Club [1971] 1 WLR 668   *126, 178*
Williams *v* A & W Hemphill Ltd 1966 SLT 259   *32, 33*
Williams *v* Reason [1988] 1 All ER 262   *297*
Willis *v* British Car Auctions [1978] 1 WLR 438   *405*
Wilsher *v* Essex Area Health Authority [1988] AC 1074; [1988] 1 All ER 871; [1987]
    2 WLR 425   *23, 119, 127, 137, 138, 139, 140*
Wilson *v* Lombank Ltd [1963] 1 WLR 1294   *404, 409*
Willson *v* Ministry of Defence [1991] 1 All ER 638   *378*
Wilson *v* Pringle [1987] QB 237; [1986] 2 All ER 440   *313, 314, 315, 316, 378,*
    404
Wilsons and Clyde Coal Co *v* English [1938] AC 57   *41*
Wimpey (George) and Co Ltd *v* British Overseas Aircraft Corporation [1955] AC
    169   *19, 20*
Winkfield, The [1902] P 42   *411, 414*
Winkworth *v* Christie, Manson & Woods [1980] Ch 496   *410*
Winterbottom *v* Wright (1842) 10 M & W 109   *45*
Wise *v* Kaye [1962] 1 QB 638   *387*
With *v* O'Flanagan [1936] Ch 575   *335*
Withers *v* Perry Chain Co [1961] 1 WLR 1314   *121*
Wood *v* Bentall Simplex Ltd (1992) The Times 3 March   *391*
Wood *v* The Law Society (1993) The Times 30 July   *66*
Woodward *v* Mayor of Hastings [1945] KB 174   *218*
Wooldridge *v* Sumner [1963] 2 QB 43   *125, 126, 176, 178*
Woollins *v* British Celanese Ltd (1966) 110 SJ 686   *216, 217*
Wright *v* British Railways Board [1983] 2 AC 773   *390*

Wright *v* Lodge and Shepherd [1993] 4 AllER 299   *156*
Wringe *v* Cohen [1940] 1 KB 229   *88, 245, 259*

X *v* Bedfordshire County Council [1993] NLJ 1783   *184*

Yachuk *v* Oliver Blais Co Ltd [1949] AC 386   *164*
Yewens *v* Noakes (1880) 6 QBD 530   *24*
Yorkshire Dale Steamship Co Ltd *v* Minister of War Transport [1942] AC 691
    136
Young and Woods *v* West [1980] IRLR 201   *25*
Youssoupoff *v* Metro-Goldwyn-Mayer (1934) 50 TLR 581   *287, 288, 289*
Yuen Kun Yeu *v* Attorney-General of Hong Kong [1988] AC 175   *48, 51, 53, 55,*
    59, 60, 107

Table of Statutes

Administration of Justice Act 1982
    s1(1)   *387, 389*
    s4(2)   *390*
    s5   *382*
    s6   *378*
Animals Act 1971   *276, 277, 278, 333*
    s1(1)   *277, 282*
    s2   *281, 282*
    s2(1)   *277*
    s2(2)   *279, 280, 281, 282*
    s3   *284*
    s4   *283, 284*
    s4(1)   *282, 283*
    s4(2)   *283*
    s5   *281*
    s5(1)   *281, 283*
    s5(2)   *174, 281*
    s5(3)   *282*
    s5(5)   *283*
    s5(6)   *284*
    s6(2)   *278, 279*
    s6(3)   *278*
    s6(4)   *278*
    s6(5)   *282*
    s7   *282, 283*
    s7(3)   *283*
    s7(5)   *283*
    s8(1)   *284*
    s8(2)   *284*
    s9   *284*
    s9(2)   *284*
    s9(3)   *284*
    s10   *281, 283*
    s11   *278, 280, 282, 283, 284*

Betting and Lotteries Act 1934
    s11(2)   *184*

Bill of Rights Act 1688   *298*
Broadcasting Act 1990
    s116   *287*
    s166   *301*
    s201   *287*

Civil Aviation Act 1982
    s76(1)   *328*
    s76(2)   *328*
Civil Evidence Act 1968
    s11   *130*
    s11(1)   *129*
    s13   *297*
Civil Liability (Contribution) Act 1978
    12
    s1   *18*
    s1(1)   *18, 36*
    s1(2)   *19*
    s1(3)   *19, 20*
    s1(4)   *20*
    s1(5)   *20*
    s1(6)   *19*
    s2   *18*
    s2(1)   *20*
    s2(2)   *20*
    s2(3)   *21*
    s3   *17*
    s4   *18*
Clean Air Act 1956   *233, 255*
Clean Air Act 1968   *233*
Companies Act 1985
    s35   *12*
Companies Act 1989   *12*
Congenital Disabilities (Civil Liability)
    Act 1976   *10, 61, 104*
    s1   *104*
    s1(3)   *10*

Congenital Disabilities (Civil Liability)
  Act 1976 (*contd.*)
    s4(5)   *11, 104*
Consumer Protection Act 1987   *196,
  200, 201, 202, 203, 262*
    s1(2)   *200, 201*
    s1(3)   *200*
    s2(1)   *200, 201, 204*
    s2(2)   *200*
    s2(3)   *201*
    s2(4)   *201*
    s2(5)   *201*
    s3(1)   *201*
    s3(2)   *202*
    s4   *202*
    s4(1)   *202*
    s4(2)   *202*
    s5(1)   *203*
    s5(2)   *203*
    s5(3)   *203*
    s5(4)   *203*
    s7   *204*
    s45(1)   *201*
    s46(4)   *201*
Control of Pollution Act 1974   *233,
  256*
Copyright Act 1956
    s21(3)   *180*
Courts and Legal Services Act 1990
    s8(1)   *307*
    s8(2)   *307*
    s62   *106*
Criminal Justice Act 1988
    ss 108–117   *323*
    s109(1)   *323*
    s109(3)   *323*
Criminal Law Act 1977
    ss6–10   *324*
Crown Proceedings Act 1947   *11*
    s2(5)   *11*
    s10   *11*
    s40(1)   *11*

Defamation Act 1952
    s2   *288*
    s3   *344*
    s4   *293, 306, 310*
    s4(5)   *293*
    s5   *297*
    s6   *305*
    s7   *301*
    s16   *287*
Defective Premises Act 1972   *60,
  201, 228, 230*
    s1   *231*
    s1(1)   *230*
    s1(2)   *230*
    s2   *231*
    s2(5)   *231*
    s3   *228*
    s3(2)   *229*
    s4   *229*
    s4(1)   *229*
    s4(2)   *229*
    s4(3)   *229*
    s4(4)   *229*

Employers' Liability Act 1880   *67*
Employers' Liability (Compulsory
  Insurance) Act 1969   *188*
    s1   *188*
Employers' Liability (Defective
  Equipment) Act 1969   *190*
    s1(1)   *190*
    s1(3)   *190*
Employment Act 1980
    s16   *259*
    s17   *367*

Factories Act 1961   *40, 165, 185*
    s14   *165, 185, 186*
Factory and Workshop Act 1878
  165, 183
Fair Trading Act 1973   *350*
Fatal Accidents Act 1976   *380, 384,
  390*

Fatal Accidents Act 1976 (*contd.*)
 s1(1) *390*
 s1(2) *390*
 s1(4) *390*
 s3(3) *391*
 s4 *391,392*
Fires Prevention (Metropolis) Act 1774
272, 274, 275
 s86 *274*

Guard Dogs Act 1975 *179, 282*
 s1(1) *281*
Gulf Oil Refining Act 1965 *246*

Health and Safety at Work Act 1974
188
 s2 *188*
Highways Act 1980 *211, 260*
 s41 *260*
 s58 *260*
 s58(1) *260*
 s58(2) *260*
Highways (Miscellaneous Provisions)
 Act 1961 *211, 260*
Housing (Homeless Persons) Act 1977
181

Infant Life (Preservation) Act 1929
105
 s1 *105*

Latent Damage Act 1986 *401, 231,*
400
Law Reform (Contributory Negligence)
 Act 1945 *159, 161, 167, 168, 220,*
247
 s1 *317*
 s1(1) *161, 168*
 s4(1) *161, 162*
Law Reform (Husband and Wife) Act
 1962 *11*
 s1(2) *11*

Law Reform (Married Women and
 Tortfeasors) Act 1935
 s6 *17*
 s6(1) *18*
Law Reform (Miscellaneous Provisions)
 Act 1934
 s1(1) *390*
Law Reform (Personal Injuries) Act
 1948
 s1 *187*
 s2 *383, 384*
 s2(4) *382*
Libel Act 1843
 s2 *306*
Libel Amendment Act 1888
 s3 *299*
Limitation Act 1939 *312*
Limitation Act 1980 *414*
 s2 *400*
 s11(1) *400*
 s11(4) *400*
 s11(5) *400*
 s14 *400*
 s33 *400*

Maritime Conventions Act 1911
 s1(1) *161*
Married Women's Property Act 1882
 s17 *11*
Medicines Act 1968
 s133 *179*
Misrepresentation Act 1967
 s2 *337*
Motor Cars (Use and Construction)
 Order 1904 *182*

National Parks and Access to the
 Countryside Act 1949
 s60 *223*
Noise Abatement Act 1960 *255*
Nuclear Installations Act 1965 *271*

Occupiers' Liability Act 1957   *12,*
  206, 207, 209, 210, 213, 219, 220,
  221, 225, 226, 227, 228, 266
    s1(1)   *206*
    s1(2)   *207, 209*
    s1(3)   *213, 221*
    s2(1)   *213, 225, 227*
    s2(2)   *213, 214*
    s2(3)   *215, 216, 219*
    s2(4)   *216, 217, 218, 225*
    s2(5)   *174, 219, 225*
    s2(6)   *211*
    s3   *220, 225*
    s3(2)   *220*
    s5   *220*
Occupiers' Liability Act 1984   *179,*
  206, 210, 221, 223, 224, 226, 227,
  228, 266
    s1(1)   *210*
    s1(3)   *223, 224*
    s1(4)   *224*
    s1(5)   *224*
    s1(6)   *225*
    s1(7)   *210*
    s1(8)   *225*
    s1(9)   *225*
    s2   *226*
Occupiers' Liability (Scotland) Act
  1960   *224*
Offices, Shops and Railway Premises
  Act 1963   *186*

Parliamentary Papers Act 1840   *298*
    s3   *300*
Partnership Act 1890
    s10   *37*
    s12   *38*
Police and Criminal Evidence Act 1984
  321, 330
    s24(4)   *321*
    s24(5)   *321*
    s24(6)   *321*

Post Office Act 1969
    s29   *14*
Powers of Criminal Courts Act 1973
  322
    s35   *384*
Prison Act 1952   *184*
    s12   *320*
Public Health Act 1936   *233, 255*

Race Relations Act 1976
    s70   *294*
Railway Fires Act 1905   *275*
Railway Fires Act 1923   *275*
Rehabilitation of Offenders Act 1974
  297
    s8(3)   *297*
    s8(5)   *297*
Rent Act 1965   *183*
Road Traffic Act 1930   *183*
Road Traffic Act 1972
    s33A   *163*
    s148(3)   *175, 177*

Sale of Goods Act 1979   *8, 197*
Slander of Women Act 1891   *288*
Social Security Act 1975   *188*
Social Security Act 1989
    s22   *383*
    Schedule 4   *384*
Social Security Administration Act
  1992
    s81(3)   *384*
    s82   *383, 384*
    s82(1)   *383*
    s85   *384*
Supreme Court Act 1981
    s32A   *378*
    s35A   *389*
    s37   *395*
    s50   *254*

Theatres Act 1968
    s4   *287*

Theatres Act 1968 (*contd.*)
    s7 *287*
Theft Act 1968   *211*
Torts (Interference with Goods) Act
    1977   *403, 407, 408*
    s1 *408*
    s2(1) *407*
    s2(2) *407*
    s3 *407*
    s3(2) *413*
    s3(3) *414*
    s3(4–8) *414*
    s4 *407*
    s5 *407*
    s5(1) *414*
    s5(2) *414*
    s5(3) *414*
    s5(4) *414*
    s5(5) *414*
    s6 *408, 413*
    s6(1) *413*
    s6(2) *413*
    s6(3) *413*
    s6(4) *413*
    s7 *407, 412*
    s7(1) *412*
    s7(2) *412*
    s7(3) *412, 414*
    s7(4) *412*
    s8 *408, 409, 411, 412, 414*
    s8(1) *411*
    s9 *408*

Torts (Interference with Goods) Act
    1977 (*contd.*)
    s10 *404, 406, 408*
    s11(1) *404, 406, 408*
    s11(2) *405*
    s11(3) *405*
    s12 *408*
    s13 *408*
    Schedule 1 *408*
Trade Union Act 1984   *367*
Trade Union and Labour Relations Act
    1974
    s2(1) *13*
    s13 *368*
    s13(1) *367*
    s13(3) *368*
    s13(4) *367*
    s15 *259*

Unfair Contract Terms Act 1977   *27,
    173, 177, 226*
    s1 *27, 226*
    s1(1) *27, 177, 226*
    s1(3) *177, 226*
    s2 *27, 177*
    s2(1) *27, 28, 177, 178, 226*
    s2(2) *27, 28, 79, 177, 178*
    s2(3) *178*
    s11 *177*
    s13 *27, 177*
    s14 *226*

Workmen's Compensation Act 1897
    188

1

Introduction

1.1 Introduction

1.2 Current difficulties in the law of tort

1.3 The interests protected

1.4 Tort and other legal subjects

1.1 Introduction

The law of tort is an exciting and fascinating subject. It is also a subject of some considerable difficulty and one which demands considerable legal skills. It is customary to commence a book on the law of tort by attempting to frame a definition of tort, but such an approach will not be adopted here because these attempts are either so vague as to be meaningless or they are too restrictive and only apply to certain torts with the result that they are downright misleading. All that will be said at this stage is that the word tort (or the Latin equivalent 'tortum') is derived from the concept of a wrong.

Instead this chapter will commence by highlighting some of the difficult issues current in tort law, then it will proceed to identify some of the interests protected by the law of tort and it will conclude by distinguishing between tort and other related legal subjects.

1.2 Current difficulties in the law of tort

There are three current difficulties in the law of tort which are worthy of some discussion. The first difficulty lies in finding acceptable control devices for the tort of negligence. This is an issue which has taxed both the judiciary and academics alike. The test laid down by the House of Lords in the case of *Anns v Merton London Borough Council* [1978] AC 728 (discussed further in chapter 6) seemed to herald the prospect of a considerable widening of the ambit of liability in negligence. In retrospect the late 1970s and the early 1980s was a period of considerable expansion for the tort of negligence. By contrast the latter half of the 1980s and the early part of the 1990s has been a period of restriction when the judiciary have refused to extend the tort of negligence in the way that was done towards the end of the 1970s. This process of restriction reached its height in *Murphy* v *Brentwood District Council* [1991] 1 AC 398 when the House of Lords overruled its own decision in *Anns*. There can be no area of law which has undergone such upheaval in recent years as has been the case with the tort of negligence.

This difficulty of drawing the line between situations where a duty of care is owed and situations where no duty is owed is an issue with which all students of the law of tort must grapple. Nor is the issue a mere academic quibble. The expansion of the law of tort in cases such as *Ross* v *Caunters* [1980] Ch 297 and *Junior Books Ltd* v *The Veitchi Co Ltd* [1983] 1 AC 520 (discussed further in chapter 7) took tort into areas which were traditionally the domain of the law of contract and these cases posed fundamental questions about the relationship between tort and contract. In particular, these cases seemed to constitute a fundamental attack upon the doctrine of privity of contract. Indeed, in *Junior Books* Lord Roskill opined that

> 'Today the proper control lies not in asking whether the proper remedy should lie in contract ... or tort ... but in the first instance in establishing the relevant principles and then in deciding whether the particular case falls within or without those principles.'

Yet the House of Lords today has chosen to re-emphasise the distinction between contract and tort. Thus, in *D & F Estates* v *Church Commissioners for England* [1989] AC 177 Lord Bridge held that a claim for the cost of repairing a defect in the product itself lay, if at all, in contract and not in tort. For him, the division between contract and tort was fundamental; it was no mere label to be applied after identifying the relevant, underlying principle. This issue of the relationship between tort and contract is one to which we shall return at various stages of the book.

The second current difficulty in the law of tort lies in ascertaining the function which lies behind the corpus of rules that make up the law of tort. *Three* principal functions may be discerned. The first is to compensate the victims of civil wrongs. Here the emphasis is upon compensation rather than upon punishment. A clear expression of this policy can be seen in the judgment of Lord Reid in *Cassell* v *Broome* [1972] AC 1027. In this case the plaintiff sought, inter alia, exemplary damages in respect of a defamatory statement published about him by the defendants. The function of exemplary damages is to punish the defendant for the wrong which he has done rather than to compensate the plaintiff for the damage done to him. The House of Lords took the opportunity to make some general observations about the availability of exemplary damages in tort. Lord Reid said that tort damages have a compensatory aim and that to grant a plaintiff an award of exemplary damages against the defendants was to confuse the function of the civil law, which was to 'compensate', with that of the criminal law, which was to 'inflict deterrent and punitive penalties'. He said that to allow the punishment of defendants in tort was to 'contravene almost every principle which has been evolved for the protection of offenders'. For example, there was no definition of the offence except that the defendant's conduct must be oppressive, the punishment was left to the jury rather than to an experienced judge, there was no limit on the punishment which could be handed out except that it must not be unreasonable and there was no effective appeal against sentence. On the other hand Lord Wilberforce took the view that it 'cannot lightly be taken for granted ... that the purpose of the law of tort is compensation' or that there is something anomalous about including within an award of damages at civil law a punitive element. He also noted that, at a practical level, the majority conceded that aggravated damages were available in a wider range of circumstances than exemplary damages and he argued that it was not clear exactly where the boundary line between exemplary and aggravated damages lay, so, he claimed, it was better to concede that exemplary damages were available rather than confuse juries by telling them they could award aggravated damages but not exemplary damages (see further 30.2).

The second principal function of the law of tort, it is said, is to deter people from committing wrongs which inflict damage upon other people or their property. In essence it teaches people that wrongful acts do not pay and, as a consequence, people will act more carefully. Certainly there are cases where the law of tort can be said to have a deterrent effect. For example the tort of defamation has an impact upon publishers and upon the conduct of the national press. The expansion of the tort of negligence has encouraged governing bodies of professions, such as the accountancy profession, to draw up codes of practice or statements of standard practice to guide their members as to what is expected of them by the tort of negligence and by the public at large. Despite these developments there are a number of criticisms which have been levelled against the idea that tort has a deterrent function.

The first such criticism is that a very general instruction, such as the duty to take reasonable care, is so vague that it has little impact upon people's standard of behaviour. The second criticism is that, in practice, the damages are usually paid by an insurer, which significantly reduces the deterrent effect on the tortfeasor (that is the person who commits the tort) because he passes on the bill to his insurer. It is true that the passing on of the bill may lead to some increased cost to the tortfeasor, in the form of higher premiums (for example, losing a no-claims bonus) but the link between higher premiums and accident prevention is rather tenuous. Thirdly, as we shall see in chapter 9, the standard of care demanded of a particular defendant may be so high that it is impossible for him to attain it. Where this is the case the law of tort does not have a deterrent effect because the tortfeasor cannot aspire to the standards required of him.

Nevertheless it is true to say that there has been renewed interest in the idea that deterrence is a function of the law of tort. This interest has largely come from American scholars, some of whom are economists, who have argued that tort law aims, or should aim, to reduce accident costs and the costs of accident prevention (see, in particular, Calabresi *The Cost of Accidents* (1970)). This theory is known as general deterrence. The essence of this argument is that the cost of accidents should be imposed on those who take part in the accident-causing activity and so that activity must bear the cost to society of carrying out that activity (for a critique of this theory see Atiyah *Accidents, Compensation and the Law* chapter 24).

Yet this dichotomy between compensation and punishment (or deterrence) may be said to be a false one because it ignores a third purpose of the law of tort, which is to prevent unjust enrichment. There are a group of cases where the remedy which has been granted to the plaintiff has sought to strip the defendant of the gain that he has made at the expense of the plaintiff as a result of the commission of a wrong or a tort. One case which is useful to consider here is *Reading* v *Attorney-General* [1951] AC 507. Sergeant Reading was in the habit of travelling on lorries in Egypt while wearing his army uniform. The reason for his doing so was to enable smugglers to get their lorries carrying illicit goods past army checkpoints. He was paid a considerable sum of money for his participation in the smuggling. After he had been caught the question arose as to who was entitled to the gains which Sergeant Reading had made; was it himself or the Crown? The House of Lords held that the Crown were entitled to the proceeds of Sergeant Reading's wrongdoing. The aim of the award of damages was therefore to deprive the defendant of his unjust enrichment and was measured, not by reference to the *loss* to the plaintiff, but by reference to the *gain* to the defendant. These damages may be called restitutionary damages. There is a clear difference here between the sum awarded and the sum which would have been awarded had the Crown sued for compensation for its loss because it is clear that the Crown had suffered no loss. It could be argued that the aim of the award of damages was to deter such conduct in the future but it is suggested that deterrence can be distinguished from the prevention of unjust enrichment. Where the aim of an award of damages is to strip the defendant of his unjust enrichment, the sum recoverable is measured definitively by the gain which the defendant has made. But, when the aim of the award of damages is to deter, the amount of the gain made by the defendant is only one factor to which the court will have regard; the amount awarded may therefore exceed the gain which the defendant has made as a result of his tort. There are a number of cases where restitutionary damages have been awarded (see generally Birks *An Introduction to the Law of Restitution* chapter X). It is beyond the scope of our present discussion to consider when restitutionary damages may be awarded by a court. But it should not be forgotten that tort is not definitively about compensation for loss; it may also be about the reversal of unjust enrichments.

The third difficulty relates to the scope of the law of tort. For example, is breach of confidence a tort? What about other equitable wrongs? One problem which we have here is an historical one; namely that our present law of tort is almost completely derived from actions at law, not actions in equity. Wrongdoing in equity is often discussed in a course on the law of trusts under the heading of constructive trusts. Yet if we say, as we do, that 'tort' simply means 'a wrong' then it is very difficult to explain why these equitable wrongs are excluded from our tort syllabus. If our subject were to be called the law of wrongs, we would be compelled to consider these equity cases. Can we continue to allow the historical division between equity and law to play tricks on us to the extent that it has fooled us into locating equitable wrongs in a course which has nothing to do with wrongs but with the institution of a trust? It is suggested that this will become a matter of hot debate in years to come.

The fourth, and final, issue of difficulty in tort law concerns the future of the law of tort. Approximately 75 per cent of cases which are set down for a hearing in the Queen's Bench Division are personal injury cases. However, of these cases, only about 1 per cent actually come to a hearing. The rest are settled out of court or are withdrawn. Of course in all these cases the plaintiff must prove that the defendant was negligent before he can recover. This raises the extremely important question of why it is necessary for the plaintiff to prove that the defendant was at fault before he can recover. The following example may help us to consider the issue.

Patrick, aged 42 and a father of four children, suffered a major heart attack in 1986 which left him an invalid who would be unable to work for the rest of his life. Patrick was a professor earning £25,000 per year. He is unable to look after himself and his wife has had to give up work to look after him.

Glanville, aged 45 and also a father of four children, was severely injured in a car crash caused by Brian, whose consciousness had been impaired by a stroke as he was driving. Glanville was so seriously injured that he will never return to work as an executive with a company which publishes law books. He is also unable to look after himself and his wife has had to give up work to look after him. Glanville's employers continue to pay his salary on an ex gratia basis. He is also in receipt of £250 per month under a personal insurance policy during the remaining period of his disability.

You should try to work out the remedies available to Glanville when you have read the chapter on damages at the end of this book. Only then will you realise the extent to which the victims of torts are placed in a privileged position in comparison with other victims of misfortune in society. In many ways the needs of Patrick and Glanville are identical, but Patrick and his family are condemned to reliance upon social security and whatever personal provision they have made for such an eventuality, whereas Glanville and his family are cushioned by the damages obtainable from a tort action. What is the justification for such a disparity of treatment?

One justification is that in tort cases the accident has been caused by the negligence of the defendant and he is under a moral and legal obligation to compensate the victim. But in our example it cannot be said that Brian was morally at fault for the injuries suffered by Glanville. Nor does the tort action have a deterrent effect upon Brian because he was in no position to prevent the accident from occurring (although it may make him more careful about resuming driving).

On the other hand it should not be thought that the tort system is ideal for Glanville. The system is expensive to operate. The Pearson Commission (*Royal Commission on Civil Liability and Compensation for Personal Injury*, Cmnd 7054, 1978) found that the cost of operating the tort system accounted for some 85 per cent of the sums paid to accident victims. The legal system is also extremely slow and cumbrous. Damages are also usually paid by means of a lump sum, which requires the courts to engage in what is no more than educated guesswork as to the future needs of the plaintiff. This can lead in some cases to significant under-compensation where the court's 'guess' is erroneous.

Dissatisfaction with the operation of the tort system in cases of personal injury reached such a height in New Zealand that the tort action was abolished in such cases and replaced by a comprehensive no-fault accident compensation scheme. This scheme covers all accidental injury, but it does not cover diseases, with the exception of occupational diseases; (on the subject of diseases see Stapleton *Disease and the Compensation Debate*). The scheme replaces the victim's financial loss at the rate of 80 per cent of his earnings before the accident. These payments are made weekly and are subject to a maximum amount. In respect of permanent injury or disability a lump sum may be payable, assessed objectively by reference to a schedule of tariffs, but these sums are low in comparison to what can be obtained in a tort action in this country. The scheme is funded by levies on motor vehicles, employers and employees and by funding out of general taxation.

The Pearson Commission did not recommend the abolition of the tort action in this way because their terms of reference did not permit them to do so. The Commission did recommend a small extension of strict liability in certain areas and proposed an extension of the existing industrial injuries scheme to motor accident victims to be funded by a tax on petrol. However there seems to be little political interest at the moment in the reform of the tort system in Britain. But with the anomalies inherent in the present system and the enormous disparities between the treatment of tort victims and other victims of misfortune in society it cannot be long before further consideration is given to the future of the tort action in Britain.

In an attempt to simplify the system and to reduce costs the Lord Chancellor has announced plans to channel most small accident claims through the Small Claims Court. The proposal is that all accident cases will be treated as small claims unless the case is worth more than £1,000, and that this limit is expected to be raised to £2,000 or £5,000 shortly.

A potential problem for litigants is that they would only be able to claim limited costs from defendants, and legal costs of the hearing would not be claimable. Thus, an employee might well face legal representatives paid for by an insurance company, and should he or she employ similar legal advisers their costs would not be claimable from the defendants and could well exceed any damages paid by the defendants.

1.3 The interests protected

The law of tort provides protection for a wide range of interests. Such protection may be obtained in one or more of three ways. The first, and most common, way is through an action for damages to compensate the victim for the loss which he has incurred. The second way in which protection may be obtained is through an application to court for injunctive relief. An injunction generally has the effect of prohibiting the defendant from doing certain acts. For example, an employer who knows that a trade union is about to engage in industrial action which will involve the commission of economic torts against him, which will result in the shut down of his factory, is likely to seek injunctive relief to prevent the strike from taking place rather than wait until the damage is done and then seek to recover damages at a later date. The third way in which a victim of a tort may obtain protection is through self help. The law of tort is, however, extremely reluctant to allow people to take the law into their own hands and so this option is only available within extremely narrow bounds. For example, the person who is the victim of the tort of battery may take reasonable steps to defend himself and a person may, in certain circumstances, take steps to abate a nuisance. The following will provide a brief account of some of the interests protected by the law of tort. These issues will be amplified in subsequent chapters of the book.

The law of tort provides protection for a person's personal security. Thus, where a person is assaulted by another then the victim may have an action in the tort of battery. Similarly where a person is injured as the result of the negligence of another the victim may have an action in the tort of negligence and recover damages in respect of his injuries. The law of tort also provides protection for a person's reputation. A person whose character is damaged by the writings or speeches of another person may have a claim against that person in defamation for libel or slander.

The law of tort provides protection for a person's property. Thus a person who interferes with another's chattel, such as his motor car, may commit one of the torts of interference with chattels, such as conversion. The torts of trespass to land and nuisance provide protection for a person in the use and enjoyment of his land.

The law of tort may also provide protection for a person's interest in the life of another. Thus where the 'breadwinner' in a family is killed due to the negligence of another, then the dependants of the victim may seek compensation in respect of the losses which they have incurred through the loss of the 'breadwinner'. Finally the law of tort provides protection for interests of a purely economic nature. As we shall see the law of tort has been reluctant to impose liability for negligently inflicted 'pure' economic loss, but the same restraint has not been shown where that loss has been inflicted intentionally. Thus employers who suffer loss as a result of the commission of economic torts during the course of industrial action may have a cause of action against those responsible for the commission of these torts.

1.4 Tort and other legal subjects

Tort and crime

Crimes are those acts and, on rare occasions, omissions which society as a whole prescribes as being completely unacceptable. Crimes are normally prosecuted by the state through the criminal courts, whereas a tort is a civil action which an individual prosecutes in a civil court at his discretion.

There are, however, torts, such as assault and battery, which may also be actionable as crimes and a civil remedy may be obtained after the completion of the criminal proceedings. The result of the criminal proceedings may be used as evidence in the civil claim and so it is often advisable for the victim to wait for the outcome of the criminal proceedings before launching his civil action. Where the person who committed the tort is acquitted in the criminal proceedings, this is not conclusive evidence in the civil action because the standard of proof in the criminal action is beyond reasonable doubt, whereas it is on the balance of probabilities in the civil action. So the fact of acquittal does not mean that the victim will not be able to prove his civil case on the balance of probabilities. The person who is the victim of a criminal offence may also seek compensation through the Criminal Injuries Compensation Scheme.

Tort and contract

Tort and contract are both matters of civil law and there is a much closer relationship between tort and contract than there is between tort and crime. The exact relationship between them is a matter of some controversy and, indeed, the distinction between the two has been denied by some who have sought to argue that English law now has a law of obligations which encompasses both tort and contract. The traditional distinction drawn between tort and contract is that obligations are imposed in tort, whereas in contract obligations are consensually assumed. This dichotomy cannot be completely accepted because some contractual terms are imposed by law (such as the implied conditions relating to title, merchantable quality etc. in the Sale of Goods Act 1979) and the standard of care in the tort of negligence can be regulated by a contract between the tortfeasor and the victim of the tort.

It is sometimes argued that contract and tort exist to protect different interests. The law of contract is supposed to protect the expectation interest, that is, an award of damages in contract is supposed to put the plaintiff in the position he would have been in had the contract been performed. On the other hand an award of damages in tort is supposed to protect the reliance interest, that is, it is supposed to put the victim of the tort in the position he would have been in had the tort never been committed. This can be seen in personal injuries cases where the object of an award of damages is to put the plaintiff in the position he would have been in, so far as this can be done by a monetary award, had the tort not been committed. But this division is not wholly acceptable either. Contract law is not committed to the wholehearted protection of the expectation interest, as doctrines such as mitigation and remoteness show. There have also been cases such as *Ross* v *Caunters* (above) and *Junior Books Ltd* v *The Veitchi Co Ltd* (above) where the effect of the tort action was to protect the expectation interest because the plaintiff was put in the position he would have been in had the defendant carried out his obligation properly. These cases are, however, a source of some controversy and they will be discussed in greater detail in chapters 6 and 7 when further consideration will be given to the relationship between contract and tort.

2

Parties to an Action in Tort

2.1 Introduction

2.2 Liability

2.3 Immunity

2.1 Introduction

As a general rule anyone may bring an action in tort. Minors may sue in tort through their 'next friend'. In *McKay* v *Essex Area Health Authority* [1982] QB 1166 the Court of Appeal held that, although no action lay in respect of negligently bringing a child into the world, a child may bring an action in tort in respect of damage done to it between conception and birth as the result of the negligence of those who are looking after its mother's health. In *Burton* v *Islington Health Authority* [1993] QB 204 the Court of Appeal affirmed that, where a child was born suffering from disabilities caused as a result of medical negligence, the child could bring a negligence claim even though the child was not a person in the eyes of the law at the time when the damage was negligently inflicted. Dillon LJ rejected the argument that the passing of the Congential Disabilities (Civil Liability) Act 1976 precluded the courts from recognising the existence of a duty of care in respect of damage suffered prior to the coming into force of the Act. But he did leave open the question whether the estate of a still-born child could recover damages in respect of damage inflicted prior to its birth.

Both *McKay* and *Burton* concerned plaintiffs who suffered damage prior to the coming into force of the Congenital Disabilities (Civil Liability) Act 1976. Now a child is given a cause of action under the 1976 Act where it is born disabled as the result of an occurrence which either affected the ability of either parent to have a normal, healthy child, or affected the mother during the pregnancy, or affected the child in the course of its birth, so that the child is born with disabilities which it would not otherwise have had. Section 1(3) further provides that the defendant is answerable to the child 'if he was liable in tort to the parent or would, if sued in due time, have been so' liable and that it is no answer to the child's claim that there could not have been such liability because the parent suffered no actionable injury. So the child's action is rather unusual in that it is derived from the defendant's

10

tortious duty to the parents. Furthermore s4(5) provides that in respect of a birth occurring after the Act came into force the Act 'replaces any law in force before its passing, whereby a person could be liable to a child in respect of disabilities with which it might be born'.

The Law Reform (Husband and Wife) Act 1962 removed the anomaly which prohibited a husband and wife from suing each other in tort. But under s1(2) of the Act the action will be stayed if no substantial benefit would accrue to either party from it or if the action would be more appropriately dealt with under s17 of the Married Women's Property Act 1882.

2.2 Liability

Subject to rules relating to immunity from tortious liability anybody may be sued in tort. The following parties are worthy of further comment.

The Crown

At common law the Crown could not be sued in tort (see *Tobin* v *R* (1864) 16 CBNS 310). However this immunity was removed by the Crown Proceedings Act 1947, which rendered the Crown liable in tort, as if it were a private person of full age and capacity, in respect of torts committed by its servants or agents. The appropriate minister of the Crown is made the nominal defendant and, where there is no appropriate minister, the Attorney-General is made the defendant.

Section 40(1) of the Act provides that the Queen herself may not be sued in tort. Section 2(5) provides a further exception in relation to anything done or omitted to be done by any person while discharging any responsibilities of a judicial nature (although the immunity does not extend to acts which are of an administrative nature: see *Welsh* v *Chief Constable of the Merseyside Police* [1993] 1 All ER 692). Finally it is provided in s10 that the Crown and members of the armed forces are immune from actions by other members of the armed forces for death or personal injury while on duty or on military premises.

Corporations

It is clearly established that a corporation, which is a legal entity separate and distinct from its members, may commit torts and have torts committed against it. However, there are certain torts which, by their very nature, cannot be committed against a corporation, such as assault or false imprisonment. Corporations are vicariously liable for the torts committed by their employees in the course of their employment. A corporation may also be personally liable where the person who commits the tort is so much in command of the company that his acts are treated as if they were the acts of the company (see *Lennard's Carrying Co* v *Asiatic Petroleum Co Ltd* [1915] AC 705). In the latter case the mere fact that the person in charge of the company has committed a tort or has committed a tort in the course of an ultra vires act will not have the effect of making the tort ultra vires the company (*Campbell* v *Paddington Corporation* [1911] 1 KB 869 and see also s35 of the Companies Act 1985 (as amended by the Companies Act 1989). Where, however, the employee has committed a tort during the course of an ultra vires act then the corporation may be able to show that the employee was acting outside the scope of his employment and so escape the imposition of liability.

Unincorporated associations

Unlike corporations, unincorporated associations have no legal personality of their own which is separate from that of their membership. Thus clubs and similar unincorporated associations cannot sue or be sued in their own right – for a recent example of this doctrine being applied see *R* v *Darlington Borough Council, ex parte The Association of Darlington Taxi Owners* (1994) The Independent 13 January. The members are themselves jointly and severally liable for their torts but only for their own torts and not for the torts of other members. In some cases a representative action may be brought against an unincorporated association where all the members have a common interest to defend (for example, where a claim is made against a club for damages under the Occupiers' Liability Act 1957 but see *Robertson* v *Ridley* [1989] 2 All ER 474).

Such an action will be brought against a representative of the club, such as the secretary or chairman. A recent example of this is *Jones* v *Northampton Borough Council* (1990) The Independent 25 May. The plaintiff slipped while playing football at the defendant council's sports centre. The cause of his slip was that water had leaked through a hole in the roof and was lying on the playing surface. Prior to the commencement of the competition in which the plaintiff was playing, the council informed the chairman of the plaintiff's sports club that there was water on the pitch. The chairman nevertheless decided to commence the competition. The council settled the plaintiff's claim and then sought a full indemnity from the club chairman under the Civil Liability (Contribution) Act 1978 (see 3.5). The chairman argued that, as a matter of law, no relevant duty of care was owed by one club member to another. The Court of Appeal rejected this argument and held that the council was entitled to a full indemnity from the chairman on the ground that he was in breach of his duty of care to the plaintiff. Ralph Gibson LJ stated that:

'... [w]here a club officer or committee member, while performing some task for other club members, learned of circumstances giving rise to risk of injury to club members acting as he knew they would if not told of the danger, then it was open to the court to find that he owed them a duty of care and, if he gave no warning, that he was in breach of it.'

The chairman therefore enjoyed no immunity from suit in tort and was liable to the plaintiff.

Trade unions

The exact legal status of trade unions is the source of some uncertainty. They are really special types of unincorporated associations who are given some of the attributes of a corporation by s2(1) of the Trade Union and Labour Relations Act 1974 (TULRA). In the famous case of *Taff Vale Railway Co* v *Amalgamated Society of Railway Servants* [1901] AC 426 it was held that registered trade unions had the capacity to sue and be sued in their own name. This principle is now embodied in s2(1)(c) of TULRA. However, in *EETPU* v *Times Newspapers Ltd* [1980] QB 585, it was held that trade unions, as unincorporated bodies, lacked the necessary legal personality to bring an action in defamation.

Minors

There is no minimum age for the existence of tortious responsibility. Minors are judged by ordinary tort principles. However a minor cannot be sued in tort where that action would have the effect of enforcing a contract which is not binding upon him. There is no general principle in English law that a parent is vicariously responsible for the torts of his children. But a parent may be liable in negligence for giving the child the opportunity to cause damage.

Thus in *Newton* v *Edgerley* [1959] 1 WLR 1031 a father was found to be liable in negligence when he gave his 12 year old son a .410 rifle without proper training and the son caused damage to the plaintiff through his use of the gun.

Insanity

The exact effect of insanity upon a defendant's liability in tort is uncertain. It is, however, clear that insanity is not recognised as a defence in tort actions. In *Morriss* v *Marsden* [1952] 1 All ER 925 the defendant attacked the plaintiff and caused him serious injury. The defendant was found unfit to plead in the resulting criminal proceedings for assault and battery but the plaintiff sued the defendant in tort. It was held that the defendant was liable because he intended to commit the attack even though he had no power to appreciate that it was wrong. What has to be ascertained is whether the defendant possessed the necessary state of mind for the tort for which he is being sued. In *Morriss* the tort was battery and it was sufficient that the defendant intended to strike the plaintiff. However if the defendant's act had been involuntary he would not have been liable (for example, if the defendant had been suffering from insane automatism which had caused him to strike the plaintiff). It is unclear whether an insane person can commit the tort of negligence.

2.3 Immunity

In certain circumstances a defendant enjoys immunity from liability in tort. The most important of these immunities are considered below.

Statutory authority

If a statute makes what was formerly a tort at common law a lawful act then that act is no longer a tortious act. Similarly a statute may give immunity to a particular body or category of persons. For example, under s29 of the Post Office Act 1969, no action lies against the Post Office for acts of employees in respect of postal packets.

Judicial immunity

Judges enjoy an immunity from action in negligence (*Anderson v Gorrie* [1895] 1 QB 668). A judge of an inferior court also enjoys such an immunity provided that he honestly believes that he is acting within his jurisdiction (*Sirros v Moore* [1975] QB 118, but see *McC v Mullan* [1984] 3 All ER 908 and *R v Manchester City Magistrates' Court, ex parte Davies* [1989] 1 All ER 90). Witnesses in legal proceedings also enjoy such an immunity (*Evans v London Hospital Medical College* [1981] 1 All ER 715; cf *Palmer v Durnford Ford (a firm)* [1992] 1 QB 483), as do those, such as arbitrators, who act in a quasi-judicial manner in resolving disputes between parties (*Sutcliffe v Thackrah* [1974] AC 727). The latter immunity has, however, been confined within narrow bounds (see *Arenson v Casson Beckman Rutley and Co* [1977] AC 405 and *Palacath Ltd v Flanagan* [1985] 2 All ER 161).

Acts of State

Foreigners normally enjoy the same rights and incur the same liabilities in tort as British nationals. However, where an Act of State is involved then the foreigner may find that he has no cause of action where he otherwise would have had one. But an Act of State is no defence against a wrong done to a British national anywhere (see *Walker v Baird* [1892] AC 491).

An Act of State may be defined as 'an act of the executive as a matter of policy performed in the course of its relations with another State including its relations with the subjects of that State unless they are temporarily within the allegiance of the Crown.'

In *Buron v Denman* (1848) 2 Exch 167 the plaintiff, a Spaniard, was a slave trader in Africa. The defendant, a British naval officer, intervened in the plaintiff's activities and set some slaves free. The defendant's action was subsequently ratified by the Admiralty. The plaintiff sued the defendant for trespass. It was held that the Admiralty's approval was a defence since it meant that the defendant's act was an Act of State.

Trade unions

Trade unions presently enjoy certain immunities from action in tort. These immunities are necessary if trade unions are to be able to engage in industrial action to defend their members' interests. The immunities have been substantially reduced since the Conservative government was elected in 1979. This is not the place to embark upon an analysis of the extent of the immunities enjoyed by trade unions and reference should be made to any of the standard works on labour law.

3

Joint and Several Tortfeasors

3.1 Introduction

3.2 Independent liability

3.3 Several liability

3.4 Joint liability

3.5 Contribution between tortfeasors

3.1 Introduction

Where two or more breaches of duty by different defendants cause the plaintiff injury, the liability of the tortfeasors (that is the persons who have committed the torts) may be: independent; several; or joint. In cases where the plaintiff has available to him the option of suing more than one tortfeasor, special rules have been laid down to deal with the possibility of successive actions by the plaintiff, and to deal with claims for contribution between defendants. We shall proceed by examining independent, several and joint liability in more detail and then conclude by examining the rules relating to contribution.

3.2 Independent liability

The plaintiff may suffer damage as the result of two entirely separate torts. In such a case the plaintiff has two completely separate causes of action against the two tortfeasors. Thus in *Baker* v *Willoughby* [1970] AC 467C (considered further at 10.7) the plaintiff suffered injury to his left leg as a result of the defendant's negligence. At a later date the plaintiff had to have the same leg amputated after he had been shot in the leg during the course of an armed robbery. It was held that each tortfeasor was liable for the injury which he caused and that the latter injury did not obliterate the liability of the first defendant. Thus the plaintiff is only entitled to sue each tortfeasor in respect of damage caused by that tortfeasor.

3.3 Several liability

Where tortfeasors act independently to cause the same damage to the plaintiff, then these tortfeasors are several (or concurrent) tortfeasors. The vital features of this form of liability are that the tortfeasors act independently and that their actions cause the same damage to the plaintiff. Each tortfeasor is separately liable in respect of the damage, but the plaintiff can only recover damages once. In *The Koursk* [1924] P 140 two ships by separate and independent negligence collided with each other. One of these ships, without further negligence, went on to collide with the plaintiff's ship. It was held that the defendants were separate tortfeasors, whose acts combined to produce a single injury and thus both were independently liable to the plaintiff.

3.4 Joint liability

Joint liability exists where two tortfeasors inflict damage on the plaintiff in furtherance of the common design of the tortfeasors. Thus in *Brooke* v *Bool* [1928] 2 KB 578 the defendant, a landlord, let premises to the plaintiff for use as a shop. The defendant remained entitled to enter the premises in the plaintiff's absence to check that the premises were secure. A lodger in the premises informed the defendant that he could smell gas coming from the shop. Both men investigated the shop. The lodger, with the consent and encouragement of the defendant, lit a match. This caused an explosion in which the plaintiff's property was damaged. It was held that the defendant was jointly liable for the damage caused by the negligence of the lodger. In such a case there is only one tort committed and so the cause of action against the tortfeasors is the same and is supported by the same evidence. Each tortfeasor is liable for the full amount, but the plaintiff can only recover once.

Joint liability does not only exist in the case of a tort committed in the course of a common design. It also exists in the case where an employer is held to be vicariously liable for the tort committed by his employee (see further chapter 4). Both the employer and the employee are, therefore, joint tortfeasors. Joint liability can also arise between a principal and an agent and between an employer and his independent contractor (where the former is under a 'non-delegable' duty – see further chapter 5).

Two principal consequences followed at common law from the finding that the parties were joint tortfeasors. The first was that judgment against one of the tortfeasors, even if it remained unsatisfied, had the effect of barring any subsequent action against the other joint tortfeasors. Judgment against one also had the effect of denying to the plaintiff the ability to continue the same action against the other tortfeasors. This rule was, however, reversed by s6 of the Law Reform (Married Women and Tortfeasors) Act 1935, 'the 1935 Act', which is now contained in s3 of the Civil Liability (Contribution) Act 1978, 'the 1978 Act'. Section 3 provides that:

'... judgment recovered against any person liable in respect of any ... damage shall not be a bar to an action, or to the continuance of an action, against any other person who is (apart from any such bar) jointly liable with him in respect of the same ... damage.'

But where the plaintiff brings an action subsequent to the first action in respect of the same damage against a joint or several (or concurrent) tortfeasor, the plaintiff will be refused his costs in the subsequent action or actions unless he satisfies the court that there was reasonable ground for bringing the subsequent action or actions (s4 of the 1978 Act).

The second principal consequence at common law of finding that liability was joint was that release of one joint tortfeasor, whether by accord and satisfaction or under seal, had the effect of releasing the other tortfeasors. The reasoning behind this rule was straightforward. In cases of joint liability only one tort was committed, so release of one tortfeasor must automatically result in the release of all (this rule never applied to several (concurrent) tortfeasors because the obligations of several tortfeasors are independent and so release of one tortfeasor leaves the others unaffected). This rule in cases of joint liability has never been reversed by statute, but its effect has been mitigated by the judiciary. What the courts have done is to draw a distinction between a release and an agreement not to sue and hold that the latter does not extinguish the obligation. It simply renders the obligation unenforceable against the tortfeasor released and so the cause of action against the other joint tortfeasors is preserved. The courts are reluctant to interpret an agreement with one joint tortfeasor as a release rather than an agreement not to sue (*Cutler* v *McPhail* [1962] 2 QB 292 and *Watts* v *Aldington* (1993) The Times 16 December) and this refinement makes it easier to avoid the conclusion that the action against the other tortfeasors is barred.

3.5 Contribution between tortfeasors

The general rule at common law was that neither joint nor several tortfeasors could recover contribution or an indemnity from other tortfeasors, in the absence of an express or implied agreement between them to the contrary. This was known as the rule in *Merryweather* v *Nixon* (1799) 8 TR 186. This rule was particularly unfortunate in its operation because it was a matter of chance, or solvency, which tortfeasor was sued and once judgment was entered against one of the tortfeasors he could not look to his fellow joint or several tortfeasors for contribution. This rule was reversed by s6(1)(c) of the 1935 Act, which is now contained in ss1 and 2 of the 1978 Act. These sections will be dealt with separately. Section 1 deals with entitlement to contribution and s2 with assessment of contribution.

Entitlement to contribution

Section 1(1) of the Act provides that '... any person liable in respect of any damage suffered by another person may recover contribution from any other person liable in respect of the same damage (whether jointly with him or otherwise)'. This, then, is the new general rule, which is interpreted very widely – see *K* v *P* [1992] 3 WLR 1015. It is further provided in s1(6) that:

> 'references ... to a person's liability in respect of any damage are references to such liability which has been or could be established in an action brought against him in England or Wales by or on behalf of the person who suffered the damage.'

The rationale behind this subsection is that a tortfeasor can only recover a contribution from someone who is, actually or hypothetically, liable to the plaintiff. The proper interpretation of s1(6) was considered by Hobhouse J in *R A Lister Ltd* v *Thomson (Shipping) Ltd* [1987] 1 WLR 1614. The defendant charterers argued that they were not 'liable' to the plaintiff cargo owners under s1(6) because the Court of Appeal had ordered the plaintiffs' action against them to be stayed because the bills of lading contained an Indonesian law and jurisdiction clause. Thus the charterers could only be sued to judgment in Indonesia and not in England. When the shipowners subsequently issued a notice declaring their intention to claim a contribution from the charterers, the charterers applied to strike out the notice. But Hobhouse J refused to strike out the notice. He held that the fact that the charterers could not be sued to judgment in England was not conclusive evidence that they were not liable to the plaintiffs because s1(6) was only concerned with whether the defendants were liable, as a matter of substantive law, to the plaintiffs. He held that it was not concerned with 'any merely procedural considerations as to how [liability] may be enforced'. All that was required was that at the time at which the plaintiffs suffered the damage there was a current and subsisting liability on the part of the charterers relating to the damage. Where the respondent is in fact outside the jurisdiction of the English courts that problem will be resolved by an application of the rules of procedure and not by adopting the charterers' interpretation of s1(6).

Section 1(2) provides that a defendant is entitled to recover contribution despite the fact that he has ceased to be liable to the plaintiff since the time when the damage occurred, provided that he was so liable immediately before the judgment or settlement in the plaintiff's favour. So if a tortfeasor settles with the plaintiff at a time when he has ceased to be liable to the plaintiff, he cannot recover contribution from the others. But if at the time of the settlement or judgment he was liable to the plaintiff then his right to contribution is subject to a two year limitation period running from the date of judgment or of the compromise.

Section 1(3) of the Act states that a party from whom contribution is sought is liable to make contribution even though he has ceased to be liable to the original plaintiff, 'unless he ceased to be liable by virtue of the expiry of a period of limitation or prescription which extinguished the right on which the claim against him in respect of the damage was based'. Thus far the clear purport of this subsection is to reverse the decision of the House of Lords in *George Wimpey and Co Ltd* v *British Overseas Aircraft Corporation* [1955] AC 169. In that case it was held that one tortfeasor could not recover from the other tortfeasor because the plaintiff's claim against the latter had been held to be time barred. The claim against the tortfeasor having been dismissed in this manner he was not 'liable' to make contribution to the other tortfeasor. Section 1(3) would appear to reverse this decision so that contribution could be recovered.

A difficulty is, however, introduced by s1(5) of the Act which states that 'judgment given in any action' brought by the original plaintiff 'against any party from whom contribution is sought under this section shall be conclusive in the proceedings for contribution as to any issue determined by that judgment in favour of the person from whom the contribution is sought'. If the phrase 'any issue' in s1(5) is interpreted so as to encompass the issue of limitation, the Act will have failed in its aim of reversing *Wimpey*, because if, in the action by the original plaintiff, the limitation issue was decided in favour of the defendants, that finding would be 'conclusive' if another defendant then sought to obtain contribution from these defendants and would prevent that other defendant from obtaining contribution.

However, it has been argued (see, for example, *Dias and Markesinis Tort Law*, 2nd ed, p580) that the phrase 'any issue' in s1(5) should be read as if it provided 'any issue as to the merits' of the original claim by the plaintiff (a similar insertion would then have to be made in s1(3) so that it read 'ceased to be liable on the merits' to the original plaintiff). The purpose behind this interpretation is to uphold the intention of the Act in reversing *Wimpey* and to hold that the issue of limitation is not a determination on the merits and therefore not 'conclusive' (except where limitation extinguishes not only the remedy, but the claim, on which see Dias and Markesinis loc cit). This interpretation was, however, approved obiter by Balcombe LJ in *Nottingham Health Authority* v *The City of Nottingham* [1988] 1 WLR 903. He held that the effect of s1(3) is to reverse *Wimpey* so that a defendant remains liable to contribute where the effect of the limitation defence is to bar the remedy but does not extinguish the right.

Lastly, s1(4) provides that a party who has made a payment under a bona fide settlement or compromise may claim contribution:

> '... without regard to whether or not he himself is or ever was liable in respect of the damage, provided, however, that he would have been liable assuming that the factual basis of the claim against him could be established.'

Apportionment

Section 2(1) of the Act provides that the amount recoverable from any person 'shall be such as may be found by the court to be just and equitable having regard to the extent of that person's responsibility for the damage in question.' There is no suggestion in the Act that the division must be on the basis of equality. Instead the court is required to take into account all the relevant circumstances, such as the degree of blameworthiness and the parties' role in bringing about the damage, and apportion the damages payable in the light of these circumstances.

Section 2(2) empowers the court either to exempt a party from having to pay contribution or to order him to make a complete indemnity. The amount which the tortfeasor can recover by way of contribution is limited to the amount which the plaintiff could have recovered from that particular defendant had the plaintiff sued him. So if the defendant from whom contribution is sought has a contract with the plaintiff which validly restricts that defendant's liability to £25, the defendant seeking contribution from that other defendant cannot recover more than £25 (s2(3)).

4

Vicarious Liability

4.1 Introduction

4.2 The rationale of vicarious liability

4.3 Who is an employee?

4.4 The employee must commit a tort

4.5 Course of employment

4.6 The master's indemnity

4.7 Principal and agent

4.8 Partnership

4.1 Introduction

Before embarking upon an analysis of the rationale behind the doctrine of vicarious liability, it is necessary to give a brief explanation of the essence of the doctrine. The effect of the doctrine of vicarious liability is to render X liable to Z for the damage done to Z by the tort of Y. The commonest example of this is the case where an employer is rendered liable for the tort committed by his employee in the course of the employee's employment. There are two essential elements to vicarious liability. The first is that there must be a relationship, such as the employment relationship, between X and Y which is sufficient to justify the imposition of liability upon X for the tort of Y. The second element is that the tort committed by Y must be referable in some particular way to the relationship between X and Y.

It is essential to note that vicarious liability is concerned with the situation where one person is rendered liable for the tort of another, not with the situation where one person is rendered liable for his own tort. Although this distinction appears to be an obvious one, it can be difficult to draw the line in practice. For example, a National Health Service patient who suffers loss as a result of a negligently performed operation may decide to sue the Area Health Authority directly for its failure to provide adequate levels of staffing in the hospital or he may elect to sue the Area Health Authority as being vicariously liable for the negligence of one of its doctors (see further *Wilsher* v *Essex Area Health Authority* [1987] 2 WLR 425, 465). While it may be difficult to draw the line in some cases, that line must be drawn if the distinction between primary and vicarious liability is to be preserved.

4.2 The rationale of vicarious liability

One of the unusual features of the doctrine of vicarious liability is that, whilst there is general agreement as to the utility of the doctrine, the doctrine has no clear rationale. A number of possible rationales have been put forward, but none are wholly convincing. These rationales are as follows:

1. The employer has control over his employee therefore he is responsible for the acts of his employee. This, however, is a demonstrable fallacy because in many cases the employee is more skilled than the employer (for example doctors and pilots) and so it cannot be said in any meaningful sense that the employer has control over his employee.
2. The employer was careless in selecting an employee who was negligent and he must accept responsibility because, by selecting a negligent employee, he set in motion the train of events which led to the negligent act of his employee. But no employee is immune from being negligent at some stage in his employment and to insist that an employer only employ non-negligent employees is to place an unreasonable and unjustified burden on the employer.
3. The employer derives benefit from the service of his employee, so it is only right that he takes the burdens as well. This justification purports to give some economic and moral basis to the imposition of liability upon the employer. It may be thought, however, that, in a society which accepts the existence of the division of labour, we often benefit from the works of others without contributing to the cost of that work and the mere fact of receipt of a benefit is not, of itself, sufficient to justify the imposition of an obligation to pay for it.
4. The employer is in a better position than the employee to compensate the victim of the tort. The employee will generally not have the funds available to meet the damages claim nor will he have an insurance policy to meet the claim, whereas an employer will normally have the latter if not the former. The employer is often in the best position to spread the loss because he can take account of the loss as a cost of the production process and thus pass the cost on as part of the cost of his product.
5. By imposing liability on the employer, the employer is thereby given an incentive to ensure that the event does not occur again and that none of his other employees do the same thing.

It is probably true to say that there is no one justification for the imposition of vicarious liability. The best conclusion may be that of Professor Williams when he said in his article Vicarious Liability and the Master's Indemnity ((1957) 20 MLR 220, 232):

' ... that vicarious liability owes its explanation, if not its justification, to the search for a solvent defendant. It is commonly felt that when a person is injured ... he ought to be able to obtain recompense from someone; and if the immediate tortfeasor cannot afford to pay, then he is justified in looking around for the nearest person of substance who can plausibly be identified with the disaster. Where there is no immediate tortfeasor at all, the same sentiment works itself out through rules of strict liability.'

So the rationale of vicarious liability may be said to lie closest to category 4. This lack of a coherent rationale for the doctrine does not appear to have troubled the judiciary. Lord Pearce in *Imperial Chemical Industries Ltd* v *Shatwell* [1965] AC 656, 685 said:

'The doctrine of vicarious liability has not grown from any very clear, logical or legal principle but from social convenience and rough justice.'

Despite this apparent lack of concern on the part of the judiciary, we shall note at various stages of this chapter that the issue is an important one and that its resolution would help to stabilise the law and give it greater coherence.

In the next three sections of this chapter we shall consider the application of the doctrine of vicarious liability to the employment relationship. We shall do so in three stages. First by considering who is an employee (4.3). Secondly by demonstrating that the employee must commit a tort (4.4) and thirdly by showing that the tort must be committed during the course of the employee's employment (4.5).

4.3 Who is an employee?

As vicarious liability arises from the employment relationship and not from the relationship of employer and independent contractor it is important to distinguish between an employee and an independent contractor. This distinction may seem an obvious one, but it has caused the courts great difficulties. These difficulties are likely to increase today because of the growth of what is called 'atypical' forms of employment, where it is difficult to tell whether the worker is an employee or not. These 'atypical' forms of employment include homeworkers, casual workers (for example, those workers who have no fixed hours of work but are called in by their employer as and when required) and those who are told by their employers when they are hired that they are self-employed so that the employer can evade the employment protection legislation. All these categories of workers are likely to present the courts with considerable problems in determining their employment status.

The original test for distinguishing between an employee and an independent contractor was the control test. This test had its origin in the judgment of Bramwell LJ in *Yewens* v *Noakes* (1880) 6 QBD 530 where he said that an employee was anyone 'who was subject to the command of the master as to the manner in which he shall do the work'. This test never meant that the employer in fact controlled the employee for every second of his working day, but that he had the right to do so. However, as we have already noted, this test became impossible to apply as many employees became more skilful, to the extent of being more skilful than their employers.

These difficulties with the 'control' test led to dissatisfaction with the test on the part of the judiciary and an attempt to find an alternative test for distinguishing between employees and independent contractors. So in *Stevenson, Jordan and Harrison Ltd* v *MacDonald* (1952) 1 TLR 101 Denning LJ formulated the 'business integration' test or the 'organisation' test. By this he meant that a worker who is an employee does his work as an 'integral part of the business' whereas an independent contractor is not 'integrated' into the business but is merely 'accessory' to it. While sounding neat in theory it was impossibly vague to apply in practice and was quickly abandoned.

The next attempt at formulating a test for distinguishing between an employee and an independent contractor occurred in *Market Investigations Ltd* v *Minister of Social Security* [1969] 2 QB 173. In this case an interviewer was hired by a research company. She was free to set her own hours of work, although the pattern of her work was set by the research company. She received no sick pay or holiday pay and she was free to work for others. It was held that she was an employee because she was not 'in business on her own account'. Although this test avoids the excesses of the 'business integration' test it is still unacceptably vague, although in *Andrews* v *King* (1991) The Times 5 July it was referred to by Browne-Wilkinson VC as 'a fundamental test'.

Another factor which has been given some weight by the courts is the parties' labelling of their own relationship. This approach reached its height in *Massey* v *Crown Life Insurance* [1978] 1 WLR 676 where a man who had agreed to be self-employed so that he could enjoy certain tax advantages sought to argue that he was an employee so that he could claim the benefits of the employment protection legislation. The Court of Appeal dismissed his claim, Lord Denning saying that 'having made his bed as being self-employed, he must lie on it'. But this approach has not been uniformly accepted. In *Young and Woods* v *West* [1980] IRLR 201 a skilled metal worker, who chose when he was hired to be treated as 'self-employed' so that he could obtain a tax saving of some £500 per year, was nevertheless held to be an employee when he presented a claim that he had been unfairly dismissed. The court held that the parties' labelling of their relationship was only one factor to be taken into account and that employees had to be protected from contracting out of their statutory employment rights. Lest it be thought that Mr West thereby made a considerable tax saving while not losing his statutory employment rights, the court undertook to inform the Inland Revenue of his true employment status, making it a somewhat hollow victory!

The approach which the courts now adopt is to abandon the search for any one factor which will be conclusive in all cases and to examine all the facts of the particular case. An early example of this is the case of *Ready Mixed Concrete (South East) Ltd* v *Minister of Pensions* [1968] 2 QB 497. MacKenna J laid down three conditions for the existence of a contract of employment:

1. the employee agrees to provide his work and skill to the employer in return for a wage or other remuneration;
2. the employee agrees, expressly or impliedly, to be directed as to the mode of performance to such a degree as to make the other his employer; and
3. the other terms of the contract are consistent with there being a contract of employment.

It should not be thought, however, that the courts confine themselves to these three factors. The courts will, in fact, consider a wide range of factors including the degree of control over the worker's work, his connection with the business, the parties' agreement, the regularity and nature of the work and methods of payment etc.

Winfield and Jolowicz argue (*Winfield and Jolowicz on Tort*, 13th ed, p562) that the distinction between an employee and an independent contractor has to be drawn for a number of different purposes and that it appears that the same answer will be given regardless of the context in which the question is posed. It is submitted that this is incorrect and that great care will have to be taken in the future in using authorities in this area. Take the case of *O'Kelly* v *Trusthouse Forte PLC* [1983] ICR 728 as an example. There the Court of Appeal held that wine butlers at the Grosvenor House Hotel, who were called 'regular' casual workers and worked in a system whereby they were called in to work when required by their employers (although they were free to refuse such work), were not employees for the purposes of the employment protection legislation. What would have been the position if one of the wine butlers had negligently spilt wine over a guest at the hotel? Surely, in such a case a court would conclude that the wine butler was an employee and that his employer was vicariously liable for his employee's negligence. (Some support for paying greater attention to the context in which it is sought to draw the distinction between an employee and an independent contractor can be found in *R* v *Callender* [1993] QB 303, 309.)

One final difficulty, which calls for comment at this stage, arises where an employer lends his employee to another employer. If that employee then commits a tort which employer is vicariously liable? The answer was provided by the House of Lords in *Mersey Docks and Harbour Board* v *Coggins and Griffith (Liverpool) Ltd* [1947] AC 1. They held that the proper test to apply was whether the hirer did or did not have the authority to control the manner in which the employee did his work and that the stipulations of the parties as to who was to be regarded as the employer were not conclusive. They held that the burden of proof was on the general employer (ie the one who hired out the employee) to show that he was not the employer and that the burden was a heavy one to discharge, and which according to Viscount Simon would only be discharged in quite exceptional cases. On the facts the general employers failed to discharge the burden on them because, although the hirers directed the employees as to what parcels they should lift with the crane, they had no authority to tell the employees how to use the crane. Other factors which may be of importance include who pays the wages, who can dismiss the employee, how long the employee is hired out for and whether machinery is also hired out. The latter factor may be important because where it is only labour which is hired out it is much easier to infer that the hirer is the employer, although even here the courts are reluctant to accept that the hirer has control (*Bhoomidas* v *Port of Singapore* [1978] 1 All ER 956). Where, however, it is the employee rather than a third party who suffers injury then the general employer remains liable on the basis that he owes a non–delegable duty of care to his employee and he cannot avoid liability for breach of that duty by delegating it to the hiring employer (see *Morris* v *Breaveglen Ltd* (1992) The Times 29 December and *Johnson* v *Coventry Churchill International Ltd* [1992] 3 All ER 14, discussed in more detail at 15.5).

Further restrictions may be placed on the ability of the general employer to transfer liability to the hiring employer by the Unfair Contract Terms Act 1977 (UCTA). In *Phillips Products Ltd* v *Hyland* [1987] 2 All ER 620 the defendants hired a JCB excavator and driver to the plaintiffs. Condition 8 of the contract stated that the driver was to be regarded as the employee of the plaintiffs and that the plaintiffs alone should be responsible for all claims arising in connection with the driver's operation of the excavator. Due to the negligence of the driver, the JCB excavator crashed into the plaintiffs' factory wall. The plaintiffs sued for damages and the defendants relied upon condition 8. The plaintiffs argued that condition 8 was caught by s2(2) of UCTA and that it failed to satisfy the requirement of reasonableness. The defendants argued that it was not caught by s2(2) on the ground that there was no negligence within the meaning of s1(1)(b) of UCTA because there had been no breach of their obligations as they had never accepted any liability for the acts of the driver. This argument was rejected by the Court of Appeal. Slade LJ asserted that in considering whether there had been a breach of duty under s1 the court must leave out of account the clause which is relied on by the defendants as defeating the plaintiffs' claim. He found support for his construction of s1(1)(b) in s13 which states that s2 also applies to terms and notices 'which exclude or restrict the relevant obligation or duty'. Having found that condition 8 was caught by s2(2) the Court of Appeal held that it failed to satisfy the reasonableness test.

An apparently conflicting conclusion was, however, reached by a differently constituted Court of Appeal in *Thompson* v *T Lohan (Plant Hire) Ltd* [1987] 2 All ER 631. Once again the case concerned the hiring of an employee and a JCB excavator and a claim arising out of the negligence of the driver. The contract term which was the subject of dispute was a new version of condition 8 (the variation is of no significance for present purposes). But this time it was held that condition 8 was not caught by s2 of UCTA. In *Thompson* the driver's negligence led to the death of Mr Thompson. Mr Thompson's widow recovered damages from the general employers and they in turn sought an indemnity from the hiring employers under condition 8. The hiring employers argued that condition 8 was caught by s2(1) of UCTA and was therefore ineffective. However it was held that condition 8 was not caught by s2(1) and therefore condition 8 was effective to transfer liability to the hiring employer. The distinction between the two cases appears to be that in *Thompson* condition 8 did not attempt to exclude liability towards Mr Thompson because he had recovered from the general employers and the issue was whether that liability could be transferred (as opposed to excluded) to the hiring employers. On the other hand condition 8 in the *Phillips* case was relied upon in an effort to exclude (rather than transfer) liability towards the hiring employers and therefore was caught by s2(2) of UCTA (for critical anlaysis of these two cases see Adams and Brownsword [1988] JBL 146).

4.4 The employee must commit a tort

This point may be said to be labouring the obvious, but it is inserted because in *Twine* v *Bean's Express Ltd* [1946] 1 All ER 202 Uthwatt J suggested that an employer could be vicariously liable even though the employee has not committed a tort. This error was, however, corrected by the House of Lords in *Imperial Chemical Industries Ltd* v *Shatwell* [1965] AC 656 where the crucial distinction between primary and vicarious liability was reaffirmed. Vicarious liability only arises where the employee commits a tort.

4.5 Course of employment

This is the most difficult issue in vicarious liability. There has been an enormous deluge of cases on this point and many of these cases are irreconcilable. All that can be said is that the courts have provided guidelines which they will use in considering whether the employee was acting within the course of his employment. The employee must, of course, have been acting within the course of his employment before the employer will be held vicariously liable for his employee's tort.

Perhaps the most famous definition of 'course of employment' is provided in the following terms by Salmond and Heuston in *The Law of Torts* (19th ed), pp 521–522:

> 'A master is not responsible for a wrongful act done by his servant unless it is done in the course of his employment. It is deemed to be so done if it is either (i) a wrongful act authorised by the master, or (ii) a wrongful and unauthorised mode of doing some act authorised by the master ... On the other hand, if the unauthorised and wrongful act of the servant is not so connected with the authorised act as to be a mode of doing it, but is an independent act, the master is not responsible: for in such a case the servant is not acting in the course of his employment, but has gone outside of it.'

This statement can be used as a basis for an analysis of the law, although it must be emphasised that it should not be taken as an exclusive statement of the law, but merely as being illustrative of the approach of the courts. It can be discussed under the following headings.

Negligent and careless acts

The fact that the mode of doing a job is wrongful and unauthorised will not prevent the employer being vicariously liable for it provided that at the time the employee was doing some act authorised by the employer. This has the effect of denying to employers the argument that the mere fact that the employee was going about his work in a negligent or mistaken manner takes the employee outside the course of his employment because the employer would not have sanctioned the commission of a negligent or mistaken act.

This can be demonstrated in its application to negligent acts by the case of *Century Insurance Co* v *Northern Ireland Road Transport Board* [1942] AC 509. The defendants employed Davison as a petrol tanker driver. While discharging petrol at a garage, Davison lit a cigarette. He threw away the lighted match, which caused a fire and an explosion in which the plaintiff's property was damaged. The House of Lords held that the defendants were vicariously liable for the tort of their employee. Although it was true that the driver had lit a cigarette for his own personal benefit and not for the benefit of his employers, this act of lighting a cigarette could not be viewed in isolation from the job he was doing at that time. At the time of the accident the driver was doing his job of discharging petrol from the tanker, albeit that he was doing his job in an unauthorised and negligent fashion.

Similar reasoning has been deployed in the case of a mistaken act on the part of an employee. Thus in *Bayley* v *Manchester, Sheffield and Lincolnshire Railway Co* (1873) LR 8 CP 148 a rather over-zealous railway porter forcibly removed the plaintiff from a train, erroneously believing that the plaintiff had got onto the wrong train. Part of the porter's job included ensuring that people got onto the correct train and so his employers were held to be vicariously liable for his tort. He was simply doing, in a mistaken manner, what he was employed to do.

A related issue concerns the situation where an employee takes steps to save his employer's property under the mistaken belief that his employer's property is threatened. In *Poland* v *John Parr and Sons* [1927] 1 KB 236 the Court of Appeal held that, as a general rule, an employee is authorised to do acts which are for the protection of his employer's property, although he is not legally 'bound' so to do. However, if the act in question had been excessive in the situation (for example, had he fired a shot at the person whom he believed to be taking his employer's property) then that would have taken the employee out of the course of his employment (see too *Warren* v *Henley's Ltd* [1948] 2 All ER 935, discussed further below).

Express prohibition

It follows from the definition provided by Salmond and Heuston that the mere fact that an employer has placed prohibitions upon the conduct of the employee will not, of itself, operate to restrict the course of employment (see to similar effect the judgment of Lord Dunedin in *Plumb* v *Cobden Flour Mills Co* [1914] AC 62, 67). It may be objected that there is no good reason why an employer should be liable where he has expressly placed prohibitions upon the employee. But such an approach would make it too easy for employers to evade the impact of the vicarious liability doctrine by prohibiting their employees from committing torts. So the law has to strike a balance between denying to employers the ability to exempt themselves from the impact of this doctrine, while avoiding the imposition of liability for acts which are wholly unconnected with the work of the employee. The approach which the law has adopted is to permit employers to limit the acts which the employee may do within the course of his employment, but to deny them the ability to restrict the mode of doing the particular act in question. Thus stated, the crucial distinction is between the mode of doing the act and the act itself. Two cases may help us to understand this distinction.

The first case is *Limpus* v *London General Omnibus Co* (1862) 1 H & C 526. Here the defendants expressly prohibited their drivers from racing with, or obstructing, other buses. Their driver, however, obstructed the plaintiff's bus to pick up two lady passengers and, in so doing, caused a collision in which several passengers were injured. It was held that the defendants were vicariously liable for the tort of their driver because at the time of the accident he was simply doing an authorised act (driving a bus) in an unauthorised manner or mode.

On the other side of the line is the case of *Conway* v *George Wimpey & Co Ltd* [1951] 2 KB 266. In this case the defendants provided transport for their employees on a construction site. The drivers were specifically told not to give lifts to employees of other companies. However, one of their drivers gave a lift to the plaintiff, who was employed by another company (although the driver was unaware of this fact). The plaintiff was injured as a result of the negligence of the driver and he sued the defendants. The Court of Appeal held that the defendants were not vicariously liable for the tort of the driver because at the time of the accident the driver was doing an unauthorised act (driving his van with an unauthorised passenger on board) and that it was not simply a case of him doing an authorised act in an unauthorised mode.

This sounds fine in theory, but it leaves us with a difficult practical problem. The problem is how do the courts define the 'act' which the employee is employed to do? For example, we could reverse the results in *Limpus* and *Conway* by redefining the act which the employee was employed to do. If in *Limpus* we said that the act which the employee was employed to do was drive buses and that at the time of the accident he was 'racing or obstructing other buses' then the driver would have been doing an unauthorised act. On the other hand, if in *Conway* we defined the act which the driver was doing at the time of the accident as driving the bus, then he would have been doing an authorised act, albeit in an unauthorised manner. It can be argued that the courts have so much discretion in defining the scope of the act that they can decide the case the way they want it to go and then select the appropriate label to justify their decision.

Further evidence of the confusion which currently exists can be discovered by comparing the decisions in *Twine* v *Bean's Express Ltd* (1946) 62 TLR 458 and *Rose* v *Plenty* [1976] 1 WLR 141. In the former case the plaintiff's husband was given a lift in a van driven by an employee of the defendants. The plaintiff's husband was killed as a result of the negligence of the driver. The driver had been told that he could only give lifts to certain passengers and the plaintiff was not one of these passengers. Furthermore there was a notice restricting the class of authorised passengers inside the van. The Court of Appeal held that the defendants were not liable for the tort of their employee. There were two grounds to the decision of the court. The first was that the deceased was a trespasser and as such was not owed a duty of care by the defendants. The second point was that the driver was not acting within the course of his employment because at the time of the accident he was doing an unauthorised act, namely giving a lift to an unauthorised person.

This case was reconsidered by the Court of Appeal in the controversial case of *Rose* v *Plenty* (above). The defendants expressly prohibited their milkmen from permitting boys to ride on their milk floats. Notices were also posted at the depot informing milkmen of this prohibition. In contravention of this order an employee allowed the plaintiff, a boy aged 13, to ride on his milk float while helping him with his deliveries and collections. As he was riding on the milk float the plaintiff was injured due to the negligence of the driver. The Court of Appeal held that the defendants were liable for the tort of their employee. Their prohibition had not affected the course of the employee's employment, it had simply affected the mode by which he could do his job. Lawton LJ dissented on the ground that he could not distinguish the present case from *Twine* and he was not prepared to say that the latter decision was wrong.

The majority, Lord Denning MR and Scarman LJ, distinguished *Twine* on two grounds. The first ground was that the deceased in *Twine* was a trespasser and was therefore owed no duty of care by the defendants. It was held that this ground of the decision could no longer stand because, since the decision of the House of Lords in *British Railways Board* v *Herrington* [1972] AC 877, it was clear that a limited duty of care is owed to trespassers (see further 17.15).

The second ground on which the majority distinguished *Twine* related to the course of employment point. Lord Denning distinguished *Twine* on the ground that there the lift was not given for any purpose beneficial to the employer (presumably because the lift was given to an employee of another company), whereas in *Rose* the plaintiff's presence on the milk float was to further the employer's business. This latter point must be regarded as doubtful because, as was pointed out by Lawton LJ, the plaintiff was not furthering the employer's business but was doing the driver's job for him and making his life an easier one. Scarman LJ dealt more fully with the case law and vainly sought to show that the case law was reconcilable. He said that in *Twine* the employer's prohibition limited the scope of the employee's employment, whereas here the employer's prohibition did not alter the scope of the employee's employment but only affected the mode by which the job was to be done. However, this reconciliation is only effective at the formal level because it does not explain how the courts define the act which the employee is employed to do, as against the mode in which he is to do the job. The more important aspect of the judgment may be that Scarman LJ argued that a broad approach should be taken to the question of the course of employment. Thus, in the recent case of *Racz* v *Home Office* [1994] 2 WLR 23 the House of Lords took a wide approach to this question and held where a prisoner sued the Home Office, alleging misfeasance in public office on the part of prison officers, that the Home Office as employers could be vicariously liable for the torts of its employee prison officers. Dicta in the speech of Lord Bridge in *R* v *Deputy Governor of Parkhurst Prison, ex parte Hague* [1992] 1 AC 58, which suggested that such actions by prison officers took them outside the course of their employment, were not followed in *Racz*.

'Frolics and detours'

Considerable difficulty has arisen with vehicle drivers who depart from authorised routes. One could argue that as soon as an employee departs from his authorised route he goes outside the course of his employment. But that would be a draconian measure for, as LP Emslie said in *Angus* v *Glasgow Corporation* 1977 SLT 206, unauthorised deviations from an authorised route are only to be expected as an incident of modern industrial life. So once again we are faced with the difficulty of devising a test to determine the extent to which an employer is responsible for the unauthorised deviations of his employee. The generally accepted test was laid down by Parke B in *Joel* v *Morrison* (1834) 6 C & P 501 in the following terms:

> 'If [the driver] was going out of his way, against his master's implied commands, when driving on his master's business, he will make his master liable; but if he was going on a frolic of his own, without being at all on his master's business, the master will not be liable.'

It is now necessary to give consideration to what constitutes a 'frolic of his own'. In *Whatman* v *Pearson* (1868) LR 3 CP 422 an employee who went home for his lunch on his horse and cart, contrary to his employer's instructions, was held to remain within the course of his employment so that his employers were liable for the damage done by the horse when, having been left unattended outside the employee's home, it ran off and damaged the plaintiff's property. On the other hand, in *Storey* v *Ashton* (1869) LR 4 QB 476, the defendant employers were held not liable when their employee, after completing his deliveries, went on a detour to visit his brother-in-law. It was held that this was a new and independent journey which had nothing to do with his employment and so was outside the course of his employment.

In *Williams* v *A & W Hemphill Ltd* 1966 SLT 259, a Scottish case which went on appeal to the House of Lords, some interesting comments were made on this area of law. The case concerned a driver who had gone on a considerable detour when driving boys home, because the boys wanted to follow some girl guides who had been camping in a nearby field. While on this detour the bus was involved in an accident and some of the boys were injured. The driver was held to be within the course of his employment. Lord Pearce said that it was a question of fact in each case whether the employee had gone on a 'frolic of his own'. He considered *Storey* and said that had the driver been carrying, at the time of the accident, some important cargo belonging to the employer then the result might have been different. In *Williams* the continued presence of the boys on the bus made it impossible to say that this was a frolic of the driver's own. This latter case suggests that it is only a new and independent journey, which is solely undertaken for the selfish purposes of the employee, that will constitute a 'frolic of his own'.

A related problem concerns the situation where the employee is travelling to or from work or between two places of work. In *Smith* v *Stages* [1989] AC 928 the plaintiff was seriously injured in a car accident which was caused by the negligence of a fellow employee, the first defendant. The two employees, who were based in Staffordshire, were sent to work in Pembroke. They worked most of the day on Sunday and worked all night. As the employees had worked all night the employers, the second defendants, agreed to pay the employees eight hours sleeping time and eight hours travelling time to enable them to return home. But they did not direct the employees as to when they should return home or even what method of travel they should adopt. Despite their exertions, the employees decided to travel home immediately after their Sunday night shift and it was on the way home that the accident occurred. The cause of the accident was the negligence of the first defendant. The House of Lords held that the first defendant was in the course of his employment when the accident occurred and that therefore the second defendants were vicariously liable. The first defendant was being paid wages to travel back to Staffordshire and so he was acting within the course of his employment when travelling home.

Lord Lowry, after engaging in a survey of the relevant case law, deduced the following prima facie propositions. The first is, that an employee who is travelling from his home to his regular place of work or from his regular place of work to his home is not within the course of his employment. But, if the employee is required by his contract of employment to use the employer's transport, then he will normally be regarded as being within the course of his employment when travelling to work. Secondly, an employee who is travelling between workplaces or in the course of a peripatetic occupation is within the course of his employment. Thirdly, receipt of wages, but not a travelling allowance, suggests that the journey is for the benefit of the employer and that the journey is within the course of employment. Fourthly, an employee is within the course of his employment if he travels in his employer's time from his home to a workplace which is not his regular workplace or to the scene of an emergency. Finally, a deviation from a journey undertaken in the course of employment, unless that deviation is merely incidental to the journey, will take the employee outside the course of his employment for the duration of the deviation. These propositions are, however, subject to two principal qualifications.

The first is that they are subject to any agreement to the contrary between an employer and his employee. The second is that these propositions are not intended to define the position of salaried employees, 'with regard to whom the touchstone of payment made in the employer's time is not generally significant'.

Intentional wrongful acts

In cases involving intentional wrongful acts the courts have adopted a much more restrictive approach to the course of employment issue. This can be seen in the following three recent cases. The first is *Heasmans* v *Clarity Cleaning Co Ltd* [1987] IRLR 286. One of the defendants' employees, who was employed to clean the plaintiff's offices, used the plaintiff's telephone to make unauthorised international calls costing £1,411. The Court of Appeal held that the defendants were not vicariously liable for the acts of their employee. Nourse LJ stated that the employee was employed to clean the telephones and not to use them. In using them he had not cleaned the telephones in an unauthorised manner, but had done an unauthorised act and so had gone outside the course of his employment. This extremely narrow approach to the course of employment issue is clearly at variance with the much broader approach found in *Rose* v *Plenty* (above). The second case is *Irving* v *The Post Office* [1987] IRLR 289. The plaintiffs claimed that the defendants had unlawfully discriminated against them on the grounds of their race. The plaintiffs lived next door to an employee of the defendants, called Mr Edwards, and they were not on speaking terms. Mr Edwards, during the course of his work sorting mail, saw an envelope addressed to the plaintiffs and wrote on the back of the envelope 'Go back to Jamaica Sambo' and drew a picture of a black smiling face. Mr Edwards was authorised to write on letters which he was sorting but only for the purpose of ensuring that the mail was properly dealt with. The plaintiffs argued that the defendants were vicariously liable for the racial abuse of Mr Edwards but it was held that, in writing racial abuse on the envelope, the employee was doing an unauthorised act and that therefore the defendants were not vicariously liable. The Court of Appeal placed strong reliance upon *Heasmans* v *Clarity Cleaning* (above) and held that the writing of the racial abuse was an act of personal malevolence by Mr Edwards, and they affirmed that it could not be assumed that, merely because the employment had provided the opportunity for the wrong, the employers were therefore liable. Fox LJ stated that 'out of fairness to employers' limits have to be set to the doctrine of vicarious liability, particularly where, as here, it was sought to make the defendants liable for the 'wilful wrongdoing' of their employee which they had in no way authorised. The third case is *General Engineering Services Ltd* v *Kingston and Saint Andrew Corp* [1989] 1 WLR 69. The plaintiffs' property was completely destroyed by fire and the damage was increased by the fact that the firemen who answered the plaintiffs' emergency call were involved in a go-slow in support of a pay claim and took 17 minutes rather than the normal three and a half minutes to reach the plaintiffs' property. The plaintiffs alleged that the defendants, who were the employers of the firemen, were vicariously liable for the acts of the firemen. The Privy Council held that the defendants were not liable because the firemen were not within the course of their employment in travelling to the plaintiff's property at such a slow speed. They were employed to travel to the scene of a fire as quickly as reasonably possible and, in travelling as slowly as possible, it could not be said that they were doing an authorised act in an unauthorised manner; they were doing an unauthorised act. Bearing in mind the restrictive tenor of the approach of the courts, we shall discuss this category under three separate headings.

Assault

Some employees, such as 'bouncers' at a discotheque, may be expected to exercise some degree of violence in the course of their employment. We have also noted that employees have some, albeit limited, authority to protect their employers' interests in an emergency (*Poland* v *John Parr* [1927] 1 KB 236). But outside these limited categories the courts have been extremely reluctant to impose liability upon employers for an assault committed by an employee. Thus in *Warren* v *Henley's Ltd* [1948] 2 All ER 935 the defendants were held not to be vicariously liable for the assault of their employee. The assault took place after the employee, who was a petrol pump attendant, had accused a customer of having tried to drive away without paying for his petrol. The customer paid his bill and said he would call the police and that he would also inform the defendants. The employee was so angry at this that he assaulted the customer. The defendants were held not to be liable because this was an act of personal vengeance and so was outside the course of his employment (see to similar effect *Deaton's Property Ltd* v *Flew* (1949) 79 CLR 370). This line of authority has been criticised convincingly by Rose (Liability for an Employee's Assaults (1977) 40 MLR 420) on the ground that an employee's personal acts cannot be viewed in isolation from the job he is doing. In *Century Insurance Co* v *Northern Ireland Road Transport Board* [1942] AC 509 the House of Lords did refuse to regard the employee's personal act of smoking in isolation from the job that he was doing but, unfortunately, such an approach has not been adopted in the case of assault.

Theft

In *Cheshire* v *Bailey* [1905] 1 KB 237 it was held that theft necessarily took the employee outside the course of his employment. But this is no longer the position today. In *Morris* v *C W Martin and Sons Ltd* [1966] 1 QB 716 the plaintiff took her fur coat to a furrier to be cleaned. With her consent, the furrier sent the coat to the defendants for cleaning, but one of the defendants' employees stole the coat. The defendants were held liable for the loss on the ground that they were in breach of their duties as bailees for reward. But the case could have been argued as one of vicarious liability and this fact was referred to by two members of the Court of Appeal. However in *Port Swettenham Authority* v *T W Wu* [1979] AC 580 Lord

Salmon rejected the 'heresy' in *Cheshire* that theft necessarily takes the employee outside the course of his employment and approved of *Morris*.

Fraud

In *Lloyd* v *Grace, Smith and Co* [1912] AC 716 the court rejected the proposition adopted in *Barwick* v *English Joint Stock Bank* (1867) LR 2 Ex 259 that the employer is only vicariously liable for the fraud of his employee when the fraud was committed for his (the employer's) own benefit. For the employer to be liable the fraudulent act must have been committed within the scope of the employee's actual or ostensible authority. This test was satisfied on the facts of *Lloyd* because the fraud arose out of a conveyancing transaction and the clerk had authority to enter into such a transaction. The test was not, however, satisfied in the case of *Armagas* v *Mundogas SA, The Ocean Frost* [1986] AC 717. An employee of the defendants entered into a contract for the charter of a ship, into which he had no authority, either actual or ostensible, to enter. The employee did represent that he had authority to enter into such a transaction but such a representation did not fall within the class of representations which a person in the position of the employee was usually authorised to perform. So the plaintiffs could not recover against the defendants because they had placed their reliance upon the employee.

The conclusion which must be drawn is that the 'course of employment' requirement has been interpreted erratically and that the category of assaults committed by employees is out of step with the other categories. This merely serves to illustrate the lack of a clear theoretical basis to the doctrine of vicarious liability.

4.6 The master's indemnity

There is no doubt that employers and employees are joint tortfeasors, with the result that when the employer is held liable for the tort of his employee, the employer has the right to recover an indemnity under s1(1) of the Civil Liability (Contribution) Act 1978. In the typical vicarious liability case this would mean that the employer could recover a complete indemnity.

In addition to this statutory right the employer may be entitled to recover an indemnity at common law, as in *Lister* v *Romford Ice and Cold Storage Co* [1957] AC 555. Here a father and son were fellow employees. The father was injured as a result of the negligence of his son. The father sued the employers in negligence and recovered from them. However the employers' insurers successfully recovered from the son as the son was in breach of his implied undertaking to take reasonable care and so they recovered the sum which had been paid to his father.

It must be doubted whether this indemnity should be permitted to continue in present circumstances. The employer is usually in the best position to bear such a loss. In most cases he is insured and it is even more undesirable to allow an insurance company, which has been paid to accept the risk, to recover from the employee when the risk, in fact, materialises. However, it is unlikely that such a case would occur again, as employers' insurers have entered into a gentleman's agreement not to take advantage of the indemnity principle unless there is evidence of collusion or wilful misconduct.

4.7 Principal and agent

A principal may be vicariously liable for torts committed by his agent in the course of his agent's employment (cf. *Winfield and Jolowicz on Tort* (13th ed) pp579–80). The main difficulty here arises with what may be called 'ad hoc' agency. These cases are really concerned with liability arising out of road traffic accidents, where the legal response is shaped by the insurance background.

The first case of significance is *Ormrod* v *Crossville Motor Services* [1953] 1 WLR 1120. The owner of a motor car asked a friend to drive the car from Birkenhead to Monte Carlo, where the owner planned to compete in the car rally. After the rally was over both parties planned to go on holiday together in the car. In the course of the journey the friend was in an accident caused by his negligence. The plaintiff's bus was damaged in the accident. It was held that the owner was liable for his friend's negligence, even though the friend was going on the journey partly for his own purposes.

However, a different result was reached in *Morgans* v *Launchbury* [1973] AC 127 where the House of Lords placed a limit on the extent to which a plaintiff can search for a defendant who has an insurance policy, irrespective of the fault of the defendant. A husband used his wife's car to go to work and when he went out drinking. The wife expressed concern about her husband's drinking habits and told him to get a friend to drive him if he had had too much to drink. One evening the husband got drunk and duly got a friend to drive him home. The friend drove off at 90 mph in the wrong direction and collided with a bus, killing the friend and the husband and injuring passengers on the bus. The passengers sued the wife, claiming that she was vicariously liable. This argument was rejected by the House of Lords on the ground that the husband could not be regarded as the wife's agent, even when he took the car to his work. Lord Wilberforce said that 'in order to fix vicarious liability on the owner of a car in such a case as the present, it must be shown that the driver was using it for the owner's purposes, under delegation of a task or duty'. If, however, the owner has permitted an uninsured driver to drive his car then he will be liable for breach of statutory duty if the driver is unable to satisfy judgment (*Monk* v *Warbey* [1935] 1 KB 175) and if the driver is uninsured then the Motor Insurers' Bureau may meet an unsatisfied judgment in respect of personal injuries.

4.8 Partnership

The vicarious liability of partners is governed by s10 of the Partnership Act 1890 which states that:

'Where, by any wrongful act or omission of any partner acting in the ordinary course of the business of the firm, or with the authority of his co-partners, loss or injury is caused to any person not being a partner in his firm, or any penalty is incurred, the firm is liable therefore to the same extent as the partner so acting or omitting to act.'

It is further provided in s12 that the liability of partners is joint and several.

5

Liability for Independent Contractors

5.1 Introduction and the general rule

5.2 Exceptions to the general rule

5.3 Conclusion

5.1 Introduction and the general rule

In addition to being liable for the torts of their employees committed in the course of their employment, employers may also, in certain circumstances, be held liable for torts committed by independent contractors which they have employed. It must be stated that none of these cases of liability for the tort of an independent contractor are examples of vicarious liability. They are all examples of primary liability of the employer. The general rule, however, is that an employer is not liable for the tort of his independent contractor. The traditional justification for this is that the employer does not control the independent contractor and so there is no justification for imposing liability upon the employer for the tort of the independent contractor. One example of this general rule is the case of *Morgan* v *Incorporated Central Council of the Girls Friendly Society* [1936] 1 All ER 404. The plaintiff suffered injury when he fell down a lift shaft on the defendants' premises. The reason for the accident was that the lift shaft had been negligently left unguarded by a firm of independent contractors. It was held that the defendants were not liable for the negligence of the independent contractors.

An interesting challenge to this rule was launched in *D and F Estates Ltd* v *The Church Commissioners for England* [1989] AC 177. The defendants were the main contractors involved in the building of a block of flats and the plaintiffs took a lease of one of the flats. After they had moved in the plaintiffs discovered that the plastering work, which had been done by a firm of independent contractors employed by the defendants, had been done defectively. So they sued the defendants for the cost of the repair and other economic loss on the ground, inter alia, that the defendants owed a duty to the plaintiffs to supervise the work of the subcontractors and that they had failed to discharge this duty properly. The House of Lords rejected the argument that the defendants owed a duty of care to the plaintiffs. The House of Lords also held that the defendants were not liable for the negligence of the subcontractors who failed to carry out the plaster work properly. Lord Bridge affirmed that 'it is trite law that the employer of an independent contractor is, in general, not liable for the negligence or other torts committed by the contractor in the course of the execution of the work'. However, Lord Bridge did acknowledge that, if the main contractor, in the course of the supervision of the subcontractor, comes to know that the subcontractor is carrying out his work in a defective and foreseeably dangerous way and if he condones the negligence on the part of the subcontractor, the main contractor would 'no doubt make himself potentially liable for the consequences as joint tortfeasor'. In the present case there was no evidence that the main contractors actually knew of the defective plastering work and, since the case did not fall within any of the exceptional cases when an employer may be liable for the tort of an independent contractor (on which see 5.2), the defendants were not liable for the negligence of the plasterers.

5.2 Exceptions to the general rule

There are a number of exceptions to the general rule that an employer is not liable for the tort of an independent contractor. These exceptions may be classified as follows.

Firstly, the employer is liable where he has authorised the independent contractor to commit a tort (*Ellis* v *Sheffield Gas Consumers Co* (1853) 2 E & B 767). In such a case the employer is liable as a joint tortfeasor with the independent contractor.

Secondly, the employer is liable if he is negligent in choosing an independent contractor who is not competent to carry out the job or if the employer fails to instruct him properly or fails to check the work where he is competent to do so (*Pinn* v *Rew* (1916) 32 TLR 451).

Thirdly, statute law may impose upon the employer a duty of care which cannot be discharged by delegating performance to an independent contractor. Whether a statute does impose such an 'absolute' obligation upon the employer is, of course, a question of construction of the particular statute. One example of a statute which imposes such an absolute obligation upon employers is the Factories Act 1961.

Fourthly, at common law certain non-delegable duties are imposed upon employers. 'Non-delegable' duty does not mean that the employer cannot, in fact, delegate performance to an independent contractor. What it means is that the employer cannot delegate responsibility for the performance of the task. There are a number of non-delegable duties which exist at common law, but there is no coherent policy behind the existence of these duties. There are six such common law duties which are worthy of consideration.

The first category consists of cases of (so called) strict liability at common law, such as the rule in *Rylands* v *Fletcher* (see chapter 20) and nuisance (chapter 18), where the employer is liable for the tort of the independent contractor. The second, and to some extent analogous, category consists of cases where the employer has employed an independent contractor to do work which is classified as being 'extra hazardous'. The operation of this principle can be illustrated by reference to the case of *Honeywill and Stein Ltd* v *Larkin Brothers Ltd* [1934] 1 KB 191. The plaintiffs were engaged to do acoustics work and employed the defendants, as independent contractors, to take photographs of the cinema as part of their work. The defendants used flash photography which, at that time, required a tray of magnesium to be ignited above the camera lens. In doing this the defendants set fire to the cinema curtains. The plaintiffs paid the damages and then sought to recover from the defendants. It was held that the plaintiffs were liable to the owners of the theatre for the damage caused by the negligence of the defendants and that they were, in turn, entitled to recover damages from the defendants for breach of contract. The operation was a hazardous one and the plaintiffs had assumed an obligation to ensure that reasonable precautions were taken so that no damage would result and this obligation could not be delegated to an independent contractor (it should be noted that the High Court of Australia in *Stevens* v *Brodribb Sawmilling Co Pty Ltd* (1986) 160 CLR 16 has refused to follow *Honeywill* on the ground that this exception cannot be justified in policy terms). This rule does not apply where the activity is not extra hazardous (*Salsbury* v *Woodland* [1970] 1 QB 342). It is not easy to say what constitutes an extra hazardous activity, but it must be something which involves the risk of special danger to others. The fact that a task is difficult does not mean that it is extra hazardous; work is only extra hazardous when, by its very nature, it involves a risk of danger to others unless done with extreme care (*Alcock* v *Wraith* (1992) 59 Build LR 16).

The third category of non-delegable duties at common law relates to liability for the escape of fire (*Balfour* v *Barty-King* [1957] 1 QB 496). The fourth category consists of cases where the work of the independent contractor is done on or over the highway, or some other place to which the public has access. Thus in *Tarry* v *Ashton* (1876) 1 QBD 314 an employer was held liable when a lamp which projected over the highway fell on the plaintiff. The employer was held liable even though he had contracted with an independent contractor for the repair of the lamp. He remained liable for the negligence of the contractor. Similarly in *Holliday* v *National Telephone Co* [1899] 2 QB 392 the contractor, a plumber, was soldering joints in telephone wires when he immersed a blowlamp in a pot of solder on the highway and it exploded, injuring the plaintiff. It was held that the defendants, who had employed the plumber, were liable because they had a duty to see that the work was carried out with due care for the protection of those who passed along the highway (in this case the defendants' duty was derived from statute).

The fifth category consists of the employer's non-delegable duty in respect of the safety of his employees (*Wilsons and Clyde Coal Co* v *English* [1938] AC 57). The sixth and final category consists of the rule that a bailee for reward, who entrusts the goods he is supposed to be looking after to an independent contractor, remains liable for any loss or damage to the goods, in the absence of any contractual provision to the contrary (see *Morris* v *CW Martin & Sons Ltd* [1966] 1 QB 716 and *British Road Services* v *Arthur Crutchley* [1967] 1 WLR 835).

Finally, the employer is not liable for the collateral or casual negligence of the independent contractor. In many cases it is difficult to discern what is meant by 'collateral negligence'. In general it can be said to mean that the negligence of the independent contractor must arise out of the very task which is delegated to him and if it is not then his negligence is collateral. Thus in *Padbury* v *Holliday and Greenwood* (1912) 28 TLR 492 the defendants employed a subcontractor to do some work on a house which the defendants were building. One of the subcontractor's employees put a tool on a window sill while he was working. A strong gust of wind blew the window and the tool fell off the sill and hit the plaintiff, who was walking along the highway. It was held that the employee's negligence was incidental to the performance of his task and so the defendants were not liable to the plaintiff.

5.3 Conclusion

Recent years have witnessed a large increase in the number of self-employed workers in this country. This increase threatens to undermine the social purposes served by the doctrine of vicarious liability because, as the law presently stands, employers are not vicariously liable for the torts of independent contractors. As yet the courts have not formed a coherent response to this problem (see generally McKendrick 'Vicarious Liability and Independent Contractors – A Re-Examination' (1990) 53 MLR 770). In some cases they have sought to extend the exceptions to the general rule of no liability (see, for example, *McDermid* v *Nash Dredging and Reclamation Co Ltd* [1987] AC 906), while in other cases they have sought to impose new forms of primary liability upon employers, such as a duty to co-ordinate third parties (see, for example, the decision of the High Court of Australia in *Stevens* v *Brodribb Sawmilling Co Pty Ltd* (1986) 160 CLR 16). One further approach which could be adopted is to abandon the generalist approach of the common law to the question of whether or not a particular worker is an employee (an example of which can be found in the judgment of Wright J in *R* v *Callender* [1993] QB 303, 309). If it was recognised that the question of whether or not a worker is an employee depends upon the context in which the question arises, then there would be room for a more flexible approach in vicarious liability cases. This is because, in such cases, the policies of loss distribution and finding a solvent defendant favour classification of a worker as an employee. One possible line of development would be for the courts to conclude that, once a person is found to be part of an organisation, in the sense that his work is an 'integral part of the business' rather than being merely 'accessory' to it, the organisation is vicariously liable for all the wrongs of that person committed within the scope of his responsibilities, whether he is an employee or an independent contractor. It must, however, be said that English law has presently set its face against the conclusion that an employer can be vicariously liable for the wrongdoing of an independent contractor (see *McDermid* (above)) but, if English law is to meet the challenge presented to it by the increase in the numbers of self-employed workers then it is suggested that it will have to reconsider its position on this issue.

6

Negligence: The Duty of Care – Some General Considerations

6.1 Introduction

6.2 The emergence of a general principle

6.3 The development of the general principle

6.4 Resiling from the general principle

6.5 A general principle or reasoning by analogy?

6.6 The incremental approach

6.7 Factors inhibiting the imposition of a duty of care

6.8 The distinction between misfeasance and non-feasance

6.9 The role of Parliament

6.10 The availability of an alternative remedy

6.11 No undermining of established principles of the common law or equity

6.12 No duty recognised before

6.13 The cost and availability of insurance?

6.14 Conclusion

6.1 Introduction

In the study of the law of tort the centre stage is occupied by the tort of negligence. The tort of negligence has been defined by *Winfield and Jolowicz on Tort* (13th ed) p72 in the following terms: '... negligence as a tort is the breach of a legal duty to take care which results in damage, undesired by the defendant, to the plaintiff'. Thus stated the tort consists of three distinct elements.

The first element is that the defendant must owe to the plaintiff a duty of care. The circumstances in which a defendant may owe a duty of care to the plaintiff will be discussed in this chapter. The second element is that the defendant must breach the duty of care which he owes to the plaintiff. This issue will be discussed in chapter 9. The third element is that the plaintiff must suffer damage as a result of the defendant's breach of his duty of care. The two main principles here are that the defendant's negligence must have caused the damage to the plaintiff (discussed in chapter 10) and the damage which the plaintiff suffered must not be too remote a consequence of the defendant's negligence (discussed in chapter 11).

This chapter will therefore discuss the principles upon which the courts decide whether or not the defendant owes to the plaintiff a duty of care. The modern source of the duty of care requirement can be found in the celebrated judgment of Lord Atkin in *Donoghue* v *Stevenson* [1932] AC 562. But, although it is now an entrenched component of the tort of negligence, it has not escaped criticism. Writing shortly after the decision of the House of Lords in *Donoghue*, Buckland stated ((1935) 51 LQR 637, 639) that the duty to take care is 'certainly a part of our law, but, as it seems to the writer, an unnecessary fifth wheel on the coach, incapable of sound analysis and possibly productive of injustice'. The requirement that the defendant owe to the plaintiff a duty of care is not logically necessary and many legal systems have survived perfectly well without it, most notably the Romans'. Nevertheless, it is of vital significance in English law because it is via the duty of care concept that the courts have sought to limit and control the circumstances in which liability may be imposed upon a defendant for the consequences of his negligence.

As is often the case in studying the law of tort we must commence our study by briefly examining the history of this issue because it is necessary to understand the history if we are to comprehend the present state of the law. We can divide the development of the duty of care into three broad stages; the first being 'the emergence of a general principle', the second being 'the development of the general principle' and the third being 'resiling from the general principle'. It must, however, be said that this tripartite division is a broad one. Cases can always be found within a particular period which appear to defy this analysis. The purpose of this division is simply to enable us to identify the broad thrust of the development of the tort of negligence.

6.2 The emergence of a general principle

A person is not liable for every negligent act which he or she commits. There has always been some control device which has identified and limited the situations in which a person may be held legally liable for the consequences of his negligence. As we have already noted, the principal control device in English law is the requirement that the defendant owe to the plaintiff a duty of care. This requirement was not articulated as a general principle until the judgment of Brett MR in the case of *Heaven* v *Pender* (1883) 11 QBD 503. At that stage in our legal development, the tort of negligence was applicable to damage caused in certain particular circumstances, such as road accidents, but was not a principle of general application. The innovation in the judgment of Brett MR was that he sought to formulate a general principle for identifying whether or not a duty of care existed, which principle could be applied to new situations as well as to the traditional categories.

But it was not until the famous case of *Donoghue* v *Stevenson* [1932] AC 562 that a general principle was firmly established for determining the existence of a duty of care. The defendants were manufacturers of ginger beer. A friend of the plaintiff purchased a bottle of ginger beer for the plaintiff. The plaintiff drank some of the ginger beer but when she poured out the remainder of the contents of the bottle a decomposed snail floated out of the bottle. The plaintiff claimed that she suffered severe shock and became very ill as a result of this incident. She was unable to proceed against the manufacturers in contract because there was no contract between the parties. So she brought an action in tort against the manufacturers. The House of Lords held that the defendants, being the manufacturers of the ginger beer, owed a duty of care to the plaintiff, as the ultimate consumer or purchaser of the ginger beer, to take reasonable care to ensure that the bottle did not contain some substance which was likely to cause injury to health. The decision of the House of Lords is important for two particular reasons.

The first reason is the judgment of Lord Atkin. His statement of principle still forms the basis of the modern law and its importance lies in its attempt to provide a general principle which could be applied in all negligence cases and, thus, could unify what had, hitherto, been a series of discrete rules. He said:

> 'In English law there must be, and is, some general conception of relations giving rise to a duty of care, of which the particular cases found in the books are but instances ... The rule that you are to love your neighbour becomes, in law, you must not injure your neighbour; and the lawyer's question, Who is my neighbour? receives a restricted reply. You must take reasonable care to avoid acts or omissions which you can reasonably foresee would be likely to injure your neighbour. Who, then, in law is my neighbour? The answer seems to be – persons who are so closely and directly affected by my act that I ought reasonably to have them in contemplation as being so affected when I am directing my mind to the acts or omissions which are called in question.'

This dicta is the general principle which has assumed enormous significance in the development of the tort of negligence.

The second point of significance was that their Lordships freed the tort of negligence from what was known as the 'contract fallacy'. According to this contract fallacy, where a manufacturer had entered into a contractual relationship with another, he could not owe a duty of care in tort to a third party who was not privy to that contract. The most oft-quoted example of this contract fallacy is the case of *Winterbottom* v *Wright* (1842) 10 M & W 109. The defendants were coachbuilders. They had a contract with the Postmaster-General to deliver a coach for the delivery of mail. The plaintiff was the driver of the coach and he was seriously injured when he fell off the coach due to a latent defect in the construction of the coach. It was held that the plaintiff could not recover from the defendants because he was not privy to the contract for the delivery of the coach. But this fallacy was exploded by the House of Lords in *Donoghue*. It was held that it was irrelevant to the plaintiff's action in tort that she was not privy to a contract with the defendants for the sale of the ginger beer. The existence of a contractual relationship with the purchaser of the ginger beer did not preclude the existence of liability in tort to the plaintiff, who was not a party to the contract. Although this contract fallacy was duly disposed of, the issue of the relationship between contract and tort has been a persistent source of difficulty.

6.3 The development of the general principle

Lord Atkin's statement of principle has come to be known as the neighbour or neighbourhood principle. As we have noted, its importance lies in providing a unifying framework for the tort of negligence and a general principle which can be applied to new situations, not falling within the traditional categories. However, some of the judiciary were reluctant to accept that this statement of principle had the effect of constituting a general principle which was applicable to new situations. As late as 1951 in the case of *Candler* v *Crane Christmas and Co* [1951] 2 KB 164 we find that the majority of the Court of Appeal were unwilling to extend liability for negligent misstatement causing economic loss. Lord Denning argued that the old authorities had to be re-examined in the light of *Donoghue* but this argument was rejected by the majority who slavishly followed the old precedents, which pre-dated *Donoghue*, and refused to subject them to fresh analysis in the light of *Donoghue*. Eventually in the landmark case of *Hedley Byrne & Co Ltd* v *Heller & Partners Ltd* [1964] AC 465 the House of Lords did extend liability for negligent misstatement, although it is crucial to note that they did not apply ordinary *Donoghue* principles for fear that it would lead to too great an ambit of liability. Instead they preferred to apply a more restrictive test. But *Hedley Byrne* is a significant decision because it demonstrated that the House of Lords were prepared to expand the ambit of liability in negligence in appropriate cases.

However in 1970 Lord Atkin's statement of principle was given explicit recognition by the House of Lords as being a statement of general principle which could be applied to all cases of negligence. In *Home Office* v *Dorset Yacht Co* [1970] AC 1004 Lord Reid said that:

> '*Donoghue* v *Stevenson* ... may be regarded as a milestone, and the well-known passage in Lord Atkin's speech should, I think, be regarded as a statement of principle. It is not to be treated as if it were a statutory definition. It will require qualification in new circumstances. But I think that the time has come when we can and should say that it ought to apply unless there is some justification or valid explanation for its exclusion.'

Lord Reid's judgment was an important one because it gave the courts significant freedom to develop the tort of negligence and to apply it to new situations.

This development of a general principle which could be applied to all cases was taken a stage further in the judgment of Lord Wilberforce in *Anns* v *Merton London Borough Council* [1978] AC 728. Lord Wilberforce said:

> 'Through the trilogy of cases in this House, *Donoghue* v *Stevenson*, *Hedley Byrne & Co Ltd* v *Heller & Partners Ltd* and *Home Office* v *Dorset Yacht Co Ltd* the position has now been reached that in order to establish that a duty of care arises in a particular situation, it is not necessary to bring the facts of that situation within those of previous situations in which a duty of care has been held to exist. Rather the question has to be approached in two stages. First one has to ask whether, as between the alleged wrongdoer and the person who has suffered damage there is a sufficient relationship of proximity or neighbourhood such that, in the reasonable contemplation of the former, carelessness on his part may be likely to cause damage to the latter, in which case a prima facie duty of care arises. Secondly, if the first question is answered affirmatively, it is necessary to consider whether there are any considerations which ought to negative, or to reduce or limit the scope of the duty or the class of persons to whom it is owed or the damages to which a breach of it may give rise.'

This two-tier approach was in many ways the high-water mark in the development of the tort of negligence. It has been frequently used in the courts. It provided a principle which could be applied to all cases and the effect of its application in some cases was to expand considerably the boundaries of the tort of negligence.

6.4 Resiling from the general principle

The broad general principle established by Lord Wilberforce in *Anns* has since come under heavy fire, both from the judiciary and from many academics. The principal judicial critics have been Lord Keith, Lord Bridge and, albeit to a lesser extent, Lord Oliver. With the benefit of hindsight, the first major judicial criticism of the two tier approach of Lord Wilberforce can be found in the judgment of Lord Keith in *Governors of the Peabody Donation Fund* v *Sir Lindsay Parkinson & Co Ltd* [1985] AC 210. Lord Keith noted the tendency to treat the passage which we have considered in Lord Wilberforce's judgment as if it was of 'a definitive character'. He went on to say that:

> 'This is a temptation which should be resisted. The true question in each case is whether the particular defendant owed to the particular plaintiff a duty of care having the scope which is contended for, and whether he was in breach of that duty with consequent loss to the plaintiff. A relationship of proximity in Lord Atkin's sense must exist before any duty of care can arise, but the scope of the duty must depend on all the circumstances of the case ... So in determining whether or not a duty of care of particular scope was incumbent upon a defendant it is material to take into consideration whether it is just and reasonable that it should be so.'

Although Lord Keith criticised Lord Wilberforce's two-tier approach, his approach, based upon what is 'just and reasonable', does not appear to be any more certain than that adopted by Lord Wilberforce, nor does it appear to be significantly different.

However, it has assumed considerable significance in subsequent cases. The most important aspect of this judgment is the emphasis on the need to have regard to all the circumstances of the case in deciding whether or not a duty of care is owed.

Further criticism was levelled against Lord Wilberforce's two-tier approach in the case of *Leigh and Sillivan Ltd* v *Aliakmon Shipping Co Ltd* [1985] 1 QB 350 (CA) and [1986] AC 785 (HL). In the Court of Appeal Oliver LJ stated that it was not correct:

> ' ... to regard *Anns* as establishing some new and revolutionary test of the duty of care, the logical application of which is going to enable the court in every case to say whether or not a duty of care exists. Nor, as it seems to me, can it properly be treated either as establishing some new approach to what the policy of the law should be or as conferring upon the court a free hand to determine for itself in each case what limits are to be set.'

This judgment adopts a much more conservative approach than did Lord Wilberforce in *Anns*. The fear which is expressed in this judgment is that the first tier of Lord Wilberforce's approach, that of proximity, is too broad and that it leaves too much to the second stage based upon policy. In particular Oliver LJ said that the courts were not free to evolve their own conception of policy without regard to established lines of authority. This reference to the need to have regard to established authorities where no duty of care has been recognised, constitutes an attack on the generality of the principle adopted in *Anns* and seems to take us back to the pre-*Donoghue* situation where a duty of care only existed in certain well-defined situations and was not to be extended. A similar approach was adopted by Lord Brandon in the House of Lords. He said that Lord Wilberforce's judgment did not provide a 'universally applicable test of the existence and scope of a duty of care'. He also said that Lord Wilberforce's judgment was given in the context of a novel factual situation and not in the context of a factual situation in which such a duty had repeatedly been held not to exist. In the latter context *Anns* was not applicable and no duty of care was owed. As Professor Hepple has noted: 'Lord Brandon's rule-orientated approach ... is reminiscent of the pre-1932 categorisations of negligence rules and of the shackled judicial reasoning before Wilberforce's emancipation' (All ER Rev 1986 p311).

A more fundamental assault was launched on the approach adopted in *Anns* in *Curran* v *Northern Ireland Co-ownership Housing Association Ltd* [1987] AC 718. Lord Bridge stated that Lord Wilberforce's judgment in *Anns*:

> ' ... may be said to represent the high-water mark of a trend in the development of the law of negligence by your Lordships' House towards the elevation of the "neighbourhood" principle derived from the speech of Lord Atkin in *Donoghue* v *Stevenson* into one of general application from which a duty of care may always be derived unless there are clear countervailing considerations to exclude it.'

To similar effect is the judgment of Lord Keith in *Yuen Kun Yeu* v *Attorney-General of Hong Kong* [1988] AC 175 when he said that Lord Wilberforce's approach 'had been elevated to a degree of importance greater than it merits, and greater perhaps than its author intended'. He added that:

'In view of the direction in which the law has since been developing, their Lordships consider that for the future it should be recognised that the two–stage test ... is not to be regarded as in all circumstances a suitable guide to the existence of a duty of care.'

Finally, in *Murphy* v *Brentwood District Council* [1991] 1 AC 398, 461 Lord Keith stated that he considered that the incremental approach adopted by Brennan J in the High Court of Australia in *Council of the Shire of Sutherland* v *Heyman* (1985) 157 CLR 424 (on which see below) was preferable to the two–stage test adopted by Lord Wilberforce in *Anns*.

6.5 A general principle or reasoning by analogy?

In understanding the reasons behind this gradual abandonment of the two–stage test in *Anns* it is very important to have regard to the judgment of Lord Bridge in *Caparo Industries plc* v *Dickman* [1990] 2 AC 605. Lord Bridge there drew a distinction between two different approaches which can be adopted when seeking to identify the existence of a duty of care. The first approach he called the traditional approach where the 'law finds the existence of the duty [of care] in different specific situations each exhibiting its own particular characteristics'. This is the approach which we noted was the predominant one prior to the judgment of Lord Atkin in *Donoghue* (see 6.2). The second approach identified by Lord Bridge, he called 'the more modern approach of seeking a single general principle which may be applied in all circumstances to determine the existence of a duty of care'. This approach found its classic expression in the judgment of Lord Reid in *Home Office* v *Dorset Yacht* (above) and in the two–stage test of Lord Wilberforce in *Anns*. But Lord Bridge noted that in a series of cases, particularly in the judgments of Lord Keith which we have already noted, the House of Lords had 'emphasised the inability of any single general principle to provide a practical test which can be applied to every situation to determine whether a duty of care is owed and, if so, what is its scope'. He continued:

'While recognising ... the importance of the underlying general principles common to the whole field of negligence, I think the law has now moved in the direction of attaching greater significance to the more traditional categorisation of distinct and recognisable situations as guides to the existence, the scope and the limits of the varied duties of care which the law imposes.'

In the light of this judgment it is now extremely difficult, if not impossible, for us to say that we have a general principle for determining the existence of a duty of care which is applicable to all cases. The courts have abandoned the attempt to frame a single general principle and have chosen instead to 'reason by analogy' with 'distinct and identifiable situations' where the law already imposes a duty of care. The difficulty with this approach is that it can easily lead to the conclusion that the categories of negligence are closed because a court may reason that, simply because the precedents are against the recognition of a duty of care, it must *necessarily* come to the conclusion that on the facts of the case before it no duty is owed. Yet such an approach would be contrary to the famous dictum of Lord Macmillan in *Donoghue* v *Stevenson* when he said that 'the categories of negligence are never closed'. This danger may be avoided if we rename the 'analogy' approach the 'incremental' approach. In his judgment in *Caparo* Lord Bridge said that the House of Lords had to recognise the wisdom contained in the judgment of Brennan J in the High Court of Australia in *Council of the Shire of Sutherland* v *Heyman* when he said that it is:

> '... preferable ... that the law should develop novel categories of negligence incrementally and by analogy with established categories, rather than by a massive extension of a prima facie duty of care restrained only by indefinable considerations which ought to negative, or to reduce or limit the scope of the duty or the class of persons to whom it is owed.'

The point to note from this quotation is the contrast between 'incrementally' and 'massive extension'. The fear which Brennan J expresses (and which is now apparently shared by the House of Lords) is that the first tier of the Wilberforce test, namely proximity, was too easily satisfied by a plaintiff and that the consequence was therefore a 'massive extension of a prima facie duty of care'. On this view the vital control device therefore became the second stage, the policy stage or, as Brennan J preferred to call it, 'indefinable considerations'. Most judges, Lord Denning apart, are reluctant to become embroiled in policy disputes, preferring to leave policy to Parliament. The 'incremental' approach has the advantage of enabling the judiciary to avoid express reliance upon broad considerations of policy by hiding their policy choices behind the finding that there was no 'proximity' between the parties or the conclusion that the existing authorities preclude the finding of a duty of care. The wisdom which lies behind this change of approach is debatable but it is incontestable that such a change has in fact taken place.

6.6 The incremental approach

How then do the courts decide whether or not to impose a duty of care upon the defendant in a particular case? A crucial factor is obviously earlier authorities. Where a duty of care has been imposed in an earlier analogous case a court will be more inclined to impose a duty on the facts of the case before it unless it is satisfied that the analogy is not properly drawn. Conversely, where the precedents are against the recognition of a duty of care a court will be reluctant to impose a duty unless it considers that the earlier cases are not directly in point or it is convinced that, reasoning incrementally and by reference to the precedents, an extension of the scope of liability is justified.

But what of the novel case, the case where there are no precedents to guide the court? What will a court do then? One possibility is that it will scour the law reports in an effort to find a case which is even remotely analogous. But such an approach would be artificial and strained. It is suggested that there are three factors which are employed by the courts in deciding whether or not to impose a duty of care in a novel case: the first is that the loss must be reasonably foreseeable, the second is that there must be a 'proximate relationship' between the plaintiff and the defendant and the third is that it must be 'fair, just and reasonable that the law should impose a duty of a given scope upon the one party for the benefit of the other' (see, for example, the judgment of Lord Bridge in *Caparo* v *Dickman* [1990] 2 AC 605, 617–618). These three factors require further comment.

The first factor does not require much by way of comment except to say that reasonable foresight of harm is a necessary requirement but that it is not of itself sufficient. It should, however, be noted that it is the foresight of the reasonable man which is used in determining liability. Thus it is not the foresight of the particular defendant which is in issue but the foresight of the reasonable man standing in the shoes of the defendant. If the plaintiff cannot show that it was reasonably foreseeable that he would suffer loss as a result of the negligence of the defendant then he cannot succeed in an action in negligence against the defendant. English law does not recognise that negligence exists 'in the air'. This can be demonstrated by reference to the case of *Bourhill* v *Young* [1943] AC 92 where the House of Lords held that no duty of care was owed to the plaintiff because injury to her was not reasonably foreseeable. The plaintiff had witnessed a motor accident caused by the negligence of the defendant and in which the defendant was killed. She claimed that she heard the accident and saw the aftermath of it and that this had caused her baby to be born stillborn. It was held that the plaintiff was so far away from the accident that she was not owed a duty of care by the defendant because it was not reasonably foreseeable that she would suffer nervous shock as a result of the accident. The fact that it was foreseeable that other people might suffer injury as a result of the defendant's negligence was irrelevant because the plaintiff could not base her case on a wrong which was done, or could have been done, to someone else.

The second element, a 'proximate relationship', does call for further comment because the meaning of this phrase is not at all clear. It will be remembered that in the first stage of his two stage test in *Anns* Lord Wilberforce spoke of a 'relationship of proximity'. The meaning of this phrase became a matter of some controversy until it was authoritatively considered by Lord Keith in his judgment in *Yuen Kun Yeu* (above). Lord Keith there identified two different interpretations of proximity. The first was that it meant simply foreseeability of harm. But Lord Keith stated that, although foreseeability of harm is 'a necessary ingredient' of liability (see above), it is not sufficient of itself automatically to give rise to a duty of care, otherwise 'there would be liability in negligence on the part of one who sees another about to walk over a cliff with his head in the air, and forbears to shout a warning'. Instead Lord Keith held that the second interpretation was the correct one, namely that proximity is a 'composite' test, 'importing the whole concept of necessary relationship between plaintiff and defendant'. In *Hill* v *Chief*

Constable of West Yorkshire [1989] AC 53 Lord Keith repeated the view that 'foreseeability of likely harm is not in itself a sufficient test of liability in negligence' and added that:

> '... some further ingredient is invariably needed to establish the requisite proximity of relationship between plaintiff and defendant, and all the circumstances of the case must be carefully considered and analysed in order to ascertain whether such an ingredient is present.'

The necessary ingredient may vary from case to case but it is now clear that what the courts are looking for is a *relationship* of proximity. One caveat must, however, be entered here, which is that in cases where a plaintiff sustains physical injury the courts do not appear to insist upon a pre-existing relationship of proximity between the plaintiff and defendant. Take an example. Suppose that I drive my car negligently and I knock you down, causing you severe injury. In such a case a court would not inquire into the nature of our relationship before the accident occurred; rather, it is the negligent infliction of physical injury which of itself *creates* the required degree of proximity. But where the loss which the plaintiff suffers is economic in character then the fact that the defendant has, through his negligence caused the loss is not, of itself, sufficient to create a relationship of proximity; the court will, in such a case, inquire into the relationship between the parties prior to the occasioning of the loss. This suggests that the requirement that there be a *relationship* of proximity between the plaintiff and defendant may not be a universal one but that it is confined to particular contexts; for example, where the plaintiff suffers economic loss or alleges that the defendant is liable for failing to prevent damage being occasioned by a third party to the plaintiff. This confinement of the proximity requirement to particular contexts suggests that considerations of policy enter into the decisions as to whether or not a relationship of proximity exists in a given case and this point was recently confirmed by Lord Oliver in *Alcock* v *Chief Constable of South Yorkshire* [1992] 1 AC 310, 410 when he said that 'no doubt "policy", if that is the right word, or perhaps more properly, the impracticability or unreasonableness of entertaining claims to the ultimate limits of the consequences of human activity, necessarily plays a part in the court's perception of what is sufficiently proximate'. He concluded: 'in the end, it has to be accepted that the concept of "proximity" is an artificial one which depends more upon the court's perception of what is the reasonable area for the imposition of liability than upon any logical process of analogical deduction.' The consequences of this approach have yet to be worked through (and they may not be shared by the other members of the House of Lords) but they do seem to call into question the division between the second and third stage of the inquiry because considerations of policy would now appear to enter into the second stage as well as the third.

The third factor is that it must be 'just and reasonable' to impose a duty of care. We have already noted the origin of this requirement in the judgment of Lord Keith in *Governors of the Peabody Donation Fund* v *Sir Lindsay Parkinson* (see 6.4) and argued that it is hard to see any difference between this test and the second of Lord

Wilberforce's two stages. But it must be conceded that the courts today tend to use the 'just and reasonable' test in preference to the second stage in *Anns*. However, it must be said that one of the welcome features of the approach adopted by Lord Wilberforce in *Anns* was that it explicitly recognised that considerations of policy play a significant role in determining whether or not a duty of care is held to exist. Lord Wilberforce was by no means the first judge to recognise that the courts were dealing with issues of policy in deciding whether or not a duty of care is owed. In *Spartan Steel and Alloys Ltd* v *Martin & Co (Contractors) Ltd* [1973] 1 QB 27 Lord Denning said that:

'Whenever the courts draw a line to mark out the bounds of duty, they do it as a matter of policy so as to limit the responsibility of the defendant.'

But judges since *Anns* seem to be more reluctant to give explicit consideration to issues of policy. In *McLoughlin* v *O'Brian* [1983] AC 410 Lord Scarman said that:

'The policy issue where to draw the line is not justiciable. The problem is one of social, economic and financial policy. The considerations relevant to a decision are not such as to be capable of being handled within the limits of the forensic process.'

This view was countered by Lord Edmund-Davies in *McLoughlin*, who described Lord Scarman's judgment as being 'as novel as it is startling'. It is probably true to say that the approach of Lord Edmund-Davies is the widely accepted approach. Nevertheless it is true to say that judges appear to be less willing to take considerations of policy explicitly into account. Oliver LJ in *The Aliakmon* (above) stated that a court did not have 'a free hand to determine for itself in each case where the limits are to be set' and in *Yuen Kun Yeu* Lord Keith said that Lord Wilberforce's second stage would rarely be used. In *Hill* v *Chief Constable of West Yorkshire* (above) Lord Keith repeated this view but he also affirmed that the second stage is capable of constituting a 'separate and independent ground' for holding that a duty of care is not owed. Therefore the just and reasonable/policy requirement has not been abolished but its role has been considerably circumscribed. However, it should not be thought that considerations of policy or of what is 'fair, just and reasonable' will cease to play an important role in determining the limits of the duty of care. As we shall see, one of the most important considerations of policy is the need to keep liability within acceptable bounds (the 'floodgates' argument) and the insistence upon the need for a *relationship* of proximity at the second stage of our inquiry reflects these policy considerations because a defendant is likely to have a relationship of proximity with a relatively small group of people. The policy issue of keeping liability within acceptable bounds is therefore addressed at the second stage without requiring a court to give explicit consideration to what is just and reasonable. Therefore what is more likely to happen is that policy choices will continue to be made but will be hidden behind a finding that there was no 'relationship of proximity' between the parties.

6.7 Factors inhibiting the imposition of a duty of care

It should now be clear that we are presently in an era in which the courts are narrowing down the scope of liability in negligence. We must now make an attempt to explain why this is so. It must be said at the outset that there is no one factor which explains the current policy of restriction; it is due to a combination of factors. In the remainder of this chapter and in chapters 7 and 8 we shall consider the various factors which together explain the reasons behind the abandonment of *Anns* and the current restrictive attitude of the appellate courts.

6.8 The distinction between misfeasance and non-feasance

One major factor which helps to explain the judicial abandonment of the two-stage test in *Anns* is the emphasis which has been placed in a number of recent cases on the distinction between misfeasance and non-feasance, a distinction which was either obscured or ignored in *Anns* itself. The argument that the *Anns* two-stage test was defective in so far as it obscured the misfeasance/non-feasance dichotomy was first accepted by the House of Lords in *Curran v Northern Ireland Co-ownership Housing Association* [1987] AC 718. Lord Bridge, in giving the judgment of the House, referred to an article written by Professors Smith and Burns (*Donoghue v Stevenson* – The Not so Golden Anniversary (1983) 46 Modern Law Review 147) and to the 'cogent criticisms' there levelled against the *Anns* two-stage test on the ground that it obscured the important distinction between misfeasance and non-feasance. The importance of this distinction lies in the fact that it is argued by critics, such as Professors Smith and Burns, that the principle enunciated in *Donoghue* applies to cases of causing damage through an act or an action (misfeasance) but that it does not apply to a failure to prevent harm from arising (non-feasance), in the absence of a positive duty to prevent harm from arising. The argument runs that a duty to prevent harm from arising is typically created by a contract between the parties (where one party promises to make the other party's position better) and that it is only exceptionally created in tort.

The distinction between misfeasance and non-feasance can be illustrated by reference to the facts of *Curran* itself. The plaintiffs bought a house, the predecessor in title of which had built an extension with the aid of an improvement grant provided by the defendants. Under the terms of the statutory regulations the defendants had to be satisfied that the property in respect of which an improvement grant was made met certain standards of habitation and the work had to be 'executed to the satisfaction' of the defendants. After purchasing the property the plaintiffs discovered that the extension had been defectively constructed. Indeed, the extent of its defects were such that the extension had to be completely rebuilt at considerable expense. In these circumstances the plaintiffs brought an action against, inter alia, the defendants, alleging that they had been negligent in the exercise of their statutory powers and that their negligence had caused the plaintiffs loss. The House of Lords held that the defendants did not owe the plaintiffs a duty of care because they held that the purpose behind the statutory regulations was to ensure that public funds were properly spent and not to protect the interest of the owner-occupier in the beneficial enjoyment of his dwelling-house. So, the statutory regulations not being enacted for the benefit of the plaintiffs, the defendants did not owe them a duty of care. The important point to note for present purposes is that *Curran* appears to be a case of non-feasance. It was the builders of the extension who were the true cause of the loss because it was their negligence which resulted in the construction of a defective building. The argument against the defendants was that they were negligent because, by virtue of their failure to carry out with reasonable care and skill their supervision of the builders' work, they had *failed to prevent* the builders from building an inadequate extension.

A similar point can be made about the decision of the Privy Council in *Yuen Kun Yeu v Attorney-General of Hong Kong* [1988] AC 175. There the plaintiffs invested money with a deposit-taking company and they lost the money which they had invested because the company had been trading fraudulently. Deposit-taking companies had to be registered and licensed under an ordinance of 1976 and the Commissioner of Deposit-taking Companies had various regulatory powers over such companies, including the power to refuse to register or to revoke the registration of a company which he considered to be not a fit and proper body to take deposits. The plaintiffs brought an action in negligence against the Attorney-General (as representing the Commissioner) alleging that the Commissioner had been negligent in the discharge of his regulatory functions on the ground that he had reason to suspect that the company was trading fraudulently and had failed to revoke its registration. However, it was held that the defendant did not owe to the plaintiffs a duty of care. Although it was reasonably foreseeable that damage would be done to persons in the position of the plaintiffs if the defendant did not carry out his duty with proper care and skill, foreseeability of harm was not sufficient of itself to justify the imposition of a duty of care. In the absence of a special relationship between the Commissioner and the plaintiff investors (the Commissioner did not oversee the day-to-day administration of these companies and it was not reasonable for the plaintiffs to rely on the defendant), it was held that there was no basis for the imposition of a duty of care. Once again this was a case in which it was argued that the Commissioner had *failed to prevent* the infliction of harm upon the plaintiffs. It was the directors of the deposit-taking company who had, by their fraudulent trading, inflicted the loss upon the plaintiffs.

The importance of the misfeasance/non-feasance dichotomy can also be seen in the general rule in English law that, in the absence of a special relationship between the parties, there is no liability in negligence for a failure to rescue another (for criticism of this general rule see Linden (1971) 34 Modern Law Review 241). Indeed, in *Yuen Kun Yeu* Lord Keith regarded it is axiomatic that there is no 'liability in negligence on the part of one who sees another about to walk over a cliff with his head in the air, and forbears to shout a warning'. It should be noted that this is a classic example of non-feasance, a failure to rescue. This explains why Lord Keith insisted that liability in negligence could not be based upon mere foreseeability of harm because the application of such a test to his cliff-top example would have led to the imposition of liability in negligence. Thus it is only where there is a relationship of proximity between the parties, that is a relationship which imposes upon the defendant a duty to take reasonable care for the safety of the plaintiff, that the defendant is under any obligation to shout a warning to the plaintiff.

Although the distinction between misfeasance and non-feasance is an important one, it is not the case that liability can never be imposed in negligence in cases of non-feasance. The point was well made by Lord Goff in his important judgment in *Smith* v *Littlewoods Organisation Ltd* [1987] AC 241. While he recognised the existence of a 'general duty to take reasonable care not to cause damage to premises in the neighbourhood', Lord Goff also held 'it is well recognised that there is no general duty of care to prevent third parties from causing such damage'. The 'fundamental reason' for this refusal to impose a general duty of care to prevent others from suffering loss or damage was, he held, that 'the common law does not impose liability for what are called pure omissions'. Thus in *Home Office* v *Dorset Yacht Co Ltd* [1970] AC 1004 Lord Diplock said that:

> 'The very parable of the good Samaritan (Luke 10:30) which was evoked by Lord Atkin in *Donoghue* v *Stevenson* ... illustrates, in the conduct of the priest and of the Levite who passed by on the other side, an omission which was likely to have as its reasonable and probable consequence damage to the health of the victim of the thieves, but for which the priest and Levite would have incurred no civil liability in English law.'

Lord Goff was prepared to concede that the refusal of English law to impose a general duty for pure omissions might 'require one day to be reconsidered especially as it is said to provoke an "invidious comparison with affirmative duties of good-neighbourliness in most countries outside the Common law orbit" (see Fleming *The Law of Torts* (6th edn, 1983) p138)'.

But, rather than seek to impose a general duty to prevent third parties from causing damage to the plaintiff, Lord Goff held that the task which lay ahead for the courts was to map out the particular circumstances in which such a liability may be imposed. He himself began this task in his judgment in *Smith* v *Littlewoods*, the facts of which neatly illustrate the distinction between misfeasance and non-feasance. The defendants purchased a disused cinema with the intention of turning it into a supermarket. They took possession of the premises on 31 May 1976 and by early July of that year it was reported that the building was no longer lockfast. Vagrants were regularly reported to be in the building and on two occasions attempts had been made to start a fire using the debris lying outside the building. These incidents were not, however, reported to the defendants or to the police. On 5 July the cinema was set on fire and as a result of the fire the plaintiffs' property was extensively damaged. They sought to recover their loss from the defendants in negligence. This was therefore a case in which it was the vandals who by their actions had caused the damage to the plaintiffs. The plaintiffs' argument was that the defendants were liable because they had *failed to prevent* the vandals from inflicting damage upon them. But it was held by the House of Lords that the defendants did not owe a duty of care to the plaintiffs of the type contended for. It was conceded by their Lordships that the defendants were under a duty to ensure that their property was not a source of danger to the neighbouring properties. But they held that this general duty could only extend to prevent damage being done by vandals where a reasonable person would foresee that, if steps were not taken to ensure that the premises were lockfast, damage would be done to neighbouring properties. On the facts, because the defendants had not known of the previous fires, it was not reasonably foreseeable that damage would be done to neighbouring properties.

Smith is an important case because the Court of Appeal had earlier experienced great difficulty in identifying the circumstances in which a defendant could be liable to a plaintiff in negligence as a result of a deliberate wrong committed by a third party (see, for example, *Lamb* v *Camden London Borough Council* [1981] QB 625, *P Perl (Exporters) Ltd* v *Camden London Borough Council* [1984] QB 342 and *King* v *Liverpool City Council* [1986] 3 All ER 544). In one case (*Lamb*) it was held that the intervention of the third party was too remote a consequence of the defendants' negligence. In another case (*Perl*) it was held that, there being no relationship of control between the defendants and the third party who inflicted the loss upon the plaintiffs, the defendants did not owe a duty of care to the plaintiffs to prevent a third party from gaining entry to their premises, thereby enabling the third party to inflict damage upon the plaintiffs. And, in a third case (*King*) it was held that the defendants were not in breach of their duty of care because it was not possible for them to take effective steps to prevent the third parties from inflicting loss upon the plaintiffs. Although the result in each of the Court of Appeal cases was the same, namely that the defendants were not liable, the justifications offered to support such a conclusion differed in each case, with duty, breach and remoteness all being invoked by the Court of Appeal. There was therefore a great need for the House of Lords in *Smith* to introduce some conceptual stability into this area.

Lord Goff sought to provide such stability by stating that, while there is a general duty to take reasonable care not to cause damage to premises in the neighbourhood, there is no general duty at common law to prevent one person deliberately inflicting damage upon another person's property. In drawing this distinction between misfeasance and non-feasance at the outset of his judgment, it is suggested that Lord Goff identified the correct starting point in seeking to enumerate the situations in which liability can be imposed upon a defendant for loss caused to a plaintiff as a result of the deliberate act of a third party.

Lord Goff therefore embarked upon the task of identifying the exceptional circumstances in which such liability could be imposed. He identified four such situations (although he conceded that there may be others). The first arose where there was a special relationship between the plaintiff and the defendant. Such was the case in *Stansbie* v *Troman* [1948] 2 KB 48. The defendant was a decorator who was held liable to the plaintiffs, who were the owners of the premises which he was decorating, because he left the premises unsecured when he went out and a thief got in and stole some of the plaintiffs' property. It was held that the contractual relationship between the plaintiffs and the defendant was sufficient to impose liability upon the defendant for the consequences of the theft committed by the third party. Whether a non-contractual relationship, such as the relationship between an occupier and a licensee, will suffice to justify the imposition of liability remains an open question. In a slightly wider context, the relationship between a plaintiff and defendant may also justify the imposition of a duty to rescue so that, for example, a parent would be liable in negligence if he stood by and let his child drown in a foot of water (an example that was given in *Carmarthenshire County Council* v *Lewis* [1955] AC 549).

The second situation which Lord Goff identified arises where there is a special relationship between the defendants and the third parties who inflicted damage. Thus in *Home Office* v *Dorset Yacht Co Ltd* (above) the defendants were held liable because the boys who damaged the plaintiffs' property had escaped from the borstal institution where they were under the control of the defendants (see also *Partington* v *Wandsworth Borough Council* (1989) The Independent 8 November).

The third situation arises 'where the defender negligently causes or permits to be created a source of danger, and it is reasonably foreseeable that third parties may interfere with it and, sparking off the danger, thereby cause damage to persons in the position of the pursuer'. Such a case was *Haynes* v *Harwood* [1935] 1 KB 146, where the defendants left horses unattended in a street and a boy threw a stone at the horses, which caused them to bolt, and the plaintiff was injured trying to save others from being injured by the horses. It was held that the defendants were liable. They had created the danger and so they were liable for the damage caused by the act of the boy.

The final exception arises where the defendant knows or has the means of knowledge that a third party is creating a danger on his property and he fails to take reasonable steps to abate the danger. But Lord Goff held that these exceptional cases did not constitute a justification for a general rule of liability in such cases because:

> 'To impose a general duty on occupiers to take reasonable care to prevent others from entering their property would impose an unreasonable burden on ordinary householders and an unreasonable curb on the ordinary enjoyment of their property.'

Unfortunately, it is not at all clear whether the judgment of Lord Goff constitutes the ratio of *Smith*, though it was applied by the Court of Appeal in *Topp* v *London County Bus (South West) Ltd* [1993] 3 All ER 448. The difficulty here stems principally from the judgment of Lord Mackay (with whom Lord Brandon agreed; Lord Griffiths took his own line, which appears to be closer to Lord Goff than to Lord Mackay, while Lord Keith managed to concur both with Lord Goff and Lord Mackay). Lord Mackay appeared either to ignore the distinction between misfeasance and non-feasance or to regard the distinction as an irrelevant one. Lord Mackay stated that 'no undue burdens are put on property occupiers' by the application of ordinary *Donoghue* principles and he held that the question to be asked in such cases was whether the damage caused was reasonably foreseeable. However, he added that:

> 'What the reasonable man is bound to foresee in a case involving injury or damage by independent human agency ... is the probable consequences of his own act or omission, but that ... a clear basis will be required on which to assert that the injury or damage is more than a mere possibility.'

In particular, where the intervening act of the third party takes the form of a burglary, Lord Mackay thought that it would be very difficult to establish that such an act was reasonably foreseeable because, by definition, the burglar will enter the premises at a time which is unannounced and unexpected. In choosing to base liability expressly upon ordinary *Donoghue* principles Lord Mackay's judgment must be taken as authority for the proposition that the distinction between misfeasance and non-feasance is here an irrelevant one and that in both cases liability can be based upon the reasonable foresight of harm.

In support of Lord Mackay it must be said that an argument can be made out to the effect that the distinction between misfeasance and non-feasance is an irrelevant one. There are two principal arguments here. The first is that, as Lord Goff noted (above), a refusal to impose a general duty in cases of non-feasance does not encourage co-operation between fellow human beings and it may be said to provoke an 'invidious comparison with affirmative duties of good-neighbourliness' in other jurisdictions. But the House of Lords, as presently constituted, is not committed to such an expansive conception of good neighbourliness. Instead a more rugged approach is being adopted and a new emphasis placed upon individual responsibility; plaintiffs should take care of their own affairs and not rely upon third parties to exercise reasonable care in looking after them. This new emphasis is best expressed in the judgment of Lord Templeman in *CBS Songs* v *Amstrad Consumer Electronics plc* [1988] AC 1013, 1059 when he said that:

> 'Since *Anns* v *Merton London Borough* put the floodgates on the jar, a fashionable plaintiff alleges negligence. The pleading assumes that we are all neighbours now, Pharisees and Samaritans alike, that foreseeability is a reflection of hindsight and that for every mischance in an accident-prone world someone solvent must be liable in damages. In *Governors of the Peabody Donation Fund* v *Sir Lindsay Parkinson Ltd* the plaintiffs were *the authors of their own misfortune* but sought to make the local authority liable for the consequences. In *Yuen Kun Yeu* v *Attorney-General of Hong Kong* the plaintiff *chose* to invest in a deposit-taking company which went into liquidation; the plaintiff sought to recover his deposit from the commissioner charged with the public duty of registering deposit-taking companies ... ' (Emphasis added.)

The second argument in favour of the approach advocated by Lord Mackay is that the line between an act and an omission simply cannot be drawn. For example, a driver who causes an accident through negligently failing to brake cannot argue that he is not liable under ordinary *Donoghue* principles because his negligence took the form of an omission. This is because the omission to brake cannot be viewed in isolation from his positive act of driving the car. But in other cases the line is more difficult to draw. For example, are *Curran* and *Yuen Kun Yeu* cases of misfeasance or non-feasance? Did the defendants cause the damage to the plaintiffs through their own negligent actions (their inadequate supervision) or was it the case that they simply failed to prevent third parties from inflicting loss upon the plaintiffs? It is conceded that these are difficult borderline examples. But it is also suggested that there is a clear distinction between the case where I punch you in the face and the case where your next door neighbour punches you in the face. In the first case I am responsible but in the second case the initial assumption must be that I am not responsible unless some particular ground can be put forward to suggest that I am under an obligation to prevent your neighbour from punching you. And so it is with the tort of negligence. I am under a general duty to take reasonable care not to cause you damage (although, even here, the existence of a 'general' duty must be in doubt, see 6.5) but I am not under a general duty to prevent third parties from causing you harm. In so far as Lord Mackay can be understood as suggesting that the distinction between misfeasance and non-feasance is an irrelevant one, it is submitted that he is incorrect. The better approach, it is submitted, is the one adopted by Lord Goff in *Smith* and Lord Bridge in *Curran*, which acknowledges the distinction between the two and begins the task of identifying the particular situations in which liability can be imposed for non-feasance.

6.9 The role of Parliament

A second factor which underpins the present restrictive approach adopted by the courts is their perception of their relationship with Parliament. We have already noted that in *McLoughlin* v *O'Brian* [1983] 1 AC 410 Lord Scarman said that 'the policy issue where to draw the line is not justiciable'. Policy is for Parliament not the courts. Although many judges would disagree with the absolute nature of Lord Scarman's statement, it is nevertheless the case that, where Parliament has intervened to regulate a particular issue, the courts are now very unwilling to impose liability at common law where, to do so, would be to go further than Parliament had been prepared to go. This conservative approach was classically demonstrated by Lord Bridge in his judgment in *D & F Estates Ltd* v *Church Commissioners for England* [1989] AC 177. He stated that he was happy to reach the conclusion that no duty was owed on the facts of the case because, had he concluded that a duty was owed, it would have resulted in the common law going further than 'the legislature were prepared to go in [the Defective Premises Act] 1972, after comprehensive examination of the subject by the Law Commission'. This judicial conservatism was also displayed in *Murphy* v *Brentwood District Council* [1991] 1 AC 398. Thus Lord Mackay stated (at p457) that:

'It is relevant to take into account that Parliament has made provisions in the Defective Premises Act 1972 imposing on builders and others undertaking work in the provision of dwellings obligations relating to the quality of their work and the fitness for habitation of the dwelling. For this House in its judicial capacity to create a large new area of responsibility on local authorities in respect of defective buildings would in my opinion not be a proper exercise of judicial power.'

And Lord Oliver stated (at p491):

'There may be very sound social and political reasons for imposing upon local authorities the burden of acting, in effect, as insurers that buildings erected in their areas have been properly constructed in accordance with the relevant building regulations. Statute may so provide. It has not done so and I do not, for my part, think that it is right for the courts not simply to expand existing principles but to create at large new principles in order to fulfil a social need in an area of consumer protection which has already been perceived by the legislature but for which, presumably advisedly, it has not thought it necessary to provide.'

Other examples can be found of such judicial conservatism (see *McNerny* v *London Borough of Lambeth* (1988) 21 HLR 188, *West Wiltshire District Council* v *Pugh* [1993] NLJ 546, *X* v *Bedfordshire County Council* [1993] NLJ 1783, *M* v *Newham London Borough Council* [1994] NLJ 357 and *Reid* v *Rush & Tompkins Group plc* [1990] 1 WLR 212, 222–223 and, indeed, this judicial conservation seems to be spreading to other areas of tort – see the judgment of Lord Goff in *Cambridge Water Co* v *Eastern Counties Leather plc* [1994] 2 WLR 53 at page 80, but contrast *Burton* v *Islington Health Authority* [1993] QB 204 where Dillon LJ rejected the argument that the passing of the Congenital Disabilities (Civil Liability) Act 1976 prevented the courts from recognising the existence of a duty of care in respect of damage suffered prior to the coming into force of the Act). There are a number of problems with this approach (see Cane (1989) 52 Modern Law Review 200, at pp210–11). The first is that it is not at all clear that consumer protection is better left to Parliament and that the intervention of Parliament should inevitably leave the common law sterile. And the House of Lords is open to the charge of inconsistency on this point because, as we shall see, their decision in *Smith* v *Eric S Bush* [1990] 1 AC 831 (discussed below at 7.6) appears to be a classic example of a court engaging in consumer protection in a negligence action. Finally, as Cane has also pointed out, the current attitude of the court

'... seems to be based on the problematic idea that once the legislature has enacted legislation on a particular subject matter ... the courts are precluded from developing the common law in that area. It also seems to be based on the misplaced faith that the legislature always does ... lay down a set of rules which are much more precise and more carefully limited and crafted than the common law can achieve.'

These assumptions are open to question and the current attitude of the House of Lords does not seem to be a particularly praiseworthy one.

6.10 The availability of an alternative remedy

The third factor which underpins the present policy of restriction is that the courts are now less willing to impose a duty of care upon a defendant where the plaintiff has an alternative remedy available to him. Thus, the availability to a plaintiff of an action on the contract against a third party contractor has been used as a justification for a refusal to impose upon the defendant a duty of care owed to the plaintiff. A neat example of this is provided by the case of *Simaan General Contracting Co* v *Pilkington Glass Ltd (No 2)* [1988] QB 758. The plaintiffs were main contractors for the construction of a new building in Abu Dhabi. The building owner (who was not a party to the proceedings) required that units of green glass be incorporated in the curtain walling of the building. The choice of colour was significant because green is regarded as the colour of peace in Islam. The plaintiffs subcontracted the supply and erection of the curtain walling to independent contractors, called Feal, who were in turn required by their contract with the plaintiffs to subcontract the manufacture of the glass units to the defendants. The glass units supplied by the defendants were not of a uniform colour of green and the plaintiffs alleged that this had caused them economic loss because performance of the building contract was disrupted. The plaintiffs elected not to bring an action in contract against Feal but to jump down the chain of contracts and bring an action in tort against the defendants. But it was held by the Court of Appeal that the plaintiffs could not bring a direct action against the defendants in the absence of a contract between them. The plaintiffs' remedy, if any, was therefore against Feal in contract and Feal's remedy, if any, was a contractual action against the defendants. The Court of Appeal could see no justification for departing from the chain of contractual claims. In the words of Bingham LJ:

> 'There is no reason why claims beginning with the [building owner] should not be pursued down the contractual chain, subject to any short cut which may be agreed on, ending up with a contractual claim against [the defendants]. That is the usual procedure. It must be what the parties contemplated when they made their contracts. I see no reason for departing from it.'

As Dillon LJ pointed out a number of very difficult practical problems would arise if such a direct action was to be permitted, which problems can be avoided by confining the parties to their ordinary contractual remedies. Yet it must be conceded that this approach has not been adopted consistently by the courts. For example, in *Junior Books Ltd* v *Veitchi Co Ltd* [1983] 1 AC 520 the availability of an action against the main contractor did not shut out the building owner's claim in tort against the subcontractor. But *Junior Books* is a problematic case (discussed in more detail at 7.7) and it belongs to the *Anns* era when the courts were prepared to expand the horizons of the tort of negligence. Now that we are in an era of restriction the courts are unlikely to follow *Junior Books* and are more likely to follow the *Simaan* line, thus preserving the structural integrity of a chain of contracts , eg *Marc Rich* v *Bishop Rock Marine* (1994) The Times 23 February. However, in exceptional circumstances, the courts are willing to find that a duty of care can co-exist with a contractual duty: *Arbuthnott* v *Feltrim* (1993) The Times 20 October.

However it should not be thought that this line of reasoning is confined to contractual claims. Thus the availability of judicial review (*Jones* v *Department of*

Employment [1989] QB 1) and the availability of an alternative statutory remedy (*Mills* v *Winchester Diocesan Board of Finance* [1989] Ch 428) have been used as justifications for a refusal to impose upon a defendant a duty of care.

6.11 No undermining of established principles of the common law or equity

Fourthly, the courts are reluctant to impose a duty of care when to do so would be to run counter to established principles of the common law or equity. Thus a duty of care will not be imposed where to do so would be to bypass or undermine the defences which exist to other torts, such as defamation (see *Spring* v *Guardian Assurance plc* [1993] 2 All ER 273 and *Petch* v *Commissioners of Customs and Excise* (1993) The Times 4 March, although contrast the approach adopted by the Court of Appeal in *Joyce* v *Sengupta* [1993] 1 WLR 337 where they emphasised that English law allows a plaintiff to take full advantage of the various remedies which the law allows for the tort which he alleges has been committed). A further example of the refusal to allow the law of tort to undermine established principles of the common law is provided by *Banque Keyser Ullmann SA* v *Skandia (UK) Insurance Co Ltd* [1990] 1 QB 665 where the Court of Appeal noted that 'our law of contract is founded' on 'the general principle of caveat emptor' so that the law of contract does not recognise the existence of a general duty to disclose information to the other party to the contract. The court held that, to recognise the existence of a general duty of disclosure in tort, would be 'to run counter' to established principles of contract law and that the law of tort would not take such a step. As Slade LJ stated: 'it should be no part of the general function of the law of tort to fill in contractual gaps'. Once again this approach has not been adopted consistently by the courts and in both *Ross* v *Caunters* [1980] Ch 297 and *Junior Books* v *Veitchi Co Ltd* [1983] 1 AC 520 the imposition of a duty of care appeared to undermine the doctrines of privity and consideration. But *Ross* and *Junior Books* both belong to the *Anns* era and must be seen in that light. One would not expect a modern court to initiate such an approach (see, for example, *Reid* v *Rush & Tompkins Group plc* [1990] 1 WLR 212), although it must be conceded that examples can still be found of a court recognising a duty of care notwithstanding the fact that in doing so it ran counter to, or even remedied gaps in, established rules of the law of contract (the most important example being *White* v *Jones* [1993] 3 WLR 730, discussed in more detail at 7.9).

The refusal to undermine principles of equity was classically illustrated by the Privy Council in *China and South Sea Bank Ltd* v *Tan* [1990] 1 AC 536. The appellant bank lent $HK30 million to a debtor. The defendant guaranteed the loan as surety. The debtor defaulted. At the time of his default the mortgaged shares would have covered the loan, but the bank did not exercise its power of sale at that moment in time. The shares subsequently became worthless. The bank sought payment from the defendant under the guarantee. The defendant refused to pay, arguing that the bank was in breach of its duty of care owed to him in failing to exercise its power of sale before the shares became worthless. The Privy Council rejected the defendant's argument. Lord Templeman stated that:

> 'The tort of negligence has not yet subsumed all torts and does not supplant the principles of equity or contradict promises or complement the remedy of judicial review or supplement statutory rights.'

It was held that it was the domain of equity to protect the surety. The creditor was not obliged to do anything to protect the surety's interest and, in particular, it was not under an obligation to exercise its power of sale at any one time. The bank had not done any act which was injurious to the defendant, nor had it acted inconsistently with the defendant's rights. So the defence that the plaintiff bank could not recover because they were in breach of a duty of care owed to the defendant failed (see also to the same effect *Downsview Nominees Ltd* v *First City Corporation Ltd* [1993] AC 295, 315–317).

6.12 No duty recognised before

The courts are also extremely reluctant to impose a duty of care where they have refused to impose a duty of care in the past. An interesting case study in this respect is provided by *Leigh and Sillivan Ltd* v *Aliakmon Shipping Co Ltd* [1986] AC 785. The plaintiffs were the consignees of goods carried by sea. They were liable to pay the price to the sellers, irrespective of the condition of the goods. But the plaintiffs were not the owners of the goods. Due to the negligence of the defendants when stowing the goods, the goods were damaged. The plaintiff buyers were bound to pay the sellers for the damaged goods and the sellers, having been paid in full for the goods, had no interest in suing the defendants for the damage to the goods. So the buyers were left to try to recover their loss from the defendants. There being no contract between the parties, the plaintiffs had to sue in tort.

The difficulty for the plaintiffs was, as Lord Brandon acknowledged, that:

> 'There is a long line of authority for a principle of law that, in order to enable a person to claim in negligence for loss caused to him by reason of loss or damage to property, he must have had either the legal ownership of or a possessory title to the property concerned at the time when the loss or damage occurred, and it is not enough for him to have only had contractual rights in relation to such property which have been adversely affected by the loss or damage to it.'

Cases in this 'long line of authority' include *Cattle* v *Stockton Waterworks Co* (1875) LR 10 QB 453 and *The Wear Breeze* [1969] 1 QB 219 and they posed a severe problem for the plaintiffs in the *Aliakmon* because, at the time of the damage, they had no possessory or proprietary interest in the goods. But in *The Irene's Success* [1982] QB 481 Lloyd J held, applying the two–stage test in *Anns*, that a person who was not the legal owner of the cargo at the time when the damage was done, could bring an action in tort, notwithstanding the line of authority which we have noted. He held that there was a relationship of proximity between the parties and that there were no reasons of policy to preclude the imposition of a duty of care. This approach was, however, rejected by the House of Lords in *The Aliakmon* and *The Irene's Success* was overruled. Lord Brandon stated that in *Anns*:

> 'Lord Wilberforce was dealing ... with the approach to the questions of the existence and scope of a duty of care in a novel type of factual situation which was not analogous to any factual situation in which the existence of such a duty had already been held to exist. He was not, as I understand the passage, suggesting that the same approach should be adopted to the existence of a duty of care in a factual situation in which the existence of such a duty had repeatedly been held not to exist.'

Thus the House of Lords affirmed the general rule that a person who, at the time of the damage, is neither an owner of the goods nor in possession of them cannot maintain an action in negligence in respect of any damage to the goods and they dismissed the plaintiffs' claim.

Another example of this type of reasoning is provided by the case of *Stephens* v *Anglian Water Authority* [1987] 1 WLR 1381. There the plaintiff alleged that the defendants had extracted water from their land or from land of a neighbouring owner with his permission and the result was that part of the plaintiff's land began to subside. The plaintiff alleged that the defendants had been negligent in that they had been warned that the consequence of their work would be that the plaintiff's land would subside. The defendants applied to have the plaintiff's action struck out on the ground that it disclosed no reasonable cause of action. The Court of Appeal agreed with the defendants and struck out the plaintiff's claim on the ground that the defendants owed no duty of care to the plaintiff. For present purposes our interest lies in the court's treatment of the decision of Plowman J in *Langbrook Properties Ltd* v *Surrey County Council* [1969] 1 WLR 167. Plowman J had held that the defendants were entitled to extract the water percolating in undefined channels under their land even though by doing so they caused damage to the property of the plaintiff. Counsel for the plaintiff in *Stephens* argued that the authorities relied upon by Plowman J in support of his decision had been decided before the development of the tort of negligence in cases such as *Home Office* v *Dorset Yacht Co Ltd* (above) and therefore had to be subjected to fresh examination. However the Court of Appeal held that the plaintiff could only succeed if she could distinguish the decision of the House of Lords in *Bradford Corporation* v *Pickles* [1895] AC 587. In the latter case it was held that the defendant, who deliberately drained his land in order to stop water supply reaching the plaintiff's land, was not liable to the plaintiff because the plaintiff had no right to the supply of water and so no right of his had been infringed. The Court of Appeal held that *Pickles* could not be distinguished because 'if a landowner has the right to abstract water from beneath his land, whatever be his motive or intention ... it cannot, in our judgment, be said that he owes a duty to his neighbour to take care in doing it'. It was irrelevant for this purpose that the plaintiff in *Stephens* suffered physical damage. The Court of Appeal was not without sympathy for the argument put forward by the plaintiff but they held that they were bound by *Pickles* and concluded that 'whether or not this state of the law is satisfactory is not for us to say'. The Appeal Committee of the House of Lords refused leave to appeal ([1988] 2 WLR 333) and so the decision of the Court of Appeal clearly represents the current state of English law.

Stephens therefore underlines the present unwillingness of the appellate courts to extend the frontiers of the tort of negligence. And it is this refusal to re-examine authorities which led Professor Hepple to argue that the approach of the House of Lords in *The Aliakmon* 'is reminiscent of the pre-1932 categorisations of negligence rules and of the shackled judicial reasoning before Wilberforce's emancipation' ([1986] All ER Rev 311). It is this very 'emancipation' to which the present House of Lords objects, preferring to reason 'incrementally' and by analogy to the existing authorities.

Thus in *Wood* v *The Law Society* (1993) Times 30 July the plaintiff sought to establish a novel duty of care, namely that a body vested with a power and duty to investigate complaints against its members owed a duty of care to a complainant, the breach of which entitled the complainant to damages. The High Court refused to recognise the existence of such a duty of care on the grounds that there was insufficient proximity between the plaintiff and the defendant, that the plaintiff was a member of an unascertained class, that the relevant function of the defendant was to prevent conduct unbecoming to a solicitor not to prevent loss to individuals and that the defendant had no power to control the day-to-day activities of the solicitors who had actually caused loss to the plaintiff.

However, in appropriate situations the courts are willing to find a duty of care in novel fact situations, eg *Kirkham* v *Chief Constable of Greater Manchester* [1990] 3 All ER 246 (police owed a duty of care to a person of unsound mind to pass on to a prison information relating to that person's suicidal tendencies); and *Ephraim* v *Newham London Borough Council* (1992) The Times 24 January (local housing authority owed a duty of care to a homeless person to ensure that premises to which it was sending her were reasonably safe for use as a bed and breakfast establishment).

6.13 The cost and availability of insurance?

Given that most tort litigation is in fact between insurance companies, it would not be surprising if the incidence and cost of insurance were relevant factors in deciding whether or not to impose upon the defendant a duty of care. Yet judges rarely make explicit reference to the incidence of insurance. Lord Denning was one of the few judges who did so (see, for example, *Spartan Steel and Alloys Ltd* v *Martin & Co (Contractors) Ltd* [1973] 1 QB 27). However the judiciary today may be more inclined to place reliance upon the incidence of insurance. Thus in *Smith* v *Eric S Bush* [1990] 1 AC 831 Lord Griffiths stated that:

'There was once a time when it was considered improper even to mention the possible existence of insurance cover in a lawsuit. But those days are long past ...'

Although the courts have not, at least until now, placed express reliance upon the availability and cost of insurance, it is arguable that they have placed implicit reliance upon these factors. Davies has recently argued (The End of the Affair: Duty of Care and Liability Insurance (1989) 9 Legal Studies 67) that the availability of liability insurance has been a critical factor in the development of the tort of negligence. He points out that such insurance was not widely available until towards the end of the nineteenth century and he argues that it can be no coincidence that Brett LJ, who was influential in procuring the passing of the Employers' Liability Act 1880 which helped create a market for liability insurance, was the same Brett MR who three years later framed the general duty of care test in *Heaven* v *Pender* (1863) 11 QBD 503 (see further 6.2), which was to prove so influential in *Donoghue* v *Stevenson*. Aware that defendants could now pay damages, the courts were more prepared to impose a duty and liability. The tort of negligence was thus able to expand its horizons, secure in the knowledge that liability insurance was readily available at reasonable cost. But the late 1980s and early 1990s has been a period in which liability insurance has not been readily available or, particularly in the case of professionals, only available at prohibitive expense. Surely it is no coincidence that the restricted availability of insurance cover is matched by a general restriction in the scope of the tort of negligence?

Although there must be a link between the development of the tort of negligence and the availability of insurance, the court is often not aware of the insurance position as between the parties. This is classically illustrated by the judgment of Lord Denning in *Lamb* v *Camden London Borough Council* [1981] QB 625. The defendants, as a result of their negligence, damaged a water main outside the plaintiff's house. This resulted in major subsidence of the house. In consequence the tenant moved out and shortly afterwards squatters moved in and inflicted substantial damage on the property. The Court of Appeal held that the plaintiff could not recover her loss from the defendants. The majority held that the loss was too remote a consequence of the defendants' negligence. But Lord Denning decided as a matter of policy that the plaintiff was responsible for the insurance of her property and that she should look to her insurers for recompense and not the defendants. The difficulty with this argument is that, as Lee and Merkin have pointed out (1981 New Law Journal 965), 'most householders' policies on contents expressly exclude coverage or loss and damage caused to a residence unoccupied for 30 consecutive days'. The plaintiff was therefore, in all likelihood, uninsured. This case demonstrates that, if the courts are to take the incidence of insurance expressly into account in reaching their decisions, it is vitally important that they be informed of the actual insurance position and not be left to make an educated guess as to the insurance position of the parties before them.

6.14 Conclusion

Thus far we have considered general factors which have been relied upon by the courts when restricting the scope of the tort of negligence. In the next two chapters we shall look at the development of the tort of negligence in particular areas. We shall do so under two headings. In chapter 7 we shall consider particular interests (such as economic loss), in relation to which the courts have been reluctant to impose a duty of care. And in chapter 8 we shall consider particular plaintiffs and defendants in relation to whom the courts have been unwilling to impose a duty of care or have only been prepared to impose a limited duty of care.

7

The Duty of Care and 'Protected Interests'

7.1 Introduction

7.2 Economic loss: introduction

7.3 Economic loss: a definition

7.4 Economic loss: the problem

7.5 Consequential economic loss

7.6 Negligent misstatement

7.7 Defective product economic loss

7.8 *Hedley Byrne* re-examined

7.9 '*Ross* v *Caunters* economic loss'

7.10 *Ministry of Housing and Local Government* v *Sharp*

7.11 *Morrison Steamship Co Ltd* v *Greystone Castle (Cargo Owners)*

7.12 Economic loss: conclusion

7.13 Psychiatric injury or 'nervous shock'

7.1 Introduction

Donoghue v *Stevenson* [1932] AC 562 was a case in which it was alleged that the plaintiff had suffered personal injury. The law of tort has never had any great difficulty in recognising that a person can recover damages for personal injury suffered as a result of the negligence of the defendant. Thus, in most road accident cases we have no problem in recognising that one road user owes another road user a duty of care. But where the loss which the plaintiff suffers is not physical injury or damage to property then difficulties can emerge in establishing the existence of a duty of care. This is particularly so where the loss which the plaintiff suffers is economic (or financial) loss. The problem can also arise where other losses are suffered, for example, where the plaintiff suffers psychiatric injury as a result of the negligence of the defendant. In this chapter we shall be concerned with economic loss and psychiatric injury because they are both interests in relation to which the courts have had difficulty in recognising the existence of a duty of care.

7.2 Economic loss: introduction

There have been a number of dicta in recent cases which suggest that the courts do not attach as much importance to the protection of a plaintiff's economic well-being as they do to his physical well-being. For example in *Murphy* v *Brentwood District Council* [1991] 1 AC 398, 487 Lord Oliver stated that:

> 'The infliction of physical injury to the person or property of another universally requires to be justified. The causing of economic loss does not.'

In *Caparo Industries plc* v *Dickman* [1990] 2 AC 605, 618 Lord Bridge said that:

> 'One of the most important distinctions always to be observed lies in the law's essentially different approach to the different kinds of damage which one party may have suffered in consequence of the acts or omissions of another. It is one thing to owe a duty of care to avoid causing injury to the person or property of others. It is quite another to avoid causing others to suffer purely economic loss.'

Other dicta can be found to the same effect in recent cases (see *Reid* v *Rush & Tomkins Group plc* [1990] 1 WLR 212, 231 and *Mariola Marine Corp* v *Lloyd's Register of Shipping, The Morning Watch* [1990] 1 Lloyd's Rep 547). The courts seem to be of the view that, while liability can be based upon reasonable foresight of harm in cases where the plaintiff suffers physical injury (such as a road accident), such a test is manifestly inappropriate in cases of economic loss, where a more restrictive test is required. If this is the case and the law of tort accords less protection to a person's economic well-being than to his physical well-being two questions must be asked. The first is: what is economic loss? And the second is: why is it more difficult to recover damages for economic loss than it is for physical damage?

7.3 Economic loss: a definition

Economic loss could be defined simply as financial loss. But such a definition is too wide. An example will illustrate the point. Suppose that I drive my car negligently and run you down. As a result of the injuries which you receive you have to give up work for a period of time and, consequently, are not paid any wages. This loss is undoubtedly financial loss but we do not experience any great difficulties in allowing such a claim to succeed. It succeeds every day in the courts. This is because it is consequential economic loss; economic loss which is a consequence of your physical injury. Where the law of tort encounters its most severe difficulties is where the plaintiff only suffers economic (or financial) loss, called 'pure' economic loss by tort lawyers.

A good example of a plaintiff suffering 'pure' economic loss is provided by the case of *Ross* v *Caunters* [1980] Ch 297. The defendant, who was a solicitor, failed to tell the testator that attestation of the will by the spouse of a beneficiary would invalidate the gift to the beneficiary. The plaintiff, whose husband had signed the will, sued the defendant in negligence for the loss of her gift under the will. This was not a case in which the plaintiff suffered physical injury or damage to her property. The only 'loss' which she suffered was that she did not receive the gift promised to her in the will. Her loss was therefore classified by Megarry VC as 'pure' economic loss which, he held, was recoverable (see further 7.9 below).

Great difficulties have, however, emerged in some cases in distinguishing between economic loss and property damage. Much of the difficulty in this respect has been caused by the decision of the House of Lords in *Anns* v *Merton London Borough Council* [1978] AC 728. In *Anns* the plaintiffs were lessees under long leases of maisonettes built by the first defendants. The second defendants were the local authority who passed the building plans for the maisonettes in 1962. In 1970 structural movements began to occur, cracks appeared in the walls and the floors began to slope. The plaintiffs issued a writ in 1972, alleging that the foundations were inadequate, being two feet six inches in depth rather than the three feet or more shown in the plans. The House of Lords held that the second defendants owed to the plaintiffs a duty of care but, for present purposes, our interest lies in the classification of the loss which the plaintiffs suffered. Lord Wilberforce stated that, if classification of the loss was required, it was 'material, physical damage'. At first sight this classification seems correct because there was physical damage to the maisonettes. But when tort lawyers talk of 'physical damage' they generally mean damage which is inflicted upon a person or upon property other than the defective product itself. A simple illustration will help us to understand the point. Let us suppose that I buy a toy for a child. The toy is defective. It explodes, injuring the child, damaging my settee and destroying the toy. The injury to the child and the damage to my settee are examples of personal injury and property damage respectively. But the damage to the toy is an example of pure economic loss. This is because, as we have noted, when tort lawyers talk about property damage, they are really talking about damage to 'other property', that is, damage to property other than the toy itself. When the toy is damaged my claim is on the contract with the vendor and the nature of my claim is that the toy did not live up to my expectations; and that is a claim in contract, not tort. It is pure economic loss because my argument is that a damaged toy is not as valuable as a toy which complies with the contractual specifications. Another example can be provided by reference to *Donoghue* v *Stevenson*. Suppose that the ginger beer had been flat. Could the plaintiff have sued in tort? The answer is 'no'. Yet, ginger beer which is flat is damaged, in the sense that it does not live up to the expectations created; but, once again, that is a claim in contract, not tort.

Now let us apply this reasoning to the facts of *Anns*. In *Anns* the only 'damage' was in the building itself but yet the House of Lords concluded that the loss was 'physical', not economic. This is difficult to understand because, in the words of Deane J in the High Court of Australia in *Council of the Shire of Sutherland* v *Heyman* (1985) 157 CLR 424, 504 '[t]he building itself could not be said to have been subjected to "material, physical damage" by reason merely of the inadequacy of its foundations since the building had never existed otherwise than with its foundations in that state'. Or, in the words of Weir (*A Casebook on Tort* (6th ed) p65), '[b]y making a bad thing you do not damage it; you damage a thing by making it worse than it was'.

So the classification of the loss in *Anns* as physical damage seemed to be contrary to fundamental principle. This was confirmed some five years later when, in *Junior Books* v *Veitchi Co Ltd* [1983] 1 AC 520, the House of Lords concluded, without apparently noticing the inconsistency with *Anns*, that the cost of repairing a defectively laid floor was a case of economic loss not physical damage. But it was not until *Murphy* v *Brentwood District Council* [1991] 1 AC 398 that the House of Lords acknowledged that the classification of the loss in *Anns* as physical damage was erroneous. In *Murphy* the plaintiff purchased a house in 1970 from builders who had constructed it in 1969. The house was built upon a single concrete raft foundation because the site had been filled in and levelled. The foundation raft was designed by a firm of civil engineers but its design was inadequate and differential settlement of the ground beneath the raft caused it to distort and caused cracks to appear in the building. When the plaintiff discovered the extent of the damage to the house he decided that it was impractical to have the necessary remedial work carried out himself and so he sold it, at a price considerably below the market price of a house which was sound, to a builder who knew the cause of the damage. The plaintiff then brought an action against the local authority alleging that they had been negligent in passing plans which were inadequate. Our interest in *Murphy* for the moment is confined to the classification of the loss which the plaintiff had suffered. It was held that his loss was economic and, in many ways, this was obvious because he had realised his loss and his claim was for the diminution in value of his property. But the fact that the loss had been realised on the facts of *Murphy* should not blind us to the fact that all cases in which a plaintiff seeks to recover the cost of repairing the defect in the product itself are cases of 'economic loss'. This point was accepted by the House of Lords in *Murphy* and it declared that the loss in *Anns* was truly economic loss, not physical damage.

7.4 Economic loss: the problem

Having identified what 'pure' economic loss is, we must now turn to the question of why it is that the courts are reluctant to compensate plaintiffs who suffer such loss. The traditional reason is the fear of the 'floodgates'; that the defendant would be exposed to indeterminate liability for an indeterminate amount to an indeterminate class. This fear of opening the floodgates could be a reference either to the exposure of the defendant to too many claims or to too much liability, or, in fact, it could be a reference to a combination of the two. The courts do not make clear exactly what they mean by the 'floodgates'. This fear of opening the floodgates does not tend to manifest itself in cases of physical injury, although in major tragedies the liability of the defendant can be enormous. But the size of the claim or the number of claimants does not, of itself, provide the defendant with a defence.

However, the 'floodgates' is frequently invoked in economic loss cases. An example will illustrate the point. Suppose that an accountant appears on national television and states that shares in a certain company are bound to be a good investment. Thousands of people go out and buy shares in the company in reliance upon the advice. Unfortunately, the accountant was careless in making his statement. Far from being a good investment, the company goes into liquidation and the investors lose all their money. The investors have all suffered pure economic loss but to allow them all to recover from the accountant would be to expose him to an indeterminate liability for an indeterminate amount to an indeterminate class. This fear of opening the floodgates was reflected in the old rule that damages are not available to compensate a plaintiff who has suffered pure economic loss as a result of the negligence of the defendant. In *Cattle* v *Stockton Waterworks Co* (1875) LR 10 QB 453 the plaintiff entered into a contract to build a tunnel under a road. The defendants negligently burst a water pipe which made it more expensive for the plaintiff to complete the contract. The plaintiff sought to recover the additional expense from the defendants in tort. It was held that the plaintiff could not recover in respect of the pure economic loss because, if liability was admitted, where would the courts draw the line? Would the workmen be able to recover for any loss of wages as a result of the defendants' negligence? This fear of opening the floodgates convinced the courts of the need to deny liability in the case of negligently inflicted pure economic loss. Although English law no longer adopts this view, the fear of opening the 'floodgates' can still be seen behind many of the present rules.

There is, however, a second objection to permitting economic loss to be recovered in a tort action. The basis of this objection is that, to do so, would be to undermine established rules and principles of the law of contract. This objection surfaced most clearly in the decision of the House of Lords in *D & F Estates Ltd* v *Church Commissioners for England* [1989] AC 177. The third defendants, Wates Ltd (referred to as 'the defendants'), were main contractors engaged in building a block of flats on land owned by the first defendants. The first plaintiffs, D & F Estates, took a lease of one of the flats and they let into occupation a Mr and Mrs Tillman (the second and third plaintiffs), the controllers of D & F. After they had moved in, the plaintiffs discovered that the plaster work, which had been done by a firm of independent contractors employed by the defendants, had been done defectively. So they sued the defendants for the cost of the remedial work, the cost of cleaning the carpets, loss of rent while the remedial work was being carried out and damages for the disturbance to the second and third plaintiffs. One of the issues argued before the House of Lords was whether the loss sustained by the first plaintiffs in renewing the plaster work was recoverable as damages in tort. The plaintiffs' claim was that the plaster itself was defective and not that the defective plaster had caused damage to other property of the plaintiffs or had caused personal injury. The claim was therefore one to recover damages for pure economic loss. After engaging in an extensive survey of British, American and Commonwealth authorities Lord Bridge concluded that damages in tort do not generally extend to the cost of repairing the defective product itself. Damages were recoverable in tort where the defective product caused personal injury or damaged other property of the plaintiff but damages were not recoverable in tort in respect of a defect in the product itself; such a claim lay, if at all, in contract. He summed up the general principle by using an illustration concerning a defect in a chattel supplied complete by a manufacturer:

> '... [if] the hidden defect in the chattel is the cause of personal injury or of damage to property other than the chattel itself, the manufacturer is liable. But if the hidden defect is discovered before any such damage is caused, there is no longer any room for the application of the *Donoghue* v *Stevenson* ... principle. The chattel is now defective in quality, but it is no longer dangerous. It may be valueless or it may be capable of economic repair. In either case the economic loss is recoverable in contract by a buyer or hirer of the chattel entitled to the benefit of a relevant warranty of quality, but is not recoverable in tort by a remote buyer or hirer of the chattel.'

It can be seen that this objection has nothing to do with the floodgates argument. It is an argument from first principle, namely that a claim for damages for the cost of repairing a defect in the product itself is a claim in contract and not tort and that, to allow such a claim to lie in tort, is to undermine fundamental contractual principles. Thus *D & F Estates* has been applied in *Preston* v *Torfaen Borough Council* (1993) The Times 21 July and *Lancashire & Cheshire Association of Baptist Churches* v *Howard & Seddon Partnership* [1993] 3 All ER 467, although in the latter case the court recognised that a duty of care could exist where the parties were in a contractual professional relationship. Yet it must be conceded that the courts have not been altogether consistent on this point. Cases, such as *Ross* v *Caunters* [1980] Ch 297 and *Junior Books Ltd* v *Veitchi Co Ltd* [1983] 1 AC 520, can be found in which the courts have permitted an action in tort to lie despite the fact that it appeared to undermine established principles of contract law, such as privity and consideration. However, the dominant attitude in the appellate courts today is to draw a clear, bright line between contract and tort and thus to deny claims in tort which seek to recover as damages the cost of repairing the defect in the product itself (although contrast the much more liberal approach adopted by the Supreme Court of Canada in *Canadian National Railway Co* v *Norsk Pacific Steamship Co Ltd* (1992) 91 DLR (4th) 289, discussed by Markesinis (1993) 109 LQR 5).

With these objections to permitting the recovery of economic loss in mind, let us now turn to examine the cases in more detail. We shall commence our analysis with situations in which such loss is recoverable and then move out into areas where it is more doubtful whether such a claim can be brought successfully.

7.5 Consequential economic loss

The first example of a situation in which a plaintiff can bring a claim for economic loss is where the plaintiff suffers 'consequential economic loss', that is, economic loss which is consequential upon physical injury or property damage. It may be objected that this is not an example of 'pure' economic loss and, of course, this is true. But it is nevertheless an area in which the courts do permit economic loss to be recovered and it is therefore worthy of note.

The general rule is that a plaintiff can recover in respect of economic loss which is consequential upon physical injury or property damage. The most obvious example in this category is a claim for loss of earnings consequential upon negligently inflicted personal injury. In the case of economic loss consequential upon property damage, the leading authority is *Spartan Steel and Alloys Ltd* v *Martin & Co (Contractors) Ltd* [1973] QB 27. In this case the defendants negligently cut through the power cable leading to the plaintiffs' factory. The power was cut off for some 14 hours. The plaintiffs had molten metal in a furnace at the time of the power cut. This molten metal suffered damage assessed at £368 and the plaintiffs lost £400 profit on the melt. They also sought to recover £1,767 in respect of profits which could have been earned on further melts which would have been made had it not been for the power cut. It was held that the plaintiffs could recover in respect of the damage to the molten metal and the £400 consequential loss of profits but that they could not recover in respect of the £1,767 loss of profits. Lord Denning reaffirmed that only 'truly consequential loss' was recoverable and that, apart from that, economic loss was irrecoverable. He said that a power cut of this nature was the type of thing which we must put up with and either insure against such loss or use a stand-by system. But Edmund Davies LJ dissented on the ground that, in his opinion, damages were recoverable for economic loss provided that such damage was a reasonably foreseeable and direct consequence of the breach of the duty of care. This approach avoided the drawing of an arbitrary distinction between the first loss of profit which was held to be recoverable and the second loss of profits which was held to be irrecoverable. Applying the test adopted by Edmund Davies LJ all the loss of profit was recoverable. But however attractive the reasoning of Edmund Davies LJ might be it does not represent the current state of English law.

7.6 Negligent misstatement

The second situation in which a plaintiff can recover damages for economic loss which he has suffered is where he can bring himself within the scope of the decision of the House of Lords in *Hedley Byrne & Co Ltd* v *Heller & Partners Ltd* [1964] AC 465. *Hedley Byrne* has now become an extremely important case because it is the one secure species of recoverable pure economic loss. The scope of this case has therefore become a matter of some considerable controversy and importance. On one interpretation it stands as authority for the proposition that pure economic loss suffered as a consequence of reasonable reliance placed upon a negligent *statement* uttered by the defendant is recoverable, at least where there is a 'special relationship' between the parties. A wider interpretation of the case is that *Hedley Byrne* is not confined to cases in which a plaintiff has suffered economic loss as a result of reliance upon a negligent statement but that it applies whenever the defendant voluntarily assumes a responsibility towards the plaintiff and the plaintiff reasonably relies upon the defendant. In this section we shall confine our attention to the narrower of these two interpretations and we shall consider the circumstances in which economic loss is recoverable where the loss has been suffered as a result of the plaintiff's reliance upon the defendant's negligent misstatement.

The leading case is of course the decision of the House of Lords in *Hedley Byrne* itself. Prior to *Hedley Byrne* such economic loss was only recoverable where there was a pre-existing contractual relationship between the parties or where there was a relationship between the parties, such as solicitor and client or doctor and patient, which equity regarded as being of a 'fiduciary' nature (see *Nocton* v *Lord Ashburton* [1914] AC 932). Beyond these narrow cases, economic loss suffered as a result of reliance upon a negligent misstatement was not recoverable (*Candler* v *Crane Christmas & Co* [1951] 2 KB 164, although contrast the dissenting judgment of Denning LJ). But *Hedley Byrne* considerably expanded the scope of liability for negligent misstatement.

The facts of *Hedley Byrne* were straightforward. The plaintiffs were advertising agents and, under one of their contracts, were personally liable if their clients failed to pay the bill. So they asked their bank to find out about the financial standing of their clients. The bank obtained a reference from the defendants which stated that the clients were good for ordinary business transactions. In fact the clients were in a bad way financially and they went into liquidation shortly afterwards. The plaintiffs sued the defendants in respect of the losses which they had suffered because they were personally liable under the contracts which they had negotiated on behalf of the clients. On the facts of the case it was held that the defendants were not liable because they had provided the reference 'without responsibility'. But, had a disclaimer not been issued by the defendants, it is clear that they would have owed a duty of care to the plaintiffs and been in breach of it.

Although the House of Lords held that, absent a disclaimer, a duty of care would have been owed by the defendants, they were not prepared to apply ordinary *Donoghue* principles because of their fear that to have done so would have been to impose too great a burden upon the makers of statements. Lord Reid stated that the law must treat negligent statements differently from negligent acts for two reasons. The first was that even careful people are likely to make statements on social occasions which may influence others, without taking the care which they would normally take in a business transaction, whereas it was highly unlikely that a person would casually put into circulation a negligently made product. The second, and more compelling, justification for treating negligent statements differently from negligent acts is that words have a greater propensity to spread (for example through newspapers and the television) than acts and so liability for statements must be confined within narrower bounds.

Before considering further the ambit of *Hedley Byrne* it should be noted that, although it is currently the only secure species of recoverable pure economic loss, the decision itself has been subjected to some criticism (see, for example Weir [1963] Cambridge Law Journal 216). The first is that the plaintiffs entered into losing business deals on the faith of a free opinion and, had they made a profit from the transaction, no part of that profit would have found its way to the defendants. The plaintiffs' case was therefore not a particularly meritorious one. The second is that the effect of the decision was, it can be argued, to give the plaintiffs, who were not privy to any contract with the defendants, the 'benefit of a relevant warranty of quality', namely that the advice would be given with reasonable care and skill. No emphasis was placed upon the fact that the plaintiffs could potentially have protected themselves against such loss by entering into a contract with the defendants to obtain such information. Yet these are the very factors which are currently being relied upon by the House of Lords in cases such as *D & F Estates* (above) and *Murphy* (above) to justify the refusal to impose a duty of care. As Stapleton has remarked ((1991) 107 Law Quarterly Review 249, 259):

> '... [r]ead today, *Hedley Byrne* comes as a shock. It can hardly be doubted that were it to be a fresh Court of Appeal decision on appeal to the current House of Lords, it would have come in for harsh criticism.'

But, despite these criticisms, *Hedley Byrne* still stands as good authority.

It is suggested that there are two central pillars upon which *Hedley Byrne* rests. The first is that the defendant must have voluntarily assumed a responsibility towards the plaintiff and the second is that the plaintiff must have reasonably relied upon the defendant. These two concepts are, in fact, closely related. If I give you advice and then tell you not to rely on it but you then do rely on it, I have not assumed a responsibility to you, nor can you say that you have reasonably relied upon my advice. But in other contexts I may reasonably rely upon the maker of a statement where he does not voluntarily assume a responsibility to me. For example, a well-known accountant may state on television that certain shares are bound to prove a good investment. If I, as a television viewer, choose to invest in these shares I may say that I have reasonably (from my point of view) relied upon his statement, but it would be difficult for me to argue that he voluntarily assumed a responsibility towards me.

However, in recent cases the House of Lords has begun to distance itself from the voluntary assumption of responsibility test. Thus in *Caparo Industries plc* v *Dickman* [1990] 2 AC 605, 637 Lord Oliver stated that while voluntary assumption of responsibility is a 'convenient phrase' it is:

> '... clear that it was not intended to be a test for the existence of the duty for, on analysis, it means no more than that the act of the defendant in making the statement or tendering the advice was voluntary and that the law attributes to it an assumption of responsibility if the statement or advice is inaccurate and is acted upon. It tells us nothing about the circumstances from which such attribution arises.'

The courts today seem to place reliance upon a number of factors in deciding whether or not to impose a duty of care. For example, in *Caparo* Lord Bridge identified the following salient features of cases in which liability has been imposed upon the defendant:

> 'The defendant giving advice or information was fully aware of the nature of the transaction which the plaintiff had in contemplation, knew that the advice or information would be communicated to him directly or indirectly and knew that it was very likely that the plaintiff would rely on that advice or information in deciding whether or not to engage in the transaction in contemplation.'

In *James McNaughten Papers Group plc* v *Hicks Anderson & Co (a firm)* [1991] 2 QB 113 Neill LJ identified the following relevant factors: (i) the precise purpose for which the statement was made; (ii) the purpose for which the statement was communicated; (iii) the relationship between the adviser, advisee and any relevant third party; (iv) the size of any class to which the advisee belongs; (v) the state of knowledge of the adviser; and (vi) the reliance by the advisee (including whether the advisee was entitled to rely on the statement, whether he did so rely, whether he should have relied upon his own judgment and whether he should have sought and obtained independent advice).

We can therefore identify a number of relevant factors, the most important of which are the knowledge of the maker of the statement, the purpose for which the statement was made and the reasonableness (or otherwise) of the plaintiff's reliance. But, before considering these factors further, we must first discuss another element which, it has been argued, is an essential ingredient of *Hedley Byrne* type liability. That factor is that the representor must be possessed of a special skill. The exact status of this requirement has been a subject of controversy since the decision of the Privy Council in *Mutual Life and Citizens Assurance Co* v *Evatt* [1971] AC 793. The plaintiff was a policyholder with the defendant insurance company. He obtained some gratuitous advice from the defendants as to the wisdom of investing in the defendants' sister company. He was assured that the sister company was financially stable and so he invested in the company. When the company crashed he brought an action against the defendants, alleging that they had been negligent in giving him advice. The Privy Council held, by a majority, that the defendants were not liable. The only duty which they owed to the plaintiff was a duty to act honestly and that duty they had fulfilled. They did not owe a duty of care under *Hedley Byrne* because the majority held that liability under *Hedley Byrne* only arose where the defendants made the statement in the course of their business. As the defendants were an insurance company and not investment advisers they were not liable to the plaintiff. The majority did, however, recognise an exception to their general rule which comes into play where the representor has a financial interest in the advice which he has given. They held that, if he does have such a financial interest, then the requirement that the defendant be in the business of giving that type of advice does not apply. It should, however, be noted that there is a degree of ambiguity about when a representor is in the business of giving advice. Can one be a professional by conduct? If so, this requirement could be interpreted liberally in such a way as to expand the application of the majority test to a considerable extent.

The status of the decision of the majority in *Evatt* is, however, unclear. It is a decision of the Privy Council and thus not technically binding on English law. The judgment of the minority, Lords Reid and Morris, has probably commanded wider support in this country. They held that a duty of care was owed by anyone who takes it upon himself to make representations knowing that another will justifiably rely upon his representation. The English courts have tended to apply the minority reasoning in preference to the reasoning of the majority. In *Esso Petroleum Co Ltd* v *Mardon* [1976] 1 QB 801 Lawson J said that the majority test was unduly restrictive and in this he was joined by Ormerod LJ. The other judges in the Court of Appeal, Lord Denning MR and Shaw LJ, were unclear which test they preferred. However, in *Howard Marine and Dredging Co* v *A Ogden and Sons (Excavations) Ltd* [1978] QB 574 both Lord Denning and Shaw LJ made it clear that they preferred the reasoning of the minority in *Evatt*. So the clear tendency is to follow the minority approach and, although *Evatt* is a Privy Council decision and as such is worthy of considerable respect, it is suggested that the majority view will not be followed and that the minority view will be preferred.

Having dismissed the *Evatt* case we must now return to consider the various factors which the courts consider in deciding whether or not it is appropriate to impose upon the defendants a duty of care. This can best be done by looking in more detail at some of the recent cases.

The two leading modern cases are *Smith* v *Eric S Bush* [1990] 1 AC 829 and *Caparo* v *Dickman* [1990] 2 AC 605. In *Smith* the plaintiff applied to a building society for a mortgage to enable her to purchase a house and the building society in turn instructed the defendant surveyor to survey the property. The plaintiff paid a fee for the survey to be carried out but the surveyor was employed by the building society, not the plaintiff. The surveyor carried out the survey negligently, failing to note that the removal of the chimney breasts had left the chimney inadequately supported. After the plaintiff had purchased the house in reliance upon the survey the chimney collapsed causing considerable damage to the house. It was held by the House of Lords that the defendant owed to the plaintiff a duty of care and that the attempt to exclude that duty by the use of a disclaimer was invalidated by s2(2) of the Unfair Contract Terms Act 1977. Lord Templeman held that the relationship between the defendant and the plaintiff was 'akin to contract' because 'the valuer knows that the consideration which he receives derives from the purchaser and is passed on by the mortgagee, and the valuer also knows that the valuation will determine whether or not the purchaser buys the home'. The plaintiff was held to be entitled to rely upon the valuer's report even though the disclaimer said that the survey was prepared for the benefit of the building society and not the plaintiff.

In *Caparo* the plaintiffs took over a company (Fidelity), allegedly in reliance upon accounts prepared by the defendants. The plaintiffs alleged that the accounts had been negligently prepared with the consequence that they had suffered financial loss. It was held that the defendants did not owe a duty of care to individual shareholders in Fidelity, nor to potential investors in Fidelity. Lord Bridge stated that the crucial factors in cases such as *Hedley Byrne* v *Heller* (above) and *Smith* v *Eric S Bush* (above) were that the defendants were:

'... fully aware of the nature of the transaction which the plaintiff had in contemplation, knew that the advice would be communicated to him directly or indirectly and knew that it was very likely that the plaintiff would rely on that advice or information in deciding whether or not to engage in the transaction in contemplation.'

But he said that the situation was entirely different in a case such as *Caparo* where the:

'... statement [the accounts] was put into more or less general circulation and may foreseeably be relied on by strangers to the maker of the statement for any one of a variety of different purposes which the maker of the statement had no specific reason to anticipate.'

So in *Caparo* the essential element of 'proximity' was missing. The statutory duties placed upon auditors for the benefit of shareholders did not extend to the imposition a duty of care upon auditors in favour of investors (see also *Al Saudi Banque* v *Clarke Pixley (A Firm)* [1990] 2 WLR 344, where Millett J held that no duty of care was owed by the defendant auditors to banks which had advanced money to a company in reliance upon accounts prepared by the defendants), whether these investors were existing shareholders or simply members of the public who had no previous connection with the company. However, Lord Bridge did suggest that a duty of care could be owed to a shareholder who sold shares in reliance upon the auditor's report, on the ground that the loss would be the 'loss of part of the shareholder's existing holding, which, assuming a duty of care owed to individual shareholders, it might sensibly lie within the scope of the auditor's duty to protect'. But no duty was owed to an individual shareholder who purchased new shares in reliance upon the auditor's report. The duty which the auditors owed to shareholders was generally a duty which was owed to the shareholders as a class but not to shareholders as individuals.

In *Morgan Crucible plc* v *Hill Samuel Bank Ltd* [1991] Ch 295 Hoffmann J, at first instance, noted the similarities between the fact situation in *Caparo* and in *Smith* v *Eric S Bush* but that in one case no duty was owed while in the other a duty was owed. He noted the following differences between the two cases. The first was that the plaintiff in *Smith* paid for the survey while the plaintiffs in *Caparo* did not pay for the audit. The second was that the plaintiff in *Smith* was a person of modest means making the most expensive purchase of her life, whereas the typical takeover bidder is an entrepreneur taking high risks for high rewards. This factor was also relevant in the case of *James McNaughten Papers Group plc* v *Hicks Anderson* (above) where it was held that the defendant accountants of a company which was the subject of a takeover bid owed no duty of care to a company which made its bid in reliance upon the draft accounts of the company. The chairman of the target company had asked the defendants to prepare draft accounts as quickly as possible so that they could be used in the negotiations for the takeover. One of the factors which persuaded the Court of Appeal to hold that no duty was owed was that the parties were experienced businessmen and that the plaintiffs had their own independent advisers. The third factor identified by Hoffmann J was that the imposition of liability upon surveyors would not be likely to result in a great increase in the insurance costs of surveyors or in the cost of surveys, whereas the same could not be said in relation to the insurance costs of accountants had *Caparo* gone the other way. Thus, on Hoffman J's analysis, it is the economic implications and the economic environment which justify the different results in *Smith* and *Caparo*. But in the Court of Appeal in *Morgan Crucible* (see above) Slade LJ was rather sceptical about the economic analysis employed by Hoffmann J on the ground that a trial judge will generally not be in a position to form more than a very broad view of the economic consequences of his decision. Despite these doubts expressed by the Court of Appeal it is suggested that there is much to be said for the view of Hoffmann J.

It is suggested that, although there are a number of factors which will be relied upon by the courts in deciding whether or not to impose a duty of care, there are in fact three principal factors to which the courts will have regard. The first is the purpose for which the statement was made. In *Smith* the court concluded that the purpose behind the survey was to enable the plaintiff to rely upon it in deciding whether or not to purchase the house, while in *Caparo* the House of Lords concluded, after examining the relevant statutes in some detail, that the purpose behind the requirement that an audit report be prepared was not to enable shareholders to sue upon it. And in *Mariola Marine Corporation* v *Lloyd's Register of Shipping, The Morning Watch* [1990] 1 Lloyd's Rep 547 it was held that a surveyor employed by Lloyds did not owe a duty of care to the purchaser of a ship which had been surveyed by the surveyor on the ground that the function of the survey was to protect life and property at sea and not to protect the economic interests of those involved in the sale and purchase of ships. This case demonstrates the importance of the court's perception of the purpose behind the statement because otherwise it is very difficult to distinguish this case from *Smith*. The fact that a duty of care is owed to the recipient of the statement does not mean that a duty is also owed to the person about whom a statement is made. Thus the author of a reference does not owe a duty of care to the subject of the reference: if the reference is false the claim of the latter lies in defamation not negligence (*Spring* v *Guardian Assurance plc* [1993] 2 All ER 273; *Petch* v *Commissioners of Customs and Excise* (1993) The Times 4 March).

The second factor of importance is the state of the defendant's knowledge. The greater the knowledge the defendant has of the plaintiff and the purpose for which he is likely to rely on his statement, the more likely it is that he will owe to the plaintiff a duty of care (contrast in this respect *Caparo* and *Smith*). The duty is not necessarily confined to the person to whom the statement is made but, as *Smith* demonstrates, can, within narrow limits, extend to the person whom the maker of the statement knew was intended as the ultimate recipient of the report (see also *Punjab National Bank* v *de Boinville* [1992] 1 WLR 1138 where it was held that the defendant insurance brokers owed a duty of care, not to their clients, but to the plaintiff bank who, to the brokers' knowledge, had actively participated in giving instructions for the insurance and who intended to become an assignee of the insurance policy which the brokers had been instructed to place).

The third factor is the reasonableness of the plaintiff's reliance upon the defendant's statement. Thus in *McCullagh* v *Lane Fox & Partners* (1994) The Times 25 January a duty was imposed on the defendant estate agent when he incorrectly advised a potential purchaser of a plot size, as the defendant knew that there would be no independent survey. *Harrison* v *Surrey County Council* (1994) The Times 27 January is an interesting novel fact situation in which a duty was imposed upon the defendant Council when it informed a mother that not only was a person a registered child-minder, but also that it would be happy for the child to be in that person's care. But there are a number of circumstances in which it may not be reasonable for a plaintiff to rely on the defendant's statement. The first is where the plaintiff has his own independent advisers upon whom he can rely (see *McNaughten* (above)). The second is that it is not generally reasonable to rely upon a representation which is made on a social occasion (*Hedley Byrne* v *Heller*, per Lord Reid). But care must be taken in establishing the existence of a 'social occasion'. This point arose in the case of *Chaudhry* v *Prabhakar* [1989] 1 WLR 29. The defendant, who was a friend of the plaintiff, offered to help her to find and purchase a suitable motor car. The defendant was not a motor mechanic but he did profess to have some knowledge of cars. The plaintiff's specification was that the car must not have been involved in an accident. The defendant found a car which had low mileage but which he knew had had its bonnet repaired or replaced. The plaintiff bought the car in reliance upon the representation of the defendant that it was suitable but it subsequently transpired that the car was unroadworthy, having been inadequately repaired after an accident. The plaintiff successfully brought an action for damages against the defendant. One of the issues discussed by the Court of Appeal was whether the defendant owed the plaintiff a duty of care on *Hedley Byrne* principles (counsel for the defendant had conceded the point but the issue was nevertheless discussed by the court). The court held that this was not a purely social relationship because of the plaintiff's reliance upon the defendant's skill and judgment and the defendant's knowledge of that reliance; indeed, he even informed the plaintiff that there was no need to have the car inspected by a mechanic. A duty of care was therefore owed on *Hedley Byrne* principles despite the fact that the plaintiff and the defendant were friends (contrast the dissenting opinion of May LJ who stated that he did not find 'the conclusion that one must impose on a family friend looking out for a first car for a girl of 26 a *Donoghue* v *Stevenson* duty of care in and about his quest, enforceable with all the formalities of the law of tort, entirely attractive' and argued that the decision 'will make social regulations and responsibilities between friends unnecessarily complex').

Thirdly, it may be the case that, in considering whether it is reasonable to rely upon a representation, the courts will draw a distinction between the passing on of information and the giving of advice; holding that it is more reasonable to rely on the latter than the former. A hint of such an approach may be gleaned from the case of *Royal Bank Trust Co (Trinidad) Ltd* v *Pampellonne* [1987] 1 Lloyd's Rep 218. The Pampellonnes alleged that the defendant bank had on two occasions given them negligent advice in relation to certain investments with the result that they lost most of the money which they had invested. The bank denied that they owed the Pampellonnes a duty of care in respect of the advice which they had given. At first instance the trial judge held that no duty of care was owed by the bank but this finding in relation to the second piece of advice was reversed on appeal to the Court of Appeal of Trinidad and Tobago. The Privy Council held that the bank was entitled to succeed in its appeal on the narrow ground that the Court of Appeal was not entitled to conclude that the trial judge had erred in finding that the Pampellonnes were not owed a duty of care by the defendants. Lord Goff pointed out the following relevant factors: (1) that the Pampellonnes' visit to the bank was without prior warnings; (2) that no fee was charged by the bank; (3) that the Pampellonnes did not inform the bank of the monies which they had available for investment; (4) that Mr Pampellonne did not sign any document relating to his alleged request for advice. Lord Goff also stated that:

'... once it was held ... that at a brief meeting the bank was prepared to do no more than provide such information as was available to them, the Judge was entitled to form the opinion on the evidence before him that no duty of care arose, other than (no doubt) to pass such information accurately to Mr Pampellonne.'

Thus the relative informality of the meeting appeared to negative the assumption of responsibility by the bank.

The minority judgment held that the defendants were experts and that Mr Pampellonne was a naive layman who, in the words of Lord Reid in *Hedley Byrne*, was 'trusting [the bank] to exercise such a degree of care as the circumstances required' and this factor was crucial to their finding that a duty of care was owed. The minority judgment certainly appears to accord more closely with the spirit of the judgments in *Hedley Byrne*. It is, however, unclear what impact the majority judgment will have on the development of the law because Lord Goff was emphatic that the 'appeal does not raise any question of law' but was confined to the question of whether or not the Court of Appeal was entitled to overturn the finding of the trial judge. Nevertheless the refusal of the majority to find the existence of a duty of care on account of the relative informality of the meeting suggests that liability will not easily attach to the passing on of information as opposed to the giving of advice (see further Clements 1987 Professional Negligence 145).

7.7 Defective product economic loss

We have already seen from our discussion of *D & F Estates Ltd* v *Church Commissioners for England* [1989] AC 177 (see 7.4) that the general rule is that damages are not recoverable in tort in respect of the cost of repairing a defect in a negligently made product. Defective product economic loss is therefore recoverable in contract, not tort. Although this rule has been firmly established as a *general* rule by cases such as *D & F Estates* and *Murphy* v *Brentwood District Council* [1991] 1 AC 398, it does admit of a number of exceptions. We will now consider three of these exceptions.

The first exception arises out of the infamous decision of the House of Lords in *Junior Books Ltd* v *Veitchi Co Ltd* [1983] 1 AC 520. The defendants were contractors who specialised in laying floors. The plaintiffs had entered into a contract with another firm of contractors for the construction of a factory. The plaintiffs nominated the defendants to lay the floor in the factory. The work of laying the floor was in fact subcontracted by the main contractors to the defendants. So there was a contract between the plaintiffs and the main contractors and between the main contractors and the defendants but there was no contract between the plaintiffs and the defendants. The plaintiffs' statement of claim alleged that the floor had been laid defectively and that they had suffered loss of in excess of £200,000 in repairing the floor and in the consequent disruption of their business. It was not alleged that the floor constituted a danger to health; it was simply a claim to recover pure economic loss (for an explanation of why this was not an economic loss case see 7.3 above).

It was held that there was such a relationship of proximity between the parties that the defendants owed a duty of care, not simply to prevent the infliction of harm upon the plaintiffs, but to avoid faults being present in the work which they had done. A number of factors were emphasised by the court as giving rise to a sufficient degree of proximity between the parties. The first was that the plaintiffs had nominated the defendants to lay the floor and so they relied upon the defendants to do the work properly. The second was that the defendants knew that the plaintiffs were relying upon their skill in laying the floor and the third factor was that the damage was a direct and foreseeable result of the negligence of the defendants.

Subsequent cases have, however, adopted an extremely restrictive interpretation of *Junior Books* (see, for example, *Tate & Lyle Industries Ltd* v *Greater London Council* [1983] 1 All ER 1159, *Muirhead* v *Industrial Tank Specialities Ltd* [1986] QB 507, *Aswan Engineering Establishment Ltd* v *Lupdine Ltd* [1987] 1 All ER 135, *Simaan General Contracting Co* v *Pilkington Glass Ltd (No 2)* [1988] QB 758 and *Greater Nottingham Co-operative Society Ltd* v *Cementation Piling and Foundations Ltd* [1989] QB 71). In *D & F Estates* Lord Bridge did not engage in a further analysis of *Junior Books* but he did state that:

'The consensus of judicial opinion, with which I concur, seems to be that the decision of the majority is so far dependent upon the unique, albeit non-contractual relationship between the pursuer and the defender in that case and the unique scope of the duty of care owed by the defender to the pursuer arising from that relationship that the decision cannot be regarded as laying down any principle of general application in the law of tort or delict.'

Indeed, in *D & F Estates* Lord Bridge stated that the dissenting opinion of Lord Brandon in *Junior Books* enunciated 'with cogency and clarity principles of fundamental importance'. Lord Brandon had dissented on the ground that the effect of *Junior Books* was to create, as between two parties who were not in a contractual relationship, obligations which were really only appropriate as between contracting parties. He noted that there was no question of any danger to the plaintiffs or to their property and argued that there was nothing to bring the case within the principles laid down in *Donoghue*. This demonstrates that we have come a long way from *Junior Books* in that, not only has the decision of the majority been largely confined to its facts, but the dissenting opinion of Lord Brandon has subsequently gained the approval of the House of Lords.

So, what are the limits of *Junior Books*? The case is dependent upon the finding of a 'unique, albeit non-contractual relationship' between the parties. What are the essential ingredients of this relationship? It is suggested that there are two such ingredients. The first is reasonable reliance upon the defendant by the plaintiff. This was easily satisfied on the facts of *Junior Books* because Junior Books nominated Veitchi to lay the floor and so they relied upon the skill of Veitchi. In many cases it will be possible to establish that the plaintiff has relied upon the defendant manufacturer. But it must be remembered that in *Junior Books* Lord Roskill distinguished the facts of *Junior Books* from the 'ordinary everyday transaction of purchasing chattels when it is obvious that in truth the real reliance was on the immediate vendor and not on the manufacturer'. But in many cases when we buy goods we decide the particular brand which we want and we place the real reliance upon the manufacturer of that brand and not upon the vendor. The House of Lords is therefore interpreting reliance, not as a matter of fact, but in the light of policy considerations, these considerations being a desire to exclude the 'ordinary everyday transaction' from the scope of *Junior Books*.

The second element in this unique, albeit non-contractual relationship is an assumption of responsibility by the defendant towards the plaintiff. It is this aspect of *Junior Books* which is particularly difficult to comprehend. In *Muirhead* v *Industrial Tank Specialities Ltd* [1986] QB 507 Robert Goff LJ clearly had difficulty in understanding the ratio of *Junior Books*. He said that the majority assumed that the defendants had accepted direct responsibility towards the plaintiffs. But, as Robert Goff LJ pointed out, this is difficult to square with the facts of the case where the parties had deliberately structured their relationships in such a way that the defendants were not legally responsible to the plaintiffs. The parties could have structured their relationships in such a way that the defendants were legally responsible to the plaintiffs. But the relationships were structured in such a way that the defendants assumed a legal responsibility towards the main contractors and the main contractors assumed a legal responsibility towards the plaintiffs. In the light of this structure, it is difficult to accept the argument that the defendants did assume a legal responsibility towards the plaintiffs.

It is this latter factor which has assumed importance in subsequent cases as plaintiffs have floundered in their attempt to establish that the defendants have assumed a responsibility towards them. It is clear from cases such as *Simaan General Contracting Co* v *Pilkington Glass Ltd (No 2)* [1988] QB 758 (discussed in more detail at 6.10) that the courts are now unwilling to allow one party to short circuit the contractual chain of actions by a direct action in tort and that, cases of physical damage apart, the assumption of a contractual responsibility by the supplier to the subcontractor will, in most cases, prevent the main contractor showing that the supplier has assumed a responsibility towards him in tort. The significance of the contractual assumption of responsibility can also be seen in the case of *Greater Nottingham Co-operative Society Ltd* v *Cementation Piling and Foundations Ltd* [1989] QB 71. The plaintiffs employed contractors to extend premises of theirs in Skegness. The defendants were nominated subcontractors who were responsible for the pile-driving. They carried out this task negligently with the result that the plaintiffs suffered economic loss which included the consequence of delay in completion of the building. There was a contract between the plaintiffs and the defendants but the contract only related to the supply of the materials and it did not extend to the manner in which the work was done. The plaintiffs originally brought an action against the defendants in both contract and tort but later abandoned the contractual action and proceeded only in tort. However, the Court of Appeal held that the defendants did not owe a duty of care to the plaintiffs because the contractual relationship between the parties precluded the existence of a duty of care in tort. The contract between the parties contained the sum total of the obligations which the defendants had accepted towards the plaintiffs. Woolf J stated that:

'Where, as here, the subcontractor has entered into a direct contract and expressly undertaken a direct but limited contractual responsibility to the building owner, I regard the direct contract as being inconsistent with any assumption of responsibility beyond that which has been expressly undertaken. This does not affect the subcontractor's normal liability in tort but does negative the existence of the exceptional circumstances needed for liability for economic loss.'

So it is clear from *Simaan* and the *Greater Nottingham* case that the assumption of a contractual responsibility by a subcontractor either to the main contractor or to the building owner will make it very difficult to show that the subcontractor has accepted an additional obligation in tort to the building owner. *Junior Books* has therefore received an extremely narrow interpretation in the appellate courts and it must now be regarded as a case decided 'on its own facts' which is only applicable where the relationship between the parties is equivalent to contract (for a different interpretation of *Junior Books* as a *Hedley Byrne* case, see 7.8 below).

The second exception is an uneasy one because it finds its origins in an explanation of the now discredited and overruled decision of the House of Lords in

Anns v *Merton London Borough Council* [1978] AC 728 where, it will be recalled, it was held that the plaintiffs could, in principle, recover from the defendants the cost of repairing the defective foundations. In *D & F Estates* both Lord Bridge and Lord Oliver hinted that *Anns* could be justified on the basis of what they called the 'complex structure theory'. On this view, if the constituent parts of a building were viewed as separate items of property which were separate and distinct from the premises as a whole, then the conflict with Lord Bridge's general principle in *D & F Estates* disappeared. We could then say that the defective foundations in *Anns* were separate and distinct from the rest of the building. There would therefore be no objection in principle to awarding damages for the repair of the cracked walls and, of course, to repair the cracked walls properly one must repair or replace the defective foundations themselves. But in *Murphy* v *Brentwood District Council* (above) the House of Lords rejected the complex structure theory as an explanation for *Anns*. For example, Lord Keith stated (at p470) that it would be 'unrealistic' to adopt the complex structure theory 'as regards a building the whole of which had been erected and equipped by the same contractor'. The significance of the 'complex structure' theory has not, however, been completely eliminated because Lords Keith, Bridge and Jauncey all clearly envisaged that a restricted role remained for the theory. Thus Lord Bridge (at p478) sought to draw a distinction between:

'... some part of a complex structure which is said to be a "danger" only because it does not perform its proper function in sustaining other parts and some distinct item incorporated in the structure which positively malfunctions so as to inflict positive damage on the structure in which it is incorporated.'

Examples which he gave in the latter category were a defective central heating boiler which explodes and damages a house or a defective electrical installation which malfunctions and sets the house on fire. In such cases Lord Bridge did not doubt that the owner of the house could recover damages on ordinary *Donoghue* principles from the manufacturer of the boiler or the electrical contractor. Lord Jauncey agreed that the complex structure theory could apply to the boiler and electrical installation examples given by Lord Bridge but he was also of the opinion (at p497) that there would be room for the operation of the theory in the case where:

'... one integral component of the structure was built by a separate contractor and where a defect in such a component had caused damage to other parts of the structure, eg a steel frame erected by a specialist contractor which failed to give adequate support to floors or walls.'

In this example it would appear, rather unusually, to be the presence of a 'separate' contractor which triggers the application of the theory.

The 'complex structure' theory therefore remains alive and well, although operating within rather narrow confines, and it should not be thought that it is only of significance in building cases. It is of general significance as can be seen from the case of *Aswan Engineering Establishment Co* v *Lupdine Ltd* [1987] 1 All ER 135. The plaintiffs bought a quantity of liquid proofing compound from the first defendants. This compound was stored in pails supplied by the second defendants. While stacked at a quayside awaiting shipment, the pails, which had been stacked some five or six high, burst and the compound was lost. The first defendants having gone into liquidation, the claim proceeded against the second defendants on two grounds. The first, with which we are not concerned, was that the pails were not of merchantable quality and the second was that the second defendants owed a duty of care in tort to provide pails which were suitable for the journey and which would preserve the compound. The claim was dismissed on both grounds. It was held that the damage to the plaintiff was not reasonably foreseeable and so the defendants were not liable. The interesting point for present purposes relates to what counts as 'other property'. The answer to this question was not entirely clear in *Aswan*. The compound was damaged by the bursting of the pails. But was the compound 'other property' of the plaintiffs? One would think not, because the plaintiffs bought the compound in the pails and property in the two passed simultaneously. But the 'provisional view' of Lloyd LJ was that there was damage to 'other property'. Lloyd LJ gave another example to illustrate his point: suppose that 'I buy a bottle of wine and find that the wine is undrinkable owing to a defect in the cork'. Once again, Lloyd LJ was of the 'provisional view' that this was a case of damage to 'other property'. These cases demonstrate that difficult issues are likely to arise in the future. But the point is an important one because, if the courts are willing to divide up 'property' in this manner then a remedy will be available to a plaintiff in a much wider range of circumstances than would be the case if the courts adopted a restrictive approach.

A third exception, of uncertain scope was recognised by Lord Bridge in *Murphy*. He stated (at p475) that:

> 'If a building stands so close to the boundary of the building owner's land that after discovery of the dangerous defect it remains a potential source of injury to persons or property on neighbouring land or on the highway, the building owner ought, in principle, to be entitled to recover in tort from the negligent builder the cost of obviating the danger, whether by repair or by demolition, so far as that cost is necessarily incurred in order to protect himself from potential liability to third parties.'

Lord Oliver was more cautious. He noted (at p489) that:

> 'Whether ... [the builder] could be held responsible for the cost necessarily incurred by a building owner in protecting himself from potential liability to third parties is a question upon which I prefer to reserve my opinion until the case arises, although I am not at the moment convinced of the basis for making such a distinction.'

In support of Lord Bridge's proposition it could be argued that the law of tort has been particularly concerned to protect users of the highway from dangers on or above the highway (see, for example, *Tarry* v *Ashton* (1876) 1 QBD 314 and *Wringe* v *Cohen* [1940] 1 KB 229, discussed further at 19.3). On the other hand, it should be noted that the possible exception identified by Lord Bridge is not confined to the highway but extends to damage to 'persons or property on neighbouring land' and, indeed, Lord Oliver talks simply of 'potential liability to third parties'. The limits or indeed the rationale of this exception remain unclear. For example, how would it apply to a case such as *Portsea Island Mutual Co-operative Society Ltd* v *Michael Brashier Associates* (1990) 6 Professional Negligence 43. There the defendant architects were employed by developers to design and supervise the construction of a supermarket. The developers were contractually obliged to repair any defects which were brought to their attention by the plaintiffs within 12 months of practical completion of the building. More than 12 months after practical completion, the plaintiffs alleged that the building was defective because some brickslips had fallen from the walls and others had had to be removed by the plaintiffs to prevent injury being inflicted upon people shopping or working in the store. The plaintiffs incurred expenditure in removing the brickslips and replacing them. The defendants denied that they had been negligent and contended, as a preliminary point, that they did not owe a duty of care to the plaintiffs. They argued that this was a *D & F Estates* pure economic loss claim because the only defect was in the product itself. But His Honour Judge Newey QC held that the plaintiffs could recover as damages the cost of removing the brickslips from the wall and any other expenditure incurred in making the property safe but he held that they could not recover the sums which they had expended in replacing the brickslips because that would be to give them the benefit of a relevant contractual warranty of quality when they were not privy to any contract with the defendants.

Could *Portsea* now be interpreted as a case falling within Lord Bridge's exception? If not, what is the difference between the position of a third party on the highway and a person entering a supermarket? Does the fact that the third party is on the land of the building owner or tenant rather than upon the highway or his own land really matter? If this exception does extend to *Portsea*, what are its limits? Does it extend to any lawful visitor entering the premises of another? Further, what would the measure of damages be? Both Lord Bridge and Lord Oliver in *Murphy* refer to the cost 'necessarily incurred in order to protect [the plaintiff] from potential liability to third parties'. Is this implicit approval of the approach adopted by His Honour Judge Newey in *Portsea*? Although there may be a public policy justification for this exception in that it is in the public interest to give building owners every incentive to ensure that buildings are repaired and not left in a state whereby they might be a danger to the safety of the public, it is difficult to square this exception with the general principle for which *Murphy* stands as authority and with the refusal of the House of Lords to protect the interest of the occupier himself in his own health and safety.

7.8 *Hedley Byrne* re-examined

It is clear that in the post-*Murphy* world *Hedley Byrne* v *Heller* (above) assumes enormous significance as the one secure species of pure economic loss. But its survival appears to throw up an anomaly. Suppose that a house is built by a builder upon inadequate foundations and some years later the house is sold to a buyer who purchases the property after having the property surveyed for the purposes of obtaining a mortgage. The surveyor fails to notice the cracks in the building and a few years later defects manifest themselves in the building. *Murphy* stands as authority for the proposition that the purchaser has no cause of action at common law against either the builder or the local authority. So why does *Smith* v *Eric S Bush* tell us that the purchaser may have a cause of action against the surveyor, especially as the surveyor has no right after *Murphy* to claim a contribution from the builder, whose primary fault it was? Further, what is the difference between a local authority inspector and a surveyor so that the latter is liable whereas the former is not? These are difficult questions which the courts must answer in the future.

A further question which arises is: how far does the net of *Hedley Byrne* extend? We have already noted that the case can be subjected to different interpretations (see 7.6). One interpretation was that the case was confined to negligent *statements*; the other view was that it was not so confined. In this connection it is interesting to note that Lord Oliver in *D & F Estates* and Lord Keith in *Murphy* classified *Junior Books* as an example of *Hedley Byrne* type liability yet *Junior Books* cannot reasonably be interpreted as a 'statements' case. This strongly suggests that *Hedley Byrne* can no longer be seen only as a statements case. Another important case in this connection is *Pirelli* v *Oscar Faber & Partners* [1983] 2 AC 1 (discussed in more detail by McKendrick (1991) 11 Legal Studies 326). There the defendants, a firm of consulting engineers, were employed by the plaintiffs to advise them in relation to the building of a new block at their factory, which included a new chimney. The defendants accepted responsibility for the design of the chimney but the concrete used for the refractory inner lining was unsuitable for its purpose and cracks began to appear in the chimney which resulted eventually in the partial demolition and replacement of the chimney itself. It was assumed in the House of Lords that the defendants owed a duty of care to the plaintiffs but this assumption appeared suspect after *D & F Estates*. The only 'damage' in *Pirelli* was damage to the chimney itself; there was no threat of damage to other property and the damages claimed were simply the cost of repairing the defect in the chimney itself which, as we have noted, is not generally recoverable in tort. But in *Murphy* Lord Keith held that *Pirelli* was a *Hedley Byrne* case and approved of it on that basis. Does this mean that there is now one principle for those who give advice but another for those who build, with the liability of the former being more extensive than the latter? How many other cases will be subjected to a process of re-interpretation and 'justified' as examples of *Hedley Byrne* type economic loss? These questions remain to be answered by the courts (the relationship between *Murphy* and *Pirelli* was considered by May J in *Nitrigin Eireann Teoranta* v *Inco Alloys Ltd* [1992] 1 All ER 854 and he stated (at p859) that *Pirelli* could not 'be read as a wide general authority that cracking damage to a chimney itself affords a cause of action against anyone concerned with its supply, manufacture or construction' because to do so 'would be plainly inconsistent with *D & F Estates* and *Murphy*').

7.9 '*Ross v Caunters* economic loss'

There remain certain cases in which economic loss has been held to be recoverable and these cases have not been overruled by the House of Lords in *Murphy*. One such case is *Ross v Caunters* [1980] Ch 297. The defendant, who was a solicitor, failed to tell the testator that attestation of the will by the spouse of a beneficiary would invalidate the gift to the beneficiary. The plaintiff, whose husband had signed the will, sued the defendant in negligence for the loss of her gift under the will. Megarry VC held that the plaintiff was entitled to recover but not on *Hedley Byrne* principles because the plaintiff had not relied upon the skill of the defendant. In finding for the plaintiff Megarry VC relied upon the judgments of Mason and Gibbs JJ in *Caltex Oil (Australia) Pty Ltd v The Dredge 'Willemstad'* (1976) 11 ALR 227. The test which they proposed was that the defendant should be held liable for economic loss caused by his negligent conduct when he can reasonably foresee that the specific plaintiff, as opposed to a general class of persons, will suffer financial loss as a result of his negligence. In *Ross* the plaintiff was a member of a limited class and therefore loss to the plaintiff as an individual could actually be foreseen by the defendant. The attraction of this test is that its adoption would not lead to indeterminate liability because a duty would only arise where the plaintiff could be foreseen as an individual.

Doubts have, however, been cast upon the utility of this test. In *Junior Books Ltd v The Veitchi Co Ltd* [1983] 1 AC 520 Lord Fraser doubted whether such an approach was the correct one to adopt. He returned to the issue in *Candlewood Navigation Corporation Ltd v Mitsui OSK Lines Ltd, The Mineral Transporter* [1986] AC 1. He said that he found it difficult to distinguish between the plaintiff as an individual and the plaintiff as a member of a class. He said that the test seemed to rest on the assumption that the class consisted of a small number of persons. What would happen where the class of persons foreseeably affected were pupils at a school? Would the issue of foreseeability really turn upon the number of pupils who attended the school? A similar criticism was levelled against this test by Robert Goff LJ in the Court of Appeal in *Leigh and Sillivan v The Aliakmon Shipping Co* [1985] 1 QB 350. He said that he did not see why a single employer should be able to recover because he was foreseeable as an individual, but that his employees should be left without a remedy because they were only foreseeable as a class and he said that he would not apply a test which led to such a conclusion.

We are therefore in the rather unusual position that the test which was used to justify the decision in *Ross* has subsequently been rejected, but the decision in *Ross* itself has not been overruled (see *Clarke v Bruce Lance and Co (a firm)* [1988] 1 All ER 364) and indeed in *Murphy* Lord Oliver (at p486) referred to it without disapproval Despite the doubts about the correctness of *Ross*, it was recently affirmed by the Court of Appeal in *White v Jones* [1993] 3 WLR 730. There a testator had quarrelled with his two daughters and so had instructed his solicitors, the defendants, to prepare a will cutting his daughters out of his estate. This was done and the will was duly executed. The testator was subsequently reconciled with his daughters and so he instructed the defendants to prepare a fresh will, in which he wished to leave £9,000 to both daughters. The defendants, however, did nothing for one month and then began the task of preparing the new will. They then made an arrangement to visit the testator one month later but, unfortunately, the testator died three days before the meeting. The distribution of his estate was covered by the old will and so the daughters were deprived of their bequests of £9,000. They brought a claim against the defendants, alleging that they had been negligent in the preparation of the new will and claimed £9,000 each by way of damages. The trial judge dismissed the plaintiffs' claim but the Court of Appeal allowed their appeal and entered judgment for £9,000. In the view of the Court of Appeal *Ross* remained good law. The defendants had argued that reliance was a prerequisite to the existence of a duty of care and that, as the plaintiffs had not relied upon the defendants, no duty of care was owed. But this argument was rejected by the court. Reliance was important but it was not the touchstone of liability. The basis upon which the court reached its conclusion that the defendants owed a duty of care to the plaintiffs was that it was 'fashioning an effective remedy for the solicitor's breach of his professional duty to his client'. Although in general a solicitor owes a duty of care to his client and to no one else, in the special circumstances of a solicitor being asked by a client to prepare a will, the payment of damages to the estate of the testator would not provide a means of recompensing the testator for the defendants' negligence. On the facts of *White*, if damages had been paid to the estate of the testator, they would have passed under the original will and so would not have been given to the plaintiffs. The only sanction that could be provided for the defendants' breach of duty was to allow the plaintiffs to bring a direct claim in tort. Rationalised on this basis, *Ross* would appear to be confined to its own special facts and it is unlikely that the courts will in future rely upon it to build some wider principle which will liberalise the rules relating to the recovery of economic loss in tort.

Thus in *Hemmens* v *Wilson Browne* [1993] 4 All ER 826 *White* was distinguished. In *Hemmens* a client instructed his solicitors to draft a document giving the plaintiff the right to call on P to pay her the sum of £110,000. The document drafted did not confer any enforceable rights on the plaintiff, although the defendant explained to the plaintiff that its effect was 'akin to a trust'. Shortly afterwards the plaintiff asked the client to fulfil his promise and he refused. The plaintiff sued the defendant in negligence and negligent misrepresentation. The High Court refused to impose a duty of care in negligence as, although damage to the plaintiff was reasonably foreseeable and there was a sufficient degree of proximity between the plaintiff and the defendant, it would not be fair, just or reasonable to impose a duty as the client was still alive and could rectify the situation, and the client had a remedy in breach of contract against the solicitor. Thus the situation differed from *Ross* and *White* where if no duty had been imposed the only person suffering loss would have had no remedy and the only person with a remedy would have suffered no loss. No duty was imposed as regards the negligent misrepresentation by the defendant as it would not be fair, just or reasonable to do so as the defendant had made it clear that he was acting for the client and not for the plaintiff and that she should not rely on the defendant's opinion regarding the legal effect of the document but should seek independent legal advice.

7.10 *Ministry of Housing and Local Government* v *Sharp*

One further case in which economic loss was recovered by the plaintiff is *Ministry of Housing and Local Government* v *Sharp* [1970] 2 QB 233. The Ministry registered planning charges in the local land charges registry so that any subsequent developer of the land could only do so after repaying a sum of money to the Ministry. Unfortunately, one of the defendants' employees failed to notice the charges when searching the register on behalf of a subsequent purchaser of the land and the search certificate which he issued failed to record the charge. The consequence was that the Ministry suffered economic loss in the form of the loss of their entitlement to have the sum repaid to them by the purchaser. The Court of Appeal held that this economic loss was recoverable from the defendants. Salmon LJ did not think that the case fell within *Hedley Byrne* principles because the Ministry had not been misled by any careless statement made to it by the defendants. The case seemed suspect after *Caparo* because it appears to be difficult to say that there was a 'relationship of proximity' between the parties. But in *Smith* v *Eric S Bush* it was referred to without disapproval and in *Murphy* Lord Oliver said (at p486) that the case may 'properly be categorised as a reliance case'. It is not at all easy to establish what Lord Oliver means here but it does underline the point that there remain certain areas of uncertain ambit where economic loss remains recoverable in a tort action.

7.11 *Morrison Steamship Co Ltd* v *Greystone Castle (Cargo Owners)*

A final case in which it is clear that economic loss remains recoverable is *Morrison Steamship Co Ltd* v *Greystone Castle (Cargo Owners)* [1947] AC 265. Two ships were involved in a collision. The plaintiffs were the owners of the cargo on one of the ships. The cargo was not damaged but the plaintiffs were required by the maritime rules of general average contribution to pay a sum of money to the owner of the ship on which the cargo was being carried. They sought to recover that sum of money from the owners of the other ship whose negligence had contributed to the collision. The House of Lords held that they were entitled to succeed in their claim. Although the case has survived as an example of the recovery of pure economic loss it has been subjected to a very narrow interpretation (although contrast the more expansive interpretation adopted by Lord Roskill in *Junior Books*). Thus in *Murphy* Lord Keith stated (at p468) that the case may 'be regarded as turning on specialties of maritime law concerned in the relationship of joint venturers at sea' while Lord

Oliver stated (at p486) that it 'clearly was not a reliance case'. Thus the case would appear to be confined to its own facts and is not of general application.

7.12 Economic loss: conclusion

In conclusion it must be said that the law relating to the recovery of pure economic loss remains in a state of uncertainty. The general restrictive trend is clear from cases such as *D & F Estates* and *Murphy* but certain cases have been allowed to survive and it is difficult to discern any principle which justifies their continued survival. The task which remains to be undertaken is to bring some coherence to the various 'exceptional' cases in which economic loss is recoverable.

7.13 Psychiatric injury or 'nervous shock'

Another type of loss or interest in respect of which the courts have been reluctant to recognise a duty of care is psychiatric injury or 'nervous shock'. This is an area of the law which classically illustrates the 'incremental' approach currently favoured by the House of Lords because, beginning with a rule of no recovery, the courts have gradually expanded the situations in which damages can be recovered in tort in respect of negligently inflicted psychiatric injury. Until the recent decision of the House of Lords in *Alcock* v *Chief Constable of South Yorkshire* [1992] 1 AC 310 (discussed by Teff (1992) 12 OJLS 440) the picture has been one of a gradual willingness on the part of the courts to allow damages to be recovered for such loss, while at the same time the courts have struggled to find an appropriate test to keep liability within acceptable bounds.

Before analysing the historical development of the law, it is necessary to say a word about what lawyers mean by the phrase 'nervous shock'. To the lawyer nervous shock means a mental injury or psychiatric illness and not simply grief and sorrow (*Brice* v *Brown* [1984] 1 All ER 997). But in recent years the courts have begun to move away from this rather misleading terminology and have begun to talk about 'psychiatric illness' rather than nervous shock (see, for example, *Attia* v *British Gas plc* [1988] QB 304). It is suggested that this approach is to be welcomed because psychiatric injury is a much more informative title and in this section of the book 'psychiatric illness' or 'injury' will be used in preference to nervous shock. It should also be noted that the psychiatric injury must be induced by the shock so that a parent who is made distraught by the wayward conduct of a brain damaged child and who suffers psychiatric injury as a consequence has no claim against the tortfeasor who caused the brain damage to the child. As Lord Ackner noted in *Alcock* v *Chief Constable of South Yorkshire Police* (above) the 'shock' must involve a sudden appreciation by sight or sound of a horrifying event and has not yet been extended to psychiatric injury caused by a process of accumulation of gradual assaults on the nervous system.

The original test applied in *Victorian Railway Commissioners* v *Coultas* (1888) 13 App Cas 222 was that no duty of care was owed in respect of psychiatric injury suffered as a result of the negligence of the defendant because it was not the type of injury which, in the ordinary course of things, would result from the negligence of another. The fear behind this approach was that, once it was admitted that a duty of care was owed, the floodgates would be opened and plaintiffs would be encouraged to make unmeritorious claims and an undue burden would be imposed upon defendants. This rigid approach was not, however, adopted for long. In *Dulieu* v *White* [1901] 2 KB 669 it was held that recovery could be granted in respect of psychiatric injury where the plaintiff was put in fear of her own safety. The plaintiff, who was pregnant, suffered psychiatric injury, which resulted in the premature birth of her baby, when an employee of the defendants negligently drove his van into a public house where the plaintiff was serving behind the bar. The plaintiff, being put in fear of her own safety, was held to be able to recover damages from the defendants.

This test did not, however, last for very long, as it was disapproved of by the Court of Appeal in *Hambrook* v *Stokes Bros* [1925] 1 KB 141. The defendant left his lorry at the top of a hill. The brakes of the lorry were not properly on. The engine was also left running with the result that the lorry started itself off and ran violently down the road. The plaintiff suffered psychiatric injury on seeing the lorry running down the hill because she had just left her children in the direction in which the lorry was travelling. It was held that the defendant was liable for the psychiatric injury suffered by the plaintiff, although the grounds of the decision are not entirely clear. Bankes LJ contented himself with saying that the injuries suffered by the mother were the normal consequences which any mother would suffer in such a situation. Sargant LJ dissented and followed the reasoning in *Dulieu*. Atkin LJ placed some emphasis on the fact that the mother was in some physical danger herself and that she perceived the accident with her own senses and not as the result of being told about it by a third party.

The next case of significance in trying to devise an appropriate test is the decision of the House of Lords in *Bourhill* v *Young* (above), the facts of which we have already considered (6.6). The House was not entirely clear as to which test it thought was applicable. Lords Thankerton, Russell and MacMillan held that the plaintiff was so far away from the scene of the accident that it was not reasonably foreseeable that she would suffer physical injury. This approach gave rise to the theory that what mattered for the recoverability in respect of psychiatric injury was that the plaintiff be within the area of physical danger. This theory was not, however, adopted by Lords Wright and Porter who argued that what was determinative of liability was the foreseeability of emotional injury and not the foreseeability of physical injury. It has been argued that this latter approach is the true ratio of *Bourhill* (see Goodhart (1953) 16 MLR 14). However, the case was so uncertain that by no means did it resolve the conflict as to which test was applicable.

Another case of significance is *King* v *Phillips* [1953] 1 QB 429 (on which see Goodhart (1953) 69 LQR 347). The defendant negligently backed his taxi cab over a small boy who had been riding on his bicycle close to the taxi cab. The boy was slightly injured as a result of the accident. The boy's mother, who was standing at her window some 70 yards away, heard her son's scream and saw her son's bicycle under the taxi cab but she could not see her son at all. In these circumstances she suffered psychiatric injury. It was held that the defendant was not liable for the psychiatric injury suffered by the plaintiff because it was held that it was not a reasonably foreseeable consequence of his negligence. The case is an important one because both Denning LJ and Singleton LJ held that the plaintiff need not be in the area of physical impact to be able to recover in respect of psychiatric injury and they held that the plaintiff need not be put in fear of her own safety to be able to recover for psychiatric injury. They held that the appropriate test to apply was that the psychiatric injury must be reasonably foreseeable, but they adopted a rather narrow test of reasonable foreseeability so as to find that the defendant was not liable to the plaintiff. It is unlikely that such a narrow approach would be adopted today (see Lord Bridge in *McLoughlin* v *O'Brian* [1983] 1 AC 410 and Lord Oliver in *Alcock* v *Chief Constable of South Yorkshire* [1991] 3 WLR 1057, 1114). Later cases such as *Schneider* v *Eisovitch* [1960] 2 QB 430 and *Boardman* v *Sanderson* [1964] 1 WLR 1317 suggested that the courts were beginning to adopt a broader approach based upon the reasonable foreseeability of the plaintiff suffering psychiatric injury.

The case which finally established the proper test for the recoverability of damages for psychiatric injury was *McLoughlin* v *O'Brian* [1983] 1 AC 410 (discussed by Teff (1983) 99 LQR 100), which was, for a number of years, the leading authority on the recoverability of damages for negligently inflicted psychiatric injury. The House of Lords held that the appropriate test to apply was whether or not it was reasonably foreseeable that the plaintiff would suffer psychiatric injury as a result of the negligence of the defendant. Although the House agreed on the general test to be applied, they did not agree on the exact ingredients of the test. In the case the plaintiff's husband and her four children were involved in a car accident which was caused by the negligence of the defendant. One of the plaintiff's children was killed in the accident and the others were severely injured. The plaintiff was informed two hours later that an accident had occurred and she went to the hospital where she saw her family and the extent of their injuries, in what were described as circumstances which were 'distressing in the extreme'. As a result of this experience the plaintiff suffered psychiatric injury. It was held that the plaintiff's psychiatric injury was a reasonably foreseeable consequence of the defendant's negligence and so she was entitled to recover damages. Two different approaches are discernible in the judgments given.

The first approach was adopted by Lord Wilberforce who held that, because shock was capable of affecting so many people, the law must place a limit upon the situations in which a plaintiff could recover in respect of psychiatric injury. Lord Wilberforce held that there were three 'elements inherent in any claim' for psychiatric injury. The first was the class of persons whose claims should be recognised. He held that, subject to the special case of a rescuer, 'so far ... the cases do not extend beyond the spouse or children of the plaintiff ... including foster children'. But at a later point in his judgment he said:

> 'Other cases involving less close relationships must be very carefully scrutinised. I cannot say that they should never be admitted. The closer the tie (not merely in relationship, but in care), the greater the claim for consideration.'

This latter dicta would appear to suggest that recovery will generally be allowed in respect of injury to close members of the family but not to ordinary bystanders. An exception to the general rule relating to bystanders is that a person who suffers psychiatric injury as a result of seeking to rescue those involved in a terrible accident may be permitted to recover in respect of the injury which he suffers (see *Chadwick v British Transport Commission* [1967] 1 WLR 912).

The second element which Lord Wilberforce identified was that of the proximity of the plaintiff to the accident. He said that the plaintiff must be both close in time and space. Such would obviously include someone who saw or heard the accident but Lord Wilberforce said that this category should not be confined to such cases. He said it should also apply to someone who came on the 'aftermath' of the accident, by which he meant 'direct perception of some of the events that go to make up the accident as an entire event'.

The third requirement related to the means by which the injury was caused. He pointed out that the injury must be caused by sight or hearing of the accident or its immediate aftermath, although he did proceed to point out that 'whether some equivalent to sight or hearing, eg through simultaneous television, would suffice may have to be considered'. He also added that there was no case in which compensation had been awarded in which the plaintiff was only told about the accident by a third party. So for Lord Wilberforce, unless these three requirements were met, there was no liability for psychiatric injury because, if it were otherwise, the floodgates would be opened to unmeritorious claims.

Lord Bridge, however, adopted a different approach. He castigated the approach adopted by Lord Wilberforce on the ground that it would impose a 'largely arbitrary limit of liability'. He gave the following instructive example to illustrate his point. He said:

> 'Take the case of a mother who knows that her husband and children are staying in a certain hotel. She reads in her morning newspaper that it has become the scene of a disastrous fire. She sees in the paper a photograph of unidentifiable victims trapped on the top floor waving for help from the windows. She learns shortly afterwards that all her family have perished. She suffers acute psychiatric illness. That her illness in these circumstances was a reasonably foreseeable consequence of the events resulting from the fire is undeniable. Yet, is the law to deny her damages as against a defendant whose negligence was responsible for the fire simply on the ground that an important link in the chain of causation of her psychiatric illness was supplied by her imagination of the agonies of mind and body in which her family died, rather than by direct perception of the event?'

The effect of the approach adopted by Lord Wilberforce would be, according to Lord Bridge, to exclude such a claim for damages and to 'freeze the law in a rigid posture' which would be productive of injustice. For Lord Bridge the vital question was whether or not psychiatric damage was a reasonably foreseeable consequence of the defendant's breach of duty.

It is extremely unfortunate that the House of Lords did not speak with one voice because, until the decision of the House of Lords in *Alcock* v *Chief Constable of South Yorkshire* [1992] 1 AC 310, first instance judges and the Court of Appeal were unsure whether to follow the reasoning of Lord Wilberforce or Lord Bridge. In *Alcock* the House of Lords followed the approach of Lord Wilberforce and held that, to the extent that Lord Bridge had suggested that reasonable foresight of psychiatric injury was sufficient, of itself, to found a duty of care, his approach was not to be followed. A plaintiff must show, not only that psychiatric injury was reasonably foreseeable, but also that there existed a relationship of proximity between the plaintiff and the defendant. The three elements relied upon by Lord Wilberforce in *McLoughlin* will obviously play a critical role in future cases and, indeed, all three were of significance on the facts of *Alcock*.

Alcock was a case which arose out of the Hillsborough disaster, where 95 football fans died as a result of overcrowding caused by the admitted negligence of the defendant, who was responsible for the policing at the stadium. Claims for damages for psychiatric injury were brought by plaintiffs who had relatives and friends at the match and who had suffered psychiatric injury as a result of the tragedy. We shall now apply the three-stage approach of Lord Wilberforce to the facts of *Alcock*.

The first element concerns the class of persons eligible to claim. The plaintiffs in *Alcock* consisted of a broad range of relatives of people present, injured or killed in the tragedy, including a wife, parents, brothers, sisters, uncles, a grandfather, a brother-in-law, a fiancee and a friend. As we have noted, Lord Wilberforce in *McLoughlin* stated that 'so far ... the cases do not extend beyond the spouse or children of the plaintiff ... including foster children' and the Court of Appeal in *Alcock* had held that the class of claimants was so restricted. But the House of Lords adopted a rather more expansive approach and held that the category of plaintiffs eligible to claim was not confined to spouses and parents but extended to all relationships which were based upon ties of love and affection and where it could be demonstrated that the love and affection for the victim was comparable to that of the normal parent, spouse or child of the victim. Remoter relationships were therefore not ruled out completely but the House held that, in the case of such relationships, the plaintiff must prove the closeness of the relationship and the court will scrutinise such claims with care. Indeed, Lord Keith, Lord Ackner and Lord Oliver went so far as to say that the claim of a bystander was not 'entirely excluded' and they suggested that a claim may be brought by a bystander where a catastrophe occurs very close to him which is particularly horrific. However, this expansive approach to the class of plaintiffs has not been followed in the Court of Appeal. In *McFarlane* v *Caledonia Ltd* [1993] NLJ 1367 it was held that a bystander to a horrific event could not recover on the grounds that the basis of the decision in *Alcock* was that the test of proximity was not simply reasonable foreseeability but that there must be a sufficiently close tie of love and affection between the plaintiff and the victim. To extend that duty to those who have no such connection would be to base the test on foreseeability alone. Returning to the facts of *Alcock* it was held that only the parents who had lost a son and the fiancee were within the category of plaintiffs eligible to bring a claim. In relation to the brothers and brothers-in-law it was held that they were excluded because there was no evidence of any particularly close ties of love and affection between themselves and their brothers or brothers-in-law. The fact of a sibling relationship is not sufficient of itself; evidence must be brought to establish that the relationship was a close and affectionate one.

Two further points must be made in relation to the class of plaintiffs eligible to claim. The first relates to the category of cases typified by *Dooley* v *Cammell Laird & Co Ltd* [1951] 1 Lloyd's Rep 271. In *Dooley* the plaintiff was a crane driver who suffered psychiatric injury after his load, without any fault on his part, fell into the hold of a ship where his colleagues were working. He thought that he must have killed or injured some of the men, although in the event no-one was hurt. His claim succeeded. Cases such as *Dooley* could have been used by the House of Lords in Alcock to widen the category of plaintiffs eligible to claim but Lord Oliver (and also, it would appear, Lord Jauncey) relied upon them to draw a distinction between cases in which the injured plaintiff was involved, either mediately or immediately, as a participant and those in which the plaintiff was no more than the passive and unwilling witness of injury caused to others. In the former category were cases such as *Dulieu* v *White* (above), *Dooley* and *Wigg* v *British Railways Board* (1986) The Times 4 February where the courts are more willing to recognise the existence of a claim because the fact that the defendant's negligence has resulted in the plaintiff being an active participant in the accident of itself establishes the existence of a proximate relationship between the plaintiff and the defendant.

The second point which must be noted in relation to the class of plaintiffs eligible to claim is that the relationship can be with the plaintiff's property. That this is so can be demonstrated by reference to the case of *Attia* v *British Gas plc* [1988] QB 304. There the defendants entered into a contract to instal central heating in the plaintiff's house. The plaintiff returned to her home to find that it was on fire as a result of the negligence of the defendants. She telephoned the fire brigade but it took them four hours to bring the fire under control. The plaintiff claimed that she had suffered psychiatric injury as a result of witnessing the extensive damage to her house. The defendants admitted that they were liable for the damage to the plaintiff's house and its contents but they denied that they owed a duty of care in respect of the plaintiff's psychiatric injury. They argued that, as a matter of law and public policy, damages could only be recovered for psychiatric injury where it was suffered as a result of fear of death or personal injury to a person closely related to the plaintiff. The argument was rejected because the court was not prepared to lay down as a rule of law that in no circumstances could damages be recovered for psychiatric injury suffered as a result of witnessing damage to property. Bingham LJ said 'suppose, for example, that a scholar's life work of research or composition were destroyed before his eyes as a result of the defendant's careless conduct, causing the scholar to suffer reasonably foreseeable psychiatric damage ... I do not think that a legal principle which forbade recovery in these circumstances could be supported'. The Court of Appeal did not say what factors would be considered in deciding whether the psychiatric injury was reasonably foreseeable but presumably they would be similar to those considered in *McLoughlin*; namely the closeness of the relationship between the plaintiff and the 'thing' damaged, the proximity of the plaintiff to the accident and the means by which the injury was caused.

The second element in Lord Wilberforce's judgment is the proximity of the plaintiff to the accident and on the facts of *Alcock* the point in issue related to the scope of the 'immediate aftermath' doctrine. Some of the plaintiffs who identified the bodies of loved ones in mortuaries sought unsuccessfully to bring themselves within the scope of this doctrine. But it was held that these cases did not fall within its scope because the earliest identification of a victim occurred eight or nine hours after the tragedy and this could not be said to be the *immediate* aftermath. Lord Jauncey also had regard to the purpose of the visit to the mortuary, which was simply the identification of the body, and stated that that was very different from the case of a relative who goes within a short time of the accident to rescue or comfort the victim. So it is now clear that the 'immediate aftermath' operates within very narrow confines and the appellate courts will be reluctant to extend it beyond the fact situation in *McLoughlin* itself.

The third element in Lord Wilberforce's judgment concerned the means by which the shock was caused and this was of vital significance on the facts of *Alcock*. Some of the plaintiffs had watched the events unfold on television but the House of Lords held that viewing the scenes of the tragedy on television was not sufficient because it could not be equated with sight or hearing of the event or its immediate aftermath. This was because viewers on television did not see recognisable individuals (such pictures being excluded by the broadcasting code of ethics). The effect of this conclusion on the facts of the case was that all the claims of the plaintiffs failed because the plaintiffs who satisfied the 'relationship' test did not satisfy this test and those who satisfied this test did not satisfy the relationship test.

Two further points should be noted about the approach of the House of Lords to the third stage. The first is that it is not necessarily the case that television viewers are excluded in all cases. Both Lord Ackner and Lord Oliver stated that they agreed with the judgment of Nolan LJ in the Court of Appeal to the effect that simultaneous broadcasts of a disaster cannot in all cases be ruled out as providing the equivalent of actual sight or hearing of the event or its immediate aftermath. Nolan LJ had given an example of a case in which television cameras 'whilst filming and transmitting pictures of a special event of children travelling in a balloon, in which there was media interest, particularly amongst the parents, showed the balloon suddenly bursting into flames'. In such a case a claim may well lie. On the other hand, Lord Jauncey refrained from making any comment on Nolan LJ's example, so it cannot be assumed that a claim will necessarily lie.

The second point is that it would appear that being told about the accident does not suffice. This can be deduced from the fact that Lord Keith, Lord Ackner and Lord Oliver stated that it must be open to serious doubt whether the first instance decisions *Hevican* v *Ruane* [1991] 3 All ER 65 and *Ravenscroft* v *Rederiaktiebogalet Transatlantic* [1991] 3 All ER 73 were correctly decided. The Court of Appeal has since heard the defendant's appeal in *Ravenscroft* and concluded that in the light of criticisms of their Lordships, the decision could not stand and so allowed the appeal ([1992] 2 All ER 470). No appeal has been heard in *Hevican* and so we shall use that case to illustrate the issues. The plaintiff was told that the minibus in which his favourite son was travelling had been involved in an accident. He was taken to a police station where he was told that his son had died. He then proceeded to the mortuary where he saw his son's body. The plaintiff was subsequently diagnosed as suffering from continuing reactive depression which rendered him unable to cope with his work. He was consequently made redundant and his illness prevented his return to the labour market. As Mantell J pointed out this case was clearly further removed from the scene of the accident than was the case in *McLoughlin* where the plaintiff came upon the 'immediate aftermath' of the accident. This was a case in which the plaintiff's trauma was the 'realisation coming to him in stages that his son was dead, in other words this was shock brought about from communication by others'. Mantell J noted that there were dicta in cases such as *McLoughlin* to the effect that there was no case in English law in which a plaintiff had recovered damages for psychiatric injury suffered as a result of being told about an accident. But he asked himself the following rhetorical question: 'can anyone doubt that it was reasonably foreseeable as a likely consequence of passengers in the minibus being killed through careless driving that the news would be communicated to their near relatives and that such news would come as a great shock ...?' However it would now appear that, in the light of *Alcock*, this approach is wrong and that such a claim should now fail. It is suggested that this conclusion will lead to ridiculous results. Suppose that in *McLoughlin* v *O'Brian* Mrs McLoughlin, after having been told that her family had been involved in a serious road accident, had collapsed and consequently suffered from some psychiatric illness. Would a court really deny her claim simply because she had not seen the injured bodies of her children and husband? It would be absurd if she could only recover damages if she was picked up, taken to the hospital, shown her children and then told 'now you can suffer your psychiatric illness'. As Deane J stated in the High Court in Australia in *Jaensch* v *Coffey* (1984) 54 ALR 417, 463:

> 'It is somewhat difficult to discern an acceptable reason why a rule based on public policy should preclude recovery from psychiatric injury sustained by a wife and mother who is so devastated by being told on the telephone that her husband and children have all just been killed that she is unable to attend at the scene while permitting recovery for the reasonably, but perhaps less readily, foreseeable psychiatric injury sustained by a wife who

attends at the scene of the accident or at its aftermath at the hospital when her husband has suffered serious but not fatal injuries.'

If, as would appear to be the case, that such a claim would now fail in the English courts, it is hard to disagree with the view of Lord Oliver in *Alcock* that the present state of the law is neither 'entirely satisfactory' nor 'logically defensible' and one can only join in his appeal for legislative intervention to put the law in this area on a sounder basis.

8

The Duty of Care and 'Protected Parties'

8.1 Introduction

8.2 The character of the plaintiff

8.3 Judges and legal representatives

8.4 Police

8.5 Negligence in the exercise of a statutory power

8.1 Introduction

In some cases the difficulty in recognising the existence of a duty of care lies not in the interest which is sought to be protected but in the character of the plaintiff or defendant. For example, the plaintiff may have been an unborn child at the time at which the damage was inflicted and the defendant may argue that no duty can be owed to a plaintiff who was not born at the time at which the damage was suffered. On the other hand, the defendant may be a barrister who maintains that he owes no duty of care to his client because of the undesirable consequences which would follow from the imposition of a duty of care. In both cases it is the character of the plaintiff or defendant which is crucial in deciding whether or not a duty of care is owed. In this chapter we shall focus upon particular examples where the character of the plaintiff or the defendant is the vital issue.

8.2 The character of the plaintiff

There are now very few plaintiffs who are not granted a cause of action in negligence as the trend in the development of the tort of negligence has been to reduce the types of plaintiffs who are not given a cause of action.

Although the law has become more liberal with the passage of time, there remain certain classes of plaintiff where the courts remain reluctant, or have had difficulty in recognising, the existence of a duty of care. One case in point is the plaintiff who suffers injury while participating in a criminal act, as a result of the negligence of the defendant. Such was the case in *Ashton* v *Turner* [1981] QB 137. The plaintiff suffered injury as a result of the negligence of the defendant who, at the time at which the plaintiff suffered injury, was driving a getaway car from the scene of a burglary in which they had both participated. Ewbank J held that, on grounds of public policy, the defendant did not owe to the plaintiff a duty of care. It is not, however, the case that participation in criminal activity will inevitably deprive a plaintiff of the protection of the law of tort; it is only where it is of sufficient gravity to invoke the maxim ex turpi causa non oritur actio that it will do so (on which see 31.3).

A second situation in which the courts have had difficulty in recognising that a duty of care is owed arises where the plaintiff was an unborn child at the time at which the damage was inflicted. We have already seen (at 2.1) that, at common law, a child who was born disabled as the result of the negligence of the defendant during the pregnancy or during birth had a cause of action (*Burton* v *Islington Health Authority* [1993] QB 204) and that right of action is now contained in s1 of the Congenital Disabilities (Civil Liability) Act 1976 (see s4(5)of the Act). But what of the plaintiff whose claim is that his deformities are such that he should not have been born at all? This question was put to the courts in the case of *McKay* v *Essex Area Health Authority* [1982] QB 1166. The infant plaintiff was born disabled as a result of her mother suffering an infection of rubella during pregnancy. The plaintiff claimed that, but for the negligence of the defendants in failing to treat the rubella, her mother would have had an abortion. It was held that the plaintiff's claim in effect was that she should not have been born at all and that such a claim was contrary to public policy on the ground that it was a violation of the sanctity of life. The other problem was that the court had no means of assessing damages for breach of such a duty, were it to exist, because damages would have to be assessed on the basis of the difference between life and the termination of life, and that the court could not calculate. *McKay* was a case decided at common law but the same position would prevail under the Congenital Disabilities (Civil Liability) Act 1976.

However, although a child cannot be heard to claim damages on the ground that he should not have been born at all, his parents may bring an action for the pain and suffering of giving birth to an 'unwanted' child and for the consequent disruption to family finances. In *Emeh* v *Kensington and Chelsea and Westminster AHA* [1985] QB 1012 the plaintiff had an abortion followed by a sterilisation operation to prevent her from becoming pregnant again (she had had three children prior to the operation). The operation was, however, performed negligently by the defendants and the plaintiff became pregnant once again and did not discover this fact until she was 20 weeks pregnant. She refused to have another abortion and she gave birth to a child which was congenitally abnormal. She claimed damages for the pain and suffering of giving birth, her loss of future earnings and the cost of maintenance of the child. It was held that the plaintiff's failure to have an abortion did not break the chain of causation and that the defendants were liable to the plaintiff. Prior to *Emeh* there had been a conflict of authority as to whether damages were recoverable for the cost of maintaining the child in the future. In *Udale* v *Bloomsbury AHA* [1983] 1 WLR 1098 Jupp J held that there were public policy objections to awarding damages for the cost of upkeep of the child because in law the birth of a child was a beneficial and not a detrimental event and there was a risk of the child finding out that he was unwanted. However, in *Thake* v *Maurice* [1984] 2 All ER 513 Peter Pain J held that there were no such public policy objections. He dismissed the idea that the birth of a child was always a blessing and equally he dismissed the argument that the fact that child might find out that he was unwanted should negate the existence of a duty of care. In *Emeh* the Court of Appeal preferred the reasoning of Peter Pain J and held that the parents could recover for all reasonable loss flowing from the tort or breach of contract, including the cost of bringing up the child (the principles to be applied in assessing the damages payable were considered by Brooke J in *Allen* v *Bloomsbury Health Authority* [1993] 1 All ER 651). But, in certain circumstances public policy may operate to defeat the parents' claim. Such was the case in *Rance* v *Mid-Downs Health Authority* [1991] 1 QB 587. The plaintiffs' son was born with severe spina bifida and hydrocephalus. The plaintiffs alleged that the defendants had, through their negligence, failed to detect the handicap when the foetus was about 26–27 weeks and that, had it been detected, the mother would have had an abortion. One of the many points which was raised in the case was whether the defendants owed the plaintiffs a duty of care. Brook J held that they did not because the plaintiffs could only have avoided their loss (which was the birth of their son) had the pregnancy been terminated. Such a termination, Brook J held, would have been unlawful under s1 of the Infant Life (Preservation) Act 1929. Using the Act as his primary reference point he held that, in enacting the 1929 Act, Parliament had made a policy decision that the sanctity of the lives of children capable of being born alive be respected and that the duty of the court was to uphold that policy and therefore to dismiss the plaintiffs' claim.

8.3 Judges and legal representatives

Having considered the position of plaintiffs in relation to whom there is a difficulty in establishing the existence of a duty of care, we must now turn to the position of defendants. There are a number of defendants who owe a limited duty of care or even enjoy an absolute immunity from suit in negligence. One such group which enjoys some form of immunity in tort is judges and, to a lesser extent, legal representatives. As we noted in chapter 2 of this book (2.3), judges enjoy immunity from suit in negligence and this immunity has been extended to witnesses in legal proceedings and arbitrators who act in a quasi-judicial capacity (see further 2.3). A preliminary point must, however, be noted. That point is that a negligence action cannot be used as a vehicle to challenge the decision of a court of competent jurisdiction. The proper method of challenge is to appeal against the decision (see *Hunter* v *Chief Constable of West Midlands* [1982] AC 529. Thus, an action cannot be brought against a barrister or a solicitor where the effect of such an action would be directly or indirectly to challenge the decision of a court of competent jurisdiction (*Somasundaram* v *M Julius Melchior* [1989] 1 All ER 129). However, this rule will only apply where the plaintiff had a full opportunity to contest the decision of the court. Where the plaintiff alleges that his legal adviser had failed to advance a point of law which might have caused a decision adverse to the plaintiff to be set aside, such an action does not amount to relitigation of a decided issue and the plaintiff may then sue his legal adviser: *Walpole* v *Partridge & Wilson* [1993] 3 WLR 1093.

Barristers and solicitors do not enjoy the same immunity from suit as do judges. But they do enjoy some immunity. In *Rondel* v *Worsley* [1969] 1 AC 191 the House of Lords held that a barrister has an immunity from suit at the instance of his client in respect of his conduct and management of a court case and in respect of the preliminary work connected with the case, such as the preparation of pleadings. In *Saif Ali* v *Sydney Mitchell and Co Ltd* [1980] AC 198 it was held by the House of Lords that the immunity declared in *Rondel* was not confined to court work but that it extended to pre-trial work provided that the pre-trial work was intimately connected with the conduct of the case before the court and that it affected the way in which the case was to be handled. A barrister does not, however, have total immunity in his or her conduct of a case. If time has been wasted by counsel during the conduct of proceedings and the court is satisfied that counsel had acted negligently, unreasonably or improperly, the court can make an order for wasted costs against the barrister: see *Antonelli* v *Wade Gery Farr* (1993) The Times 29 December.

The immunity of a barrister may, however, be more extensive than the immunity of a solicitor. In *Somasundaram* v *M Julius Melchior & Co* (above) the plaintiff alleged that the defendant solicitors had been negligent in overpersuading him to plead guilty to a charge of the unlawful and malicious wounding of his wife. The advice was given at a conference with counsel, but no action was brought against counsel. The defendant solicitors claimed a *Saif Ali* type immunity because they were advising the plaintiff as to his plea, which was work intimately connected with the conduct of the case before the court. The Court of Appeal held that, although barristers enjoyed an immunity in advising a plaintiff as to his plea and that the same immunity was extended to solicitors when they were acting as advocates, they were not prepared to 'extend the immunity that protects barristers and solicitors qua advocates any further than is necessary in the interests of justice and public policy'. Therefore the court refused to strike out the claim against the defendants on the ground that the defendants enjoyed an immunity from suit. But, as May LJ pointed out, in practice the plaintiff will not be able to succeed against the solicitor because of the rule that a negligence action cannot be used to challenge the decision of a court of competent jurisdiction and because, as a matter of causation, the advice of counsel as to the plea is likely to break the chain of causation between the solicitor's advice and the plaintiff's plea. The immunity accorded to those who act qua advocates has been confirmed by s62 of the Courts and Legal Services Act 1990 which states that a person who is not a barrister but who lawfully provides any legal services in relation to any proceedings shall have the same immunity from liability for negligence in respect of acts or omissions as he would have if he were a barrister lawfully providing these services.

The immunity of barristers and solicitors is not founded upon the lack of foreseeability of harm but on considerations of public policy and Lord Keith recently stated in *Yuen Kun Yeu* v *Attorney-General of Hong Kong* [1988] AC 175 (see 6.6) that *Rondel* was one of the few cases where considerations of policy (or of what is 'just and reasonable') will operate to deny the existence of a duty of care. The considerations of policy are that a barrister must be able to carry out his duty to the court fearlessly, negligence actions against barristers would make a retrial of the original action inevitable and so lengthen proceedings and that a barrister has to accept any client, however difficult he may be. These factors combined to persuade the courts to give barristers and solicitors the immunity described above (for criticism of these policy considerations see Whelan and Veljanovski (1983) 46 MLR 700).

The reluctance of the courts to impose a duty of care arising out of the conduct of litigation is not confined to cases involving barristers and solicitors, as can be seen from the case of *Business Computers International Ltd* v *Registrar of Companies* [1988] Ch 229. The defendant served a winding-up petition on the plaintiffs at the wrong address. The result was that the winding-up petition was made before the plaintiffs were aware of its existence. The plaintiffs alleged that the defendant owed them a duty of care to ensure that the winding-up order was correctly served at the plaintiffs' registered office and that that duty had been breached. They claimed damages of £8,000 in respect of having the winding-up order set aside and £90,000 in respect of the loss of goodwill caused as a result of the winding-up order. Scott J held that the defendant did not owe to the plaintiffs a duty of care in respect of the conduct of litigation. He held that it was not 'just and reasonable' to impose a duty of care in a case such as the present where the parties were antagonists in an adversarial system of litigation and where the safeguards against impropriety were to be found in the rules and procedures that control litigation and not in any remedy in tort.

Where, however, there are no rules which act as a safeguard against impropriety a court may be more inclined to hold that it is just and reasonable to conclude that a duty of care should be owed. In *Welsh* v *Chief Constable of the Merseyside Police* [1993] 1 All ER 692 the Crown Prosecution Service (CPS) agreed to notify the magistrates' court that the plaintiff accused's offences had been taken into consideration by the Crown Court. Unfortunately, it failed to so inform the magistrates and, when the plaintiff did not appear before the magistrates' court to answer the charges which he thought had been dealt with, they issued a warrant for his arrest. The plaintiff was subsequently arrested and kept in custody for a period of time. He brought a claim for damages and the CPS applied to strike out the claim against them as an abuse of process of the court. Tudor Evans J refused to strike out the claim. He held that there was no authority which unambiguously stated that proof of malice was an integral part in an action which touched upon the judicial process and the factors which had troubled Scott J in *Business Computers* were not present on the facts of this case. Although the parties were antagonists in adversarial litigation, Tudor Evans J thought that it was highly arguable that the CPS were not in the same position as solicitors acting at arm's length in civil litigation. For example, prosecutors are under a duty to make available to the defence witnesses who can give material evidence. So the fact that the parties were antagonists in the litigation was not a conclusive bar to the existence of a duty of care.

Even within the context of civil litigation, there may be exceptional cases in which a court may be prepared to conclude that a duty of care is owed in the context of hostile litigation. That this is so can be illustrated by reference to the case of *Al-Kandari* v *JR Brown & Co* [1988] QB 665. The defendant solicitors were acting for their client in custody proceedings involving their client and the plaintiff, who was the former wife of their client. The defendants' client was granted access to the children after the defendants gave an undertaking to the court that they would retain their client's passport (the passport covered the children as well as the defendants' client). Their client had previously taken the children to Kuwait and refused to return them, so the undertaking was given in circumstances where there was a real risk that if their client obtained his passport he would abduct the children and flee the country. The defendants' client then informed the defendants that he wished to have the names of the children removed from his passport. To achieve this it was necessary to return the passport to the Kuwaiti embassy. The defendants arranged for the passport to be taken to the embassy but they had to leave it there while the necessary amendments were being made. The defendants told the embassy that they were not to give the passport to their client, but they did not inform the plaintiff that the passport was out of their control. Their client obtained his passport from the embassy by deception, he beat up the plaintiff, kidnapped the children and fled with them to Kuwait. The plaintiff sued the defendants for the injuries which she suffered and for the fact that she had not seen her children since they had been abducted. The defendants denied that they owed a duty of care to the plaintiff.

The Court of Appeal affirmed that in a 'hostile litigation' public policy would usually require, for the reasons given in *Rondel* v *Worsley* (above), that a solicitor be protected from a claim in negligence by his client's opponent. But in the present case the defendants had 'stepped outside their role as solicitors' and had accepted a responsibility towards the plaintiff and her children. In particular they had accepted a responsibility to keep their client's passport in safe custody. They were held to be in breach of this duty and were liable in damages to the plaintiff.

Where the considerations of policy discussed in *Rondel* are not present, in other words where the negligence does not relate to the conduct of the case in court, then a solicitor or barrister may owe a duty of care to the plaintiff (see *Ross* v *Caunters* [1980] Ch 297, the facts of which are discussed at 7.9). But it should not be assumed that *Ross* stands for the proposition that a solicitor will inevitably owe a duty of care to someone who is not his client. Thus in *Clarke* v *Bruce Lance and Co (a firm)* [1988] 1 All ER 364 the Court of Appeal held that the defendant solicitors did not owe a duty of care to the plaintiff who was not their client. A testator executed a will which was drawn up by the defendants and under which the plaintiff was a devisee of a service station owned by the testator. The testator subsequently granted a lease of the service station to a third party for 21 years and later varied the lease to grant the third party an option to purchase the service station for a fixed price of £28,000. The defendants also acted for the testator in the variation of the lease. The plaintiff argued that the solicitors had been in breach of their duty to the testator and to himself in failing to advise the testator that a fixed price option was commercially imprudent. The plaintiff based his case, to a large extent, on *Ross* v *Caunters* (above).

The Court of Appeal held that there may be situations in which a solicitor owes a duty of care to someone other than his client. They were prepared to assume that *Ross* was correctly decided, although the point was not necessary for the resolution of the present case. But it was held that *Ross* was distinguishable on its facts. In *Ross* there was a very close proximity between the plaintiff and the defendant but here there was no such close proximity. Secondly in *Ross* the drawing up of the will had as its purpose the benefit of the plaintiff, whereas in the present case it could not be said that the purpose behind the grant of the fixed price option was to benefit the plaintiff. On the contrary, the granting of the option affected the plaintiff's interests detrimentally. Thirdly it was held that to hold that the defendants owed a duty of care to the plaintiff would expose solicitors to a liability in 'an indeterminate amount for an indeterminate time to an indeterminate class'. Finally it was held that the testator had a cause of action against the defendants and that to allow the plaintiff a cause of action as well would be to open up the possibility of the defendants having to pay damages twice over for the same wrong. Such a possibility could arise because any damages awarded to the estate of the testator would enure for the benefit of the residuary beneficiary, who could be a person other than the plaintiff. Thus, had the defendants been liable to the plaintiff, they could have been liable both to the plaintiff and to the residuary beneficiary under the testator's will. This the Court of Appeal held to be unacceptable and so they held that the defendants did not owe to the plaintiff a duty of care. Thus, where there is a conflict between the interest of the client and the interest of the plaintiff, it is unlikely that the solicitor will be held to owe a duty of care to the plaintiff (see to the same effect *Gran Gelato Ltd* v *Richcliff (Group) Ltd* [1992] Ch 560 where Sir Donald Nichols VC stated that in 'normal conveyancing transactions solicitors who are acting for a seller do not in general owe the would-be buyer a duty of care when answering enquiries before contract or the like'; cf *Edwards* v *Lee* (1991) 141 NLJ 1517).

8.4 Police

A number of interesting recent negligence cases have been reported in which the defendants have been members of the police force. However, it must be said at the outset of our discussion that the police do not enjoy a general exemption from the ordinary law of the land (see *Marshall* v *Osmond* [1983] QB 1034). Thus the police have been held liable in negligence when they have negligently inflicted damage in the course of their work (see *Rigby* v *Chief Constable of Northamptonshire* [1985] 1 WLR 1242 and *Kirkham* v *Chief Constable of Greater Manchester Police* [1990] 2 QB 283, discussed in more detail at 13.4). Two particular problems have, however, arisen in relation to actions brought against members of the police force; the first is the role of public policy in denying the existence of a duty of care and the second is whether, and if so when, the police can be held liable for the deliberate wrongdoing of third parties.

The role of public policy can be illustrated by reference to two recent cases. The first is *Calveley* v *Chief Constable of the Merseyside Police* [1989] AC 1228. Three police officers alleged that the defendant chief constable was vicariously liable for the negligence of investigating officers who were responsible for carrying out investigations into complaints made by members of the public who had been arrested by the plaintiff officers. The plaintiffs alleged that the investigating officers had been negligent in failing to proceed expeditiously with their investigations and in failing to provide them with written notice of the complaints which had been made against them as soon as possible. The House of Lords dismissed the plaintiffs' claim, holding that no duty of care was owed by the investigating officers to the plaintiffs. The anxiety, ill-health and loss of reputation allegedly suffered by the plaintiffs were not a reasonably foreseeable consequence of the alleged negligence. Nor had the plaintiffs suffered any reasonably foreseeable economic loss because they had been suspended on full pay during the investigations. The House of Lords also held that it would be contrary to public policy to recognise the existence of such a duty because there was a public interest in the full and free investigation of such complaints and the imposition of a duty of care might impede such investigations. Lord Bridge also held that no duty is owed to a civilian suspect by a police officer who is investigating a suspected crime.

The second case is *Hughes* v *National Union of Mineworkers* [1991] 4 All ER 278. The plaintiff police officer suffered injury while seeking to maintain order at a colliery during the bitter mineworkers' dispute in the early part of the 1980s. At one point a vast number of pickets surged forward and struggled with the police; the plaintiff was knocked over and eight to ten pickets fell on him, occasioning him injury. The plaintiff brought an action against the Chief Constable of North Yorkshire, alleging that he had deployed his forces negligently, leaving the plaintiff in an unsupported and unprotected position. May J struck out the claim on the ground that the proceedings disclosed no reasonable cause of action. It was held that it was not in the public interest that a senior police officer, who was charged with the task of deploying police officers to control a serious public disorder, should have to make critical decisions in the knowledge that they might be the basis for a claim in negligence (although May J did acknowledge that there may be exceptions to this general rule, for example *Knightley* v *Johns* [1982] 1 WLR 349, discussed at 11.8).

The second issue is whether the police can be liable to a plaintiff for loss suffered as a result of the deliberate wrongdoing of a third party. This raises the misfeasance/non-feasance issue (discussed in more detail at 6.8). The leading case is *Hill* v *Chief Constable of West Yorkshire* [1989] AC 53. The claim arose out of one of the murders committed by the 'Yorkshire Ripper'. The plaintiff was the mother of Jacqueline Hill, who was the last victim of the 'Yorkshire Ripper'. The plaintiff argued that the defendant had failed to exercise all reasonable care and skill in seeking to apprehend the perpetrator of these murders and that, had he exercised proper care and skill, the perpetrator would have been apprehended earlier and her daughter would not have been murdered. The defendant applied to have the action struck out on the ground that it disclosed no reasonable cause of action. The House of Lords held that the claim disclosed no cause of action and it was struck out. The House of Lords held that it was foreseeable that if a violent criminal was not apprehended a citizen could suffer injury, but it was also held that foreseeability of harm did not of itself establish the existence of a duty of care. While at common law police officers owe to the general public a duty to enforce the criminal law which is enforceable, in an appropriate case, by mandamus (*R* v *Commissioner of Police of the Metropolis, ex parte Blackburn* [1968] 2 QB 118 that duty could not be translated into a general duty of care to identify and apprehend an unknown criminal. Even in the case where a criminal escapes (as in *Home Office* v *Dorset Yacht* [1970] AC 1004) it was held that the duty of care only extends to those who are at special risk in the course of the escape (as was the case with the yacht owners in *Dorset Yacht*) and that it does not extend to members of the public who suffer injury when the criminal resumes his general criminal career. In the present case it could not be said that Miss Hill was at a special risk and so no duty of care was owed. Lord Keith also added that public policy negated the existence of a duty of care because the imposition of a duty of care could lead to police discretion being exercised in a 'detrimentally defensive frame of mind' and because any investigation by the court would be a 'significant diversion of police manpower and attention from their most important function, that of the suppression of crime' (contrast the wider view of Lord Templeman).

Hill has been applied in a number of recent cases. In *Clough* v *Bussan (West Yorkshire Police Authority, third party)* [1990] 1 All ER 431 the plaintiff was injured in a road accident, which occurred at a road junction where the traffic lights were malfunctioning (the lights showing green in both directions). The police were informed of the malfunction some 35 minutes before the accident occurred but took no steps to alert motorists. The plaintiff brought an action in negligence against the driver of the other car who, in turn, issued a third party notice against the police authority. The police authority applied to strike out the third party notice on the ground that it disclosed no reasonable cause of action. It was held that the police did not owe a duty of care to the plaintiff. Although the police were under a general duty to preserve law and order and to protect life and property, there was nothing to show that they owed a particular duty of care to this particular plaintiff. The fact that the police had been informed of the malfunction was not sufficient, of itself, to justify the imposition of a duty of care 'to every motorist who might thereafter use the junction'. In *Alexandrou* v *Oxford* [1993] 4 All ER 328 the plaintiff owned a shop and installed a burglar alarm which, when activated, raised an alarm to a local police station. One evening the alarm was activated and the police checked the front of the premises. They failed to check the rear of the shop where the burglars had forced entry and were hiding. The burglars later, when the police had left, removed a large amount of goods from the shop. The Court of Appeal held that the defendants owed no duty of care to the plaintiff. If such a duty were held to exist it would be owed to all 999 callers. There was no special relationship between the parties, as in *Home Office* v *Dorset Yacht* (above), and, following *Hill*, it was held not to be just and reasonable to impose upon the defendants a duty of care.

Similar reasoning was applied by the Court of Appeal in *Osman* v *Ferguson* [1993] 4 All ER 344, where a schoolteacher formed an unhealthy attachment to a 15-year-old male pupil and harassed the boy by making a series of untrue sexual allegations. The teacher changed his surname to that of the boy and damaged property belonging to the boy's family. He was dismissed from his job but continued the harassment. The police were aware of these facts and the teacher even told a police officer that he feared that he would do something criminally insane. Later the teacher deliberately rammed a vehicle in which the boy was a passenger. The police, as a result, laid an information alleging driving without due care and attention but it was not served. Finally, the teacher shot and severely injured the boy and killed his father. An action was brought against the police alleging negligence in that although the police had been aware of the teacher's activities for nearly a year they had failed to apprehend him or interview him or charge him with a more serious offence before the shooting. The court held that it was arguable that a very close degree of proximity amounting to a special relationship existed between the boy's family and the police, but it was against public policy to impose a duty of care, following *Hill* and *Alexandrou*.

8.5 Negligence in the exercise of a statutory power

The final type of defendant who may owe a limited duty of care is a defendant who commits a tort in the course of the exercise of a statutory power. Where the defendant fails to exercise a statutory duty, that failure may of itself give rise to an action in tort (see further chapter 14). Different considerations arise where the negligence lies in the exercise or non-exercise of a statutory *power*. The difficulty which arises in the latter type of case is that the courts must reconcile the principles of the tort of negligence with public law doctrines relating to the control by the courts of the exercise of statutory powers and the exercise of discretion conferred by Parliament.

The problem can be illustrated by reference to the case of *Sheppard* v *Glossop Corporation* [1921] 3 KB 132 (the whole issue is fully discussed by Craig (1978) 94 LQR 428. The defendants were empowered to install street lighting but, in the exercise of their discretion, they decided to turn the lamps off at 9 pm. The plaintiff was injured when he fell in the street in the dark. He brought an action in negligence against the defendants. The Court of Appeal held that the defendants could not be held liable in negligence when they had decided, in the exercise of their discretion, not to light the streets or only to light them for a certain time. To allow such an action would be to second guess the defendants in the exercise of their discretion and have the effect of exercising for the defendants the discretion which Parliament had conferred upon the defendants (see too *East Suffolk Rivers Catchment Board* v *Kent* [1940] 1 KB 319 (CA) and [1941] AC 74 (HL).

The issue was further considered by the House of Lords in *Home Office* v *Dorset Yacht Co* [1970] AC 1004. The plaintiff's yacht was damaged when it was rammed by some boys, who had escaped from a borstal training camp and boarded a yacht. The boys had escaped because the men in charge of them had gone to sleep and left the boys unsupervised. The defendants, who were the employers of the officers who let the boys escape, argued that they owed no duty of care to the plaintiff because they were acting in pursuance of a discretion which had been conferred on them by Parliament. They argued that, in the exercise of their discretion as to the control to be exercised over the boys, they had decided to institute a system of open borstals, where emphasis was placed upon the training of the boys. A finding for the plaintiff would result in stricter discipline and the operation of a closed borstal system rather than an open one and thus an undermining of the discretion which had been conferred upon the defendants. The preliminary point which was argued in the House of Lords was whether the defendants owed any duty of care to the plaintiff.

It was held that the defendants could owe a duty of care to the plaintiff but that in considering the duty of care owed by the defendants to the plaintiff account had to be taken of the statutory powers. Lord Diplock held that where the defendants made a decision of policy in the exercise of their discretion it must be shown that the public body had acted ultra vires before a claim in negligence could succeed. However where the negligence was at the level of the implementation of these policies, referred to as the operational level, then the defendants would not enjoy an immunity from suit because there the imposition of liability in tort would not conflict with the exercise of the defendants' discretion.

In *Anns* v *Merton London Borough Council* [1978] AC 728 further consideration was given to the approach adopted by Lord Diplock in *Dorset Yacht*. Before entering into a discussion of this aspect of *Anns* it must be recalled that *Anns* has since been overruled by the House of Lords in *Murphy* v *Brentwood District Council* [1991] 1 AC 398 (discussed further at 7.3). In *Murphy* it was held that the loss which the plaintiffs suffered in *Anns* was truly economic loss and that the local authority owed no duty of care to the plaintiffs in respect of that pure economic loss. However it remains unclear whether local authorities owe any duty of care to house purchasers arising out of their exercise of their statutory powers to secure compliance with the building by-laws. In *Murphy* the defendant council did not seek to argue that they owed no duty of care at all to persons who might suffer injury through their failure to take reasonable care to secure compliance with the relevant building by-laws; they were content to accept that such a duty existed but argued that it did not extend to pure economic loss. But Lords Mackay, Bridge, Keith and Jauncey all expressly reserved their opinion on the correctness of the defendants' assumption. So the point must be regarded as an open one. Although the House of Lords in *Murphy* held that *Anns* was incorrect in relation to the particular by-laws at issue, *Murphy* itself does not cast doubt on the policy/operational dichotomy with which we are here concerned.

Returning to the facts of *Anns*, the plaintiff bought a flat in a two storey block of maisonettes. By 1970 cracks had appeared in the walls and the floors had begun to slope. The reason for this damage occurring was that the houses were built on an inadequate foundation. So the plaintiffs brought an action in negligence against the builders and the local authority. The action against the latter alleged that they had been negligent in approving the foundations of the property because the foundations were only made to a depth of 2 feet 6 inches and not the 3 feet which was required under the by-laws. The defendants had a statutory discretion to decide whether or not to inspect the premises and they argued that the existence of this statutory discretion precluded the existence of a duty of care towards the plaintiff. Lord Wilberforce had no difficulty in concluding that there was a sufficient degree of proximity between the parties to found a duty of care; the problem was as to the effect of the statutory discretion on the existence of a duty of care.

Lord Wilberforce adopted the distinction we have noted between a policy decision and an operational decision. He said that, in making a decision as to which buildings to inspect, the defendants were making a decision of policy but that they 'are under duty to give proper consideration to the question whether they should inspect or not. Their immunity from attack, in the event of failure to inspect ... though great is not absolute'. However he did not make it clear whether the action which he envisaged would be available was a public law action seeking judicial review or an action in the tort of negligence. On the other hand Lord Salmon was of the opinion that, were such a cause of action to exist, it could take the form of an action in negligence. Lord Wilberforce said that, where the negligence existed at the operational level, then it would be easier to superimpose a common law duty of care than in the case of negligence at the policy level. Even at the operational level it must be remembered that the case must be interpreted against the statutory background and that it must be shown that the defendants did not act within the limits of their discretion, bona fide exercised.

The policy/operational dichotomy has, however, come under criticism from the Privy Council in *Rowling* v *Takaro Properties Ltd* [1988] AC 473 (see Craig (1988) 104 LQR 185). In giving judgment Lord Keith noted the academic criticism which had been levelled against the dichotomy (see Craig *Administrative Law* pp534–538 and Bowman and Bailey [1986] CLJ 430) and stated that the distinction did not provide a 'touchstone of liability'. Instead he said that the dichotomy expressed a need to exclude discretionary decisions as to the allocation of scarce resources from the scope of a negligence action. Thus Lord Keith appears to be saying that the crucial question is whether or not the issue is justiciable in the sense that it is unsuitable for judicial resolution because, for example, it concerns the exercise of a discretion which Parliament has entrusted to the local authority. But he said that a conclusion that the decision was not within the 'policy' category did not mean that a duty of care will necessarily exist. All the facts had to be examined carefully before such a conclusion was to be reached.

The negligence in *Rowling* was alleged to consist of a negligent interpretation by the Minister of Finance of his statutory powers. The plaintiff had earlier been granted judicial review of the minister's decision and the decision was quashed on the ground that it was based upon an irrelevant consideration. By the time that the defendants' appeal against the grant of judicial review was dismissed, the plaintiff had suffered extensive and irremediable financial loss and he sought to recover these losses from the defendants.

The Privy Council was prepared to assume for the purposes of argument that the minister owed a duty of care to the plaintiff but found that, on the facts, there had been no breach of duty. But the Privy Council also pointed to the existence of a number of factors which militated against the imposition of a duty of care in a case such as the present. These factors are likely to be of considerable importance in future cases where it is alleged that a duty of care is owed in the exercise of a statutory power. The first is that in many cases the plaintiff will be able to obtain judicial review within a short space of time and so the only damage which will be suffered is the cost of delay, which is unlikely to be large. The second is that it will be very difficult to establish that an error in interpreting a statute is negligent, because a misconstruction of a statute can be severely criticised without it being held to be negligent. Thirdly the court must bear in mind the danger of overkill in that the imposition of liability may result in the cautious civil servant going to extreme lengths before making a decision in order to escape liability in negligence (see, for example, the judgment of the Court of Appeal in *Martine* v *South East Kent Health Authority* (1993) The Times 8 March where this criterion was invoked). Finally it will be very difficult to establish a case in which the minister is under an obligation to seek legal advice as to the extent of his statutory powers. Of particular importance is the third factor and a regard to the consequences of the finding that a duty of care is owed may lead courts to conclude that no duty of care is owed in the exercise of a statutory power (see too *Jones* v *Department of Employment* [1989] QB 1, where it was held that an adjudication officer did not owe a duty of care to a claimant for unemployment benefit unless it could be shown that the officer was guilty of misfeasance and that the remedy, if any, for a claimant was by way of judicial review).

Although the courts are now undoubtedly more reluctant to conclude that a defendant owes a common law duty of care when exercising a statutory power, this does not mean that a negligence claim can never lie in such circumstances. That this is so can be demonstrated by reference to the case of *Lonrho plc* v *Tebbit* [1992] 4 All ER 280. The case arose out of the long-running dispute between Lonrho and the Al-Fayed brothers over the takeover of the House of Fraser group. In 1981 the plaintiffs, Lonrho, gave an undertaking to the Secretary of State for Trade and Industry that they would not acquire more than 30 per cent of House of Fraser's share capital (when they gave the undertaking they owned 29.9 per cent of the shares) while a reference was made to the Monopolies and Mergers Commission (MMC). In November 1984 the plaintiffs sold the vast majority of their shares in House of Fraser to a company controlled by the Al-Fayed brothers. On 14 February 1985 the MMC reported that the proposed merger between the plaintiffs and House of Fraser would not be contrary to the public interest. On 4 March the company controlled by the Al-Fayed brothers made a public offer for the remaining shares in House of Fraser which enabled them to acquire more than 50 per cent of its shares. On 14 March the Secretary of State released the plaintiffs from their undertaking, but it was then too late for the plaintiffs to make a successful bid for House of Fraser. So the plaintiffs brought an action against the Secretary of State, Mr Tebbit, alleging that he had been negligent in the exercise of his statutory power because of his delay in releasing the plaintiffs from their undertaking. At first instance, Sir Nicolas Browne-Wilkinson VC refused to strike out the plaintiffs' claim and the defendants appealed to the Court of Appeal.

The defendants argued that they did not owe a duty of care in private law to the plaintiffs and that the issues which arose on the facts of the case all belonged within the domain of public law. Both arguments were rejected by the Court of Appeal. A central plank in the defendants' argument was that there was no precedent for holding that a minister owed a duty of care sounding in private law as a result of his exercise of public law powers, and that there was no precedent for holding a minister liable in damages (particularly for economic loss) because in good faith he had misconstrued his legal position. But Dillon LJ rejected this argument on the basis that the public interest in the *release* of the undertaking was considerably smaller than in its imposition. In light of the factors set out by Lord Keith in his speech in *Rowling* (above), the court acknowledged that the plaintiffs' case faced a number of difficulties but concluded that these were not sufficient to warrant striking out the claim. Dillon LJ stated that it did not appal him that it should be suggested that the Secretary of State should assume a private law duty to the plaintiffs to release the undertaking when it was no longer needed and the restriction on the plaintiffs' freedom to conduct their business no longer had a rationale.

9

Negligence: Breach of the Duty

9.1   Introduction

9.2   The reasonable man

9.3   Foreseeability

9.4   Magnitude of the risk

9.5   Utility of the defendant's activity

9.6   The practicality of precautions

9.7   Common practice

9.8   Children

9.9   Sport

9.10 Emergencies

9.11 Professionals

9.12 Proof of the breach

9.13 Res ipsa loquitur

9.1 Introduction

Having established that the defendant owes to the plaintiff a duty of care, the second thing which must be established is that the defendant breached that duty of care. Professor Fleming has said of negligence that it is 'conduct falling below the standard demanded for the protection of others against unreasonable risk of harm' (*The Law of Torts* (7th ed) p96). The important point to note is that the standard required of the defendant is an objective one, that is it depends on the standard of care which would have been adopted by the reasonable man in the circumstances. The most famous description of this objective standard was provided by Alderson B in *Blyth* v *Birmingham Waterworks Co* (1856) 11 Ex 781, 784 when he said:

117

'Negligence is the omission to do something which a reasonable man, guided upon those considerations which ordinarily regulate the conduct of human affairs, would do, or doing something which a prudent and reasonable man would not do.'

Although the standard is an objective one, the question whether a particular defendant has breached the standard of care is largely a question of fact. There are, however, certain principles which the court will apply in considering whether the defendant has breached the standard of care. We shall consider these principles in this chapter. We shall commence by giving further consideration to the reasonable man standard, then we shall consider the various factors which the courts balance in deciding whether the defendant has breached his duty of care. We shall then consider various situations in which difficulties have arisen in identifying the requisite standard of care. Finally we shall examine the issues which arise in attempting to prove that the defendant was negligent.

9.2 The reasonable man

As we have already noted the standard which is applied in considering whether the defendant has been negligent is the standard of the reasonable man. The requirements of the reasonable man standard were clearly articulated by the House of Lords in *Glasgow Corporation* v *Muir* [1943] 2 AC 448. The manageress of the defendants' tearoom gave a church party permission to use the tearoom when rain prevented them from eating their food outside. Two of the leaders of the church party were carrying a tea urn down a narrow passage when one of them, for some unexplained reason, let go of one of the handles of the urn, with the result that tea poured out and some children were badly scalded. The plaintiffs sought to recover damages from the defendants on the ground that the manageress was negligent in giving permission for the tea urn to be brought down the narrow passage. One of the issues argued before the House of Lords concerned the standard of care owed by the defendants. Lord MacMillan provided the following analysis of the reasonable man standard:

'The standard of foresight of the reasonable man is in one sense an impersonal test. It eliminates the personal equation and is independent of the idiosyncrasies of the particular person whose conduct is in question. Some persons are by nature unduly timorous and imagine every path beset with lions; others, of more robust temperament, fail to foresee or nonchalantly disregard even the most obvious dangers. The reasonable man is presumed to be free both from over-apprehension and from over-confidence.'

However Lord MacMillan did concede that the test did contain a subjective element because the standard of the reasonable man had to be applied to the facts of the case and to what the reasonable man, in the position of the particular defendant, ought to have foreseen. It was held on the facts that the defendants were not negligent because they could not have foreseen that such an accident would occur.

The application of this objective reasonable man test can be seen in the case of *The Lady Gwendolen* [1965] P 294. Two ships were involved in a collision in foggy conditions. The accident was caused by the negligence of the defendants, who were a firm of brewers who used the ship to carry stout from Dublin to Liverpool. The defendants argued that they should be judged by the standard of the reasonable brewers who happened to hire a ship and not according to the standards of the reasonable shipowner. This argument was rejected by the court. The standard of care which was owed by the defendants was the same as the standard of care owed by every other shipowner. Winn LJ stated that 'the law must apply a standard which is not relaxed to cater for [the defendants'] factual ignorance of all activities outside brewing: having become owners of ships, they must behave as reasonable shipowners'. We will see the same principle at work when we consider the standard of care required of professionals. In *Wilsher* v *Essex Area Health Authority* [1987] 2 WLR 425 the Court of Appeal held that the standard of care required of a doctor was not tailored to the particular doctor but to the act which he chose to perform. The argument that this put too high a burden upon young doctors was met by Mustill LJ in the following terms:

> 'It would be a false step to subordinate the legitimate expectation of the patient that he will receive from each person concerned with his care a degree of skill appropriate to the task which he undertakes to an understandable wish to minimise the psychological and financial pressures on hard-pressed young doctors.'

Another well known example of the objective standard of care is provided by cases involving car drivers. The most well known case is *Nettleship* v *Weston* [1971] 2 QB 691. The plaintiff, who was an experienced driver, agreed to give driving lessons to the wife of one of his friends. On her third lesson, with the plaintiff moving the gear lever and the defendant steering the car, the defendant panicked and the car, moving at walking pace, mounted the pavement and struck a lamp-post. The plaintiff suffered a broken knee cap and sought to recover from the defendant. The defendant denied that she had been negligent. The Court of Appeal held that the defendant was negligent. They held that the standard of care required of a learner driver was the same as the standard required of an experienced driver; that standard being the standard of the reasonably competent and experienced driver. Lord Denning said that, while the defendant was not morally at fault, she was legally required to be insured and therefore the risk should fall on her. Megaw LJ stated that, if it was accepted that the standard of care was a variable one, it could not logically be confined to car drivers and would have to be a principle of universal application. The adoption of a variable standard, he said, would lead to unpredictability, uncertainty and the impossibility of arriving at fair and consistent decisions. So he concluded that a general standard was preferable to 'the vagaries of a fluctuating standard'.

A similar approach was adopted in the case of *Roberts* v *Ramsbottom* [1980] 1 All ER 7. The defendant argued that he was not liable to the plaintiff, whom he had knocked down, because he had suffered a stroke 20 minutes before the accident occurred and that his driving had been impaired by the stroke. It was accepted by the court that, after the stroke, the defendant was, through no fault of his own, unable to control the car properly. However it was held that this was not sufficient to free the defendant from liability unless the facts established a defence of automatism, that his actions were wholly beyond his control. On the facts it was held that the defendant retained some control over his actions, although that control was admittedly imperfect, and therefore the standard of the reasonably competent driver was applicable and the defendant was in breach of it. These two decisions were obviously influenced by the fact that the defendants were insured and so were in a better position to bear the loss, but it would be a mistake to dismiss them solely on that ground. As Megaw LJ stated, if it was accepted that the standard required was a variable one, then this would lead to enormous uncertainty and difficulty in practice. It is for this reason that the courts have set their face against a variable standard of care.

Having considered what the objective standard of the reasonable man involves, consideration will now be focused upon the different factors to which the courts have regard in considering whether or not the defendant was negligent.

9.3 Foreseeability

The standard of care is based upon what the reasonable man would have foreseen in the circumstances. The defendant may not be liable because the harm to the plaintiff was not foreseeable. Such was the case in *Roe* v *Minister of Health* [1954] 2 QB 66. In 1947 the plaintiff went into hospital for a minor operation. He was paralysed because a spinal anaesthetic which he was given became tainted with phenol when it was in a syringe which was stored in phenol. At the time it was not known that the phenol could seep into the syringe through invisible cracks in the syringe. It was held that the defendants were not negligent. Denning LJ said that the court could not look at the accident which occurred in 1947 'with 1954 spectacles'. In 1947 it was not known that harm to the plaintiff could occur in this way and so the defendants were not liable.

9.4 Magnitude of the risk

Although harm to someone may be foreseeable, the risk of that harm being inflicted may be so unlikely that the defendant will not be required to take precautions against it happening. Such was the case in *Bolton* v *Stone* [1951] AC 850. The plaintiff, who was standing on the road close to a cricket ground, was hit by a cricket ball which had been hit for six straight out of the ground. There was a fence around the ground which was seven feet high and, due to the slope of the ground, the top of the fence was some 17 feet above the level of the pitch. The fence was located some 80 yards from where the batsman stood, so it was an exceptional hit. There was evidence that cricket balls had been hit out of the ground on about six occasions in the previous 30 years. It was held that the likelihood of a person outside the ground suffering injury in this way was so slight that the defendants were not negligent in continuing to play cricket there without taking additional precautions. Lord Oaksey said that the standard of the reasonable man did not require a man to take precautions against 'every foreseeable risk' and that 'life would be almost intolerable if [the ordinarily careful man] were to attempt to take precautions against every risk which he can foresee'.

Bolton v *Stone* was distinguished in the case of *Hilder* v *Associated Portland Cement Manufacturers Ltd* [1961] 1 WLR 1434. The defendants were the occupiers of land and they permitted some small boys to play football on their land. The land was close to a road and one of the boys kicked the ball on to the road and caused the plaintiff's husband to have an accident, in which he was killed. It was held that the defendants were negligent. The risk of injury to a road user was much greater than the risk in *Bolton*. The land was only some 15 yards from the road and the risk of injury was not one which the reasonable man would have disregarded.

In *Haley* v *London Electricity Board* [1965] AC 778 the House of Lords was impressed by the statistical evidence of the likelihood of an accident occurring. The defendants dug a hole in the pavement. They took sufficient steps to warn a sighted person of the hole but they took insufficient steps to warn a blind person. The plaintiff, who was blind, fell into the hole, through no fault of his own. As a result of the fall he became deaf. The House was provided with evidence of the number of blind people in London and of the proportion of the population who were blind and concluded that the likelihood of a blind person falling into the hole was not so small that the defendants could ignore it and that therefore the defendants were negligent. It should not be thought, however, that statistical evidence is a regular feature of negligence cases. Even where it is adduced and the court has regard to it, it will only be one factor among many to be weighed in the balance.

Where the harm which is likely to be done if the risk materialises is serious, then more will be required of the defendant. This requirement can be demonstrated by reference to the case of *Paris* v *Stepney Borough Council* [1951] AC 367. The plaintiff, who only had one eye, was employed by the defendants in a job which involved some risk of injury to his eye. Had the plaintiff had two eyes the risk of injury would not have required the defendants to supply the plaintiff with goggles. But the fact that the plaintiff only had one eye meant that the consequences of an injury to his eye were so serious that the reasonable man would have supplied the plaintiff with goggles. When the plaintiff suffered injury to his eye at work, which rendered him blind, the defendants were held to have been negligent in not supplying the plaintiff with goggles.

On the other hand a different result was reached by the court in *Withers* v *Perry Chain Co* [1961] 1 WLR 1314. The plaintiff was particularly susceptible to dermatitis on coming into contact with grease. The defendants, who were her employers, put her on the most 'grease-free' job they could find, but the plaintiff still contracted dermatitis. It was held that the defendants were not liable for the dermatitis which the plaintiff contracted. The defendants had done all they could to avoid the plaintiff contracting dermatitis and the only thing which they could have done to ensure that the plaintiff did not contract it was to dismiss her. It was held that the defendants were not negligent in failing to dismiss the plaintiff, as such a step would not have been in the interest of any of the parties.

So the court will consider the likelihood of the risk materialising and the seriousness of the injury which will be suffered if the risk does, in fact, materialise.

9.5 Utility of the defendant's activity

The social utility of the defendant's conduct is a relevant factor in considering whether the defendant was negligent. The greater the social utility of the defendant's conduct, the less likely it is that the defendant will be held to be negligent. As Asquith LJ stated in *Daborn* v *Bath Tramways* [1946] 2 All ER 333:

> 'If all the trains in this country were restricted to a speed of five miles an hour, there would be fewer accidents, but our national life would be intolerably slowed down. The purpose to be served, if sufficiently important, justifies the assumption of abnormal risk.'

A similar result was reached in the case of *Watt* v *Hertfordshire County Council* [1954] 1 WLR 835. The plaintiff, who was a fireman, was injured when travelling to rescue a woman who had been reported to have been trapped under a heavy lorry. Two of the plaintiff's colleagues threw a jack, in haste, into the lorry in which they were travelling. The jack was needed to save the woman's life. The lorry was not equipped for carrying the jack and the plaintiff was injured when the driver of the lorry braked suddenly and the jack fell on him. It was held that the defendant employers were not negligent because the need to act speedily in an attempt to save the woman's life outweighed the risk to the plaintiff. But Denning LJ said that if the accident had occurred in a commercial enterprise the plaintiff would have recovered. He said that 'the commercial end to make profit is very different from the human end to save life or limb'. However it should not be thought that drivers of fire engines have carte blanche in their rush to get to the scene of a fire. In *Ward* v *London County Council* [1938] 2 All ER 341 a driver of a fire engine was held to have been negligent in driving through a traffic light which was at red.

9.6 The practicality of precautions

If the cost of eliminating the risk is exorbitant or out of all proportion to the benefit obtained by its elimination, then it will not generally be negligent to fail to eliminate the risk. An example of this principle at work is the case of *Latimer* v *AEC Ltd*

[1953] AC 643. The floor of the defendants' factory was flooded by an exceptionally heavy rainstorm. One of the consequences of the flooding was that oil which was normally kept in troughs was washed out on to the floor. The defendants put sawdust on the floor in an effort to prevent their employees from falling but there was not enough sawdust to cover the whole factory floor. Despite these efforts the plaintiff fell and broke his ankle. It was held that the defendants were not liable for the injury suffered by the plaintiff. They had done all they could, short of closing the factory, to prevent injury arising to their employees. Although this case illustrates the principle that the practicability of precautions is one factor to be taken into account, the decision has been criticised on the ground that commercial profitability was given so much prominence over the employees' interest in their personal security and the fact that no consideration was given to the practicability of other precautions such as roping off the area where no sawdust had been put down.

9.7 Common practice

Where there is a common practice in the activity with regard to which the defendant is alleged to have been negligent, conformity with that common practice by the defendant is very good evidence that the defendant has not been negligent. It is not, however, conclusive evidence that the defendant has not been negligent because the common practice itself may be negligent (*Lloyd's Bank Ltd* v *E B Savory & Co* [1933] AC 201).

On the other hand failure to conform to the common practice, without good reason, is good evidence that the defendant has been negligent. Once again, however, a failure to conform with common practice is not conclusive evidence that the defendant has been negligent. In *Brown* v *Rolls Royce Ltd* [1960] 1 WLR 210 the plaintiff contracted dermatitis at work and she claimed that this was caused by the negligence of the defendants, her employers. Although the defendants provided adequate washing facilities at the work place they did not supply a barrier cream which was commonly supplied by other employers who were engaged in the same type of work. But, while this cream was in common use in the type of work in which the plaintiff was involved, there was conflicting evidence about its efficacy and it was not proved that, had the defendants supplied the cream, the plaintiff would not have contracted dermatitis. It was held that the defendants were not negligent in failing to supply the cream because it was not proved that it would have prevented the plaintiff from contracting dermatitis.

The role of common practice is likely to assume greater importance in negligence cases involving professionals. Some professional bodies have issued guidelines or statements of standard practice in an effort to provide guidance for their members who are concerned about being sued in negligence. For example, the governing bodies of the accountancy profession have drawn up some 'Statements of Standard Accountancy Practice' (SSAP) in an effort to provide some guidance to their members as to the standards expected of them. How much weight will be accorded to such statements by the courts in considering whether a defendant has been negligent? Some indication of the answer to this question may be gleaned from the case of *Lloyd Cheyham & Co Ltd* v *Littlejohn & Co* QBD 30 September 1985 (Unreported). The case turned upon whether the defendants had complied with the requisite standard of care. The plaintiffs argued that the defendants were negligent because they had failed to comply with the standards laid down in SSAP 2. Woolf J rejected the plaintiff's argument and held that the defendants had not been negligent. During the course of his judgment he said that the SSAPs were:

> '... not conclusive, so that a departure from their terms necessarily involves a breach of the duty of care and they are not ... rigid rules. They are very strong evidence as to what is the proper standard which should be adopted and unless there is some justification a departure from this will be regarded as constituting a breach of duty.'

It is clear that these and other standards laid down by the professions will assume growing significance in negligence actions. In considering whether a professional has been negligent the courts make allowance for the existence of differing views within the profession and will not choose between the different schools of thought, holding one to be negligent and the other not (*Maynard* v *West Midlands Health Authority* [1984] 1 WLR 634 (discussed at 9.11) and *Luxmoore-May* v *Messenger May Baverstock* [1990] 1 All ER 1067).

A problem may, however, arise in identifying an appropriate comparator for the purpose of assessing the common practice. Such was the case in *Knight* v *Home Office* [1990] 3 All ER 237. The deceased was detained in a remand prison after pleading guilty to a charge of wounding with intent to cause grievous bodily harm. He was known to have suicidal tendencies and was put in a cell where prison officers observed him at intervals of not less than 15 minutes but he was not put in the hospital wing because of his violent tendencies. He committed suicide in his cell and his personal representatives brought an action in negligence against the Home Office. The plaintiffs argued that the defendants were negligent because they had not complied with the standard required of a psychiatric hospital outside prison. Pill J rejected the analogy and held that the Home Office were not in breach of their duty. He held that a psychiatric hospital outside prison was not an appropriate comparator because such a hospital provides a specialist service in treating mental illness whereas the central function of a prison is to detain persons deprived of their liberty by the operation of law. Pill J did not accept that the plaintiffs' only remedy was a political one but he was of the opinion that the fact that the resources available for the public service were limited was a factor which was relevant in considering whether or not there had been a breach of the duty of care (see 9.6 above). Although it was possible for the prison officers to watch the deceased on a continuous basis, the decision to observe him at 15 minute intervals was one which a skilled medical member of staff could make and therefore it could not be said to have been a negligent decision.

These factors which we have discussed at 9.2–9.7 are the principal factors to which the courts will have regard in deciding whether a defendant was or was not negligent. No one factor predominates to the exclusion of the others. In each case a court will balance the different factors and come to a conclusion on the facts. There are, however, certain particular cases to which special rules are applicable. We shall now consider these special cases.

9.8 Children

Where it is alleged that a child has been negligent the question arises as to the standard of care required of the child. Is it the standard of the reasonable man or is it some lesser standard? Strangely, there is no authority on this point in England. There is, however, Australian authority on the point. In *McHale* v *Watson* [1966] ALR 513 the High Court of Australia rejected the application of the reasonable man standard to cases involving children. The plaintiff, who was a nine-year-old girl, was injured when she was struck in the eye by a steel rod thrown by the defendant, a twelve-year-old boy. The defendant was throwing the rod at a post, but it glanced off the post and struck the plaintiff who was standing nearby. Kitto J said it was 'absurd ... to speak of normality in relation to persons of all ages taken together'. The standard to be applied was the standard of a child of a corresponding age. The test remained an objective one, however, and so it was 'no answer for him ... to say that the harm he caused was due to his being abnormally slow-witted, quick-tempered, absent-minded or inexperienced'. Applying that standard it was held that the boy was not negligent. Although there is no authority directly in point in England, the courts, in contributory negligence cases, have been prepared to take account of the special position of children (see 12.6) and so it is submitted that an English court would follow the decision in *McHale*.

9.9 Sport

The courts have had occasion to consider the standard of care owed by sportsmen to each other and to spectators. The most famous of these cases is *Wooldridge* v *Sumner* [1963] 2 QB 43. The defendant was an experienced horseman taking part in a competition. He galloped his horse so fast round a corner that his horse went out of control after completing the turn and plunged out of the arena and the plaintiff, who was a photographer, was injured in the ensuing chaos. It was held by the Court of Appeal that the defendant's failure to control his horse was not negligence but was simply an error of judgment. It was further held that the relationship between a competitor and a spectator was a special one and that a spectator took the risk of any damage done to him during the course of the game, even though his injury resulted from an 'error of judgment' on the part of a competitor. It was only where the competitor deliberately intended to injure the spectator or demonstrated a reckless disregard for the safety of the spectator that the spectator would have a cause of action in respect of the damage done.

This is an extremely restrictive conception of the standard of care required of sportsmen. The emphasis on the need to show that the sportsman was 'reckless' is at odds with the general reasonable man standard. Thus the decision has been subjected to severe and cogent criticism. Professor Goodhart has argued ((1962) 78 LQR 490, 496) that the proper standard to apply was not one based upon recklessness but one based upon the following question:

> 'Is a competitor to be held liable for an injury to a spectator caused by an error of judgment that a reasonable competitor, being the reasonable man of the sporting world, would not have made?'

The adoption of such a standard would preserve the coherence of the reasonable man standard while avoiding the imposition of excessive liability upon sportsmen.

It is not yet clear whether the courts have adopted the test advocated by Professor Goodhart. In *Wilks* v *Cheltenham Cycle Club* [1971] 1 WLR 668 the approach in *Wooldridge* was followed rather reluctantly. However, Phillimore LJ did affirm that the test remained simply one based upon 'negligence' and Edmund-Davies LJ referred to *Wooldridge* as a 'puzzling case'. Further, in the more recent case of *Condon* v *Basi* [1985] 2 All ER 453 the Court of Appeal had to consider the standard of care owed by one sportsman to another. The plaintiff was injured during a football match when the defendant, who was playing for the opposing side, tackled him and broke his leg. The defendant was held to be negligent. The finding of fact that the tackle was made in a 'reckless and dangerous manner' meant that the court did not have to resolve the conflict over the status and interpretation of *Wooldridge*. However it was held that the standard required was an objective one and that a higher standard would be required of a First Division footballer than would be required of a footballer in a local league. This latter statement suggests that the court would have applied the standard based upon the reasonable sportsman rather than the approach based upon recklessness and that this will be the approach adopted in the future (see Hudson (1982) 98 LQR 545 and Hepple [1985] All ER Rev 300).

9.10 Emergencies

Where the defendant acts in an emergency or in the heat of the moment, the standard of care is adjusted to take account of the dilemma in which the defendant is placed (*Ng Chun Pui* v *Lee Chuen Tat* [1988] RTR 298, see further 9.13). Provided that the decision which the defendant makes is a reasonable decision in the circumstances, he will not be held to have been negligent, even though with hindsight he would have adopted another course of action (see *Jones* v *Boyce* (1816) 1 Stark 493, discussed further at 12.9).

9.11 Professionals

A person who claims to have a special skill is judged, not according to the standard of the reasonable man in the street, but according to the standard of the reasonable person enjoying the skill which he claims to possess. We have already seen that compliance with common practice is good, but not conclusive, evidence that the defendant has not been negligent (see 9.7). Generally the same rule applies in cases of alleged professional negligence (*Edward Wong Finance* v *Johnson, Stokes & Master* [1984] AC 296), although practically it is extremely difficult to show that standard professional practice is negligent. This is especially so in cases of alleged medical negligence where the medical profession appears to have been allowed to set its own standard of care (see Grubb [1988] CLJ 12, contrast Jones *Textbook on Torts,* (3rd ed) pp113–114). The ground rules were laid down by McNair J in *Bolam* v *Friern Hospital Management Committee* [1957] 1 WLR 582 in the following terms:

> 'Where you get a situation which involves the use of some special skill or competence, then the test as to whether there has been negligence or not is not the test of the man on the top of the Clapham omnibus, because he has not got this special skill. The test is the standard of the ordinary skilled man exercising and professing to have that special skill ... he is not guilty of negligence if he has acted in accordance with a practice accepted as proper by a responsible body of medical men skilled in that particular art.'

Some confusion was caused by the judgment of the Court of Appeal in *Whitehouse* v *Jordan* [1980] 1 All ER 650. The court drew a distinction between an error of clinical judgment and negligence. Lord Denning warned against what he saw as the dangers of imposing too high a standard of care upon doctors. Using the United States of America as his exemplar, he said that to impose too high a standard of care on doctors would lead to colossal damages awards, high insurance premiums, experienced practitioners refusing to treat certain patients and even to some young men being deterred from entering the profession because of the standard of care demanded of them. The decision of the Court of Appeal was, however, reversed by the House of Lords ([1981] 1 WLR 246). The House rejected Lord Denning's distinction between an error of clinical judgment and negligence saying that:

> 'To say that a surgeon committed an error of clinical judgment is wholly ambiguous, for, while some such errors may be committed consistent with the due exercise of professional skill, other acts or omissions in the course of exercising "clinical judgment" may be so glaringly below proper standards as to make a finding of negligence inevitable.'

So it was reaffirmed that the standard of care is that of the reasonably competent professional man professing to have the standard and type of skill which the defendant held himself out as having. In *Wilsher* v *Essex Area Health Authority* [1987] 2 WLR 425 the Court of Appeal held that there was no concept of team negligence, so that each member was required to observe the standard demanded of the unit as a whole. Each member was required to observe the standard of his or her own profession. The court also rejected the argument that a junior, inexperienced doctor owes a lesser standard of care than a more experienced doctor. They did hold, however, that an inexperienced doctor who was required to do a task requiring specialist skill could satisfy the standard of care required of him by seeking the help and advice of his superiors.

The importance of common practice in cases of medical negligence can be seen by contrasting the following two cases. In *Clark* v *MacLennan* [1983] 1 All ER 416 the defendant was held to have been negligent when he failed to conform to the general practice. On the other hand in *Maynard* v *West Midlands Health Authority* [1984] 1 WLR 634 the defendant was able to show that he had followed one school of thought in preference to another. The House of Lords held that the court was not required to choose as between the schools of thought. As long as the defendant could show that he acted in accordance with a standard which was accepted as proper by professional and competent people within his profession then the defendant would not be negligent.

So it is clear that the *Bolam* standard applies in the context of diagnosis and treatment, but does it apply to the risks involved in a course of treatment which a doctor should be required to disclose to a patient? An argument could be made out to the effect that it should not, because each individual is entitled to decide for himself whether or not to undergo an operation or course of treatment, and that sufficient information must be disclosed to enable the patient to give his 'informed consent' to the operation (for discussion of the issue of 'informed consent' see Robertson (1981) 97 LQR 102, Teff (1985) 101 LQR 432 and Brazier (1987) 7 Legal Studies 169). The issue was considered by the House of Lords in *Sidaway* v *Bethlem Royal Hospital Governors* [1985] AC 871. The plaintiff was advised by her surgeon to have an operation on her spinal column because of the pain which she was experiencing in her neck and shoulders. The surgeon did not warn the plaintiff that there was a risk, assessed at less than 1 per cent, of damage being done to her spinal cord due to the fact that he would be operating within less than three millimetres of her spinal cord. The plaintiff consented to the operation which was carried out by the surgeon with all due care and skill. But the risk of damage to her spinal cord materialised and the plaintiff was left severely disabled. She alleged that the surgeon had been negligent in failing to disclose to her the risk of damage to her spinal cord. The House of Lords dismissed the plaintiff's claim. They held, Lord Scarman dissenting, that English law did not require a doctor to disclose sufficient information to enable the plaintiff to give an informed consent to the operation. But there the unanimity ends and it is not altogether clear what is the ratio of *Sidaway*. Two principal speeches were given. The first was given by Lord Diplock and he held that the proper test to apply was the *Bolam* test, that is to say, the test in all cases was whether a reasonable doctor would have acted as the defendant had done. Thus it was for the medical profession to set the appropriate standards of disclosure. He held that a distinction should not be drawn between, on the one hand, diagnosis and treatment and, on the other hand, the disclosure of risks to patients; all cases were to be governed by the *Bolam* test. But Lord Bridge, with whom Lord Keith agreed, was prepared to override the *Bolam* test in certain cases. He said that the judge 'might in certain circumstances come to the conclusion that the disclosure of a particular risk was so obviously necessary to an informed choice on the part of the patient that no reasonable prudent medical man would fail to make it'. The type of case which he had in mind was an operation involving 'a substantial risk of grave adverse consequences,) as for example the 10 per cent risk of a stroke from the operation'.

Further consideration was given to *Sidaway* by the Court of Appeal in *Gold* v *Haringey Health Authority* [1988] QB 481. The plaintiff underwent a sterilisation operation but was not told of the risk of the operation failing; nor was she told that the failure rate for sterilisation was higher than the failure rate for a vasectomy. The sterilisation was not a success and the plaintiff subsequently became pregnant. She brought a negligence action against the defendant health authority. The trial judge found for the plaintiff ([1987] 1 FLR 125), holding that *Bolam* only applied to advice given in a therapeutic context and that it did not apply in a non-therapeutic context.

The Court of Appeal rejected this argument and held that *Bolam* applied in both contexts. Applying *Bolam* they held that the defendants were not liable because there was a substantial body of medical opinion which in 1979 would not have warned the plaintiff of the risk of failure. Both Lloyd LJ and Stephen Brown LJ relied on the judgment of Lord Diplock in *Sidaway* and, although the court was not asked to choose between the approaches adopted by Lord Diplock and Lord Bridge in *Sidaway*, it would seem that the former approach has gained the approval of the Court of Appeal. However, it is unfortunate that the Court of Appeal did not consider the conflicting opinions delivered in *Sidaway*, and its uncritical reliance upon the judgment of Lord Diplock is likely to be subjected to some re-examination in the future (see Grubb [1988] CLJ 12 and Lee (1987) 103 LQR 513).

9.12 Proof of the breach

The plaintiff bears the burden of proof of showing that the defendant was negligent. He must prove his case on the balance of probabilities (the problems of proof which arise where there are difficulties in showing that the defendant's negligence was the cause of the damage to the plaintiff will be discussed at 10.6).

There are certain cases where the legal burden of proof can be switched to the defendant. Section 11(1) of the Civil Evidence Act 1968 permits a plaintiff to lead evidence that the defendant was convicted of a criminal offence arising out of the act which is the subject of the civil action. So where the defendant has been convicted of careless driving and that careless driving caused the accident in which the plaintiff was injured, the plaintiff may succeed in an action in negligence simply by proving that the defendant was convicted of the offence of careless driving, unless the defendant can discharge the onus of proving that he was not negligent. In *Wauchope* v *Mordecai* [1970] 1 WLR 317 the plaintiff, who was riding his bicycle, was injured when the defendant suddenly opened the door of his parked car and hit the plaintiff. The defendant was convicted of an offence arising out of this incident and it was held that the effect of s11 of the 1968 Act was to shift the burden of proof to the defendant in the negligence action to show that he was not negligent.

9.13 Res ipsa loquitur

The phrase res ipsa loquitur means that the thing speaks for itself. Where the maxim applies the court is prepared to draw the inference that the defendant was negligent without hearing detailed evidence of what the defendant did or did not do. The application of the maxim can be illustrated by reference to the case of *Scott* v *London and St Katherine Docks Co* (1865) 3 H & C 596. The plaintiff was passing the defendant's warehouse when six bags of sugar, which were being hoisted by the defendant's crane, fell on the plaintiff and caused him injury. The only thing which the plaintiff could prove was that the bags fell on him and caused him injury. It was held that the facts were sufficient to give rise to an inference of negligence on the part of the defendant and so the maxim was applicable. There are three conditions which must be satisfied before res ipsa loquitur is applicable.

The first condition which must be satisfied is that the defendant must be in control of the thing which caused the injury to the plaintiff. Here two cases are customarily contrasted. The first case is *Gee* v *Metropolitan Railway* (1873) LR 8 QB 161. The plaintiff leaned against the door of an underground train shortly after it left the station. The door flew open and the plaintiff fell out of the train, suffering serious injury. It was held that the door had recently been in the control of the defendants because the train had just left the station and so there was evidence of negligence on the part of the defendants. On the other hand a different result was reached in the case of *Easson* v *LNE Railway* [1944] 2 KB 421. In this case the plaintiff, who was a four year old boy, fell through the door of a corridor train and was severely injured. At the time of the accident the train was seven miles from its last stopping place. It was held that res ipsa loquitur did not apply because the door was not under the control of the defendants. The train was sufficiently far away from the station for the door to have been opened by a passenger rather than by one of the defendants' employees.

The second condition which must be satisfied for res ipsa loquitur to apply is that the accident must be of such a nature that it would not have occurred in the ordinary course of events without negligence. This requirement can be demonstrated by reference to the facts of *Scott* v *London and St Katherine Docks* (above) because bags do not normally fall from a height from cranes without negligence on the part of somebody. Similarly in *Byrne* v *Boadle* (1863) 2 H & C 722 the plaintiff was able to invoke the maxim when a barrel of flour fell on him as he was passing underneath the defendant's upstairs window. Similarly the maxim was invoked in *Mahon* v *Osborne* [1939] 2 KB 14. The plaintiff went into hospital for an abdominal operation. He died and on examination it was discovered that the surgeon had left a swab in his body. It was held that the plaintiff was entitled to call expert evidence to demonstrate that the accident would not have occurred without negligence. If it were otherwise the plaintiff would be severely handicapped in his attempt to invoke the maxim.

The third condition which must be satisfied is that there must be no explanation for the accident. This requirement is not of any great practical significance because all that it means is that, where the facts are sufficiently known, there is no need to invoke the maxim because the plaintiff can prove what actually happened (see *Barkway* v *South Wales Transport Co Ltd* [1950] 1 All ER 392).

Once these three conditions for the application of the maxim are satisfied, the question arises as to what effect the maxim has on the case. This question has given rise to some controversy (on which see Atiyah (1972) 35 MLR 337). There are basically two schools of thought relating to the effect of res ipsa loquitur. The first is that, while the maxim raises an inference that the defendant was negligent, if the defendant rebuts that inference then the plaintiff has to prove that the defendant was negligent. In other words the legal burden of proof rests on the plaintiff throughout. The second school of thought takes a broader view of the effect of the maxim. According to them, the maxim reverses the burden of proof so that the legal burden of proof passes to the defendant so that, once the plaintiff has made out a prima facie case of negligence, the defendant then bears the burden of proving on the balance of probabilities that he was not negligent.

The first view appeared to be adopted by the House of Lords in *Colvilles Ltd* v *Devine* [1969] 1 WLR 475 where Lord Donovan said that the maxim had no effect on the legal burden of proof. However a year later the House of Lords took a different approach in the case of *Henderson* v *Henry E Jenkins & Sons* [1970] AC 282. An employee of the defendants was driving one of the defendants' lorries down a hill when the brakes suddenly failed. As a result of the brake failure the lorry careered into a van, killing the plaintiff's husband. The brake failure was caused by the corrosion of the pipe carrying brake fluid. The defendants had had the lorry maintained but the pipe which had corroded could only be seen by dismantling the pipe and this was not recommended by the manufacturers until the lorry had done a certain mileage. The plaintiff raised a prima facie case of negligence on the part of the defendants. The defendants then showed that the vehicle had been properly maintained, that the corrosion could only be seen by removing the pipe and that such a practice was not recommended by the manufacturers. Despite these arguments the House of Lords held that the defendants had failed to rebut the inference of negligence. It was held that they should have gone on to show that there was nothing in the history of the vehicle that would have caused abnormal corrosion or required special treatment or inspection. They had therefore failed to displace the inference that their negligence had been the cause of the accident. Although the language of the judgments was not entirely clear, their effect appeared to be to apply the view of the second school of thought, namely that the effect of res ipsa loquitur is to switch the legal burden of proof to the defendant (see also *Ward* v *Tesco Stores Ltd* [1976] 1 WLR 810).

But the issue has been reconsidered by the Privy Council in *Ng Chun Pui* v *Lee Chuen Tat* [1988] RTR 298. A coach skidded across the central reservation of a dual carriageway and collided with a bus which was travelling on the opposite carriageway, injuring the plaintiffs who were passengers on the bus. The plaintiffs alleged that the accident was caused by the negligence of the first defendant, who was the driver of the coach. At the trial of the action the plaintiffs called no oral evidence but invoked the doctrine of res ipsa loquitur. The first defendant led evidence to the effect that a car had cut out in front of the coach, which had forced him to swerve to avoid that car, and, in doing so, the coach had skidded across the central reservation. The trial judge found for the plaintiffs, on the ground that the defendants had failed to discharge the burden of disproving negligence. The trial judge was reversed by the Court of Appeal of Hong Kong and the plaintiffs appealed to the Privy Council. The Privy Council dismissed the appeal.

Lord Griffiths, giving the judgment of the Privy Council, stated that res ipsa loquitur is no more than a maxim 'to describe a state of the evidence from which it is proper to draw an inference of negligence'. Crucially he stated that:

> 'It is misleading to talk of the burden of proof shifting to the defendant in a res ipsa loquitur situation. The burden of proving negligence rests throughout the case on the plaintiff.'

Where, as in a case such as *Scott* v *London and St Katherine Docks* (above), the plaintiff suffers injury as a result of an accident which should not have occurred if the defendant had taken due care, it is possible for a court to draw the inference from the facts of the case that, on a balance of probabilities, the defendant failed to exercise reasonable care. In such a case, where the defendant adduces no evidence, he will have failed to rebut the inference of negligence and the plaintiff will have proved his case. On the other hand, the defendant can lead evidence in an effort to rebut the inference of negligence. Lord Griffiths stated that:

> 'Loosely speaking this may be referred to as a burden on the defendant to show that he was not negligent, but that only means that faced with a prima facie case of negligence the defendant will be found negligent unless he produces evidence that is capable of rebutting the prima facie case. Resort to the burden of proof is a poor way to decide a case; it is the duty of the judge to examine all the evidence at the end of the case and decide whether on the facts he finds to have been proved and on the inferences he is prepared to draw he is satisfied that negligence has been established. In so far as resort is had to the burden of proof, the burden remains at the end of the case as it was at the beginning upon the plaintiff to prove that his injury was caused by the negligence of the defendants.'

Applying this approach to the facts of the case, it was held that the evidence of the defendants displaced any inference of negligence by the driver of the coach. Although a decision of the Privy Council is not technically binding, it is suggested that future English courts will follow *Ng Chun Pui* and conclude that res ipsa loquitur does not reverse the burden of proof; the burden remains upon the plaintiff throughout.

10

Negligence: Causation

10.1 Introduction

10.2 But for test

10.3 Pre-existing condition

10.4 Omissions

10.5 Multiple causes

10.6 Proof of causation

10.7 Successive causes

10.1 Introduction

A defendant is not liable in negligence unless the plaintiff's loss has been caused by the negligence of the defendant. Sometimes when discussing causation a distinction is drawn between causation in fact and causation in law. The former is concerned with whether, as a matter of fact, the defendant's negligence was a cause of the plaintiff's loss. The test which has been adopted here is whether the plaintiff's loss would have occurred 'but for' the defendant's negligence. The latter concept of causation, causation in law, is concerned with whether, as a matter of law, the defendant is to be held liable for the damage which he has, in fact, caused. Thus causation in law is concerned with the situation where the defendant's negligence has in fact caused loss to the plaintiff and the question which arises is whether the law will attribute the damage which has arisen to the negligence of the defendant. This latter form of causation is really concerned with remoteness of damage and will be dealt with in chapter 11. Here we will concentrate upon causation in fact.

10.2 But for test

In considering whether the defendant's act or omission was a cause of the plaintiff's loss the test which is generally adopted is called the 'but for' test. In *Cork* v *Kirby MacLean Ltd* [1952] 2 All ER 402 Lord Denning said that 'if the damage would not have happened but for a particular fault, then that fault is the cause of the damage; if it would have happened just the same, fault or no fault, the fault is not the cause of the damage.'

The application of the 'but for' test can be seen in the case of *Barnett* v *Chelsea and Kensington Hospital Management Committee* [1969] 1 QB 428. The plaintiff's husband went to a casualty department of a hospital complaining that he had been vomiting. The doctor refused to examine him and he was told to go home and consult his own doctor in the morning. The plaintiff's husband was, in fact, suffering from arsenical poisoning and he died some five hours later. The plaintiff sued the hospital alleging that they had been negligent in the treatment given to her husband and that as a result of their negligence her husband had died. It was held, however, that the defendants were not liable to the plaintiff as their negligence had not caused her husband's death. Even if the doctor had examined her husband and treated him her husband would still have died from the poisoning and so the doctor's negligence was not a cause of the husband's death.

In the vast majority of cases the 'but for' test gives rise to no legal problems but, in the following cases, it has given rise to considerable difficulty.

10.3 Pre-existing condition

If the damage is attributable to a pre-existing condition rather than to the negligence of the defendant then the defendant will not be liable for the full extent of the damage. In *Cutler* v *Vauxhall Motors Ltd* [1971] 1 QB 418 the plaintiff suffered a graze to his right ankle in an accident caused by the negligence of the defendants. Shortly after the accident it was discovered that the plaintiff had a pre-accident condition of varicosity in the veins of both of his legs. Because an ulcer had formed on the site of the graze it was decided to operate immediately to cure the varicose condition of his legs. As a result of the operation the plaintiff suffered pain and discomfort and a loss of earnings of £173. He sought to recover this sum from the defendants. It was held that the plaintiff was entitled to damages for the graze but that he could not claim for the losses due to the operation. The condition of varicosity was not connected with the negligence of the defendants and it would have required treatment at some time in the future. So the plaintiff would have suffered such a loss at some time in the future and the defendants' negligence was not a cause of the plaintiff's loss.

Russell LJ stated that the maxim, that the tortfeasor must take his victim as he finds him, can work to the advantage of the tortfeasor when the victim suffers from a pre-existing condition. He found support for this argument in the case of *Performance Cars* v *Abraham* [1962] 1 QB 33. The defendant negligently crashed into the plaintiff's Rolls-Royce and caused damage to the wing and bumper of the Rolls-Royce. The damage would normally have required a respray but the Rolls-Royce had previously been involved in another accident caused by the negligence of a third party and the damages which had been awarded as a result of the latter accident included the cost of a respray. So it was held that the plaintiff could not recover the cost of the respray from the defendant as well because the defendant had 'damaged' an already damaged car and so had not caused any loss to the plaintiff. Had the plaintiff been allowed to recover the cost of the respray from the defendant it would have resulted in the plaintiff being compensated twice for the same loss.

10.4 Omissions

It is extremely difficult to apply the 'but for' test where the negligence of the defendant takes the form of an omission to act. This difficulty can be demonstrated by reference to the case of *McWilliams* v *Sir William Arrol & Co Ltd* [1962] 1 WLR 295. The plaintiff, who was a steel erector, fell to his death at work. At the time of the accident the plaintiff was not wearing a safety belt. The defendants were in breach of their statutory duty in failing to supply safety belts but there was evidence that the plaintiff had rarely, if ever, worn such a safety belt in the past and so the defendants argued that he would not have worn a safety belt even if one had been made available. A crucial point to note here is that the onus of proof is on the plaintiff to show, on a balance of probabilities, that the defendant's negligence is a cause of the damage which he has suffered. It was held that the defendants were not liable because it was probable that the plaintiff would not have worn a safety belt and so would have fallen to his death even if the defendants had provided safety belts. In this type of case the court is engaged upon a hypothetical inquiry and has to speculate, in the light of all the evidence, as to what would have happened on a given state of facts. Lord Reid in *McWilliams* said that the 'natural' and 'almost inevitable' inference was that the plaintiff would not have worn a safety belt and that 'that inference is strengthened by the general practice of other men not to wear belts'. This decision has been criticised on the ground that it does not give any incentive to employers to ensure that safety belts are worn (see Atiyah *Accidents, Compensation and the Law* (4th ed) pp97–8) but there is no doubt that the principle laid down in *McWilliams* remains good law.

10.5 Multiple causes

Where there is more than one cause of the damage to the plaintiff the 'but for' test can run into difficulties. An example given by Professor Atiyah illustrates the point (*Accidents, Compensation and the Law* (4th ed) p99). Two fires started independently by A and B unite and spread to C's house which is destroyed. The 'but for' test would appear to acquit both parties because if the question is asked 'would the damage have occurred but for the negligence of A?' the answer would be 'yes' and the same answer would be given if the question is asked 'would the damage have occurred but for the negligence of B?' This absurd result would not, however, be reached by the courts. Judges in such cases decide issues of causation upon ideas of common sense rather than metaphysics. As Lord Wright said in *Yorkshire Dale Steamship Co Ltd* v *Minister of War Transport* [1942] AC 691 'causation is to be understood as the man in the street, and not as either the scientist or the metaphysician, would understand it.' Thus in *Galoo* v *Bright Grahame Murray* (1994) The Times 14 January the Court of Appeal held that in tort cases which were analogous to a breach of contract the court had to decide whether the breach was the cause of the loss or merely the occasion of the loss on the basis of the application of common sense.

A similar problem arises where it is not apparent which of two parties has caused the loss to the plaintiff. There is no clear English authority on this point, but the issue arose in the Canadian case of *Cook* v *Lewis* [1952] 1 DLR 1. The plaintiff was injured by a gun shot. It was unclear which of the two defendants had caused injury to the plaintiff as they had both fired shots simultaneously. It was held that both defendants were liable because the burden of proof lay on them to show that they had not been negligent and they failed to discharge the burden. It is submitted that this approach is preferable to dismissing the plaintiff's claim against the defendants. As Professor Fleming has argued the 'law prefers a 50 per cent chance of doing justice to the certainty of doing injustice' (*The Law of Torts* (7th ed) p288). It is clear that this type of case gives rise to problems concerning the proof of causation and these problems are such that they are worthy of separate treatment.

10.6 Proof of causation

Considerable difficulty arises where it is unclear whether or not the damage to the plaintiff has been caused by the negligence of the defendant. In such a case the standard of proof of causation assumes enormous significance. This area of law has, for many years now, been dominated by the case of *McGhee* v *National Coal Board* [1973] 1 WLR 1. The proper interpretation of *McGhee* has, however, been the subject of considerable controversy. We shall commence our analysis by examining the decision of the House of Lords in *McGhee* itself; then we shall see how it was expansively interpreted by the Court of Appeal and finally we shall conclude by noting the rejection of this expansive interpretation by the House of Lords in three recent cases.

In *McGhee* the pursuer worked in brick kilns, where the working conditions were extremely hot and dirty. Despite this fact the pursuer had to cycle home in his dirty clothes because there were no washing facilities at his place of work. He contracted the skin disease dermatitis. The defenders admitted that they had been negligent but they argued that their negligence was not the cause of the pursuer contracting dermatitis. The pursuer pleaded that, had the defenders provided washing facilities, he would not have contracted the disease. The House of Lords held that the medical evidence did not prove that the pursuer would not have contracted the disease had the defenders provided the washing facilities, but that the pursuer was entitled to recover damages on the ground that the defenders had materially increased the risk of the pursuer contracting the disease. Their Lordships held that it did not expect the pursuer to show on a balance of probabilities that the defenders' breach was actually the cause of his disease, but merely that it materially increased the risk of his contracting the disease. The unusual feature of this case is that, in effect, the pursuer succeeded without ever showing that the defenders' negligence caused him any damage. All that he did show was that the defenders had increased the risk of him suffering damage. Lord Wilberforce justified the conclusion which he reached on the ground that the defenders, by their negligence, had created the risk of a particular damage occurring and when that risk became reality they were not allowed, on grounds of policy, to hide behind the evidential difficulty of showing what had caused the damage to the pursuer. As between the two parties it was the defenders who had to shoulder the evidential difficulty.

McGhee was interpreted liberally by the Court of Appeal in the case of *Wilsher* v *Essex Area Health Authority* [1987] 2 WLR 425. When the plaintiff was born prematurely he suffered from, inter alia, oxygen deficiency. Due to the negligence of one of the doctors employed by the defendants, the plaintiff was given an excess of oxygen. The plaintiff alleged that the excess of oxygen in his bloodstream caused incurable damage to his retina with the result that he was almost blind. The Court of Appeal held that the defendants were negligent and, by a majority, they held that the defendants' negligence caused the damage to the plaintiff. The difficulty on the causation point was that, while medical evidence showed that an excess of oxygen was a factor which caused blindness in premature babies, it was not the only factor which caused blindness in these babies. Mustill LJ applied the reasoning of the House of Lords in *McGhee* and found for the plaintiff. He noted that there was a difference in approach in the judgments of the House in *McGhee*, with Lord Wilberforce arguing that the effect was to shift the burden of proof to the defendants, whereas the rest of their Lordships were of the opinion that once it was shown that the defendants' breach of duty increased the risk of damage, that established a sufficient connection between the negligence and the damage. Mustill LJ did not, however, attempt to resolve this conflict because he held that excess of oxygen could cause or contribute to blindness and so *McGhee* was applicable. However, Mustill LJ held that there was a difference between *McGhee* and the instant case. The difference was that in *McGhee* there was only one risk in operation, namely that the heat and dust would lead to dermatitis, whereas in the present case there were a number of factors at work and what the defendants had done was to add to the list of factors which might cause blindness, by giving the plaintiff an excess of oxygen. Mustill LJ held that this difference was without substance because where the defendant, by his negligence, has increased the risk of damage then the defendant is liable, even though the defendant's negligence is but one of the factors which could have led to the damage. Glidewell LJ held that while the factual situation in the present case was more complex, the legal principle was the same as in *McGhee*. Browne-Wilkinson VC dissented on the ground that *McGhee* was an illogical decision which was not to be extended. He held that, until the plaintiff could show that his condition was caused by an excess of oxygen, it was impossible to argue that the case was covered by *McGhee*, where it was clear that the dust and heat was the cause of the dermatitis (a liberal approach was also adopted by the Court of Appeal in *Fitzgerald v Lane* [1987] QB 781. It should be noted that when the case was appealed to the House of Lords ([1989] AC 328) there was, rather strangely, no appeal against this aspect of the decision of the Court of Appeal).

The second case in which the Court of Appeal adopted an expansive interpretation of *McGhee* is the case of *Fitzgerald v Lane* [1987] QB 781. The plaintiff suffered serious injury as the result of a motor accident. The plaintiff had walked on to the road when the pelican crossing was at red for pedestrians and green for traffic. He was struck by the first defendant's car and was then struck by the second defendant's car. Both the defendants were held to have been driving negligently at the time of the accident. It was held that all three parties were equally to blame for the accident and damages were apportioned accordingly. The point which is of interest here, however, concerns the argument of the second defendant that the plaintiff had failed to prove that his (the second defendant's) negligence had caused the serious injuries which the plaintiff had sustained, because regard had to be had to the effect of the first accident, which may have been the sole cause of the damage to the plaintiff. In other words, the plaintiff could have already suffered the damage before he came into contact with the second defendant's car. This argument was rejected by the Court of Appeal, who held that the second defendant had created a risk of physical injury to the plaintiff by his negligent driving, or he had increased the existing risk that such an injury would take place. The Court of Appeal held that the principle laid down in *McGhee* was applicable and they also approved of the judgment of Mustill LJ in *Wilsher* and the extension to *McGhee* which he formulated there.

Perhaps the most significant aspect of these two cases is the recognition by Mustill LJ in *Wilsher* and by Slade LJ in *Fitzgerald v Lane* [1987] QB 781 that the decision in *McGhee* is ultimately one which is based upon policy. Slade LJ in *Fitzgerald* said that:

> 'If considerations of broad justice demanded that the respective plaintiffs should succeed against the respective defendants in both *McGhee*'s case and *Wilsher*'s case, I find it hard to see why the plaintiff in the present case should fail in his claim against the negligent second defendant merely because ... he cannot positively prove that his collision with the second defendant's car ... caused or materially contributed to his tetraplegia.'

So, as Mustill LJ demonstrated in *Wilsher*, the decision of the House of Lords in *McGhee* 'mitigated the rigour of the rule that the plaintiff must prove that the breach caused the loss'.

However, as we have noted the House of Lords has not shared the Court of Appeal's enthusiasm for an expansive interpretation of *McGhee*. Nor has it approved of the considerations of policy noted by Mustill LJ and Slade LJ. In a line of three cases, culminating in the overruling of the decision of the Court of Appeal in *Wilsher*, the House of Lords has adopted a much more restrictive interpretation of *McGhee*.

The first of these three cases is *Kay v Ayrshire and Arran Health Board* [1987] 2 All ER 417. Here the plaintiff's son, who at the time was suffering from pneumococcal meningitis, was given an overdose of penicillin as a result of the negligence of one of the doctors employed by the defendants. After recovering from the meningitis the plaintiff's son was found to be deaf. Deafness is a common consequence of meningitis, but the plaintiff argued that the deafness was caused by the defendants' negligence in giving him an overdose of penicillin. There was no established medical evidence that an overdose of penicillin could lead to deafness, and the deafness was held to have been caused by the meningitis and the claim against the defendants was dismissed. It was held that, had there been medical evidence that an overdose of penicillin was known to create an increased risk that the meningitis would result in deafness, then *McGhee* would have been applicable. However the law could not presume that the defendant's negligence was responsible for the plaintiff's injury, in the absence of evidence to show that the defendant's negligence was capable of causing damage to the plaintiff. In this case the issue was relatively clear; there was no medical evidence of a link between the negligence of the defendants and the damage to the plaintiff and so the plaintiff's case was dismissed.

The second decision is *Hotson v East Berkshire AHA* [1987] AC 50. The plaintiff injured his hip when he fell out of a tree. He was taken to a hospital run by the defendants but the injury to his hip was not diagnosed and it was not until some five days later that the injury to his hip was discovered. The effect of the hip injury was to leave the plaintiff with a severe and permanent disability by the time that he was 20. Had the hospital discovered the damage to his hip when he was first admitted then the plaintiff would have had a 25 per cent chance of recovery, but the effect of the delay in diagnosis was that the plaintiff lost his 25 per cent chance of a recovery. The trial judge awarded the plaintiff a sum by way of damages which equalled 25 per cent of the full damages awardable. That decision was affirmed by the Court of Appeal but was reversed by the House of Lords. The crucial principle which was relied upon by their Lordships was that the plaintiff must prove his case on a balance of probabilities. It was held that the plaintiff failed to prove his case on a balance of probabilities. On a balance of probabilities the injury was caused when the plaintiff fell out of the tree. Neither party placed reliance upon *McGhee* and Lord Mackay recognised that '*McGhee* [was] far removed on its facts from the circumstances of the present appeal'. Nevertheless, the emphasis placed upon the need for the plaintiff to prove his case on a balance of probabilities threw some doubt on the standing of *McGhee*, and in particular upon the decision of the Court of Appeal in *Wilsher*.

It therefore came as little surprise when, in the third and final case, the House of Lords in *Wilsher v Essex Area Health Authority* [1988] AC 1074 reversed the decision of the Court of Appeal. It was held that in all cases the plaintiff bears the burden of proving on a balance of probabilities that the damage was caused by the negligence of the defendants. Further Lord Bridge stated that *McGhee:*

> '... laid down no new principle of law whatever. On the contrary it affirmed the principle that the onus of proving causation lies on the plaintiff. Adopting a robust and pragmatic approach to the undisputed facts of the case, the majority concluded that it was a legitimate inference of fact that the defenders' negligence had materially contributed to the pursuer's injury. The decision, in my opinion, is of no greater significance than that and the attempt to extract from it some esoteric principle which in some way modifies, as a matter of law, the nature of the burden of proof of causation which a plaintiff ... must discharge once he has established a relevant breach of duty is a fruitless one.'

Lord Bridge also held that, in so far as Lord Wilberforce in *McGhee* had suggested that the burden of proof of causation switched to the defendant, this was a minority opinion which found no support in the other speeches in *McGhee*. *McGhee* was treated as a case where an inference was drawn that the 'consecutive periods' (that is while he was at work and when he was cycling home) when the brick dust was on the pursuer's body contributed cumulatively to the causation of the dermatitis. That inference could not be drawn in *Wilsher* where the possible causal factors operated concurrently and it could not be ascertained which of the possible causal factors had in fact caused the blindness. The House of Lords therefore ordered a re-trial on the issue of causation, and the relevant question for the trial judge was whether the plaintiff could prove on a balance of probabilities that the negligence of the defendants was the cause of the damage which he had suffered.

By way of conclusion it is important to note the contrasting perceptions of the policies at work here. We have already noted that in the Court of Appeal in *Wilsher* the judges sought to mitigate the rigour of the rule that the plaintiff must prove that the breach of duty caused the loss which he suffered. This view was not, however, shared by Lord Bridge in *Wilsher*. He stated that:

> 'Whether we like it or not, the law, which only Parliament can change, requires proof of fault causing damage as the basis of liability in tort. We should do society nothing but disservice if we made the forensic process still more unpredictable and hazardous by distorting the law to accommodate the exigencies of what may seem hard cases.'

It is therefore clear that, in future, plaintiffs will have to show that, on the balance of probabilities, the defendant's breach of duty caused the loss which he (the plaintiff) suffered.

10.7 Successive causes

Where the plaintiff suffers successive injuries, one of these injuries being caused by the negligence of the defendant, then difficulty arises because of the relationship between two decisions of the House of Lords.

The first decision is *Baker* v *Willoughby* [1970] AC 467. The plaintiff was knocked down by the defendant while he was crossing the road. As a result of the accident the plaintiff suffered injuries to his left leg, which caused him some pain and discomfort and also detrimentally affected his earning power. The plaintiff took up a new job after the accident, but while he was at work he was shot in the same leg during an armed robbery. As a result of this second incident the plaintiff's left leg had to be amputated. The defendant argued that his liability to the plaintiff in respect of the injury to his left leg had to be reduced in the light of the robbery because the plaintiff's left leg had to be amputated as a result of the shot fired during the robbery and so the effect of his negligence had been obliterated.

This argument was rejected by the House of Lords. They rejected the argument that the plaintiff's loss had been diminished as a result of the shooting. Lord Reid said that the plaintiff is not compensated for the physical injury itself but for 'the loss he suffers as a result of that injury'. The shooting incident had not diminished the plaintiff's pain and suffering, nor had it diminished the plaintiff's loss of his earning capacity. The second reason for rejecting the defendant's argument was that, had the plaintiff sued the robbers, the robbers would have been able to take advantage of the rule that a tortfeasor takes his victim as he finds him and so would only have been liable for the damage which they had caused to an already damaged leg. So to refuse the plaintiff a remedy in respect of the damage done by the defendant would be to leave the plaintiff under-compensated because he would not be able to recover in respect of that damage from the robbers. So, to do justice on the facts of the case, the defendant was held liable to the plaintiff.

A different result was, however, reached by the House of Lords in the case of *Jobling* v *Associated Dairies* [1982] AC 794. The plaintiff suffered injury to his back at work in 1973. This injury was caused by the defendants' breach of statutory duty and the effect of the injury was to compel the plaintiff to take a less strenuous job, with the result that his earning capacity was reduced by 50 per cent. Before the action against the defendants was tried in 1979 it was discovered in 1976 that the plaintiff was suffering from a crippling back disease called myelopathy. The effect of the latter disease was to render him totally unfit for work by the end of 1976. There was no connection between the myelopathy and the defendants' negligence. It was held that the defendants were not liable for any loss of earnings suffered by the plaintiff after 1976 when the myelopathy rendered the plaintiff totally unfit for work.

The House of Lords in *Jobling* were critical of the judgments handed down in *Baker*. Lord Edmund-Davies criticised *Baker* on the ground that it failed to take account of the fact that the plaintiff could have received some compensation from the Criminal Injuries Compensation Scheme. So a finding that the defendant was not liable would not necessarily have left the plaintiff under-compensated. This criticism is not, however, entirely accurate. The Criminal Injuries Compensation Board, in assessing the sum payable, proceeds upon a similar basis to a court and so would have taken account of the existing disability and there would have been no double compensation.

Baker was also criticised on the ground that it took no account of the vicissitudes of life. Lord Wilberforce stated that in assessing damages payable the court took account of the vicissitudes of life and reduced the damages payable accordingly. It was then argued that if a court reduced damages on account of the possibility that the plaintiff might suffer some misfortune which was not attributable to the negligence of another, then surely it should also reduce damages when that possibility became a reality. Thus the House appeared to suggest that the contraction of another independent disease would count as a vicissitude and would have the effect of reducing the damages payable, but that the commission of another tort was not a vicissitude of life and so would not reduce the damages payable. But, as has been pointed out, 'it is just as much a contingency of life that one might get knocked down by a negligently driven car as it is that one might suffer some disabling illness' (Evans (1982) 45 MLR 329, 332). So this distinction is hardly a satisfactory one.

There is also a conflict of policy between *Baker* and *Jobling*. The policy behind *Baker* is to prevent the plaintiff from being left under-compensated. But the policy behind *Jobling* is the oppposite one of preventing the plaintiff from being over-compensated. In fact it increases the possibility of the plaintiff being under-compensated because no inquiry was made as to whether or not the plaintiff was entitled to receive state benefits in respect of the injury to his back. Despite this complete conflict of policy it is possible to rationalise *Baker* and *Jobling* on the act of a third party: whereas in *Jobling* the supervening event was an inherent rather unsatisfactory ground, in *Baker* the supervening event was the tortious disease. So, where the supervening event is not the result of the commission of a tort, the defendant's liability to the plaintiff falls to be reduced accordingly, but where the supervening event is the commission of a tort the defendant's liability does not fall to be reduced.

11

Negligence: Remoteness of Damage

11.1 Introduction

11.2 *Polemis* and the directness test

11.3 *Wagon Mound* and foreseeability

11.4 Damage to the person

11.5 Damage to property

11.6 *Polemis* and *Wagon Mound* contrasted

11.7 Cases where the reasonable foresight test does not apply

11.8 Intervening acts (novus actus interveniens)

11.1 Introduction

Having established that the defendant owes the plaintiff a duty of care, and that duty was breached causing loss to the plaintiff, it must now be considered whether the loss which the plaintiff has sustained is one which is recoverable in negligence. The defendant is not liable for all the loss which flows from his breach of his duty of care. The law places limits upon the extent to which a plaintiff can recover in negligence. We have already noted in chapter 10 that the plaintiff must show that the defendant's negligence was the cause of his loss. Here we shall consider the limits placed upon the damages recoverable by the rules relating to remoteness of damage. We shall also note that there is a degree of overlap between the rules relating to remoteness and the rules relating to causation.

The legal position in relation to remoteness of damage has been dominated by two different cases and the rules laid down in these cases. These two cases are *Re Polemis and Furness, Withy & Co* [1921] 3 KB 560 and *Overseas Tankship (UK) Ltd v Morts Dock & Engineering Co (The Wagon Mound (No 1))* [1961] AC 388. We shall consider the tests laid down in these cases before proceeding to examine the present state of the law.

11.2 *Polemis* and the directness test

The first case of importance is the case of *Re Polemis* (above) and the test laid down in this case held sway for a considerable period of time before it was displaced in 1961.

In *Re Polemis* the charterers of a ship loaded a quantity of benzine on board the ship. The benzine leaked, causing the hold of the ship to fill with vapour. A stevedore, employed by the charterers, negligently dropped a wooden plank into the hold of the ship. This dropping of the plank caused a spark, which ignited the vapour, and the ship exploded. The owners of the ship sued the charterers in negligence in respect of the damage done by their servant. The charterers defended the action on the ground that the loss caused to the owners by the negligence of their servant was too remote to be recovered in a negligence action. The Court of Appeal held that the charterers were liable for the negligence of the stevedores and that the loss was not too remote.

Although the ratio of the decision is not entirely free from doubt (for consideration of the different interpretations see Clerk and Lindsell on *Torts* (16th ed) para 10–151), the generally accepted view is that as long as some damage to the plaintiff is foreseeable, the defendant is liable for all the damage that directly results from the negligence. It was once thought that *Polemis* stood for the proposition that a defendant was liable for all the damage directly resulting from his negligent behaviour and even to a plaintiff who was not within the reasonable foresight of the defendant. Such a proposition is, however, clearly in conflict with the neighbour principle laid down in *Donoghue* v *Stevenson* and has been properly rejected. So the crucial determinant of liability in *Polemis* has been perceived to be the issue of directness, as compared with the standard of reasonable foresight which was employed in *The Wagon Mound (No 1)* (above).

Although the decision in *Polemis* is said to rest on the proposition that the damage to the plaintiff must arise 'directly' from the negligence of the defendant, the unusual feature of the case is that nobody seems to know what was meant by the word 'directly' in *Polemis*. All that was said in *Polemis* was that 'indirect' meant damage due to the 'operation of independent causes having no connection with the negligent act, except that they could not avoid its results' (per Scrutton LJ).

So it is submitted that the crucial element in determining the scope of *Polemis* lies not in the element of directness but in the meaning of the requirement that 'some damage to the plaintiff must be foreseeable'. In considering whether damage to the plaintiff is foreseeable, one could say that the fact that any sort of damage to the plaintiff is foreseeable is sufficient. But the law has not adopted such an approach. Instead *Polemis* may be said to draw a distinction between damage to property, damage to the person and economic damage. What *Polemis* seems to suggest is that once a defendant can foresee some damage to the plaintiff within one of these categories then damage is foreseeable and the defendant is liable. Thus in *Polemis* it did not matter that the type of property damage which in fact occurred was different in kind from what was reasonably foreseeable. In other words, it did not matter that the damage caused by the dropping of the wood was an explosion rather than a dent in some part of the ship.

This proposition is subject to the qualification that economic damage seemed to be treated differently from damage to the person or damage to property. This can be seen from the case of *Liesbosch Dredger* v *SS Edison* [1933] AC 449. In this case the 'Edison' negligently struck the dredger 'Liesbosch' in a harbour and as a result the 'Liesbosch' sank. At the time of the accident the 'Liesbosch' was under contract and the owners, as a result of the delay caused by the accident, had insufficient time to complete the work under the contract. Being short of money, they did not have the cash to purchase a new dredger to complete the work and so they hired a dredger, at an exorbitant price, to complete the work under the contract. The plaintiffs sought to recover the money they had expended on the hire of the dredger from the defendants. It was held that the plaintiffs were only entitled to the cost of the new dredger which, but for their own impecuniosity, they would have been able to purchase at the earlier date. It was held that the plaintiffs' impecuniosity was an extraneous factor for which the defendants were not liable. Lord Wright specifically distinguished *Polemis* on the ground that the losses suffered there were the 'immediate physical consequences of the negligent act'. Had the House of Lords applied *Polemis* the owners would surely have recovered damages because economic damage was foreseeable and the fact that the economic damage was of a greater size than was anticipated would not have mattered. However, in *Mattocks* v *Mann* (1992) The Times 19 June the Court of Appeal noted that the law of damages had not stood still since 1933, and that in *Perry* v *Sidney Phillips & Son* [1982] 1 WLR 1297 Kerr LJ had stated that the authority of what Lord Wright said in *Liesbosch* was consistently being attenuated in more recent decisions. In *Mattocks* the court stated that 'in the varied web of affairs after an accident, only in exceptional circumstances was it possible or correct to isolate impecuniosity of a plaintiff as a separate cause and as terminating the consequences of a defendant's wrong'.

11.3 *Wagon Mound* and foreseeability

A different approach was, however, adopted by the Privy Council in *The Wagon Mound (No 1)*(above). This decision was heralded as introducing a new approach to the issue of remoteness in English law. Due to the negligence of the defendants' employees, furnace oil leaked from the defendants' ship, the 'Wagon Mound', and into Sydney harbour. The furnace oil floated across the harbour to the plaintiffs' wharf where welding was taking place. The plaintiffs had sought scientific advice as to the likelihood of the oil igniting during their welding operations and they were assured that there was no danger of the oil igniting. So they resumed their welding. Two days later, however, the oil did in fact ignite and the plaintiffs' wharf and the ships on which the plaintiffs were working were damaged in the blaze. The plaintiffs sought to recover from the defendants in respect of their losses. The Privy Council held that the defendants were not liable for the destruction of the wharf because they could not have foreseen the risk of damage by fire. The expert opinion of that time was that it was impossible to set furnace oil alight while it was on water. Therefore the defendants could not have foreseen that the oil which they negligently discharged was likely to go on fire. It should be noted, however, that the defendants could have foreseen the risk of damage to the property of the plaintiffs. They could have foreseen that the furnace oil would cause damage to the plaintiffs' wharf through pollution. But the Privy Council held that damage by fire was different in kind from damage by pollution and that therefore the damage which occurred was not reasonably foreseeable. The vital factor emphasised by the Privy Council was that the kind of damage must be reasonably foreseeable, although neither the extent of the damage nor the precise manner of its occurrence need be reasonably foreseeable.

The essential difference between the test laid down in *The Wagon Mound (No 1)* and the test laid down in *Polemis* is said to be that *Polemis* only requires that the damage be a direct consequence of the defendant's negligence, whereas under *Wagon Mound* the kind of damage must have been a reasonably foreseeable consequence. But how does 'foreseeability' differ from 'directness'? In *The Wagon Mound* Lord Simonds said that it was the foresight of the reasonable man which alone can determine responsibility. However, as was the case with directness in *Polemis*, there does not appear to be any definition of exactly what constitutes reasonable foresight and how it differs from directness. In *The Wagon Mound* the Privy Council did say that a reasonably foreseeable risk was a real risk and was one which would occur to the mind of the reasonable man. It did not, however, extend to a risk which the reasonable man would dismiss as being far-fetched. Nevertheless it is a noticeable feature of the case that there was no extended analysis of what constitutes reasonable foresight.

It will be remembered that in discussing *Polemis* we noted that there was a three-fold division of the kind of damage employed; damage to property, damage to the person and economic damage. We noted that under the rule in *Polemis* it was sufficient that damage to the plaintiff's person or property be foreseeable and that these interests were not sub-divided. We shall examine the categories of damage to the person and damage to property to see how, if at all, the standard adopted in *The Wagon Mound (No 1)* differs from the standard adopted in *Polemis*.

11.4 Damage to the person

A strong argument can be made that the law does not divide up damage to the person as a category and that as long as damage to the person is foreseeable it does not matter that the consequences of the damage are unforeseeable. This can be seen in what has come to be known as the 'egg-shell skull' rule. In *Dulieu* v *White & Sons* [1901] 2 KB 669, 679 Kennedy J stated that 'if a man is negligently run over or injured in his body, it is no answer to the sufferer's claim for damages that he would have suffered less injury, or no injury at all, if he had not had an unusually thin skull or an unusually weak heart.'

The impact of the egg-shell skull rule can be demonstrated by reference to the case of *Smith* v *Leech, Brain & Co* [1962] 2 QB 405. Here the defendants failed to provide adequate protection for the plaintiff's husband as he was working with molten metal in their factory. Some of the molten metal splashed out of the tank at which he was working and burnt him on the lip. This burn induced cancer, which developed at the site of the burn. It was not known at the time of the accident that the plaintiff's husband had any form of pre-malignant cancer. The plaintiff's husband died from the cancer three years after the accident. He might never have developed the cancer had it not been for the burn. The defendants argued that they were not responsible for the death of the plaintiff's husband because his death was not a reasonably foreseeable consequence of their negligence. This argument was rejected by the court. It was held that a tortfeasor must take his victim as he finds him. Lord Parker CJ stated that the test was not whether the defendants could have foreseen that the burn would induce cancer which in its turn would kill the plaintiff's husband, but whether the defendants could have reasonably foreseen that the plaintiff's husband would be burnt. The answer to this question was 'yes' and so the defendants were liable.

Three further cases illustrate the operation of the egg-shell skull rule. The first is the case of *Bradford* v *Robinson Rentals* [1967] 1 WLR 337. The plaintiff was required to drive a van for his employers from Bedford to Exeter on one exceptionally cold day in winter. There was no heater in the van and the plaintiff was held up on his journey on several occasions on account of the weather. As a result of the journey the plaintiff suffered frostbite, which was virtually unknown in Britain. It was held that the defendants were liable for the frostbite suffered by the plaintiff. It did not matter whether or not the plaintiff was abnormally susceptible to frostbite because the defendant had to take his victim as he found him.

The second case which illustrates the operation of the egg-shell skull rule is *Robinson* v *Post Office* [1974] 1 WLR 1176. Here the plaintiff, who was employed by the Post Office, fell down a ladder in the course of his employment. The cause of his fall was some oil which had been left on one of the steps. As a result of the fall the plaintiff cut his leg and when he visited the doctor some eight hours later he was given an anti-tetanus injection. The doctor did not test for any allergy to such an injection but, even if he had, there would have been no indication of any allergy. As a consequence of the injection the plaintiff contracted encephalitis, which is an inflammation of the brain. The defendants argued that they were only liable for the injury to the plaintiff's shin and not for the encephalitis. This argument was rejected by the court on the ground that the defendant must take his victim as he finds him and that the need for an anti-tetanus injection was a reasonably foreseeable consequence of the plaintiff's fall. Professor Atiyah (*Accidents, Compensation and the Law* (4th ed) p115) has used this case in an effort to demonstrate how 'generous' the law of tort is prepared to be to tort victims. He argues that a case such as *Robinson* is 'in a sense, a bridgehead between liability for fault and strict liability. While initial negligence must be proved, the plaintiff recovers damages for what most people would regard as nothing but an accident.'

The third, and most important, case is the decision of the House of Lords in *Hughes* v *Lord Advocate* [1963] AC 837. Some employees of the Post Office left a manhole in Edinburgh uncovered, with only an erected tent and some paraffin lamps surrounding the manhole. While the employees were away on their tea-break, the plaintiff, a ten year old boy, climbed down the manhole. He took one of the paraffin lamps with him. When he was climbing back up out of the manhole, the paraffin lamp fell back into the hole. Due to an extremely rare combination of circumstances, there was a violent explosion in which the plaintiff was badly burned. He brought an action against the defendants in respect of the injuries which he had suffered. The defendants disputed liability on the ground that the explosion was too remote to be foreseen by them, so they argued that they were not liable for the injuries suffered by the plaintiff as a result of the explosion. This argument was rejected by the House of Lords on the ground that as long as injury by burning was foreseeable it did not matter that the method by which the burning occurred was unforeseeable. Lord Reid stated that:

> 'A defender is liable, although the damage may be a good deal greater in extent than was foreseeable. He can only escape liability if the damage can be regarded as differing in kind from what was foreseeable.'

So the mere fact that the damage is greater in extent than could have been foreseen will not act as a defence. It must be shown that the damage which occurred was of a different kind to the damage which was foreseeable. In *Hughes* it was held that damage caused by the explosion was not different in kind from the damage which was foreseeable, as it was foreseeable that a child might be burned by one of the paraffin lamps.

These cases suggest that a broad approach is taken by the law to the issue of injury to the person and that as long as injury to the plaintiff is foreseeable it does not matter that the extent or precise manner by which the injury was inflicted is unforeseeable. Such a position is consistent with the aim of tort law which is to protect a plaintiff's interest in his personal safety and to uphold the principle of full compensation for tort victims. But there are two cases which cast doubt on the proposition that the mere fact that injury to the plaintiff is foreseeable is sufficient to enable the plaintiff to recover for his injuries.

The first case is *Doughty* v *Turner Manufacturing Co* [1964] 1 QB 518. The plaintiff was standing close to a cauldron of molten metal when an employee of the defendants carelessly let an asbestos cement cover fall into the molten metal. The sudden increase in temperature caused chemical changes in the asbestos and a few minutes later it caused an explosion in which the plaintiff was very badly burned. The possibility of an explosion occurring in this way was unknown at the time of the accident. The Court of Appeal held that, even if injury to the plaintiff had been foreseeable due to a splash from the molten metal, the plaintiff would not have been able to recover because injury by splashing was different in kind from injury by explosion. So here the Court of Appeal appears to be saying that the mere fact that injury to the plaintiff is foreseeable is not, of itself, sufficient to establish liability. The injury to the plaintiff must be foreseen with a greater degree of specificity. This approach appears to be much narrower than the approach adopted by the House of Lords in *Hughes* v *Lord Advocate* (above). However, it is submitted that these remarks of the Court of Appeal were obiter as the asbestos cover slid into the molten metal at such an oblique angle that injury to the plaintiff, even by a splash, was unforeseeable. So there was, in fact, no injury to the plaintiff foreseeable at all and therefore no liability to the plaintiff.

The second case which appears to take a much narrower approach to injury to the person is *Tremain* v *Pike* [1969] 1 WLR 1556. The plaintiff, who was an employee of the defendants, contracted a disease called Weil's disease while working for the defendants. The disease is contracted through coming into contact with rats' urine. Such a disease is very rare in human beings and there was no evidence that farmers knew that such a disease could be contracted by human beings coming into contact with rats. The plaintiff alleged that he contracted the disease through handling hay or washing in water which had been contaminated by rats' urine. It was held that the plaintiff could not recover damages in respect of the disease because the damage was too remote. Although it was reasonably foreseeable that the plaintiff would suffer injury as a result of rat bites or through contamination of his food it was not foreseeable that the plaintiff would contact Weil's disease. Weil's disease was an extremely rare disease and was held to be 'entirely different in kind' from other diseases which can be contracted through coming into contact with rats. This formulation requires that the particular injury to the plaintiff be foreseen rather than simply having to foresee that the plaintiff might be injured. However, this case must be considered doubtful in the light of the decision of the Court of Appeal in *H Parsons (Livestock) Ltd* v *Uttley Ingham & Co Ltd* [1978] QB 791. In that case the plaintiff's pigs contracted a rare disease as a result of being fed with mouldy nuts supplied by the defendants. The defendants were held to be in breach of contract in supplying the plaintiff with these mouldy nuts. It was held that as long as some risk of the pigs contracting some kind of disease was foreseeable, it did not matter that the particular disease which the pigs contracted was of an unforeseeably rare kind. Although this case was concerned with remoteness of damage in contract, Lord Denning stated that the issue of foreseeability was the same in contract and tort and so the case may be of persuasive value in this context and it is a good indicator of the fact that the approach adopted in *Tremain* is unlikely to be followed. It is submitted that the approach which was applied by the Court of Appeal in *Parsons* is more consistent with the aim of tort in protecting a plaintiff's interest in his personal security.

11.5 Damage to property

This category of damage is more difficult to deal with than damage to the person. It is clear that it is not sufficient that some damage to the plaintiff's property be foreseeable because in *The Wagon Mound (No 1)* damage to the plaintiff's property through fouling was foreseeable but this was not sufficient to ground liability. Thus the Privy Council clearly envisaged a narrower definition of foreseeability in cases of damage to property than the simple requirement that some damage to the plaintiff's property must be reasonably foreseeable. It was held that damage to property by fire was different in kind from damage to property by fouling or pollution. But how was it different?

In answering this question it is necessary to consider the decision of the Privy Council in *The Wagon Mound (No 2)* [1967] 1 AC 617. In this case the owners of the two ships which were being repaired at the wharf of the plaintiffs in *The Wagon Mound (No 1)* sued the owners of the 'Wagon Mound' in respect of the damage done to their ships. This time the defendants were held to be liable to the plaintiffs. The vital difference between the two *Wagon Mound* cases concerns a finding of fact at first instance. In *The Wagon Mound (No 2)* the trial judge found that there was a bare possibility of fire as a result of the oil spillage. The trial judge held that the likelihood of fire was so remote that the defendants were entitled to ignore it. The trial judge was, however, reversed by the Privy Council on this point and it was held that as long as the fire was foreseeable as a kind of damage by the defendants they were liable in respect of it, even though the possibility of a fire occurring was remote.

Dias and Markesinis conclude (*Tort Law* (2nd ed) p136) that 'in effect, therefore, *Wagon Mound (No 2)* reversed *Wagon Mound (No 1)*'. But it is submitted that the inconsistency is a factual one, turning on the different findings of fact at first instance relating to whether or not it is foreseeable that the oil would catch fire, and that there is no inconsistency in the legal principle which is applicable. Had the finding of fact at first instance in *The Wagon Mound (No 2)* been different it is certain that the Privy Council would have followed their previous decision in *The Wagon Mound (No 1)*.

Dias and Markesinis seek to support their argument that *The Wagon Mound (No 2)* has overruled *The Wagon Mound (No 1)* by reference to the case of *Vacwell Engineering* v *BDH Chemicals Ltd* [1971] 1 QB 88. The defendants manufactured a chemical which was liable to explode if it came into contact with water. They did not, however, give any warning of this fact. The plaintiffs purchased some of this chemical. One of the plaintiffs' scientists placed a consignment of the chemical in the sink and a violent explosion then occurred. The scientist was killed and extensive damage was done to the plaintiffs' property. The defendants were held to be liable to the plaintiffs for the damage which was done. Rees J held that it was foreseeable that some damage would be done to the plaintiffs' property and that it did not matter that the extent of the damage was not foreseeable. But it is submitted that this case does not take us very far because the kind of damage, that is damage by explosion, was foreseeable and it was merely the extent of the damage which was unforeseeable. This case does not stand as authority for the proposition that the mere fact that damage to the plaintiff's property is foreseeable is sufficient to render the defendant liable to the plaintiff (however for a broad approach to the issue of foreseeability in cases of damage to property see the decision of the Court of Appeal in *Muirhead* v *Industrial Tank Specialities Ltd* [1986] QB 507).

So it appears that kind of damage is divided into a narrower category than damage to property simpliciter. It is submitted that there are two major policy reasons behind this narrower approach in the case of damage to property. The first policy reason is that the plaintiff whose property is damaged is much more likely to be insured against such damage than is the person who is injured as the result of the defendant's negligence. So the plaintiff, in the case of property damage, is often in a better position to bear the loss. The second policy reason is that the measure of damage in a case of property damage can be far greater than in a case of personal injury, for example where, as in *The Wagon Mound*, the negligence leads to extensive damage to a ship. Where this is the case there is a reluctance on the part of the court to find the defendant liable for the whole of the loss, especially when, as we have already noted, the plaintiff is likely to be insured against such a loss.

So it is submitted that there are good reasons behind the courts' narrower approach to damage to property. The difficult question which remains is how we divide up property damage. We could say that the vital question is whether the events which have occurred are within the 'risk' which has been created by the defendant. This does not take us very far unless a definition is provided of the risk which was created by the defendant. For example what was the risk created by the defendants in the *Wagon Mound* cases? Another approach is to say that the distinction depends on the nature of the impact of the damage. This approach can explain *The Wagon Mound (No 1)* because it can be said that the damage was done by the impact of fire whereas the foreseeable impact was damage by fouling. But it is doubtful whether or not it is applicable to all cases and again much depends on how impact is defined.

It is submitted that the instability here is reflective of the insecure terminology which is used in this area. According to the test laid down in *The Wagon Mound (No 1)* the kind of damage must be foreseeable but neither the manner nor the extent need be foreseeable. This view was reiterated by the House of Lords in *Hughes* v *Lord Advocate*. However it is submitted that there is no clear-cut distinction between the kind of damage and the manner by which the damage occurs. For example it could be said that in *The Wagon Mound (No 1)* the kind of damage was damage to property and that the manner of damage was by fire rather than by fouling and so the defendants were liable. Equally it could be said that in *Hughes* the kind of damage was damage by fire and that damage by explosion was different in kind from damage by fire and so the defendants were not liable. What the courts do not tell us is how they go about defining the 'kind' of damage as opposed to the 'manner' in which the damage has occurred. Until we know how the courts set about that task the present test appears to be capable of almost infinite expansion or contraction as the courts enjoy considerable discretion in deciding what is the kind of damage. However it is submitted that the courts are correct in taking a narrower approach in the case of damage to property because tort law is generally less assiduous of interests in property than it is in a person's interest in his personal security and because of the availability of insurance in cases of damage to property.

11.6 *Polemis* and *Wagon Mound* contrasted

The traditional explanation of the difference between *Polemis* and *Wagon Mound* is that the former only requires that the damage be a direct result of the defendant's negligence whereas the latter requires that the damage be a reasonably foreseeable consequence of the defendant's negligence. The analysis offered here suggests that the traditional explanation is not entirely accurate. The real difference between the two can be best illustrated by reference to the following diagrams.

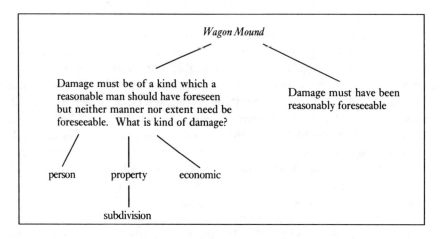

It can be seen from the diagrams that the real difference between the two lies on the bottom line of each diagram and not in the directness/reasonable foreseeability distinction. There does not appear to be any difference between the two rules in relation to damage to the person. The difference appears to lie in the rules applicable to damage to property because *Wagon Mound* adopts a narrower approach than the one which was adopted in *Polemis* (see 11.5).

11.7 Cases where the reasonable foresight test does not apply

There are a number of situations where the reasonable foresight test does not apply. The test does not apply where the defendant intended to inflict harm upon the plaintiff. In *Quinn* v *Leatham* [1901] AC 495 Lord Lindley stated that 'the intention to injure the plaintiff ... disposes of any question of remoteness of damage' (see too *Doyle* v *Olby (Ironmongers) Ltd* [1969] 2 QB 158).

Similarly it appears, although the position is not absolutely clear, that the reasonable foresight test does not apply in cases of strict liability under the rule in *Rylands* v *Fletcher*. The reasonable foresight test also does not apply in cases of breach of statutory duty because, since by virtue of the nature of the action the Act must have been passed for the benefit of the plaintiff, it is difficult to conceive of his loss being too remote.

11.8 Intervening acts (novus actus interveniens)

Novus actus interveniens simply means that an act or event has intervened to break the chain of causation which was set in motion by the defendant's negligence. It is at this stage that the close link between the rules relating to remoteness and the rules relating to causation becomes apparent. Some commentators include novus actus interveniens within the section of their book on causation; others include it in the section on remoteness of damage. We are considering novus actus interveniens at this stage because, having considered the rules relating to both causation and remoteness, we are now in a position to assess whether these rules are properly part of the rules relating to remoteness of damage or whether they are part of the rules relating to causation. The argument that will be put forward at the end of this section will be that they are best regarded as part of the rules relating to causation. The cases on novus actus interveniens can be split into the following three categories.

Intervening act of the plaintiff

The defendant will not be liable where the conduct of the plaintiff has amounted to a novus actus interveniens. The plaintiff's conduct may amount to a novus actus interveniens when his conduct has been so careless that his injury can no longer be attributed to the negligence of the defendant. But it is not every act of carelessness on the part of the plaintiff which amounts to a novus actus interveniens. Sometimes it is held to be simply contributory negligence on the part of the plaintiff, which has the effect of reducing the damages payable to the plaintiff, rather than an event which completely breaks the link between the defendant's negligence and the damage to the plaintiff. The distinction between these two types of case is illustrated by reference to the following two cases.

The first case is the decision of the House of Lords in *McKew* v *Holland & Hannen & Cubitts (Scotland) Ltd* [1969] 3 All ER 1621. The pursuer was injured as a result of the negligence of the defenders. His injury was only a slight one but it caused him occasionally to lose control of his left leg. Despite this weakness in his left leg the pursuer went down a steep flight of stairs which had no handrail. On his way down the stairs his left leg gave way and he fell and broke his ankle. It was held that the pursuer's act of going down a steep flight of stairs which had no handrail was unreasonable and that its effect was to break the chain of causation. So the defenders were not liable in damages for the injury caused by the plaintiff falling down the stairs. Lord Reid stated that 'if the injured man acts unreasonably he cannot hold the defender liable for injury caused by his own unreasonable conduct.'

On the other hand a different conclusion was reached in the case of *Wieland* v *Cyril Lord Carpets* [1969] 3 All ER 1006. The plaintiff suffered injury as a result of the negligence of the defendants. As a consequence of the injury a surgical collar was fitted to her neck, which restricted her ability to move her head, and she was unable to use her bi-focal spectacles with her customary skill. While in this condition the plaintiff fell down a flight of stairs. It was held by Eveleigh J that the defendants were liable for the injury which the plaintiff sustained when she fell down the stairs. Eveleigh J said that this was not a case where the plaintiff had been unreasonable in continuing to wear bi-focals. This was a case where the plaintiff had been left, as a result of the accident, unable to cope with the vicissitudes of life and the defendants were liable for the further injury which she received while in this condition.

The distinction between *McKew* and *Wieland* lies in the fact that the conduct of the pursuer in *McKew* was unreasonable, whereas the conduct of the plaintiff in *Wieland* was held to be reasonable. It is not altogether clear why *McKew* was not treated as a contributory negligence case. It seems that the pursuer's conduct was held to be so unreasonable that it was more than being contributorily negligent and that it broke the chain of causation. It is largely a matter of conjecture as to when a plaintiff's conduct will be held to transcend the boundaries of contributory negligence and constitute a novus actus interveniens.

Intervening act of nature

If the damage suffered by the plaintiff is the result of an act of nature which is independent of the negligence of the defendant, the defendant is not liable. The operation of this rule can be demonstrated by reference to the decision of the House of Lords in *Carslogie Steamship Co* v *Royal Norwegian Government* [1952] AC 292. The plaintiffs' ship was damaged in a collision caused by the negligence of the defendants. Temporary repairs were done to the ship which restored her to a seaworthy condition. She then set out on a voyage to America. She would not have made this trip had it not been for the negligence of the defendants. During the voyage the ship suffered extensive damage in a storm. The plaintiffs sought to recover, inter alia, the cost of repairing the damage done by the storm. It was held that the defendants were not liable for the cost of the repairs because, although the ship would not have been caught in the storm but for the negligence of the defendants, this 'was not in any sense a consequence of the collision, and must be treated as a supervening event occurring in the course of a normal voyage'. It should be noted that this was not a case where the negligence of the defendants left the ship unseaworthy. Had this been the case then different principles would have come into play.

Intervening act of a third party

If it is the act of a third party which is the true cause of the damage to the plaintiff then the general rule is that the defendant is not liable to the plaintiff. This is, in many ways, one of the most interesting areas of the law of tort, partly because there are a number of different conceptual devices, such as the existence of a duty of care, causation and remoteness, which can all be used in an attempt to resolve these problems.

A case which illustrates the problems which can arise here is *The Oropesa* [1943] P 32. Two ships were in a collision as a result of the negligent navigation of the defendants' ship, the 'Oropesa'. The captain of the other ship involved in the collision, the 'Manchester Regiment', in an effort to save his ship, set out in rough seas in a lifeboat with 16 of his crew. The lifeboat overturned in the rough seas and some of the crew were drowned. It was held that the defendants were liable for the deaths of the members of the crew and that the captain's decision to take out the lifeboat was a reasonable action taken in an attempt to save the ship and so did not break the chain of causation. Lord Wright said that:

'To break the chain of causation it must be shown that there is something which I will call ultroneous, something unwarrantable, a new cause which disturbs the sequence of events, something which can be described as either unreasonable or extraneous or extrinsic.'

So the defendant remains liable where the act of the third party is not truly independent of the defendant's negligence, as was the case in *The Oropesa*. The defendant will also remain liable where the act of the third party was an involuntary one. Thus in *Scott* v *Shepherd* (1733) 2 Wm Bl 892 the defendant threw a lighted squib into a market place. The stall holders, to avoid injury, threw the squib from stall to stall until eventually it exploded, blinding the plaintiff. It was held that the defendant was liable and that the actions of the stall holders in ridding themselves of the squib did not break the chain of causation because their actions were instinctive in an effort to save themselves from injury. It should finally be noted in this context that the defendant remains liable where he intentionally procures the third party to do the intervening act.

Difficulty has also arisen in relation to the negligent intervention of third parties. The difficulties which arise here can be seen by contrasting the following two cases. In *Knightley* v *Johns* [1982] 1 WLR 349 the defendant's negligent driving caused an accident which had the effect of blocking a busy tunnel. The second defendant, a police officer, forgot to seal off the tunnel and, in breach of police standing orders, sent the plaintiff, a police motor cyclist, back into the tunnel against the flow of traffic. While travelling through the tunnel the plaintiff was injured when he was involved in a collision with another driver. It was held that the second defendant was negligent in not closing the tunnel when the initial accident occurred and so the first defendant was not liable for the injuries sustained by the plaintiff. The court held that 'negligent conduct is more likely to break the chain of causation than conduct which is not' and that there were so many errors and 'departures from the common sense procedure' that the chain of causation was broken.

On the other hand a different result was reached in the case of *Rouse* v *Squires* [1973] QB 889. The first defendant, through his negligent driving, caused an accident, in which his lorry jack-knifed across the road. A few minutes later the second defendant negligently collided with the vehicles involved in the first accident and killed the plaintiff. It was held that the first defendant's negligence was an operative cause of the plaintiff's death and so he was held to be 25 per cent responsible for the plaintiff's death. Here the second accident was a natural and probable consequence of the first accident and was foreseeable, therefore it did not amount to a break in the chain of causation.

Where the intervention of the third party takes the form of a reckless act, then it is more likely to break the chain of causation. That this is so can be demonstrated by reference to the case of *Wright* v *Lodge and Shepherd* [1993] 4 All ER 299. The second defendant's car broke down in the nearside lane of an unlit dual carriageway one foggy night. While she was attempting to start the car a lorry driven by the first defendant crashed into the back of her car and seriously injured, one of the plaintiffs who was sitting in the back of the car. The lorry then veered out of control across the central reservation and came to rest on its side on the other carriageway, where it was struck by three cars and a lorry. The driver of one of the cars was killed and another was injured, and the latter and the personal representatives of the former brought a claim in damages against the defendants. The trial judge found that the first defendant was driving recklessly and was liable to the plaintiffs. He ordered that the second defendant pay a contribution of 10 per cent in relation to the claim by the passenger in her car but dismissed the contribution claims in relation to the claims of the other plaintiffs. The first defendant appealed to the Court of Appeal, arguing that the second defendant should be ordered to pay a 10 per cent contribution in respect of the other claims. The Court of Appeal dismissed his appeal. The sole cause of the lorry being on the other side of the carriageway was the reckless driving of the first defendant, for which the second defendant could not be responsible. The court held, relying in part upon the judgment of Cairns LJ in *Rouse* v *Squires*, that the trial judge was entitled to distinguish between the consequences of deliberate or reckless driving which causes the obstruction into which other vehicles subsequently collide and the consequences which would have occurred even as a result of negligent driving. The former does break the chain of causation, while the latter does not.

The most difficult issue of all arises where the intervention of the third party takes the form of a wilful wrong towards the plaintiff. We have already considered these cases in chapter 6 where we noted that the general principle is that the defendant is not liable to the plaintiff for the loss wilfully inflicted upon the plaintiff by a third party over whom the defendant has no control. Reference should be made to the discussion of these cases at 6.8 as we shall not go over the same ground here but will confine ourselves to the comments made by the judiciary in these cases on the subject of novus actus interveniens.

The starting point is the judgment of Lord Reid in *Home Office* v *Dorset Yacht Co Ltd* [1970] AC 1004 when he said that:

'Where human action forms one of the links between the original wrongdoing and the loss suffered by the plaintiff, that action must at least have been something very likely to occur if it is not to be regarded as a novus actus interveniens.'

Thus Lord Reid clearly envisaged that a defendant would only be liable for the wilful wrong of a third party in restricted circumstances and that, in the vast majority of cases, the intervention of the third party would break the chain of causation.

However, as we noted in chapter 6.8 when discussing the case of *Smith* v *Littlewoods Organisation Ltd* [1987] AC 241, the courts have recently preferred to resolve these cases on the ground that no duty of care exists rather than on the ground of a break in the chain of causation. Nevertheless some interesting comments have been made about remoteness and causation in this context. In *Lamb* v *Camden London Borough Council* [1981] QB 625 Lord Denning said that:

'the truth is that all these three, duty, remoteness and causation, are all devices by which the courts limit the range of liability for negligence and nuisance ... All these devices are useful in their way. But ultimately it is a question of policy for the judges to decide.'

While one may disagree with Lord Denning's heavy reliance upon policy, it is difficult to refute his argument relating to the similarities of these doctrines. Indeed in *P Perl (Exporters) Ltd* v *Camden London Borough Council* [1984] QB 342 Oliver LJ stated that:

'I think that the question of the existence of a duty and that of whether the damage brought about by the act of a third party is too remote are simply two facets of the same problem; for if there be a duty to take reasonable care to prevent damage being caused by a third party then I find it difficult to see how damage caused by the third party consequent on the failure to take such care can be too remote a consequence of the breach of duty.'

As has been pointed out elsewhere (see Jones (1984) 47 MLR 223), the problem really lies in 'the overworked concept of reasonable foreseeability', which can come into the duty issue, remoteness and causation.

So then we have a number of different doctrines competing for a role to play in resolving these problems. In relation to the wilful intervention of third parties the courts have chosen the duty issue as their preferred method of solution. But which doctrine lies at the root of novus actus interveniens? We could say that it is remoteness because where the intervening act is foreseeable it generally will not break the chain of causation and so we are really concerned here with events which are not reasonably foreseeable and therefore too remote. The solution advocated here is, however, to treat novus actus interveniens as part of the rules relating to causation on the ground that, while there are similarities with the rules relating to remoteness, 'it ... seems sensible to maintain a distinction between cases of multiple cause, where the question is which cause is to be treated as having legal significance, and cases where on any view the defendant's negligence was the cause of the harm, but it is thought to be unfair to hold him responsible because it occurred in some unusual or bizarre fashion' (Jones *Textbook on Torts* (3rd ed) p143).

12

Contributory Negligence

12.1 Introduction

12.2 The position at common law

12.3 The 1945 Act – the general rule

12.4 Fault

12.5 The standard of care

12.6 Children

12.7 Workmen

12.8 Rescuers

12.9 Emergencies

12.10 Causation

12.11 Apportionment

12.1 Introduction

Where the damage which the plaintiff has suffered has been caused partly by his own negligence and partly by the negligence of the defendant then the damages which the plaintiff can recover from the defendant may well be reduced because of the plaintiff's contributory negligence. The damages payable to the plaintiff may fall to be reduced under the Law Reform (Contributory Negligence) Act 1945. This Act was introduced to reverse the rule at common law which was that contributory negligence was a complete defence which precluded the plaintiff from recovering anything. Before examining the provisions of the 1945 Act, it is necessary to give a brief explanation of the common law rules which prevailed before the enactment of the 1945 Act.

12.2 The position at common law

As has been noted, the general rule at common law was that if the plaintiff was responsible, whether in whole or in part, for the injury which he sustained his claim against the defendant failed and he recovered nothing on the ground that he had been guilty of contributory negligence. The case which is generally cited as illustrative of the common law rule is *Butterfield* v *Forrester* (1809) 11 East 60. The defendant, who was repairing his house, wrongfully obstructed the highway by leaving a pole lying across the road. The plaintiff was injured when he collided with the pole as he was riding along the road. The defendant had, undoubtedly, been negligent in leaving the pole lying across the road but the plaintiff was held to be unable to recover from the defendant because the pole was visible at a distance of 100 yards but the plaintiff had not seen it as he was riding his horse so violently. Had he been riding with ordinary care he might have seen the pole and avoided the accident. He had therefore been guilty of contributory negligence and was unable to recover.

Such a rule might be thought to work fairly where both parties were equally to blame for the damage which occurred. In *Butterfield* Lord Ellenborough CJ said that 'one person being at fault will not dispense with another's using ordinary care'. But even if this argument is accepted, it was clear that the rule was capable of great injustice where the negligence of the plaintiff was insignificant or slight in comparison with the negligence of the defendant. So it is hardly surprising that the courts were prepared to create exceptions to the general common law rule.

One such exception was known as the rule of last opportunity. According to this rule a plaintiff could recover from the defendant, notwithstanding his own negligence, if the defendant was the party who had the last opportunity to avoid the damage and he had not done so. This rule was applied in the case of *Davies* v *Mann* (1842) 10 M & W 546. The plaintiff fettered the forefeet of his donkey and negligently left it on the highway. The defendant, who was driving his wagon and horses faster than he should have done, collided with the donkey and the donkey was killed. It was held that the defendant was liable because, by driving his wagon and horses more carefully, he could have avoided the donkey and so he had the last opportunity to avoid the accident.

In pursuance of their policy of avoiding the hardships which would have been caused by the application of the general common law rule, the courts extended the rule of last opportunity to cases of 'constructive' last opportunity. In such a case the defendant was treated as having had the last opportunity and the plaintiff was able to recover in full from the defendant. This rule was applied by the Privy Council in the case of *British Columbia Electric Railway* v *Loach* [1916] 1 AC 719. The plaintiff was in a cart being driven over a railway level crossing when an oncoming electric car collided with the cart and killed the plaintiff. It was held that the driver of the cart was negligent in not seeing that the road was clear but that the defendants, who were responsible for the electric cars, were negligent on the ground that the car could have been stopped, thus avoiding the accident, if the brakes of the car had been in good repair. So the defendants were held liable. Although this rule mitigated some of the hardships imposed by the general common law rule, it led to complicated arguments about causation and who had had the last opportunity to avoid the accident. More important, perhaps, was the fact that, at the end of the day, the court had to make a finding in favour of one or other party. Either the plaintiff recovered nothing or he recovered everything. The common law had set its face against apportionment of damages.

It was not until statute intervened in 1911 that the principle of apportionment was introduced into English law, but then only as regards collisions at sea. Section 1(1) of the Maritime Conventions Act 1911 provided that:

> 'Where, by the fault of two or more vessels, damage or loss is caused to one or more of those vessels, to their cargoes or freight, or to any property on board, the liability to make good the damage or loss shall be in proportion to the degree in which each vessel was at fault.'

In *Admiralty Commissioners* v *SS Volute* [1922] 1 AC 129 the House of Lords were critical of the state of the common law and noted that there were no such complications under admiralty law. Given these, and other criticisms, it was not surprising that Parliament intervened to overhaul the common law.

12.3 The 1945 Act – the general rule

The new general rule is now contained in section 1(1) of the Law Reform (Contributory Negligence) Act 1945 which provides that:

> 'Where any person suffers damage as the result partly of his own fault and partly of the fault of any other person or persons, a claim in respect of that damage shall not be defeated by reason of the fault of the person suffering the damage, but the damage recoverable in respect thereof shall be reduced to such extent as the court thinks just and equitable having regard to the claimant's share in the responsibility for the damage.'

This section is now the source of the general rule relating to contributory negligence. Two points should be noted about this section. The first point is that the section only applies to a person who suffers damage. 'Damage' is defined in s4(1) as including 'loss of life and personal injury'. It is generally agreed that the Act also applies to property damage, as such damage was covered by the common law. The second point to note is that a claim only arises out of damage caused partly by the 'fault' of the defendant and partly as the result of the 'fault' of the plaintiff. 'Fault' is defined in s4(1) as meaning 'negligence, breach of statutory duty or other act or omission which gives rise to liability in tort or would, apart from this Act, give rise to the defence of contributory negligence'. Thus the Act applies to nuisance and cases under the rule in *Rylands* v *Fletcher* as well as negligence actions. It remains unclear whether or not it applies to trespass to the person (see further 24.2). It is also unclear whether the Act applies to an action for breach of contract. But the Act does not apply to cases of intentional interference with chattels, nor does it apply to deceit.

In order to make out the defence of contributory negligence the defendant must prove two things. The first thing he must prove is that the plaintiff was at fault. This requirement contains two distinct elements which will be considered separately.

The first relates to the meaning of the word 'fault' (12.4) and the second relates to the standard of care required of the plaintiff (12.5–12.9). The second thing which the defendant must prove is that the plaintiff's negligence was a cause of the damage which he suffered (12.10).

12.4 Fault

We have already noted the definition of fault in s4(1) of the Act and that the effect of that definition is that the Act only applies to those torts committed by the defendant which come within the meaning of the word 'fault'. Here we are concerned with the meaning of the word 'fault' as it is applied to the plaintiff. Does it mean that the plaintiff must be held to owe a duty of care to the defendant? The answer to that question is 'no'. In *Nance* v *British Columbia Electric Railway Co Ltd* [1951] AC 601 Viscount Simon said:

> 'When contributory negligence is set up as a defence, its existence does not depend on any duty owed by the injured party to the party sued and all that is necessary ... is to prove to the satisfaction of the jury that the injured party did not in his own interest take reasonable care of himself and contributed, by this want of care, to his own injury.'

The fact that the plaintiff need not owe a duty of care to the defendant means that the plaintiff's fault may simply consist of failing to look after himself properly. Thus in *Davies* v *Swan Motor Co* [1949] 2 KB 291 the plaintiff's damages fell to be reduced on the ground of contributory negligence, even though the plaintiff owed no duty of care to the defendant. The plaintiff's husband was riding on the offside steps of a dust-cart, knowing of the dangers of such a practice. As the dust-cart was being overtaken by one of the defendants' buses a collision occurred and the plaintiff was killed. It was held that the driver of the bus, the driver of the dust-cart and the plaintiff were all negligent: the bus driver because he had overtaken on a bend; the driver of the dust-cart because he had turned across the road without signalling; and the plaintiff because of the dangerous manner in which he was riding on the dust-cart. It was held that the bus driver was guilty of negligence, but that the plaintiff was guilty of contributory negligence. The Court of Appeal affirmed that negligence in this context did not mean breach of the duty of care, but simply that the plaintiff had been careless.

Where it cannot be shown that the plaintiff was at fault, the plaintiff is entitled to recover in full. Thus in *Tremayne* v *Hill* [1987] RTR 131 the plaintiff was able to recover in full because the defendant was unable to show that the plaintiff had been at fault. The plaintiff was held to be under no duty to keep a look-out for cars when the traffic lights were at red and the defendant had gone through the lights when they were at red and collided with the plaintiff. It was held that a pedestrian was not under a duty either to keep a look-out for traffic going through red lights nor was he under a duty to use a pedestrian-controlled crossing. Although the Court of

Appeal spoke of the pedestrian not being 'under a duty' it is submitted that they simply meant he was not careless and it should not be read as referring to the duty of care in the *Donoghue* sense.

12.5 The standard of care

In *Jones* v *Livox Quarries Ltd* [1952] 2 QB 608 Lord Denning said that:

> 'A person is guilty of contributory negligence if he ought reasonably to have foreseen that, if he did not act as a reasonable, prudent man, he might be hurt himself; and in his reckonings he must take into account the possibility of others being careless.'

It can be seen from this statement that, in considering whether the plaintiff has acted with reasonable care, the courts take account of similar factors to those which they take account of when they consider whether the defendant has acted with reasonable care. Like the standard of care in establishing that the defendant was negligent the test for want of care by the plaintiff is an objective one and one which varies depending upon the facts of the case. It may, however, be the case that the courts expect less from a plaintiff in complying with the standard of reasonable care than they do of defendants.

The standard of care may be adjusted to meet changing conditions as in the case of seat-belts. In *Froom* v *Butcher* [1975] 3 WLR 379 the plaintiff's car was in collision with the defendant's car. The collision was caused by the negligence of the defendant. The plaintiff was not wearing a seat-belt at the time of the accident because he did not like to do so and he had seen a number of accidents where the driver had been trapped in the car as the result of wearing a seat-belt. The plaintiff's injuries were worse than they would have been had he been wearing a seat-belt. The Court of Appeal held that the damages which should be awarded to the plaintiff should be reduced by 20 per cent on account of the contributory negligence of the plaintiff. The court affirmed that the standard of care demanded of a plaintiff was to be judged objectively and they held that a prudent man would always wear a seat-belt unless there were exceptional circumstances, for example where the person concerned was a pregnant woman. This case should now be read in the light of s33A of the Road Traffic Act 1972 which made the wearing of seat-belts mandatory (see also the Motor Vehicle (Wearing of Seat Belt) Regulations 1982 (SI 1982 No 1203)).

There are, however, four situations where particular problems arise in establishing the requisite standard of care. We shall now discuss these four situations.

12.6 Children

It is not entirely clear whether or not there is an age below which a child cannot be held to be guilty of contributory negligence. The standard textbooks, such as *Winfield and Jolowicz*, state that 'while it is not possible to specify an age below which, as a matter of law, a child cannot be guilty, of contributory negligence, age of the child is a circumstance which must be considered in deciding whether it has been guilty of contributory negligence' (*Winfield and Jolowicz on Torts* (13th ed) p162). This view was accepted in Scotland in the case of *McKinnell* v *White* 1971 SLT (Notes) 61 where a child of five years of age was held to have been guilty of contributory negligence.

But in the case of *Gough* v *Thorne* [1966] 1 WLR 1387 Lord Denning cast doubt on whether such a proposition represents the current state of English law. Three children, aged 17, 13 1/2 and 10, crossed a road in front of a lorry. The lorry driver indicated to the children that they could cross the road and he put out his hand to warn the traffic which was coming up the road. But a 'bubble' car, which came up too fast from behind, overtook the lorry and seriously injured the 13 1/2 year old plaintiff. It was held that the child was not guilty of contributory negligence. She had been beckoned to cross the road by the lorry driver and she had done so. She had done everything which could have been expected of a child of her age. During the course of his judgment Lord Denning said that:

> 'A very young child cannot be guilty of contributory negligence. An older child may be; but it depends on the circumstances. A judge should only find a child guilty of contributory negligence if he or she is of such an age as reasonably to be expected to take precautions for his or her own safety: and then he or she is only to be found guilty if blame should be attached to him or her.'

Hence in *Adams* v *Southern Electricity Board* (1993) The Times 21 October the Court of Appeal found an intelligent 15-year-old boy to be guilty of contributory negligence where he knew that what he did was wrong and dangerous, and in *Morales* v *Eccleston* [1991] RTR 151 an 11-year-old boy was held to be guilty of contributory negligence.

Another example of the more benevolent English approach is the case of *Yachuk* v *Oliver Blais Co Ltd* [1949] AC 386. A nine-year-old boy purchased from the defendants a quantity of petrol, falsely stating that his mother wanted the petrol for her car. In fact he used the petrol to play with and as a result of doing so he was badly burned. It was held that the defendants were negligent in supplying petrol to such a young child. But the boy was not guilty of contributory negligence because he neither knew, nor could be expected to know, of the dangers of petrol. So while it may, nominally, be the case that there is no age below which a child cannot be guilty of contributory negligence, in practice it is extremely difficult and, in cases involving very young children, almost impossible, to show that the child was guilty of contributory negligence.

It should also be noted that a child will not be 'identified' with the negligence of his parent or guardian. In *Oliver* v *Birmingham and Midland Omnibus Co* [1933] 1 KB 35 the plaintiff, a four-year-old boy, was injured when crossing the road with his grandfather. A bus belonging to the defendants approached them without warning. The grandfather was so startled that he let go of the plaintiff's hand. The boy ran onto the road and was struck and injured by the defendants' bus. It was held that the defendants were liable to the plaintiff in negligence and that the plaintiff was not prevented from recovering from the defendants on account of the negligence of his grandfather.

12.7 Workmen

Where a workman sues his employer for breach of statutory duty, or possibly in negligence, the court is more reluctant to find that the employee has been guilty of contributory negligence. The reason for this is that statutes, such as the Factories Acts, have been introduced for the protection of employees and the courts have held that such protection should not be undermined by a finding that the employee cannot recover damages, or that his damages should be reduced, on the ground that he was guilty of contributory negligence.

In considering whether the workman has been guilty of contributory negligence the court will have regard to the fact that the workman's sense of danger has been dulled by factors such as repetition, noise, fatigue and confusion. In *Caswell* v *Powell Duffryn Associated Collieries Ltd* [1940] AC 152 Lord Wright stated that:

'What is all important is to adapt the standard of negligence to the facts, and to give due regard to the actual conditions under which men work in a factory or mine, to the long hours and the fatigue, to the slackening of attention which naturally comes from constant repetition of the same operation, to the noise and confusion in which the man works, to his pre-occupation in what he is actually doing at the cost perhaps of some inattention to his own safety.'

It is unclear whether this leniency also applies to cases where the employer is sued for negligence and not for breach of statutory duty. The cases are heavily influenced by the desire to avoid the undermining of the statutory regulations and it is not clear that it will be extended to cases where the courts are not influenced by the statutory background.

It should not be thought that this lenient approach means that a workman cannot be guilty of contributory negligence. In *Jayes* v *IMI (Kynoch) Ltd* [1985] ICR 155 the plaintiff, who was a very experienced worker, was cleaning a machine of which the safety guard had been removed when his hand was pulled into the moving machinery and he lost the tip of his finger. He claimed that the defendants were in breach of their absolute statutory duty under s14 of the Factories Act 1961. But he admitted that what he had done was very foolish and he was held to have been guilty of 100 per cent contributory negligence (although it should be noted that a reduction of 100 per cent could not now be supported according to the Court of Appeal in *Pitts* v *Hunt* [1991] 1 QB 24, see 12.11). Similarly, where the workman fails to comply with the statutory regulations placed upon him, he may be found to be guilty of contributory negligence. In *Bux* v *Slough Metals Ltd* [1974] 1 All ER 262 the plaintiff, who was a die-caster employed in the defendants' iron foundry, was given a pair of goggles which he was told to wear at work. The plaintiff refused to wear the goggles because he found that they misted up when in use. He did, however, ask if any better goggles were available, but he got no reply. The plaintiff sued the defendants after molten metal splashed up into his eyes, causing him injury. It was held that the defendants were liable in negligence for failing to ensure that the plaintiff wore the goggles, but that the plaintiff was also guilty of contributory negligence in failing to comply with the regulations requiring him to make 'full and proper use' of equipment provided for his protection.

12.8 Rescuers

In *Sayers* v *Harlow UDC* [1958] 1 WLR 623 it was established that damages can be reduced on the ground that a rescuer is guilty of contributory negligence if the rescuer is negligent in carrying out a rescue. The courts are reluctant, however, to hold that a rescuer has been guilty of contributory negligence. This reluctance can be seen in the case of *Harrison* v *British Railways Board* [1981] 3 All ER 679. The plaintiff, who was a guard on a train, was injured in attempting to pull a passenger onto a moving train. His instructions from his employers were that, in such a case, he was to pull on the brake rather than attempt to pull the passenger onto the train. If the guard had pulled on the brake he may not have been so severely injured or possibly he may not have been injured at all. The plaintiff was held to be guilty of contributory negligence and his damages were reduced by 20 per cent.

12.9 Emergencies

Where the plaintiff is placed in a position of imminent danger by the negligence of the defendant, the courts are more sympathetic towards the plaintiff who makes a wrong decision in the heat of the moment. This can be demonstrated by reference to the case of *Jones* v *Boyce* (1816) 1 Stark 493. The plaintiff was a passenger on top of the defendants' coach. The coupling ring of the coach broke and the coach was in imminent danger of overturning. Thinking that the coach was about to overturn and, in order to save himself, the plaintiff jumped from the top deck of the coach and broke his leg. In fact the coach did not overturn and, when the plaintiff sued the defendants in respect of his injuries, the defendants argued that he had been guilty of contributory negligence. Lord Ellenborough CJ directed the jury that the plaintiff was not guilty of contributory negligence if he selected the more perilous of the two alternatives with which he was confronted by the defendant's negligence, provided that the plaintiff had acted as a reasonable and prudent man would have done. The jury found for the plaintiff.

12.10 Causation

It is not necessary that the plaintiff's negligence contribute to the accident. What is essential is that the plaintiff's negligence must contribute to the damage which he has suffered. Thus in *Froom* v *Butcher* (above) the plaintiff's damages were reduced because his negligence, in not wearing a seat-belt, contributed to the damage which he suffered, even though his negligence in no way contributed to the accident. A plaintiff's damages may also fall to be reduced where a motorcyclist fails to wear a crash helmet (see *O'Connell* v *Jackson* [1972] 1 QB 270) or fails to fasten the chin strap of a crash helmet (*Capps* v *Miller* [1989] 2 All ER 333). Equally damages may fall to be reduced where a person accepts a lift in a car when he knows that the driver has consumed substantial quantities of alcohol (see *Owens* v *Brimmell* [1977] QB 859).

This principle can also be illustrated by reference to the case of *Jones* v *Livox Quarries Ltd* [1952] 2 QB 608. The plaintiff was riding on the towbar of a 'traxcavator' in breach of safety instructions which he had been given. The driver of the traxcavator was unaware of the presence of the plaintiff on the vehicle and he stopped suddenly so that he could change gear. A dumper truck, which was following behind the traxcavator, collided with the back of the traxcavator and injured the plaintiff. It was found that the plaintiff was guilty of contributory negligence and his damages were reduced by 20 per cent. It was held that the plaintiff's position on the vehicle was one of the causes of his damage. It had been argued that the plaintiff's negligence had not been the cause of damage to himself because it was only foreseeable that the plaintiff would suffer injury as the result of falling off the traxcavator and not from being run into from behind. This distinction was rejected by the court and it was held that the plaintiff's negligence had been a cause of the damage which he suffered. Lord Denning did, however, say that 'if the plaintiff, whilst he was riding on the towbar, had been hit in the eye by a shot from a negligent sportsman, I should have thought that the plaintiff's negligence would in no way be a cause of his injury'. In other words, Lord Denning is saying that the damage must not be too remote and that the plaintiff's negligence must have exposed him to the particular risk of the type of damage suffered.

The 1945 Act did not alter the rules for determining whether or not contributory negligence exists, nor did it deal with the issue of whether the plaintiff's negligence was so overwhelming as to be the sole effective cause of his loss. Some difficult questions relating to causation can still arise as was demonstrated by the case of *Stapley* v *Gypsum Mines Ltd* [1953] AC 663. The plaintiff's husband worked in the defendants' gypsum mine. He was told that he and another worker were to bring down a roof in the mine which was unsafe before they recommenced their normal work. After making unsuccessful attempts to bring down the roof the plaintiff's husband and his mate decided to give up and return to their normal work. The roof later collapsed and the plaintiff's husband was killed. In these circumstances the plaintiff brought an action against the defendants. The court had to decide whether the damage had been done solely as a result of the negligence of the plaintiff's husband or whether the negligence of his mate was also a cause of his death. In answering this question the House of Lords had to resort to the common law of causation, as the 1945 Act does not deal with the problem of causation, although, as Lord Porter noted, the 1945 Act does enable the court:

> '... to seek less strenuously to find some ground for holding the plaintiff free from blame or for reaching the conclusion that his negligence played no part in the ensuing accident in as much as owing to the change in the law the blame can now be apportioned equitably between the two parties.'

Approaching the issue of causation in a 'common sense manner' the House of Lords held that the other workman had been negligent in disobeying orders and that the plaintiff's husband had not been the sole cause of his own death. However they also held that her husband had been guilty of contributory negligence and her damages were reduced by 80 per cent.

It should also be noted in this context that a distinction must be drawn between contributory negligence and novus actus interveniens. The latter breaks the chain of causation with the result that the defendant ceases to be liable for the damage which occurs after the chain of causation is broken. The former is covered by the 1945 Act and the court has the power to apportion the damages under s1(1) of the Act (see further *McKew* v *Holland & Hannen & Cubitts* [1969] 3 All ER 1621, discussed in greater detail at 11.8).

12.11 Apportionment

Under s1(1) of the Act damages awarded to the plaintiff who has been contributorily negligent are to be reduced 'to such extent as the court thinks just and equitable having regard to the claimant's share in the responsibility for the damage'. The apportionment of damage is regarded by the courts as a matter of fact. In assessing what is 'just and equitable' the courts have regard to the extent to which the plaintiff's and the defendant's negligence was the cause of the damage which the plaintiff sustained, but the more important factor is the comparative blameworthiness or culpability of the parties. The Act presupposes that the person suffering the damage will recover at least some damages and so damages cannot be reduced by 100 per cent on the ground that the plaintiff was guilty of contributory negligence (*Pitts* v *Hunt* [1991] 1 QB 24).

Where there is more than one defendant the position should be considered separately between the plaintiff and each defendant. Thus, in *Fitzgerald* v *Lane* [1989] AC 328 the plaintiff and two defendants were held to be equally to blame for the plaintiff's injuries. As each party was equally at fault the House of Lords held that the plaintiff could only recover half of his damages from each defendant and so the plaintiff was entitled to half of the total award of damages, with each defendant being liable to make an equal contribution to the amount recoverable by the plaintiff (for analysis see Chandler and Holland [1989] LMCLQ 30).

Where the accident is a common one the court may produce guidelines to be used in apportioning damages. Thus in *Froom* v *Butcher* (above) it was suggested that the courts should proceed on the basis that, where the injuries could have been completely prevented by the wearing of a seat-belt, damages should be reduced by 25 per cent, but that, where the wearing of a seat-belt would simply have reduced the severity of the plaintiff's injuries, then damages should be reduced by 15 per cent. Such an approach has the merit of providing some certainty and consistency, but it has not been widely used by the courts (although in *Capps* v *Miller* [1989] 2 All ER 333 Croom-Johnson LJ stated that, 'ordinarily [these guidelines] should be adhered to because it is of the greatest importance that they should be generally kept for the sake of the swift conduct, and it may be settlement, of litigation.').

13

Volenti Non Fit Injuria

13.1 Introduction

13.2 The intentional infliction of harm

13.3 The negligent infliction of harm

13.4 Voluntariness

13.5 Agreement

13.6 Knowledge

13.7 Volenti and exclusion clauses

13.8 Volenti and the standard of care

13.1 Introduction

Volenti non fit injuria or volenti, as it is more usually called, is a complete defence to the plaintiff's action. It is a defence the scope of which and, indeed, the nature of which is the subject of some controversy. As we shall see it can be difficult to distinguish between volenti and contributory negligence and it is also difficult to ascertain the relationship between volenti and the standard of care. The defence is said to apply when the defendant can prove that the plaintiff knew of the risk of harm or injury and had voluntarily submitted to that risk.

It should be noted that volenti only comes into play where it has been demonstrated that the defendant has committed a tort. Volenti has a role to play in the case of both the intentional infliction of harm and the negligent infliction of harm. Salmond and Heuston (*The Law of Torts* (19th ed) p556) suggest that a distinction should be drawn between the role of consent in the intentional infliction of harm and the negligent infliction of harm. We shall adopt this suggestion and consider the intentional infliction of harm and the negligent infliction of harm separately.

13.2 The intentional infliction of harm

In relation to the intentional infliction of harm, consent negatives what would otherwise be a tort. Thus consent negatives what would otherwise be a trespass; whether that trespass be trespass to the person (chapter 24) or trespass to land (chapter 25). So the doctor who performs an operation after the plaintiff has signed a consent form consenting to the operation does not commit the tort of battery because the plaintiff has given him permission to carry out the operation.

13.3 The negligent infliction of harm

It is in relation to the negligent infliction of harm that the defence of volenti has given rise to the greatest difficulty. There are a number of conditions which must be made out for the defence to apply and we shall now give consideration to these conditions (13.4–13.6).

13.4 Voluntariness

The plaintiff must have voluntarily submitted to the risk of injury. This requirement was clearly articulated by Scott LJ in the case of *Bowater* v *Rowley Regis Corporation* [1944] KB 476 when he said that:

> 'A man cannot be said to be truly "willing" unless he is in a position to choose freely, and freedom of choice predicates, not only full knowledge of the circumstances on which the exercise of choice is conditioned, so that he may be able to choose wisely, but the absence from his mind of any feeling of constraint so that nothing shall interfere with the freedom of his will.'

This element was not always rigidly insisted upon in the nineteenth century when the defence of volenti was at its widest. In many cases concerning the employment relationship it was not recognised that the employee was under pressure from his employer and so was not simply free to refuse to accept a particular practice.

But a more relaxed and realistic approach was adopted by the House of Lords in the case of *Smith* v *Baker* [1891] AC 325. The plaintiff was employed by the defendants. He worked in a quarry, drilling in the rock face. While he did this a crane worked overhead and, as both he and his employers knew, there was a risk that a heavy stone would fall from the crane. The plaintiff was never warned as to when the crane would be operating. A stone fell from the crane and injured the plaintiff. It was held that, although the plaintiff knew of the risk of injury and incurred it as part of his job, the defence of volenti was not made out because the plaintiff was threatened with the loss of his job if he objected to the crane working overhead. So it could not be shown that the plaintiff had voluntarily consented to the risk of injury. This decision is a welcome one in so far as it recognises the industrial realities of the employment relationship.

Where, however, the employee is not under pressure at his work and he adopts a dangerous method of work which causes damage to himself, the courts are more willing to hold that the defence of volenti is applicable. This can be demonstrated by reference to the case of *Imperial Chemical Industries Ltd* v *Shatwell* [1965] AC 656. The plaintiff and his brother, James, were working as shotfirers in the defendants' quarry. Both were employees of the defendants. In breach of the instructions given to them by the defendants and in breach of certain statutory regulations, they decided to test some detonators without standing in a shelter which had been provided for them. While they were testing the detonators without using the shelter the plaintiff was injured. He sued the defendants on the ground that he claimed that they were vicariously liable for the negligence of his brother, James. It was held that the plaintiff and his brother were fully aware of the risk of injury and that they were volens as regards the injury because it had been caused by their conduct in deliberately not using the shelter when there was a risk of injury from the explosion.

Where the plaintiff attempts to rescue another, the courts have not accepted that the plaintiff has thereby voluntarily accepted the risk of injury. This principle can be traced back to the case of *Haynes* v *Harwood* [1935] 1 KB 146. The plaintiff, who was a policeman on duty, was injured attempting to prevent some horses, which had bolted, from injuring bystanders. The plaintiff sought to recover in respect of his injuries from the defendant, who was the owner of the horses and who had negligently left his horses unattended. It was held that the defendant could not rely on the defence of volenti because the plaintiff, as a policeman, was under a duty to try to stop the horses and therefore had not acted voluntarily.

The principle is not, however, confined to cases where the plaintiff's job is to try to prevent injury being inflicted on others. It applies to anyone who attempts to rescue another. Thus in *Chadwick* v *British Transport Commission* [1967] 1 WLR 912 the plaintiff suffered nervous shock as the result of leaving his home, which was near a railway line, to go to help in a rescue operation after a major railway accident. It was held that the defendants were liable for the injury suffered by the plaintiff because it was their negligence which had caused the accident and the plaintiff's injury was a reasonably foreseeable consequence of the defendants' negligence. The plaintiff was not volens. If it had been held that the plaintiff was volens it would, to a large extent, have undermined the rule that a duty of care is owed to a rescuer (on which see 8.2).

Where, however, there is no real danger, the plaintiff who attempts a rescue may be held to be volens in respect of any injury which he receives. Such was the case in *Cutler* v *United Dairies* [1933] 2 KB 297. The defendant, who was a milkman, carelessly left his horses unattended with the result that they bolted. The plaintiff was injured when he tried to stop the horses and the milk cart in a meadow. It was held that the horses were not a source of danger to anyone when they were in the meadow and so the plaintiff could not recover in respect of his injuries as he was held to be volens.

Finally, it is difficult to establish that a plaintiff was volens when, at the relevant time, he was of unsound mind. In *Kirkham* v *Chief Constable of Greater Manchester Police* [1990] 2 QB 283 the plaintiff's husband, who was known by the police to have suicidal tendencies, was taken into police custody. The police failed to inform the prison authorities of his suicidal tendencies and he subsequently committed suicide in the remand centre to which he had been sent. The plaintiff alleged that the defendants were negligent in failing to pass on to the prison authorities the information relating to her husband's suicidal tendencies. The defendants argued, inter alia, that the plaintiff's claim must fail because her husband was volenti. Lloyd LJ conceded that volenti could be invoked against a person of sound mind who committed suicide. But he held that, where the person who committed suicide was of unsound mind, it could not be said that he was volens because his judgment was impaired and he could not be said to have 'waived or abandoned any claim arising out of his suicide'. On the other hand, 'impairment' of mind which is induced by alcohol will not necessarily result in the conclusion that the plaintiff is not volens. In *Morris* v *Murray* [1991] 2 QB 6 the plaintiff was a passenger in an aeroplane which crashed because the pilot was drunk. The plaintiff was an active participant in the whole enterprise. He had been out drinking with the pilot, had driven him to the airport and assisted him in the preparations for the flight. The plaintiff brought a claim against the estate of the deceased pilot claiming damages for the personal injury which he suffered in the crash. An autopsy on the pilot showed that he had consumed the equivalent of 17 whiskies and the plaintiff had been drinking on a similar scale. One of the issues which was before the Court of Appeal was whether or not the plaintiff was volens. The court held that he was volens because he was not so drunk that he was incapable of appreciating the risks involved in the flight and this was evidenced by the fact that he had driven the car to the airport and had assisted in the preparations for the flight.

13.5 Agreement

It is clear that the defence is applicable where the plaintiff agrees with the defendant that he, the plaintiff, will accept the risk of injury. Where the parties expressly agree in advance that the defendant shall not be liable to the plaintiff for any future act of negligence which he commits it is clear that the defence of volenti is applicable. This is subject to the caveat that where the parties agree in advance that the defendant shall not be liable for his breach of duty then that agreement will probably amount to an exclusion clause which must then satisfy the provisions of the Unfair Contract Terms Act 1977 (see further 13.7). The courts are also prepared to concede that, in an appropriate case, the parties may have impliedly agreed that the defendant will not be liable to the plaintiff for future acts of negligence. But the courts are reluctant to spell out an implied agreement that the plaintiff will accept the risk of injury. This has been particularly evident in cases involving persons who accept a lift in a car from a driver whom they know to be incapable of driving, for example, through intoxication. In such cases the courts have not generally held that the person accepting the lift has impliedly agreed to waive his right to sue in respect of any act of negligence by the driver (see *Dann* v *Hamilton* [1939] 1 KB 509 (discussed further below) and *Nettleship* v *Weston* [1971] 2 QB 691 cf *Ashton* v *Turner* [1981] QB 137). Such an implied agreement was, however, held to exist on the facts of *ICI* v *Shatwell* (above). The two employees had expressly agreed that the dangerous act of testing the detonators be done without using the shelter and from this express agreement it was not difficult to imply an agreement that they accepted the risk of any injury resulting from this dangerous practice.

Although it is clear that the parties may agree expressly or impliedly to forego a claim in respect of a future act of negligence by the defendant, two further problems remain and it is to these problems that we now turn. The first problem relates to whether the defence of volenti can be made out when there is no agreement between the parties. The second problem concerns whether an agreement that the defendant will not be liable can validly be made between the parties after the negligent act has been committed.

The first problem concerns whether agreement is an essential element in the defence of volenti. Professor Williams has stated (*Joint Torts and Contributory Negligence* p308) that:

> 'To constitute a defence, there must have been an express or implied bargain between the parties whereby the plaintiff gave up his right of action for negligence.'

Support for such a view can be found in the judgment of Lord Denning in *Nettleship* v *Weston* [1971] 2 QB 691 when he said that:

> 'Nothing will suffice short of an agreement to waive any claim for negligence. The plaintiff must agree, expressly or impliedly, to waive any claim for any injury that may befall him due to the lack of reasonable care by the defendant.'

This view has not, however, been accepted in other cases. One such case is *Dann* v *Hamilton* [1939] 1 KB 509. The defendant, the plaintiff and two other people went out drinking and the defendant, who was the driver of the car, was rather drunk by the end of the evening. They all nevertheless went home in the defendant's car. One of the three passengers later got out of the car close to his home and he stated to the other two passengers that they had more pluck than he had in staying in the car with the defendant. The plaintiff replied 'You should be like me. If anything is going to happen, it will happen.' A few minutes later the defendant crashed the car. The defendant was killed and the plaintiff was injured. The plaintiff sued the defendant's estate in respect of the injuries which she suffered. It was held that the plaintiff could recover and that the defence of volenti did not apply in such a case. But Asquith J held that the type of case in which the plaintiff comes into a situation where the danger has already been created by the negligence of the defendant was the type of case to which the defence of volenti was applicable. It has also been pointed out (Jaffey [1985] CLJ 87, 92–5) that certain statutory provisons appear to assume that the defence can be made out by showing that the plaintiff encountered an already existing danger created by the defendant's negligence (see, for example, s2(5) of the Occupiers' Liability Act 1957 and s5(2) of the Animals Act 1971).

Although Asquith LJ accepted that volenti could apply to a case in which a plaintiff came into a situation in which the danger had already been created by the negligence of the defendant, his conclusion that, on the facts of the case, the plaintiff was not volenti has been subjected to considerable criticism. In defence of Asquith J it should be noted that contributory negligence was not pleaded as a defence in *Dann* (despite the suggestion by Asquith J that the pleadings should be amended to incorporate the defence) and so *Dann* does not prevent a defendant invoking contributory negligence in an analogous case. Nevertheless in relation to the volenti point, *Dann* has been subject both to judicial criticism and a narrow interpretation in recent years. The first case which we can note here is *Pitts v Hunt* [1991] 1 QB 24. The plaintiff was a pillion passenger on a motor cycle and the first defendant was the motor cyclist. The plaintiff knew that the first defendant did not have a driving licence and that he was uninsured. Immediately prior to the accident, both the plaintiff and the first defendant had been drinking and the plaintiff encouraged the first defendant to drive in a reckless manner by weaving in and out of the white lines in the centre of the road. While driving in this reckless manner the motor cycle was in collision with a car driven by the second defendant. The first defendant was killed and the plaintiff was seriously injured in the accident. It was held that the second defendant had not been negligent and so the plaintiff's claim against him was dismissed. At first instance and in the Court of Appeal it was held that the plaintiff's claim against the first defendant must also fail because at the time of the accident they were both involved in the commission of a criminal offence which was of sufficient gravity to bring the maxim ex turpi causa non oritur actio into play (see further 31.3). But at first instance ([1989] 3 WLR 795, 805–808) Judge Fallon QC also noted the criticisms which have been levelled against the decision of Asquith J in *Dann* and he stated that it 'has not been approved of universally', thereby suggesting that it may yet be open to re-examination in the appellate courts. However it was not necessary for him to engage in such a re-examination on the facts of *Pitts* because he was able to distinguish *Dann*. He held that volenti was established on the facts of this case because the first defendant was so obviously drunk that the case was distinguishable from *Dann*. However, on the facts of the case, he held that the first defendant could not invoke volenti successfully because s148(3) of the Road Traffic Act 1972 had the effect of precluding reliance upon volenti in such road accident cases. The Court of Appeal in agreeing with Judge Fallon QC was more circumspect. Although *Dann* was cited to them, they did not discuss it in their judgments. They simply stated (at p556) that, while the plaintiff had voluntarily accepted the risk of injury by taking part in such a foolhardy, risky and illegal activity, such a voluntary acceptance of risk did not relieve the first defendant of liability because of the operation of s148(3) of the 1972 Act.

A second case which subjected *Dann* to a narrow interpretation is *Morris v Murray* (above) where, it will be recalled, the plaintiff was a passenger in an aeroplane which crashed because the pilot was drunk. The Court of Appeal held that the plaintiff's claim must fail because he was volens. It was held that *Dann* was distinguishable because in *Morris* the pilot's drunkenness was extreme and glaring and the journey was fraught with danger from its very inception (which was not the case in *Dann* because there the driver did not get drunk until a later stage in the social outing at a time when it might not have been very easy for the plaintiff 'to extricate herself without giving offence'). Sir George Waller was also of the opinion that there was a fundamental difference between driving a car and piloting an aeroplane, the latter being more risky and requiring greater accuracy of control than the former. Although *Dann* has survived this scrutiny by the Court of Appeal it is now clear that its sphere of application is limited and that it has no application where the driver of the vehicle is obviously and glaringly drunk.

Despite this doubt about the application of the principle laid down in *Dann* to the facts of the case, the majority view appears to be that an agreement is not necessary and that the defence can be established where the plaintiff encounters a danger which has already been created by the defendant's negligence. However, a powerful argument has been made that this should not be the case. Jaffey ([1985] CLJ 87) argues that, where there is no agreement between the parties, then all that has happened is that the plaintiff has done the act in question knowing of the risk of injury. He argues that, where the plaintiff unreasonably accepts the risk of injury, this should be treated as a case of contributory negligence and not volenti. A defendant who unreasonably takes a risk is treated as being negligent, so why should a plaintiff who unreasonably takes a risk be treated not as contributorily negligent but as volenti so that he has no cause of action at all against the defendant? He argues that such cases should be treated as cases of contributory negligence (or perhaps novus actus interveniens) and that the standard of the plaintiff's conduct could then be taken into account in apportioning the loss.

The second problem concerns whether an agreement between the plaintiff and the defendant, under which the plaintiff agrees to accept the risk of injury, can be made after the defendant has committed the negligent act which caused the damage to the plaintiff. Once again there is no clear authority on this point (in *Titchener* v *British Railways Board* [1983] 1 WLR 1427 Lord Fraser appeared to accept that such an agreement could be made but this view was not shared by Diplock LJ in *Wooldridge* v *Sumner* [1963] 2 QB 43), but there is academic support for the argument that such an agreement may be made (Clerk and Lindsell on *Tort* (16th ed) para 1–161). However it has been argued that the defence should not be applicable in such a case (Jaffey [1985] CLJ 87, 88–91). Jaffey's argument is that volenti operates as a kind of estoppel in that, where the agreement was made before the defendant committed the negligent act, the defendant can argue that he would not have committed the act had it not been for the agreement of the plaintiff and so it would be unfair to impose liability upon him in such a case. No such argument can be used, however, where the agreement was entered into after the defendant had committed the negligent act and so, he argues, there is no reason for giving effect to the agreement. Attractive though this argument is, it remains unclear whether or not it will find favour with the judiciary.

13.6 Knowledge

Mere knowledge of the danger is not sufficient, of itself, to establish the defence of volenti. As has frequently been pointed out the maxim is *volenti* non fit injuria not *scienti* non fit injuria (see, for example, *Dann* v *Hamilton* (above) where the plaintiff had knowledge of the risk of injury but was held not to have accepted the risk of injury). It must be proved that the plaintiff consented to the risk, not simply that he had knowledge of the risk.

Having said that, knowledge of the risk does play a role within the defence of volenti because for the defence to be applicable it must be known that the plaintiff had knowledge of the danger. The test of knowledge is a subjective one (see *Smith* v *Austin Lifts Ltd* [1959] 1 WLR 100). Where the plaintiff was not aware of the danger in a situation where he ought to have been aware of it, the defence of volenti is not made out and the defendant should rely instead on the argument that the plaintiff was guilty of contributory negligence.

13.7 Volenti and exclusion clauses

Although the plaintiff may conclude an agreement with the defendant that he (the plaintiff) will accept the risk of injury, that agreement may constitute an exclusion clause, the validity of which may be affected by the Unfair Contract Terms Act 1977. Here we are concerned with s2 of the Act which regulates attempts to exclude or restrict liability for negligence. Section 2(1) provides that:

> 'A person cannot by reference to any contract term or to a notice given to persons generally or to particular persons exclude or restrict his liability for death or personal injury resulting from negligence.'

A number of points should be noted about this subsection. The first is that it only applies to attempts to exclude or restrict liability and does not apply to clauses which merely define the obligations between the parties (unless such clauses are caught by s13 of the Act). The second point is that the subsection only applies to attempts to exclude or restrict business liability (defined in s1(3) of the Act). The third point to note is that it only applies to 'negligence' (which is defined in s1(1) of the Act).

Section 2(2) of the 1977 Act provides that:

> 'In the case of other loss or damage, a person cannot so exclude or restrict his liability for negligence except in so far as the term or notice satisfies the requirement of reasonableness.'

Once again this subsection only applies to attempts to exclude or restrict liability, business liability and negligence. In considering what constitutes reasonableness regard should be had to the general guidelines provided in s11 of the Act.

In relation to road traffic legislation it is provided in s148(3) of the Road Traffic Act 1972 that a clause in a contract or a notice which purports to exclude liability in circumstances where compulsory insurance is required is of no effect.

Finally the exact wording of s2(3) of the Unfair Contract Terms Act 1977 should be noted. It provides that:

> 'Where a contract term or notice purports to exclude or restrict liability for negligence a person's agreement to or awareness of it is not of itself to be taken as indicating his voluntary acceptance of any risk.'

It has been pointed out by Jaffey ([1985] CLJ 87, 95) that this subsection envisages that the defence of volenti may exist in the absence of an agreement between the parties (see 13.5). This is because, where there is an agreement between the parties, the case will be covered either by s2(1) or by s2(2), so s2(3) of the Act can only apply where there is no agreement between the parties and it therefore supports the argument of those who maintain that the defence of volenti may be made out in the absence of an agreement between the parties.

13.8 Volenti and the standard of care

We have already discussed cases such as *Wooldridge* v *Sumner* [1963] 2 QB 43 and *Wilks* v *Cheltenham Cycle Club* [1971] 1 WLR 668 (see 9.9), which were cases where spectators were injured by competitors in a sporting activity. We have noted that the courts, in deciding the standard of care owed by the competitor to the spectator, took account of the fact that the spectator took the risk of any damage done to him during the course of the game. It has been argued that a similar result could have been achieved by analysing these cases in terms of volenti. One could say that the spectator is aware of the risk of injury and, by attending the sporting event with knowledge of the danger, has agreed to accept the risk of injury. However this was not the analysis which the court adopted in the case of *Wooldridge*. Diplock LJ stated that:

> 'The spectator takes the risk because such an act involves no breach of the duty of care owed by the participant to him. He does not take the risk by virtue of the doctrine expressed or obscured by the maxim volenti non fit injuria.'

However, it has been argued that such a case can be analysed in terms of volenti (see Jaffey [1985] CLJ 87, 107–8, but compare Jones *Textbook on Torts* (3rd ed) pp370–371). The argument is that there is an implied agreement between the parties that the spectator shall accept the risk of injury caused by the competitor acting in accordance with the rules. Such an implied agreement could also be inferred where the two parties to the action are both participators in the competition. It is true that these cases could be analysed in terms of volenti and that in most cases such an analysis would not have affected the result of the case. But problems would arise in cases where the spectator was a child because of the difficulty of showing that the child entered into an agreement, even an implied agreement, with the competitor that he (the spectator) would accept the risk of injury. Because of this difficulty it is submitted that the courts should continue to analyse these cases in terms of the standard of care owed by competitors to spectators.

14

Breach of Statutory Duty

14.1 Introduction

14.2 Does the breach confer a right of action in tort?

14.3 The remedy provided in the Act

14.4 Statutes for the benefit of a class

14.5 Public rights and special damage

14.6 Ambit of the statute

14.7 Defences

14.1 Introduction

A breach by the defendant of his statutory duty may give the plaintiff a cause of action in tort. The difficulty which arises with breach of statutory duty lies in discerning which statutes, in their breach, give rise to a cause of action in tort. Sometimes this can be clear, as when the statute is enacted for the very purpose of giving the plaintiff a cause of action in tort in a situation in which he would not have had a cause of action before (see, for example, the Occupiers' Liability Act 1984, discussed at 17.15) or where the statute expressly excludes a cause of action in respect of a failure to comply with its provisions (see, for example, s133 of the Medicines Act 1968 or s5 of the Guard Dogs Act 1975). But in the vast majority of cases the statute is completely silent as to whether or not breach gives rise to a cause of action in tort. So we must look to the cases to see the principles which the courts have applied in considering whether breach of statutory duty gives rise to a cause of action in tort.

The standard required of the defendant in a particular case depends on the wording of the statute. The statute may, in effect, impose absolute liability upon the defendant or it may require that the defendant be guilty of negligence before its provisions are breached (see further 14.6).

14.2 Does the breach confer a right of action in tort?

In deciding whether the breach of statutory duty confers upon the plaintiff a cause of action in tort the general approach which the courts adopt is one of construction; that is, does the Act, on its true construction, confer upon the plaintiff a right of action in tort in respect of the breach of the statute (*Cutler* v *Wandsworth Stadium Ltd* [1949] AC 398; *R* v *Deputy Governor of Parkhurst Prison ex parte Hague* [1992] 1 AC 58). As we have noted the Act is generally silent on this issue and so it is left to the courts to discern the intention of Parliament. In the recent decision of the House of Lords in *Lonrho Ltd* v *Shell Petroleum Co Ltd (No 2)* [1982] AC 173 Lord Diplock stated that the initial presumption was that, where the statute created an obligation and a means of enforcing that obligation, such as a criminal penalty, then the obligation cannot be enforced in any other way (see the statement of principle by Lord Tenterden CJ in *Doe d Bishop of Rochester* v *Bridges* (1831) 1 B & Ad 847, 849). Lord Diplock held that there were two main exceptions to this initial presumption. The first arose where the statute was enacted for the benefit of a particular class of individuals and the second was where the statute created a 'public right' and the plaintiff had suffered 'special damage', which was damage over and above the damage suffered by the public at large.

The importance of these presumptions can be seen in the decision of the Court of Appeal in *CBS Songs Ltd* v *Amstrad Consumer Electronics plc* [1988] Ch 61 (affirmed by the House of Lords [1988] AC 1013). The defendants manufactured a twin-deck tape-recording machine which could be used to copy directly from one tape on to another. The plaintiffs, who were three record companies who were also representing other copyright owners in the music industry, alleged that the defendants had advertised the machines in such a way as to incite members of the public to commit the criminal offence of taping copyright material in breach of s21(3) of the Copyright Act 1956. The plaintiffs sought an injunction to restrain the defendants from selling the machines unless they ensured that the plaintiffs' copyright material would not thereby be infringed. The Court of Appeal, by a majority, refused to grant the injunction.

Nicholls LJ held that Lord Diplock's judgment in *Lonrho* was a comprehensive one. He held that in the present case the plaintiffs did not come within either of the two exceptions to the initial presumption so that they could not maintain an action in tort for breach of statutory duty. He rejected the idea that there was a third exception under which a court could in equity grant an injunction to a plaintiff to restrain a breach of the criminal law. He conceded that the court might grant such an injunction where the defendant's crime infringed a property right of the plaintiff, but he held that such a jurisdiction arose out of a concern to protect the property rights of the plaintiff and not out of a desire to ensure that the criminal law was enforced. The remedy open to the plaintiffs was not an action in tort but a private prosecution against the defendants.

We shall adopt the approach of Lord Diplock in analysing the law. First we shall consider whether the Act itself makes any provision for a remedy for its breach (14.3), then we shall consider the two exceptions, relating to statutes enacted for the benefit of a class (14.4) and the 'public right' exception (14.5).

14.3 The remedy provided in the Act

One of the crucial issues in determining whether breach of the statute gives rise to a cause of action in tort is the remedies provided, or not provided, in the Act for breach of its provisions. Where the Act imposes a duty upon the defendant, but provides no remedy for breach of that duty, then the presumption is that breach does give rise to a cause of action in tort. Thus in *Thornton v Kirklees Metropolitan Borough Council* [1979] QB 626 the defendants were in breach of the Housing (Homeless Persons) Act 1977 and the plaintiff suffered loss thereby. There was no provision in the Act for a remedy for breach of the Act's provisions and so the court held that a cause of action lay in tort in respect of the defendants' failure to comply with their statutory obligations (cf *Cocks v Thanet District Council* [1983] 2 AC 286 and Buckley (1984) 100 LQR 204, 217–20).

On the other hand, where the statute itself provides a remedy for breach of its provisions, then it is much harder to show that the breach also gives rise to a cause of action in tort. It is not, however, impossible to show that the plaintiff still has a cause of action. Thus in *Groves v Lord Wimborne* [1898] 2 QB 402 the defendants were subject to a fine of £100 for breach of their statutory duty in failing to put a fence around their machinery. The plaintiff was injured by the unfenced machinery. But AL Smith LJ pointed out that 'not one penny of a fine imposed under the sections [of the Act] need ever go into the pocket of the person injured'. He held that the object of the fine was to inflict a punishment upon the employer for his breach of duty and that the compensation of the victim of the employer's failure to comply with his obligation was an entirely separate issue. The fine imposed on the offender under the Act could also have been a small one in comparison with the injury to the plaintiff. It was held that there was no reason why the plaintiff should be bound by this limitation and this was held to be another reason for not denying to the plaintiff a cause of action in respect of the breach of the Act.

Again, a different approach was taken in the case of *Atkinson v Newcastle Waterworks Co* (1877) 2 Ex D 441 (cf *Read v Croydon Corporation* [1938] 4 All ER 631). The defendants, who supplied water to Newcastle, were statutorily required to keep their pipes at a certain pressure level. Failure to do so could result in a fine of £10, no part of which was payable to the person affected by the defendants' failure to comply with their obligations. The plaintiff's premises caught fire and, due to the pressure in the pipes being insufficient, there was no water to extinguish the fire and the premises were burnt down. It was held that the penalty imposed in the statute was an exclusive one and that it could not have been intended that the defendants would become, in effect, an insurer that sufficient water would be available to put out a fire. The fact that the fine, which was payable in respect of the breach, did not go into the pocket of the individual but was a 'public' penalty was held to be evidence that the Act did not give a cause of action to an individual in respect of a breach of its provisions and that the purpose behind the fine was simply to impose a security for performance of the statutory duty (cf *Groves* v *Lord Wimborne* (above)).

It is not entirely clear how the cases of *Groves* and *Atkinson* are to be reconciled. It may be that the latter case is the one that will be followed today and that *Groves* will be distinguished on the ground that it was a case of a statute enacted for the benefit of a class (see further 14.4 below). Whichever way the cases are eventually reconciled, it is clear that it is difficult to show that a plaintiff has a cause of action in tort where the statute provides another remedy for its breach (for a recent example see *Wentworth* v *Wiltshire County Council* [1993] 2 WLR 175). These cases also show that it cannot necessarily be assumed that the mere fact that the statutory penalty is inadequate will lead a court to conclude that the plaintiff has available to him a cause of action in tort in respect of the damage which he has suffered as a result of the breach.

It should also be noted in this context that the fact that the plaintiff had available to him a remedy at common law may affect the willingness of the court to conclude that the plaintiff also has available to him a tort action in respect of the breach of statutory duty. In *Phillips* v *Britannia Hygienic Laundry Co Ltd* [1923] 2 KB 832 the defendants were in breach of the Motor Cars (Use and Construction) Order 1904 because their vehicle was in a defective condition. The reason for it being in a defective condition was the negligence of the people to whom they had entrusted the car for repair. While the defendants were using the vehicle in this defective state, it was involved in an accident in which the plaintiff's van was damaged. The plaintiff claimed damages in respect of the breach of statutory duty. The regulations made provision for a criminal penalty in respect of their breach but were silent as to a civil remedy. It was held that the duty owed under the regulations was a public one and that it did not give a member of the public, and therefore the plaintiff, a cause of action in respect of its breach. Atkins LJ stated that:

> 'The obligations of those who bring vehicles upon highways have already been well provided for and regulated by the common law. It is not likely that the legislature intended by these regulations to impose upon the owners of vehicles an absolute obligation to make them roadworthy in all events, even in the absence of negligence.'

However, it should not be thought that the availability of an alternative remedy makes it impossible to show that the plaintiff also has a cause of action in respect of the breach of statutory duty. Cases such as *Groves* v *Lord Wimborne* show that it is possible to bring such a cause of action where an alternative remedy is available. Winfield and Jolowicz (*Winfield and Jolowicz on Tort* (13th ed) pp176–7) suggest that:

> 'The courts will, in the absence of clear indications to the contrary, lean against a statutory duty which would contradict the general pattern of liability in a particular area of activity but will find one which will support or supplement it.'

They then use this rationalisation to explain the case of *Monk* v *Warbey* [1935] 1 KB 175, which is a case which has seemed to defy explanation. The defendant, in breach of the Road Traffic Act 1930, gave permission to an uninsured driver to drive his car. The negligence of the latter caused an accident in which the plaintiff was injured. The plaintiff was unable to recover from the driver because he was not worth suing. So he sued the defendant and was held to be entitled to recover. The effect of the judgment was to reinforce the commitment of the common law to those injured as the result of the negligence of another because it created another means by which such people could enforce judgment. On the other hand, had the defendants been held liable in *Phillips* v *Britannia Hygienic Laundry* (above), that would have run counter to the development of the common law because it would have had the effect of imposing liability in the absence of fault rather than imposing liability where it could be shown that the defendant was at fault.

14.4 Statutes for the benefit of a class

The first exception to the initial presumption which was identified by Lord Diplock in *Lonrho* v *Shell Petroleum* (above) concerned statutes which were passed for the benefit of a class. If the Act was intended to protect the plaintiff himself, or a class of persons to which the plaintiff belongs, then the plaintiff has a cause of action in tort. The difficulty with this formulation is to ascertain what exactly constitutes a class of persons. Employees are generally regarded as a class of persons in relation to industrial safety legislation. This can be seen in the case of *Groves* v *Lord Wimborne* (above). The plaintiff lost an arm when it was caught in some machinery in the defendants' factory. At the time of the accident the machine was unfenced, which was a breach of the regulations passed under the Factory and Workshop Act 1878. That Act imposed criminal sanctions upon the employer for breach of its requirements but it made no mention of any civil remedy. It was held that the Act was 'passed for the benefit of workmen in factories, by compelling the masters to do certain things for their protection'. So the plaintiff was held to have a cause of action against the defendants.

Employees have been treated generously by the courts in respect of a breach of the industrial safety legislation and the courts have been ready to find that they constitute a class for whose benefit the legislation was enacted. The courts have, however, been much more reluctant to create civil liabilities out of the road traffic legislation and have held that the public using the highway is not a class (*Phillips* v *Britannia Hygienic Laundry Co Ltd* (above) and *Coote* v *Stone* [1971] 1 WLR 279, but contrast *London Passenger Transport Board* v *Upson* [1949] AC 155). A similar reluctance was evident in the case of *McCall* v *Abelesz* [1976] QB 585 where it was rather surprisingly held that a group of residential tenants was not a class of persons for whose benefit the Rent Act 1965 had been passed. In *R* v *Deputy Governor of*

Parkhurst Prison ex p Hague [1992] 1 AC 58 the House of Lords held that a breach of the Prison Rules 1964 did not give to a prisoner a private law claim for damages. The Prison Rules and the Prison Act 1952 were designed to deal with the administration of prisons and the management and control of prisoners; they were not intended to create private law rights of action. Another example of this more restrictive approach is the case of *Cutler* v *Wandsworth Stadium* [1949] AC 398. The plaintiff, who was a bookmaker, was unable to find a space where he could carry out his trade at the defendants' dog track. He sued the defendants for breach of statutory duty, alleging that the defendants had caused him loss through their breach of s11(2) of the Betting and Lotteries Act 1934, which provided that the occupier of the track should ensure that there was 'available space for bookmakers on the track'. It was held that the purpose behind the legislation was to regulate the conduct of bookmakers, but that the legislation was not passed for their benefit but for the benefit of the race-going public. As the Act was not passed for the benefit of the plaintiff it was held that he had no cause of action in tort in respect of the alleged breach of the statute. In a recent spate of cases this approach has been followed. In *West Wiltshire District Council* v *Pugh* [1993] NLJ 546 a district auditor employed to audit the accounts of the local authority in accordance with the Local Government Finance Act 1982 owed a statutory duty not to the officers of the authority but to the authority itself, since the purpose of the audit was to protect the authority; and in *X* v *Bedfordshire County Council* [1993] NLJ 1783 an infant plaintiff was denied the right to sue a local authority for breach of statutory duty in failing to discharge its duties under child care legislation as it was not the intention of Parliament to confer a right of action. A similar decision was reached in relatively similar circumstances in *M* v *Newham London Borough Council* [1994] NLJ 357 and in *T* v *Surrey County Council* [1994] NLJ 319 the court concurred in the reasoning in *X* (above).

These cases demonstrate a rather variable approach to the issue of what constitutes a class of persons for whose benefit the legislation was passed. There does not appear to be any discernible consistency in the approach which the courts have adopted and much depends on the facts of each case.

14.5 Public right and special damage

In *Lonrho* v *Shell Petroleum* (above) Lord Diplock said that the second case in which the initial presumption did not arise was:

> ' ... where the statute creates a public right (ie a right to be enjoyed by all those of Her Majesty's subjects who wish to avail themselves of it) and a particular member of the public suffers what Brett J in *Benjamin* v *Storr* (1874) LR 9 CP 400 at 407 described as "particular, direct and substantial" damage other and different from that which was common to all the rest of the public.'

It was held on the facts of *Lonrho* that the statutory prohibition upon supplying oil to Southern Rhodesia did not create a public right to be enjoyed by all Her Majesty's citizens. It did the opposite, by prohibiting the members of the public from doing what had previously been lawful for them to do. Therefore no cause of action arose in respect of the defendants' breach of their statutory duty. This distinction between statutes which create public rights and statutes which merely prohibit what was previously lawful activity does not seem to be a satisfactory distinction or to be one which is based upon any obvious coherent principle. Nevertheless it must be conceded that, at present, it does represent the current state of English law.

14.6 Ambit of the statute

Since the plaintiff's action is based upon the defendant's breach of his statutory duty it is obvious that the plaintiff's action is heavily dependent upon the wording of the particular statute which he claims that the defendant has breached. For example, the plaintiff must show that the act which he alleges has caused him damage is one which is regulated by the statute and that he is one of the people whom the Act was intended to protect. The plaintiff must also show that the injury or damage which he has suffered is of a kind which the statute was intended to prevent. The operation of this latter principle can be demonstrated by reference to the case of *Gorris* v *Scott* (1874) LR 9 Exch 125. The defendant shipowner was statutorily required to provide pens for cattle on board his ship. The reason for this was to lessen the risk of cattle catching a contagious disease called murrain. The plaintiff's sheep were swept overboard because they were not in pens and he brought an action against the defendants in respect of their breach of statutory duty. It was held that the defendants were not liable because the purpose behind the statute was to protect cattle from murrain and not to protect them from being swept overboard.

Since the plaintiff's action is so heavily dependent upon the wording of the statute, it is the particular statute that is in issue to which we must look to ascertain the standard required of the defendant. Thus the statute may impose an absolute duty upon the defendant or it may require proof that he was negligent. For example some of the provisions contained in the Factories Act 1961 impose absolute standards, such as the duty in s14 'that every dangerous part of any machinery ... shall be securely fenced unless it is in such a position or of such construction as to be as safe to every person employed or working on the premises as it would be if securely fenced'. That breach of this section is not dependent upon the defendant having been negligent can be demonstrated by reference to the case of *John Summers & Sons Ltd* v *Frost* [1955] AC 740. The plaintiff's thumb was injured when it was in contact with a revolving grinding wheel which belonged to the defendants. The plaintiff alleged that, in failing to fence the machine, the defendants had breached s14. He alleged that the section had been breached even though the effect of fencing the machine would have been to render the machine useless. It was held that the machine was indeed a dangerous one and that s14 required it to be 'securely fenced' and that, therefore, the machine must be so fenced even though the consequences of doing so would be to render the machine inoperable. On the other hand the statute may impose a standard which is closer to the common law negligence standard in that it only requires the defendant to do that which is practicable or reasonably practicable. In such a case the statutory obligation has little effect upon the obligations owed by the defendant at common law.

Lastly it must be shown that the defendant's breach of his statutory duty was the cause of the plaintiff's loss. This can give rise to difficult problems of causation where the defendant's breach of statutory duty takes the form of an omission, such as the failure to provide safety belts (see, for example, *McWilliams* v *Sir William Arrol & Co Ltd* [1962] 1 WLR 295 and the discussion of this particular issue at 10.4).

14.7 Defences

The defence of volenti is not available where an employer has breached his statutory duty and in consequence one of his employees suffers damage, unless the case falls within the narrow confines of *Imperial Chemical Industries Ltd* v *Shatwell* [1965] AC 656. It is not entirely clear whether the defence is available in all other cases. The majority view among commentators is that the defence is available, although an argument can be made out to the effect that any attempt to contract out of a statutory duty is void (see further chapter 15).

The defence of contributory negligence is also available in an appropriate case, but the courts tend to be rather reluctant to accept it, especially when an employee is suing his employer and the employer alleges that the employee was guilty of contributory negligence. In *Westwood* v *Post Office* [1974] AC 1 the plaintiff, who was a Post Office employee, entered the lift room of the telephone exchange. He was, in fact, forbidden to go in there. While there he fell through a defective trap door and was killed. It was alleged that the defendants had breached their statutory duty under the Offices, Shops and Railway Premises Act 1963. The defendants alleged that the plaintiff had been guilty of contributory negligence. It was held that the plaintiff was not guilty of contributory negligence. The fact that he was a trespasser did not have the effect of entitling the defendants to act in breach of their statutory duty and the plaintiff was entitled to assume that the defendants would comply with their statutory obligations (see further chapter 12).

Finally it should be noted that, as a general rule, a person who is the subject of a statutory duty cannot discharge that duty by entrusting responsibility for its performance to someone else.

15

Employers' Liability

15.1 Introduction

15.2 Competent staff

15.3 Proper plant and equipment

15.4 Safe place of work

15.5 Safe system of work

15.6 The economic welfare of employees

15.7 Defences

15.1 Introduction

Employers owe certain duties to their employees. These duties are derived from both common law and statutory sources. We have noted that an employer may be vicariously liable for the torts of his employee (see chapter 4). Here we are concerned, not with the case where the employee negligently causes loss to a third party, but with the liability of an employer for the injury suffered by one of his employees. This area of law was for many years troubled by the doctrine of common employment which had the effect of reducing the liability of an employer towards his employees. According to this doctrine, an employer was not liable where injury was negligently inflicted on one employee by another employee on the ground that the employee had consented to the risks involved in his employment, including the risk that one of his fellow workers would be negligent (see *Bartonshill Coal Co* v *Reid* (1858) 3 Macq. 266 (HL)). This doctrine was finally abolished by s1 of the Law Reform (Personal Injuries) Act 1948. However the doctrine of common employment has left its mark on the development of this area of law. This is particularly so in relation to the personal non-delegable duties which are owed by employers to their employees. These personal non-delegable duties were introduced in an effort to mitigate the rigours of the common employment doctrine because, where it could be shown that the employer was in breach of his own duty to his employee, the employer could not rely on the doctrine of common employment because that doctrine only came into play where the cause of the injury was the negligence of a fellow employee. So at common law it was crucial to distinguish between the employer's breach of his own personal duty, for which the employer was liable, and the breach of duty by one of his employees, for which the employer was not vicariously liable.

But now that the doctrine of common employment has been abolished, the employer may be liable either vicariously for the negligence of his employee committed in the course of his employment or for breach of his own personal non-delegable duty. It is still important to keep the two forms of liability separate because one is vicarious liability, whereas the other is primary. The rules applicable may therefore differ depending on whether we are dealing with primary liability or vicarious liability. For example, in vicarious liability, it is necessary to show that the employee committed the tort in the course of his employment, but there is no such limitation in the case of primary liability. Similarly vicarious liability only arises as between an employer and an employee, it does not extend to an independent contractor; whereas an employer may be in breach of his primary duty where he entrusts the work to an independent contractor. So, although the distinction is no longer as crucial as it once was, it is a distinction which still must be drawn because different rules are applicable depending on whether we are dealing with primary or vicarious liability.

In addition to these two common law sources of liability, statute has intervened to impose certain obligations upon employers in relation to the safety of their employees. The principal example of such legislative intervention is the Health and Safety at Work Act 1974, which, in s2, imposes a general duty upon 'every employer to ensure, so far as is reasonably practicable, the health, safety and welfare at work of all his employees'. We shall not, however, be concerned with these statutory obligations in this chapter but shall confine our attention to the common law duties imposed upon employers. In so far as failure to comply with these statutory obligations gives rise to an action in tort this issue has been considered in chapter 14 when discussing breach of statutory duty.

Before embarking upon an analysis of these common law duties, it is necessary to give brief mention to the statutory Industrial Injuries Scheme. Today many accidents at work are covered by this scheme. Ever since the first Workmen's Compensation Act in 1897 there has been in existence a statutory scheme which operates upon a no-fault basis and which compensates those injured in an accident 'arising out of and in the course of insurable employment'. The scheme is now administered by the Department of Health and Social Security under the Social Security Act 1975. It is to this scheme that most employees injured at work will look for compensation and the Pearson Commission noted that only 12½ per cent of those injured at work obtain any compensation through a tort action. It should also be noted that it is compulsory for employers to have insurance for personal injury to their employees under the Employers' Liability (Compulsory Insurance) Act 1969. It is, however, important to note that the Act only applies to liability for bodily injury or disease which is sustained by employees 'arising out of and in the course of their employment in Great Britain' (s1, see also *Reid v Rush & Tompkins Group plc* [1990] 1 WLR 212, discussed below at 15.6).

We shall now consider the four principal duties which employers owe to their employees. It is important to note that these duties are personal non-delegable duties and so an employer cannot discharge his responsibility simply by entrusting the performance of the work to an employee or to an independent contractor. We shall start by considering the employer's duty to provide competent staff.

15.2 Competent staff

At common law an employer owes a duty to his employees to select competent employees. The operation of this principle was considered in the case of *Hudson* v *Ridge Manufacturing Co Ltd* [1957] 2 QB 348. There it was held that an employer was liable for the foolish prank committed by one employee upon another in the course of his employment. The employer was held to be in breach of his personal duty because the employee's readiness to involve himself in such pranks had been known to them for a considerable period of time and they failed to take proper steps to put an end to these pranks. However, the position may be different where the employer has no cause to know that the employee has violent tendencies. (In such a case it may also be very difficult for the injured employee to argue that the employee who assaulted him was acting in the course of his employment because of the reluctance of the courts to hold an employer vicariously liable for an assault committed by his employee. See further 4.5.)

Hudson should be contrasted with the case of *Smith* v *Crossley Brothers Ltd* (1951) 95 Sol Jo 655. The plaintiff was injured at work when a fellow apprentice approached him from behind and placed a compressed air pipe near his rectum and signalled to another apprentice to turn on the compressed air. As a result the plaintiff suffered severe internal injuries. The plaintiff's action against the defendant employers failed because he could not show that they had failed to take reasonable care for his safety; they could not have foreseen that the apprentices would do such a thing.

15.3 Proper plant and equipment

The employer owes a duty to his employees to provide properly maintained plant and equipment. This can be seen in the case of *Smith* v *Baker* [1891] AC 325. There Lord Herschell said that:

> 'The contract between employer and employed involves on the part of the former the duty of taking reasonable care to provide proper appliances, to maintain them in proper condition, and so to carry on his operations as not to subject those employed to unnecessary risk.'

In *Davie* v *New Merton Board Mills Ltd* [1959] AC 604 the House of Lords held that the defendant employers were not liable for the injury to the plaintiff, one of their employees, which was caused by a defective tool which the defendants had purchased from a third party. It was held that the defendants were not liable because they had purchased the tool from a reputable firm of manufacturers and the defect was not discoverable on a reasonable inspection of the tool. So the defendants had fulfilled their duty to the plaintiff. This decision was, however, reversed by the Employers' Liability (Defective Equipment) Act 1969 which provided that where the defective equipment is supplied to the employer then the employer may be vicariously liable for the supplier's negligence. Section 1(1) of the 1969 Act states that:

> 'Where ... an employee suffers personal injury in the course of his employment in consequence of a defect in equipment provided by his employer for the purposes of the employer's business and the defect is attributable wholly or partly to the fault of a third party (whether identified or not) the injury shall be deemed to be also attributable to negligence on the part of the employer.'

The meaning of the word 'equipment' was recently considered by the House of Lords in *Coltman* v *Bibby Tankers Ltd* [1988] AC 276. A ship sank in 1980 with the loss of all the crew. The plaintiff, who represented the estate of one of the crew members, brought an action against the defendants under s1(1) of the 1969 Act. The defendants argued that the 1969 Act was not applicable because a ship was not 'equipment' for the purposes of the Act. 'Equipment' is defined in s1(3) of the Act as including 'any plant and machinery, vehicle, aircraft and clothing'. The Court of Appeal had held that a ship was not equipment because equipment was ancillary to something else and did not encompass the workplace itself. But in the House of Lords Lord Oliver held that there was no warrant for holding that equipment is restricted to parts of a larger whole. Their Lordships conceded that the strongest argument for the defendants was the omission of ships from the definition in s1(3). Lord Oliver said that the omission was 'certainly curious', but it was held that Parliament could not have intended to exclude ships from the ambit of the Act. To adopt such a narrow construction of the Act would require a court to draw a distinction between machinery on a ship which was not part of the ship and machinery which was actually part of the ship itself; an almost impossible task. Lord Oliver held that the purpose behind the Act was to render the employer liable for defective equipment of every type and, adopting a purposive construction of the Act, he held that there was no reason to exclude ships from the ambit of the Act.

The need for a purposive interpretation of 'equipment' was also emphasised by the House of Lords in *Knowles* v *Liverpool City Council* [1993] 4 All ER 321. The plaintiff suffered personal injury in the course of his employment when the flagstone which he was handling broke. The defendants, his employers, argued that the flagstone was not 'equipment' but was 'material upon which the employee used the equipment'. In rejecting this argument Lord Jauncey stated that it was necessary to adopt a broad approach to the construction of the Act, bearing in mind its broad purpose, rather than engage in a precise construction of its terms.

15.4 Safe place of work

The employer is under a duty to provide a safe place of work for his employees. It should be noted that this obligation is not an absolute one but is one which demands that the employer take reasonable steps to provide a safe place of work. In *Latimer* v *AEC* [1953] AC 643 (discussed further at 9.6) it was emphasised that the employer's obligation to provide a safe place of work only required the employer to do what was reasonable to eliminate the risk and that, where the cost of eliminating the risk was exorbitant by comparison with the benefit obtained by the elimination of the risk, then it was not generally negligent to fail to eliminate the risk (see also *Gitsham* v *CH Pearce & Sons plc* (1991) The Times 11 February).

15.5 Safe system of work

The employer is also under a duty to provide his employees with a safe system of work. What constitutes a safe system of work depends on the facts of each case. This can be demonstrated by reference to the case of *General Cleaning Contractors* v *Christmas* [1953] AC 180. The plaintiff, who was a window cleaner, was employed by the defendants to clean windows. He was informed that he should use the 'sill' method of cleaning the upper windows, which involved standing on the window ledge and holding the window sash while cleaning the windows. While he was cleaning the upper windows in this way, a window fell on his fingers and he fell to the ground and suffered various injuries. It was held that the defendants could not have provided the plaintiff with safety ropes as there was nothing on the building to which they could have been attached. But it was held that they should have told the plaintiff to test the window sashes to see whether they were loose and that they could have provided him with wedges for the windows. So it was held that in all the circumstances the defendants had failed to supply a safe system of work. In considering all the relevant circumstances regard should also be had to the character and attributes of the plaintiff. Thus in *Paris* v *Stepney Borough Council* [1951] AC 367 the employers were held to have been negligent in failing to provide their employee with goggles because the employee only had sight in one eye and so the consequence of any eye injury to him was much greater than if he had sight in both eyes (see further 9.4). Where the employer has adopted the standard practice in the industry, that is good, but not conclusive, evidence that the employer has provided a safe system of work (see *Thompson* v *Smiths Shiprepairers (North Shields) Ltd* [1984] 1 All ER 881).

In *McDermid* v *Nash Dredging and Reclamation Co Ltd* [1987] AC 906 the defendants employed the plaintiff, who was an inexperienced 18 year old, as a deckhand and, while he was working under the control of another company (who were the parent company of the defendants), he was seriously injured and his leg had to be amputated. The plaintiff brought an action for damages against the defendants. The House of Lords held that the defendants were under a non-delegable duty to ensure that a safe system of work was provided for the plaintiff and that that system was operated safely. It is important to note that the duty encompasses both the *devising* of a safe system of work and the *operation* of a safe system of work (for criticism of this extension see McKendrick 'Vicarious Liability and Independent Contractors – a Re-examination' (1990) 53 MLR 770, esp pp773–774). Lord Brandon said that the essential feature of a non-delegable duty is that:

> 'If it is not performed, it is no defence for the employer to show that he delegated performance to a person, whether his servant or not his servant, whom he reasonably believed to be competent to perform it. Despite such delegation the employer is liable for the non-performance of the duty.'

There are two vital factors which limit the scope of *McDermid*. The first is that, in accordance with general principle, the obligation of the employer is not strict but requires only the exercise of reasonable care. This can be illustrated by reference to the case of *Cook* v *Square D Ltd* [1992] ICR 262. The plaintiff was sent by the defendants, his employers, to work as a computer consultant in Saudi Arabia. While working there he slipped into a small hole in the tiled floor of the control room and suffered injury. The plaintiff relied upon *McDermid* but the Court of Appeal rejected the analogy and held that there had been no breach of duty by the defendants. The site was some 8,000 miles away and both the site occupiers and the general contractors were reliable companies who were aware of their responsibility for the safety of workers on site. The court did not, however, rule out the possibility that circumstances might require employers in the UK to take steps to satisfy themselves as to the safety of foreign sites, for example, where a number of their employees are going to work on a foreign site or where one or two employees are going to work there for a considerable period of time (but contrast *Johnson* v *Coventry Churchill International Ltd* [1992] 3 All ER 14, discussed below).

The second factor is that the plaintiff must be an employee of the defendant employers. In *Watts* v *Lowcur Ltd* (Queen's Bench (Commercial Division) 11 February 1988) the plaintiff had been employed by the first defendants but was hired by them to the second defendants (who worked on the same building site) so that the latter became his employers. The plaintiff was injured as a result of the second defendants' breach of statutory duty in failing to provide him with a suitable and safe access to his place of work. It was held that the plaintiff could not recover damages from the first defendants. *McDermid* was distinguished on the ground that the plaintiff in *Watts* was no longer in the employment of the first defendants and so they ceased to be under a duty to provide him with a safe place or a safe system of work.

Watts should, however, be contrasted with the recent decision of the Court of Appeal in *Morris* v *Breaveglen Ltd* (1992) The Times 29 December. The plaintiff was employed by the defendants and was sent by them to work at Dartmoor Prison farm pursuant to a labour only sub-contract which the defendants had entered into with the main contractors at the site. Under the terms of the sub-contract, the defendants accepted that they were liable to observe and perform all safety obligations imposed by statute or common law and to maintain employers' liability insurance in respect of their employees. The trial judge found that, while the plaintiff was working on the site, it was the main contractors who had the right to control what he did and how he did it. The plaintiff volunteered to drive the main contractors' dumper truck but while doing so he suffered serious injury when the truck went over the edge of the site. The trial judge found that the accident was caused by an unsafe system of work and by the plaintiff's lack of instruction in the use of the truck and held that the defendants were liable in damages to the plaintiff. The defendants appealed, arguing that it was the main contractors who were liable to the plaintiff and not themselves. This argument was rejected by the Court of Appeal. The court held that a vital distinction had to be drawn between two types of claim. The first arises where the sub-contracted employee causes damage to a third party, in which case the employer responsible for the damage is the one who has the right of control over the employee (see *Mersey Docks and Harbour Board* v *Coggins & Griffiths (Liverpool) Ltd* [1947] AC 1, discussed at 4.3). The second type of claim arises when it is the subcontracted employee himself who is injured. In such a case it is the general employer who remains liable because he is personally liable for the performance of his duty to the employee and cannot avoid liability by delegating it to a main contractor (see *McDermid* v *Nash Dredging & Reclamation Ltd* (above)). Therefore the Court of Appeal held that, on the present facts, the defendants were liable to the plaintiff.

So, where the general employer remains the employer of the sub-contracted employee, a non-delegable duty of the type recognised in *Morris* will be in play. But where, as in *Watts*, the employment relationship is terminated by the hiring, the original employer's non-delegable duty will also come to an end. It may, however, be no easy task to persuade a court that the employment relationship has been terminated as a result of the hiring of the employee, as can be seen from the recent case of *Johnson* v *Coventry Churchill International Ltd* [1992] 3 All ER 14. The plaintiff fell while working on a building site in Germany and suffered serious injury. He brought a claim in negligence against the defendants, who were an employment agency recruiting personnel to work abroad, arguing that he was their employee and that they were in breach of their duty to provide him with a safe system of work. The defendants argued that they were not his employers because his contract with them was described as a 'sub-contract', and that his employers were the owners of the site in Germany where he had been sent to work by the defendants. It was held that, having regard to the realities of the relationship between the parties, the plaintiff was an employee of the defendants and that he had not been transferred to the employment of the German employers. It was held that there would have to be 'clear and cogent evidence' that the plaintiff had knowingly accepted a transfer before such a conclusion could be reached. The evidence established that the defendants remained his employers: they continued to pay him and generally acted as if they were his employers. The adoption of this approach will make it very difficult for a general employer to argue that the employee is no longer its employee.

15.6 The economic welfare of employees

The cases which have been discussed thus far are all cases in which a duty had been imposed upon the employer to protect the employee's physical safety or well-being. But does the duty imposed upon employers extend to the economic welfare of the employee? That was the critical question considered by the Court of Appeal in *Reid v Rush & Tompkins Group plc* [1990] 1 WLR 212. The plaintiff was employed by the defendants and was sent by them to work in Ethiopia, where he suffered serious injury in an accident caused by the negligence of an unidentified driver. There was no equivalent to the Motor Insurers' Bureau in Ethiopia and so the plaintiff had no effective means of recovering compensation from the other driver. So he alleged that the defendants were negligent either in failing to take out insurance on his behalf or in failing to advise him of the need to take out such insurance. The Court of Appeal held that the defendant employers were not under a duty to take out insurance on his behalf, nor were they under a duty to advise him of the need to take out such insurance. Ralph Gibson LJ held that, while a duty may be imposed upon an employer to warn a prospective employee of the physical risks he would expose himself to if he accepted the job (*White v Holbrook Precision Castings Ltd* [1985] IRLR 215), the duty imposed upon employers 'has hitherto not been extended to the taking of reasonable care to protect the servant from economic loss' (see *Deyong v Shenburn* [1946] KB 227 and *Edwards v West Herts Group Hospital Management Committee* [1957] 1 WLR 415). Although such a duty does not arise out of the general relationship of employer and employee, it may arise on a particular set of facts (for example, it may arise from an express or implied term of the contract of employment or from a voluntary acceptance of responsibility (in the *Hedley Byrne* sense) by the employer for the employee's economic welfare).

15.7 Defences

The defence of volenti (see further chapter 13) is applicable to employers' liability. In *Smith v Baker* [1891] AC 325 the House of Lords recognised the economic realities of the employment relationship in applying the doctrine of volenti to employment situations. It was held that the mere fact that the employee had continued to work in dangerous circumstances did not mean that he was volens because knowledge of the danger is not the same as consenting to the risk of danger. Unless it can be clearly shown that the employee voluntarily accepted the risk of injury the defence will not be applicable (see further 13.4).

The damages payable to the employee may fall to be reduced on the ground that the employee was guilty of contributory negligence. In the case of *Bux* v *Slough Metals Ltd* [1974] 1 All ER 262 the damages payable to the plaintiff employee fell to be reduced by 40 per cent on the ground that the employee was guilty of contributory negligence. However it should be noted that the courts tend to be more lenient in applying the doctrine of contributory negligence to cases concerning the liability of employers towards their employees (see further 12.7).

16

Product Liability

16.1 Introduction

16.2 Historical development

16.3 Defects in the common law

16.4 The Consumer Protection Act 1987

16.1 Introduction

The subject of liability in tort for dangerous or defective products has undergone considerable change as the law of tort has developed. This form of liability has now been transformed as a result of the enactment of the Consumer Protection Act 1987. The first part of this Act renders a producer strictly liable to a consumer when a defective product causes personal injury or damage to property of the consumer. Before analysing the provisions of this Act, it is necessary to give consideration to the development of the common law for two reasons. The first is that the Act has not repealed the common law rules and the second is that the deficiencies in the common law were a factor which influenced the pressure for reform of this particular area of law.

16.2 Historical development

Prior to *Donoghue* v *Stevenson* [1932] AC 562 the ambit of liability was extremely narrow due to the operation of what has become known as the 'contract fallacy' (see further 6.2). According to this fallacy there was no duty of care owed by a manufacturer to any person who was not a party to a contract with him and who was injured or otherwise suffered loss as a result of a defect in the manufacturer's goods. As we have noted (see 6.2) this contract fallacy was exploded by the decision of the House of Lords in *Donoghue* v *Stevenson* (above). In *Donoghue* Lord Atkin laid down the following statement of principle:

'A manufacturer of products, which he sells in such a form as to show that he intends them to reach the ultimate consumer in the form in which they left him with no reasonable possibility of intermediate examination, and with the knowledge that the absence of reasonable care in the preparation or putting up of the products will result in an injury to the consumer's life or property, owes a duty to the consumer to take that reasonable care.'

Although this statement of principle constituted a major step forward in the development of the law, it is the subject of a number of restrictions. The first is that the statement, as originally explained by Lord Atkin, was only applicable to manufacturers. It has since, however, been extended to repairers (*Haseldine* v *Daw* [1941] 2 KB 343), erectors (*Brown* v *Cotterill* (1934) 51 TLR 21) and builders (*Sharpe* v *E T Sweeting & Sons Ltd* [1963] 1 WLR 665). This category of persons to whom the principle has been extended are characterised by the fact that they created the danger or were responsible for the creation of the danger. The difficulty which then arises is whether the principle should also be applied to the vendor of the defective goods. Here, of course, the situation is different because the vendor has not created the danger, he has simply sold the product to the consumer. Of course, such a vendor could be liable to the consumer in contract and the consumer would be able to claim the benefit of the protection afforded by the Sale of Goods Act 1979 where the subject matter of the contract between the parties was goods. But can the supplier also be liable in tort? It seems that he may be liable in tort where he fails to inspect the goods and he is under a duty so to inspect the goods. Such a duty to examine the goods does not arise in every case, it only arises where the supplier could reasonably be expected to carry out such an examination. Winfield and Jolowicz (*Winfield and Jolowicz on Tort* (13th ed) p241) put the issue in the following way:

'A second-hand car dealer may be expected to discover a patent defect in the steering mechanism of one of his cars … but a retail grocer, for example, cannot be expected to institute inspections to discover whether his tinned food is contaminated.'

So the obligation imposed upon suppliers does not arise in every case and, even where it does arise, it is not an onerous obligation and it can even be discharged by selling the goods 'as seen and with all its faults and without warranty' (see *Hurley* v *Dyke* [1979] RTR 265).

The second qualification in Lord Atkin's judgment is that it only applies to 'products'. However the principle, as interpreted, is not confined to items such as food and drink. It has been applied, for example, to tombstones (*Brown* v *Cotterill* (above)) and to cars (*Andrews* v *Hopkinson* [1957] 1 QB 229). Nor is it confined to consumers in the strict sense; it applies to the ultimate user of the product as well as to persons within close proximity of the product.

The third qualification is that the manufacturer must intend the goods to reach the consumer in the form in which they left him. This is not to say that they must be in exactly the same form. For example in *Grant* v *Australian Knitting Mills Ltd* [1936] AC 85 the defendants were held to be liable to the plaintiff, who contracted dermatitis as a result of wearing underwear which had been manufactured by the defendants and which contained an excess of sulphite. The defendants argued that they were not liable to the plaintiff because the underwear left their factory in packs of six and only two had been sold to the plaintiff, so somebody could have tampered with them when they were in the shop being unpacked. This argument was rejected by the Privy Council who held that the mere possibility of someone else tampering with the goods was insufficient to discharge the liability of the defendants. But the Privy Council did concede that, where there was the possibility of someone else tampering with the goods, the difficulties of proof may be greater for the plaintiff because the plaintiff must provide sufficient evidence that the defect existed when the product left the possession of the defendants (see *Evans* v *Triplex Safety Glass Co Ltd* [1936] 1 All ER 283).

The fourth qualification is that Lord Atkin's original statement of principle was confined to the case where there was 'no real possibility of intermediate examination' by the consumer. So where the plaintiff is actually aware of the defect the principle does not apply. In *Kubach* v *Hollands* [1937] 3 All ER 907 some manufacturers sold a chemical to the second defendants, with an express warning that the chemical had to be tested before use. The second defendants then mistakenly sold the chemical to a school teacher but did not supply the warning relating to the need to test before use. The plaintiff, a schoolgirl, was injured when the chemical exploded in an experiment. The plaintiff was unsuccessful in her attempt to recover damages from the school (the first defendants), but she did succeed against the second defendants. The second defendants then sought to claim an indemnity from the manufacturers. It was held that they were not entitled to such an indemnity because they had been given adequate warning by the manufacturers of the danger and had chosen to ignore it.

It is not, however, the case that the mere fact that there was a possibility of intermediate examination is sufficient, of itself, to exonerate the defendant (see, for example, *Griffiths* v *Arch Engineering Co* [1968] 3 All ER 217). In *Andrews* v *Hopkinson* (above) the plaintiff bought a car on hire purchase from the defendant. The car was second-hand and the defendant had taken no steps to ensure that the car was roadworthy, although the car had been in his possession for a week. The car had a defective steering mechanism and, as a result, the plaintiff was involved in an accident shortly after he took possession of the car. It was held that this was the type of defect of which the plaintiff should have been warned by the defendant and that it was not the type of defect which the plaintiff was expected to discover upon a reasonable examination of the car. So the defendant was held to be liable to the plaintiff.

The fifth qualification contained in Lord Atkin's statement of principle relates to the nature of the loss recoverable. It is clear from his judgment that damages are recoverable in respect of 'injury to the consumer's life or property'. But caution must be exercised in relation to the recovery of damages in respect of property damage. It is submitted that what Lord Atkin had in mind was not a claim in tort on the ground that the goods which the consumer had bought were less valuable than he had anticipated, but a claim in tort on the ground that the goods had damaged other property of the consumer (see the judgment of Lloyd LJ in *Aswan Engineering Establishment Co* v *Lupdine Ltd* [1987] 1 All ER 135, discussed at 7.7). Where the plaintiff's claim is that the defect in the product has simply rendered the goods less valuable then, subject to the principle laid down in *Junior Books Ltd* v *The Veitchi Co Ltd* [1983] 1 AC 520 (see further 7.7), his claim lies in contract and not in tort.

The sixth and final qualification in the judgment of Lord Atkin relates to the nature of the defendant's obligation. It is simply an obligation to take reasonable care and the burden is on the plaintiff to show that the defendant has failed to exercise reasonable care. This can be done by showing that the product was defective and that, on the balance of probabilities, that defect arose during the course of the manufacturing process. In *Mason* v *Williams & Williams Ltd* [1955] 1 WLR 549 the plaintiff was injured when using a cold chisel which had been manufactured by the defendants. The chisel was too cold for the purpose for which it was intended and it was held that the plaintiff had established that the defendants were negligent by demonstrating that nothing could have happened to the chisel after it left the defendants' possession which could have caused the excessive hardness of the chisel.

16.3 Defects in the common law

Although Lord Atkin's statement of principle, as subsequently developed, was an improvement on the state of the law pre-1932, it did suffer from certain defects. The first defect was the difficulty which could be experienced in showing that the defect occurred during the manufacturing process. This can be demonstrated by reference to the case of *Evans* v *Triplex Safety Glass Co Ltd* (above). The plaintiff purchased a new Ford car which was fitted with a 'Triplex Toughened' windscreen. A year after the car was purchased the windscreen suddenly shattered for no apparent reason and injured the occupants of the car. It was held that the defendants were not liable to the plaintiff for the injuries which he and his family had received because the plaintiff could not show that the defect existed in the windscreen at the time at which it left the defendants' possession. The defect could have arisen when the windscreen was screwed in place on the assembly line or have been due to some event which occurred during the year in which the plaintiff used the car.

The second difficulty arises where the damage was purely economic in the sense that the plaintiff's complaint was that the product was simply less valuable than he had anticipated. It has been argued that such a claim properly lies in contract and not in tort and that, while in many cases the Sale of Goods legislation will provide the plaintiff with adequate protection, there may be cases where the plaintiff cannot rely upon the Sale of Goods legislation, for example, because he was given the goods as a gift (see also *Daniels* v *R White & Sons Ltd* [1938] 4 All ER 258 cf *Hill* v *James Crowe (Cases) Ltd* [1978] 1 All ER 812).

The third difficulty is the problem which we have noted of establishing a claim in tort against the suppliers of the goods, although once again, in the majority of cases, the plaintiff will have available to him a contractual action in respect of the losses which he has suffered.

The final difficulty concerns the practical problem of showing that the manufacturer was at fault. The manufacturer may be able to show that it was not financially reasonable to take the safety precautions advocated by the plaintiff or be able to show that the state of knowledge at the time of the alleged negligence was not sufficient to enable the manufacturer to avoid injury to the plaintiff.

These defects led to strong arguments for reform. Advocates of reform included the Pearson Commission (Cmnd 7594) and the Law Commisson (No. 82 Liability for Defective Products (1977)). Finally the European Economic Community produced a Directive on product liability (Directive 85/374/EEC) which gave member states three years from 25 July 1985 to introduce national laws which complied with the terms of the Directive. It was this Directive which was one of the main influences behind the Consumer Protection Act 1987 and the Act is intended to bring English law into line with the provisions of the Directive (for consideration of some of these proposals for reform see Stapleton (1986) 6 OJLS 392).

16.4 The Consumer Protection Act 1987

Here we shall simply outline the main provisions of the Act, as a detailed analysis is beyond the scope of this book (for further details see R Merkin *A Guide to the Consumer Protection Act 1987*). The general principle is contained in s2(1) of the Act which provides that:

> 'Where any damage is caused wholly or partly by a defect in a product, every person to whom subsection (2) ... applies shall be liable for the damage.'

This statement of principle can be broken down into a number of separate elements. The first element relates to the persons to whom s2(2) applies. These persons are the producer of the product, any person who holds himself out as being a producer of the product, the importer of the goods into the EEC and, in more limited circumstances, the supplier of the product. The 'producer' of the product is defined in s1(2) as the person who manufactured the product, where the substance is 'won or abstracted' the person who won or abstracted it, or, in the case of a product which has been neither manufactured nor won or abstracted 'but essential characteristics of which are attributable to an industrial or other process having been carried out ... the person who carried out that process'. Where a defective product, such as a defective tyre, is contained in a car, it appears that both the manufacturer of the car and the manufacturer of the tyre may be liable (s1(3)). A person holds himself out as being the producer of the product where he puts his name on the product or uses a trade mark or 'other distinguishing mark in relation to the product' (s2(2)(b)). This definition would catch a supermarket chain which had its own logo upon a product and which held itself out as being the manufacturer of the product. The supplier is only liable where the person who suffered the damage requests the supplier (within a reasonable time of the damage and when it is not practicable for him to identify the producer, the person who has acted as the producer or the importer of the goods into the EEC) to identify one of those persons who may be liable and the supplier fails to comply with the request or to identify the persons who supplied the products to him (s2(3)). Thus the liability of the supplier is a secondary liability which may be discharged by him identifying his producer and it is only where he fails to do this that he will be liable. It should be noted that the supplier can discharge his liability by identifying his supplier, even if that supplier is bankrupt or otherwise unable to satisfy judgment. The liability of these persons is joint and several (s2(5)).

The second element which should be noted is that the principle contained in s2(1) only applies to a 'product'. 'Product' is defined in s1(2) as:

' ... any goods or electricity and (subject to subsection (3)) includes a product which is comprised in another product, whether by virtue of being a component part or raw material or otherwise.'

Goods is further defined in s45(1) as including:

' ... substances, growing crops and things comprised in land by virtue of being attached to it and any ship, aircraft or vehicle.'

A number of difficulties are likely to arise in the interpretation of the word 'product', particularly in the context of intellectual products, such as books and computer programmes, where it remains wholly unclear whether such products are caught by the Act (see further Whittaker 'European Product Liability and Intellectual Products' (1989) 105 LQR 125). Although buildings are not expressly excluded from the scope of the Act, it is provided in s46(4) of the Act that references to supplying goods shall not include references to supplying goods comprised in land where the supply is effected by the creation or disposal of an interest in the land. So where the builder sells the building that sale lies outside of the scope of the 1987 Act, although it may be caught under the Defective Premises Act 1972 (see further 17.19). Agricultural products (defined in s1(2) as any produce of the soil, of stock-farming or of fisheries) are also outside the scope of the Act, provided that they have not undergone an 'industrial process' (s2(4)).

The third point to note about the statement of principle is that the product must suffer from a defect. It should be noted that there are broadly two approaches which could be adopted to the issue of 'defectiveness' (see Clark 'The Conceptual Basis of Product Liability' (1985) 48 MLR 325). On one view it could be said that a product is defective when it does not live up to the expectations of consumers ('the contract standard'). On the other hand, a product could be said to be defective when the product is unreasonably dangerous to people or to their property ('the tort standard').. The 1987 Act adopts the tort standard rather then the contract standard because s3(1) states that a defect is contained in the product where:

' ... the *safety* of the product is not such as persons generally are entitled to expect.'

The Act does not require that the product be absolutely safe; it suffices that the product is reasonably safe. The Act does not contain an exhaustive definition of 'safety', but it does provide a list of factors to be taken into account in considering what is meant by 'safety'. The Act provides in s3(2) that 'all the circumstances shall be taken into account' including:

1. the manner in which, and purposes for which, the product has been marketed, its get-up, the use of any mark in relation to the product and any instructions for, or warnings with respect to, doing or refraining from doing anything with or in relation to the product;
2. what might reasonably be expected to be done with or in relation to the product; and
3. the time which the product was supplied by its producer to another.

These then are the specific factors to which the courts are directed to have regard, but they are not the only factors to which the courts can have regard. It is not yet clear whether the courts will have regard to the cost of making the product safe or the cost of the product itself (see further on the meaning of a defect Newdick (1987) 103 LQR 288).

The Act also contains some defences in relation to products which would otherwise be held to be defective. These defences are extremely important in setting the limits of the ambit of liability. These defences are contained in s4 of the Act. It should be noted that in all cases the burden of proof is on the defendant to establish the defence. The defences include a defence that the defect was attributable to 'compliance with any requirement imposed by or under any enactment or with any Community obligation' and that the defect did not exist in the product at the 'relevant time' (defined in s4(2)(a)). The most important and controversial defence is, however, the development risks defence which is contained in s4(1)(e) in the following terms:

> ' ... that the state of scientific and technical knowledge at the relevant time was not such that a producer of products of the same description as the product in question might be expected to have discovered the defect if it had existed in his products while they were under his control.'

This version of the 'development risks' defence differs in significant respects from the wording of Article 7 of the EEC Directive which states that a producer shall not be liable if he proves:

> ' ... that the state of scientific and technical knowledge at the time when he put the product into circulation was not such as to enable the existence of the defect to be discovered.'

The vital difference between the Act and the Directive concerns the scope of the inquiry relating to knowledge. Under the Act the inquiry is limited to producers of 'products of the same description as the product in question' but no such limitation is contained within the Directive. The European Commission is, however, likely to institute infringement proceedings against Great Britain, arguing that we have failed to comply with the requirements of Article 7 of the Directive.

The inclusion of the 'development risks' defence in both the Directive and the Act has been the subject of considerable criticism. The Directive in fact gave to member states the option whether or not to include the defence within the implementing legislation and the British government elected to incorporate it into the Act. The defence is likely to assume great significance in cases involving drug manufacturers where the manufacturers will, in many cases, argue that the state of scientific knowledge did not enable them to discover that the drug had the particular side effect which has caused the damage which the plaintiff has suffered (for an excellent analysis of the development risks defence see Newdick 'The Development Risks Defence of the Consumer Protection Act 1987' [1988] CLJ 455). The effect of this defence may well be to bring the law back to a standard which approximates more closely to liability for negligence than to strict liability. This is because this defence, as contained in the 1987 Act, appears to make a defendant manufacturer liable only where other producers of products of the same description had the relevant knowledge but the defendant did not; an inquiry very similar to the one which would be carried out in a negligence action. The only difference is that s4 makes it clear that the burden is upon the defendant to establish the defence, whereas at common law the burden rests on the plaintiff throughout.

The fourth point to note is that the factor of causation plays a crucial role in determining the ambit of liability. The plaintiff must show that the damage was caused wholly or partly by the defect in the product. There is no requirement that the loss be a foreseeable one; simply that it was caused by the defect in the product. Nor need the defect be the sole cause of the damage to the plaintiff. It is sufficient that it was partly responsible for the damage which occurred.

The fifth point to note is that the Act only applies to certain types of losses which are suffered by the plaintiff. Damage is defined in s5(1) as meaning 'death or personal injury or any loss of or damage to any property (including land)'. Damage to business property is outside the scope of the Act. A claim may only be made under the Act where, at the time of the damage, the property was 'of a description of property ordinarily intended for private use, occupation or consumption' and it was 'intended by the person suffering the loss or damage mainly for his own private use, occupation or consumption' (s5(3)). There is, however, a crucial limitation in s5(2) which provides that a defendant shall not be liable in respect of 'the loss of or damage to the product itself or for the loss of or any damage to the whole or any part of the product which has been supplied with the product in question comprised in it'. So, as at common law, the plaintiff can recover in respect of damage to other property of his, but not in respect of the defective product itself. There is also a minimum amount of damages which must be payable before the Act can apply. Section 5(4) provides that damages shall not be awarded under the Act in respect of damage to property where the amount which would be awarded, apart from interest, could not exceed £275. The aim of this requirement is clearly to exclude the possibility of the courts and insurers being flooded with masses of small claims. There is no ceiling on the limit of liability imposed in the Act. Finally it is provided in s7 of the Act that liability under s2(1) of the Act 'shall not be limited or excluded by any contract term, by any notice or by any provision'.

The Act constitutes a significant improvement upon the common law and is a real improvement for consumers. In this respect the Act is to be welcomed. However it is by no means the case that the Act has removed all the problems which existed at common law. The Act does not remove the difficulty of recovering in respect of the defect in the product itself. The defence that the defect did not exist in the product at the relevant time may also leave the consumer with considerable problems of proof, but, as compared with the common law, these problems may be alleviated by the fact that the burden is on the defendant to prove the defence rather than the burden being upon the plaintiff. Finally the inclusion of the state of the art defence may undermine, to a considerable degree, the claim of the Act to have introduced a regime of strict liability which is applicable to defective products. While it must be remembered that an increase in the extent of liability brings with it increased costs, in the form of higher insurance premiums, the cost of which is passed on to the public, the inclusion of this defence in the Act may prove a significant flaw in the legislation and it is likely to lead, at some time in the future, to still further calls for reform of the law relating to product liability.

17

Occupiers' Liability

17.1   Introduction

17.2   The scope of the 1957 Act

17.3   Who is an occupier?

17.4   Visitors

17.5   Premises

17.6   The common duty of care

17.7   Children

17.8   Common calling

17.9   Warning of danger

17.10 Independent contractors

17.11 Volenti

17.12 Contributory negligence

17.13 Contractors

17.14 Damage to property

17.15 Trespassers

17.16 Exclusion of the occupier's duty

17.17 Liability of independent contractors who are not occupiers

17.18 Liability of vendors and lessors

17.19 Liability of builders

17.1 Introduction

In many ways this area of law is but a specialised aspect of common law negligence. The vital difference, however, is that it is governed by statute, namely the Occupiers' Liability Acts of 1957 and 1984, rather than by purely common law principles. This calls for a different approach in analysing problems concerned with occupiers' liability because very close attention must be paid to the *exact words* used by Parliament as these are the words which set the limits to the ambit of liability.

Before embarking upon an analysis of these Acts it is necessary to make a few points about the pre-1957 law. The common law distinguished between different categories of entrant who came on to the land and held that occupiers owed a different duty to each category. The highest standard of care was owed to a contractor because here the occupier's freedom to use his land as he saw fit had to be balanced against the contractual rights of the contractor. Invitees, who were people invited on to the occupiers' land because they had some mutual interest of a business, or other material nature, with the occupier, were owed the next highest standard of care. The next category of visitors was licensees, who were persons who had permission to enter on to the land for some purpose of their own. They were owed a still lesser standard of care. The last category was trespassers, who were those persons who came on to the land without the consent of the occupier. They were owed the lowest standard of care of all.

Considerable criticism was directed against this classification, especially the narrowness of the distinction between the second and third categories. Criticism was also levelled against the idea that the occupier should be as free as possible in the use of his land and it was argued that greater weight should be given to the interests of those who come on to the land. It was in these circumstances that, in 1957, the Law Reform Committee reported on the urgent need to reform the law and it was their report which formed the basis of the 1957 Act.

The following discussion will concentrate upon the Occupiers' Liability Act 1957 ('the 1957 Act'), and the Occupiers' Liability Act 1984 ('the 1984 Act') will be discussed primarily in paragraph 17.15.

17.2 The scope of the 1957 Act

Before the enactment of the 1957 Act, a distinction was drawn between damage arising as a result of an activity carried out on the premises (the 'activity duty') and damage occurring due to the state of the premises (the 'occupancy duty'); the former being governed by *Donoghue* v *Stevenson* principles, while the latter was governed by a separate line of authority solely applicable to occupiers' liability. It is unclear whether this distinction has survived the Act. Section 1(1) of the Act states that the Act shall apply 'in respect of dangers due to the state of the premises *or to things done or omitted to be done on them*'. The latter part of the subsection clearly envisages that the Act shall apply to the 'activity duty'. But in s1(2) it is provided that the Act shall 'regulate the nature of the duty imposed by law in consequence of a person's occupation or control of premises'. This subsection does not appear to encompass the 'activity duty'. There is no authoritative decision on the point, but the weight of academic opinion is that the Act only applies to the 'occupancy duty' (see *Winfield and Jolowicz on Tort* (13th ed) p208). In *Ogwo* v *Taylor* [1987] 2 WLR 988 Stephen Brown LJ stated that he did not think that injury suffered by the plaintiff fireman while fighting a fire on the defendant's premises, which was started by the defendant's negligence, was 'strictly a case for consideration in the context of the Occupiers' Liability Act' because the injury did not result from a defect in the premises. Neither of the other judges commented on this issue and Stephen Brown LJ's dicta was strictly obiter, but it is submitted that, as it is consistent with the majority of academic opinion, it should be taken to represent the law. However, in practice, the issue is not of great importance because there is little, if any, difference between the standard of care owed at common law and the standard of care owed under the 1957 Act.

17.3 Who is an occupier?

Section 1(2) of the Act states that the definition of 'occupier' remains the same as at common law, so it is necessary to go back and consider common law authorities. The original test for identifying an occupier focused on the fact of control over the premises, in the sense of having the power to control entry to the premises (*Cavalier* v *Pope* [1906] AC 428). But the test was rejected by the House of Lords in *Wheat* v *E Lacon and Co Ltd* [1966] AC 522.

In *Wheat* the defendants owned a public house, which was managed by one of their employees, Richardson. Richardson and his wife occupied the first floor of the public house as their private dwelling, but they did not have any interest in the premises. Indeed, under an agreement with the defendants, it was provided that there was not even a tenancy agreement between the parties. Richardson's wife was given permission to take in paying guests in a part of the first floor which they occupied. There was no direct access from the first floor to the public house, but there was an outside staircase which went to the rear of the premises. The handrail of this staircase terminated directly above the third step and the staircase was not lit because someone had stolen the bulb. The plaintiff and her husband were paying guests of the Richardsons. One night the plaintiff's husband fell down the stairs and fractured his skull. He died from his injuries. It was held that both the Richardsons and the defendants were occupiers of the staircase, but that the defendants were not in breach of their duty of care because the staircase was normally safe and they were not responsible for the act of a stranger in removing the bulb.

The most influential judgment was given by Lord Denning. He said that:

'Wherever a person has a sufficient degree of control over premises that he ought to realise that any failure on his part to use care may result in injury to a person coming lawfully there, then he is an "occupier" and the person coming lawfully there is his "visitor".'

Lord Denning then divided the law up into four categories, which form a useful basis for analysis. These categories were as follows:

1. Where a landlord lets premises by demise the landlord is regarded as having parted with all control over the premises so that the tenant is the occupier.
2. Where a landlord lets part of a building but retains other parts, such as the common staircase, then the landlord remains liable as an occupier for the parts of the building which he has retained (for an example of this see *Miller* v *Hancock* [1893] 2 QB 177).
3. Where a landowner licenses a person to occupy his premises on terms which do not amount to a demise and the owner still has the right to enter on to the premises to do repairs then the owner remains sufficiently in control to be an occupier (see *Wheat* itself).
4. Where an occupier employs independent contractors to do some work on his premises, the owner is generally still sufficiently in control to be an occupier. The difficulty really lies in determining whether or not the independent contractors are also occupiers. It should be noted that there is no requirement that control be exclusive, so that there can be more than one occupier at the same time, as in *Wheat*. Independent contractors were held to be occupiers in *AMF International Ltd* v *Magnet Bowling Ltd* [1968] 1 WLR 1028. The plaintiffs' timber was damaged by rainwater while it was on the first defendants' premises. The rainwater got in through an unfinished doorway. The plaintiffs only brought the timber on to the land, after the first defendants and the second defendants, who were a firm of independent contractors, had confirmed that the property was ready for installation of the timber. It was held that both defendants were sufficiently in control to be occupiers (see too *Collier* v *Anglian Water Authority* (1983) The Times 26 March).

This four-tier approach is useful but it is not exhaustive, as was confirmed by the Court of Appeal in *Harris* v *Birkenhead Corporation* [1976] 1 WLR 279. The first defendants, in pursuance of a slum clearance policy, issued a compulsory purchase order over a house owned by the second defendant. They then issued her with a notice of entry under the Housing Acts, which entitled them to take over the premises after 14 days. The house was not, however, vacated for another several months. After the house was vacated the first defendants took no steps to have the house boarded up, even though they knew that failure to do so was likely to lead to vandalism. The plaintiff, a child of four and a half, wandered into the house through an unsecured door and suffered serious injuries when he fell from a second floor window. Megaw LJ analysed the four-fold classification of Lord Denning and concluded that actual physical possession was not a necessary ingredient of control. In this case the fact that the first defendants had, by virtue of their having served a notice of entry, the legal right to control the premises made them the occupiers to the exclusion of the second defendant, even though the first defendants had not, actually or symbolically, taken possession of the premises. In all cases the question of sufficiency of control is one of fact.

17.4 Visitors

The duty owed by an occupier under the 1957 Act is owed to those who are his 'visitors'. Once again resort must be had to the common law because s1(2) states that a lawful visitor is, for the purposes of the Act, either an invitee or a licensee. It should be noted that the Act only applies to persons who come on to the occupier's premises; it has no application to someone who remains outside the premises. In considering who is a visitor it is helpful to divide the issue up into the following categories.

Express permission

This is the easiest category of all and simply depends on proof that the occupier did, in fact, give permission.

Implied permission

The onus of proving the existence of implied permission rests on the person who alleges that it exists. Many of the cases under this category concern policemen seeking entry to a private dwelling house. One such case is *Robson* v *Hallett* [1967] 2 QB 393. There it was laid down that a person who enters upon the premises of the occupier for the purpose of communicating with the occupier is treated as having the occupier's implied permission to be there until the visitor knows or ought to know that his permission has been revoked. Once his permission has been revoked he has a reasonable time to leave the premises before becoming a trespasser.

Another problem which has troubled the courts has arisen where the occupier knows that persons are in the habit of coming on to his land. Does this knowledge, of itself, operate to convert that other person into his visitor? In *Lowery* v *Walker* [1911] AC 10 the public had been in the habit of taking a short cut across the defendant farmer's land for some 35 years. The defendant had never taken legal proceedings to stop them, however, because many of them were his customers. One day he put a wild horse into the field. The plaintiff, who was taking a short cut, was injured by the horse. It was held that the plaintiff was not a trespasser but, by virtue of the long use of the short cut to the knowledge of the defendant, was a licensee. Care must be used in relying upon this case as it was decided at a time when the courts were very willing to classify plaintiffs as licensees because the duty which was owed by an occupier to a trespasser was so minimal (see paragraph 17.15). Now that trespassers are covered by the 1984 Act there is no longer the same need to adopt such a benevolent approach.

The issue was, however, reconsidered by the House of Lords in *Edwards* v *Railway Executive* [1952] AC 737. The plaintiff, a nine-year-old boy, was seriously injured by a train after he had fallen on the railway line. He had got on to the railway line by climbing through the boundary fence in order to retrieve his ball which had gone on to the railway line. The defendants knew that the boundary fence was frequently broken by children who then made their way on to the railway line, but they repaired the fence whenever they discovered that it had been broken. The plaintiff argued that this step was not sufficient to keep children out and so the plaintiff was not a trespasser but was a licensee. The House of Lords unanimously rejected this argument. Lord Goddard stated that some of the earlier cases appeared to be decided out of sympathy for the plaintiff rather than upon sound legal principle. He affirmed that repeated trespass does not, of itself, turn a person into a licensee. There must be evidence of the landowner's express consent or conduct on his part which is such that he cannot be heard to say that he did not give permission. *Lowery* was distinguished on the ground that the defendant was not entitled to let loose a horse which he knew to be dangerous without giving any warning whatsoever. So while knowledge of a person's presence is not sufficient, of itself, to give that person a licence to be present, an occupier who is aware that people are in the habit of coming on to his land should take positive and regular steps to ensure that these people know that they are not welcome.

Public and private rights of way

In *Holden* v *White* [1982] 2 WLR 1030 it was held that persons lawfully exercising a private right of way were not 'visitors' for the purposes of the 1957 Act. Oliver LJ noted that the purpose behind the 1957 Act was to remove the old common law categorisations, but he said that the purpose behind the Act was not to extend the category of persons to whom a duty was owed. As a person lawfully exercising a right of way was not an invitee or licensee at common law he could not be covered by the 1957 Act. This decision has now been reversed by s1(1)(a) of the Occupiers' Liability Act 1984 and such people are now owed a duty of care under that Act but it must be stressed that the duty owed under the 1984 Act is different from the duty owed under the 1957 Act (see 17.15 below). One problem remains here and it concerns who the occupier is. In the Law Commission Report *Liability for Damage or Injury to Trespassers and Related Questions of Occupiers' Liability* (paras. 42–56) it was assumed that it would be the occupier of the servient land and this point was conceded by counsel in *Holden*. But Oliver LJ doubted whether this concession was correct and thought that it was the occupier of the dominant land who was the occupier. So the position is unclear at the moment.

In *Greenhalgh* v *British Railways Board* [1969] 2 QB 286 the Court of Appeal held that persons lawfully exercising a public right of way were not visitors for the purposes of the 1957 Act. Section 1(7) of the 1984 Act states that they are not covered by that Act either. So they are only protected by the common law which states that the occupier is liable for negligent misfeasance but not for negligent nonfeasance. In other words the occupier is not liable for a failure to repair the right of way. However, in *Thomas* v *British Railways Board* [1976] QB 912 there was a suggestion that an occupier owed a duty similar to that owed to trespassers, but it remains to be seen how far this will be developed. In practice this anomalous rule only applies to public rights of way not maintainable at public expense because the Highways Acts impose liability upon the highway authorities for both negligent misfeasance and non-feasance.

It is submitted that the law here is in an unsatisfactory state, reflecting the pre-1957 state of the law, where persons lawfully coming on to the land are classified according to their status.

Lawful authority

Section 2(6) of the 1957 Act expressly provides that persons who enter premises for any purpose in the exercise of a right conferred by law are to be treated as having permission by the occupier to be there for that purpose, whether they in fact have permission or not.

Limitations on permission

The occupier may give the visitor permission to enter the premises, but may elect to limit that permission in one of three ways.

The first limitation relates to space. An occupier may give a visitor permission to enter some parts of his premises but not others. In *The Calgarth* [1927] P 93 Scrutton LJ said that 'when you invite a person into your house to use the stairs, you do not invite him to slide down the bannisters'. In *Gould* v *McAuliffe* [1941] 2 All ER 527 the plaintiff got lost looking for the outside lavatory in a public house. She went through an open gate and was attacked by a dog. The defendants argued that the plaintiff was a trespasser. This was rejected by the court on the ground that the gate was not locked, there was no notice that the yard was private or that a dangerous dog was there. So, if an occupier wishes to place limitations upon the visitor, then he must take steps to bring the limitation to the visitor's attention.

The second limitation relates to the purpose for which the visitor comes on to the land. This was considered in the criminal case of *R* v *Smith and Jones* [1976] 1 WLR 672. In this case a son broke into his father's house and stole a television set. At the son's trial the father said that the son would never be a trespasser in his house. It was held that, for the purposes of the Theft Act 1968, the son was a trespasser because he knew when he entered the house that he was entering in excess of the permission given to him or he was reckless whether his entry was in excess of that permission.

The third limitation relates to the time at which the visitor may come on to the premises. In *Stone* v *Taffe* [1974] 1 WLR 1575 the plaintiff's husband died when he fell down the stairs outside a public house after attending a party, held by the manager of the public house, which had continued after licensing hours. The widow sued the owners of the public house, who claimed that the deceased was a trespasser. Stephenson LJ held that an occupier who intends to permit a person to enter his premises for a limited period of time only must give that person a clear indication that his permission to be on the premises is subject to a time limit. On the facts the deceased had not been given any indication that his permission to be on the premises was subject to a time limit and so the deceased was not a trespasser. The deceased did not know that the manager of the public house was only entitled to hold a private party out of hours if prior permission had been given by the owners and the police had been notified.

Multiple occupiers

Where there is more than one occupier the possibility arises of a plaintiff being a visitor in relation to one occupier and a trespasser as regards the other occupier. Such a possibility was considered by the House of Lords in *Ferguson* v *Welsh* [1987] 3 All ER 777. The occupiers of the land were the defendant council. They had accepted a tender from an independent contractor, Spence (S), to demolish a building. It was a condition of the tender that the work was not to be subcontracted without the permission of the council. Notwithstanding this prohibition S subcontracted the work to Welsh Brothers (W) who in turn employed the plaintiff to demolish the building. The plaintiff was injured because of an unsafe system of work employed by W. The plaintiff brought an action against W, S and the council. The difficulty for the plaintiff was that W were men of straw and S was unlikely to have sufficient funds to meet the plaintiff's claim, which was for £150,000. So the claim against the council was of crucial significance to the plaintiff. The council conceded that both they and S were occupiers of the building. The House of Lords held that the council were not liable to the plaintiff (see 17.6 and 17.10). A preliminary point concerned whether or not the plaintiff was a visitor in relation to the defendant council. Lord Keith, with whom Lord Brandon and Lord Griffiths concurred, held that there was evidence capable of establishing that the plaintiff was a visitor vis-a-vis the council. Despite the terms of the contract between the council and S, the council had placed S in control of the building for the purpose of its demolition and therefore S had been clothed with ostensible authority to invite W and their employees on to the land. However Lord Goff could not see any difficulty in an appropriate case in holding that the plaintiff was a lawful visitor as against S but a trespasser as against the council. He said that the answer to the question whether or not the plaintiff was a visitor as against the council must depend on whether S, as an occupier, had authority from the council (whether that authority be actual (express or implied) or ostensible) to allow a third party on to the land of the council. On the fact he was prepared to assume for the purpose of the appeal that S did have ostensible authority.

17.5 Premises

The 1957 Act applies to an occupier of 'premises'. There is no exhaustive definition of premises in the Act. It obviously includes land, houses and buildings. Some guidance is afforded by s1(3)(a) which states that the Act shall regulate 'the obligations of a person occupying or having control over any fixed or moveable structure, including any vessel, vehicle or aircraft'. In *Wheeler* v *Copas* [1981] 3 All ER 405, the plaintiff, who was constructing a house on the defendant's land, borrowed a ladder from the defendant, without asking whether the ladder was suitable for his purpose. The ladder was not suitable for his purpose and he fell and was injured. It was held that the defendant was not liable to the plaintiff under s1(3)(a) because, although the Act might in appropriate circumstances apply to a ladder, it could not be said that in this case the defendant was still the occupier of the ladder once he handed it to the plaintiff. The defendant was, however, liable to the plaintiff in negligence.

17.6 The common duty of care

One of the major innovations of the 1957 Act was to enact a common duty of care which is owed to all visitors. Section 2(1) of the Act states that:

> 'An occupier of premises owes the same duty, the 'common duty of care', to all his visitors, except in so far as he is free to and does extend, restrict, modify or exclude his duty to any visitor or visitors by agreement or otherwise.'

This common duty of care is defined in s2(2) in the following terms:

> ' ... a duty to take such care as in all the circumstances of the case is reasonable to see that the visitor will be reasonably safe in using the premises for the purposes for which he is invited or permitted by the occupier to be there.'

A number of points may be made about this definition. The first is that the visitor must be reasonably safe 'in using the premises for the purposes for which he is invited or permitted by the occupier to be there'. In *Ferguson* v *Welsh* (above) Lord Goff held that plaintiff's action against the defendant council must fail because it could not be said that the plaintiff was not 'reasonably safe in using the premises for the purposes for which he was invited to be there'. Rather his injuries arose because of the 'manner in which he carried out his work on the premises' and such injuries were not caught by s2(2). However Lord Keith, with whom Lord Brandon and Lord Griffiths agreed, stated that the safety referred to in s2(2) was safety 'not only from dangers due to the state of the premises but also known dangers due to things done or permitted by the occupier to be done on them'. Thus he held that s2(2) was applicable, although he found that there had been no breach of the common duty of care (see 17.10). The second is that it is the *visitor*, not the premises, which must be reasonably safe. The third is that the duty to take such care as is reasonable in the circumstances involves consideration of issues similar to those involved in a common law negligence action. This can be demonstrated by reference to the case of *Sawyer v H and G Simonds Ltd* (1966) 197 EG 877. The plaintiff was injured when he slipped at the bar of the defendants' hotel and hurt his hand on some broken glass on the floor. Veale J held that it was not proved that the defendants had failed to keep a reasonable look-out for broken glass and so the defendants had discharged the duty which they owed. The court considered the nature of the danger, the length of time that the danger was in existence, the steps necessary to remove the danger and the likelihood of injury resulting. These are the very factors which would be taken into account in a common law negligence action. As in all negligence actions, each case in which it is alleged that the defendant has breached his duty of care depends ultimately on the application of an established principle to the facts of the case. Thus *Sawyer* can be contrasted with the recent case of *Murphy* v *Bradford Metropolitan Council* (1991) The Times 11 February. The plaintiff teacher fell on a path leading to a school run by the council and she suffered injury. The path was notoriously slippery but on the morning of the accident the school caretaker had cleared the path of snow at 6.30 am and treated it with rock salt and done so again at 8 am, on being told that the path was still slippery. Despite these efforts the plaintiff still slipped on the path half an hour later. The trial judge held that the defendants had not discharged their duty under s2(2) because the path was a likely place for an accident to occur and they had failed to lay grit and cinders on it. This finding was upheld by the Court of Appeal.

It should also be noted that an occupier may be in breach of his duty of care to a visitor as a result of his failure to control the activities of a third party on his land. This was the case in *Cunningham* v *Reading Football Club Ltd* (1991) The Independent 20 March. The plaintiffs were police officers on duty at a league football match played at the defendants' football ground and were injured by missiles thrown by fans attending the match. The defendants had failed to maintain their ground with the result that it was possible to break off pieces of concrete from the structure of the ground and use the pieces of concrete as missiles. The defendants knew both that it was possible to break off lumps of concrete and that fans in the past had used them as missiles. It was held that the defendants were liable because they knew of the condition of their ground, they knew that it was 'very probable' that such missiles would be used (see *Home Office* v *Dorset Yacht* [1970] AC 1004, discussed at 11.8) and they had therefore failed to discharge the common duty of care owed to the plaintiffs.

The fourth, and final, point to note about s2(2) is that, where there is more than one occupier of the premises at the one time, it may be that the standard of care required of each occupier is different.

But it must be noted that the Act differs from the common law in that specific provision is made in the Act for particular situations. These provisions will be considered in paragraphs 17.7 to 17.10.

17.7 Children

Section 2(3)(a) of the 1957 Act provides that 'an occupier must be prepared for children to be less careful than adults'. This sentiment was echoed by Hamilton LJ in *Latham v R Johnson and Nephew Ltd* [1913] 1 KB 398, 415 when he said:

> 'In the case of an infant, there are moral as well as physical traps. There may accordingly be a duty towards infants not merely not to dig pitfalls for them, but not to lead them into temptation.'

There have been numerous cases reported involving an application of this principle. Two cases will be discussed here to illustrate its application. The first case is *Glasgow Corporation v Taylor* [1922] 1 AC 44. A child aged seven died after eating poisonous berries which he had picked off a bush in a public park. The berries resembled blackberries and were very tempting to the child. The bush was not fenced off in any way, nor was there any warning of the dangerous nature of the berries. It was held that the defendants were liable (see too *Moloney v Lambeth* LBC (1968) 198 EG 895).

On the other hand in *Liddle v Yorks (North Riding) CC* [1934] 2 KB 101 the defendants were not liable to the child plaintiff. Here the defendants left a heap of soil close to a wall so that it was possible to climb up the soil and on to the wall. The plaintiff, a boy aged seven who had previously been warned off by the defendants, climbed up the soil on to the wall and, in trying to show his little friends how bees flew, fell off the wall and was injured. It was held that the defendants were not liable because the danger of falling off the wall was obvious, even to the child plaintiff.

A particular problem which has emerged concerns particularly young children, as there is hardly anything which is not a danger to such children. The position was authoritatively considered by Devlin J in *Phipps v Rochester Corporation* [1955] 1 QB 450. Here a boy aged five fell into a trench and broke his leg. Children were in the habit of using this area as a play area and this fact was known to the defendants, but they took no steps to prevent the children from playing there. It was held that the defendants were not liable to the plaintiff. Devlin J held that, in cases involving children of 'tender years', account must be taken of the fact that: reasonable parents will not permit children to be sent into danger without protection; guardians of the child and the place of the accident must both act reasonably; and each is entitled to assume that the other will act reasonably.

In *Phipps* the five-year-old plaintiff was only accompanied by his seven-year-old sister and there was no evidence of any breach of duty by the defendants (see too *Simkiss v Rhondda Borough Council* (1983) 81 LGR 460).

17.8 Common calling

Section 2(3)(b) provides that 'an occupier may expect that a person, in the exercise of his calling, will appreciate and guard against any special risks ordinarily incident to it, so far as the occupier leaves him free to do so'. This subsection was considered by the Court of Appeal in *Roles* v *Nathan* [1963] 1 WLR 1117. Here two chimney sweeps were killed by carbon monoxide fumes while sealing up a sweep-hole in the vertical chimney shaft of a furnace on the occupier's premises. Lord Denning thought that s2(3)(b) applied here because a householder can reasonably expect a sweep to take care of himself in respect of dangers arising out of the flue. Harman LJ doubted whether s2(3)(b) applied on the facts of the case because it was the occupier who created the danger by lighting the furnace when he had been told not to. Pearson LJ thought that s2(3)(b) was inapplicable because this was not a risk which was 'ordinarily incident' to the sweeps' calling, as was shown by the repeated warnings which the sweeps received.

The fact that the visitor is possessed of a particular skill is not sufficient, of itself, to discharge the duty of care owed to the visitor. Thus, in *Salmon* v *Seafarer Restaurants Ltd* [1983] 3 All ER 729 it was held that an occupier owes the same duty of care to a fireman as to any other visitor and the argument that the duty was limited to protecting the fireman from special risks not associated with normal fires was rejected. *Salmon* was approved by the House of Lords in *Ogwo* v *Taylor* [1988] AC 431. The House of Lords dismissed the argument that a duty of care was owed only in relation to exceptional risks which were greater than the 'ordinary' risks inherent in fire-fighting. In all cases they held that the appropriate question was whether the injury to the fireman was reasonably foreseeable. The person who starts a fire negligently is, however, entitled to expect that the fireman will act in accordance with standard practice in fighting the fire and not expose himself to 'unnecessary' risks in a 'foolhardy' manner.

This phrase 'ordinarily incident' was important in the case of *Bird* v *King Line* [1970] 1 Lloyds Rep 349. Here a foreman scaler, who tripped over an empty bottle lying on the deck of a ship, was held to be entitled to recover from the defendants because the risk of tripping over an empty bottle was not 'ordinarily incident' to the work of a foreman scaler (see too *Woollins* v *British Celanese Ltd* (1966) 110 SJ 686).

17.9 Warning of danger

It is provided in s2(4)(a) that, in determining whether an occupier has discharged his duty of care, regard is to be had to all the circumstances so that, for example:

> 'Where damage is caused to a visitor by a danger of which he has been warned by the occupier, the warning is not to be treated without more as absolving the occupier from liability, unless in all the circumstances it was enough to enable the visitor to be reasonably safe.'

This subsection was considered by the Court of Appeal in *Roles* v *Nathan* (above). In this case the sweeps were given a warning of the danger of fumes by a heating engineer. The sweeps were repeatedly told not to stay in the flue for too long and that the boiler was not to be turned on until the sweep-hole was sealed. Lord Denning said that this was a clear case for the application of s2(4)(a) as the warnings given were sufficient to enable the sweeps to be reasonably safe and that what happened was entirely the sweeps' own fault. Harman LJ agreed with Lord Denning on this point, but Pearson LJ dissented on the ground that it was the occupier's agents themselves who, in disregard of the warning, did the dangerous act of lighting the fire before the access had been sealed and so the warning did not enable the sweeps to be reasonably safe.

It should be noted that, for the purposes of s2(4)(a), the warning must be given by the occupier. This was satisfied in *Roles* because the heating agent who gave the warning was treated as the agent of the occupier.

If a warning is given then it should be given in clear terms because an inadequate warning may lead to the imposition of liability. This is because the fact that the occupier has gone to the trouble of putting up a warning notice suggests that he is aware of the existence of the danger and his failure to take sufficient steps to bring the danger to the attention of the visitor is a breach of duty on his part (see *Woollins* v *British Celanese Ltd* (above)). It should also be noted that s2(4)(a) states that a warning shall not, without more, absolve the occupier from liability. This suggests that a warning may, in combination with some other factor such as a handrail, be sufficient to discharge the duty upon the occupier.

17.10 Independent contractors

It is provided in s2(4)(b) that:

> 'Where damage is caused to a visitor by a danger due to the faulty execution of any work of construction, maintenance or repair by an independent contractor employed by the occupier, the occupier is not to be treated without more as answerable for the danger if in all the circumstances he had acted reasonably in entrusting the work to an independent contractor and had taken such steps (if any) as he reasonably ought in order to satisfy himself that the contractor was competent and that the work had been properly done.'

This subsection was introduced to reverse the decision of the House of Lords in *Thomson* v *Cremin* [1956] 1 WLR 103 that an occupier owes a personal non-delegable duty to his invitees to take reasonable care and that he cannot discharge this duty by entrusting the work to independent contractors.

A number of points may be made about this subsection. The first is that it only applies to the 'faulty execution of any work of construction, maintenance or repair'. This phrase was interpreted liberally by Mocatta J in *AMF International Ltd* v *Magnet Bowling Ltd* [1968] 1 WLR 1028. There it was argued that the independent contractors had simply failed to prevent the flooding arising and that no faulty work had been done. However, Mocatta J managed to find that some very minor work had been done and this was sufficient to make the subsection applicable. He went on to say that, if a builder failed to take adequate steps against flooding in the course of the construction of a building and damage resulted, it would be 'too technical' to hold that this was not within s2(4)(b). So a narrow approach will not be taken to the construction of this subsection. This liberal approach is further evidenced by the judgment of Lord Keith in *Ferguson* v *Welsh* (above). He held that by a 'broad and purposeful construction' of s2(4)(b) works of demolition could be included within 'construction'. With the greatest respect to his Lordship it is difficult to see how construction can encompass demolition; demolition is the very opposite of construction. Where a contractor is employed to demolish a building prior to constructing a new one it is conceded that such demolition work should be caught by s2(4)(b), but the same reasoning should not apply where, as in *Ferguson*, the contractors were employed only for the purpose of demolition.

The second point to note is that it must be reasonable for the occupier to entrust the work to an independent contractor. It is submitted that it is reasonable to do so whenever the work requires special skill or it is commercial practice to engage an independent contractor in the circumstances. The third point to note is that the occupier must take reasonable care to ensure that the contractors, to whom he entrusts the work, are competent to carry the work out.

The fourth, and final, point to note about this subsection is that the occupier must take reasonable care to check, where possible, that the work 'had been properly done'. It should be noted that, although the subsection actually states that 'the work had been properly done', it was held in *Ferguson* v *Welsh* (above) that the subsection did not depend for its application upon the work having been completed but that it could apply where the work was still being done and had not been completed. In general it may be said that the more technical the work, the less reasonable it is to require the occupier to supervise the work. This can be demonstrated by reference to the following cases. In *Haseldine* v *Daw* [1941] 2 KB 343 the plaintiff was killed, when the lift in which he was travelling fell to the bottom of the shaft. This happened because of the negligence of a firm of contractors employed by the defendants to repair the lift. It was held that, in employing a competent firm of contractors to keep the lift in repair, the defendants had discharged their duty to the plaintiff. To go further and impose liability upon them would be to make them insurers of the safety of the lift.

On the other hand the defendants were held liable in *Woodward* v *Mayor of Hastings* [1945] KB 174. The plaintiff, a school pupil, was injured when he slipped on an icy step at the school. The step was in an icy condition because it had been negligently cleaned by a cleaner. Assuming that the cleaner was an independent contractor, it was held that the defendants were still liable under s2(4)(b) because they had failed to take reasonable steps to inspect the cleaner's work. Du Parcq LJ said that the 'craft of the charwoman may have its mysteries, but there is no esoteric quality in the nature of the work which the cleaning of a snow-covered step demands'.

One final problem arises where the employee of an independent contractor is injured on the premises of the occupier as the result of an unsafe system of work used by the independent contractor. In such a case can the injured party bring an action against the occupier? In *Ferguson* v *Welsh* Lord Keith, with whom Lord Brandon and Lord Griffiths concurred, held that it would not ordinarily be reasonable to expect an occupier of premises, who has engaged an independent contractor whom he had reasonable grounds to believe was competent, to supervise the contractor's activities in order to ensure that the independent contractor was discharging his duty to his employees to use a safe system of work. However he did indicate that, in exceptional cases, such as where the occupier knows or has reason to suspect that the independent contractor is using an unsafe system of work, it might well be reasonable to expect the occupier to take reasonable steps to see that the system is made safe. This proposition was, however, doubted by Lord Goff. He thought that the knowledge of an occupier that an independent contractor was using an unsafe system of work was not ordinarily sufficient to impose liability on the occupier in an action under the 1957 Act or in a common law negligence action. He gave the example of a householder who employs an electrician to do some repair work. He held that if the electrician then sends an employee to do the work, and the employee uses an unsafe system of work established by his employer, then 'I cannot see that, in ordinary circumstances, the householder should be held liable under the 1957 Act, or even in negligence, for failing to tell the man how he should be doing his work'. He concluded by saying that there may be exceptional cases where the occupier may be liable for failing to warn the employee, but he held that in such a case the liability of the occupier would be as a joint tortfeasor with the independent contractor. Lord Oliver agreed with Lord Goff that in such a case the liability of the occupier would be as a joint tortfeasor.

17.11 Volenti

It is provided in s2(5) of the 1957 Act that:

> 'The common duty of care does not impose upon an occupier any obligation in respect of risks willingly accepted as his by the visitor (the question whether a risk was so accepted to be decided on the same principles as in other cases in which one person owes a duty of care to another).'

John if
visitor

For an example of the courts' approach in this area see *Simms* v *Leigh Rugby FC* [1969] 2 All ER 923.

17.12 Contributory negligence

In s2(3) of the 1957 Act it is provided that in considering the common duty of care the circumstances relevant include the 'degree of care, and of want of care, which would ordinarily be looked for in such a visitor'. So it is clear that the apportionment provisions of the Law Reform (Contributory Negligence) Act 1945 are applicable. In *Stone* v *Taffe* [1974] 1 WLR 1575, for example, the plaintiff's damages were reduced by 50 per cent on the ground of contributory negligence (discussed further in chapter 12).

17.13 Contractors

Specific provision is made in the 1957 Act for those who enter an occupier's premises in pursuance of a contract with the occupier. Section 5 provides that:

> 'Where persons enter or use, or bring or send goods to, any premises in exercise of a right conferred by contract with a person occupying or having control of the premises, the duty he owes them in respect of dangers due to the state of the premises or to things done or omitted to be done on them, in so far as the duty depends on a term to be implied in the contract by reason of its conferring that right, shall be the common duty of care.'

However, s5 does not apply to:

> '... obligations imposed on a person by or by virtue of any contract for the hire of, or for the carriage for reward of persons or goods in, any vehicle, vessel, aircraft or other means of transport, or by virtue of any contract of bailment.'

The position of third parties to the contract is governed by s3 of the Act. That section provides that:

> 'Where an occupier of premises is bound by contract to permit persons who are strangers to the contract to enter or use the premises, the duty of care which he owes to them as his visitors cannot be restricted or excluded by that contract, but (subject to any provision of the contract to the contrary) shall include the duty to perform his obligations under the contract, whether undertaken for their protection or not, in so far as those obligations go beyond the obligations otherwise involved in that duty.'

The effect of this section is twofold. The first is that the occupier cannot reduce his obligation to a visitor who is a stranger to the contract below that contained in the common duty of care. Secondly, if the contract imposes some higher duty on the occupier, then the visitor shall have the benefit of that provision.

Section 3(2) provides that:

> 'A contract shall not by virtue of this section have the effect, unless it expressly so provides, of making an occupier who has taken all reasonable care answerable to strangers to the contract for dangers due to the faulty execution of any work of construction, maintenance or repair or other like operation by persons other than himself, his servants and persons acting under his direction and control.'

17.14 Damage to property

Section 1(3)(b) makes it clear that the Act applies to 'damage to property, including the property of persons who are not themselves his visitors'. The Act does not, however, create a liability where none existed at common law (see *Tinsley* v *Dudley* [1951] KB 18).

17.15 Trespassers

It is essential to note that the duty owed by an occupier to a trespasser is regulated by the Occupiers' Liability Act 1984. Although we shall commence our analysis with a consideration of the common law, this is done for the sole purpose of giving a background to the development of the law and to shed light on the likely interpretation of the 1984 Act. It is the 1984 Act which now forms the basis of the law.

A trespasser was defined by Lord Dunedin in *Robert Addie and Sons (Collieries) Ltd* v *Dumbreck* [1929] AC 358 in the following terms as:

' ... he who goes on to the land without invitation of any sort and whose presence is either unknown to the proprietor or, if known, is practically objected to.'

But it must be stressed that not every trespasser is a criminal or an immoral person. A person who overstays his welcome could be a trespasser as could a child who wanders innocently on to someone else's land. In truth it covers both the 'wicked' and the 'innocent'.

The duty originally owed to trespassers, which was laid down by the House of Lords in *Addie* v *Dumbreck* (above), was an extremely narrow one. It only arose where the trespasser's injury was due to some wilful act on the part of the occupier, which was done either with the intention of doing harm to the trespasser or was done with reckless disregard of the presence of the trespasser. The decision reflected two particular policy considerations. The first was that the property rights of the occupier were sacrosanct and could only be interfered with in meritorious situations. The second was that trespassers were wrongdoers who were not worthy of such protection.

These policy reasons are no longer so persuasive as they were in 1929 and so some judges sought to escape from this restrictive ruling. They did so in one of two ways. The first was to classify the entrant as an implied licensee rather than a trespasser. This approach can be seen in the case of *Lowery* v *Walker* (above) and in many cases involving children. The second approach was adopted in a case called *Videan* v *British Transport Commission* [1963] 2 QB 650, where an attempt was made to confine *Addie* to breaches of the 'occupancy duty' and hold that it had no application to the 'activity duty'. This approach was, however, rejected by the Privy Council in *Commissioner for Railways* v *Quinlan* [1964] AC 1054.

Surprisingly trespassers were omitted from the coverage of the 1957 Act and they had to wait until 1972 for the judiciary to intervene to alleviate their position. This was done in *British Railways Board* v *Herrington* [1972] AC 877. The plaintiff, a six-year-old boy, climbed through a gap in a fence beside an electrified railway track run by the defendants and was seriously injured when he was burnt on the live wire. The fence was in a dilapidated condition so that it was relatively easy to get on to the railway line. It had been in this state for some time and it had been reported to the defendants that people were using the gap as a short cut, but the defendants had done nothing about it. The House of Lords held that *Addie* was no longer an exclusive statement of the law and, in particular, they considered that the two policies which we noted underpinned the decision no longer held good. Yet the House was not prepared to impose full *Donoghue* v *Stevenson* liability because it was thought that this would place too onerous a burden upon occupiers. It is not clear exactly what test the House intended to impose because the five judgments given were not a model of clarity. It is sometimes referred to as the duty of 'common humanity' and is a duty in between that imposed in *Addie* and the *Donoghue* standard. There would appear to be two principal differences between the *Herrington* standard and the *Donoghue* standard.

The first difference is that, in most cases, the presence of the trespasser will not be reasonably foreseeable. Lord Reid said that the occupier must have knowledge of a 'substantial probability' of the presence of the trespasser. Lord Diplock was the most extreme in saying that the occupier must actually know that the trespasser is present or have actual knowledge of the facts from which a reasonable person would infer that a trespasser was present on his land. This test is much more subjective than the *Donoghue* standard. The second point of difference is that the standard of care required of an occupier towards a trespasser is less onerous than that required in relation to a lawful visitor. The most controversial aspect here was the dicta of Lords Reid, Wilberforce and Diplock that the resources of the particular occupier were to be taken into account in assessing what it was reasonable for the occupier to do. Once again this is a much more subjective test than that which prevails under *Donoghue*.

In practice, however, there was not much of a difference between the *Herrington* standard and the *Donoghue* standard (see for example *Pannett* v *McGuinness* [1972] 2 QB 599). The distinction between the two standards became even harder to discern after the decision of the Privy Council in *Southern Portland Cement Ltd* v *Cooper* [1974] AC 623 (valuably discussed by Spencer [1974] CLJ 202). There the Privy Council appeared to eradicate the two differences noted above between *Herrington* and *Donoghue*. In relation to the need for some subjective knowledge of the presence of the trespasser, Lord Reid rejected the view that 'no duty was owed unless the advent of the trespasser is extremely probable', although he did concede that an occupier could ignore a bare possibility. In relation to the second point, Lord Reid suggested that the duty of common humanity may not be entirely subjective where the occupier creates the danger by his own activity, rather than simply failing to deal with a danger which had arisen from another source. This tendency to synthesise the *Donoghue* and *Herrington* standards can also be seen in *Harris* v *Birkenhead Corporation* (above).

The uncertainties in the judgments in *Herrington* and the subsequent interpretation of the decision were the subject of much criticism and debate. Yet it should be noted that in *Leakey* v *National Trust* [1980] QB 485 Megaw LJ saw no difficulty in applying the *Herrington* standard to a nuisance action concerning the liability of a landowner for the natural condition of his land which has caused damage to his neighbour's land (see 18.10). Despite this latter point the Law Commission reported on the decision in *Herrington* and their report formed the basis of the 1984 Act.

The 1984 Act applies to 'persons other than ... visitors' and so it encompasses not only trespassers, but also persons entering pursuant to a private right of way (see paragraph 17.3) and persons who enter land in the exercise of rights conferred by an access agreement or order under the National Parks and Access to the Countryside Act 1949 s60. The Act determines:

'a) whether any duty is owed by a person as occupier of premises to persons other than his visitors in respect of any risk of their suffering injury on the premises by reason of any danger due to the state of the premises or to things done or to be done on them; and
b) if so, what that duty is.'

Thus the Act would appear to apply to the 'activity' duty as well as the 'occupancy' duty. In the remainder of this section we shall apply this Act to trespassers, but it should be borne in mind that the Act applies to the wider category of non-visitors.

In considering the duty of care that is owed to trespassers, the 1984 Act adopts a two-stage approach. Section 1(3) of the Act provides that an occupier of premises owes a duty of care to a non-visitor if:

'a) he is aware of the danger or has reasonable grounds to believe that it exists;
b) he knows or has reasonable grounds to believe that the other is in the vicinity of the danger concerned or that he may come into the vicinity of the danger (in either case, whether the other has lawful authority for being in that vicinity or not); and
c) the risk is one against which, in all the circumstances of the case, he may reasonably be expected to offer the other some protection.'

Paragraph (c) was in the Law Commission's draft Bill but paragraphs (a) and (b) were not. It is not clear whether the test contained in this subsection is supposed to be subjective or objective. This lack of clarity is particularly unfortunate because of the confusion we have noted under *Herrington* over whether the standard was subjective or objective. The words 'he knows' suggest a subjective test, but the words 'has reasonable grounds to believe' suggest an objective test. It may be that what is intended is that the Act shall apply to the situation where the occupier knows or is aware of the primary facts but fails to draw the reasonable inference from the known facts (for such an approach see the judgment of Lawton LJ in *Harris* v *Birkenhead Corporation* (above)). It is difficult to see how the Act could apply to the situation where the occupier is unaware of the primary facts in circumstances where the reasonable occupier would have been so aware. This difficulty is compounded by the lack of case law. There is apparently only one decided case under the Act. That case is *White* v *St Albans City and District Council* (1990) The Times 12 March (noted by

Mullis [1991] Conveyancer 54). The plaintiff took a short cut across the defendants' land and fell down a trench which he had not seen. The defendants were aware of the danger and so the plaintiff could satisfy s1(3)(a). The difficulty arose over the proper interpretation of s1(3)(b). The plaintiff argued that, once it was demonstrated that the occupier had taken steps to prevent people getting on to his land, it followed that the occupier had reason to believe that someone was likely to come into the vicinity of the danger and so the requirement of s1(3)(b) was satisfied. The court rejected this argument and held that the question had to be answered in the light of the actual state of affairs on the premises when the injury occurred and that the vital question was the simple one of whether the occupier had reasonable grounds to believe that someone would come into the vicinity of the danger. On the facts the Court of Appeal held that the trial judge was justified in reaching the conclusion that the defendant council had no reason to believe that the plaintiff would be in the vicinity of the danger; the fence which had been put up by the defendants was insufficient to prevent all but the elderly and disabled from entering the land and there was no evidence that people tended to use the land as a short cut. On the wider view of whether the Act imposes an objective test of knowledge the court did not speak with one voice. Both Neill and Nicholls LJJ thought that an occupier could be liable where he had actual knowledge of the trespasser's presence from which a reasonable man would draw the inference that a trespasser was in the vicinity or was likely to come into the vicinity, whereas Bingham LJ appeared to adopt a wholly objective test. The issue therefore remains an open one.

The second stage of the inquiry is contained in s1(4) which provides that the duty is:

> ' ... to take such care as is reasonable in all the circumstances of the case to see that the non-visitor does not suffer injury on the premises by reason of the danger concerned.'

This appears to be the familiar negligence standard and there is no reference to the resources of the particular occupier.

It is submitted that the 1984 Act is structurally unsound and that it confuses the type of duty owed with the standard of care required to fulfil the duty in a particular case. It must be remembered that reasonable care is a flexible and not a fixed standard. What the 1984 Act should have done is to provide that the occupier owes the same duty of care to the non-visitor as he does to the visitor, namely the common duty of care. Then the courts, in considering what constitutes reasonable care, could have taken account of the fact that the plaintiff was a trespasser and held that the standard required of an occupier in such a case is less than it would be in the case of a visitor. This is what was done in Scotland in the Occupiers' Liability (Scotland) Act 1960 and that Act has not given rise to as many problems as the English Act (see Spencer [1974] CLJ 202).

One or two other points may be made about the 1984 Act. The first is that s1(5) provides that the occupier can discharge the duty by taking such steps as are reasonable in all the circumstances of the case to give warning of the danger concerned, or to discourage persons from incurring the risk. Section 1(6) preserves the defence of volenti. The final point concerns the situation which arises where the property of the trespasser is damaged. The Law Commission in their report considered whether recovery should be allowed in respect of the clothes which the trespasser was wearing when he entered the premises, but considered that this would be illogical. So the definition of injury in s1(9) is confined to death or personal injury, including disease and any impairment of physical or mental condition and s1(8) provides that the occupier's duty does not extend to any loss of or damage to property. In the absence of statutory protection the trespasser must look to the common law for any available protection. It is unlikely that the *Herrington* standard of 'common humanity' is applicable to property damage because it is a test designed to deal with personal injuries. The only remaining option, if option there be, is the standard laid down in *Addie*.

17.16 Exclusion of the occupier's duty

Separate consideration will be given to the ability of an occupier to exclude liability towards a visitor and to his ability to exclude liability towards a trespasser. Visitors will be considered first.

One of the problems with the 1957 Act is that it has a number of provisions which appear to overlap here. The first is s2(4)(a) which concerns warnings (considered in paragraph 17.9). A warning is, however, different from an exclusion clause. The latter simply seeks to exclude liability on the happening of a specified event, while the former seeks to inform the visitor of a danger so that he can take steps to avoid it (see the approach of Buckley and Roskill LJJ in *White* v *Blackmore* [1972] QB 651). The second provision which overlaps is s2(5) which deals with volenti (discussed in paragraph 17.11). Volenti looks at the issue from the perspective of the visitor and asks whether he has assumed the risk of injury, while an exclusion clause is concerned with the steps taken by the occupier to bring the exclusion clause to the attention of the visitor. So, in some ways, the two look at the same thing from different perspectives.

The provision of the 1957 Act which deals with exclusion clauses is s2(1). So far as material the section states that the occupier owes the common duty of care to all his visitors 'except in so far as he is free to and does extend, restrict, modify or exclude his duty to any visitor or visitors by agreement or otherwise'. The words 'by agreement or otherwise' demonstrate that liability may be excluded by a non-contractual notice. Thus effect was given, in the 1957 Act, to the decision of *Ashdown* v *Samuel Williams and Sons Ltd* [1957] 1 QB 409 (criticised by Gower (1956) 19 MLR 532 and (1957) 20 MLR 181).

But the critical qualification in s2(1) is that the occupier may only exclude or restrict his duty 'in so far as he is free to do so'. There are three restrictions on the occupier's freedom. The first is contained in s3 of the 1957 Act which provides that an occupier cannot by contract with one person exclude or restrict the common duty of care which he owes to third parties (see 17.13).

The second, and major, restriction upon the freedom of an occupier to exclude or modify his obligations under the 1957 Act is the Unfair Contract Terms Act 1977 (UCTA). Here we are concerned with the controls in UCTA directed at attempts to exclude or restrict liability for negligence. The definition of negligence in s1 of UCTA includes, in s1(1)(c), the common duty of care under the 1957 Act. However, UCTA only places controls upon attempts to exclude or restrict 'business liability'. The latter phrase is defined in s1(3) as liability for breach of an obligation or duty arising:

> '... from things done or to be done by a person in the course of a business (whether his own business or another's) or
> ... from the occupation of premises used for business purposes of the occupier.'

'Business' is defined in s14 as including 'a profession and the activities of any government department or local or public authority'. This rather vague definition led to difficulties in the situation where a fee was charged for entrance on to the land, but the proceeds were devoted to a charitable purpose (see, for example, the fact situation in *White* v *Blackmore* [1972] QB 651). To take account of this point the definition of 'business liability' in s1(3) was amended (by s2 of the 1984 Act) by the addition of the following words:

> ' ... but liability of an occupier of premises for breach of an obligation or duty towards a person obtaining access to the premises for recreational or educational purposes, being liability for loss or damage suffered by reason of the dangerous state of the premises, is not a business liability of the occupier unless granting that person access for the purposes concerned falls within the business purposes of the occupier.'

This addition will relieve some of the uncertainty, but it still does not provide us with a definition of 'business' (for further consideration of this amendment see Bragg and Brazier (1986) 130 SJ 251 and 274).

Section 2(1) of UCTA makes attempts to exclude or restrict liability for death or personal injury resulting from negligence void and in the case of other loss or damage such attempts are subject to a reasonableness test.

The third and final restriction upon the ability of an occupier to exclude or restrict liability exists, or may exist, at common law. Winfield and Jolowicz argue (*Winfield and Jolowicz on Tort* (13th ed) p222) that the *Herrington* standard, based as it is upon 'common humanity', represents a minimum legal standard which cannot be excluded by agreement or by notice. There is, however, no authority for or against such a proposition.

In relation to trespassers there is a logical difficulty in imposing conditions upon the terms of entry of a trespasser because in the vast majority of cases the occupier will be unaware of the trespasser, so he can hardly impose terms on his entry. However UCTA does not apply in the case of a trespasser because the definition of negligence in s1 of UCTA only includes the common duty of care under the 1957 Act; it makes no mention of the duty owed under the 1984 Act.

A number of arguments can be adduced in favour of holding that the duty owed under the 1984 Act is unexcludable. The first is that there is some authority for the proposition that an agreement to contract out of a statutory duty is void. The second point is that s2(1) of the 1957 Act makes provision for contracting out, so the failure to include such a provision in the 1984 Act is surely significant, especially when provision was made in the Law Commission's Draft Bill, which formed the basis of the Act, for contracting out. The third argument is that, since the duty owed to trespassers is the very minimum imposed by law, it should not, as a matter of public policy, be excludable. Lastly, if the argument of Winfield and Jolowicz is accepted, and the *Herrington* standard is held to be unexcludable, then some symmetry is produced with the 1984 Act because the standard adopted by *Herrington* or the 1984 Act becomes a minimum which cannot be excluded in any case. However, the point remains to be resolved (see Jones (1984) 47 MLR 713 and Buckley [1984] Conv. 413).

17.17 Liability of independent contractors who are not occupiers

Once again we must distinguish between the duty which is owed to visitors and the duty which is owed to trespassers. In relation to visitors it is clear that it is ordinary *Donoghue* v *Stevenson* principles which are applicable and not the standards applicable under the Occupiers' Liability Act 1957, although it has been noted that there is little difference between the two standards (see *A C Billings and Sons Ltd* v *Riden* [1958] AC 240).

The position in relation to trespassers is more complex. In *Buckland* v *Guildford Gas Light and Coke Co* [1949] 1 KB 410 ordinary *Donoghue* principles were applied by Morris J. However, in *Herrington*, Lords Pearson and Wilberforce suggested that no distinction should be drawn between occupiers and non-occupiers in relation to the duty owed to trespassers and that 'common humanity' be applied in all cases involving trespassers. But it is clear that independent contractors, who are not occupiers, are not caught by the 1984 Act because that Act only applies to occupiers. So it is a straight choice between applying *Herrington* or *Donoghue*. Since the purpose behind the 1984 Act was to replace *Herrington* it would be odd if *Herrington* were to be resurrected in this context and it is submitted that the approach adopted in *Buckland* is the preferable one.

17.18 Liability of vendors and lessors

In this section consideration is given to the liability of vendors and lessors of defective premises. Here we are dealing with the situation where a vendor or a lessor creates a danger or defect in his premises and then sells or lets the property to another person who then suffers injury as a result of the danger or defect. Vendors and lessors do not fall within the ambit of the Occupiers' Liability Acts if they are not occupiers of the premises. So some other action must be used if liability is to be imposed on the vendor or lessor.

One possibility is a contractual action by the purchaser against the vendor or by the lessee against the lessor. The difficulty here is that the implied obligations as to the quality of the premises are much less extensive than in the case of a contract for the sale of goods. The rule in relation to the sale or letting of land is 'caveat emptor' (but see Gleeson and McKendrick in The Rotting Away of Caveat Emptor? [1987] Conv 121). So a contractual action offers little prospect of hope.

An action in tort used to provide little comfort either. The reason was that vendors and lessors enjoyed extensive immunities from suit in tort. In *Cavalier* v *Pope* [1906] AC 428 the immunity of a landlord from suit in tort in respect of dangerous premises was established (cf *Cunard* v *Antifyre* [1933] 1 KB 551). In *Bottomley* v *Bannister* [1932] 1 KB 458 a similar immunity was extended to vendors. So at this stage in our legal development vendors and lessors enjoyed immunity for their own acts or omissions before letting or selling the premises.

An attack was launched upon *Cavalier* v *Pope* in the case of *McNerny* v *London Borough of Lambeth* (1988) 21 HLR 188 (noted by Smith [1989] Conv 216). But the Court of Appeal rejected the argument that *Cavalier* had to be re-examined in the light of the expansion of the tort of negligence which began with *Donoghue* v *Stevenson* [1932] AC 562. So *Cavalier* remains good law. But the Court of Appeal did note that there are two exceptions to the rule in *Cavalier*. The first is that it does not apply to furnished lettings and the second is that it does not apply to cases in which the landowner is the builder of the house and the house has been built negligently (see *Rimmer* v *Liverpool City Council* [1984] 1 All ER 930, recently followed by the Court of Appeal in *Targett* v *Torfaen Borough Council* [1992] 3 All ER 27, who rejected the argument that *Rimmer* could no longer be regarded as good law in the light of the decision of the House of Lords in *Murphy* v *Brentwood District Council* [1991] 1 AC 398).

A more successful attack on the immunity of vendors and lessors was begun in *Dutton* v *Bognor Regis UDC* [1972] 1 QB 373. The Court of Appeal stated, obiter, that the principle of *Donoghue* v *Stevenson* applied to realty as well as to personalty. This statement was approved by the House of Lords in *Anns* v *Merton London Borough Council* [1978] AC 728 and was applied by the Court of Appeal in *Batty* v *Metropolitan Realisations Ltd* [1978] QB 554 (but doubted by the House of Lords in *D & F Estates Ltd* v *The Church Commissioners for England* [1989] AC 177).

The major assault on the immunities of the vendor and lessor are to be found, however, in the Defective Premises Act 1972. Section 3 of that Act provides that:

'Where work of construction, repair, maintenance or demolition or any other work is done on or in relation to premises, any duty of care owed, because of the doing of the work, to persons who might reasonably be expected to be affected by defects in the state of the premises created by the doing of the work shall not be abated by subsequent disposal of the premises by the person who owed the duty.'

This section, which is subject to exceptions in s3(2), virtually restates the position which the courts have reached at common law and in some ways it, or the decisions at common law, could be said to be superfluous.

In relation to landlords, s4 of the 1972 Act is a much more far-reaching provision. It states that:

'(1) Where premises are let under a tenancy which puts on the landlord an obligation to the tenant for the maintenance or repair of the premises, the landlord owes to all persons who might reasonably be expected to be affected by defects in the state of the premises a duty to take such care as is reasonable in all the circumstances to see that they are reasonably safe from personal injury or from damage to their property caused by a relevant defect.

(2) The said duty is owed if the landlord knows (whether as the result of being notified by the tenant or otherwise) or if he ought in all the circumstances to have known of the relevant defect.'

'Relevant defect' is defined in s4(3). These provisions apply to the landlord who has a power, express or implied, to enter and repair the premises as well as to the landlord who is under an obligation to repair (s4(4), the scope of which was discussed by the Court of Appeal in *McAuley* v *Bristol City Council* [1992] 1 QB 134). But no duty is owed in respect of a defect which has arisen out of a failure by the tenant to carry out his express obligations under the tenancy agreement (s4(4)).

17.19 Liability of builders

A builder may be liable to his 'employer' (that is the person who has contracted with the builder for the commission of the work) in contract. In many ways the liability of builders here involves the application of ordinary contractual principles, although there are certain terms which are implied into such contracts, but these are beyond the scope of this book. The position in tort is more complex. In *Bottomley* v *Bannister* [1932] AC 458 it was held that the builder on land who owned the land upon which the building was constructed was not liable in negligence for personal injury or damage to property caused by the defective state of the premises. This immunity was not, however, enjoyed by builders who built on someone else's land. Such a builder was subject to *Donoghue* principles.

The immunity of the builder/vendor or builder/lessor was removed by the Court of Appeal in *Dutton* v *Bognor Regis UDC* [1972] 1 QB 373. Lord Denning said that there was no sense behind the distinction which was drawn at common law because:

'... it would mean that a contractor who builds a house on another's land is liable for negligence in constructing it, but that a speculative builder, who buys land and himself builds on it for sale, and is just as negligent as the contractor, is not liable. That cannot be right. Each must be under the same duty of care and to the same persons.'

In *Anns* v *Merton London Borough Council* [1978] AC 728 the House of Lords approved of this dictum of Lord Denning. However, since *Anns* the common law liability of the builder has been considerably circumscribed. In *D & F Estates* v

Church Commissioners for England [1989] AC 177 it was held that a claim for the cost of repairing a defect in the building itself did not lie against a builder in tort, only in contract, and this approach was affirmed by the House of Lords in *Murphy* v *Brentwood District Council* [1991] 1 AC 398, which itself overruled *Anns*. The effect of this cutting back upon the scope of common law liability is to attach much greater significance to the Defective Premises Act 1972. Indeed, in *D & F Estates* Lord Bridge said that he was happy to reach the conclusion that the cost of repairing the defect in the building itself was not recoverable in tort because, had he decided otherwise, it would have resulted in the common law going further than 'the legislature were prepared to go in 1972, after comprehensive examination of the subject by the Law Commission'. He concluded that 'consumer protection is an area of law where legislation is much better left to the legislators'. The common law is therefore unlikely to be extended beyond the scope of the 1972 Act. Section 1(1) of the Act provides that:

> 'A person taking on work for or in connection with the provision of a dwelling (whether the dwelling is provided by the erection or by the conversion or enlargement of a building) owes a duty: (a) if the dwelling is provided to the order of any person, to that person; and (b) without prejudice to paragraph (a) above, to every person who acquires an interest (whether legal or equitable) in the dwelling, to see that the work which he takes on is done in a workmanlike or, as the case may be, professional manner, with proper materials and so that as regards that work the dwelling will be fit for habitation when completed.'

The scope of s1(1) was recently considered by the Court of Appeal in *Andrews* v *Schooling* [1991] 1 WLR 783. The third defendants granted the plaintiff a 199-year lease of a ground floor flat, including a cellar. Extensive work had been done to the flat itself but the only work which had been done in the cellar was the painting of the walls. The plaintiff later discovered that the flat suffered from penetrating dampness which she alleged emanated from the cellar. She claimed damages from the defendants, alleging that they were in breach of the duty which they owed to her under s1. The defendants argued that they were not liable because they had not done any relevant work on the flat so that it could not be said that they had 'taken on work' in relation to the cellar. Thus they argued that the Act applied only to cases of misfeasance and not non-feasance. This argument was rejected by the Court of Appeal and damages were awarded to the plaintiff. It was held that a dwelling was unfit for habitation when it was without some essential attribute when the works were completed, even though the problems arising therefrom had not then been patent. The requirement that the dwelling be fit for habitation when completed is not part of the duty itself but is the intended consequence of the proper performance of the duty. So a plaintiff who cannot show that the dwelling is unfit for habitation cannot bring a claim under s1(1) of the Act (*Thompson* v *Clive Alexander & Partners* (1992) 28 Con LR 49).

A defence is provided for builders in s1(2) which states that:

> 'A person who takes on any such work for another on terms that he is to do it in accordance with instructions given by or on behalf of that other shall, to the extent to

which he does it properly in accordance with those instructions, be treated for the purposes of this section as discharging the duty imposed on him by subsection (1) above except where he owes a duty to that other to warn him of any defect in the instructions and fails to discharge that duty.'

The operation of s1 is also limited by the fact that in s2 it is provided that s1 does not apply to dwelling houses covered by an 'approved scheme'. The National House Builders Protection Scheme (NHBPS) is such an approved scheme. Under this scheme the builder warrants that the house is properly constructed and that he will obtain NHBC insurance cover for the dwelling, which will cover any unfulfilled judgment or arbitration award against a builder.

It should be noted that this section only applies to dwellings. The section also suffers from the drawback that the six year limitation period runs from the date of completion of the dwelling, or, if further work was done on the dwelling after the dwelling was completed, the period begins to run from the date of completion of that work (s2(5)). However, the plaintiff may be able to enjoy the longer limitation period under the Latent Damage Act 1986 (see 31.5).

18

Private Nuisance

18.1 Introduction

18.2 The interests protected

18.3 Conduct amounting to a private nuisance

18.4 The duration of the nuisance

18.5 Abnormal sensitivity

18.6 Character of the neighbourhood

18.7 Utility of the defendant's conduct

18.8 Malice

18.9 Fault?

18.10 Who can be sued in nuisance?

18.11 Types of harm

18.12 Defences

18.13 Remedies

18.14 The future of the nuisance action

18.1 Introduction

A well-known American jurist called Dean Prosser once wrote of nuisance that 'there is perhaps no more impenetrable jungle in the entire law than that which surrounds the word nuisance' (*Prosser on Torts* (4th ed) p571). But the difficulty with nuisance appears to lie more in applying the legal principles to the facts of a particular case. Nuisance cases are so infinite in their variations that it is often difficult to discern any general principles at work. This tort is not difficult in the same way that negligence is difficult, where the complexities are often conceptual (for example, the role of reasonable foreseeability in determining the existence of a duty of care). Ironically the only real conceptual difficulty which arises in the law of nuisance concerns the role of negligence within nuisance.

Nuisance is basically concerned with unreasonable interference with a person's use or enjoyment of his land or some right in connection with his land. Thus it concerns disputes between neighbours relating to their respective uses of their land. But nuisance can also apply to environmental disputes, for example, when large manufacturing concerns pollute the atmosphere. In the latter context statute has intervened to regulate activities which harm the environment (see, for example, the Control of Pollution Act 1974, the Clean Air Acts 1956 and 1968 and the Public Health Act 1936). Within these statutes nuisance sometimes has a role to play in defining the offence but, since these Acts are largely enforced by public bodies, they do not fall within the scope of this book. Some have gone so far as to suggest that the nuisance action is in crisis and that it is incapable of handling modern environmental issues and so the action should be abolished. This is an issue to which we shall return at a later date.

Nuisance can be divided into two categories; public and private nuisance. We shall deal with the former in chapter 19. Here we are only concerned with private nuisance. Private nuisance has been defined by *Winfield and Jolowicz on Tort* (13th ed) p378 as 'an unlawful interference with a person's use or enjoyment of land, or some right over, or in connection with it'. The essence of the tort is said to be found in the maxim sic utere tuo alienum non laedas (that no man is allowed to use his property in such a way as to injure another). But the law of nuisance does in fact allow one person to use his land in such a way as to injure another. What is struck at by the law of nuisance is the unreasonable use of land by one person which causes damage to another. So nuisance really seeks to balance two competing policies. The first is the interest of the landowner in using his land as he sees fit and the second is the interest of the neighbour in the quiet enjoyment of his land. As we shall see throughout this chapter these two policies are constantly in tension.

18.2 The interests protected

Since we have defined private nuisance in terms of the unlawful interference with a person's use or enjoyment of land, it follows that only those who have an interest in the land affected can sue in nuisance. Thus in *Malone* v *Laskey* [1907] 2 KB 141 the defendant let a house to a tenant who sublet it to a company. The managing director of the company and his wife then lived in the house. The water cistern fell off the wall while the wife was using the lavatory. The causes of the fall of the cistern were vibrations from adjacent premises caused by machinery belonging to the defendant and the negligent repairs done to the cistern by the defendant's employees or agents. It was held that the wife was unable to sue in private nuisance as she had no proprietary or possessory interest in the land (this case was decided in the days when it was not common for property to be held in joint names). *Malone* therefore stands as authority for the proposition that a plaintiff must have an interest in the land or a legal right of occupation before he or she can bring an action in private nuisance (see also *Metropolitan Properties Ltd* v *Jones* [1939] 2 All ER 202). Thus guests staying in the family home or children of the owners of the property would appear to be unable to bring an action in nuisance because they lack the necessary interest in land.

However, a different approach has been adopted by the New Brunswick Court of Appeal in *Devon Lumber Co Ltd* v *MacNeill* (1988) 45 DLR (4th) 300. Dust emanating from the defendants' cedar mill unreasonably interfered with the ordinary use and enjoyment of the home of Mr and Mrs MacNeill and their two children. The majority of the court held that, although the children had no legal title to the property, their right to occupy the family home with their parents was sufficient to ground a cause of action in nuisance. Quoting from Professor Fleming's textbook (*The Law of Tort* (7th ed) p395), Stratton CJNB said that it would be 'senseless discrimination' to deprive the children of a right of action simply because they had no legal title to the property. Rice JA dissented, adopting the orthodox approach that the 'original character' of the nuisance action was based upon the invasion of an interest in land and that therefore only those with an interest in land could bring an action in nuisance. The issue therefore is whether the English courts should follow the approach adopted in *Devon Lumber* or whether they should adhere to *Malone* (see further *Kodilyne* (1989) 9 Legal Studies 284). It can be argued that the requirement that the plaintiff possess an interest in land is justifiable if nuisance is a tort whose function is to protect land and the enjoyment of land, but otherwise it appears rather difficult to justify. Some indication of the approach which the English courts are likely to adopt can be gleaned from the decision of the Court of Appeal in *Khorasandjian* v *Bush* [1993] 3 WLR 476. The plaintiff was the victim of nuisance telephone calls from a former boyfriend. When the plaintiff informed the defendant that she wanted nothing more to do with him, the defendant refused to accept it and began to harass her. He assaulted her, threatened and abused her and began to make nuisance telephone calls to her at her parents' home. In these circumstances the plaintiff sought an injunction to restrain the defendant from persisting with this conduct. The trial judge granted the plaintiff an injunction restraining the defendant from 'harassing, pestering or communicating with' the plaintiff. The defendant appealed, arguing that these words did not reflect any tort known to the law. The defendant argued that the plaintiff was only a licensee in her parents' home and so did not have a sufficient interest in the land to maintain an action in private nuisance to complain of these unwanted telephone calls. Dillon LJ accepted that it was correct, historically, to state that the tort of private nuisance was developed initially to protect private property or rights of property in relation to the use or enjoyment of land. But, after considering the decision of the Alberta Supreme Court in *Motherwell* v *Motherwell* (1976) 73 DLR (3d) 62 where it was held that the wife of the owner of the land could maintain an action in private nuisance to restrain unwanted telephone calls, he held that the court had to reconsider earlier decisions, such as *Malone* v *Laskey*, in the light of 'changed social conditions'. He concluded that, if the wife of the owner of the land could maintain an action in *Motherwell*, then there was no reason to conclude that a child living at home with her parents could not also bring a claim. It was therefore held that the plaintiff was entitled to bring a claim in private nuisance. *Khorasandjian* thus now stands as authority for the proposition that an interest in land is not always necessary to found an action in private nuisance. Rose LJ agreed with Dillon LJ but Peter Gibson J dissented and distinguished *Khorasandjian* from *Motherwell,* holding that in *Motherwell* the person allowed to sue had a right to live in the property and thus had sufficient occupancy to sue, whereas the plaintiff in *Khorasandjian* had no such right. Hence even the dissenting judgment suggests that in appropriate circumstances the classic interest required by *Malone* is no longer necessary.

A further limitation was introduced in *Bridlington Relay Ltd* v *Yorkshire Electricity Board* [1965] Ch 436. The plaintiffs sought an injunction to restrain the defendants from operating a new overhead power line on the ground that it would cause electrical interference which would detrimentally affect the reception on their broadcasting system. The defendants argued that the plaintiffs' use was an extremely sensitive one and that the plaintiffs were seeking a higher degree of interference-free reception than the ordinary man would require. Buckley J refused to grant an injunction and one of his reasons was that, for the purpose of the tort of nuisance, recreational considerations were on a different level from considerations of health and physical comfort. So he held that occasional, if recurrent and severe, electrical interference affecting only one of the available programmes did not constitute a nuisance. Once again a different approach has been adopted in the Canadian courts. In *Nor-Video Services Ltd* v *Ontario Hydro* (1978) 84 DLR (3d) 221 the defendants located their electrical power station close to the plaintiffs' cable television station. This resulted in considerable interference with the reception and transmission of the broadcast signals, which, in turn, compelled the plaintiffs to halt transmission of one channel to a town of 6,000 people, 80 per cent of whom were subscribers to the television network. It was held that the plaintiffs in these circumstances could bring an action in nuisance. It is suggested that the reasoning of the Canadian court is more persuasive than the reasoning in *Bridlington Relay*, especially in a society in which individuals spend on average 30 hours per week watching television (see further Kidner [1989] Conv 279).

18.3 Conduct amounting to a private nuisance

This is where the difficulties arise in the application of the law to the many situations which come before the courts. A convenient starting point is the case of *St Helens Smelting Co* v *Tipping* (1865) 11 HL 642. In this case the plaintiffs bought an estate in a manufacturing area of town. The defendant operated a copper smelting works close to the plaintiffs' estate and the vapours from the defendant's factory caused damage to the plaintiffs' trees. The defendant argued that he was not liable to the plaintiffs because his factory was located in an industrial area and so the vapours were acceptable. This argument was rejected by the House of Lords and the plaintiffs recovered damages. In reaching their decision the House of Lords held that there was a distinction between an action in nuisance which alleged that the nuisance caused material damage to property and an action in nuisance which alleged that the nuisance produced personal discomfort in the use or enjoyment of the land. In the former case it is easier to establish nuisance because the locality of the nuisance is only a relevant consideration in the latter case (see further paragraph 18.6). Dias and Markesinis (*Tort Law* (2nd ed) pp301-2) put forward three justifications for this distinction drawn by the House of Lords. The first is that property generally receives greater protection from the law of tort than does the enjoyment of the use of that property. But as they point out there is no clear cut distinction between property and enjoyment of that property. The second justification is that property damage can be said to be more easily identifiable and assessable than interference with enjoyment of that property. But as they point out the difficulty of assessment has not really troubled the courts in cases of personal injury so it is difficult to see why it should be conclusive here. The third justification is that it may represent an attempt to reconcile two conflicting earlier decisions (*Hole* v *Barlow* (1858) 4 CBNS 334 and *Bamford* v *Turnley* (1860) 3 B & S 62). It should not be thought, however, that there is a rigid distinction between these two categories. Although the point is not altogether clear, it is submitted that the courts will balance roughly the same factors in cases of property damage as in cases of interference with enjoyment of the land, except that in cases of injury to property the nature of the locality is not a relevant factor.

In considering what constitutes an unreasonable user of land the courts have to balance a wide range of factors in reaching their decision. The most important of these factors are considered in paragraphs 18.4 to 18.9.

18.4 The duration of the nuisance

The shorter the duration of the interference, the less likely it is that the use will be found to be unreasonable. In *Harrison* v *Southwark and Vauxhall Water Co* [1891] 2 Ch 409 it was held that the actions of the defendants in sinking a shaft in the land adjoining the plaintiff's land did not constitute a nuisance because of the temporary nature of the work. Professor Fleming has stated that 'the temporary nature of the harm is only one, but by no means a conclusive, factor in deciding whether the injury is too trivial to qualify as a nuisance' (*The Law of Torts* (7th ed) p389). The temporary nature of the harm is more important in a case where the plaintiff seeks an injunction because courts tend to be reluctant to grant an injunction where the harm is of a temporary nature and is unlikely to continue or to recur. But where the plaintiff's claim is for damages the mere fact that the harm is temporary will not, where the other factors also point in the direction of the existence of an actionable nuisance, deny to the plaintiff the ability to claim damages.

A related question concerns whether an isolated or a single escape can constitute a nuisance. There is a conflict of authority on this point. In *Bolton* v *Stone* [1949] 1 All ER 237 Oliver J stated that a nuisance must 'be a state of affairs, however temporary, and not merely an isolated happening'. So the isolated escape of a cricket ball from a cricket ground was held not to constitute a nuisance. But in *Midwood* v *Manchester Corporation* [1905] 2 KB 597, where there was a gas explosion, this was held to be an actionable nuisance on the basis that, although it was an isolated event, it was due to a pre-existing state of affairs (ie the build up of gas in the main). The generally accepted view now is that the event must be attributable to a 'state of affairs' before it will constitute a nuisance. So if a cricket ball is hit out of the ground often enough then there can be said to be a dangerous state of affairs which can ground an action in nuisance (see *British Celanese* v *A H Hunt Ltd* [1969] 1 WLR 959 and *SCM (United Kingdom) Ltd* v *W J Whitall and Son Ltd* [1970] 1 WLR 1017).

18.5 Abnormal sensitivity

A man cannot increase his neighbour's liability merely because he puts his land to some special use. Thus in *Robinson* v *Kilvert* (1889) 41 Ch D 88 the defendant, who was the tenant of a cellar in a house, heated up the cellar to a temperature of 80 degrees fahrenheit. The heat had the effect of causing damage to some sensitive paper which was stored upstairs on the floor of the plaintiff's premises. It was held that the heat was not of such a character as would ordinarily interfere with the normal use of the rest of the house. A similar result was reached in the case of *Heath* v *Mayor of Brighton* (1908) 98 LT 718 where a church minister sought to obtain an injunction to restrain the noise which emanated from the defendant's electrical power station. There was no evidence that any member of the congregation was upset by the noise, the minister was not prevented from conducting his services and there was no evidence of any decline in the attendance at the church because of the noise, so the court refused to grant an injunction.

18.6 Character of the neighbourhood

We have already noted that the case of *St Helens Smelting Co* v *Tipping* (above) stands as authority for the proposition that the character of the neighbourhood is not a relevant factor in cases of physical damage to property. So here we are only concerned with cases of interference with enjoyment or use of land. The classic statement on this point was given by Thesiger LJ in *Sturges* v *Bridgman* (1879) 11 Ch D 852 when he said that 'what would be a nuisance in Belgravia Square would not necessarily be so in Bermondsey'.

It should not be thought, however, that the character of the neighbourhood is always the decisive factor. It is but one factor to be weighed in the balance. Thus in *Roshmer* v *Polsue and Alfieri Ltd* [1906] 1 Ch 234 a milkman, who had lived and managed a dairy for eighteen years in a neighbourhood in which he was the only resident and which was largely dedicated to printing, sought and obtained an injunction restraining the defendants from using a new machine in their printing press at night because it interfered with the milkman's sleep. It was held that the noise of this machine at night was too great even for an area largely dedicated to printing.

18.7 Utility of the defendant's conduct

As nuisance seeks to identify what is an unreasonable use of land, it is not unnaturally the case that some attention is given to the utility of the defendant's conduct. The more reasonable and useful it is, the more likely it is that the plaintiff's action will be unsuccessful. For example the construction of houses necessitates the making of a certain amount of noise but the noise is only temporary and it is necessary to achieve the desirable social goal of constructing houses, so it is less likely to constitute a nuisance.

However in the Irish case of *Bellew* v *Cement Co* [1948] Ir R 61 the court granted an injunction for a nuisance which had the effect of closing down Ireland's only cement factory for three months at a time when it was urgently needed. So once again this factor cannot be treated as a conclusive factor.

18.8 Malice

In a sense this category bears a strong resemblance to the issues discussed in paragraph 18.7 because where the defendant's acts are malicious they are devoid of social utility and so are less deserving of protection. Two cases illustrate the approach of the courts here. The first is *Christie* v *Davey* [1893] 1 Ch 316. Here the plaintiff was a teacher of music whose house was separated from the defendant's house by a party wall. The defendant became so fed up with the constant noise made by the plaintiff's pupils trying to play the piano that he took to interrupting the lessons by beating on trays, whistling and shrieking. It was held that, in making these noises, the defendant was acting maliciously and so an injunction was granted restraining him from making these noises.

Another example of the approach of the courts is the case of *Hollywood Silver Fox Farm Ltd* v *Emmett* [1936] 2 KB 468. Here the defendant deliberately caused guns to be fired on the boundary of his own land. The boundary was very close to the plaintiffs' land and the purpose behind firing the shots was to scare the plaintiffs' silver foxes during their breeding time. These types of vixens were extremely nervous during breeding time and any loud noise was likely to deter them from breeding, produce miscarriages or cause them to kill and devour their young. It was held that the plaintiffs were entitled to an injunction and damages, even though the shooting took place on the defendant's land, where he was entitled to shoot. This case shows the importance which a malicious motive may have on the outcome of a case because, in the absence of malice, the injunction would probably have been refused on the ground that the plaintiffs were using their land for an abnormally sensitive purpose.

It should also be noted in this context that it must be shown that the defendant maliciously interfered with a right of the plaintiff. If no such right is interfered with then no cause of action sounds in nuisance. Thus in *Bradford Corporation* v *Pickles* [1895] AC 587 the defendant, who deliberately drained his land in order to stop the water supply reaching the plaintiffs' land, was not liable to the plaintiffs because the plaintiffs had no rights in relation to the supply of water and so no right of theirs had been infringed (see too *Home Brewery plc* v *William Davis and Co (Loughborough) Ltd* [1987] QB 339).

18.9 Fault?

One of the most vexed issues in the law of nuisance is whether or not it is necessary to prove that the defendant was negligent before a plaintiff can succeed in a nuisance action. In many ways the dominance of the tort of negligence has become such that the common law is reluctant to impose liability in the absence of fault. But if the plaintiff can show that the defendant was negligent then he can plead negligence and there is no need to rely upon the tort of nuisance. Thus stated the tort of nuisance is in danger of becoming redundant and being swallowed up by the tort of negligence.

Lord Reid contributed to the confusion here in *The Wagon Mound (No 2)* [1967] 1 AC 617, 639 when he said that 'negligence is not an essential element in nuisance. Nuisance is a term used to cover a wide variety of tortious acts or omissions and in many negligence in the narrow sense is not essential'. He then went on to qualify this by saying that 'although negligence may not be necessary, fault of some kind is almost always necessary and fault generally involves foreseeability'. This statement could be understood as referring to the tests for remoteness of damage in both negligence and nuisance (see Dias [1967] CLJ 62) but it is more likely that Lord Reid was talking about the standard of liability in both negligence and nuisance.

It is submitted that he was saying that the tests for the standard of liability in negligence and nuisance are not the same. Although nuisance is concerned with unreasonable use of land and negligence with failing to take reasonable care and therefore both tests are based upon the standard of reasonableness, it is submitted that reasonableness means different things in the two torts. In negligence reasonableness is concerned with the foreseeable harm to which a reasonable man would not expose others, while reasonableness in nuisance focuses upon the character of the harm caused rather than upon harm which the reasonable man could foresee.

Reasonableness also differs in the two contexts because it is not necessarily a defence to a nuisance action that the defendant took all reasonable care, or even all possible care, to ensure that the nuisance did not occur.

So the fact that reasonableness is used in different senses in the different contexts suggests that the boundaries of nuisance and negligence are not coterminus. But this is not to say that there is no substantial overlap between the two torts. For example, if I bring pigs into my garden in a residential area of town and these pigs cause a smell which annoys the neighbours and interferes with their enjoyment of their land, is this nuisance or negligence? We would tend to classify this as nuisance because such disputes tend to form the basis of nuisance actions, but could we not also say that people are under a duty not to permit the escape of such a noxious nature that the plaintiff cannot reasonably be expected to tolerate it? The fact that there is a substantial overlap between the two torts is borne out by the fact that cases such as *Bolton* v *Stone* [1949] 1 All ER 237 and [1950] 1 KB 201, *The Wagon Mound (No 2)* [1967] 1 AC 617 and *Leakey* v *National Trust* [1980] QB 485 were pleaded in both nuisance and negligence.

Nevertheless there remains a body of opinion which suggests that liability in nuisance is strict; in other words it is based upon the fact of causation rather than upon the fact of fault. It is true that liability is strict in the sense that it is not necessarily a defence to show that the defendant has taken all reasonable care to abate the nuisance. However it is not true to say that the mere fact that the nuisance has emanated from the defendant's land is sufficient to attach the defendant with liability (see *R* v *Shorrock* [1993] 3 WLR 698). The authorities establish that the defendant must either be the creator of the nuisance or else he must have continued it with knowledge that it has taken place (see paragraph 18.10).

Winfield and Jolowicz on Tort (13th ed) pp381-2 draws a distinction between cases where the plaintiff seeks an injunction and cases where the plaintiff seeks damages. They argue that, in cases where the plaintiff seeks an injunction, the court is concerned with the wider issue of whether in all fairness an injunction should be granted and that the foreseeability of the harm is not in issue because the defendant knows what has happened. But they argue that in cases where the plaintiff seeks damages the courts will take account of the negligence, or lack of negligence, on the part of the defendant because the courts are reluctant to impose liability in damages in the absence of fault. It is not clear why the need to show the existence of negligence should depend on the remedy which is sought and it is submitted that this is a wholly arbitrary distinction and one which should be rejected.

18.10 Who can be sued in nuisance?

The creator of the nuisance

The person who creates a nuisance by some positive act on his part (misfeasance) rather than by nonfeasance may be sued in respect of the nuisance. The generally accepted view is that the creator may be sued whether or not he is the occupier of the land from which the nuisance came (*Southport Corporation* v *Esso Petroleum Co* [1953] 3 WLR 773 per Devlin J and [1954] QB 182 per Morris LJ cf Denning LJ).

The occupier of the land

It is clear that the occupier of the land where the nuisance exists is liable when he creates the nuisance. The occupier is also vicariously liable where it is his employee who creates the nuisance in the course of his employment. The occupier may also be liable for the nuisance created by his independent contractor where the occupier is under a non-delegable duty (see further chapter 5) or where the occupier could reasonably have foreseen, from the instructions which he gave to the independent contractor, that a nuisance was likely to occur. Thus in *Bower* v *Peate* (1876) 1 QBD 321 the plaintiff and defendant were the owners of adjoining properties. The plaintiff was entitled to the support for his house of the defendant's soil. The defendant employed an independent contractor to demolish, excavate and rebuild his house. The contractor took the risk under the contract to shore and support the plaintiff's house during the works. The plaintiff's house was damaged during the works because of the means used by the contractor to support the plaintiff's house. It was held that the defendant was liable. The undertaking concerning shoring up and support did not exclude the defendant from liability for nuisance.

The difficulty arises here where the act creating the nuisance is done by a trespasser or it arises as the result of an act of nature. The position in relation to the acts of trespassers was considered by the House of Lords in *Sedleigh-Denfield* v *O'Callaghan* [1940] AC 880. A local authority trespassed on to the defendant's land without the defendant's knowledge or consent and placed a culvert in a ditch on the defendant's land. The culvert was placed in the wrong place with the result that a risk of flooding was created which was likely to spread to the plaintiff's land. The defendant, through his employees, came to know of the work that had been done by the local authority. He did nothing about it, although he should have realised that it created a risk of flooding on the plaintiff's land. During a heavy rainstorm the ditch flooded because of the local authority's work and the plaintiff's land was damaged. The plaintiff sued to recover damages for his loss. The House of Lords held that the defendant was liable to the plaintiff because he knew or ought to have known of the risk of flooding and he had done nothing to prevent the plaintiff's land from becoming flooded. Viscount Maugham rejected the argument that an occupier of land is necessarily free from liability where the nuisance was created by a trespasser. Instead he held the cases held that an occupier was liable where he either 'continued' or 'adopted' the nuisance created by the trespasser. He then went on to say that:

> 'An occupier of land "continues" a nuisance if, with knowledge or presumed knowledge of its existence, he fails to take any reasonable means to bring it to an end, though with ample time to do so. He "adopts" it if he makes use of the erection, building, bank or artificial contrivance which constitutes the nuisance.'

Lord Atkin said that the occupier was not an insurer of the premises and that there must be some element of personal responsibility on his part. This element of personal responsibility existed where the occupier either continued or adopted the nuisance. On the facts in *Sedleigh-Denfield* the defendant was held to have both continued and adopted the nuisance.

So *Sedleigh-Denfield* settled the position at an early date in relation to the liability for the acts of trespassers, but it was not until much later that the position was settled in relation to the liability of occupiers for nuisance arising out of the natural condition of the land. The first major attempt at dealing with this issue can be found in the decision of the Privy Council in *Goldman* v *Hargrave* [1967] 1 AC 645. A very large redgum tree on the defendant's land was struck by lightning and caught fire. The defendant had the land in the immediate vicinity of the tree cleared and got a tree feller to cut the tree down. The defendant did not take any steps to have the fire put out but chose to let the fire burn itself out. Unfortunately the temperature increased rather than decreased and a strong wind sprang up. This caused the fire to spread extremely rapidly from the defendant's land and on to the plaintiffs' lands, where extensive damage was done. The plaintiffs sued to recover damages for the damage done. The Privy Council held that the risk of the fire spreading was a foreseeable one and that the defendant was liable for failing to take adequate steps to prevent the fire from spreading. Lord Wilberforce recognised that occupiers of land were not simply under a duty to refrain from causing damage to the plaintiffs, but could be under a positive duty to take steps to prevent such harm from arising. However he did not say whether this duty existed in nuisance or negligence.

The issue was further considered by the Court of Appeal in *Leakey* v *National Trust* [1980] QB 485. The defendants owned and occupied land, which included a conical shaped hill called 'Burrow Mump'. This hill had a steep side overlooking the plaintiffs' houses. During a period of drought in the summer of 1976 there appeared large cracks in the hill adjacent to the plaintiffs' property. The hot summer of 1976 was followed by a very wet autumn. In September of 1976 the plaintiffs pointed out to the defendants that a large crack had opened in the side of the hill and that there was a risk of a major collapse. The defendants, however, said that they were not under a duty to do anything because the danger arose from the natural condition of the soil for which they were not responsible. So they did nothing. At a later date the earth duly fell on the plaintiffs' houses. The defendants were prepared to permit the plaintiffs to come on to their land to remove the debris but the defendants were not prepared to contribute anything to the cost of the work. In these circumstances the plaintiffs brought an action against the defendants seeking injunctions requiring the defendants to remove the soil and to take steps to prevent further falls. The defendants were held to be liable to the plaintiffs. The Court of Appeal held that a person on whose land a hazard occurred naturally, whether that hazard was in the soil itself or was in something on or growing on the land, and which encroached or threatened to encroach on another's land thereby causing or threatening to cause damage, was under a duty, if he knew or ought to have known of the risk of encroachment, to do what was reasonable in the particular circumstances to prevent or minimise the risk of known or foreseeable damage to the other person or his property, and was liable in nuisance if he did not take such steps. It has been noted that this decision represents a change of policy in English law because it moves away from the laissez-faire idea that each landowner is autonomous and under no obligation to come to the aid of his neighbour towards the goal of accident prevention under which positive duties may be owed towards one's neighbours (see Markesinis [1980] CLJ 259).

So the Court of Appeal has clearly held that such positive duties are owed under the tort of nuisance and that a plaintiff will not be prejudiced by his failure to plead negligence. However *Leakey* does not hold out the prospect of us all being under an obligation to go to the aid of our neighbours, regardless of the cost of so doing. This is because of the standard of care which the Court of Appeal held to be appropriate in such a case. The court held that the hypothetical reasonable man standard of *Glasgow Corporation* v *Muir* [1943] 2 AC 448 was not the appropriate standard. The court held that the appropriate standard was a subjective one and that regard was to be had to the abilities and resources of the particular defendant. This standard was directly derived from the decision of the House of Lords in *British Railways Board* v *Herrington* [1972] AC 877. The court, however, deprecated a minute analysis of the financial standing and abilities of the defendant. Megaw LJ said that where substantial expenditure was required to prevent or minimise the risk of damage then the resources of the occupier, assessed upon a broad basis, were a relevant factor in deciding what was reasonably required of the occupier to discharge the duty imposed upon him and that the neighbour's ability to protect himself from damage, also considered on a broad basis, might similarly be a relevant factor to be taken into account depending on the circumstances of the particular case.

These authorities were recently considered by Piers Ashworth QC in the case of *Home Brewery PLC* v *William Davis and Co (Loughborough) Ltd* [1987] QB 339. The defendants bought land for the purpose of developing it for housing. In pursuance of their development plans the defendants filled in two clay pits and, at a later date, they filled in an osier-bed. The effect of this was that the water which had previously drained from the plaintiffs' land on to the defendants' land could no longer escape and the plaintiffs had to install pumps to clear the flooding. The plaintiffs brought an action seeking damages for the cost of installing the pumps. It was held that the defendants were under no obligation to permit the water from the plaintiffs' land to pass over their land and that they were entitled to take reasonable steps, which were consistent with the reasonable user of their land, to prevent the water coming on to their land, even if, by so doing, they caused damage to someone else's land. It was held that the defendants had acted reasonably in filling in the two clay pits in pursuance of their development plans and that the plaintiffs had no cause of action in respect of the damage caused by the filling in of these pits. Piers Ashworth QC said that he did not understand the judgment of Megaw LJ in *Leakey* to apply to a case 'where all the landowner is doing is exercising his right to reject water coming on to his land and is doing so in a reasonable manner'. But it was held that the plaintiffs were entitled to recover, either in nuisance or in trespass, in respect of the damage done by the filling in of the osier-bed because it was reasonably foreseeable that the filling in of the bed would cause damage to the plaintiffs. So it appears that *Leakey* has now become the accepted standard to be applied in cases of nuisance arising as the result of an act of nature, subject to the caveat noted by Piers Ashworth QC in the *Home Brewery* case.

Landlords

The liability of a landlord in nuisance is not altogether easy to state. The general rule is that a landlord who has relinquished possession and control of premises which he has demised is not liable for any nuisance which is committed on the demised premises. There are, however, three situations where a landlord may be liable for a nuisance committed on demised premises.

The first situation where a landlord may be liable arises in relation to a nuisance which existed before the landlord demised the premises. A landlord may be liable for a nuisance which existed before the date of the grant of the tenancy and before the landlord went out of possession if the landlord knew or ought to have known of the nuisance. In this situation, however, the landlord may escape liability to the tenant for such a nuisance by covenanting with the tenant, under the lease, that the tenant will take steps to discontinue or prevent the nuisance (see *Gandy* v *Jubber* (1865) 9 B & S 15). In the case of a third party, the landlord cannot escape liability in respect of a known pre-existing nuisance by contracting with the tenant that the tenant shall bear the responsibility for the repair of the premises because the landlord is not permitted to rid himself of his obligation to the third party in this way.

The second situation in which a landlord may be liable for nuisance which occurs on demised premises arises where a landlord lets premises to a tenant for purposes which are, in themselves, a nuisance. Thus in *Harris* v *James* (1876) 45 LJQB 545 a landlord let land to a tenant for the purpose of carrying out blasting operations and lime-burning. The landlord was held to be liable in nuisance because he knew of and permitted these activities to take place on his land. Similarly in *Tetley* v *Chitty* [1986] 1 All ER 663 it was held that the defendant council were liable in nuisance to the plaintiffs. The defendants had granted permission to a go-kart club to use their land for the purpose of using go-karts. The plaintiffs, who lived close to the go-kart track, complained of the noise made by the go-karts. The defendants argued that they were not liable in nuisance because they had not created the nuisance nor had they permitted the go-kart club to cause a nuisance. This argument was rejected by McNeill J on the ground that the noise made by the go-karts was an 'ordinary and necessary' consequence of the use of go-karts and therefore the defendants were held to have consented, either expressly or impliedly, to the commission of the nuisance.

The third situation in which a landlord may be liable for the commission of the tort of nuisance on demised premises arises where a landlord expressly or impliedly reserves to himself the right to enter and repair the premises. In such a case the landlord will be liable to a third party or, in some cases, the tenant for damage caused by the nuisance. In *Payne* v *Rogers* (1794) 2 H Bl 350 Heath J appeared to suggest that the tenant would not be liable where a third party was injured and that it was the landlord who was liable, but in *St Anne's Well Brewery Co v Roberts* (1928) 140 LT 1 it was held that the tenant could also be liable and that the tenant's obligation to the third party could not be discharged simply because the landlord was under an obligation to repair the premises. In *Wringe v Cohen* [1940] 1 KB 229 the gable end of a house belonging to the defendant fell onto the highway during a heavy fall of rain and caused damage to the plaintiff's shop. The defendant's premises had been in a state of disrepair for three years. The defendant, who was the landlord of the premises, argued that, although he was under an obligation to repair the premises, he would only be liable if, as a matter of fact, he knew or ought to have known of the disrepair. It was held that the defendant was liable whether or not he knew or ought to have known of the danger because he had accepted an obligation to repair the premises. This obligation to repair gave him the control of the premises and gave him the right to enter the premises to maintain them. The landlord is not, however, liable where the nuisance has been created by a trespasser or by an act of nature, unless the principles established in *Sedleigh-Denfield v O'Callaghan* (above) or *Leakey v National Trust* (above) have been satisfied. It should be noted that in addition to his liability in nuisance a landlord may also be subject to the controls laid down in s4 of the Defective Premises Act 1972 (discussed at 17.18).

18.11 Types of harm

It is not possible to classify every type of harm which may be actionable in nuisance. Three broad categories can, however, be identified.

Encroachments

This category includes physical objects which actually interfere with the plaintiff's land, for example, tree roots which damage the plaintiff's house (*Davey v Harrow Corporation* [1958] 1 QB 60), trees which overhang a neighbour's land (*Lemon v Webb* [1895] AC 1) and landslides on to the plaintiff's land (*Leakey v National Trust* [1980] QB 485).

Physical damage to the plaintiff's land

This category includes overflows from blocked drains and culverts (*Sedleigh-Denfield v O'Callaghan* [1940] AC 880), dilapidated buildings falling onto neighbouring property (*Wringe v Cohen* [1940] 1 KB 229) and vibrations *(Hoare and Co v McAlpine* [1923] 1 Ch 167).

Acts interfering with a neighbour's enjoyment of his own property

This category mainly consists of non-physical injuries to the enjoyment of property such as noise (*Halsey v Esso Petroleum Co* [1961] 1 WLR 683), smell (*Adams v Ursell*

[1913] 1 Ch 269) and fumes, heat and dust (*Matania* v *National Provincial Bank Ltd* [1936] 2 All ER 633), harassing telephone calls (*Khorasandjian* v *Bush* [1993] 3 WLR 476) and using premises in a residential area as a sex shop (*Laws* v *Florinplace Ltd* [1981] 1 All ER 659).

18.12 Defences

There are a number of defences to a nuisance action. The most important of these defences are dealt with below.

Prescription

Continuance of a nuisance for 20 years will, by prescription, legalise a private nuisance (but not a public one). The crucial point to note is that the time does not begin to run for this purpose until the plaintiff is aware of the existence of the nuisance. If it were otherwise the plaintiff might find that he had lost his right of action before he even knew that it existed. But this rule can have rather odd effects in practice. In *Sturges* v *Bridgman* (1879) 11 Ch D 852 the defendant, who was a sweet manufacturer, had for more than 20 years used certain machinery in the manufacture of sweets. The plaintiff, who was a doctor, bought property nearby in 1865. In 1873 the plaintiff built his consulting rooms in his garden, adjacent to the defendant's premises. The noise from the defendant's machines disturbed the plaintiff in the use of his consulting rooms. In the plaintiff's nuisance action the defendant claimed that he had acquired a right to make the noise by 20 years' prescription. It was held that there was no nuisance until the consulting rooms were built in 1873 and that time did not begin to run until that date and so there had been no 20-year prescription.

Statutory authority

If the act which gave rise to the nuisance was authorised by statute, that statutory authority will afford the defendant a defence only if it can be shown that the interference with the plaintiff's rights was, either expressly or impliedly, permitted by the wording in the statute. The scope of this defence was recently considered by the House of Lords in *Allen* v *Gulf Oil Refining Ltd* [1981] AC 1001. The defendants were authorised by the Gulf Oil Refining Act 1965 to construct an oil refinery on certain lands at Milford Haven, together with railways, jetties and harbours to serve the refinery. The refinery was built very close to a small village where the plaintiffs lived. The operation of the refinery caused noxious fumes to be emitted over the plaintiffs' village and the plaintiffs brought an action in nuisance in respect of the noxious odours, vibrations, continuous roars, high-pitched noises and flames from burning waste gases. The defendants argued that their activities did not constitute a nuisance because they had statutory authority for their activities. The Act under which they claimed that they had statutory authority empowered the defendants to construct the refinery but it conferred no express authority to use the refinery once built.

The majority of the House of Lords held that Parliament had, by necessary implication, authorised the operation and use of the refinery. Parliament could not have intended the refinery to stand unused as an 'adornment' of the countryside. In adopting this approach the House of Lords approved of the approach adopted by Lord Dunedin in *Corporation of Manchester* v *Farnworth* [1930] AC 171 when he said that:

> 'When Parliament has authorised a certain thing to be made or done in a certain place, there can be no action for nuisance caused by the making or doing of that thing if the nuisance is the inevitable result of the making or doing so authorised. The onus of proving that the result is inevitable is on those who wish to escape liability for nuisance.'

In *Allen* this onus was satisfied by those committing the nuisance and it was held that they had immunity from any non-negligent interferences with the enjoyment of, or damage to, the plaintiffs' property.

Lord Keith dissented and took an extremely literal approach to the interpretation of the statute upon which the defendants purported to rely. He said that the Act only authorised the construction of the refinery. It made no mention of the use of the refinery and so, in using the refinery, the defendants could not claim the authorisation of the statute. The difficulty with this view lies in seeing how the refinery was to operate at all because Parliament surely could not have intended that the refinery, once built, would lie unused.

Lord Denning, in the Court of Appeal in *Allen*, sought to find a solution to this problem by formulating a new principle to be applied in cases where statutory authority was invoked as a defence to a nuisance action. He said that, even where the statutory defence was applicable, the plaintiff should not be left without a remedy when the use and enjoyment of his property had been interfered with. However, he argued that the plaintiff should not be granted an injunction because that would be to allow private rights to prevail over valuable public projects. But he did argue that the plaintiffs were entitled to damages in respect of the damage they had suffered as a result of the nuisance. This may produce the fairest result because it would not prevent the operation of the refinery, yet it would not leave the plaintiffs without a remedy in respect of the damage which they had suffered. This approach was, however, rejected by the House of Lords on the ground that it was inconsistent with established authorities.

Other defences

The Law Reform (Contributory Negligence) Act 1945 is applicable to nuisance and, therefore, is a defence. Agreement to the existence of the nuisance is also a defence. Act of God and act of a stranger may also constitute a defence, unless the defendant has 'adopted' or 'continued' the nuisance. Inevitable accident is a defence in cases where negligence is of the essence of liability. Ignorance of the nuisance may in certain cases amount to a defence. For example, in *Noble* v *Harrison* [1926] 2 KB 332 a branch of a tree overhung a highway. The fact that it overhung did not make it a nuisance. It fell due to a latent defect, not discoverable by any reasonably careful inspection, on to the plaintiff's car. It was held that the defendant was not liable. The branch fell due to a latent crack caused 'by a secret and unobservable operation of nature' for which the defendant was not liable.

The following are NOT defences to a nuisance action.

Coming to the nuisance

As a general rule it is no defence to show that the plaintiff came to the nuisance, that is to say the defendant cannot argue that he was making the nuisance before the plaintiff moved into the area. We have already seen the operation of this rule in *Sturges* v *Bridgman* (above). The doctor built his consulting room after the defendant had been using the offending machinery, but it was held that this fact did not give the defendant a good defence to the doctor's action. This may seem to be unfair to the defendant because the doctor chose to put his consulting rooms close to the defendant's machinery and so he should take the consequences. But if the law did adopt such an approach its effect would be to freeze the use of land and this is undesirable. The rule is also mitigated in its application by the locality principle, under which the plaintiff must, in relation to interference with the enjoyment of his property, accept the standard of noise, smell etc customary in that particular area.

Although this particular rule is well established in terms of age it was not viewed with great favour by the Court of Appeal in *Miller* v *Jackson* [1977] QB 966. Houses were built on the edge of a cricket ground. Cricket had been played there for some considerable time before the houses were built. Cricket balls kept on landing in the gardens of these houses or even in the houses themselves. The cricket club did what they could. They built a fence around the boundary line and they even asked batsmen to try to hit fours rather than sixes. But still the balls kept on landing in the houses. The plaintiffs, who owned the houses, brought an action against the cricket club in nuisance. Lord Denning, in a robust judgment, upheld the values of playing cricket and said that the damage was due to the building of the houses and not to the playing of cricket. He held that *Sturges* was no longer binding today and so found for the defendants. But long established authority cannot simply be brushed aside in such a manner. The other judges were more circumspect. Geoffrey Lane LJ said that, had the matter been an open one, he would have found for the defendants but he felt constrained by authority to find for the plaintiffs. Having said that, this fact that the houses were built at a time when cricket was already being played on the ground was used to justify refusing to grant an injunction to the plaintiffs and so their claim was relegated to a damages claim. So *Sturges* may yet be open to re-examination in the House of Lords.

Usefulness is not, in itself, a defence

The mere fact that the defendant's activity is socially useful is not, of itself, a defence to a nuisance action. The case most commonly cited in this connection is the case of *Adams* v *Ursell* [1913] 1 Ch 269. Here the defendant opened a fish and chip shop in what had been, hitherto, a rather 'well-to-do' residential part of a street. The argument that the granting of an injunction to stop the nuisance created by the smell would cause hardship to the defendant's business and to the 'less well off' who were his regular customers was rejected. The defendant should have located his shop in the area where his customers resided, presumably because they would not be offended by the smell emanating from the shop.

No defence that it is due to many

It is no defence to an action in nuisance that the nuisance was caused by many people acting together and that the defendant's act, taken alone, would not have amounted to a nuisance. In assessing what is a reasonable user the courts will take account of all the surrounding circumstances, including the conduct of other people.

18.13 Remedies

There are three basic remedies in English law which are available to a plaintiff in a nuisance action. These three remedies are an injunction, damages and abatement. Since an injunction is the most important remedy, consideration will be given to this remedy first.

Injunctions

An injunction is an extremely powerful weapon because it gives to the court the power to order the defendant to stop the activity which has given rise to the nuisance. The order may require the defendant to halt the activity immediately or it may give him a reasonable time in which to comply with the court order. The court in a nuisance action will generally grant a prohibitory injunction, that is an injunction requiring the defendant to stop the particular activity which is the subject of the action.

   An injunction is a discretionary remedy. The general rule in relation to the granting of injunctions is that an injunction may be granted where damages are inadequate. In many cases it is not difficult for a plaintiff to show that damages are inadequate because, once he can show that the nuisance is a continuing one and that the damage will therefore continue, damages are presumed to be inadequate because the plaintiff would have to keep coming back to court for more damages as the nuisance continued. Until 1977 it could be said with some confidence that an injunction would be available as a matter of course to restrain a continuing nuisance.

This was largely because of the high value placed by the English judiciary upon property rights and their refusal to countenance the interference with these property rights. Thus in *Pride of Derby* v *British Celanese Ltd* [1953] Ch 149 an injunction was granted restraining the defendants from polluting a river with untreated sewage and the plaintiff club's private interest in fishing in the river was allowed to prevail over the interest of the town in having its sewage cheaply and easily disposed of. But in *Miller* v *Jackson* (above) Lord Denning adopted a different approach. He said that:

> 'There is a contest here between the interest of the public at large and the interest of the private individual. The public interest lies in protecting the environment by preserving our playing fields in the face of mounting development, and by enabling our youth to enjoy all the benefits of outdoor games such as cricket and football. The private interest lies in securing the privacy of [the plaintiff's] home and garden without intrusion or interference by anyone ... As between their conflicting interests I am of the opinion that the public interest should prevail over the private interest.'

This approach was heralded by some commentators (see, for example, Ogus and Richardson 'Economics and the Environment – A Study of Private Nuisance' [1977] CLJ 284 and also Tromans 'Nuisance – Prevention or Payment?' (1982) 41 CLJ 87) as proclaiming the dawn of a new era in the law of nuisance when judges would have regard to the public interest and issues of public policy in adjudicating upon nuisance cases.

However in the later case of *Kennaway* v *Thompson* [1981] QB 88 the Court of Appeal refused to follow the approach adopted by the court in *Miller*. In *Kennaway*, the plaintiff, who was an old lady, lived in a house close to a lake. Her enjoyment of her property was spoilt by power boat racing which was held by the defendant club on the lake. Some of these races were very important races (for example national championship races were held there) but the boats were also extremely noisy. The plaintiff sought an injunction and damages against the defendant club. The Court of Appeal reaffirmed that in cases where there was a continuing actionable nuisance the court's jurisdiction to award damages instead of an injunction was only to be exercised very sparingly and that the public interest did not prevail over the private interest. Lord Denning's judgment in *Miller* was said to be inconsistent with the principles laid down by the House of Lords in *Shelfer* v *City of London Electric Lighting Co Ltd* [1895] 1 Ch 287 and was not followed. So there remains a conflict of authority on this point, but it must be conceded that the approach adopted by the court in *Kennaway* represents the traditional view in English law (the cases are usefully discussed by Tromans (above) and by Tettenborn and Markesinis (1981) 131 NLJ 108).

This conflict of authority requires us to examine the arguments for and against granting injunctions as a matter of course in cases of continuing nuisances. There are two principal reasons why English law has favoured the granting of injunctions as a matter of course. The first reason lies in the difficulty of assessing the quantum of damages, especially in cases where the nuisance is alleged to take the form of interference with the enjoyment of property. The second, and more compelling, reason is the unwillingness of the courts to, in effect, expropriate, without the sanction of Parliament, the plaintiff's interest in the enjoyment of his land by legalising a nuisance. The unwillingness of the courts to undermine the property interests of plaintiffs can be clearly seen in the judgments of the Court of Appeal in *Kennaway*.

There are, however, some arguments against an injunction being granted as a matter of course. The first is that the grant of an injunction may have a disastrous effect on the defendant (especially if he is ordered to halt the nuisance immediately) or on the public at large. This argument can be met to some extent by the court granting the injunction on terms (for a good example of this see the terms of the injunction granted in *Kennaway* which, in fact, permitted the defendants to hold certain power boat races provided that certain conditions were met) or by the court suspending the injunction for a short period to allow the defendant to take the necessary steps to comply with the terms of the injunction. However, in considering the merits of this argument it should not be thought that the granting of an injunction has, as a necessary consequence, the cessation of the activity which is the subject of the injunction. In a valuable article (Property Rules, Liability Rules and Inalienability: One View of the Cathedral (1972) 85 Harv LR 1089) Calabresi and Melamed point out that the effect of the granting of an injunction is to shift the entitlements as between the plaintiff and defendant. The injunction gives the plaintiff the right to insist on the injunction being carried out according to its terms or it gives him the option of selling the injunction to the defendant at the price of his own choosing. Thus in the case of *Allen* v *Gulf Oil Refining Ltd* (above) the granting of the injunction would not necessarily have had the effect of closing down the refinery but would have given to the plaintiffs the right to sell their injunction to the defendants at a price of their own choosing so that they were properly compensated for the nuisance created by the operation of the refinery. Similarly the analysis of Calabresi and Melamed suggests that the refusal by a court to grant an injunction does not necessarily mean that the nuisance-causing activity will go on as before. What the refusal does do is to throw the onus upon the plaintiff to bargain with the defendant over the terms on which the defendant may be prepared to stop the activity in question. This time, in the bargaining, it will be the defendant who has the entitlement, and therefore the stronger bargaining position, because the court has refused to grant the plaintiff his injunction. This analysis, in terms of different entitlement, should be borne in mind whenever it is argued that the grant of an injunction will necessarily have a disastrous effect on the defendant because he will have to cease the nuisance-causing activity immediately. This is not strictly true. The defendant does have an option. He can bargain with the plaintiff to see whether the plaintiff is prepared to come to an agreement on the terms on which the injunction may be discharged.

The second argument against the granting of injunctions as a matter of course is the effect which such an approach has on the substantive law of nuisance. For example, it could be argued that the decision of the House of Lords in *Allen* v *Gulf Oil Refining Ltd* (above) was heavily influenced by the fear which the effect of granting an injunction would have on the operation of the refinery. Thus the scope of the substantive right was dictated by the remedial consequences. However, the case has not really been made out that the fear of the remedial consequences has shaped the scope of the substantive right to any great extent.

So it is submitted that English law has been correct in adopting the rule that injunctions should be granted as a matter of course and that the law of nuisance should be protective of the property rights of individuals. We should leave the wider issues, such as those considered by Lord Denning in *Miller* v *Jackson* (above), to the law relating to planning and not leave such issues to be decided according to the subjective whims of judges such as Lord Denning.

Abatement

As we noted in chapter 1 of this book the law of tort is extremely reluctant to allow a plaintiff to take the law into his own hands. An exception to this can be found in the willingness of the law to permit a plaintiff to abate a nuisance. This remedy can, however, only be resorted to within narrow confines. In particular, three conditions must be met.

In the first place, before any attempt is made to abate the nuisance, notice should be given to the defendant (that is, the person committing the nuisance) to remedy the nuisance, unless the nuisance can be abated without obtaining entry to the defendant's premises or the security of life or property is at risk and time does not permit the giving of notice (see *Lemon* v *Webb* [1895] AC 1). The nuisance can be abated without going on to the defendant's land where, for example, the branches from the defendant's tree hang over into the abator's land, in which case the abator can simply lop off the offending branches while standing on his own property.

The second condition which must be complied with is that the abator must not do unnecessary damage to the defendant's property when abating the nuisance. The third, and final, condition is that where there is more than one way of abating the nuisance, the method which involves the least cost to the defendant should be employed unless the adoption of that method would have a detrimental effect on the interests of innocent third parties or on the public at large.

Damages

In many ways damages is the residuary remedy in the tort of nuisance because in most cases the plaintiff will want an injunction to put a stop to the nuisance. But there are cases where a plaintiff will want damages, for example where the nuisance is not continuous or where the plaintiff's property has been damaged by the nuisance.

The easiest way for a plaintiff to show that he has suffered damage is to show that his property has diminished in value as a result of the nuisance. However, it is not necessary to show the existence of damage in all cases. Thus in *Fay* v *Prentice* (1845) 1 CB 828 the plaintiff was able to recover without showing the existence of damage. The defendant erected a cornice on his house which projected over the plaintiff's garden, with the result that water dripped from it on to the plaintiff's garden. It was held that the cornice was a nuisance and that the plaintiff did not have to show that damage had been caused. So the fact that it had not rained was irrelevant because when it did rain damage of some kind could be presumed.

The approach to the award of damages in cases of interference with the enjoyment of property was demonstrated by the Court of Appeal in *Bone* v *Seale* [1975] 1 All ER 787. The defendants owned a pig farm which was adjacent to the plaintiff's property. The storage of pig manure and the boiling of pig-swill emitted intolerable smells, both day and night. The plaintiff sought an injunction and damages in respect of these smells. It was held that, on the facts, there was no pecuniary loss to the plaintiff, there was no damage to his property and no interference with his health. So the court awarded damages on a basis analagous to that adopted in cases of loss of amenity in personal injuries cases. The court awarded damages of £1,000, being similar to the sum which would have been awarded in a personal injury case for loss of the sense of smell.

There is little explicit authority on the question whether economic loss is recoverable in nuisance. In *British Celanese Ltd* v *A H Hunt Ltd* [1969] 1 WLR 959 Lawton J was prepared to concede that economic loss was recoverable in nuisance, but this is only an obiter remark (although in *Ryeford Homes Ltd* v *Sevenoaks District Council* (1989) 16 Con LR 75 Judge Newey QC said that, on the facts of the case, if economic loss was held to result from the commission of the tort of nuisance, then he thought that such loss was 'probably recoverable'. There is no English authority which expressly affirms or denies the existence of a right to bring an action for damages for personal injury in a nuisance action. Canadian authority can, however, be found to support the proposition that damages for personal injury can be recovered in a nuisance action (*Devon Lumber Co Ltd* v *MacNeill* (1988) 45 DLR (4th) 300, discussed at 18.2). It can be argued that the plaintiff in a case such as *Devon Lumber* ought to be able to bring an action for damages because his injury is suffered qua occupier (that is to say, it arises because he or she lives next door to the cedar mill). But, where the injury which is suffered is incidental to the plaintiff's enjoyment of land (for example, where the vibrations from the defendants' factory cause a heavy object to fall and hit the plaintiff), it is arguable that such a claim can only be brought in negligence because, given that the injury could equally have been suffered by a visitor to the premises, 'it would be anomalous and unfair if the occupier could plead strict liability in nuisance whilst a visitor, equally affected, could only sue in negligence' (Kodilyne (1989) 9 Legal Studies 284 at 290).

The loss must not be too remote, or else it will be irrecoverable. In *The Wagon Mound (No 2)* [1967] 1 AC 617 the House of Lords held that the test for remoteness of damage was reasonable foreseeability of the kind of damage, as it is in the case of negligence.

Where the court refuses, in the exercise of its discretion, to grant an injunction then the court may award damages in equity in lieu of (in place of) an injunction.

But the court uses this power to grant damages in lieu of an injunction very sparingly. The relevant principles were laid down by the Court of Appeal in *Shelfer v City of London Electric Lighting Co Ltd* [1895] 1 Ch 287. The court held that damages should only be awarded where: the injury to the plaintiff's legal rights is small; the damage is capable of being estimated in money; the damage can be adequately compensated by a small money payment; and the case is one in which it would be oppressive to the defendant to grant an injunction.

This power to award damages in lieu of an injunction is now contained in s50 of the Supreme Court Act 1981.

18.14 The future of the nuisance action

It is clear that measures to protect the environment and anti-pollution measures are here to stay. What is the role of the nuisance action in all these developments? It is unlikely that the tort of nuisance will have a great role to play in these types of disputes. This is especially so when it is noted that the courts are reluctant to give priority to considerations of public policy in deciding whether or not to issue an injunction. The tort of nuisance is too wedded to the protection of private property rights to be of great assistance in resolving such disputes.

The control of pollution is likely to remain in the hands of regulatory legislation. This is not to say that nuisance should have no part to play in setting the standards for such legislation. It may have some role to play in setting the appropriate standards. Nor is it to say that the nuisance action should be abolished. The action still has a role to play in resolving disputes between neighbours and in filling in the gaps in the regulatory legislation. But, although the action should be retained, its importance should not be over-emphasised in modern society.

19

Public Nuisance

19.1 Introduction

19.2 The elements of the tort of public nuisance

19.3 Public nuisance and the highway

19.1 Introduction

Public nuisance is generally given separate consideration from private nuisance on the ground that public nuisance is a crime as well as a tort. Indeed in many ways its primary significance is as a crime rather than as a tort. It is a crime of somewhat uncertain ambit. *Archbold's Criminal Pleading and Practice* ((42nd ed) para 27–44) defines a public nuisance in the following terms:

> 'Every person is guilty of an offence at common law, known as public nuisance, who does an act not warranted by law, or omits to discharge a legal duty, if the effect of the act or omission is to endanger the life, health, property, morals, or comfort of the public, or to obstruct the public in the exercise of enjoyment of rights common to all Her Majesty's subjects.'

After noting that a person who commits a public nuisance incurs liability to life imprisonment and unlimited fines, Spencer concludes (Public Nuisance – A Critical Examination [1989] CLJ 55) that '[w]ith such a broad concept in existence, backed with such broad remedies, what need have we of any other criminal offence? – or torts? ...' He further notes that almost everything about public nuisance runs contrary to 'modern notions of certainty and precision in criminal law – and, indeed, in civil law as well'. Thus it is no surprise to learn that at common law a wide variety of activities could constitute a public nuisance. They included the selling of food which was unfit for human consumption, obstructing a public highway, keeping a brothel, displaying one's naked body in public and throwing fireworks in the street. Statute has, however, intervened to amend this list, sometimes regulating activities, such as brothel-keeping, which were public nuisances at common law and on other occasions statute has supplemented the common law by making certain activities a public nuisance. The Public Health Act 1936 has made certain activities a public nuisance, for example to permit insanitary water tanks to be used for domestic purposes. Similarly the Noise Abatement Act 1960, the Clean Air Act 1956 and the Control of Pollution Act 1974 have intervened to regulate activities which were previously governed by the common law. However, cases of public nuisance are still prosecuted – see *R* v *Shorrock* [1993] 3 WLR 698 for a modern example of the use of this action as a crime.

One interesting question concerns the relationship between public nuisance and such modern regulatory legislation. One facet of this issue was discussed by Buckley J in *Gillingham Borough Council* v *Medway (Chatham) Dock Co Ltd* [1993] QB 343 when he was asked to consider the relationship between public nuisance and planning legislation. The defendants were lessees of a port. The plaintiffs alleged that the use of the roads around the port at night by numerous heavy goods vehicles (HGVs) constituted a public nuisance. The evidence established that in 1988 there were approximately 750 HGV 'movements' every night and that the sleep and comfort of the residents in the vicinity of the port were disturbed. The defendants conceded that these conditions constituted a substantial interference with the residents' enjoyment of their property up to June 1990 and that, subject to defences, enough residents were affected to constitute a public nuisance. However, the defendants argued that they had been given planning permission to operate a commercial port, that such a port could operate viably only on a 24-hour basis, that no limits had been placed on the volume of traffic in the vicinity when they had been granted planning permission and that their estimate of the likely throughput of traffic had been remarkably accurate. Buckley J noted that planning legislation had been enacted by Parliament in an effort to balance the interests of the community and the interests of individuals likely to be adversely affected by the plans being put forward. He then asked himself the question whether residents can defeat the planning legislation by bringing an action in nuisance. His conclusion was that 'where planning consent is given for a development or change of use, the question of nuisance will thereafter fall to be decided by reference to a neighbourhood with that development or use and not as it was previously'. So planning permission is not, of itself, a defence to a nuisance action but it is a factor to be taken into account in identifying the character of the neighbourhood. So, on the facts of the present case, account had to be taken of the fact that planning permission had been given to use the dockyard as a commercial port. In the light of this fact, Buckley J held that the disturbance experienced by the residents of the area was not an actionable nuisance.

19.2 The elements of the tort of public nuisance

There are two basic elements which must be established in showing that the tort of public nuisance has been committed. The first is that it must be shown that the persons affected by the nuisance constituted the public or a section of the public. The intention behind this requirement is to distinguish a public nuisance from a private nuisance. In *Attorney General* v *PYA Quarries* [1957] 2 QB 169 the defendants argued that the persons affected by the blasting operations at their quarry were not sufficiently numerous to constitute a section of the public. The only persons affected by their blasting operations, and the dust and vibrations created thereby, were the residents who lived close to the quarry. So they argued that, at worst, they had committed the tort of private nuisance. The Court of Appeal held that a public nuisance was a nuisance which 'materially affects the reasonable comfort and convenience of life of a class of Her Majesty's subjects'. Lord Denning declined to answer the question how many people were needed to constitute a 'class of Her Majesty's subjects'. He indicated that it was not simply a question of numbers but that regard had to be had to the effect of the nuisance. He held that a public nuisance was a nuisance which was so widespread that it was not reasonable to expect one individual to bring an action to put a halt to it, but rather that it was the responsibility of the whole community to bring the action. The trial judge had held that the residents were a 'class of Her Majesty's subjects'. The Court of Appeal held that this question was, in all cases, a question of fact for the trial judge and that they would not interfere with his finding. So the defendants' appeal was dismissed and they were held to be liable to the plaintiffs and injunctions were granted in the plaintiffs' favour.

The second element which a plaintiff must establish in an action in public nuisance is that he suffered special damage. The plaintiff must establish that he suffered particular damage over and above the annoyance and inconvenience suffered by the public at large. This requirement of special damage prevents a multiplicity of actions arising out of the one event and so it operates as a limitation upon the damages for which the defendant may be liable. In *Rose v Miles* (1815) 4 M & S 101 the defendant moored his barge across a canal in such a way as to block the canal. The plaintiff was put to considerable extra expense because he had to unload his barge and carry his cargo by land because the blockage of the canal meant that he could not continue down the canal. It was held that the obstruction had caused the plaintiff special damage because of the extra expense which he had incurred and so the defendant was liable in public nuisance.

Apart from these two particular requirements there is much in common between public and private nuisance and the courts balance roughly similar factors in each case. There are, however, one or two other differences between the torts. Private nuisance is concerned with the protection of interests in land and so it is arguable that the plaintiff must have an interest in the land affected (see 18.2) but there is no such limitation in cases of public nuisance. Prescription is not a defence to a public nuisance, whereas it is a defence to a private nuisance. Exemplary damages may be recovered in private nuisance but are not available in public nuisance (*AB v South West Water Services Ltd* [1993] 2 WLR 507). There are also certain special rules which have grown up in relation to public nuisances and the highway. We will now consider some of these rules.

19.3 Public nuisance and the highway

There has been considerable case law concerned with public nuisance and the highway. It is a public nuisance to obstruct the highway or to create a danger on, or close to, the highway. We shall consider first the law relating to obstruction of the highway.

Obstruction of the highway

The highway does not have to be completely blocked before a public nuisance may be committed. It is sufficient if the highway is unreasonably obstructed. However it is not necessarily a nuisance to leave a vehicle stationary on the road for a period of time. But in *Dymond* v *Pearce* [1972] 1 QB 497 it was held that the defendant had committed a public nuisance in leaving his lorry parked on the highway. It was a large lorry but he had left it with its parking lights on and the lorry was visible from a distance of 200 yards. Despite this the plaintiff, who was on his motor cycle, collided with the lorry. It was held that the defendant, in leaving the lorry on the public highway for his own convenience, had committed a public nuisance. The defendant was not, however, liable for the injuries to the plaintiff because they were caused entirely by the negligence of the plaintiff and not by the defendant leaving his lorry on the highway. However, the case might have been decided differently if the reason for the defendant leaving his lorry on the highway was that it had broken down. It was held that the leaving of the lorry on the highway could be a public nuisance even though there was no foreseeable risk of injury. But as Sachs LJ pointed out, where the leaving of the lorry does not create a foreseeable risk of injury, it is unlikely that it will be the cause of the injury to the plaintiff, as *Dymond* itself demonstrates. It is submitted, however, that these cases could be more appropriately dealt with as cases of negligence (see Newark (1949) 65 LQR 480). Where stationary vehicles are left where they may foreseeably be a source of danger to others then it could be said that the defendant has been negligent in leaving his vehicle on the highway. Thus liability would only be imposed in respect of the creation of a foreseeable risk of injury and resort would not have to be had to the awkward issues of causation discussed in *Dymond* when the risk of injury is not foreseeable.

A public nuisance can also be created where the obstruction of the highway is of a temporary nature. Thus in *Barber* v *Penley* [1893] 2 Ch 447 it was held that a queue waiting to get into the defendants' theatre was a public nuisance when it made it difficult for the plaintiff to gain access to his premises (see too *Lyons* v *Gulliver* [1914] 1 Ch 631).

In *Hubbard* v *Pitt* [1976] QB 142 the defendants were picketing on the highway outside an estate agent's shop. The Court of Appeal held that picketing on the highway may constitute a public nuisance (see too *Thomas* v *NUM (S Wales Area)* [1985] 2 All ER 1, where Scott J invented a tort of unreasonable harassment which, he claimed, was committed by pickets on the highway). However, it should be noted that where the picketing occurs in the course of a trade dispute the defendants will be able to claim some immunity in tort in relation to certain torts committed during the course of the picketing (see s15 of the Trade Union and Labour Relations Act 1974 as amended by s16 of the Employment Act 1980).

Dangers on the highway

A public nuisance may also be created where a danger is created on the highway. Almost anything which is left on the highway may be a source of danger. A pile of rubble left on the highway may constitute such a danger (see *Clark* v *Chambers* (1878) 3 QBD 327), as may a vehicle which is left on the highway (see *Dymond* v *Pearce* (above)).

Dangers close to the highway

The danger may not actually be on the highway but be very close to the highway. The occupier of premises close to the highway may thus come under a duty to members of the public using the highway to keep his premises in repair. Thus in *Tarry* v *Ashton* (1876) 1 QBD 314 the defendant was held to be liable in public nuisance when a lamp which overhung his premises fell and injured the plaintiff, who was a passer-by. The defendant had argued that he was not liable because he had employed an independent contractor to repair the lamp and so he claimed that he had discharged the duty upon him. But it was found that the lamp was insecure because it had not been properly repaired. It was held that the defendant was under a duty to keep the lamp in good repair, that he had been in breach of that duty because the duty was a non-delegable one and so he was liable to the plaintiff.

In *Wringe* v *Cohen* [1940] 1 KB 229 it was held that the occupier of premises on the highway was under a duty to keep the premises in repair whether he knew of the danger or not. This principle laid down by the Court of Appeal in *Wringe* appears to be a principle of strict liability (see Friedmann (1940) 3 MLR 305). However the court said that the rule would not apply where the damage resulted from the 'secret and unobservable operation of nature' or from the unforeseeable act of a trespasser. These exceptions have been seized upon in subsequent cases to narrow the scope of the principle laid down in *Wringe*. One example of this restrictive interpretation is *British Road Services Ltd* v *Slater* [1964] 1 WLR 498. A large oak tree on the defendant's land overhung the highway. A branch of the tree which overhung the highway caused a package to be knocked off a lorry which was travelling along the highway. The package fell on to the road and the lorry which was travelling behind was damaged when it had to swerve to avoid the package. It was held that the defendant landowners were not responsible for the damage done to the plaintiff's lorry. The branch was not a foreseeable source of danger and it was only through 'fortuitous circumstances' that the damage had been done to the plaintiff's lorry.

It seems that the rule in *Wringe* creates a liability in between strict liability and liability for fault. Once the plaintiff demonstrates that the defendant had control over the premises and that he (the plaintiff) was injured, then the onus seems to switch to the defendant to show that the accident was an inevitable one which could not have been prevented by taking all reasonable care to keep the premises in good repair. The point was made by Denning LJ in *Mint* v *Good* [1951] 1 KB 517 when he said that 'when structures fall into dangerous disrepair' then 'there must be some fault on the part of someone or other for that to happen' and that it is the defendant who is legally held responsible for the damage which ensues.

The condition of the highway

At common law the highway authorities were only liable for misfeasance and not non-feasance. In other words they were liable for a repair which they had carried out negligently but not for a mere failure to repair. This immunity from suit in respect of negligent non-feasance was removed by the Highways (Miscellaneous Provisions) Act 1961. The law is now stated in the Highways Act 1980.

It is provided in s41 of that Act that the highway authorities are under a duty to maintain the highways. Under s58(1) of the Act the highway authorities are provided with a defence where they have taken reasonable care in all the circumstances to ensure that 'the part of the highway to which the action relates was not dangerous for traffic'. In s58(2) it is provided that in considering what constitutes reasonable care regard is to be had to, amongst other things, the character of the highway, the appropriate standard of maintenance and what constitutes a reasonable standard of repair. Note that although s41 does not require the highway authority to carry out work on land which does not form part of the highway, the authority does owe a common law duty of care to all road users to alleviate known dangers impairing visibility on land adjoining the highway: see *Stovin* v *Wise* (1994) The Times 8 March.

Some controversy has arisen as to what is the correct interpretation of what is now s58 of the 1980 Act. In *Griffiths* v *Liverpool Corporation* [1967] 1 QB 374 Diplock and Salmon LJJ were of the opinion that s58 imposed an absolute liability upon the highway authorities subject to the defence provided in s58(1), whereas Sellers LJ thought that negligence was an essential ingredient in the cause of action. This conflict has not yet been resolved but it appears that where the plaintiff can show that the highway is not in a proper state of repair the onus is on the highway authority to show that their statutory obligations have been discharged (see too *Littler* v *Liverpool Corporation* [1968] 2 All ER 343 and *Heydon* v *Kent County Council* [1978] QB 343). In *Wentworth* v *Wiltshire County Council* [1993] 2 WLR 175 the Court of Appeal held that the right to recover damages from the highway authority for breach of statutory duty was limited to users who suffered damage to property or the person, and did not cover economic loss.

20

The Rule in *Rylands* v *Fletcher*

20.1   Introduction

20.2   The rule

20.3   Accumulation

20.4   Non-natural user

20.5   Dangerous things?

20.6   Escape

20.7   Occupation

20.8   'His own purposes'

20.9   Foreseeability of damage

20.10 Protected interests

20.11 Defences

20.1 Introduction

We have noted in earlier chapters the dominant role played by the fault principle in the law of tort in England. Nevertheless, negligence has never succeeded in taking over the whole of the law of tort. There have always been pockets of tort law where the progress of negligence has been resisted. There are some cases where a defendant is held to be strictly liable for the consequence of his activities. A word of explanation is required about the phrase 'strict liability'. It does not necessarily mean that liability is absolute, admitting of no defence whatsoever. As we shall see, 'strict liability' is a somewhat ambiguous phrase and that it can admit of defences to a greater or to a lesser degree.

The classic example of strict liability in English law is the rule in *Rylands* v *Fletcher* (1868) LR 3 HL 330, affirming (1866) LR 1 Ex 265. Until recently it was thought by most lawyers that this rule was anomalous and not to be extended. But strict liability appears to be regaining its popularity. The EEC proposed to extend it to areas such as product liability (for consideration see Finch (1986) 2 PN 53) and these proposals have been put into effect by the Consumer Protection Act 1987. Even within the tort of negligence there have been cases where the standard of care required by the courts has been so high that, in practice, it has really amounted to the imposition of strict liability (see for example *Nettleship* v *Weston* [1971] 2 QB 691) although as we shall see later both negligence and the rule in *Rylands* v *Fletcher* now require the foreseeability of damage, so the term 'strict liability' is rather misleading.

20.2 The rule

It is now time to consider the rule that was actually laid down in the case of *Rylands* v *Fletcher*. First it is necessary to examine the facts of the case. The defendants were mill owners who wished to improve the water supply to their mill. In order to do this they employed some independent contractors, who were apparently competent, to construct a reservoir on their land, which would supply the defendants with water. During the course of their work the independent contractors discovered some underground passages and mines on the land where the reservoir was to be constructed. They did not seal these mines and shafts properly with the result that, when the reservoir was filled with water, the water burst through into the mines and shafts and flooded the plaintiff's coal mine, causing damage agreed at £937. The defendants were held liable for the damage.

Dias and Markesinis, in their book *Tort Law* (2nd ed) p344, helpfully considered whether the court could have decided the case on the existing law rather than develop a new principle of liability. They concluded that the plaintiff could not have succeeded in an action in trespass because the damage caused by the flooding was not a direct and immediate consequence of the defendants' activities. Nor could it have amounted to a nuisance since the damage was not continuous or recurring (but see *British Celanese* v *A H Hunt* [1969] 1 WLR 959). Although it was clear that the independent contractors had been at fault it was not clear whether they should have foreseen that their conduct could cause damage to the plaintiff. Similarly it was unclear whether the defendants would have been held liable for the negligence of the independent contractors. So it was unlikely that the plaintiff would have succeeded in negligence.

Therefore the traditional view was that the court had to develop a new principle of liability in order to find for the plaintiff. However, it should be noted that, in the Court of Exchequer Chamber, Blackburn J did not appear to be aware of the fact that he was extending the law in any significant way when he stated:

> 'We think that the true rule of law is, that the person who for his own purposes brings on to his lands and collects and keeps there anything likely to do mischief if it escapes, must keep it in at his peril, and, if he does not do so, he is prima facie answerable for all the damage which is the natural consequence of its escape.'

However, the whole scope of the rule in *Rylands* was reviewed and the rule analysed and restated by the House of Lords in *Cambridge Water Co* v *Eastern*

Counties Leather plc [1994] 2 WLR 53. Lord Goff, with whose judgment all the other Law Lords agreed, stated that Blackburn J had not stated any new principle of law but merely extended the law of nuisance to cases of an isolated escape.

Although this is the crucial statement of principle which has emerged from the case it should be noted that it was given by Blackburn J who was a member of the Court of Exchequer Chamber. The case was, in fact, appealed to the House of Lords where Lord Cairns LC gave the leading judgment and explicitly approved of the judgment of Blackburn J. He did, however, add a crucial addition that in *Rylands* the defendants made a 'non-natural' use of their land. This addition has assumed great significance in subsequent cases. The present scope of the rule in *Rylands* can be discussed under the following nine headings (paragraphs 20.3 to 20.11).

20.3 Accumulation

It should be noted that in his judgment Blackburn J referred to 'bringing' things on to the defendant's land. Thus he clearly intended to distinguish between things which are naturally on the land and things which are brought on to the land; only the latter being caught by the rule in *Rylands*. Thus in cases such as *Smith* v *Kenrick* (1849) 7 CB 515, *Pontardawe RDC* v *Moore-Gwyn* [1929] 1 Ch 656 and *Giles* v *Walker* (1890) 24 QBD 656 no liability was imposed under the rule in *Rylands* because the 'thing' which caused the damage either grew naturally on the land (thistle seed in *Giles* v *Walker*) or it accumulated naturally on the land (rain water as in *Smith* v *Kenrick*). It should not be assumed, however, that because the plaintiff cannot succeed under *Rylands* that he has no cause of action at all. It may be that he has a cause of action in nuisance or negligence (see *Leakey* v *National Trust* [1980] QB 485, discussed at 18.10).

20.4 Non-natural user

This requirement has caused many problems. As we have already noted this requirement did not appear in Blackburn J's statement of principle, but was introduced as a gloss by Lord Cairns LC in the House of Lords. In an important article (Non-Natural User and *Rylands* v *Fletcher* (1961) 24 MLR 557) Professor Newark has examined the use of the words 'natural' or 'naturally' in the judgments in *Rylands*. In the judgment of Blackburn J, the words 'natural' or 'naturally' occurred eight times. On six occasions they related to the type of consequence for which the defendants would be liable (ie 'natural and foreseeable consequences'). On one occasion it related to the capacity of the dangerous thing to do damage (ie 'will naturally do damage if it escapes'). On the other occasion it related to the circumstances in which the dangerous thing came to be on the land (ie it had to be brought onto the land, see paragraph 20.3). So for Blackburn J the word 'natural' simply meant something which was naturally there or something which was there by nature. In his examination of the judgment of Lord Cairns LC, Professor Newark demonstrates that Lord Cairns also meant by the use of the word 'natural' something which was naturally on the land.

Professor Newark then demonstrates that, starting with the case of *Farrer* v *Nelson* (1885) 15 QBD 258 and culminating in the famous case of *Rickards* v *Lothian* [1931] AC 263, the courts misconstrued the use of the word 'natural' in *Rylands* so that it came to mean not 'natural' in the sense of according to nature, but came to mean 'ordinary' or 'usual', thus narrowing the scope of the rule.

In *Rickards* v *Lothian* (above) the plaintiff leased second-floor offices in premises occupied by the defendants. One morning the plaintiff discovered that his offices had been flooded and that his stock-in-trade had been damaged by the water. The water had come from a fourth-floor lavatory basin, which had been plugged with nails, soap, pen-holders and string and whose tap had been fully turned on. The jury found that the defendants had been careless in failing to provide an overflow pipe, but that the plugging of the outlet and the turning on of the tap had been the 'malicious act of some person'. The Privy Council held that the defendants were not liable to the plaintiff. Lord Moulton stated that it was not every use of land which brought the rule in *Rylands* into play; he continued:

> 'It must be some special use bringing with it increased danger to others, and must not merely be the ordinary use of the land or such a use as is proper for the general benefit of the community.'

In *Cambridge Water* Lord Goff agreed that by 'natural' Blackburn J meant something which is there by nature and stated that Lord Moulton's expression 'ordinary use of land' was lacking in precision. Lord Goff particularly criticised the alternative criterion 'or such use as is proper for the general benefit of the community' as introducing doubt and being interpreted in a way that would not keep the exception within reasonable bounds. Lord Goff expressly rejected the finding of the judge at first instance that the use of the land by the defendants created employment and thus constituted a natural or ordinary use of land.

Lord Goff continued, however, by stating that he did not need in the instant case to redefine natural or ordinary use. Strictly speaking, therefore, his judgment on this criterion could be considered obiter, but in view of the House's root and branch reconsideration of the rule his views must be of great persuasive authority. Lord Goff went on to state that he felt 'that the storage of substantial quantities of chemicals on industrial premises should be regarded as an almost classic case of non-natural use'.

Given the views of Lord Goff on non-natural use, the judgment of Mackenna J in *Mason* v *Levy Auto Parts of England Ltd* [1967] 2 QB 530 can be reconciled. Here the defendants stored on their land crates and a large quantity of combustible materials which ignited in mysterious circumstances. The resulting fire spread to and damaged the plaintiff's premises. The defendants were held liable under *Rylands*. The factors which persuaded the judge to hold that this was a non-natural user of land were:

1. the quantities of combustible material which the defendants brought on to their land;
2. the way in which the materials were stored; and
3. the character of the neighbourhood.

The later case of *British Celanese* v *A H Hunt* [1969] 1 WLR 959 now seems suspect. In *British Celanese* the defendants used an industrial estate to manufacture electrical components. Lawton J held that the use was natural because the defendants were using the land for the very purpose for which it was designed and that the goods manufactured were needed for the general benefit of the community. Although the actual decision in *British Celanese* may be correct, the ratio decidendi cannot be justified in the light of *Cambridge Water*.

20.5 Dangerous things?

As originally formulated in *Rylands* the rule purported to apply to 'anything likely to do mischief if it escapes'. But it has been pointed out that there are few, if any, objects which do not give rise to a risk of danger if they escape (see Stallybrass 'Dangerous Things and the Non-Natural User of Land' (1929) 3 CLJ 376). But reference can still be seen in the cases to the dangerousness of the thing which has escaped (see *Hale* v *Jennings* [1938] 1 All ER 579 and *Perry* v *Kendrick Transport Ltd* [1956] 1 WLR 85). However, it was not mentioned at all in *British Celanese* v *A H Hunt* (above) and in *Read* v *Lyons Ltd* [1947] AC 156 where Lord MacMillan said that it would be impracticable to devise a legal framework which distinguished between dangerous things and non-dangerous things, attaching liability to the former but not to the latter. The Law Commission in its report on Civil Liability for Dangerous Things and Activities (1970) (Law Com No 32) came to a similar conclusion. So it is submitted that there is no longer a separate requirement that the thing which escapes be dangerous, but that this requirement has been subsumed within the non-natural user test and that the more dangerous a thing is, the more likely it is that it will be held to constitute a non-natural use.

20.6 Escape

It is clear from the judgment of Blackburn J that the thing must escape from the defendant's land. This requirement was of vital significance in the case of *Read* v *Lyons Ltd* (above). The plaintiff was employed as an inspector at the defendants' munitions factory during the war. She was injured in the course of her employment at the factory by the explosion of a high explosive shell. She sued the defendants, but made no allegation of negligence. It was held that the defendants were not liable under the rule in *Rylands* because there was no escape of the dangerous thing from their premises; the explosion was confined within their premises. Lord Porter conceded that the ruling would produce strange results, but sought to justify this on the ground that the rule in *Rylands* was anomalous and that it ought not to be extended. Only Lord Uthwatt attempted to find a principled basis for this distinction. He argued that a person who comes on to the occupier's land is subject to the dominion of the occupier and that the dominion of the occupier would not be overridden by the rule in *Rylands*. Where, however, the person was not on the occupier's land he was not subject to the occupier's dominion and his right to be on the adjoining land was worthy of protection under the rule in *Rylands*. This justification is unlikely to be accepted today because the Occupiers' Liability Acts have, to a large extent, undermined the dominion of the occupier and required that the interests of those coming on to the land be given consideration and, in most cases, protection. Professor Fleming in his text book *The Law of Torts* (7th ed) at pp314–15 has convincingly criticised *Read* on the ground that it has prematurely stunted the development of a coherent theory of strict liability in England.

20.7 Occupation

In his judgment in *Rylands* Blackburn J referred to the defendant bringing the thing on to 'his lands'. Thus he clearly envisaged that the defendant would be in occupation of the land from which the thing escaped. But in the Australian decision of *Benning* v *Wong* (1969) 122 CLR 249 gas escaped from a leaking pipe under a public street. The defendants had no title in the public street, but they were responsible for the maintenance of the pipe. Windeyer J, who dissented, rejected the argument that this took the defendants outside of the rule in *Rylands*. For him the critical question was whether the defendants had control of the place from which the thing escaped. It is unclear whether this approach would be followed in England.

20.8 'His own purposes'

The reference to 'his own purposes' in the judgment of Blackburn J suggests that the rule only applies where the landowner brings the thing on to his land for his own purposes and that whenever the thing is brought on for the purposes of someone else the rule does not apply. The position was considered by the House of Lords in *Rainham Chemical Works* v *Belvedere Fish Guano Co* [1921] 2 AC 465. Two parties, F and P, entered into an agreement for the tenancy of a factory, which they wished to use for the purpose of manufacturing explosives. They covenanted, inter alia, not to assign the premises without the prior consent of the landlords. In fact, at a later date, F and P assigned the benefit of the tenancy, without obtaining the prior consent of the landlords, to a private company which they had formed. An explosion then occurred at the factory and the plaintiff's property was damaged. The House of Lords held that F and P were liable under *Rylands* because they had not effectively divested themselves of their occupation under the terms of the tenancy agreement. Lord Parmoor, however, was of the opinion that if the private company had become tenants in exclusive occupation of the premises then it, and not F and P, would have been liable.

An owner who is not in occupation of the land at the time when the thing escapes may be liable if he has authorised the accumulation which has escaped (see *Rainham* above).

20.9 Foreseeability of damage

Perhaps the most fundamental change to the rule in *Rylands* v *Fletcher* was made by the House of Lords in *Cambridge Water Co* v *Eastern Counties Leather plc* [1994] 2 WLR 53 when, after an extensive historical survey of the scope of the rule and its application, the House held that, as in nuisance, foreseeability of damage was an ingredient of the cause of action under *Rylands*.

The effect of this aspect of the judgment is that, as mentioned in paragraph 20.2 above, the rule in *Rylands* is in many respects merely the law of nuisance extended to cover the situation of an isolated escape. The House of Lords held that the earlier case of *West* v *Bristol Tramways Co* [1908] 2 KB 14 and *Rainham Chemical Works Ltd* v *Belvedere Fish Guano Co* [1921] 2 AC 465, which suggested that no foreseeability of damage was required, did not provide a firm enough basis to reject the requirement as stated by Blackburn J in his original judgment, and that the point was open for consideration by the House in the instant case.

20.10 Protected interests

In considering whether a plaintiff can recover damages under *Rylands* it is important to ascertain what his interest in the land (if any) is and the type of injury in respect of which he is suing. It is important to distinguish between damage to property, physical injury and economic loss, as shown in the following five categories.

An owner of land suffers property damage on his land

This is the clearest category of all because it is clear from *Rylands* itself that an owner may recover in respect of such damage.

The owner of land suffers property damage but at the time of the damage the property was not on his land

This might arise where the land owner's car is damaged while it is parked on a public street. Surprisingly, there is no clear decision on the point. However, in *Halsey* v *Esso Petroleum Ltd* [1961] 1 WLR 683, the plaintiff was allowed to recover damages under *Rylands* in respect of damage to his car while it was on a public street, although no authorities were considered by Veale J on this point. It is submitted that this approach is the preferable one and that it should be followed.

Personal injury suffered by the owner of land

This point was considered by the Court of Appeal in *Hale* v *Jennings Bros.* (above). The defendant had a licence to use certain ground for a fun fair. He erected chair o'planes. While these were in operation one day, a chair, with its occupant, became detached from the chair o'plane and landed in a shooting gallery belonging to the plaintiff, severely injuring the plaintiff. The defendant was held liable to the plaintiff. Scott LJ thought that the point that *Rylands* applied to personal injury to be so obvious that it was not worth arguing. However the position has been complicated by the restrictive decision of the House of Lords in *Read* v *Lyons Ltd* (above). Although the House decided the case on the escape point, they proceeded to consider whether *Rylands* could apply to personal injuries. Viscount Simon and Lord Simonds reserved their opinion on the point and Lord Uthwatt made no mention of the point. Lord Porter considered that any suggestion that *Rylands* applied to personal injuries was an extension of the original principle formulated by Blackburn J and as such would have to be considered carefully. Lord MacMillan adopted the most restrictive approach. He considered that the rule in *Rylands* was confined to conflicts between neighbouring landowners relating to property damage and, because of its anomalous nature, it would not be extended to apply to personal injury. It should be noted here, that in his leading judgment in *Cambridge Water* (above), Lord Goff referred to Professor Newark's 'seminal' article 'The Boundaries of Nuisance' (1949) 65 LQR 480. In particular Lord Goff quoted a passage which reads: 'They [the legal profession] rashly jumped to two conclusions ... and secondly that the Rule could be used to afford a remedy in cases of personal injury'. Professor Newark was of the clear opinion that *Rylands* should not apply to personal injuries, but Lord Goff did not consider this point at all. In view of the House of Lords' acceptance of the basis of Professor Newark's article, however, recovery for personal injuries under *Rylands* must be considered an arguable or questionable point.

Personal injury suffered by persons who are not owners of the land

This is the most difficult category of all because it is here that *Read* is directly in point because the plaintiff who was injured was merely in the position of an invitee and was not the owner of the land. Prior to *Read* there had been an obiter remark in a case called *Shiffman* v *Order of St John* [1936] 1 All ER 557 to the effect that damages were recoverable in such a situation. The case was in fact decided on the ground of negligence. However it is true to say that *Read* is not a popular decision. Thus in *Perry* v *Kendrick Transport Ltd* [1956] 1 WLR 85 the Court of Appeal held that *Rylands* did apply to personal injury. This view was followed by Veale J in *Halsey* v *Esso Petroleum Ltd* (above) and by the High Court of Australia in *Benning* v *Wong* (above) and it is submitted that these cases should be followed.

Economic loss

Once again there is no clear authority on the point. In *Weller* v *Foot and Mouth Disease Research Institute* [1966] 1 QB 569 Widgery J held that the defendants could not be liable to the plaintiffs under the rule in *Rylands* because the plaintiffs, who were cattle auctioneers who lost business as a result of an outbreak of foot and mouth disease, had no interest in any land to which the virus had escaped. But in the second and fourth categories above it has already been argued that a proprietary interest is not essential to recovery under *Rylands*, so this reasoning is not convincing. On the other hand, in *Ryeford Homes Ltd* v *Sevenoaks District Council* (1989) 16 Con LR 75 Judge Newey QC stated that whether economic loss could be a 'sufficiently direct result' of an escape 'must I think be a question of fact'. It is submitted that economic loss is, in principle, recoverable under *Rylands*, although it could be argued that it should be no more recoverable under *Rylands* than in negligence itself.

20.11 Defences

The scope of the defences is vitally important in determining the nature of the action in *Rylands* because, if wide defences are admitted, the less likely it is that the action will be one of strict liability. In fact, the defences have been remarkably wide and have stopped only just short of actually admitting absence of negligence as a defence. The defences are as follows:

Act of God

This was defined in *Tennant* v *Earl of Glasgow* (1864) 2 M (HL) 22, 26–7 as:

> ' … circumstances which no human foresight can provide against, and of which human prudence is not bound to recognise the possibility, and of which when they do occur, therefore, are calamities that do not involve the obligation of paying for the consequences that may result from them.' – per Lord Westbury.

The difficulty lies in determining what constitutes an Act of God. In *Nichols* v *Marsland* (1876) 2 Ex D 1 some artificial lakes had been created by the damming up of a natural stream. An extraordinary rainstorm occurred, the artificial banks burst, and the plaintiff's property was damaged in the ensuing flood. The defendants were excused after the jury found that the defendants could not reasonably have anticipated such an extraordinary storm. But a different view was taken by the House of Lords in *Greenock Corporation* v *Caledonian Railway Co* [1917] AC 556. The Corporation constructed a paddling pool for children in the bed of a stream, by diverting the natural course of the stream and obstructing the natural flow of water. After an extremely heavy rainstorm, the stream overflowed and in the flood created thereby the plaintiff's property was damaged. It was held that the Corporation was liable because the rainfall was not an Act of God. The court held that the criterion to be applied in determining whether there has been an Act of God is not, as in *Nichols*, whether the event could reasonably have been anticipated but whether or not human foresight and prudence could reasonably recognise the possibility of such an event.

Default of the plaintiff

If the damage has been caused by an act or default of the plaintiff himself then he has no remedy. Thus in *Ponting* v *Noakes* [1894] 2 QB 281 the plaintiff was unable to recover when his horse reached over his neighbour's boundary fence and ate some poisonous berries, as a result of which the horse died. The damage was due to the intervention of the horse and not to any escape from the defendant's land.

Consent of the plaintiff

If the plaintiff consents, expressly or impliedly, to a dangerous thing being brought on to the defendant's land which may cause him damage if it escapes, he cannot recover damages unless he can show that the damage was caused by the negligence of the defendant. In *Kiddle* v *City Business Premises Ltd* [1942] 2 All ER 216 the plaintiff leased a shop to the defendants in an arcade. A part of the roof of the arcade also formed the roof of part of the defendants' premises and sloped towards the plaintiff's shop. As a consequence of wartime bombing the gutter became clogged with dust and the plaintiff's shop was flooded. It was held that the plaintiff had impliedly consented to the water drainage system and that he was unable to succeed in his action in the absence of proof of negligence.

Common benefit

Where the source of the danger is maintained for the common benefit of both the plaintiff and the defendant, the defendant is not liable for any escape in the absence of negligence on his part. This defence was also relevant in the case of *Kiddle* (above).

Independent act of a third party

This is the defence which has played the greatest role in enabling a comparison to be made between negligence and the rule in *Rylands*. It is difficult to reconcile this defence with the existence of strict liability because it provides that if the act of the third party was not foreseeable the defendant is not liable and, when we move into the language of foreseeability, we move very close to, if not into, the language of negligence. Thus in *Rickards* v *Lothian* (above) the defendants succeeded in showing that it was third parties, for whom the defendants bore no responsibility, who were responsible for the escape.

In *Perry* v *Kendrick Transport Ltd* (above) two boys ignited the empty fuel tank of a disused bus. The plaintiff, a boy aged ten, who was near to the bus, was seriously injured by the resulting explosion. The Court of Appeal held, assuming that *Rylands* applied to cases of personal injury, that the plaintiff had failed to show that the act of a stranger in removing the petrol cap was the type of action which the defendant could have reasonably anticipated and guarded against. The claim therefore failed. The crucial factors here appear to be knowledge of the risk and control over the situation (see too *North Western Utilities* v *London Guarantee and Accident Co* [1936] AC 108). An independent contractor employed by the defendant does not constitute a third party for these purposes (*E Hobbs (Farms) Ltd* v *The Baxenden Chemical Co Ltd* [1992] 1 Lloyd's Rep 54).

Statutory authority

If a dangerous thing is operated or maintained under a statutory authority, liability will not arise under the rule in *Rylands* unless negligence is established. The question whether a statute exempts a defendant from liability is a question of construction in each case. Thus in *Green* v *Chelsea Waterworks* (1894) 70 LT 547 a main, which belonged to a company which was statutorily authorised to lay mains, burst without any negligence on the part of the defendants. It was held that the defendants were not liable since they were authorised by statute to lay mains and since they were under a statutory duty to maintain a continuous supply of water, the statute, by necessary implication, exempted them from liability where there was no negligence on their part. In certain cases, rather than create defences to strict liability actions, Parliament has created absolute liability for the escape of dangerous things, rendering all of these defences useless (see, for example, the Nuclear Installations Act 1965).

21

Fire

21.1 Introduction

21.2 Liability at common law

21.3 Defences at common law

21.4 The Fires Prevention (Metropolis) Act 1774

21.5 The railway statutes

21.1 Introduction

We noted at the outset of chapter 20 that there are pockets of tort law where the progress of negligence has been resisted and liability is imposed in the absence of fault. One such 'pocket', where it has been argued that liability was strict, is liability for damage caused by fire. It has never, however, been clear whether liability was strict or whether it was based on fault. It has also been noted that the extent of liability for fire has undergone considerable change as the law of tort has developed (see Ogus [1969] CLJ 104). We shall commence our analysis by considering liability at common law for the damage done by the escape of fire before considering the various statutory interventions in this area.

21.2 Liability at common law

At common law liability for the escape of fire was probably established originally by an action on the case for negligently permitting a fire to escape (see Winfield (1926) 42 LQR 42). The existence of such liability has been traced back as far as the decision in *Beaulieu* v *Finglam* (1401) YB Pasch 2 Hen 4 f 18 pl 6). It should be noted that, although this liability may originally have been an example of strict liability, it is a form of liability which pre-dates the rule in *Rylands* v *Fletcher* and much confusion has arisen in ascertaining the relationship between liability for fire and the rule in *Rylands*.

The relationship between liability at common law for fire and the rule in *Rylands* was considered by MacKenna J in *Mason* v *Levy Auto Parts of England Ltd* [1967] 2 QB 530 (the facts of which are discussed at 20.4). MacKenna J started his analysis by discussing the judgment of Bankes LJ in *Musgrove* v *Pandelis* [1919] 2 KB 43, where Bankes LJ said that there were three alternative heads of liability at common law for damage done by a fire which started on a person's property. The first was liability 'for the mere escape of the fire', the second was an action in negligence in respect of the fire and the third was an action under the rule in *Rylands*. It was argued by MacKenna J that, in making a distinction between the first head of liability and the third head, Bankes LJ was 'making a distinction unknown to the common law'. MacKenna J pointed out that liability for fire cannot be based exactly upon the rule in *Rylands* because the 'thing' has not escaped from the defendant's land (see 20.6). So he held that there were two alternatives open to him. The first alternative was to require the plaintiff to prove:

'(1) that the defendant had brought something onto his land likely to do mischief if it escaped; (2) that he had done so in the course of a non-natural user of the land; and (3) that the thing had ignited and that the fire had spread.'

The alternative was to require the plaintiff to show that:

'(1) the defendant brought onto his land things likely to catch fire, and kept them there in such conditions that if they did ignite the fire would be likely to spread to the plaintiff's land; (2) he did so in the course of some non-natural use; and (3) the things ignited and the fire spread.'

MacKenna J preferred to adopt the latter approach on the ground that the first alternative was not 'very sensible' because it made 'the likelihood of damage if the thing escapes a criterion of liability, when the thing had not in fact escaped but had caught fire'. So, although involving considerations similar to those in a *Rylands* case, the test to be applied is the slightly different one adopted by MacKenna J in *Mason*.

The plaintiff who suffers damage as the result of a fire on the defendant's land or a fire which was started by the defendant may also be able to bring an action in either nuisance or negligence. The plaintiff may be able to bring an action in nuisance where the fire interfered with his use or enjoyment of his property or where it damaged his property (see *Spicer* v *Smee* [1946] 1 All ER 489 and *Goldman* v *Hargrave* [1967] 1 AC 645). Finally the plaintiff may be able to bring an action in negligence where it can be shown that the defendant failed to take reasonable care to prevent the fire from doing damage to his neighbour (see *Musgrove* v *Pandelis* (above) and see also *Ogwo* v *Taylor* [1987] 3 All ER 961).

21.3 Defences at common law

There are certain defences which exist at common law in relation to liability for fire. In *Mason* v *Levy Auto Parts of England Ltd* (above) MacKenna J said that at common law 'a person from whose land a fire escaped was held liable to his neighbour unless he could prove that it had started or spread by the act of a stranger or of God'. Thus these two defences are clearly established and the principles involved in these defences have already been discussed at 20.11 (see too *HN Emanuel Ltd* v *GLC*

[1971] 2 All ER 835 on the act of a stranger defence). Other defences which are available at common law include default of the plaintiff, consent of the plaintiff and statutory authority (see further the discussion of these defences at 20.11).

21.4 The Fires Prevention (Metropolis) Act 1774

One of the principal statutory controls upon liability for fire is the Fires Prevention (Metropolis) Act 1774. Section 86 of that Act provides that:

> ' ... no action, suit, or process whatever, shall be had, maintained, or prosecuted against any person in whose house, chamber, stable, barn or other building, or on whose estate any such fire shall ... accidentally begin, nor shall any recompense be made by such person for any damage suffered thereby, any law, usage, or custom to the contrary notwithstanding.'

The effect of this section is to place a strict limit on the extent of liability for damage caused by fire by providing that the defendant shall not be liable for a fire which was begun 'accidentally'. This section appears to proceed on the assumption that liability at common law for the escape of fire was strict.

The meaning of the word 'accidentally' was considered by the court in *Filliter* v *Phippard* (1847) 11 QB 347. The defendant lit a fire on his land to burn weeds. He then neglected the fire and the fire spread to the plaintiff's land, damaging the plaintiff's hedge. It was held that the defendant could not rely on the Act because the fire did not begin 'accidentally'. It began negligently. It was held that a fire was only begun 'accidentally' where the fire was produced by 'mere chance' or 'was incapable of being traced to any cause'. So the important principle was established that the Act did not apply to a fire which was started negligently (see too *Mulholland* v *Baker* [1939] 3 All ER 166).

A similar interpretation has been adopted where the fire started accidentally but was then negligently allowed to spread. This can be demonstrated by reference to the case of *Musgrove* v *Pandelis* (above). The plaintiff let part of his garage, which was below his flat, to the defendant. The plaintiff's flat was damaged by a fire which was started when the petrol in the carburettor of the defendant's car suddenly caught fire. Although the fire in the carburettor did indeed begin 'accidentally', the defendant's chauffeur was negligent in failing to prevent the fire from spreading. He could have prevented the fire from spreading to the plaintiff's flat by taking immediate steps to turn off the tap connecting the petrol tank with the carburettor. It was held that the fire which damaged the plaintiff's flat was not the fire which began accidentally in the carburettor but the fire which the defendant's chauffeur had negligently permitted to spread. These two fires were thus treated as different fires for the purposes of the Act and so the Act was held to be inapplicable. A similar result was reached in the case of *Goldman* v *Hargrave* (above, the facts are discussed at 18.10) where the fire was initially caused by lightning (an Act of God), but was allowed to spread through the negligence of the defendant. It was held that in such a case the 1774 Act was not applicable.

The logical consequence of the ruling in *Musgrove* is that, where the fire is started intentionally but then spreads accidentally and it is the fire which spreads which causes the damage to the plaintiff, then the defendant should be able to claim the protection of the Act. This is because, according to *Musgrove*, the two fires are separate and the fire which caused the damage to the plaintiff was one which was begun accidentally and therefore covered by the Act. This was held to be the case in *Sochacki* v *Sas* [1947] 1 All ER 344 where liability was not imposed when damage was caused by a fire which was lit in a grate and then for some unknown reason spread and caused damage to the plaintiff's property.

The second point which was established in *Musgrove* was that the Act did not apply where the defendant is liable under the rule in *Rylands* v *Fletcher*.

21.5 The railway statutes

Legislation has also been enacted to deal with the liability for fires started by sparks from railway engines. In the nineteenth century railways were constructed and operated under statutory powers and, at that time, railway engines were in the habit of shooting out sparks and fire, which could damage the land adjacent to the railway line and to things growing on that land. As statute had generally authorised the use of the railway line by such engines, liability could not be imposed in respect of such use in the absence of negligence on the part of the railway owners. Thus it was very difficult, if not impossible, for landowners to recover their losses from the railway owners in respect of such fires. This can be illustrated by reference to the case of *Vaughan* v *Taff Vale Railway Co* (1860) 5 H & N 679. Sparks from an engine belonging to the defendants set fire to a wood which belonged to the plaintiff. Extensive damage was done to the wood. The defendants had been statutorily authorised to use the railway in this manner and it was held that they could not be held liable for so acting, in the absence of negligence on their part. As they had taken all possible steps to avoid such damage occurring they were not negligent and so the plaintiff was not entitled to succeed.

On the other hand, where the defendant was not able to rely upon statutory authority for the operation of his railway, the task of the plaintiff was made much easier. This can be seen in the case of *Jones* v *Ffestiniog Railway Co* (1868) LR 3 QB 733 where the defendants were held liable under the rule in *Rylands* v *Fletcher* when a spark from one of their engines set the plaintiff's haystack alight and destroyed it. It was held that the defendants were liable because they had no statutory authorisation to use locomotive engines.

However, where the defendants did have such statutory authorisation it remained very difficult for landowners to recover any compensation for the damage done to their land and so, in an effort to restore the balance, the Railway Fires Acts of 1905 and 1923 were enacted. The effect of these Acts is to create liability for the fire damage caused by such sparks but to limit that liability to £200 in respect of damage to the land or crops.

22

Animals

22.1 Introduction

22.2 Liability at common law

22.3 Dangerous animals

22.4 Non-dangerous animals

22.5 Defences

22.6 Straying livestock

22.7 Straying on to the highway

22.8 Protection of livestock against dogs

22.1 Introduction

A person may be liable for the damage caused by an animal both at common law and under statute law. The most significant intervention in this area is the Animals Act 1971 and it is upon this Act that most attention will be focused in this chapter. We shall, however, commence our analysis with an examination of the liability which exists at common law and then the remainder of the chapter will be devoted to an analysis of the 1971 Act.

22.2 Liability at common law

A person may be liable under ordinary principles of tort law for acts he has done through the agency of an animal which he owns or which is in his possession. A person may commit the tort of nuisance through permitting his animals to block the highway (*Cunningham* v *Whelan* (1917) 52 Ir LT 67), or by allowing the stench created by his pigs (*Aldred's case* (1610) 9 Co 57b) or the noise created by the crowing of his cockerels (*Leeman* v *Montagu* [1936] 2 All ER 1677) to unreasonably affect his neighbours' enjoyment of their property. A person who sets his dog on to someone else may commit the tort of battery (see chapter 24) and a person who teaches his parrot to utter defamatory statements commits the tort of defamation. Similarly the person who permits his animal to trespass on the land of another may commit the tort of trespass (see chapter 25). Finally it should be noted that a person may be liable under ordinary principles of negligence where he fails to exercise reasonable care over his animal and as a result the plaintiff suffers damage. Such was the case in *Draper* v *Hodder* [1972] 2 QB 556. The defendant was the owner of some Jack Russell terriers. He failed to take reasonable precautions to prevent them from escaping and when they escaped they mauled the plaintiff, causing him serious injury. There was no evidence that these terriers had ever attacked a person before, but there was evidence that such terriers were known to be dangerous when they were in a pack and permitted to roam free. It was held that the defendant was negligent in failing to take reasonable precautions to prevent the terriers from escaping because it was foreseeable that they would do such damage if a pack of them escaped and were permitted to roam free.

So far we have been considering the applicability of ordinary tort principles to damage which is caused by an animal. It should, however, be noted that the common law also possessed a form of action which was specifically applicable to damage caused by animals. This was an action on the case for damage done by savage or dangerous animals and was known as the 'scienter' action. In this action the plaintiff had to show that the defendant, who was the keeper of the animal, knew or ought to have known that the animal was of a dangerous character. He could do this in one of two ways. The first was to show that the animal belonged to a class which was known as ferae naturae (ie was of a dangerous species), in which case the defendant was deemed to know of its dangerous character. The second way was to demonstrate that the animal belonged to a class known as mansuetae naturae (ie they were not of a dangerous species) and liability was established here where it could be shown that the defendant knew of the animal's dangerous or vicious characteristics. Once one of these two hurdles was overcome by the plaintiff the liability which was imposed on the defendant was strict. This common law action has now, however, been replaced by the provisions of the Animals Act 1971 (see s1(1)(a)).

22.3 Dangerous animals

The Animals Act 1971 (referred to as 'the 1971 Act') follows the common law approach in drawing a distinction between dangerous animals (which were known at common law as ferae naturae) and non-dangerous animals (which were known at common law as mansuetae naturae). In this section we will deal with dangerous animals, while non-dangerous animals will be dealt with at 22.4.

Section 2(1) of the 1971 Act contains the following statement of general principle:

'Where any damage is caused by an animal which belongs to a dangerous species, any person who is a keeper of the animal is liable for the damage, except as otherwise provided by this Act.'

This section makes the keeper of the animal strictly liable for the damage done by an animal which falls within the ambit of this section. The liability is not, however, absolute (see further 22.5 on defences). There are two crucial phrases in this section which require further explanation.

The first relates to the meaning of the word 'keeper'. Section 6(3) of the Act states that a person is a keeper of an animal if:

'a) he owns the animal or has it in his possession; or
b) he is the head of a household of which a member under the age of sixteen owns the animal or has it in his possession;
and if at any time an animal ceases to be owned by or to be in the possession of a person, any person who immediately before that time was a keeper thereof by virtue of the preceding provisions of this subsection continues to be a keeper of the animal until another person becomes a keeper thereof by virtue of those provisions.'

It is provided in s6(4) that a person is not to be deemed to be a keeper of an animal simply because he has taken possession of the animal for the purpose of preventing it from causing damage or for the purpose of restoring the animal to its owner.

The second, and more important, phrase which requires some explanation is 'dangerous species'. 'Dangerous species' is defined in s6(2) as a species:

'a) which is not commonly domesticated in the British Islands; and
b) whose fully grown animals normally have such characteristics that they are likely, unless restrained, to cause severe damage or that any damage that they may cause is likely to be severe.'

This definition of dangerous species is likely to be considerably wider than the category of ferae naturae which existed at common law. A number of points should be noted about the wording of s6(2). The first is that 'species' is defined in s11 as including 'sub-species and variety'. The second is that damage is defined in s11 as including 'the death of, or injury to, any person (including any disease and any impairment of physical or mental condition)'. Thus property damage is not expressly covered by the Act, although it has been argued that, because the definition of damage in s11 does not purport to be exhaustive, then the Act does, in fact, cover damage to property (see *Winfield and Jolowicz on Tort* (13th ed) p458 n26).

The third point to note about this section is that it is the 'species' which must be dangerous and not the particular animal which did the damage. So if the animal which was the cause of the damage was tame, but happened to be a member of a species which is dangerous, it is no defence to show that the animal was not dangerous but was tame. The fourth point to note is that it is probably a question of law and not a question of fact whether or not a particular species is dangerous (see *Behrens* v *Bertram Mills Circus Ltd* [1957] 2 QB 1, which, although decided at common law, is presumed to represent the position under the Act).

The fifth point which should be noted is that the requirement in s6(2)(a) is that the animal be of a type which is not commonly domesticated in the British Islands and, for the purpose of this inquiry, it is irrelevant that the animal happens to be one, such as a camel, which is commonly domesticated in another country. Finally it should be noted that s6(2)(b) is worded in the alternative; that is to say it is satisfied *either* by showing that the animal was likely to cause severe damage *or* by showing that, if it were to do damage, that damage was likely to be severe.

22.4 Non-dangerous animals

Non-dangerous animals are covered by s2(2) of the Act which provides that:

'Where damage is caused by an animal which does not belong to a dangerous species, a keeper of the animal is liable for the damage ... if
a) the damage is of a kind which the animal, unless restrained, was likely to cause or which, if caused by the animal, was likely to be severe; and
b) the likelihood of the damage or of its being severe was due to characteristics of the animal which are not normally so found in animals of the same species or are not normally found except at particular times or in particular circumstances; and
c) those characteristics were known to that keeper or were at any time known to a person who at that time had charge of the animal as that keeper's servant or, where that keeper is the head of a household, were known to another keeper of the animal who is a member of that household and under the age of sixteen.'

In applying s2(2) to the facts of any given case it is essential that the requirements of paragraphs (a), (b) and (c) be considered separately. However, it must be noted that the drafting of this subsection was subjected to severe criticism by Stuart-Smith and Nourse LJJ in *Curtis* v *Betts* [1990] 1 All ER 769.

It is important to note that paragraph (a), like s6(2)(b) (on which see 22.3), is worded in the alternative; that is to say, it can be satisfied either by showing that the damage was of a kind which the animal was likely to cause unless restrained or by showing that the damage was of a kind which, if caused by the animal, was likely to be severe. The plaintiff in *Curtis* was attacked by a bull mastiff which was owned by his neighbours, the defendants. The plaintiff had known the dog since it was a puppy and had been very friendly with it. But, on one occasion, the plaintiff approached the dog while it was being loaded into a Land Rover owned by the defendants, when the dog leapt at the plaintiff, biting him on the face. Slade LJ stated that the requirement of paragraph (a) was satisfied because, although the damage was not of a kind which the dog, unless restrained was likely to cause (the dog was lazy and docile), it was damage of a kind which, if caused by the dog, was likely to be severe. The court rejected an argument, based upon Professor North's book (*The Modern Law of Animals* p56), to the effect that the latter requirement was only satisfied where 'the animal had such abnormal characteristics that it was likely that, if it did cause damage, the damage would be severe' because it was pointed out that the abnormal characteristic requirement is contained in paragraph (b), not paragraph (a).

Paragraph (b) gives rise to more difficult problems of interpretation. Nourse LJ stated that the words 'the likelihood of the damage or of its being severe' were 'inept' and were probably attributable to the fact that the draftsman had reproduced the wrong part of s2(2)(a) in paragraph (b). All that was required was the use of the words 'the damage' so that the paragraph read 'the damage was due to characteristics of the animal etc'. Stuart-Smith LJ was equally critical of the drafting of paragraph (b). He was of the opinion that the words 'the likelihood of' suggested that the damage must be foreseeable, whereas paragraph (b) without these words dealt with causation. Although he found it difficult to give a meaning to the words 'the likelihood of' he concluded that paragraph (b) required that there be a causal link between the characteristic and the damage.

On the facts of *Curtis* it was held that the requirements of paragraph (b) were satisfied because the dog had a characteristic which was not normally found in bull mastiffs except at particular time or at particular places. That characteristic was a tendency to act in a frightening and aggressive manner when protecting its own territory, which, in this case, included the back of the Land Rover.

At common law, under the old scienter action, it was held that, for liability to arise in relation to non-dangerous animals, the plaintiff must show that the animal had a vicious or mischievous propensity to attack people or other animals (see *Fitzgerald* v *Cooke Bourne (Farms) Ltd* [1964] 1 QB 249). However it was held by Park J in *Wallace* v *Newton* [1982] 1 WLR 375 that this requirement, that the animal have a vicious propensity to attack others, was not incorporated into s2(2) of the 1971 Act. He held that all that need be shown is that the animal was possessed of a characteristic not normally found in an animal of the same species. On the facts in *Wallace* the plaintiff was held to be entitled to recover damages in respect of her injuries. The plaintiff, who was a groom employed by the defendants, was seriously injured when a horse, which she was loading into the trailer, suddenly and without any warning became violent and uncontrollable. It was held that, because the horse was known to be unreliable and unpredictable, it was possessed of characteristics which were not normally found in horses and so the requirements of s2(2)(b) were satisfied. Similarly in *Kite* v *Napp* (1982) The Times 1 June it was held that the plaintiff was entitled to recover damages in respect of his injuries when he was bitten by a dog which had a propensity to attack people carrying bags. It was held that such a propensity constituted a characteristic not normally so found in animals of the same species under s2(2)(b) of the Act. In *Hunt* v *Wallis* (1991) The Times 10 May it was held that, in deciding whether a dog (a border collie) which had caused injury to the plaintiff had characteristics which were not normally found in 'animals of the same species' the relevant comparison was with other dogs of the same breed (border collies) and not with dogs generally. Pill J held that, given the interpretation of 'species' in s11 of the Act as including 'sub-species and variety', where an identifiable breed existed, such as border collies, the relevant comparison should be made with that breed and not with dogs generally.

The exception in paragraph (b) relating to characteristics which are only found in such species 'at particular times and in particular circumstances' has the effect of making normal behaviour in an animal at a particular stage of its development actionable under s2(2). Thus a female animal which bites to protect her young would appear to be caught under this provision notwithstanding the fact that such behaviour is normal in an animal at that stage. This exception was considered by the Court of Appeal in *Cummings* v *Grainger* [1977] QB 397 in a case in which the plaintiff was attacked by a guard-dog (it should, however, be noted that since 1975 it has been a criminal offence under s1(1) of the Guard Dogs Act 1975 to use or permit the use of a guard-dog on premises without the guard-dog being at all times under the control of a handler). The plaintiff, who was a young barmaid, entered a scrapyard next to the bar in which she worked. She knew that the defendant, who was the owner of the yard, kept an untrained Alsatian dog in the yard. She also knew that there were 'Beware of the dog' notices on the gate of the yard. While the plaintiff was standing in the yard she was attacked and bitten by the dog. She brought an action against the defendant under s2(2) of the 1971 Act claiming that the defendant was liable for the damage done by the dog. It was held that the plaintiff had made out a prima facie case under s2(2)against the defendant (but see further 22.5 on defences). It was held that the requirement of s2(2)(a) was satisfied because the damage done by a bite from an Alsatian dog was likely to be severe. It was held that s2(2)(b) was also satisfied because Alsatians were not normally vicious except 'in the particular circumstance' of their being kept as guard-dogs. So, although this dog was acting 'normally' for an Alsatian which had been trained as a guard-dog, it was nevertheless covered by s2(2)(b) because it was not a normal characteristic of dogs as a species, but only an Alsatian dog in the 'particular circumstances' of having been trained as a guard-dog. The requirement of s2(2)(c) was also satisfied because the keeper knew of these characteristics in the Alsatian.

Finally it should be noted that the liability under s2(2) is qualified by the need to show that the keeper has actual knowledge, as opposed to constructive knowledge, of these characteristics of the animal. It should be noted that the two exceptions contained in s2(2)(c) are tightly drawn. The servant of the keeper must have 'charge' of the animal before his knowledge becomes relevant and the knowledge of the member of the household who is under 16 is only relevant where that person is the keeper, unless that knowledge is communicated to the keeper.

22.5 Defences

The liability which is imposed on the keeper of the animal by virtue of s2 is strict, but this is not to say that there are no defences to the action. There are a number of defences contained in s5 of the Act. A person is not liable where the damage is due 'wholly to the fault of the person suffering it' (s5(1)). Where the damage is not wholly, but only partly, the fault of the person suffering the damage then reliance cannot be placed on s5(1) but the defendant may be able to argue that the plaintiff was guilty of contributory negligence (s10). A person is not liable where the person who suffered the damage has voluntarily accepted the risk of such damage (s5(2)).

However a person is not treated as having voluntarily accepted the risk where he is employed by the keeper of an animal and incurs a risk incidental to his employment (s6(5)).

A person is not liable under s5(3) for any damage caused by an animal:

'... kept on any premises or structure to a person trespassing there, if it is proved either –
a) that the animal was not kept there for the protection of persons or property; or
b) (if the animal was kept there for the protection of persons or property) that keeping it there for that purpose was not unreasonable.'

The scope of this defence was considered by the Court of Appeal in *Cummings* v *Grainger* (the facts of which are considered at 22.4 above). The defendant claimed that he was not liable on the ground that he was entitled to the protection contained in s5(3). As we have already noted the plaintiff had made out a prima facie case under s2(2), but her case failed because the defendant was able to rely on the defences contained in both s5(2) and s5(3). The plaintiff was held to have known of the risk created by the dog and to have accepted that risk so as to bring her within the defence in s5(2). The Court of Appeal also held that the defendant could have relied upon the defence contained in s5(3) because the plaintiff was a trespasser and keeping a guard–dog for the purpose of seeking to protect the defendant's property in the yard was not unreasonable (although see now the Guard Dogs Act 1975). Lord Denning said that the only way of protecting the place was to have a guard–dog since the yard was 'in the East End of London where persons of the roughest type come and go'.

Neither an act of God nor an act of a stranger constitute a defence to any of the liabilities contained in s2 of the 1971 Act.

22.6 Straying livestock

At common law the owner of cattle was strictly liable for the damage done by his cattle when they strayed on to the land of his neighbour. This common law action has now been abolished (s1(1)(c) of the Animals Act 1971) and has been replaced by s4(1) of the 1971 Act which provides that:

'Where livestock belonging to any person strays on to land in the ownership or occupation of another and –
a) damage is done by the livestock to the land or to any property on it which is in the ownership or possession of the other person; or
b) any expenses are reasonably incurred by that other person in keeping the livestock while it cannot be restored to the person to whom it belongs or while it is detained in pursuance of section 7 of this Act, or in ascertaining to whom it belongs;
the person to whom the livestock belongs is liable for the damage or expenses, except as otherwise provided by this Act.'

'Livestock' is defined in s11 as 'cattle, horses, asses, mules, hinnies, sheep, pigs, goats and poultry and also deer not in the wild state'. Once again damage is defined in s11 as including 'the death of, or injury to, any person (including any disease and any impairment of physical or mental condition)'. The incorporation of this definition of damage into s4 is rather unusual because it is clear that s4(1)(a) is directed at damage to property and not personal injury. It is submitted that the better view is that, despite the incorporation of s11, damages for personal injury are not recoverable under s4. For the purposes of s4 livestock belongs to the person who has possession of the livestock (s4(2)). The livestock must also 'stray' on to the land of another, so it is necessary to show that there was some degree of entry on to the plaintiff's land (see *Ellis* v *Loftus Iron Co* (1874) LR 10 CP 10).

Section 7 empowers an occupier of land to detain livestock which has strayed on to his land and to sell the livestock to recover for the damage to his property and expenses he has incurred in detaining the animal. This power can only be exercised, however, within certain rigidly defined constraints (s7(3)). The right to detain the livestock ceases to exist:

'a) after 48 hours has elapsed unless both the police and the person to whom the livestock belongs (provided that he knows to whom the livestock belongs) have been informed; or
b) an amount to satisfy his claim under s4 has been tendered; or
c) where there is no claim under s4 and the person entitled to possession of the livestock claims them.'

The occupier who detains livestock is liable for any damage caused to the livestock by his failure to exercise 'reasonable care' or by his failure to supply the livestock with 'adequate food and water'. Where the net proceeds of any sale exceed the value of the claim for damages and expenses which the detainer had against the possessor of the livestock, the excess is recoverable from the detainer by the person who would be entitled to the livestock but for their being sold (s7(5)).

It is a defence to show that the damage was due wholly to the fault of the plaintiff (s5(1)), or to show that the plaintiff was guilty of contributory negligence (s10). It is also provided in s5(5) of the Act that:

'A person is not liable under section 4 of this Act where the livestock strayed from a highway and its presence there was a lawful use of the highway.'

This section was thought to give effect to the rule at common law contained in *Tillet* v *Ward* (1882) 10 QBD 17. The defendant was driving his ox to market when it entered the open door of the plaintiff's property and did considerable damage to that property before it was finally removed from the property. It was held that the defendant was not liable for the damage because he was not negligent and he was making a reasonable use of the highway. The scope of the defence in s5(5) was recently considered by the Court of Appeal in *Matthews* v *Wicks* (1987) The Times 25 May. The defendants were the owners of sheep and they had a right to let them graze on common land. They also left them free to wander at will on to the highway. One night the sheep got into the plaintiff's garden where they did extensive damage. The defendants sought to rely upon s5(5) as a defence to the plaintiff's claim. It was held that permitting livestock to wander at will on to the highway did not constitute a 'lawful use of the highway' and so the defendants were held to be unable to rely on the defence contained in s5(5).

It is also provided in s5(6) that damage shall not be treated as being due to the fault of the person who has suffered the damage on the sole ground that he could have prevented the damage from occurring by fencing the land. However, there is no liability under s4 where it is proved that the straying of the livestock on to the land would not have occurred but for a breach of duty by any other person, being a person having an interest in the land, of a duty to fence.

22.7 Straying on to the highway

Where animals stray on to the highway the person who is responsible for the animals will be liable under s8(1) of the 1971 Act if he did not take reasonable care to prevent them from straying on to the highway. The practical effect of s8(1) is to place an obligation upon keepers to keep their animals fenced in. However where the damage is caused by animals which have strayed from unfenced land on to the highway, s8(2) provides that the person who placed the animals on that land will not be regarded as having breached his duty of care by placing them there if:

'a) the land is common land, or is land situated in an area where fencing is not customary, or is a town or village green; and
b) he had a right to place the animals on that land.'

22.8 Protection of livestock against dogs

Section 3 of the 1971 Act provides that a keeper is strictly liable 'where a dog causes damage by killing or injuring livestock'. This liability does not depend upon it being shown that the defendant was negligent so it is no defence for the defendant to show that he had no reason to believe that his dog would attack livestock. 'Livestock' is defined in s11 of the Act (see 22.6 above).

In certain circumstances it may be lawful for the owner of livestock to kill or injure a dog to protect his livestock. This right was originally recognised at common law (see *Cresswell* v *Sirl* [1948] 1 KB 241) and is now enshrined in s9 of the 1971 Act. Section 9 provides that it is a defence to any civil proceedings against a person (referred to as the defendant) for killing or causing injury to a dog to prove that: the defendant acted for the protection of his livestock and was entitled so to act; and the officer in charge of a police station was informed of the incident within 48 hours of its occurring.

The defendant is deemed to have been entitled to act for the protection of his livestock only if 'the livestock or the land on which it is belongs to him or to any person under whose express or implied authority he is acting' (s9(2)(a)). A person shall be deemed to be acting for their protection under s9(3) only if:

'a) the dog is worrying or is about to worry the livestock and there are no other reasonable means of ending or preventing the worrying; or
b) the dog has been worrying livestock, has not left the vicinity and is not under the control of any person and there are no practical means of ascertaining to whom it belongs.'

23

Defamation

23.1 Introduction

23.2 The distinction between libel and slander

23.3 Who may be defamed?

23.4 What is defamatory?

23.5 Refers to the plaintiff

23.6 Publication

23.7 Defences

23.8 Consent

23.9 Justification or truth

23.10 Absolute privilege

23.11 Qualified privilege

23.12 Fair comment

23.13 Apology and amends

23.14 Remedies

23.15 Conclusion

23.1 Introduction

The tort of defamation seeks to protect the interest of an individual in his reputation. Where a defendant makes an untrue defamatory statement about the plaintiff, the plaintiff will have a right of action against the defendant unless the defendant can establish one of the many defences available in a defamation action. The courts here are required to balance the interest of the individual in the protection of his reputation against the freedom of speech of the person who makes the allegedly defamatory statement. We have no constitutionally protected freedom

285

of speech in this country, so the courts do not often expressly consider the freedom of speech implications of a ruling in a defamation case. It may seem at first sight that the maker of a defamatory statement should not be able to claim the benefit of a constitutionally protected freedom of speech because his statement is of little value, but it should be remembered that some statements which are alleged to be defamatory are statements which are critical of the government or public figures or statements on matters of public interest. Thus a person who is in fear of being sued in a defamation action will be discouraged from criticising the government or from making statements on matters of public interest and a fundamental principle of democracy will be undermined. Of course not all defamatory statements are on matters of public interest and so worthy of protection, but it should be remembered that the easier it is for a plaintiff to succeed in a defamation action, the more likely it is that significant inroads will be made into the protection of freedom of speech.

As a tort, defamation is unusual in that it is one of the few civil actions still tried before a jury. It is the jury which assesses the damages payable by the defendant and concern has been expressed about the apparently excessive awards made by some juries, especially in the light of the award of damages of £600,000 to Mrs Sonia Sutcliffe. There has also been considerable criticism levelled against some of the substantive rules of the tort and the law was subjected to a review and report by the *Report of the Faulks Committee on Defamation* (Cmnd 5909, 1975). We shall return to a consideration of that report and the future of defamation after analysing the substantive law.

23.2 The distinction between libel and slander

Defamation consists of two categories; libel and slander. The difference between the two is historical in origin. Libel evolved from the old Court of Star Chamber in Tudor times as a criminal action and it remains, in certain circumstances, a criminal offence. Slander, on the other hand, developed out of the ecclesiastical courts and the common law courts. The Star Chamber was eventually abolished and its jurisdiction was assumed by the common law courts, who also have jurisdiction in slander cases, but the distinction between libel and slander has never been abolished.

Libel is a defamatory statement which is contained in a permanent form. The commonest way in which libel is committed is by writing. However it may be committed in other ways as long as it is in a permanent form. Thus in *Monson v Tussauds Ltd* [1894] 1 QB 671, the defendants were held to have libelled the plaintiff in displaying a waxwork effigy of him near the 'Chamber of Horrors' in their wax-works. It was held that a waxwork could be a libel as it was in a permanent form. Lopes LJ stated that, although libels:

' ... are generally in writing or printing, ... this is not necessary; the defamatory matter may be conveyed in some other permanent form. For instance, a statue, a caricature, an effigy, chalk marks on a wall, signs, or pictures may constitute a libel.'

Slander, on the other hand, is a defamatory statement which is not in a permanent form, such as a spoken statement. Although the distinction between libel and slander is easy to state in the abstract, it can be difficult to apply in practice. Sometimes Parliament has intervened to resolve the problem and, for example, it is provided in ss166 and 201 Broadcasting Act 1990 and s16 Defamation Act 1952 that television and radio broadcasts are treated as a libel and s4 of the Theatres Act 1968 provides, subject to the exceptions contained in s7, that a theatre performance is a libel.

However, Parliament has not resolved all of the problems in distinguishing between libel and slander. For example, if I dictate a defamatory statement to my typist, do I commit libel or slander? The answer appears to be that the dictation of the defamatory statement to the secretary is slander, but that the sending of the letter is libel. However, rather unusually, it appears that a person who reads out defamatory matter from a written document to a third party publishes a libel and not a slander (*Forrester* v *Tyrell* (1893) 9 TLR 257).

There are other cases where it can be difficult to distinguish between libel and slander. Does sky-writing constitute libel? What if I make a record which contains defamatory material, is that libel or slander? In *Youssoupoff* v *Metro-Goldwyn-Mayer* (1934) 50 TLR 581 the plaintiff claimed damages from the defendants for an alleged libel when, in a sound film, it was alleged that the plaintiff had been seduced by Rasputin. The Court of Appeal held that a defamatory statement contained in a film was libel. Slesser LJ stated that, because 'the photographic part of the exhibition' was in a permanent form, then it was the proper subject of an action for libel. He said that the speech part of the film was merely 'ancillary' to the film; being 'part of the surroundings explaining that which is to be seen'. However, it is not entirely clear whether Slesser LJ would have regarded the sound alone, without the vision, as being a libel and so it remains uncertain whether a defamatory statement contained on a record is libel or slander.

The difficulty of distinguishing between libel and slander does little credit to the law. But this difficulty of distinguishing between these two categories is only of relevance where there is a difference between the rules relating to libel and slander. In fact there are some crucial differences between libel and slander. Libel can be a crime as well as a tort. Slander is only a tort, although the spoken words may constitute a crime, for example, blasphemy. Libel is actionable per se but the general rule is that slander is only actionable where the plaintiff can show that he has suffered special damage. Special damage requires that the plaintiff suffer loss which is capable of being estimated in money. Loss of friendship is not capable of being estimated in money terms and so does not constitute special damage, but loss of hospitality or loss of marriage prospects may constitute special damage (*Roberts* v *Roberts* (1864) 5 B & S 384).

Although the plaintiff in a slander action must generally show that he has suffered special damage, there are certain exceptional cases where this is not so. These exceptional cases are as follows.

Imputation of a crime

Where the defendant implies that the plaintiff has committed a crime which is punishable by imprisonment then the plaintiff need not show that he has suffered special damage (*Hellwig* v *Mitchell* [1910] 1 KB 609). However where the imputation is that the plaintiff has committed a crime which is not punishable by imprisonment, but is punishable by a fine, then the plaintiff must show that he has suffered special damage.

Imputation of unchastity in women

Under the Slander of Women Act 1891 the imputation of unchastity in women is actionable without proof of special damage. Such imputations include an imputation of lesbianism (*Kerr* v *Kennedy* [1942] 1 KB 409) and an imputation that the plaintiff had been raped (*Youssoupoff* v *Metro-Goldwyn-Mayer* (above)).

Imputation of disease

Where there is an imputation that the plaintiff suffers from an infectious or contagious disease, such as venereal disease, which is likely to prevent other persons from associating with the plaintiff, then such a slander is actionable without proof of special damage (*Bloodworth* v *Gray* (1844) 7 Man & G 334).

Imputation of unfitness to one's trade or calling

This is the most important category where it is not necessary for the plaintiff to show that he has suffered special damage. This exception is now enshrined in s2 of the Defamation Act 1952 which provides that:

> 'In an action for slander in respect of words calculated to disparage the plaintiff in any office, profession, calling, trade or business held or carried on by him at the time of the publication, it shall not be necessary to allege or prove special damage, whether or not the words are spoken of the plaintiff by way of his office, profession, calling, trade or business.'

The wording of this section would appear to be wide enough to encompass any slander which is reasonably capable of injuring the plaintiff in his office and it need not be shown that the slander was referable to the plaintiff in the capacity of his office (as was the case at common law in *Jones* v *Jones* [1916] 2 AC 481).

These exceptions considerably reduce the distinction between libel and slander, and there are, in fact, many common elements. These are that the statement of the defendant must be defamatory, it must be published to others and it must be understood as being referable to the plaintiff. We shall discuss these separate elements after discussing who can be defamed.

23.3 Who may be defamed?

It is only a living person who can bring an action in defamation. A dead person cannot be defamed, no matter how distressing the defendant's statement is to the deceased's relatives. Corporations, whether trading or non-trading, have personality for this purpose so that they can sue for defamatory statements made affecting their corporate reputation (*Metropolitan Saloon Omnibus Co v Hawkins* (1859) 4 H & N 87, approved by the House of Lords in *Derbyshire County Council v Times Newspapers Ltd* [1993] 2 WLR 449). Different considerations have been held to apply to local authorities because of the fact that a local authority is a democratically elected government body which must be open to uninhibited public criticism. Therefore it has been held that a local authority is not entitled to bring a claim in defamation (*Derbyshire County Council v Times Newspapers Ltd* (above)). The same principle applies to those departments of central government, such as the Department of the Environment, which are statutory corporations. Individual councillors who are defamed may, of course, bring an action in their own name, but the only legitimate response of a council which is subject to public criticism is to defend itself by public utterances and by debate in the council chamber. Finally, it has been held that trade unions, because they are unincorporated associations, do not to have any personality for this purpose and so cannot maintain an action in defamation (*Electrical, Electronic, Telecommunication & Plumbing Union v Times Newspapers Ltd* [1980] QB 585).

23.4 What is defamatory?

The words which are used by the defendant must be words which are defamatory. The definition of defamatory is an issue of considerable difficulty. The difficulty is not only the legal one of framing a satisfactory definition of the word, but it is also a troublesome issue of policy. Lord Atkin in *Sim v Stretch* [1936] 2 All ER 1237 said that defamatory words were 'words which tend to lower the plaintiff in the estimation of right thinking members of society generally'. The statement may lower the plaintiff in the estimation of right thinking people by exposing him to 'hatred, contempt or ridicule' (*Parmiter v Coupland and Another* (1840) 6 M & W 105). But the statement need not have that effect. Thus it has been held in *Youssoupoff v Metro-Goldwyn-Mayer* (1934) 50 TLR 581 to be defamatory to impute that the plaintiff had been raped. The fact that the plaintiff was said to have been raped would not have exposed her to 'hatred, contempt or ridicule' but it may have caused people to shun her or to avoid or lose confidence in her. However deplorable we feel that this attitude to the victims of rape may be, defamation takes people as they are and not as they ought to be.

   This test, based as it is upon the opinion of 'right thinking members of society', begs a number of questions. For example, who is a 'right thinking' member of society? Would the 'right thinking' person consider it defamatory to call a person who refuses to participate in industrial action a 'scab'? In answering this question regard may be had to the case of *Byrne* v *Deane* [1937] 1 KB 818. The plaintiff reported to the police that the defendants' club unlawfully kept some automatic gambling machines on their premises. After these machines had been removed by the police, a typewritten message was put on the wall of the club premises which stated that 'he who gave the game away may he burn in hell and rue the day'. It was held that to allege that the plaintiff had reported a crime to the police was not defamatory because it would not be so regarded by a 'good and worthy subject of the King'. It did not matter for this purpose that the plaintiff would be less well thought of by his fellow club members. So the fact that the section of the public with which the plaintiff has the closest contact thinks less of him is not conclusive that the statement is defamatory if the views of that group are not consistent with our right thinking member of society. So it may not be defamatory to allege that a person is a 'scab'.

Some guidance as to the approach to be adopted in deciding whether a particular statement was defamatory was provided in the case of *Hartt* v *Newspaper Publishing plc* (1989) The Times 7 November where it was held that, in deciding whether or not a statement was defamatory, the approach which should be adopted is that of the hypothetical ordinary reader who was neither 'naive' nor 'unduly suspicious' but who 'could read in an implication more readily than a lawyer, and might indulge in a certain amount of loose thinking'. On the other hand, the hypothetical ordinary reader was not someone who was 'avid for scandal' and he was not someone who selected one bad meaning where other, non-defamatory meanings were available. The publisher of an alleged defamatory document is entitled to have the publication looked at in full and in the proper context. The plaintiff cannot select part of the statement to justify his claim. Thus in *Charleston* v *News Group Newspapers* (1994) The Times 12 January, where two well known actors had their faces superimposed in pornographic photographs in a newspaper, and the accompanying text stated that they were innocent and unknowing participants, no action in defamation lay. The Court of Appeal, however, stated that the law might some time be required to consider the impact of photographs on the readers of tabloid newspapers in particular.

In considering whether a statement is defamatory regard must be had to all the circumstances of the case. Words must be interpreted in the context in which they were spoken or written. Thus where a book describes statements made in the 1960s the question as to whether or not they are defamatory must be decided on whether they would have been defamatory in the cultural context and circumstances of the time: see *Mitchell* v *Book Sales Ltd* (1994) The Independent 25 March. Additionally it is sometimes said that vulgar abuse is not defamatory. But this is not entirely accurate. Much depends on the manner in which the words were spoken. Were they slanderous or merely vituperative? In *Fields* v *Davis* [1955] CLY 1543 the defendant called the plaintiff, who was a married woman, a 'tramp'. It was held that the words were not defamatory because they were uttered by the defendant in a fit of temper and were understood by those around as being mere vulgar abuse. Where the words are written they will not be interpreted as mere vulgar abuse because the defendant has time for consideration of the words before writing them and the reader has no way of knowing that the words were merely vituperative rather than libellous.

It need not be shown that the defendant intended to defame the plaintiff. In *Cassidy* v *Daily Mirror Newspapers Ltd* [1929] 2 KB 331 the defendants published a picture of the plaintiff's husband and another woman in their newspaper and under the photograph were the words 'Mr M Corrigan, the race horse owner and Miss X, whose engagement has been announced'. The plaintiff was, in fact, married to her husband, although they did not live together, except on the rare occasion that he stayed with her. She claimed that she had suffered damage through the imputation that she lived in immoral cohabitation with her husband. The defendants published the article in all good faith, not knowing that it was in any way defamatory and they argued that it would amount to a great hardship if liability was to be imposed upon them. However, it was held that the defendants had libelled the plaintiff. Russell LJ stated that 'liability for libel does not depend on the intention of the defamer, but on the fact of defamation'.

The fact that the defendant has an innocent motive is not, therefore, a defence to a defamation action, but, by the same token, the fact that the words are, on the face of it, innocent, does not mean that the statement cannot be defamatory. The words may, on a natural and ordinary interpretation, contain nothing of a defamatory nature, but may be defamatory when combined with some extrinsic facts known to readers of the publication. This is called innuendo. An example will help to illustrate what is meant by innuendo. In *Tolley* v *JS Fry & Sons Ltd* [1931] AC 333 the plaintiff was the English amateur golf champion and he was featured, without giving his consent, on a poster advertising the defendants' chocolate bar. The text of the poster compared the excellence of the chocolate bar with the excellence of the plaintiff's swing. The plaintiff alleged that this constituted an innuendo because it implied that he had agreed to feature in the poster for financial gain and that he had flouted the rules relating to his amateur status. It was held that the innuendo was made out and that the plaintiff was entitled to succeed in his action against the defendants.

However, a distinction must be drawn between a 'false' innuendo and a 'true' innuendo. A 'false' innuendo arises where the plaintiff alleges that the words, in their ordinary and natural meaning, bear a particular meaning which is discernible without the need for additional evidence. On the other hand, a 'true' innendo arises where the plaintiff has to adduce additional evidence to establish the meaning which he alleges that the words should be given. The distinction is an important one because an innuendo must be distinctly pleaded and proved. A case which illustrates this distinction is *Lewis* v *Daily Telegraph Ltd* [1964] AC 234. It was reported by the defendants in their newspaper that the Fraud Squad were investigating the plaintiff's firm. It was argued that the words 'Fraud Squad Probe City Firm' were defamatory because they indicated that the plaintiff was guilty of fraud or was, at least, suspected of fraud by the police. It was held that the statement that a person was being investigated for fraud was not the same thing as saying that he was guilty of fraud. It was therefore held that the words were not in their ordinary meaning defamatory and it was only by pleading additional facts, which the plaintiff did not do, that he could have proved that the statement was defamatory. On the other hand *Tolley* was a case of true innuendo because the plaintiff had to plead additional evidence of his amateur status to prove that the statement was defamatory.

It is the task of the jury to decide whether or not a given statement is defamatory. However, the judge retains the prior task of deciding whether or not there is a case for the jury to consider and whether, as a matter of law, the defendant's words are capable of bearing a defamatory meaning. This role can be seen in the case of *Capital & Counties Bank Ltd* v *Henty & Sons* (1882) 7 App Cas 741. The defendants quarrelled with the manager of one of the plaintiffs' banks and then sent out a circular letter to their own customers, who in turn showed it to other people, which stated that the defendants would not accept as payment any cheque which was drawn on the plaintiff bank. The plaintiff bank alleged that this circular letter was defamatory because it implied that they were insolvent. It was held that the words were not, in their ordinary and natural meaning, defamatory and that a reasonable man would not infer any innuendo that the plaintiffs were insolvent (but see the criticism of the application of this test on the facts in *Slim* v *Daily Telegraph Ltd* [1968] 2 QB 157). So it was held that there was no case to go to the jury and judgment was entered for the defendants.

23.5 Refers to the plaintiff

The statement uttered by the defendant must be shown to have referred to the plaintiff. This requirement is easily satisfied where the plaintiff is referred to by name by the defendant. Where the plaintiff is expressly referred to by the defendant, the plaintiff need not show that the defendant intended to refer to him. This can be seen in the case of *Hulton* v *Jones* [1910] AC 20 (cf *Blennerhassett* v *Novelty Sales Services Ltd* (1933) 175 LT 393). The defendants published an article in their newspaper which purported to describe a motor festival in Dieppe. In the article they described the activities of one Artemus Jones, who was a churchwarden in Peckham and who was described as 'the life and soul of a gay little band that haunts the Casino and turns night into day, besides betraying a most unholy delight in the society of female butterflies'. The plaintiff, who was called Artemus Jones but was a barrister rather than the churchwarden at Peckham, brought a libel action against the defendants. Neither the writer of the article nor the editor of the paper had heard of the plaintiff and neither intended to refer to him, but the plaintiff produced witnesses who said that they thought that the article referred to him. It was held by the House of Lords that if reasonable people understood the language of the article as being defamatory of the plaintiff, it was irrelevant that the defendants did not intend to defame the plaintiff.

A defendant may also be liable where his statement is true of one person but is, in fact, defamatory of another person of the same name or same description, who was not known to the defendant, and who suffered injury as a result of the publication of the statement. Such was the case in *Newstead* v *London Express Newspapers Ltd* [1940] 1 KB 377. An article in the defendants' newspaper entitled 'Why do people commit bigamy?' referred to a self-confessed bigamist called 'Harold Newstead, a thirty-year-old Camberwell man'. The plaintiff, who was of the same name and lived in Camberwell, brought a libel action against the defendants. The defendants argued that they had not intended to refer to the plaintiff but to another Harold Newstead who lived in Camberwell. It was held that the defendants were liable to the plaintiff because they should have taken greater care to ensure that their article could not have been taken as referring to someone else.

However, there is no requirement that the plaintiff be expressly referred to by the defendant. It is sufficient if the statement impliedly referred to the plaintiff (*Le Fanu* v *Malcolmson* (1848) 1 HL Cas 637) and it can also be satisfied where the defendant's statement does not make any obvious reference to the plaintiff. Such was the case in *Morgan* v *Odhams Press Ltd* [1971] 1 WLR 1239. The plaintiff claimed that he had been libelled by the defendants in an article concerned with a dog-doping gang which had allegedly kidnapped a certain Miss Murray. At the time Miss Murray was staying in the plaintiff's flat and the plaintiff produced six witnesses who testified that they thought that the article was referring to the plaintiff and that he was involved with this dog-doping gang. It was held by the House of Lords that there was sufficient evidence to go to the jury because the ordinary reader who had special knowledge of the circumstances would conclude that the article referred to the plaintiff.

However s4 of the Defamation Act 1952 has intervened to mitigate the rigours of the common law, as far as defendants are concerned. This section applies to any defamatory words which are innocently published and s4(5) provides that words are innocently published where the following conditions are satisfied:

'a) that the publisher did not intend to publish them of and concerning that other person, and did not know of the circumstances by virtue of which they might be understood to refer to him; or
b) that the words were not defamatory on the face of them, and the publisher did not know of circumstances by virtue of which they might be understood to be defamatory of that other person
and in either case that the publisher exercised all reasonable care in relation to the publication ...'

Section 4(5)(a) would apply to a case such as *Hulton*, whereas s4(5)(b) would apply to a case such as *Cassidy*. Where the section is applicable the defendant can discharge his liability by making an offer of amends (see further 23.14).

In considering whether a defamatory statement referred to the plaintiff, regard may be had to subsequent statements which shed light on the person to whom the defamatory article referred (*Hayward* v *Thompson* [1982] QB 47).

One important issue is whether a group can sue where it is alleged that the group as a whole has been defamed. This issue was considered by the House of Lords in *Knupffer* v *London Express Newspapers Ltd* [1944] AC 116. The plaintiff was a Russian refugee and was a member of the 'Young Russian Party', which had 24 members in this country and several thousand members abroad. The article alleged that this group were Nazis. The House of Lords held that the plaintiff could sue in respect of this statement if he could prove that the statement was capable of referring to him and that it was in fact understood as referring to him. It was held that the plaintiff could not show that the article was capable of referring to him as it referred mainly to the activities of the group overseas and so his action was dismissed. This ruling makes it extremely difficult for a plaintiff to sue in respect of a group libel unless the group which is alleged to have been libelled is very limited in size, so that the statement can be understood as referring to the plaintiff (*Browne* v *DC Thompson* 1912 SC 359). This can have detrimental civil liberties implications where the group which has been defamed is an oppressed minority group with little other hope of obtaining redress (but see s70 of the Race Relations Act 1976 and, in America, *Beauharnais* v *Illinois* 343 US 250 (1952)).

23.6 Publication

The defendant must publish the defamatory statement about the plaintiff because it is the plaintiff's reputation in the eyes of others which is protected and not the plaintiff's pride. For this purpose a communication between the defendant and his spouse does not constitute publication (*Wennhak* v *Morgan* (1888) 20 QBD 635). However a communication to the spouse of the plaintiff does constitute publication for this purpose (*Wenman* v *Ash* (1853) 13 CB 836). The handing back of a defamatory statement by the printer to the author of the statement does not constitute publication, although, of course, there is a publication where the author hands the defamatory material to the printer for printing (*Eglantine Inn Ltd* v *Smith* [1948] NI 29).

The defendant need not have intended that the defamatory statement be communicated to any particular person. It is sufficient that the publication to that person could have been reasonably anticipated. This can be seen in the case of *Theaker* v *Richardson* [1962] 1 WLR 151. The defendant wrote a defamatory letter to the plaintiff, accusing her of being a whore and a brothel keeper. The plaintiff was a married woman and was a fellow local councillor with the defendant. The defendant put the defamatory letter through the plaintiff's letterbox in a manilla envelope, similar to the type used for election addresses. The plaintiff's husband picked up the envelope and, believing it to contain an election address, he opened it and read its contents. The jury found that the defendant was liable because it was a reasonable and probable consequence of the defendant's method of delivery of the letter that the plaintiff's husband would open it and read it and the Court of Appeal upheld this finding. The limits of this rule can, however, be seen in the case of *Huth* v *Huth* [1915] 3 KB 32. The defendant sent a defamatory letter to his wife, from whom he was separated, stating that they were not married and that their children were illegitimate. The letter was opened by a curious butler who read its contents. It was held that there was no publication of the letter because the defendant could not reasonably have anticipated that an inquisitive butler would open his wife's mail.

Every time that the defamatory statement is repeated, the tort is committed again and a fresh cause of action arises. In *Cutler* v *McPhail* [1962] 2 QB 292 a defamatory letter was written to a newspaper and the letter was subsequently published by the newspaper. It was held that the writer of the letter was liable for the libel which he had written, but the publishers of the newspaper were also liable for the libel which was published. The maker of a defamatory statement may also find himself liable for the damage caused by the repetition of the defamatory statement by a third party, at least where that repetition was reasonably foreseeable. In *Slipper* v *British Broadcasting Corporation* [1991] 1QB 283 the plaintiff alleged that he was libelled by a film which was broadcast by the defendants. The plaintiff argued that, in assessing general damages, regard should be had to reviews of the film in national newspapers which repeated the sting of the libel because the defendants had invited the press to review the film, they knew that the film would be reviewed by the national press and that people would read the reviews who would not have seen the film. The defendants applied to strike out the plaintiff's claim in so far as it related to the reviews in the national press on the ground that they could not be liable for the repetition of the libel which was not authorised by them and which was made by an independent third party. The Court of Appeal held that the law relating to republication was an aspect of novus actus interveniens and that the critical question was therefore whether or not there was a break in the chain of causation. Slade LJ was prepared to accept that prima facie a court will regard an unauthorised repetition of a libel by an independent third party as a novus actus interveniens but, on the facts, the court refused to strike out the claim. The court regarded it as 'plainly arguable' that the defendants could reasonably foresee and anticipate as a natural and probable consequence of the film that the sting of the libel would be repeated in the reviews in the national press.

However, in an effort to lessen the hardship which the application of this principle would give rise to, the courts have drawn a distinction between the publishers of a defamatory statement (who are its author, printer and publisher) and the person who merely disseminates the publication (such as a bookseller, public library etc.). The disseminator will only be liable where it can be shown that he knew that the publication was in some way defamatory or that he was negligent in not knowing that the publication was defamatory (*Sun Life Assurance Co of Canada* v *WH Smith & Son Ltd* (1934) 150 LT 211, cf *Goldsmith* v *Sperrings Ltd* [1977] 1

WLR 478). This principle can be seen at work in the case of *Vizetelly* v *Mudie's Select Library Ltd* [1900] 2 QB 170. The defendants, who were the owners of a circulating library, failed to return books which the publishers had asked to be returned on the ground that they might contain libellous material. It was held that the defendants were liable because they knew that the books might contain libellous material (compare *Bottomley* v *Woolworth & Co* (1932) 48 TLR 521).

23.7 Defences

There are a number of defences to the tort of defamation. In many ways these defences are the most important aspect of the law of defamation because they are frequently relied upon by defendants.

23.8 Consent

It is a defence to show that the plaintiff consented to the publication of the statement which would otherwise be defamatory. In *Chapman* v *Lord Ellesmere* [1932] 2 KB 431 the plaintiff, who was a trainer of horses at Newmarket, was given a licence by the Jockey Club to train horses and his licence was the subject of a number of conditions. One of these conditions was that the Jockey Club could withdraw his licence and publish this in the *Racing Calendar*. The plaintiff accepted his licence on these conditions. At a subsequent race a horse was found to have been doped and the plaintiff, as its trainer, was given a warning which was published in the *Racing Calendar* and in *The Times*. The plaintiff sued both publications for libel. It was held that the defendant had consented to the publication of the warning in the *Racing Calendar* when he accepted his licence and so he had no cause of action against the *Racing Calendar*. However the plaintiff was able to succeed against *The Times* on the ground that he had not consented to publication in that paper.

23.9 Justification or truth

Where the defendant can show that his statement was true then no action in defamation lies. It is for the defendant to prove that his statement was true and not for the plaintiff to show that the statement was false. The fact that the defendant was inspired by malice is irrelevant if the statement is true. The defendant must prove that the statement was actually true. Where a defendant repeats a defamatory statement he must prove that the statement is true and not simply that it is true that such a statement was made to him (*'Truth' (NZ) Ltd* v *Holloway* [1960] 1 WLR 997). It is no defence that he reasonably believed that the statement was true if, in fact, it was false.

The defendant need not show that his statement is literally true; it is sufficient if the substance of it is true. In *Alexander* v *North Eastern Railway Co* (1865) 6 B & S 340 the defendants stated that the plaintiff was fined £9, or three months' imprisonment in default of paying the fine, for riding on the railway without a ticket. In fact the plaintiff had been fined £9 but was only given a sentence of two weeks' imprisonment in default of paying the fine. It was held that this was a sufficiently minor inaccuracy for the defence to succeed. It should also be noted that s5 of the Defamation Act 1952 provides that, where there is more than one distinct charge against the plaintiff:

'A defence of justification shall not fail by reason only that the truth of every charge is not proved if the words not proved to be true do not materially injure the plaintiff's reputation having regard to the truth of the remaining charges.'

In proving the truth of a statement it should be noted that, under s13 of the Civil Evidence Act 1968, evidence of a conviction in a criminal court is conclusive evidence of guilt. Under the Rehabilitation of Offenders Act 1974 a conviction becomes spent after a period of time and cannot be used in judicial proceedings, but this is subject to the caveat that, under s8(3) of the Act, a spent conviction may be proved for the purpose of establishing the defence of justification, fair comment or qualified privilege, unless the publication is proved to have been with malice (s8(5)).

The defendant may wish to argue that the words bear a less defamatory meaning than that alleged by the plaintiff and that in this less defamatory sense they are true. Conversely, he may wish to argue that the words should be understood as imparting a general charge of dishonesty rather than an allegation of dishonesty confined to a particular event. The latter issue was considered by the Court of Appeal in *Williams* v *Reason* [1988] 1 All ER 262. The plaintiff, a well-known amateur rugby football player, brought an action against the defendants alleging that they had libelled him in publishing an article claiming that he had breached the rules relating to his amateur status by writing a book for money during his career. The defendants sought leave to bring new evidence to the effect that the plaintiff had accepted 'boot money' during his career. It was held that the defendants were entitled to lead this evidence. The sting of the libel was that the plaintiff was guilty of 'shamateurism' and it was held that evidence that the plaintiff had accepted 'boot money' was relevant to the charge of 'shamateurism'. It was held that the defendants could lead evidence of facts which were capable of justifying the words in a wider sense than that pleaded by the plaintiff provided that the words which the defendants sought to justify were capable of bearing that meaning. In *Prager* v *Times Newspapers Ltd* [1988] 1 All ER 300 the Court of Appeal affirmed that the defendants were entitled to plead justification of any alternative meaning which the words which had been published were capable of meaning, and that they were not restricted to attempting to justify the meaning which the plaintiff had pleaded.

The defendant who pleads that his statement was justified must particularise the meaning of the words which he alleges to be justified. In *Lucas-Box* v *News Group*

Newspapers Ltd [1986] 1 WLR 147 the plaintiff brought a libel action against the defendants in respect of a newspaper article which inferred that she had knowingly associated with Italian terrorists. The defendants' original defence was that the article could not, in its ordinary and natural meaning, be understood as being defamatory of the plaintiff. Two years after the defences were served the defendants obtained leave to amend their defences so as to plead the defence of justification (for consideration of the principles to be applied in considering an amendment to plead justification at a late stage see *Atkinson* v *Fitzwalter* [1987] 1 All ER 483). The plaintiff argued that it was not clear in what respect the defendants were seeking to justify their statements. It was held that the defendants were under an obligation to make clear the respect in which they were seeking to rely on the defence of justification and the meaning which they were seeking to justify (but see *Viscount De L'Isle* v *Times Newspapers* [1987] 3 All ER 499). This achieves some degree of parity between the parties because it is settled practice for a plaintiff to plead the meaning which he alleges that the words which he used mean where the meaning of the words is not clear.

23.10 Absolute privilege

It is a defence for the defendant to show that his statement was absolutely privileged. There are certain cases in which English law recognises that a statement made by the defendant enjoys absolute privilege from suit in defamation. It does not matter how untrue or how outrageous the statement is, it still enjoys absolute privilege. The cases where a statement enjoys absolute privilege are as follows.

Statements in Parliament

Any statement made by a member of either of the Houses of Parliament during the course of parliamentary proceedings enjoys an absolute privilege (Bill of Rights Act 1688). The privilege extends to statements made during debates in the House, to proceedings in committee, but not to statements made by MPs outside the House. In *Church of Scientology of California* v *Johnson-Smith* [1972] 1 QB 522 the plaintiffs alleged that a statement which had been made about them was made maliciously and to substantiate their claim that the defendant was motivated by malice, they sought to refer to a statement which the defendant had made in Parliament. It was held that the plaintiffs could not use statements made by the defendant in the House as evidence of malice because such statements enjoyed absolute privilege. The absolute privilege is extended by the Parliamentary Papers Act 1840 to cover reports, papers and proceedings authorised to be published by Parliament.

Judicial proceedings

Statements made during the course of judicial proceedings are also the subject of absolute privilege. The privilege is a wide one and extends to statements made by judges, counsel, parties and witnesses during the court proceedings (*Royal Aquarium and Summer and Winter Garden Society* v *Parkinson* [1892] 1 QB 431). The courts have taken a wide view of what constitutes judicial proceedings for this purpose and it has been held to extend to other hearings, such as a military court of inquiry or a professional disciplinary committee (*Addis* v *Crocker* [1961] 1 QB 11). However in *Hasselblad (GB) Ltd* v *Orbinson* [1985] 1 All ER 173 it was held that proceedings before the Commission of the European Communities were administrative rather than judicial so that absolute privilege did not apply to documents used as evidence before the Commission in a restrictive practices case under Article 85 of the Treaty.

Although the privilege applies to statements made during judicial proceedings the statement which is the subject of the defamation action must, in some way, be connected with the case. The defendant cannot use the occasion of judicial proceedings to make defamatory statements totally unconnected with the case and then claim absolute privilege (*More* v *Weaver* [1928] 2 KB 520).

It is unclear whether absolute privilege also extends to statements made between a solicitor and his client. If the communication is made in relation to the judicial proceedings then it is the subject of absolute privilege. The uncertainty relates to communications which are not related to the judicial proceedings. In *More* v *Weaver* (above) the privilege was held to be absolute, but the point was expressly left open by the House of Lords in *Minter* v *Priest* [1930] AC 558. If it is held that these communications are not deserving of absolute privilege, it does not mean that these statements enjoy no privilege at all; they still enjoy qualified privilege (on which see 23.11).

Absolute privilege is also extended to fair and accurate reports of judicial proceedings in the United Kingdom by s3 of the Libel Amendment Act 1888 which states that a:

> ' ... fair and accurate report in any newspaper of proceedings publicly heard before any court exercising judicial authority shall, if published contemporaneously with such proceedings, be privileged: provided that nothing in this section shall authorise the publication of any blasphemous or indecent matter.'

Official communications

A communication made by one officer of state to another in the course of his official duties is the subject of absolute privilege (*Chatterton* v *Secretary of State for India* [1895] 2 QB 189). The rationale behind this protection is said to be that a minister of state must be free to carry out his duties without fear of being the subject of a defamation action. It is, however, unclear how far this exception extends. The courts have not given altogether consistent signals on this point. In *Szalatnay-Stacho* v *Fink* [1946] 1 All ER 303 it was held that the exception did not extend below the rank of minister and in *Merricks* v *Nott-Bower* [1965] 1 QB 57 it was held that it probably did not extend to a memorandum written by a deputy commissioner of the Metropolitan Police to the Commissioner. On the other hand in *Dawkins* v *Lord Paulet* (1865) LR 5 QB 94 it was held that the exception did apply to a report about a lieutenant-colonel written by a major-general to the Adjutant-General. The extent of this privilege was recently in issue in *Fayed* v *Al-Tajir* [1987] 2 All ER 396. The plaintiff was criticised in a memorandum, for which the defendant was responsible, and he claimed that it libelled him. The defendant claimed that the memorandum was the subject of absolute privilege because it was prepared at a time at which he was acting as the ambassador of the United Arab Emirates and the memorandum was of an inter-departmental nature. It was held that the memorandum was protected by absolute privilege because public policy required that the interference with the affairs of a foreign sovereign be kept to a minimum and because Article 24 of the Vienna Convention on Diplomatic Relations required embassy documents to be treated as inviolable.

23.11 Qualified privilege

There are certain types of statements which, although not qualifying for absolute privilege, nevertheless are entitled to what is known as qualified privilege. This protects the maker of the statement from suit in defamation provided that he acted honestly and without malice. It is for the plaintiff to prove that the defendant was actuated by malice. Malice simply means that the defendant has no honest belief in the truth of his statement (see *Horrocks* v *Lowe* [1975] AC 135). It is sometimes said that the defendant has acted in excess of privilege. However this seems to mean simply that the privilege is not available on the facts because the case does not fall within one of the categories in which the privilege is available. The defence cannot be bypassed or outflanked by resort to an action in negligence (*Spring* v *Guardian Assurance plc* [1993] 2 All ER 273). Qualified privilege is applicable in cases under the following categories.

Privileged reports

This category encompasses such things as fair and accurate reports of parliamentary proceedings, including extracts of reports, papers etc published by order of Parliament (see s3 of the Parliamentary Papers Act 1840). Other reports which enjoy qualified privilege include fair and accurate reports of judicial proceedings which the public may attend. This qualified privilege applies to any court and, unlike absolute privilege, is not confined to contemporaneous reports or to newspaper reports. This privilege does not extend to such reports of proceedings in foreign courts, unless the public interest requires their publication (*Webb* v *Times Publishing Co* [1960] 2 QB 535).

Qualified privilege also extends to certain fair and accurate reports published in a newspaper or broadcast from a station in the UK. Section 7 of the Defamation Act 1952 provides that the publication in a newspaper or by means of a television or radio broadcast (s166(3) of the Broadcasting Act 1990) of any report contained in the Schedule of the Act 'shall be privileged unless the publication is proved to be made with malice'. The reports contained in the Schedule of the Act are divided into two categories; statements which are privileged without explanation or contradiction and statements which are privileged subject to explanation or contradiction.

Statements which are privileged without explanation or contradiction include a fair and accurate report of any proceedings:

1. in public of the legislature of any part of Her Majesty's dominions outside Great Britain;
2. in public of an international organisation or conference of which the United Kingdom is a member;
3. in public of an international court;
4. before a court exercising jurisdiction throughout any part of Her Majesty's dominions outside the UK;
5. in public of a body or person appointed to hold a public inquiry by the government or legislature in any part of Her Majesty's dominions outside the UK.

The following statements are some of those which enjoy privilege subject to explanation or contradiction; in other words the defendant is not entitled to rely on the defence where he failed to publish, in an appropriate manner, any letter or statement of the plaintiff which explains or contradicts the defendant's statement. This category includes fair and accurate reports of proceedings:

1. at public meetings;
2. of a local authority;
3. of the general meeting of a public company;
4. any association formed in the UK for the purpose of promoting or encouraging the exercise of or interest in any art, science, religion, learning, trade, business, industry, profession, game, sport or pastime and empowered by its constitution to exercise control over or adjudicate upon matters of interest or concern to the association, or the actions or conduct of any person subject to such control or adjudication.

It is for the jury to strike a balance between the rights of the press and the rights of individuals and it is only in the clearest of cases that a judge should withdraw the issue of the fairness and accuracy of the report from the jury (*Kingshott* v *Associated Kent Newspapers Ltd* [1991] 1 QB 88).

Statements made in furtherance of a duty

Where the defendant was under a legal, moral or social duty to communicate the information to the recipient of the information, the statement enjoys a qualified privilege. In *Watt* v *Longsden* [1930] 1 KB 130 an overseas manager of a company wrote to the defendant, who was one of the company directors, informing him that the plaintiff, the overseas managing director, was dishonest and was leading an immoral and drunken life. The defendant showed the report to the company chairman and to the plaintiff's wife. The report proved to be false and the plaintiff brought a libel action against the defendant. It was held that the statements made between the company officers were all privileged because they all had a common interest in the running of the company and they were all entitled to discuss the plaintiff's behaviour. However, it was held that the communication to the plaintiff's wife was not protected by privilege because the defendant had no duty to inform the wife of these allegations. The test for such a duty was laid down in the following terms in *Stuart* v *Bell* [1891] 2 QB 341:

'Would the great mass of right-minded men in the position of the defendant have considered it their duty under the circumstances to make the communication?'

Common interest

Where the statement is made pursuant to a common interest between the parties then the statement may enjoy qualified privilege. An employer and an employee have a common interest in the conduct of the employee which is capable of leading to dismissal or other disciplinary sanction (*Watt* v *Longsden* (above) and *Bryanston Finance Ltd* v *De Vries* [1975] QB 703). However, if a plaintiff makes a valid criticism of the defendant's business, the defendant cannot defame the plaintiff and claim qualified privilege as a defence: see *Fraser-Armstrong* v *Haddow* (1994) The Times 21 January.

Protection of an interest

A defendant may make a statement in his own defence or the defence of his property and still claim the benefit of qualified privilege. This can be seen in *Osborne* v *Boulter* [1930] 2 KB 226. The plaintiff alleged that the defendant's beer was of poor quality. The defendant dictated a letter to his typist defending his beer and stating that the beer was of poor quality only because the plaintiff watered it down. It was held that the latter statement was privileged because it was made as part of company business in protection of their interests. Qualified privilege also extends to statements made to the proper authorities for the redress of a public grievance.

23.12 Fair comment

The defence of fair comment is frequently invoked in the courts, especially by the press, and it is one of the defences which is important in setting the limits of free speech in this country. Nevertheless it is a defence which can only be invoked within certain rather rigid confines. A defendant who invokes the defence of fair comment must plead the comment which is relied upon as constituting the defence with sufficient precision to enable the plaintiff to know the case which he has to meet (*Control Risks Ltd* v *New English Library Ltd* [1990] 1 WLR 183). The defendant must show that the matter to which his statement referred was one of public interest, that his comment was an opinion based upon true facts, that the comment was fair and that it was made without malice. We shall consider these four elements separately.

Public interest

The defendant's comment must relate to a matter of public interest. The question whether a matter is one of public interest is a question to be decided by the judge, but the courts have chosen to define public interest fairly widely. In *London Artists Ltd* v *Littler* [1969] 2 QB 375 Lord Denning stated that:

> 'Whenever a matter is such as to affect people at large, so that they may be legitimately interested in, or concerned at, what is going on; or what may happen to them or others; then it is a matter of public interest on which everyone is entitled to make fair comment.'

The case itself concerned a letter published by the defendant which alleged that the plaintiffs had plotted to bring a successful play to an end by enticing the four principal performers to terminate their contracts. The defendant pleaded fair comment as a defence on the ground that the closure of a successful play was a matter of public interest. It was held, applying the test noted above, that people were legitimately interested in what went on in the theatre and that people in the show business industry welcomed publicity and so the matter was one of public interest. Lord Denning said that the test could also be satisfied where people had a legitimate concern in what was going on, rather than a legitimate interest. He gave as an example of legitimate concern the case of *South Hetton Coal Co Ltd* v *North-Eastern News Association Ltd* [1894] 1 QB 133. It was alleged that cottages, which were owned by the plaintiffs and which constituted the majority of housing in a village, were in an insanitary condition. It was held that this was a matter of public interest because it was one in which people were legitimately concerned. Public interest would also include comments concerning public figures and politicians, theatres and plays, and the reviews of books etc.

Statement of opinion

The defendant's statement must be a statement of opinion and not one of fact. It is, however, very difficult in many cases to distinguish between a statement of fact and one of opinion. This is so for two principal reasons. The first is the inherent difficulty involved in drawing the distinction. One case in which it was difficult to draw the line was *Dakhyl* v *Labouchere* [1908] 2 KB 325. The plaintiff described himself as a 'specialist for the treatment of deafness, ear, nose and throat diseases'. The defendant, however, referred to him as a 'quack of the rankest species'. It was held that this was a statement of opinion and not one of fact. Winfield and Jolowicz pose the question (*The Law of Torts* (13th ed) p325) whether calling a person 'immoral' or a 'sinner' is a statement of opinion or a statement of fact? No clear answer can be given to this question.

The second difficulty lies in the extent to which the court should have regard to the wider context of the statement in deciding whether it is one of fact or of opinion. This was one of the issues which was before the House of Lords in *Telnikoff* v *Matusevitch* [1992] 2 AC 343. The plaintiff, a Russian emigre, wrote an article in the *Daily Telegraph* in which he argued, inter alia, that the BBC Russian Service failed to distinguish between Russia on the one hand and Communism on the other and that the service was staffed almost entirely from Russian speaking minorities of the Soviet Union. The defendant, who was also a Russian emigre, responded by writing a letter to the same newspaper which imputed racialist and anti-semitic opinions to the plaintiff. The plaintiff brought a claim for damages for libel and the defendant invoked the defence of fair comment. The point which separated the parties (and the House of Lords) was not whether the court should have regard to the wider context of the defendant's statement in deciding whether it was a statement of fact or opinion, but whether that context included the original article written by the plaintiff. The plaintiff argued that, in deciding whether or not the statements in the defendant's letter were fact or comment, the jury should have regard only to the words of the defendant and not to the original article written by the plaintiff. The majority of the House of Lords agreed and held that the context did not include the contents of the original article written by the plaintiff because many of the readers of the defendant's letter would not have read the article or, even if they had read it, its contents would not have been fully to their minds. This provoked a vigorous dissent from Lord Ackner. He argued that the freedom to comment on matters of public interest was vital to the functioning of a democratic society and that the defence was available to a defendant who had done no more than express an honest opinion on publications put before the public. He stated that it was sufficient for the defendant to have identified the publication on which he was commenting without having to set out such extracts from it as would enable his readers to judge for themselves whether they agreed with his opinion or not. This argument was, however, refuted by the majority. Lord Keith stated that the writer of a letter to a newspaper had a duty to take reasonable care to make clear that he was writing comment and not making misrepresentations about the content of the original article and Lord Templeman asserted that a critic must in future simply make clear that he is not quoting the plaintiff but is commenting on the words which the plaintiff had uttered (see further Sutherland (1992) 55 MLR 278).

Although the defendant's statement must be one of opinion and not one of fact, the opinion must be stated upon the basis of facts which are true. In *London Artists Ltd* v *Littler* (above) Lord Denning said that the commentator must get his 'basic facts right', by which he meant those facts which go to the 'pith and substance of the matter'. The defendant in *Littler* failed to establish one of these basic facts because he could not prove that the plaintiffs had plotted to close the play (see too *Merivale* v *Carson* (1887) 20 QBD 275). This must be read subject to s6 of the Defamation Act 1952 which provides that:

'A defence of fair comment shall not fail by reason only that the truth of every allegation of fact is not proved if the expression of opinion is fair comment having regard to such of the facts alleged or referred to in the words complained of as are proved.'

Although the facts upon which the defendant made his comment must be true there is no requirement that all the facts be contained in the alleged libellous statement. It is sufficient that the facts are stated in such a way as to make clear the facts upon which the comment is based. In *Kemsley* v *Foot* [1952] AC 345 the defendant, Michael Foot, attacked the Beaverbrook Press and said that it was 'lower than Kemsley'. Kemsley, who was the owner of another newspaper, brought a libel action against the defendant on the ground that his statement implied that his newspapers were of low character. It was held that the article had sufficient factual content about the conduct of the plaintiff's newspaper for the defendant to be entitled to plead the defence of fair comment.

Fairness

Thirdly it must be shown that the comment was, in all the circumstances fair. In considering the fairness of the comment it has been held that the honesty of the defendant is the 'cardinal test' (per Lord Denning in *Slim* v *Daily Telegraph Ltd* [1968] 2 QB 157). Where the comment is based upon improper motives then the comment will be unfair. The test of fairness is an objective one and, once a defendant shows that his comment is objectively fair, the court will presume that his statement of opinion is honest unless the plaintiff can plead and prove express malice (*Telnikoff* v *Matusevitch* [1992] 2 AC 343).

Where the defendant's comment consists of an allegation that the plaintiff is actuated by some corrupt or dishonest motive then it is much more difficult for the defendant to rely on this defence. This point can be seen in the case of *Campbell* v *Spottiswoode* (1863) 3 B & S 769. The defendant alleged that the plaintiff's purpose behind starting a scheme to spread Christianity among the Chinese was to promote the sale of his own newspaper. It was held that, although the defendant honestly believed that what he had said was true, he was not entitled to rely on the defence of fair comment because there was no reasonable basis of fact for his allegations. In such cases it is not the case that the defence is not available to the defendant, it is simply the case that he must show the existence of reasonable grounds for his belief.

Absence of malice

The defendant's comment must not be inspired by malice, which for this purpose consists of spite, ill-will or any other improper motive. It is for the plaintiff to show that the defendant was actuated by malice. Malice was successfully shown in the case of *Thomas* v *Bradbury Agnew* [1906] 2 KB 627. The Court of Appeal held that the hostility of the book review written by the defendant, combined with the hostility which he displayed in the witness box, showed that he was actuated by malice and so was not entitled to rely on the defence of fair comment. It appears to be the case that where the writer of the statement acted maliciously but the publisher did not, then the publisher will not be tainted with the malice of the writer and will remain entitled to rely on the defence of fair comment (*Lyon* v *Daily Telegraph Ltd* [1943] KB 746).

23.13 Apology and amends

Where the defendant apologises for a defamatory statement which he has made, it is not a complete defence to the defamation action but it will have the effect of mitigating the damages for which he is liable. Section 2 of the Libel Act 1843 provides that where a statement was inserted in a newspaper without actual malice or gross negligence and the defendant has inserted a full apology for the libel either before or at the earliest possible moment after the commencement of the action then the defendant is entitled to rely on the defence of apology. The apology must be accompanied by a payment into court of a sum of money by way of amends.

Where the defendant has innocently published a defamatory statement so that he complies with the requirements of s4 of the Defamation Act 1952, then the defendant must offer to publish a suitable apology and correction and he must take reasonable steps to notify the distributors. Where this is done and the apology and amends are accepted no action will lie in libel or slander against the person who has issued the apology. Where the apology is not accepted then a defence is provided in s4 as long as the apology and amends were made as soon as possible and not withdrawn.

23.14 Remedies

The primary remedy for defamation is damages and the principles upon which damages are awarded is discussed in chapter 30. It should be noted that it is for the jury to assess the damages payable. It should also be noted that exemplary damages may be available in a suitable case (see chapter 30). At common law the ability of the appellate courts to review the award of juries is strictly limited (see *Cassell* v *Broome* [1972] AC 1027) and the unpredictability and lack of reality in many jury awards has been a major cause of concern. These issues were classically illustrated by the case of *Sutcliffe* v *Pressdram Ltd* [1991] 1 QB 153. The plaintiff, Sonia Sutcliffe, who was the wife of the 'Yorkshire Ripper', was awarded damages of £600,000 by a jury in respect of a libel published by the defendants, Private Eye. The defendants appealed to the Court of Appeal on a number of grounds, one of which was that the damages awarded by the jury was excessive. The Court of Appeal agreed. While being careful to affirm that the assessment of damages was the province of the jury and that the courts should not interfere unless the sum awarded was substantially in excess of any sum which the jury could reasonably have awarded, they held that the sum was, indeed, excessive and should be set aside. The Court of Appeal suggested that juries could properly be invited to consider the weekly or monthly sum which would be yielded by investing the capital sum or, in the case of smaller sums of money, to consider what they could buy with the sum of money. Nourse LJ added that the judge should in appropriate cases warn the jury of the possible consequences of awarding an excessive sum, in the sense that any appeal would expose the plaintiff to more delay, expense and anxiety. The hope was that, in doing so, juries would be more 'realistic' in their assessment of damages. But, despite these guidelines, juries in certain well publicised cases continued to set damage awards at spectacular levels and Parliament was forced to intervene. Section 8(2) of the Courts and Legal Services Act 1990 states that:

'... rules of court may provide for the Court of Appeal, in such classes of case as may be specified in the rules, to have power, in place of ordering a new trial, to substitute for the sum awarded by the jury such sum as appears to the court to be proper.'

For this purpose 'case' means 'any case where the Court of Appeal has power to order a new trial on the ground that damages awarded by a jury are excessive or inadequate' (s8(1)). The scope of s8(1) and 8(2) was considered by the Court of Appeal in *Rantzen* v *Mirror Group Newspapers* [1993] 3 WLR 953 (discussed by Milmo [1993] NLJ 550). Prior to the enactment of the 1990 Act, the Court of Appeal could only interfere where the award of the jury was so excessive as to be 'divorced from reality' (*McCarey* v *Associated Newspapers Ltd* [1964] 1 WLR 855). However, it was held that this barrier against intervention should be lowered because the grant of an almost 'limitless discretion to a jury' did not satisfy the requirements of Article 10 of the European Convention for the Protection of Human Rights and Fundamental Freedoms, which exists to protect the right to freedom of expression. So the court held that the critical question to be asked in considering the scope of the jurisdiction of the Court of Appeal was: 'could a reasonable jury have thought that this award was necessary to compensate the plaintiff and to re-establish his reputation?'. On the facts the court held that the sum awarded (£250,000) was excessive and exercised its power to substitute the sum of £110,000. The court also held that, in giving guidance to a jury on the assessment of damages in a defamation claim, the judge may direct the jury to consider awards made by the Court of Appeal under s8(1) in the hope that 'in the course of time a series of decisions of the Court of Appeal will establish some standards as to what are ... "proper" awards.' But the jury should not be directed to consider previous jury awards in defamation cases or to conventional awards in personal injury cases.

Note that where a case is settled out of court rather than allowed to proceed to trial, the defendants are not entitled to say in a statement made on behalf of the plaintiff that the payment into court of a substantial sum of money was done for commercial reasons. The inclusion of such an explanation detracts from the value of the payment in as being in itself a vindication: *Charlton* v *EMAP plc* (1993) The Times 11 June.

An interlocutory injunction may also be granted in an appropriate case to restrain the publication of a defamatory statement, but the courts are very reluctant to grant such an injunction where the defence of qualified privilege, justification or fair comment is pleaded by the defendant, unless the plaintiff can show that the defendant dishonestly and maliciously proposes to publish the statement when he knows that it is untrue. In *Gulf Oil (GB) Ltd* v *Page* [1987] Ch 327 the Court of Appeal held that the rule that a plaintiff is not entitled to an interlocutory injunction to restrain the publication of defamatory material when the defendant pleads the defence of justification is not an absolute rule, but that it does admit of an exception. That exception arises where the defamatory material is published in the course of a conspiracy by the defendants which has as its sole or dominant purpose the infliction of injury upon the plaintiff (although even in such a case a court may refuse an application for an interlocutory injunction where to accede to the application would be to interfere to an unacceptable extent with freedom of speech, see *Femis-Bank (Anguilla) Ltd* v *Lazar* [1991] Ch 391). The court did not think that such a ruling had undesirable implications for freedom of speech. Parker LJ thought that it would only be in the 'rarest of cases' that the evidence would establish that the sole or dominant purpose behind the publication of, for example, a newspaper article was the infliction of injury upon the plaintiff. Thus where the plaintiff alleges that the defendants have conspired to cause him injury he need only satisfy the court that there is a serious question to be tried on the combination and the intent to injure to obtain his interlocutory injunction.

23.15 Conclusion

The Faulks Committee report (see 23.1) made some far-reaching proposals for the reform of the law relating to defamation, but no attempt has been made to implement these proposals and it is highly unlikely that they will now be enacted. But reform of the law relating to defamation has become a more important issue in recent years. A number of factors account for this. The first is the controversy surrounding the role of the jury in assessing damages in defamation actions (see *Sutcliffe* v *Pressdram Ltd* (above)). The second is the lack of protection afforded by the law of tort to an individual's interest in the protection of his own privacy. English law at present does not recognise any tort of invasion of privacy and justification is a defence to a defamation action, no matter how unreasonably or maliciously the defendant has acted. The Court of Appeal has recently urged that this issue be examined so that greater protection can be afforded to the individual whose privacy is unreasonably violated (see *Kaye* v *Robertson* [1991] FSR 62, discussed by Markesinis (1990) 53 MLR 802, Prescott (1991) 54 MLR 451, Markesinis (1992) 55 MLR 118).

The third factor is that legal aid is not available for defamation actions. This essentially turns defamation into a rich man's tort because the costs involved in defamation litigation are so great that it is unlikely that anyone other than the very rich will hazard their life savings and risk bankruptcy to clear their reputation. There is therefore a need to provide a cheap accessible forum in which individuals can clear their name and their reputation (see, for example, the experiment with the ombudsmen who have recently been appointed by national newspapers to consider complaints from aggrieved persons). Some plaintiffs have sought to get round the legal aid hurdle by bringing their claim on some other basis. The most notable example of this is provided by *Joyce* v *Sengupta* [1993] 1 WLR 337. The defendants published an article in which they asserted that the plaintiff had stolen intimate letters belonging to the Princess Royal and that she had handed them to a national newspaper. These assertions were false and were capable of generating a claim for defamation. But the plaintiff elected not to bring such a claim because of the unavailability of legal aid. Instead, she chose to bring a claim in malicious falsehood and thus obtained legal aid. The defendants applied to strike out the claim for malicious falsehood as an abuse of the process of the court. The Court of Appeal refused to strike it out. The defendants argued that the plaintiff was seeking to invoke a 'secondary tort', here malicious falsehood, and that one consequence of her so doing was that they were deprived of their absolute constitutional right to trial by jury. A 'secondary tort' was defined as a 'tort which would not be relied upon save for the plaintiff's need to secure a collateral purpose unrelated to the merits of her claim'. The Court of Appeal rejected this argument on the ground that English law allows a plaintiff to take full advantage of the various remedies which the law allows for the tort of which she claims. Nor was the plaintiff seeking to avoid a trial by jury because she said that she would not oppose any application the defendants might wish to make for trial by jury. Thus it can be seen that a plaintiff who chooses to take this route does obtain an advantage in that the legal aid hurdle is avoided. But other obstacles will be encountered which would not ordinarily be met in a defamation action. The plaintiff must prove that the statement was false, that the defendant was actuated by malice and she must show that she has suffered financial loss as a result of the defendant's statement (see further 27.2–27.4 and the discussion of some of these points in the judgments of the Court of Appeal in *Joyce*). None of these hurdles will be easy to overcome and so, at the end of the day, *Joyce* v *Sengupta* may prove to be a very small victory for plaintiffs.

Fourthly, the legal procedures used in defamation cases are convoluted and expensive. In *Morrell* v *International Thomson Publishing Ltd* [1989] 3 All ER 733

May LJ noted that the pleadings in defamation cases do not appear to seek to inform the other side of the case which has to be met but rather seek to hide as much as possible. He said that the result was that defamation litigation was too complicated, lengthy and costly. He argued that defamation litigation now requires swift and firm consideration by the Law Commission and the Rule Committee.

The process of reform may, however, be close at hand. In December 1992 the Lord Chancellor announced his intention to reform the law of defamation. His proposals are far-reaching. The principal reforms suggested include the repeal of s4 of the Defamation Act 1952 and its replacement by a new procedure for an 'offer of amends' defence where damages will be fixed by a judge rather than a jury, a new summary procedure which will enable plaintiffs to claim damages up to a fixed ceiling and the abolition of the rule which prevents defendants from bringing evidence of specific discreditable acts by the plaintiff in an attempt to mitigate the damages payable. But, when considering these proposals for reform it is important to bear in mind the free speech implications of expanding the scope of the tort of defamation (or of creating a new tort of invasion of privacy). It is arguable that English law at present gives too much weight to the reputation of the individual at the expense of free speech considerations. There are, however, signs of a change of heart. In both *Derbyshire County Council* v *Times Newspapers Ltd* [1992] QB 770 and *Rantzen* v *Mirror Group Newspapers* [1993] 3 WLR 953 the Court of Appeal invoked Article 10 of the European Convention for the Protection of Human Rights and Fundamental Freedoms to place fresh limits on the tort of defamation and these cases may herald the beginning of a new, more restrictive approach by the appellate courts to the development of the tort of defamation. At the very least they emphasise that the cost of giving any further protection to the reputation of the individual may be to undermine our commitment to the protection of freedom of speech to an extent which is considered undesirable.

24

Trespass to the Person

24.1 Introduction

24.2 Battery

24.3 Assault

24.4 False imprisonment

24.5 The rule in *Wilkinson* v *Downton*

24.6 Conclusion

24.1 Introduction

Trespass to the person comprehends the torts of battery, assault and false imprisonment as well as what is sometimes referred to as the rule in *Wilkinson* v *Downton*. These torts provide us with some further evidence of the role of the law of tort in protecting a person's interest in his personal security. They also demonstrate an overlap with the criminal law as the acts which give rise to the tortious liability of the defendant may also give rise to criminal sanctions (this is an issue to which we shall return at 24.6). These torts are also of interest because of the question of the role of negligence within these torts. This latter issue has been of some considerable interest in the tort of battery and it is with that tort that we begin our analysis.

24.2 Battery

The tort of battery has been defined by Trindade ((1982) 2 OJLS 211,216) in the following terms:

'A battery is a direct act of the defendant which has the effect of causing contact with the body of the plaintiff without the latter's consent.'

This definition of the tort is a helpful one because it highlights most of the essential ingredients of the tort. There are five ingredients of the tort and these ingredients are as follows.

Direct act

The act of the defendant must be the direct cause of the damage to the plaintiff. The most famous example of this principle is the case of *Scott* v *Shepherd* (1773) 2 W Bl 892. The defendant threw a lighted squib into a market place. The first 'recipient' of this squib instinctively threw the squib to the next stall where it was once again picked up and thrown to another part of the market where it exploded and injured the plaintiff. It was held that the defendant was liable for the injuries suffered by the plaintiff because they were a direct result of the act of the defendant. The acts of the stall holders in passing on the squib were instinctive and did not break the direct link between the act of the defendant and the injury to the plaintiff. This requirement of directness serves the function of marking off the limits of liability in a way done by the rules relating to remoteness of damage in negligence.

Intentional act

The act of coming into contact with the person of the plaintiff must be an intentional act. At one time it was probably the case that trespass to the person was actionable even where the contact with the plaintiff was accidental, in the sense that it was not negligent, but this view was rejected by Denman J in *Stanley* v *Powell* [1891] 1 QB 86 when he held that trespass to the person was not actionable in the absence of either intent or negligence. The view of Denman J may now be too wide because it is not clear whether trespass to the person may be committed negligently. It is clear from cases such as *Stanley* v *Powell* and *NCB* v *Evans* [1951] 2 KB 861 that it was once the case that it could be committed negligently.

However, this traditional view was challenged by Lord Denning in the case of *Letang* v *Cooper* [1965] 1 QB 232. The plaintiff was sunbathing on an area of grass which was also used as a car park. While she was sunbathing, the defendant negligently drove his car over the plaintiff's legs and injured her. She brought an action against the defendant more than three years after the incident. The defendant argued that her claim was time barred because, under the Limitation Act 1939, an action in 'negligence, nuisance or breach of duty' had to be brought within three years of the cause of action arising. The plaintiff argued that her cause of action did not lie in 'negligence' or 'breach of duty' but in battery and that in battery the limitation period was six years. The Court of Appeal, however, disagreed and held that the plaintiff's action was statute barred because it was based upon the defendant's failure to take reasonable care and so it was, for the purposes of the Limitation Act, an action in 'negligence' even though it could also be called an action in trespass to the person.

Lord Denning, with whom Danckwerts LJ concurred, took a broader view and held that, where the act causing the damage was intentional, then the cause of action lay in trespass to the person but that, where the act causing the damage was a negligent one, then the cause of action lay in negligence. Thus he was of the opinion that there was no overlap between the tort of negligence and trespass to the person. He repeated this view in *Miller* v *Jackson* [1977] QB 966 where he said that where the damage-causing act was unintentional then no cause of action lay in trespass to the person but only in negligence. This view that trespass to the person cannot be committed negligently was apparently accepted by the Court of Appeal in *Wilson* v *Pringle* [1987] QB 237.

Diplock LJ was not as forthright as Lord Denning and he was not prepared to affirm that where the act causing the damage was unintentional the cause of action must lie in negligence. Yet, while he was not prepared to hold that trespass could not be committed negligently, the effect of his judgment was to eliminate the practical differences between these two torts so that where damage is inflicted unintentionally, there is no real advantage in electing to proceed in trespass rather than negligence. For example one of the major differences between trespass and negligence was that in negligence it was the plaintiff who had the burden of proof of showing that the defendant was negligent, whereas in trespass the burden was on the defendant to show that he was not negligent. Thus an action in trespass offered a considerable advantage to a plaintiff. But in *Fowler* v *Lanning* [1959] 1 QB 426 Diplock J, as he then was, held that the plaintiff in a trespass action bore the burden of showing that the defendant was negligent. In terms of history, this decision may well be questionable because there was a considerable body of opinion that, in cases which were not concerned with accidents on the highway, the burden was on the defendant to show that he was not negligent. Diplock J held, however, that there was no reason to confine the cases which held that the burden was on the plaintiff to cases involving accidents on the highway and so he held that they were not so confined and were of general application (for criticism of this decision see Trindade (1971) 30 ICLQ 706). Another important difference between trespass and negligence was thought to be that trespass was actionable per se, whereas negligence depended upon proof of damage. However in *Letang* Diplock LJ said that 'actual damage ... is a necessary ingredient in unintentional as distinct from intentional trespass to the person' (also criticised by Trindade (above)). Thus he removed what had previously been one of the most important differences between trespass and negligence. *Letang* also removed another advantage of proceeding in trespass rather than negligence by holding that, where the plaintiff's action was based upon the defendant's failure to take reasonable care, the plaintiff could not take advantage of the longer period of limitation applicable to trespass to the person. Thus the only remaining differences between trespass and negligence may be that the rules relating to remoteness of damage are different (being based upon foreseeability in negligence but upon directness in trespass, although see the discussion in chapter 11 on the narrowness of the distinction between foreseeability and directness), that contributory negligence may not be a defence in the case of trespass (but see to the contrary *Barnes* v *Nayer* (1986) The Times 19 December) and that trespass has no duty element (but where the courts have held that, for reasons of policy, there is no duty of care owed in negligence, it is unlikely that they will then permit the plaintiff to proceed in trespass).

So even if Lord Denning's approach is rejected as being contrary to the weight of authority (see *Street on Torts* (7th ed) p13–14 where such a view is expressed), the plaintiff is unlikely to benefit from electing to proceed in trespass rather than negligence because the practical advantages of such an election have been largely removed and such differences as may remain are of little practical importance.

Hostility?

In the recent case of *Wilson* v *Pringle* (above) it was held that it was the act of touching the plaintiff which had to be intentional and that that touching had to be proved to be a 'hostile touching'. The aim behind this requirement is clearly to exclude from the ambit of the tort the ordinary everyday contact which is part of life. Such contact had previously been thought not to be a battery because the plaintiff consented to such contact (see further paragraph on Defences below). The Court of Appeal rejected such an approach and held that it was the element of hostility which was missing from such contact. However they held that hostility was not the same thing as ill-will or malevolence and that in each case the question of the existence of hostility was an issue of fact for the court to decide. Where the act of touching which gave rise to the action did not, of itself, display hostility then the Court of Appeal held that the plaintiff must plead the facts which he claims demonstrate that the touching was a hostile one.

But the authority of *Wilson* must now be viewed with some suspicion. In *re F (mental patient: sterilisation)* [1990] 2 AC 1, 72–73 Lord Goff doubted, obiter, whether *Wilson* was correct. He argued that the requirement that the touching be a 'hostile' one was difficult to reconcile with the principle that any touching of another's body is, in the absence of lawful excuse, capable of amounting to a battery. He stated that a prank which gets out of hand, an over-friendly slap on the back or surgical treatment by a surgeon who mistakenly thinks that the patient has consented to it may all constitute a battery, without the touching being characterised as hostile. Due regard must also be paid, in cases of medical treatment, to the libertarian principle that 'every human being of adult years and sound mind has a right to determine what shall be done with his own body' (*Schloendorff* v *Society of New York Hospital* (1914) 211 NY 125, 126 per Cardozo J). The requirement that the touching be a hostile one failed to give sufficient weight to this libertarian principle. It is suggested that the approach adopted by Lord Goff is, in fact, the correct one and that *Wilson* should be overruled. The requirement that the touching be a 'hostile' one threatened to deflect the inquiry from the real issue, which is whether the touching was consented to by the plaintiff, into irrelevant inquiries into the motives of the defendant.

Contact with the plaintiff

There must be contact with the person of the plaintiff before there can be an action in the tort of battery. In *Cole* v *Turner* (1704) 6 Mod 149 it was said that the 'least touching of another in anger is a battery'. The reference to touching in 'anger' should be noted because it was one of the authorities relied upon by the court in *Wilson* v *Pringle* [1987] QB 237 in holding that the plaintiff had to show that the touching was 'hostile'. The contact with the person of the plaintiff must be an active contact. So, for example, the person who blocks a doorway so that the plaintiff cannot get through does not commit the tort of battery when the plaintiff bumps into him in his effort to get through the doorway. The simple requirement that the contact be an active one means that something which is relatively trivial, such as an unwanted kiss, may be a battery. It is not necessary that the plaintiff be aware that contact has been made with his or her person. It is therefore a battery to kiss a person while he or she is asleep, but evidence would have to be led that, had the plaintiff been awake, he or she would not have consented to the kiss.

Defences

There are a number of defences to the tort of battery. One of the principal defences is that the plaintiff consented to the contact with his person. Thus the doctor or dentist who makes contact with the person of the plaintiff during an operation or other examination does not commit the tort of battery because the plaintiff will have signed a form under which he consents to the operation being performed. In *Chatterton* v *Gerson* [1981] QB 432 the plaintiff suffered a trapped nerve after a hernia operation. She went to see the defendant, who was a specialist, about her trapped nerve. He performed an operation to free the trapped nerve but, as a result of the operation, the plaintiff lost all sensation in her right leg. She sued the defendant in battery on the ground that she had not truly consented to the operation because its effect had not been properly explained to her. Her claim was rejected because it was held that an action in battery could only succeed where her consent to the operation was not real and that provided the doctor had informed her in general terms of the nature of the operation, which he had, she had no cause of action. The House of Lords in *Sidaway* v *Bethlem Royal Hospital Governors* [1985] AC 871 held that English law did not recognise the existence of the doctrine of informed consent. They held that the question to be asked in each case was not whether sufficient information had been disclosed to the plaintiff to enable her to make an informed choice about whether or not to undergo the operation but whether a reasonable doctor would have acted as the defendant had done in only releasing a certain amount of information.

The defence of consent may also be applied to participants in sports which involve physical contact. As long as the contact takes place in accordance with the rules of the game, then no action in battery will lie. But where the contact is not in accordance with the rules of the game, as when a person who does not have the ball is punched during a game of rugby, then an action in battery will lie (*R* v *Billinghurst* [1978] Crim LR 553).

It was once thought that the defence of consent explained why no action in battery lay when two people bumped into each other in the street. In *Cole* v *Turner* (above)

Holt CJ said that 'if two or more meet in a narrow passage, and without any violence or design of harm, the one touches the other gently, it will be no battery'. In *Collins* v *Wilcock* [1984] 3 All ER 374 Robert Goff LJ sought to rationalise the defences on the ground that they are all part of the 'physical contact which was generally acceptable in the ordinary conduct of daily life'. This rationalisation was, however, rejected by the Court of Appeal in the case of *Wilson* v *Pringle* (above). Croom Johnson LJ said that it was not 'practicable' to define the tort of battery in terms of 'physical contact which is not generally acceptable in the ordinary conduct of daily life'. Instead it was held that it was the hostility of the touching which determined the existence of a contact which amounted to a battery. So, according to the Court of Appeal in *Wilson*, where two people bump into each other in the street or in a supermarket no action in battery arises unless it can be shown that one party had a hostile intent in bumping into the other. But, as was noted above, Lord Goff in *F* v *West Berkshire Health Authority* cast doubt upon the authority of *Wilson* and sought to restore the test which he had adopted in *Collins* v *Wilcock*; namely that the touching is not actionable when it is 'generally acceptable in the ordinary conduct of everyday life'.

Self defence also constitutes a defence to the tort of battery. Reasonable force may be used to resist an unlawful attack. The defence is only available where the steps taken in self-defence are not out of all proportion to the threatened harm (see *Lane* v *Holloway* [1968] 1 QB 379).

It is not entirely clear whether the plaintiff's damages can be reduced on the ground that he was guilty of contributory negligence. Some authority can be found for the proposition that damages are not reducible (see *Fontin* v *Katapodis* (1962) 108 CLR 177), but a contrary view may be gleaned from the cases of *Lane* v *Holloway* [1968] 1 QB 379 and *Murphy* v *Culhane* [1977] QB 94. However, this issue was recently considered by the Court of Appeal in *Barnes* v *Nayer* (1986) The Times 19 December. The defendant killed the plaintiff's wife with a machete, almost severing her head from her body. He was convicted of manslaughter by reason of diminished responsibility. His defence to the plaintiff's civil law claim was that he had been provoked by the deceased who had 'goaded' their respective sons into fighting each other and had then threatened the defendant's son with further violence. The defendant argued that the plaintiff's claim was barred on three grounds. The first was that it was barred by the maxim *ex turpi causa non oritur actio* (that no cause of action arises out of the wrong of the plaintiff). May LJ held that *ex turpi causa* could apply in an appropriate case to battery and that it would afford a complete defence to the plaintiff's action when it was applicable. But he held that the defence was not made out on the facts. The second ground was that the defence of volenti (see chapter 13) was applicable because the plaintiff willingly accepted the risk of injury. Once again May LJ held that the defence could apply to battery and that where it did apply it would afford a complete defence. But he held that the defence was not made out on the facts. The third ground relied upon by the defendant was that the plaintiff had been guilty of contributory negligence. May LJ established the important point that, in his opinion, the plaintiff's contributory negligence could constitute 'fault' under sl of the Law Reform (Contributory Negligence) Act 1945 so as to reduce the damages awardable by an appropriate degree (compare Hudson (1984) 4 Legal Studies 332 where, after much fuller consideration of the authorities, he concluded that contributory negligence is not a defence to battery). May LJ held that the defence was not applicable on the facts of the case because the defendant's response was out of all proportion to any act of the plaintiff so that no judge or jury could conclude that the plaintiff was guilty of contributory negligence. The plaintiff was therefore held to be entitled to recover in full from the defendant. Finally May LJ held that the defence of provocation could apply to battery but that the 'better view' was that its only effect was to reduce the exemplary damages payable and that it did not affect the compensatory damages payable.

24.3 Assault

The tort of assault may be defined as a direct threat made by the defendant to the plaintiff which has the effect of putting the plaintiff in reasonable apprehension of immediate physical contact with his person. It is important that the distinction between assault and battery be borne in mind. If I clench my fist in such a way as to put someone in reasonable apprehension of imminent contact with their person then I commit the tort of assault, but, if I actually punch that person, then I commit the tort of battery.

There is no requirement that the fear of imminent physical contact be produced by the words of the defendant. Indeed, in the example which we considered above, the fear of physical contact was produced by the clenching of the fist and not by any spoken words (for an example of the tort being committed without any words being spoken see *Mortin* v *Shoppee* (1828) 3 C & P 373). There is more controversy over whether the tort can be committed by words alone. The difficulty can be traced back to dicta of Holroyd J in *R* v *Meade and Belt* (1823) 1 Lew CC 184 when he said that 'no words or singing are equivalent to an assault'. The absurdity of this view has been demonstrated by commentators (see Trindade (1982) 2 OJLS 211, 231–2 and Handford (1976) 54 Can Bar Rev 563). For example, it means that the tort of assault cannot be committed in darkness where the plaintiff is put in fear of a battery by words which he hears but which are uttered by a person whom he cannot see. The better view, it is submitted, is that, where the words are sufficient of themselves to put the plaintiff in reasonable apprehension of a battery, then the tort of assault has been committed. Support for such a proposition can be found in the case of *R* v *Wilson* [1955] 1 WLR 493.

While it is unclear whether words alone can constitute an assault, words can negative what would otherwise be an assault. Such was the case in *Tuberville* v *Savage* (1669) 1 Mod Rep 3. The plaintiff and the defendant were involved in a heated argument. The defendant, while placing his hand on his sword, said that 'if it were not assize time, I would not take such language from you'. It was held that no assault had been committed by the defendant because his words negatived the apprehension of immediate contact which was aroused by him placing his hand on his sword. The statement made in *Tuberville* must be distinguished from a conditional threat because the latter may be actionable as an assault. For example if I said 'I'll break your neck unless you give me ten pounds' that could constitute an assault because it is a conditional threat and one which could give rise to reasonable apprehension of a battery (see *Read* v *Coker* (1853) 13 CB 850).

Although the plaintiff must be in reasonable apprehension of physical contact there is no requirement that he actually be afraid of the defendant. It is sufficient that he expects physical contact to take place. The apprehension of physical contact must be a reasonable one and it must be one of imminent contact. Thus the tort is not committed where the defendant does not have the capacity to carry out the battery. So, where the defendant threatens the plaintiff as the former's train leaves the station, the plaintiff cannot sue the defendant for assault because the fact that the train is leaving the station removes the defendant's present capability of carrying out a battery.

It is clearly an assault to place a loaded gun at the head of another, but what is the position where the pistol is unloaded? In *Blake* v *Barnard* (1840) 9 C & P 626 Lord Abinger CB was of the opinion that if the pistol was unloaded then no assault was committed. However in the criminal case of *R* v *St George* (1840) 9 C & P 483 Parke B stated that it was his opinion that to point an unloaded gun at another could constitute an assault at common law. It is submitted that the latter view is the preferable one and that provided that the plaintiff reasonably believes that the gun is loaded and that he is in danger of being shot then the tort has been committed.

In *Stephens* v *Myers* (1830) 4 C & P 349 it was held that the tort of assault had been committed when the defendant sought to punch the plaintiff but was physically restrained by a third party. It was held that, although the defendant was unsuccessful in his attempted battery, the tort of assault had been committed because the plaintiff was put in fear of a battery and, but for the intervention of the third party, the defendant had the means to carry out the battery.

24.4 False imprisonment

This tort is committed when the defendant intentionally causes the plaintiff's freedom to be totally restrained or causes the plaintiff to be confined within a particular limited area. The tort can be committed by making a wrongful arrest, by detaining someone for longer than is justifiable or simply by preventing someone from leaving a room.

For many years there has been some controversy as to whether or not the plaintiff must be aware of the restriction upon his freedom. There were two conflicting cases on the point. The first case was *Herring* v *Boyle* (1834) 1 Cr M & R 377. A headmaster refused to allow a mother to take her son home for the school holidays because she had not paid his fees for the term. It was held that the tort of false imprisonment was not committed because there was no evidence that the boy was aware of any restriction upon his freedom.

On the other hand a different result was reached in the case of *Meering* v *Graham-White Aviation Co* (1919) 122 LT 44. The plaintiff was suspected of stealing some varnish from the defendants' factory. He was taken to the defendant company's offices and two of the works policemen remained close to him while he was questioned. In an action for false imprisonment the defendants argued that the plaintiff was unaware that he had been imprisoned and so it was impossible for the tort to have been committed. This argument was rejected by the Court of Appeal. Atkin LJ stated that:

> 'A person could be imprisoned without his knowing it. I think that a person can be imprisoned while he is asleep, while he is in a state of drunkenness, while he is unconscious, and while he is a lunatic ... Of course, the damages might be diminished and would be affected by the question whether he was conscious of it or not.'

This conflict of authority was, however, finally resolved (albeit obiter) by the House of Lords in *Murray* v *Ministry of Defence* [1988] 2 All ER 521. Lord Griffiths said that *Herring* was an 'extraordinary' case and that he could not believe that the case would be decided the same way today. He expressly approved of the judgment of Atkin LJ in *Meering*, stating that it was not difficult to envisage circumstances in which a plaintiff would suffer harm from false imprisonment even though he was unaware of the fact that he had been imprisoned (for example the case of a two–day–old baby locked in a bank vault). The knowledge of the plaintiff is therefore not relevant to the existence of the cause of action but to the recoverability of damages. Where the plaintiff is unaware of the fact that he has been falsely imprisoned and has suffered no harm he will normally only recover nominal damages. Lord Griffiths considered redefining the scope of the tort by adopting the rule contained in the American Law Institute's Restatement of the Law of Torts ((1965) s35 p52) that the plaintiff must be conscious of the confinement or be harmed by it, but he rejected this saying that:

> 'The law attaches supreme importance to the liberty of the individual and if he suffers a wrongful interference with that liberty it should remain actionable even without proof of special damage.'

The tort is only committed where the plaintiff's liberty is totally restrained. In *Bird* v *Jones* (1845) 7 QB 742 the defendant wrongfully roped off a section of the public footpath at Hammersmith Bridge. The plaintiff was stopped by the defendant and told that he could not climb over the ropes as he made his way along the footpath. He brought an action for false imprisonment. His action was unsuccessful because his liberty had not been completely restrained. Only part of the footpath was roped off and the plaintiff was free to go back the way he had come, cross the road and then proceed in the direction in which he was travelling.

Although the tort is not committed when the plaintiff has an avenue of escape open to him, that means of escape must be a reasonable one. The means of escape will not be reasonable if it involves danger to the plaintiff.

The restriction upon the liberty of the plaintiff must be unlawful before the tort can be committed. This requirement has given rise to difficulty in cases where prisoners have been confined in their cells in breach of prison rules. The Court of Appeal in *Weldon* v *Home Office* [1990] 3 WLR 465 held that, although it is true to say that a prisoner has been, to a large extent, deprived of his liberty upon imprisonment, he does retain a residual liberty which is to be exercised in accordance with prison rules and he can therefore bring an action for false imprisonment when that residual liberty is intentionally and without justification denied to him. But on appeal the House of Lords rejected the approach adopted by the Court of Appeal and held ([1992] 1 AC 58) that a prisoner does not have a residual liberty because his whole life is regulated by the prison regime. Although the conditions under which he is detained may be changed this does not deprive the prisoner of any liberty which he had not already lost when initially confined. This principle may, however, be the subject of two exceptions. The first is that both Lord Ackner and Lord Bridge held that a prisoner may have a residual liberty as against a fellow prisoner so that he can bring a claim for false imprisonment if he is locked in a confined space by a fellow prisoner (Lord Jauncey left this particular point open). Secondly, Lord Bridge stated that a prison officer who acted in bad faith by deliberately subjecting a prisoner to restraint which he knew he had no authority to impose may render himself personally liable to an action for false imprisonment because he lacks the authority of the governor and does not have the protection of s12 of the Prison Act 1952. The Home Office would not, however, be vicariously liable for such deliberate wrongdoing of the officer. The House of Lords also held that an otherwise lawful imprisonment could not be rendered unlawful because of the intolerable conditions of detention (thus disapproving of the dictum of Ackner LJ in *Middleweek* v *Chief Constable of Merseyside* [1992] 1 AC 179 which was to the contrary). But they held that, where the conditions of life were intolerable, the plaintiff would have available to him a public law remedy in the form of judicial review and may also have private law remedies in the form of an action in negligence (although see *H* v *Home Office* (1992) The Independent 5 May where the plaintiff's negligence claim failed), assault or misfeasance in the exercise of a public office (provided the requirements of these torts are satisfied). But no action will lie in false imprisonment.

The requirement that the restriction upon the liberty of the plaintiff be unlawful has given rise to difficulty in cases where occupiers purport to place restrictions upon the terms on which people can leave their premises. The law does, however, allow an occupier of premises lawfully to impose certain restrictions upon persons leaving his premises. Thus, in *Robinson* v *Balmain Ferry Co Ltd* [1910] AC 295 the defendants charged one penny on entry to their ferry and one penny on exit. The plaintiff paid his penny to enter the ferry but changed his mind about travelling on the ferry. But he refused to pay the penny to get off the ferry and so the defendants refused to allow him to leave. It was held that this refusal to allow the plaintiff to leave without paying the penny was not false imprisonment because the condition that a penny be paid was a reasonable one to impose. It should not be thought, however, that occupiers have carte blanche to lay down any conditions they please as to the terms on which a visitor may leave the premises. In *Sunbolf* v *Alford* (1838) 3 M & W 248 an innkeeper was held to have committed the tort of false imprisonment when he locked the plaintiff in when he refused to pay his bill.

A similar issue was at stake in the case of *Herd* v *Wearsdale Steel, Coal and Coke Co Ltd* [1915] AC 67. The plaintiff, who was a coal miner, refused, in breach of contract, to continue with his work and he demanded that he be taken up to the surface immediately. The defendants, who were his employers, refused to do this until it was time for the cage to come back to the surface at the end of the shift. As a result the plaintiff had to wait some time to get back to the surface and he alleged that this constituted false imprisonment. It was held that there was no false imprisonment as the plaintiff had voluntarily gone down the mine and the defendants were under no obligation to bring him back up until the end of the shift. This case could also be explained on the ground that it was sought to make the defendants liable for an omission and this could not be done in the absence of a positive duty on the defendants to come to the aid of the plaintiff. But both this case and the *Robinson* case have been criticised on the ground that they allow plaintiffs to be imprisoned on the ground of a mere breach of contract (see Dias and Markesinis *Tort Law* (2nd ed) pp242–3).

There are a number of defences to the tort of false imprisonment. It is a defence to show that the plaintiff consented to his confinement (see on consent the discussion at 24.2). The major defence is, however, that the plaintiff was lawfully arrested. The powers of arrest are contained within the Police and Criminal Evidence Act 1984. By s24(4) anyone may arrest without warrant anyone who is in the act of committing an arrestable offence, or anyone he reasonably suspects to be committing such an offence. This power does not extend to the situation whee the offence has actually been committed, but s24(5) allows any person to arrest without warrant anyone who has committed the offence or anyone he reasonably believes committed the offence. Thus s24(5) provides a defence where the arrester arrests the wrong person, provided that an arrestable offence has actually been committed. Sub-section 24(4) and 24(5) apply to any person, but by s24(6) a police officer has wider powers in that he may arrest without warrant anyone he reasonably suspects of committing an arrestable offence, even though no offence has been committed. Thus PACE preserves the trap in *Walters* v *W H Smith Ltd* [1914] 1 KB 595 in that a private person who arrests another after the offence has been committed must prove not only reasonable suspicion but that someone (not necessarily the person arrested) committed the offence. So, for example, a store detective may be liable in false imprisonment if he arrests a person on reasonable suspicion of theft and that person is subsequently acquitted in the criminal trial. The recent case of *R* v *Self* [1992] 1 WLR 657 is an example of the trap in action.

Note that a person is not liable for false imprisonment when he merely gives information to the police, and does not himself instigate or procure it. Thus in

Davidson v *Chief Constable of North Wales Police* (1993) The Times 26 April a store detective who incorrectly informed police that the plaintiff had been involved in shoplifting was not liable where the officers, in the exercise of their own discretion, had arrested and detained the plaintiff.

24.5 The rule in *Wilkinson* v *Downton*

In the case of *Wilkinson* v *Downton* [1897] 2 QB 57 the defendant, in pursuance of a practical joke, falsely told the plaintiff that her husband had been in an accident and that both his legs had been broken. The plaintiff believed that this story was true and was greatly upset and, in consequence, suffered nervous shock. The defendant was held liable for this nervous shock. In finding the defendant liable Wright J made the following statement of principle:

> 'The defendant has ... wilfully done an act calculated to cause physical damage to the female plaintiff, ie, to infringe her legal right to personal safety, and has thereby in fact caused physical harm to her. That proposition, without more, appears to me to state a good cause of action, there being no justification alleged for the act.'

The only case in which this principle has been applied in England is the case of *Janvier* v *Sweeney* [1919] 2 KB 316, so it is difficult to establish the limits of the principle. However it is clear that the defendant must have intended to cause some shock to his victim, although it is no defence to show that the shock was greater than was anticipated. It must also be shown that the defendant's act was reasonably likely to cause shock to a normal person, unless the defendant knew of the plaintiff's particular susceptibility, and that the plaintiff's shock is objectively verifiable.

24.6 Conclusion

There is obviously a considerable degree of overlap with the criminal law in relation to these torts concerned with trespass to the person. There has, however, been a relative decline in the number of tort actions being brought in respect of trespass to the person. There are a number of possible reasons for this. One is that, if the trespass is committed unintentionally, the plaintiff is likely to bring an action in negligence rather than trespass. Another reason is that, where the sum of money at stake is rather trivial, the plaintiff may decide not to bother with bringing an action, especially where the defendant is not worth pursuing. The criminal court also has a discretion under the Powers of Criminal Courts Act 1973 to make a direct compensation order in favour of the victim when a person has been convicted of an offence. Lastly account must be taken of the existence of the Criminal Injuries Compensation Scheme. This scheme operated for many years on an ex gratia basis, making payments, in certain cases, to the victims of violent crimes. But far-reaching reforms have been introduced in ss108–117 of the Criminal Justice Act 1988, which puts the scheme on a statutory basis, giving to those applicants who fall within the scope of the Act an enforceable legal right to claim compensation (discussed by Duff (1989) 52 MLR 518).

It is not all crimes which give to victims a right to claim compensation under the Act. In an effort to provide some degree of certainty, s109(3) lists certain offences (such as rape or assault) which, in principle, give rise to a claim for compensation and, added to that list, is any other offence which 'requires proof of intent to cause death or personal injury or recklessness as to whether death or personal injury is caused' (s109(1)(a)(ii)). Thus injury received as a result of criminal damage to property will not generate a claim under the Act. It should be noted that the claimant must satisfy the Criminal Injuries Compensation Board, not the police or the court, that a relevant offence has been committed or that the injuries have been suffered as a result of the commission of such an offence. Thus compensation may be claimed even though no-one has been convicted or charged with the relevant offence. The availability of these alternative remedies obviously makes the pursuance of a civil remedy less attractive to the victims of crimes.

However, it has been argued that we should not abolish the civil action because it still plays a valuable role in compensating victims. Trindade points out ((1982) 2 OJLS 211, 214–6) that to rely exclusively upon the Criminal Injuries Compensation Board may be a retrograde step because the Board may conclude that there was no crime when there clearly was a civil battery and he has pointed out that the sums payable to the victims of crime by the Board tend to be lower than the sums which would be awarded in a civil action. These arguments adduced by Trindade depend for their force upon the defendant being able to meet the judgment, but Professor Atiyah has estimated that the number of defendants able to satisfy judgment is perhaps as low as one in a thousand (*Accidents, Compensation and the Law* (4th ed) p291). So the arguments put forward by Trindade are not particularly persuasive. However it is submitted that the reason for retaining these torts lies not in connection with the criminal law, but in relation to their constitutional significance. Some of the recent cases, such as *Collins* v *Wilcock* (above), have concerned the limits placed upon the power of police officers to interfere with the liberty of the subject and we have had cause to note, during the course of this chapter, the paramount importance which must be attached to the preservation of individual liberty. It is submitted that these torts must be preserved for their role (which admittedly at times is a small role) in preserving individual liberty.

25

Trespass to Land

25.1 Introduction

25.2 Possession

25.3 Interference with possession

25.4 Nature of the interference

25.5 Defences

25.6 Remedies

25.1 Introduction

Trespass to land is a tort which has existed in England for many centuries. It is often thought of as a crime rather than as a tort, but its primary significance is, in fact, as a tort. It is only exceptionally that a trespass to land constitutes a criminal offence (see ss6–10 of the Criminal Law Act 1977).

Trespass to land has been defined by Winfield and Jolowicz (*Winfield and Jolowicz on Tort* (13th ed) p359) as the 'unjustifiable interference with the possession of land'. It is a tort which is actionable per se, which means that it is not dependent upon the plaintiff showing that he has suffered damage as the result of the trespass of the defendant. In protecting the plaintiff's interest in the peaceful enjoyment of his property, trespass performs a function similar to that of the tort of nuisance (see chapters 18 and 19). The two torts differ in that damage is normally an essential element in nuisance, whereas it is not in trespass and trespass is concerned with direct interference with the plaintiff's enjoyment of his property, whereas nuisance is concerned with indirect or consequential damage to his property.

25.2 Possession

Trespass to land is founded upon interference with the plaintiff's possession of his property. It should be noted that it is not ownership which gives rise to a cause of action in trespass, but possession. One consequence of the requirement that the plaintiff be in possession of the land is that, where the plaintiff is a lessor of land who has given up possession both in fact and at law, he can only bring an action in trespass where the damage which is done to the property does permanent damage to the property with the result that damage is done to his reversionary interest in the property (*Jones v Llanrwst UDC* [1911] 1 Ch 393). However, where the owner brings an action in trespass against a wrongdoer who claims to be in possession, the courts are willing to hold that the slightest action by the owner which evinces an intention to take possession is sufficient to maintain an action in trespass (see *Ocean Estates Ltd* v *Pinder* [1969] 2 AC 19).

The fact that a right of action is based upon possession means that use of the land is not sufficient of itself to constitute possession. The person who has a licence to occupy the land does not possess the land for the purposes of the tort of trespass, he simply has the use of the property (*Hill v Tupper* (1863) 2 H & C 121). Nor does it appear that a lodger or a guest in a hotel has possession for this purpose (*Allan* v *Liverpool Overseers* (1874) LR 9 QB 180).

The plaintiff's possession of the land need not amount to possession at law, it can be satisfied by possession in fact. Possession in fact does not require that the plaintiff be in possession of the property for 24 hours of every day. So, for example, the plaintiff who leaves the property to go out on an errand or to go to work still remains in possession in fact. Possession in fact covers cases where the plaintiff has no actual property interest in the land affected but does actually have possession of the land or is otherwise in control of it. Thus a plaintiff who had possession under a lease which was wholly void by statute was held to have possession for the purpose of the tort of trespass (see *Graham* v *Peat* (1861) 1 East 244).

Where the true owner does not have possession of the land then the owner cannot bring an action in trespass, subject to the rule laid down in *Ocean Estates Ltd* v *Pinder* (above). However, once the person who has the immediate right to possess actually takes possession of the property then, by virtue of the doctrine of trespass by relation, his possession is back-dated to the date at which he acquired the right to possess, so as to give him the right to sue in respect of trespasses which were actually committed while he was out of possession (*Dunlop* v *Macedo* (1891) 8 TLR 43).

25.3 Interference with possession

There must be some interference with the plaintiff's possession of the property. This interference can occur in many ways. However, the interference must cause direct and immediate interference with the plaintiff's possession of the property. The most common way of committing the tort is for the defendant to enter on to the land of the plaintiff without the plaintiff's permission. The tort can even be committed by placing something on the plaintiff's land; for example the placing of a ladder against the plaintiff's wall without his permission has been held to be a trespass (*Westripp* v *Baldock* [1938] 2 All ER 799, see also *Gregory* v *Piper* (1829) 9

B & C 591). It is not necessary that the defendant's initial entry be without the permission of the plaintiff; the tort can be committed by a person who abuses his permission to be on the land or who refuses to leave the land when asked to do so (see *Robson v Hallett* [1967] 2 QB 393, discussed further at 25.5).

The interference which constitutes the trespass need not be of a 'one-off' nature; it can be of a continuing nature. Where the trespass is of a continuing nature, then it gives rise to a new cause of action from day to day for as long as the trespass lasts. This can be seen in the case of *Holmes v Wilson* (1839) 10 Ad & El 503. The defendants installed buttresses to prop up a road which they had noticed was sinking, but to install the buttresses they had to trespass on the plaintiff's land and the buttresses were actually installed on the plaintiff's land. The plaintiff sued the defendants in trespass and obtained £25 damages. He then brought a further action when the defendants failed to remove the buttresses but was met with the claim that his action was time barred. This argument was rejected by the court. It was held that this was a case of continuing trespass, which continued for as long as the buttresses were on the land, and so the plaintiff could bring an action in trespass until the buttresses were removed. It is also a continuing trespass to fail to remove something which was initially on the land lawfully but has ceased to be there lawfully, for example, because the permission to keep it there had expired (see *Konskier v Goodman Ltd* [1928] 1 KB 421).

These are the general principles to be applied in considering whether an interference with possession constitutes a trespass. However, it is necessary to give separate consideration to some particular forms of interference which have given rise to difficulty.

Trespass on the highway

A person can use the highway for the purpose of passage and for travelling from one point to another. However, where the highway is used for some purpose which is not reasonably incidental to the purpose of passage, the user of the highway may commit the tort of trespass against the person who is in possession of the highway. This can be seen in the case of *Hickman v Maisey* [1900] 1 QB 752. The defendant, who was a 'racing tout', was in the habit of walking up and down a short stretch of the highway and watching trials of racehorses taking place on the plaintiff's land so that he could see the form of the horses. It was held that the defendant was abusing his right of passage on the highway and that, as the plaintiff was the owner of the subsoil under the highway, he could maintain an action in trespass against the defendant. In *Harrison v Duke of Rutland* [1893] 1 QB 142 the defendant stood on the highway close to the plaintiff's pheasant shoot and opened and shut his umbrella and waved his handkerchief so as to scare the pheasants away. It was held that the defendant was liable to the plaintiff for trespass because his activities were not reasonably incidental to the purpose of passage and the plaintiff was the possessor of the highway.

Trespass to the subsoil

The trespass need not be committed against the surface of the land itself; it can also be committed against the subsoil. This can be seen in the case of *Cox* v *Moulsey* (1848) 5 CB 533, where the defendant was held to be liable in trespass to the plaintiff when he drove a stake into the subsoil which was owned by the plaintiff. So where the possession of the surface and the subsoil is in the hands of different persons it is only the owner of the subsoil who can maintain an action in respect of trespass to the subsoil and vice versa.

Trespass to airspace

It was once thought to be the case that trespass could not be committed in the airspace above a person's land unless there was contact with the plaintiff's land (see *Pickering* v *Rudd* (1815) 4 Camp 219). This view was, however, rejected in the case of *Kelsen* v *Imperial Tobacco Co Ltd* [1957] 2 QB 334. The defendant erected an advertising sign over his own property but the sign also overhung the plaintiff's property by some eight inches. It was held that a trespass had been committed and the defendant was therefore ordered to remove the sign.

However, it is not every intrusion into the plaintiff's airspace that will give rise to an action in trespass. It must be shown that the intrusion was at such a height that it interfered with the ordinary use and enjoyment of the property and the structures erected on the property. In *Lord Bernstein of Leigh* v *Skyviews & General Ltd* [1978] QB 479 the plaintiff, who was the owner of a country house in Kent, brought an action in trespass against the defendants, who were in the business of taking aerial pictures of property and who had taken an aerial photograph of the plaintiff's property. The plaintiff asserted that he was the owner of the airspace above his property and that he had not given the defendants permission to enter that airspace. The plaintiff relied upon the Latin maxim cujus est solum ejus est usque ad coelum et ad infernos, which means that the owner of the land owns the space above it up to heaven and the space below it down to hell. However, Griffiths J was unable to find authority for the proposition that a landowner's rights in respect of the airspace above his property extended to an unlimited height. He said that the Latin maxim, if applied literally, would lead to the 'absurdity of a trespass being committed by a satellite every time it passes over a suburban garden'. So it was held that the plaintiff's rights only extended to such a height as was necessary for the ordinary use and enjoyment of his property and that it did not extend to the flight of an aeroplane many hundreds of feet above his property.

In *Anchor Brewhouse Developments Ltd* v *Berkley House (Docklands Developments) Ltd* [1987] 2 EGLR 173 Scott J gave further consideration to the judgment of Griffiths J in *Bernstein*. The defendants, while developing a prestigious site in London, hired some cranes, the booms of which hung over into the plaintiffs' airspace. The defendants argued that it was 'virtually essential' for the commercial development of the site for such cranes to be used. Nevertheless the plaintiffs sought an injunction to restrain the instrusion of these booms into their airspace. Scott J held that the invasion of these booms did indeed constitute a trespass and that the plaintiffs were entitled to their injunction. The defendants had argued that, as in *Bernstein*, the plaintiffs' rights only extended to such a height as was necessary for the enjoyment of their property and that on the facts the intrusion of the cranes did not interfere with the plaintiffs' ordinary use and enjoyment of their property. However, Scott J held that *Bernstein* was confined to the particular issue of overflying aircraft and that it could not be applied to the case where a static structure on the defendants' land hung over on to the land of the plaintiffs. In the latter case Scott J held that the extent of proprietary rights enjoyed by landowners ought to be clear and that this could best be achieved by holding that, apart from the special case of overflying aircraft, every unauthorised intrusion into the airspace of another constitutes a trespass (see further McKendrick (1988) NLJ 23).

It should, however, be noted in this context that s76(1) of the Civil Aviation Act 1982 provides that no action in trespass or nuisance shall lie:

' ... by reason only of the flight of an aircraft over any property at a height above the ground which, having regard to wind, weather and all the circumstances of the case is reasonable, or the ordinary incidents of such flight ...'

However s76(1) must be read in the light of s76(2) which provides that:

'Where material loss or damage is caused to any person or property on land or water by, or by a person in, or an article, animal or person falling from, an aircraft while in flight, taking off or landing, then unless loss or damage was caused or contributed to by the negligence of the person by whom it was suffered, damages in respect of the loss or damage shall be recoverable without proof of negligence or intention or other cause of action, as if the loss or damage had been caused by the wilful act, neglect, or default of the owner of the aircraft.'

Trespass ab initio

Where the defendant's entry on to the plaintiff's land is with the authority of the law (rather than with the authority of the plaintiff) and the defendant subsequently abuses that right, there is an old rule of the common law which states that he becomes a trespasser ab initio, that is from the moment he enters on to the plaintiff's land. The rule is well established in the older authorities and only applies to wrongful acts and does not apply to non-feasance (see *The Six Carpenters' Case* (1610) 8 Co Rep 146a and *Elias* v *Pasmore* [1934] 2 KB 164). However this rule was recently considered by the Court of Appeal in *Chic Fashions (West Wales) Ltd* v *Jones* [1968] 2 QB 299. The police entered the plaintiffs' shop with a warrant to look for particular merchandise which was believed to be stolen. They did not find these goods but they did find other goods which they erroneously believed to have been stolen. The plaintiffs brought an action in trespass against the police officers in removing the goods not covered by the warrant. The action was unsuccessful on the ground that it was held that the police had the authority, when entering premises with a warrant, to remove anything which they believed to have been stolen. Lord Denning went further and criticised the doctrine of trespass ab initio on the ground that it rendered unlawful an act which was lawful at the time at which it was done. So the doctrine has been subjected to some criticism recently but it is unlikely to be abandoned and, indeed, Lord Denning himself applied the doctrine in the later case of *Cinnamond* v *British Airports Authority* [1980] 2 All ER 368.

25.4 Nature of the interference

Trespass is a tort of intention in the sense that the defendant must have intended to enter upon the land where the trespass was committed; it is not a tort of intention in the sense that the defendant must have intended to commit the tort of trespass. Therefore it is no defence to show that the defendant was unaware that the land on to which he had entered was land which belonged to someone else (*Conway* v *George Wimpey & Co Ltd* [1951] 2 KB 266).

However where the defendant can show that he had no intention of entering upon the land then he has not committed the tort. Thus the tort was not committed in *Smith* v *Stone* (1647) Style 65 where the defendant was dumped on the plaintiff's land by a gang of men. It was held that he had not committed the tort because there was no voluntary act on his part. Where the defendant enters the plaintiff's land under duress the tort can still be committed because his act in going on to the plaintiff's land remains a voluntary one (*Gilbert* v *Stone* (1647) Style 72).

It remains unclear whether trespass to land can be committed negligently, but, as was the case in trespass to the person (see 24.2), there is a trend in favour of holding that such actions must be brought in negligence and that an action in trespass may only be brought where the defendant's act was an intentional one (*Letang* v *Cooper* [1965] 1 QB 232). However, in *League Against Cruel Sports Ltd* v *Scott* [1985] 2 All ER 489, Park J appeared to be of the opinion that trespass could be committed negligently. The plaintiffs, who were opposed to blood sports, owned a sanctuary for wild deer and refused the defendant permission to come on to their land during a local hunt. Despite this fact the hunt strayed on to the plaintiffs' land on seven occasions and so the plaintiffs sought an injunction to restrain this trespass. It was held that the master of the hunt was liable in trespass if he knew that there was a real risk of hounds entering on to the plaintiffs' land and if he intentionally or negligently permitted the hounds to enter the plaintiffs' land. If this decision is correct then it means that trespass to land can be committed negligently and that the approach of Lord Denning in *Letang* does not apply to all forms of trespass.

25.5 Defences

There are a number of defences to the tort of trespass. The principal defences are as follows.

Licence

There is no trespass committed where the defendant enters on to the plaintiff's land with the plaintiff's express or implied permission. Such a person is deemed to have a licence to enter upon the land of the plaintiff and it is only where that licence is exceeded by the defendant or the licence is lawfully revoked by the plaintiff that trespass can be committed. Even where the defendant's licence has been lawfully revoked by the plaintiff, the defendant has a reasonable time in which to leave the premises before he becomes a trespasser (see *Robson* v *Hallett* (above)).

The extent to which the defendant's licence can be lawfully revoked depends on the type of licence which the defendant has. Where his licence is a gratuitous one then it is clear that it may be revoked at any time on the giving of reasonable notice. The position is less clear where the defendant has a contractual right to be on the premises because the contractual licence may or may not be revocable. A licence may be irrevocable where a breach of the licence by the grantor would be restrained by granting an equitable remedy to the licensee. Where the licence is revocable the licensee will be confined to an action for breach of contract, but where the licence is held to be irrevocable any attempt to remove the licensee may give rise to an action in battery and the possibility of substantial damages. Where the defendant's licence is for a limited period of time and for a specific purpose, such as watching a film, then the licence is likely to be irrevocable for that limited period or particular purpose. Such was the case in *Hurst* v *Picture Theatres Ltd* [1915] 1 KB 1. The plaintiff paid to enter the defendant's cinema. When he sat down in the seat which he had paid for he was asked to leave the premises by one of the defendant's employees, who believed that he had not paid for his seat. The plaintiff refused to leave and was eventually ejected by the defendant's doorman. It was held that the defendant had no right to eject the plaintiff in this manner. The contract between the parties gave the plaintiff an irrevocable licence to be in the cinema for the duration of the performance and the defendant could not revoke the plaintiff's licence unless the plaintiff had exceeded the terms of the licence, which he had not. A licence will also be irrevocable where it is combined with an interest in the land (*Thomas* v *Sorrell* (1672) Vaughan 330).

Lawful authority

Where the defendant has lawful authority to enter upon the land of the plaintiff then the defendant does not commit a trespass. For example the police have powers under the Police and Criminal Evidence Act 1984 to enter premises and to search them. Another example of a person having lawful authority to enter upon the land of the plaintiff arises where the defendant enters the land pursuant to a public right of way. The defendant may also have a right at common law to enter upon the plaintiff's land, for example, to abate a nuisance or the power of a landlord to enter premises to distrain for rent.

Necessity

It is a defence to show that it was necessary for the defendant to enter upon the plaintiff's land. The scope of this defence was considered by Taylor J in *Rigby* v *Chief Constable of Northamptonshire* [1985] 2 All ER 985. The police fired a canister of CS gas into a building in order to force a dangerous psychopath to come out of the building so that he could be arrested. As the result of the use of the CS gas the plaintiff's shop was burnt out. It was held that the defence of necessity was available in an action in trespass provided that there was no negligence on the part of the defendant in contributing to the state of necessity. The defendant was, therefore, entitled to rely on the defence of necessity because of the need to arrest the psychopath. However, the plaintiff was held to be entitled to recover damages on the ground that the defendant had been negligent in firing the CS gas canister without any fire-fighting equipment being present.

25.6 Remedies

The plaintiff has available to him a number of remedies against a defendant who has committed a trespass. The principal remedies are as follows.

Damages

The plaintiff may seek a remedy in damages but, where the trespass is a trivial one, then damages will be nominal. Where damage is done to the plaintiff's land then the measure of damages is the diminution in value of the plaintiff's land and not the cost of restoring the land to the state it was in before the trespass. There is a possibility that the plaintiff may be able to recover aggravated or exemplary damages where the case is an appropriate one for the grant of such a remedy. Such was the case in *Drane* v *Evangelou* [1978] 1 WLR 455 where the plaintiff was thrown out of his lodgings after obtaining a reduction in his rent through the Rent Officer and the defendant calculated that it was cheaper to refuse to comply with any injunction than to take the plaintiff back. It was held that this was an appropriate case for the granting of £10,000 exemplary damages to teach the defendant a lesson.

Injunction

Where the trespass is of a continuing nature or the trespass has been threatened but not yet committed then the plaintiff may seek an injunction to restrain the trespass or to restrain any further trespasses. The general rule is that the plaintiff is prima facie entitled to an injunction in the case of a continuing trespass. This gives rise to difficulty in a case such as *Anchor Brewhouse Developments Ltd* v

Berkley House (Docklands Developments) Ltd (above) where the present rules enable a plaintiff whose airspace has been invaded to hold a property developer to ransom. Scott J was clearly worried about the practical implications of his judgment, and he concluded by saying that it would be 'convenient if the Court had power, in order to enable property developments to be expeditiously and economically completed, to allow, on proper commercial terms, some use to be made by the developers of the land of neighbours'. However, he did not think that such a reform was within the competence of the courts, and he was of the opinion that resort would have to be had to Parliament to implement such a reform. On the other hand, it is arguable such a reform is within the competence of the courts, and that it could be achieved by the courts demonstrating a greater willingness to exercise their discretion to award damages in lieu of an injunction (see further McKendrick (1988) NLJ 23 and 30.23).

Re-entry

A person who is entitled to possession may re-enter the land either personally or through an employee or agent and will not incur liability in tort where reasonable force is used to remove the other party or his property (*Hemmings* v *Stoke Poges Golf Club* [1920] 1 KB 720). However, where the plaintiff forcibly obtains re-entry to his land then a criminal offence may be committed under s6 of the Criminal Law Act 1977. In *Burton* v *Winters* [1993] 1 WLR 1077 the Court of Appeal held that self-redress for trespass to land by encroachment was a summary remedy that was only justified in clear and simple cases or in an emergency.

Mesne profits

The plaintiff who has been wrongfully dispossessed of his land may claim in an action for mesne profits for the profits which the defendant has obtained from his occupation of the plaintiff's property, for damages for the deterioration of the property and for the reasonable costs of obtaining possession. The plaintiff need not show that he would have profited by renting the land out to someone else during the period of the defendant's occupation (*Swordheath Properties Ltd* v *Tabet* [1979] 1 All ER 240). The plaintiff can bring an action for possession and mesne profits in the same action (RSC Ord 15 r1), or he can sue for mesne profits after obtaining possession of the land or he can claim for mesne profits alone where his interest in the land has since been terminated.

Ejection

A person who has been dispossessed may bring an action for ejectment. A plaintiff is only entitled to such an order where he can establish that he has an immediate right to possession (see further *Winfield and Jolowicz on Tort* (13th ed) pp371–2).

Distress damage feasant

If a chattel is unlawfully on the plaintiff's land and has done actual damage to the plaintiff's property, the plaintiff may retain the property until the owner pays, or offers to pay, compensation for the damage which was done. This action has been abolished in relation to animals by the Animals Act 1971 (see further chapter 22). This remedy does not give the plaintiff the right to sell the property, nor does it give him the right to use the property. When the defendant tenders a reasonable sum by way of compensation then the plaintiff must accept the sum and return the chattel to the defendant.

26

Deceit

26.1 Introduction

26.2 False statement of fact

26.3 Knowledge of the falsity of the statement

26.4 Intention that the statement be acted upon

26.5 The plaintiff must act on the statement

26.6 Damage to the plaintiff

26.1 Introduction

In *Pasley* v *Freeman* (1789) 3 TR 51 it was established that a defendant who wilfully or recklessly makes a false statement to another with the intention that the other shall act in reliance upon the statement, and the person does so rely upon the statement to his injury, the defendant is liable to the plaintiff in the tort of deceit. The imposition of liability in the tort of deceit is separate from the liability which is imposed for negligent mis-statement (on which see 7.6). The latter is a liability which is truly based upon negligence, whereas deceit is concerned with the imposition of liability for misrepresentation which is made fraudulently.

There are five separate elements to the tort of deceit, which will be discussed in the remainder of this chapter.

26.2 False statement of fact

The plaintiff must show that the defendant made a false representation of fact. There are two separate elements to this requirement.

False representation

The first is that the representation must be false. This element can be split into two parts. The first is that the representation must be false, which is a question of fact.

The second is that there must be a representation. The representation may be by speech or by conduct. Thus in *R* v *Barnard* (1837) 7 C & P 784 the defendant went into a shop in Oxford wearing a gown and mortar board and by his appearance obtained credit. It was held that the defendant had, by conduct, represented that he was a member of the University. He was therefore held to be guilty of obtaining credit by false pretences when it was discovered that he was not a member of the University.

The requirement that there must be a representation underlines the fact that there is generally no duty of disclosure in English law and that liability is not imposed for failing to speak (see *Wales* v *Wadham* [1977] 1 WLR 199). However a duty of disclosure may arise in certain exceptional cases and liability imposed in deceit for a failure to speak.

The first situation where a duty of disclosure may exist is where a representation, which was initially true, later becomes false to the knowledge of the maker of the original statement. Such was the case in *With* v *O'Flanagan* [1936] Ch 575. The parties were involved in negotiations for the sale by the defendant to the plaintiff of the defendant's medical practice. When the negotiations commenced in January the practice was said to be worth £2,000. However, by the time that the contract was signed in May, the practice was virtually worthless because of the illness of the defendant in the intervening period. The defendant did not disclose this fact to the plaintiff at the time of signing the contract. The contract of sale was set aside on the ground that the vendor was under an obligation to disclose the change of circumstances to the plaintiff. It is unclear why there should be an obligation to disclose a change of circumstances when there is no general duty of disclosure. One justification may be that, once the defendant has started to speak, he must tell the whole story. This, however, does not work where the defendant makes the initial representation by conduct rather than by words. The only justification which can be offered for the principle laid down in *With* is that the representation, once made, is deemed to be a continuing representation, so that it becomes a misrepresentation when the defendant fails to correct the representation when it becomes false.

The second situation where a person may become under a duty of disclosure arises where the defendant's statement was literally true but was, in fact, misleading. Such was the case in *Notts Patent Brick and Tile Co* v *Butler* (1886) 16 QBD 778. The defendant's solicitor, in response to a question from the plaintiff purchaser, said that he did not know of any restrictive covenant which affected the land. Although it was true that he did not know of any restrictive covenant, this was because he had not bothered to look. It was held that this was a misrepresentation which entitled the plaintiff to rescind the contract because the statement was so misleading that it amounted to a misrepresentation.

The third situation where a person may come under a duty of disclosure arises in contracts uberrimae fidei. These contracts are contracts of the utmost good faith, such as insurance contracts, and there is imposed an obligation to disclose all material facts. The final case arises where there is a fiduciary relationship between the parties which is sufficient to impose a duty of disclosure upon the defendant.

Representation of existing fact

The second element is that the representation must be one of existing fact. Generally it can be assumed that a representation is one of existing fact unless it falls within one of the four following categories. The first is where the statement is a mere puff, such as slogan used by an advertiser to sell his products. It is a difficult question to determine whether such a statement is a statement of fact or whether it is a mere puff. In the case of *Dimmock* v *Hallett* (1866) LR 2 Ch App 21, the statement that land was 'fertile and improveable' was held to be a mere puff which could not constitute a statement of fact unless the circumstances of the case were extreme and a considerable part of the land was irredeemable. The second category is where the statement is one of opinion. Once again it can be difficult to distinguish between a statement of fact and a statement of opinion. In *Bisset* v *Wilkinson* [1927] AC 177 the statement by the vendor of land that he believed that the land which he was selling would support 2,000 sheep was subsequently found to be erroneous and the purchaser sought to rescind the agreement to sell the land on the ground that the defendant had misrepresented the carrying capacity of the land. It was held that he could not do so because the vendor's statement was one of opinion and not one of fact. The land had never been used for sheep farming before and the defendant's statement had simply been his opinion as to the number of sheep which the land could support. However, where the maker of the statement has special knowledge of the situation, then the court is likely to hold that the defendant must know of reasonable grounds to support his opinion and that a failure to possess such grounds may constitute a misstatement of fact. Thus in *Brown* v *Raphael* [1958] Ch 636 the defendant's solicitors stated that the annuitant was 'believed to have no aggregable estate', but they had no reasonable grounds for this statement. It was held that this statement was one of fact and not one of opinion because the statement was an extremely important one and also because the defendant's solicitors could have found out the true state of affairs themselves, whereas the plaintiff, who was the purchaser of the trust fund, was in no position to discover this information for himself. Where the defendant misrepresents what his true opinion is then this constitutes a misstatement of existing fact (see *Smith* v *Land and House Property Corporation* (1884) 28 Ch D 7).

Thirdly, a statement of intention does not constitute a statement of existing fact. However, if the defendant misrepresents his present intention then he makes a misrepresentation of existing fact. This can be seen in the case of *Edgington* v *Fitzmaurice* (1885) 29 Ch D 459. The defendants, who were company directors, stated in a company prospectus that their purpose behind issuing a subscription for debentures was to improve the company buildings and to expand the company business. The money was, in fact, required to pay off some of the company's debts. It was held that the defendants had misstated their purpose in issuing the debentures and that this constituted a misrepresentation of fact and so the defendants were held to be liable in deceit.

Fourthly, a statement of law does not constitute a statement of fact and so does not give rise to liability in deceit. However, it is not altogether clear in many cases whether the defendant has misstated the law or whether he has misstated a fact and the courts are likely to lean in favour of construing the misstatement as a misstatement of fact (see *West London Commercial Bank Ltd* v *Kitson* (1884) 13 QBD 360).

26.3 Knowledge of the falsity of the statement

The defendant must know that the statement is false or be reckless whether it be true or false. This was established in the famous decision of the House of Lords in *Derry* v *Peek* (1889) 14 App Cas 337, where it was held that a distinction must be drawn between unreasonableness of belief as a ground of action and unreasonableness of belief as evidence of dishonesty. The directors of a company issued a prospectus which stated that they had the right to run their trams on steam power. At that time it was necessary to get Board of Trade approval before it was possible to use steam power. The directors honestly believed that Board of Trade approval would be given as a matter of course. But the Board of Trade refused to give its approval and, as a consequence, the company was wound up. The plaintiff, who had bought shares in the company on the faith of the prospectus, brought an action against the directors in deceit. It was held by the House of Lords that the plaintiff did not have a cause of action in deceit. Lord Herschell stated that, in order to bring an action in deceit, fraud must be proved and nothing short of fraud would do. He then went on to say that fraud is proved when it is shown that a false statement has been made (i) knowingly, (ii) without belief in its truth, or (iii) recklessly, careless whether it be true or false.

The House in *Derry* took a very restrictive approach to the definition of fraud and made deceit a tort which it is very difficult to prove. In many cases it is easier for a plaintiff to bring an action in negligent misrepresentation at common law or to bring an action under s2 of the Misrepresentation Act 1967 than it is to bring an action in deceit. To bring an action in deceit it must therefore be shown that the defendant did not believe that his statement was true or was reckless whether it was true or false. Two points should be noted here. The first is that, in considering whether the defendant believed that his statement was true, the unreasonableness of his belief is only evidence that he did not believe that his statement was true; it is not a ground of action in itself. The second point relates to the meaning of the phrase 'reckless, careless whether it be true or false'. This phrase was considered by the Court of Appeal in *Angus* v *Clifford* [1891] 2 Ch 449. The defendants were company directors who purchased a gold mine and then issued a prospectus in which they stated that a report on the mine had been prepared by an engineer for the directors when, in fact, it had been prepared for the vendors of the mine. The defendants were held not to be liable to the plaintiff because they did not appreciate the importance of the words 'prepared for the directors'. Bowen LJ stated that 'careless whether it be true or false' did not mean careless in the duty of care sense. He said careless meant indifference to the truth or wilful disregard of the importance of the truth. Here the Court of Appeal can be seen to be attempting to draw a clear distinction between negligence and fraud and holding that carelessness, in the sense of a breach of the duty of care, does not give rise to a cause of action in deceit.

The last point which should be noted about the definition of fraud adopted by the House of Lords in *Derry* is that, once fraud is proved, the motive of the person who made the statement is irrelevant. This can be seen in the case of *Polhill* v *Walter* (1832) 3 B & Ad 114. The defendant purported to accept a bill of exchange on behalf of his principal, although he knew that he had no authority so to do. So the defendant knew that his statement was false but he had no intention of making a profit for himself; he simply believed that his principal would ratify his act. It was held that the defendant was liable in deceit because he had made a knowingly false representation and it did not matter that his motive in making that statement was an innocent one.

26.4 Intention that the statement be acted upon

The defendant must have made the false statement with the intention that it be acted upon. The only persons entitled to act on the statement are those persons or the class of persons whom the maker of the statement intended would act upon the statement. It is not, however, necessary to show that the defendant personally knew of the plaintiff. The easiest way of satisfying this requirement is to show that the statement was made to the plaintiff directly. This may, however, give rise to difficulty where the statement was made to a class of persons. This can be seen by contrasting the following two cases. The first one is *Peek* v *Gurney* (1873) LR 6 HL 377. The defendants issued a prospectus which misstated the true condition of the company. The plaintiff purchased shares in the company, but he did not purchase any shares in the first allotment made as the result of the issue of the prospectus. Instead he bought the shares at a later date on the Stock Exchange. It was held that the plaintiff was not entitled to succeed because the misstatement in the company prospectus was exhausted by the time that the plaintiff purchased his shares. The misstatement was only made to those persons who purchased shares in the initial allotment because it was to them, and only to them, that the prospectus was directed. A different approach was, however, taken in the second case of *Andrews* v *Mockford* [1896] 1 QB 372. The defendants made a false statement in a company prospectus and repeated that statement in a newspaper advertisement. The plaintiff bought the shares on the faith of the advertisement which, he believed, confirmed what was contained in the prospectus. When the company turned out to be a sham he brought an action in deceit against the defendants. It was held that the plaintiff was entitled to succeed because the statements contained in the prospectus were continuing ones which sought to impress upon the public that this company was a real one and not a sham. It was held that *Peek* was distinguishable on the ground that the statements there served a much more limited purpose than the prospectus in *Andrews*. So in this area much turns upon the court's interpretation of the defendant's purpose in making the statement.

In considering whether the defendant made the statement with the intention that it be acted upon, there is no need to show that the statement was made directly to the plaintiff. It can be satisfied by showing that the statement was made with the intention that it be passed on to the plaintiff (see *Commercial Banking Co of Sydney v RH Brown & Co* [1972] 2 Lloyd's Rep 360).

26.5 The plaintiff must act on the statement

It must be shown that the plaintiff acted on the false statement of fact made by the defendant. In other words the defendant's false statement must have been relied upon by the plaintiff. The defendant's false statement need not be the sole factor or even the decisive factor in persuading the plaintiff to act as he did. This can be seen in the case of *Edgington* v *Fitzmaurice* (above). The defendants' misstatement was said by the plaintiff to have been an influence upon him in deciding to invest in the company but he also said that he would not have advanced the money had he not believed, erroneously as it turned out, that the money was advanced on the basis of a charge upon the property of the company. It was held by the court that the plaintiff was still entitled to succeed with his action. It was held that the statement need not have been the sole inducement, it is sufficient that it was a material one, and that it was a material one if it was actively present to the plaintiff's mind when he invested the money (see too *JEB Fasteners* v *Marks, Bloom and Co* [1983] 1 All ER 583).

The plaintiff will be unable to show that he relied upon the misstatement of the defendant when he was unaware of the existence of the representation (*Horsfall* v *Thomas* (1862) 1 H & C 90), where he regarded the representation as being unimportant (*Smith* v *Chadwick* (1884) 9 App Cas 187) or where he relied upon his own judgment (*Atwood* v *Small* (1838) 6 Cl & Fin 232). However, the mere fact that the plaintiff had the opportunity to discover that the defendant's statement was false does not mean that the plaintiff did not rely, or was not entitled to rely, upon the statement of the defendant. This can be seen in the case of *Redgrave* v *Hurd* (1881) 20 Ch D 1. The defendant was induced to purchase the plaintiff's practice and house on the basis of a misrepresentation made by the plaintiff as to the value of the practice. The defendant had asked the plaintiff about the value of the practice and the plaintiff had shown him some papers which he claimed evidenced the value of the practice. Had the defendant examined these papers he would have discovered that the business was worthless. He did not examine the papers. When he discovered the true condition of the business the defendant refused to go through with the contract and the plaintiff sought an order of specific performance. The defendant argued that such an order should be refused on the ground of the plaintiff's misrepresentation. The court refused to grant the plaintiff such an order, saying that it was no defence to a fraudulent misrepresentation to show that the defendant might, with reasonable diligence, have discovered the truth.

26.6 Damage to the plaintiff

Finally the plaintiff must show that he suffered damage as the result of the defendant's false statement. It was established in *Doyle* v *Olby* [1969] 2 QB 158 (noted by Treitel (1969) 32 MLR 526) that the proper measure of damages is the reliance measure, which is generally calculated by comparing the price which the plaintiff paid with the actual value of the thing which he obtained from the defendant in return (see further chapter 30). In other words, the award of damages seeks to put the plaintiff in the position which he would have been in had the misrepresentation not been made. Where the deceit has the consequence that the plaintiff is deprived of his goods, the court will generally award damages by reference to the market value of these goods, without reference to their cost of production (*Smith Kline & French Laboratories Ltd* v *Long* [1989] 1 WLR 1). In *Doyle* v *Olby* the Court of Appeal refused to apply the reasonable foresight test (as established in *The Wagon Mound* [1961] AC 388) as the criterion for considering whether a loss was too remote. Lord Denning held that the defendant was liable for all losses directly flowing from his fraudulent inducement, whether or not that loss was reasonably foreseeable and he justified this conclusion on the ground that it does not lie in the mouth of a fraudulent person to argue that the loss was not recoverable because it could not reasonably be foreseen (see also *East* v *Maurer* [1991] 1 WLR 461). It remains unclear whether or not exemplary damages can be recovered for the tort of deceit. In *Archer* v *Brown* [1985] 1 QB 401 Peter Pain J noted that there was a conflict of authority on this point, but he refused to attempt to resolve the conflict and held that the plaintiff was not entitled to exemplary damages on the facts. He did, however, award the plaintiff aggravated damages (see further chapter 30).

27

Malicious Falsehood

27.1   Introduction

27.2   Falsehood

27.3   Malice

27.4   Damage

27.1 Introduction

This tort is called malicious falsehood by some commentators and judges, while others refer to it as injurious falsehood (in this chapter it will be referred to as malicious falsehood). This tort is a tort of respectable antiquity and it consists of the making of a false statement, with malice, to a person other than the plaintiff, with the result that the plaintiff suffers damage.

The tort which we now call malicious falsehood was originally referred to as 'slander of title' because the first cases in which it was recognised were cases which involved one person making a false statement about the plaintiff's title to land with the result that the plaintiff was unable to sell the land or only able to sell it with greater difficulty than would otherwise have been the case (*Bliss* v *Stafford* (1573) Owen 37 and *Banister* v *Banister* (1583) 4 Co Rep 17a). However the scope of the tort has gradually expanded. It was also applied to cases of 'slander of goods', which was similar to 'slander of title' except that the defendant made an attack on the plaintiff's goods (*Kerr* v *Shedden* (1831) 4 C & P 528). The tort was also applied in cases of 'passing off' (discussed in chapter 28). By the time of the decision of the Court of Appeal in *Ratcliffe* v *Evans* [1892] 2 QB 524 it was clear that the tort was not confined to cases of slander of title, slander of goods and passing off, but was a principle of general application. In *Ratcliffe* the defendant, who was a newspaper proprietor, maliciously and falsely implied in an article published in his newspaper that the plaintiff's firm had gone out of business. As a result of this publication the plaintiff suffered a considerable loss of business and he sought to recover from the defendant. It was held that the plaintiff was entitled to recover damages in respect of the defendant's malicious falsehood. Bowen LJ stated that an action would lie for written or oral falsehoods:

'... not actionable per se nor even defamatory, where they are maliciously published, where they are calculated in the ordinary course of things to produce, and where they do produce, actual damage.'

So by 1892 it was established that this tort was a tort of general application. Before examining the constituent elements of this tort it is necessary to distinguish this tort from the torts of deceit and defamation. Malicious falsehood can be distinguished from deceit on the ground that deceit is concerned with a false statement made by the defendant to the plaintiff which causes loss to the plaintiff, whereas malicious falsehood is concerned with a false statement about the plaintiff made to a third party as a result of which the plaintiff suffers damage. Malicious falsehood can be distinguished from defamation on the ground that defamation is concerned with attacks on the plaintiff's reputation, whereas malicious falsehood is not so confined and is generally concerned with attacks on the plaintiff's business or property (although a plaintiff who would otherwise have brought a claim in defamation may elect to bring a claim for malicious falsehood in order to get round the fact that legal aid is unavailable in defamation cases, see *Joyce* v *Sengupta* [1993] 1 WLR 337).

There are three basic elements to the tort of malicious falsehood. The first is that the defendant must have made a false statement to someone other than the plaintiff (27.2). The second is that the defendant must have made that statement with malice (27.3) and the third element is that the statement must have caused damage to the plaintiff (27.4).

27.2 Falsehood

As was the case in the tort of deceit, the falsehood must be a false statement of fact. It cannot be a false statement of opinion, nor can it be a mere puff. The same difficulties are experienced in this tort as are experienced in the tort of deceit in distinguishing between a statement of fact and a statement of opinion.

Particular difficulties have been experienced here in distinguishing between a trade puff and an actionable misrepresentation. This can be seen in the following cases. In *White* v *Mellin* [1895] AC 154 the defendant, who was the owner of a shop, stuck labels on the food produced by the plaintiff to the effect that the defendant's food was better in a number of respects than the food produced by the plaintiff. It was held that this was not actionable because the defendant was merely seeking to boost up his own product. Where, however, the defendant makes disparaging remarks about the plaintiff's goods, rather than contenting himself with boosting his own goods, then it is much more likely that the defendant's statement will be held to be actionable. This can be seen in the following two cases. In *Lyne* v *Nichols* (1906) 23 TLR 86 the defendant newspaper proprietor stated that the circulation of his paper was 'twenty to one of any other weekly paper in the district'. It was held that this statement was not a mere puff but was intended to be taken seriously and so was actionable upon proof of actual damage. The second case is *De Beers Products* v *Electric Co of New York* [1975] 1 WLR 972. The parties were both manufacturers of diamond abrasives for cutting concrete. As part of a sales drive the defendants published a pamphlet which incorporated a supposed laboratory report which had been conducted to compare the performance of the goods manufactured by the plaintiffs and the defendants. The pamphlet contained adverse statements about the standard of the product produced by the plaintiffs and stated that the defendants' product was superior. The plaintiffs brought an action for slander of goods but the defendants claimed that the statement contained in the pamphlet was a mere puff. It was held by Walton J that the test to apply was whether the reasonable man would interpret the defendants' statement as being a serious one. It was held that the reasonable man would take the defendants' statement seriously because it was supposed to be a properly conducted scientific report. Walton J held that a trader was entitled to puff his own goods. He thought that the defendants were entitled to make a statement such as 'our goods are better than those which are produced by the plaintiffs' even though that statement may be seen as denigrating the goods of the plaintiffs. He held that the defendants were not, however, entitled to say that 'our goods are better than those of the plaintiffs because the plaintiffs' goods are rubbish', unless of course he can establish that the plaintiffs' goods are indeed rubbish.

27.3 Malice

The plaintiff must prove that the defendant's statement was made maliciously; that is, that the defendant acted out of some improper motive such as spite or a desire to injure the plaintiff. The burden of proving malice lies on the plaintiff. The test of what constitutes malice in the tort of malicious falsehood is the same as the test in relation to the torts of libel and slander (*Spring* v *Guardian Assurance plc* [1993] 2 All ER 273, 288). Where the defendant makes the statement knowing that it is false or reckless whether it be true or false then he has acted out of malice. In *Greers Ltd* v *Pearman & Corder Ltd* (1922) 39 RPC 406 the defendants falsely alleged that the plaintiff had infringed their trade mark for chocolates, which included the words 'Bouquet Brand'. However, the defendants had frequently stated in the past that they had no right to the exclusive use of these words. It was held that the fact that the defendants had made these allegations that the plaintiff had infringed their trade mark when they knew that this was untrue was sufficient to establish that they had acted out of malice. If it is proved that the defendants had acted out of malice it is irrelevant that the reason for their action was an attempt to further their business interests rather than an attempt to denigrate the business of the plaintiffs. Thus in *Joyce* v *Motor Surveys Ltd* [1948] Ch 252 the defendants were held to have acted maliciously in telling the Post Office that the plaintiff, who was their tenant, had moved out of their premises and in telling the plaintiff's trade association that he had gone out of business so that they (the defendants) could sell the business with vacant possession.

However, where the defendant honestly believes a statement is true but in fact it is false the defendant has not acted out of malice. This is also the case where the defendant makes the statement carelessly but without any intention of injuring the plaintiff (*Balden* v *Shorter* [1933] Ch 247).

27.4 Damage

The plaintiff must show that he suffered pecuniary damage as a result of the defendant's statement. The plaintiff must prove that he has suffered special damage, but where the defendant intended to cause harm to the plaintiff this is usually easily established by showing that the plaintiff suffered a general loss of business as a result of the defendant's false statement (see *Ratcliffe* v *Evans* (above)). The need to prove special damage has been dispensed with in certain cases by s3 of the Defamation Act 1952 which provides that:

'... it shall not be necessary to allege or prove special damage –
a) if the words upon which the action is founded are calculated to cause pecuniary damage to the plaintiff and are published in writing or other permanent form; or
b) if the said words are calculated to cause pecuniary damage to the plaintiff in respect of any office, profession, calling, trade or business held or carried on by him at the time of publication.'

The purpose of s3 has been held to be one of giving 'the plaintiff a remedy in malicious falsehood despite the difficulty of proving actual loss' and so it cannot be the case that an award of damages under s3 must necessarily be nominal (*Joyce* v *Sengupta* [1993] 1 WLR 337, 347). As has been noted, damages are not recoverable in respect of non-pecuniary loss, such as distress and injury to feelings. But, once a plaintiff has established that he has suffered pecuniary loss or that he has a claim under s3, it may be the case that he is entitled to recover damages in respect of the whole of his loss, including damages for mental distress (per Parker LJ in *Joyce* v *Sengupta* [1993] 1 WLR 337, 348–349, but the contrary view is taken by Sir Michael Kerr at pp351–353).

28

Passing Off

28.1 Introduction

28.2 Methods of passing off

28.3 Made by a trader in the course of a trade

28.4 Remedies

28.1 Introduction

The tort of passing off is committed where the plaintiff's goods are passed off by the defendant as being his own (that is, the defendant's) goods. The person whose goods have been passed off in this manner may have an action in tort in respect of any losses which he has incurred. Although this tort has been recognised for a number of years now, commentators continue to disagree on its classification. We noted in chapter 27 that there is a link between passing off and the tort of malicious or injurious falsehood and that some have argued that passing off is part of malicious falsehood. There is also a link between passing off and the tort of deceit as the person who passes off his goods as belonging to another deceives the public. But it should be noted that the plaintiff in the passing off action is not the member of the public who has been deceived but the person whose goods have been passed off and he has not been deceived. On the other hand, as we shall note in chapter 29, passing off could be classified as part of the economic torts because the subject matter of the tort of passing off is the protection of the plaintiff's financial interest in his property. It could also be classified as part of the law relating to intellectual property and ranked alongside copyright, trademarks and patents.

Despite this confusion as to the classification of the tort of passing off, it is included in a textbook on tort because it has been consistently recognised as part of the law of tort and because it differs from other types of intellectual property on the ground that the basis of the law lies in the common law and not in statute law.

The classic definition of the tort of passing off can be found in the judgment of Lord Diplock in *Erven Warnink BV* v *J Townend & Sons (Hull) Ltd* [1979] AC 731. Lord Diplock identified the five essential elements of the tort when he said that it is:

'... possible to identify five characteristics which must be present in order to create a valid cause of action for passing off: (1) a misrepresentation, (2) made by a trader in the course of trade, (3) to prospective customers of his or ultimate consumers of goods or services supplied by him, (4) which is calculated to injure the business or goodwill of another trader (in the sense that this is a reasonably foreseeable consequence) and (5) which causes actual damage to a business or goodwill of the trader by whom the action is brought or (in a quia timet action) will probably do so.'

These five elements must be proved to exist in any passing off action. Most of these elements are self-explanatory and require no further comment, so attention will be focused instead on the different ways in which this tort can be committed.

The crucial point of reference is the point of sale. Hence an identical appearance, revealed only after a purchaser had removed opaque wrapping, does not even furnish an arguable case: see *Bostik Ltd* v *Sellotape GB Ltd* (1993) The Times 11 January.

28.2 Methods of passing off

The passing off of the plaintiff's goods as if they were the defendant's goods can take place in a number of different ways. The principal ways in which goods may be passed off are.

A direct statement that the goods belonging to the plaintiff in fact belong to the defendant

In *Lord Byron* v *Johnson* (1816) 2 Mer 29 the defendant, who was a publisher, advertised some poems which he had published as being written by Lord Byron when, in fact, they were written by someone else. It was held that the defendant had committed the tort of passing off.

Imitating the appearance of the plaintiff's goods

In *White Hudson & Co Ltd* v *Asian Organisation Ltd* [1964] 1 WLR 1466, the plaintiffs manufactured 'Hacks' cough sweets in Singapore, which they sold in red cellophane wrappers and which came to be known as 'red paper cough sweets'. The plaintiffs were, at that time, the only persons who sold cough sweets in such form in Singapore. The defendants then started to import into Singapore cough sweets called 'Peckos' which were also sold in red paper wrappers. The plaintiffs proved that most of the customers in Singapore could not read English and simply asked for red paper cough sweets. It was held that the court would protect the plaintiffs' interest in the appearance of their product and that the plaintiffs would be granted an injunction to restrain the defendants from passing off their sweets as if they were the goods of the plaintiffs. Innocence is no defence to a passing-off action: *Gillette UK Ltd* v *Edenwest Ltd* (1994) The Times 9 March.

In *Cadbury-Schweppes Pty Ltd* v *Pub Squash Co Pty Ltd* [1981] 1 WLR 193 the

Privy Council held that a cause of action could lie, not only in respect of the physical appearance of the goods, but also in respect of the way in which they are advertised. Here the plaintiffs had launched an advertising campaign which sought to associate their drink with a virile, sporting image. Shortly afterwards the defendants launched a similar advertising campaign. It was held that the plaintiffs were not entitled to an injunction because they had not established that a virile, sporting image was associated by the public exclusively with their product. However, the Privy Council held that, had the plaintiffs been able to establish this association, then an action in passing off could have succeeded in respect of the passing off of their advertising campaign.

Using a name similar to the plaintiff's goods

In *Reddaway v Banham* [1896] AC 199, the plaintiffs were manufacturers of camel hair belting which they sold abroad. The belting contained a design with a camel and the words 'Camel Hair Belting' on it. The defendants also made camel hair belting with the words 'Camel Hair Belting' on it, but without the camel. The defendants argued that these words were simply a description of the goods which they were selling and not a passing off. It was held that the defendants had committed the tort of passing off because when the plaintiffs' goods were sold abroad the words 'Camel Hair Belting' were not simply a description of the goods but were a trade mark of the plaintiffs.

The description of the goods was also in issue in four further cases. The first is *J Bollinger v Costa Brava Wine Co Ltd* [1960] Ch 262. The plaintiffs, who were champagne producers from the Champagne district of France, sought an injunction to restrain the defendants, who were wine merchants from Spain, from manufacturing a wine which was not produced in Champagne under the title of 'Spanish Champagne'. It was held that the word 'champagne' referred to the particular area where the wine was produced and that the producers from that area were entitled to protect the goodwill of the word 'champagne' and an injunction was granted accordingly. Similarly, in *Taittinger v Allbev Ltd* (1993) The Times 26 June it was held by the Court of Appeal that a non-alcoholic sparkling fruit drink marketed under the name 'Elderflower Champagne' which was neither champagne nor had any connection with its producers eroded the goodwill in the distinctiveness and exclusivity of the name 'champagne' and a similar injunction was granted. The third case is *Erven Warnink BV v J Townend and Sons (Hull) Ltd* (above). The plaintiffs were manufacturers of a drink called 'advocaat', which was made from eggs and spirits. They had sold the drink for a number of years in England and the name 'advocaat' had acquired a considerable reputation and goodwill. The defendants then began to manufacture a drink made from sherry and eggs which they called 'Old English Advocaat'. The plaintiffs sought an injunction to restrain the defendants from using the name advocaat. It was held that the name which was used by the plaintiffs was a name which distinguished the plaintiffs' product from the products of others and it was held that the plaintiffs were entitled to an injunction to protect that name. Where, however, the name which the plaintiff is seeking to protect is a name which does not distinguish his goods but is given to a class of goods then an injunction will not be granted (see *British Vacuum Cleaner Co Ltd* v *New Vacuum Cleaner Co Ltd* [1907] 2 Ch 312).

The final case is *Mothercare UK Ltd* v *Penguin Books Ltd* (1987) The Times 8 July. The plaintiffs sought an injunction to restrain the defendants from using the words 'Mother Care' in a book which they had published called 'Mother Care/Other Care'. The book was written by two academics and was somewhat polemical and the plaintiffs said that it was their policy to avoid all such matters of controversy and to confine themselves to useful and practical advice to mothers. However, Dillon LJ was unable to see how the book, taken as a whole, indicated in any way that the plaintiffs were associated with it. So he found that the plaintiffs had not overcome the first of Lord Diplock's hurdles in *Erven Warnink* in showing that the defendants had misrepresented that the plaintiffs were in any way involved in the production of the book and so the injunction was refused.

Using the plaintiff's name

Where the defendant uses the plaintiff's name, as opposed to the name of the plaintiff's products, the tort may be committed. This can be seen in the case of *Maxim's Ltd* v *Dye* [1977] 1 WLR 1155. The plaintiff was the owner of a famous restaurant called Maxim's in Paris and he sought an injunction to restrain the defendant from opening a French restaurant in Norwich with the same name. The restaurant in Norwich did not operate to the same standard as the restaurant in Paris and so the plaintiff was granted an injunction, even though he did not have any business in this country, because the conduct of the defendant was injuring the goodwill of the plaintiff's restaurant in Paris (contrast *Bernadin et Cie* v *Pavilion Properties Ltd* [1967] RPC 581).

Using the defendant's name

As a general rule the defendant is entitled to use his own name to advertise his products but this is subject to the qualification that the defendant cannot do so where that would be to mislead the public. This can be seen in the case of *Parker-Knoll Ltd* v *Knoll International Ltd* [1962] RPC 265. Both parties were furniture manufacturers, the plaintiffs being a well-known company which traded in Great Britain, while the defendants traded in America. When the defendants started to trade in this country, the plaintiffs sought an injunction to restrain the defendants from using their name on their furniture without distinguishing it from the products of the plaintiffs. It was held by a majority of the House of Lords that the plaintiffs were entitled to their injunction because they had established that their name had come to be associated with goods made by themselves alone and that the use by the defendants of their own name was likely to cause confusion among the public. It was not necessary for the plaintiffs to show that the defendants intended to deceive the public, it was sufficient if it was likely that the public would be deceived by the defendants' use of their own name.

28.3 Made by a trader in the course of a trade

Where the parties are not in the same trade, it is much harder for the plaintiff to show that the public is likely to be confused by the defendant's alleged passing off of the property of the plaintiff. This can be seen in the case of *Granada Group Ltd* v *Ford Motor Co Ltd* [1972] FSR 103. The plaintiffs, who were a major entertainment organisation, sought to restrain the defendants from calling their new car 'Granada'. It was held that they were not entitled to an injunction because there was no risk of confusion in the minds of the public between the defendants' car and the plaintiffs' entertainment company. Similarly the plaintiff was unsuccessful in *McCullough* v *May* [1947] 2 All ER 845. The plaintiff, who was a well-known children's broadcaster called 'Uncle Mac', sought to prevent the defendants from calling their breakfast cereal 'Uncle Mac's Puffed Wheat'. He failed on the ground that there was no common trading activity between the parties and so there was no risk of confusion in the minds of the public (cf *Henderson* v *Radio Corporation Pty Ltd* [1960] NSWR 576).

28.4 Remedies

In many cases the remedy which the plaintiff will seek is an injunction to restrain the defendant from continuing to pass off his goods as if they were the plaintiff's. The injunction may be granted on terms, such as where the defendant is permitted to continue to manufacture the goods as long as he distinguishes his goods from those of the plaintiff. In deciding to grant an injunction a judge may take into account the behaviour of the parties and refuse to grant an injunction if the plaintiff has failed to respond to reasonable enquiries and the defendants have, as a result, expended much time and expense in marketing their product: see *Dalgety Spillers Foods Ltd* v *Food Brokers Ltd* (1993) The Times 2 December. The plaintiff may also seek a remedy in damages for the loss which he has suffered as a result of the defendant's activities, or he may seek from the defendant an account of the profits which he has made as a result of the passing off.

29

The Economic Torts

29.1 Introduction

29.2 The ground rules

29.3 Conspiracy

29.4 Inducing breach of contract

29.5 Intimidation

29.6 Economic duress?

29.7 Interference with trade by unlawful means

29.8 The statutory immunities

29.9 Conclusion

29.1 Introduction

The economic torts are concerned with the intentional, rather than the negligent, infliction of economic harm on another. In fact many of the cases which we shall discuss are concerned with the legal consequences of industrial action, although some are concerned with alleged unlawful competition. The common law has never developed a principle that commercial parties must trade fairly (see *Associated Newspapers Group plc* v *Insert Media Ltd* [1988] 1 WLR 509 where Hoffmann J rejected the proposition that 'any intentional act which is calculated to cause damage to the plaintiffs' business or goodwill is actionable per se' and, while he accepted that the law in relation to unfair trading is not static, he refused to recognise the existence of a tort of 'unfair trading') and so, until the intervention of statutes such as the Fair Trading Act 1973, the common law regulation of trade and competition was left to the economic torts.

It is possible to divide the economic torts into four different nominate torts, but the adoption of such an approach has the consequence of ignoring the threads which are common to all the economic torts. So we shall discuss the economic torts in one chapter and compare and contrast them. There has also been some debate recently as to whether or not the torts are in fact all part of the one innominate tort, called interference with trade or business by unlawful means. This issue is one to which we shall return after discussing the ground rules.

29.2 The ground rules

The foundation rules which are applicable to the economic torts were laid down at the end of last century and the beginning of this century. Through a trilogy of cases the House of Lords was given the opportunity to put the law on a coherent basis. Unfortunately they failed to set out any clear or principled approach and the consequences of this failure can still be seen in our law today.

The first of the three cases was *Mogul Steamship Co Ltd* v *McGregor, Gow & Co* [1892] AC 25. In this case the defendants sought to obtain a monopoly in the tea trade, which was at that time extremely profitable. They sought to obtain a monopoly by, amongst other things, cutting the price of tea so as to drive the plaintiffs, who were shipowners involved in the tea trade, out of business. The defendants were successful in driving the plaintiffs out of the trade and so the plaintiffs brought an action against the defendants alleging that the defendants had conspired to injure them. The House of Lords held that the plaintiffs had no cause of action against the defendants. They held that such a cause of action would only arise where the defendants had committed an unlawful act against the plaintiffs. No such unlawful act had been committed. Competition, however vigorous or unfair, was not, of itself, an unlawful act.

In electing to impose liability when the defendant committed an unlawful act the House of Lords made an important choice. There were, in fact, two avenues open to the House. The first, and the one which the House chose, was to impose liability when the defendant commits an unlawful act. The second avenue open to them was to impose liability when one person, without justification, intentionally inflicts harm upon another. The adoption of such an approach might have achieved a different result on the facts of *Mogul*. It was at least arguable that the defendants had acted unfairly vis-a-vis the plaintiffs. But the adoption of this approach would have led the courts into troubled waters. Let us take an example to illustrate the point. Suppose that several small traders have traded on a housing estate for a number of years and provided the residents with a satisfactory service. However, the owners of a large chain of supermarkets think that they can provide a better and cheaper service for the residents of the housing estate and for residents of nearby estates. They open up a large new store nearby and offer their products at a significantly lower price than those in the local stores, in an effort to attract the residents of the estate who previously were customers of the small traders. The traders lose money and some are forced out of business. Can these traders bring an action against the supermarket owners on the ground that the supermarket owners have intentionally inflicted economic loss upon them without justification? Had the

House of Lords based liability in *Mogul* upon the fact that the defendants had acted without justification, then the traders could have argued that they had a case. This would have involved the courts in adjudicating upon what are acceptable and what are unacceptable forms of competition. Such an approach would have required the courts to make difficult policy choices, which could be dubbed as being 'political' choices. It is perhaps for this reason that the courts refused to adopt this approach. The line between what is lawful and what is unlawful does not require the courts to make such explicit choices of policy and provides a more certain guideline for subsequent courts and for legal advisers. However, as we shall note at different points in this chapter, the line between what is lawful and what is unlawful is, to some extent, an arbitrary one and it has produced some rather strange results in the cases.

The second case in the trilogy is *Allen* v *Flood* [1898] AC 1. The case centred around a dispute between two trade unions. The ironworkers' union objected to members of the woodworkers' union doing certain work which they claimed had always been done by members of the ironworkers' union. An official of the ironworkers' union informed the employers of the woodworkers that they would stop work unless the woodworkers were dismissed. The employers gave in to this threat and dismissed the woodworkers, who brought an action against the official of the ironworkers' union who had threatened the strike unless the plaintiffs were dismissed. This time the House of Lords was divided, but the majority held that the plaintiffs had no cause of action against the defendant because the defendant had not done an unlawful act. The act of informing the employers that his members would go on strike unless the plaintiffs were dismissed did not constitute an unlawful act because the members of the ironworkers' union were employed under contracts which were determinable at will and so, in threatening to bring them out on strike, there was no threat of the commission of an unlawful act. Nor had the contracts of the plaintiffs been unlawfully interfered with because the employers had lawfully determined their contracts. So the principle laid down in *Mogul* was applied and the plaintiffs were held to have no cause of action. The fact that the defendant was alleged to have acted out of spite was irrelevant because spite or malice could not, of itself, turn what was otherwise a lawful act into an unlawful act.

The final case in the trilogy is *Quinn* v *Leatham* [1901] AC 495. This case has given rise to considerable difficulty because it obscures the clear principle which was established in *Mogul* and *Allen*. The plaintiff was the owner of a fleshing business. He employed non-union men. The defendants, who were trade union officials, sought to persuade the plaintiff not to employ non-union men. The plaintiff was prepared to permit his employees to join the union but he was not prepared to require them to join the union as a condition of continued employment. So the defendants instructed their members who worked for a butcher, who was the plaintiff's principal customer, not to handle the plaintiff's meat. As a result of this action the plaintiff suffered loss and he brought an action against the defendants, alleging that they had conspired to injure him. The defendants had not committed an unlawful act against the plaintiff because, in instructing their members not to handle the plaintiff's meat, they had not instructed their members to breach their contracts. So an application of the principle laid down in *Mogul* required that the plaintiff's action be dismissed. But this was not the approach adopted by the House of Lords. The House held that the defendants had conspired unjustifiably to inflict loss on the plaintiff and so the defendants were liable. The jury had found that the defendants had acted out of malice and that they had no justification for their action and this finding was upheld by the House of Lords.

The obvious difficulty to which this case gives rise is how to reconcile it with the reasoning adopted in *Mogul* and *Allen*. On the face of it they appear to adopt totally inconsistent approaches. In *Mogul* and *Allen* the House of Lords held that a cause of action lay in respect of the unlawful infliction of harm and not in respect of simply unjustified infliction of harm, while in *Quinn* the House held that a cause of action does lie in respect of the unjustified infliction of harm. The accepted, if unprincipled, distinction between the cases is that in *Allen* there was only one defendant, whereas in *Quinn* there was more than one. So, where defendants conspire together to inflict harm on another, without having any justification for so doing, their lack of justification may turn an otherwise lawful act into one which is actionable in tort. The supposed rationale behind this distinction is that collective pressure is greater than the pressure which can be exerted by a single individual. The absurdity inherent in this approach was demonstrated by Lord Diplock in *Lonrho v Shell Petroleum Co Ltd (No 2)* [1982] AC 173. He pointed out that the fact that the law regards a limited company as a legal person destroys the argument that collective pressure is inevitably greater than the pressure exerted by a single individual. In the example which we considered above, involving the supermarket and the small traders, it is obvious that the supermarket can exert greater pressure than the small traders and to suggest otherwise and to treat the supermarket more favourably than the small traders is ludicrous.

So the principle established in *Quinn*, that the motive of a group of persons acting together can render an otherwise lawful act actionable, is an anomalous one and one which the House of Lords held in *Lonrho* was not to be extended. It is a rule which is confined to cases of conspiracy to injure and it does not undermine the general principle in English law that liability is based upon the unlawfulness of the defendant's actions.

Having examined the general principle which runs through the cases we shall now consider the separate nominate torts which have been recognised in English law and then we shall conclude by considering whether there is, in fact, one innominate tort which unifies these nominate torts. We shall commence by considering the anomalous tort of conspiracy.

29.3 Conspiracy

The tort of conspiracy is a tort of respectable antiquity. A useful definition of the tort was provided by Willes J in *Mulcahy* v *R* (1868) LR 3 HL 306, 317 in the following terms:

> 'A conspiracy consists not merely in the intention of two or more, but in the agreement of two or more to do an unlawful act, or to do a lawful act by unlawful means.'

It is clear from this definition that there are, in fact, two different types of conspiracy. The first type consists of a conspiracy to commit an unlawful act. This type of conspiracy conforms to the general principle which requires that the defendant commit an unlawful act. The second type of conspiracy consists of a conspiracy to do acts which, if done by an individual would be lawful, but which, by virtue of the fact that they are done in combination, become unlawful and actionable. This is the anomalous tort and the one which does not conform to the general principle requiring that the defendant commit an unlawful act. Although the tort of conspiracy has these two distinct branches there are some factors common to both branches and we shall consider these common elements before analysing the two branches of the tort.

There are three elements common to both branches of the tort. The first is that there must be two or more persons involved in the conspiracy. This requirement generally gives rise to no difficulties. However it should be noted that a company is treated as a legal person for this purpose and so a company can conspire with its directors (*Belmont Finance Corpn* v *Williams Furniture Ltd (No 2)* [1980] 1 All ER 393). This may need qualification in the case where it is alleged that the conspiracy is between a 'one man' company and the controller of that company because of the difficulty of showing that there were two minds involved in the conspiracy (*R* v *McDonnell* [1966] 1 QB 233, although it should be noted that this was a criminal case). There is an old rule of criminal law that a husband and wife cannot conspire together, but this rule has been held to be inapplicable to the tort of conspiracy (see *Midland Bank Trust Co Ltd* v *Green (No 3)* [1982] Ch 529 where it was held that the fictional unity of husband and wife did not apply to liability in the tort of conspiracy).

The second common element is that there must be a combination between the parties. The word combination has been preferred to agreement on the ground that the latter may be thought to require an agreement of a contractual kind when, in fact, all that is required is that the parties combine together with a common purpose (see *Belmont Finance Corpn* v *Williams Furniture Ltd* (above) p404). There is no requirement that the conspirators all join the conspiracy at the same time. It is sufficient that at some stage they combined together. Nor need the conspirators have exactly the same aim in joining the conspiracy but, the wider the difference in aim, the less likely it is that there will be a combination.

The third common element is that there must be damage to the plaintiff because damage is of the very essence of the tort. Once these three common elements are established, it must be considered which of the two branches of the tort has been committed. We shall consider unlawful means conspiracy first and then consider conspiracy to injure by lawful means.

Unlawful means conspiracy

This branch of the tort is consistent with the general principle which requires that the defendant commit an unlawful act. The only problem which arises here concerns what constitutes unlawful means. It is clear that conspiracy to commit a crime constitutes unlawful means and a conspiracy to commit a tort can constitute unlawful means (see the judgment of Lord Dunedin in *Sorrell* v *Smith* [1925] AC 700, 729–30). It is not, however, clear whether a breach of contract constitutes unlawful means for this purpose. In *Rookes* v *Barnard* [1964] AC 1129 Lord Devlin expressly left this particular point open, but the majority view amongst commentators is that it may constitute unlawful means (see *Clerk and Lindsell on Torts* (16th ed) para 15–23).

The most important recent case on unlawful means conspiracy is *Lonrho Ltd* v *Shell Petroleum Co Ltd (No 2)* [1982] AC 173. Shell, the defendants, built an oil refinery in Southern Rhodesia. Lonrho built the pipe-line to the refinery from a port in Mozambique and the expectation of the parties involved in the enterprise was that the pipe-line would be used to get the oil to the refinery. However, in 1965 the government of Rhodesia unilaterally declared independence (UDI) and the response of the British government was to pass the Southern Rhodesia (Petroleum) Order 1965 which made it a criminal offence to supply oil to Southern Rhodesia. Thus the pipe-line ceased to be used. But the plaintiffs alleged that the defendants secretly conspired to maintain the supply of oil to Southern Rhodesia, without using the pipe-line, and that this continued the illegal declaration of independence and so increased the plaintiffs' loss because it increased the length of time for which the pipe-line was out of use. It was held that the plaintiffs did not have an action in tort in respect of the defendants' breach of the sanctions order because the mere prohibition upon members of the public doing what was otherwise lawful in trading with Southern Rhodesia was not enough, of itself, to found a cause of action for breach of statutory duty. More significantly, perhaps, the judgment of Lord Diplock was subsequently interpreted as authority for the proposition that, to establish a cause of action in unlawful means conspiracy, it must be shown not only that the defendants intended to injure the plaintiff but that, as in the case of conspiracy to injure by lawful means, the predominant purpose of the conspirators must have been to injure the plaintiff rather than further their own interests (see, for example, *Metall und Rohstoff AG* v *Donaldson Lufkin & Jenrette Inc* [1990] 1 QB 391). But the House of Lords in *Lonrho plc* v *Fayed* [1992] 1 AC 448 overruled the decision of the Court of Appeal in *Metall und Rohstoff* and held that, in cases of unlawful means conspiracy, it is not necessary to show that the defendants had as their predominant purpose an intention to injure the plaintiff; it suffices that they had intent to injure the plaintiff. The predominant purpose to injure test is therefore confined to the anomalous tort of conspiracy to injure by lawful means (see below). In *Lonrho plc v Fayed (No 5)* [1993] 1 WLR 1489 the Court of Appeal held that actual pecuniary loss could be recovered in an action for conspiracy, but that damages for injury to reputation and injury to feeling could only be recovered in defamation.

Conspiracy to injure by lawful means

This is the anomalous form of the tort which is derived from *Quinn v Leatham* (above). Since it is a highly anomalous tort its ambit has been severely restricted. The most famous case concerned with this branch of the tort is *Crofter Hand Woven Harris Tweed Co Ltd v Veitch* [1942] AC 435. The case concerned the production of Harris tweed on the Isle of Lewis. Originally the tweed was made from hand spun yarn produced on Lewis. But, by 1930, many mill owners on Lewis were importing machine spun yarn from the mainland as it was much cheaper to do this. Some mill owners, however, persisted in using the local hand spun yarn. When the trade unions which represented the employees at the latter's mills sought a pay rise they were told that the mill owners could not afford it because of the competition provided by the importation of machine spun yarn from the mainland. So the trade union officials ordered the dockers, who were also members of the union, not to handle imported yarn, with the object of driving out the competition and enabling the mill owners to raise the wages. The dockers did this without breaking their contracts of employment. The plaintiffs, who suffered loss as a result of this embargo upon the importation of machine spun yarn, brought an action against the defendant trade union officials alleging that they had conspired to injure them without justification.

It was held that the plaintiffs had no cause of action against the defendants because the predominant purpose behind the defendants' actions was to defend the interests of their members and not to inflict loss on the plaintiffs. This case established the important point that the pursuit of self-interest constitutes a justification for the tort of conspiracy to injure by lawful means. Although the pursuit of self-interest or selfish goals constitutes a justification, the defendant may not be able to rely on the defence when his actions are motivated by spite or vindictiveness. Such was the case in *Huntley v Thornton* [1957] 1 WLR 321. The defendant trade union officials hounded the plaintiff out of every job which he obtained in their district. It was held that their purpose in driving the plaintiff out of a job was not to defend the interests of the union but to uphold 'their own ruffled dignity'. This was held to be an unjustified purpose and the plaintiff was able to recover damages from the defendants (contrast *Scala Ballroom (Wolverhampton) Ltd v Ratcliffe* [1958] 1 WLR 1057 where the refusal of union members to play at a ballroom which operated a colour bar was held to be justified).

29.4 Inducing breach of contract

This is the major economic tort and the one which is most commonly committed in the course of industrial disputes. The tort has its origins in the case of *Lumley* v *Gye* (1853) 2 El & Bl 216. The plaintiff was a theatre owner and he claimed that he had entered into a contract with a famous opera singer, Miss Wagner, under which she was to sing only at his theatre for a period of time. The defendant, who was the owner of a rival theatre, procured Miss Wagner to break her contract with the plaintiff by promising to pay her more than she was receiving from the plaintiff. When Miss Wagner, in breach of contract, refused to continue to perform at the plaintiff's theatre, he brought an action against the defendant alleging that the defendant had induced Miss Wagner to break her contract with him and that this had caused him loss. It was held that the plaintiff was entitled to maintain an action for damages in respect of the wrong done to him by the defendant inducing Miss Wagner to break her contract with him. This tort has since given rise to a considerable body of case law and it can be analysed in the following five stages.

The forms of the tort

In the case of *DC Thomson & Co Ltd* v *Deakin* [1952] Ch 646 Jenkins LJ described the three different ways in which this tort can be committed. The first way is by directly persuading one of the contracting parties to break his contract. *Lumley* is a case within this category. The courts formally distinguish between persuasion to break the contract and the mere giving of advice that the contract will be broken, the latter not being actionable. However, the courts have been willing to find that the defendant has persuaded the party to break his contractual obligations. This willingness can be seen in the case of *Square Grip Reinforcement Co Ltd* v *MacDonald* 1968 SLT 65 where Lord Milligan said that, where the defendant was 'desperately anxious' to achieve a particular result, then a court was likely to construe a 'suggestion' made by the defendant as being persuasion but that, where the defendant was not 'really interested' in the result, then a court was not likely to construe a 'suggestion' as amounting to persuasion. This test is hardly a difficult one for the plaintiff to satisfy. It appears that the only person who can sue in respect of such direct persuasion is the contracting party who is harmed by the other party's breach of contract. The duty of the party who receives the inducement is to resist the inducements and so he cannot bring an action in tort in respect of any loss which he incurs as a result of the breach of contract (per Upjohn LJ in *Boulting* v *Association of Cinematograph, Television and Allied Technicians* [1963] 2 QB 606, 639–40).

The second way in which this tort may be committed arises where the defendant prevents performance of the contract taking place by some other direct and wrongful means. An example given by Jenkins LJ in *Thomson* was of a defendant wrongfully taking the contracting party's tools so that he could not carry out his contractual obligations. The intervention of the defendant here must be wrongful in itself.

The third way in which this tort can be committed is where the defendant (referred to as 'A') induces a third party, such as an employee of a customer of the plaintiff, to break his contract with his employer (referred to as 'B') with the result that his employer (B) is unable to perform his contractual obligations with the plaintiff (referred to as 'C'). The four requirements of this limb of the tort were laid down by Jenkins LJ in *Thomson* v *Deakin* (above). The first was that the defendant (A) must have known of the contract between the plaintiff (C) and the other contracting party (B). The second was that the defendant (A) must have intended to breach the contract between C and B by inducing the employees of B to break their contracts of employment. The third requirement is that the employees so induced must have broken their contracts of employment and finally the breach of the contract between B and C must have ensued as a necessary consequence of the breach by the employees of B of their contracts of employment. This form of the tort was the form which was in issue in *Thomson* v *Deakin* (above). The plaintiffs were newspaper publishers who only employed non-union labour. The defendant trade union officials tried to compel the plaintiffs to stop employing non-union labour and, in seeking to do this, they told their members to boycott the plaintiffs' supplies. Bowaters, who supplied the plaintiffs with paper, refused to carry out their contracts with the plaintiffs because of the fear of a dispute with their own employees if they continued to supply the plaintiffs with paper. The plaintiffs sought an injunction to restrain what they believed to be the unlawful acts of the defendants. The Court of Appeal refused to grant an injunction on the ground that there was no evidence that the employees of Bowaters had breached their contracts of employment. This failure to show such a breach was fatal to the plaintiffs' action because unlawful means is of the essence of the tort. The indirect procurement of a breach of contract by means which are not in themselves unlawful is not actionable.

Although these three forms of the tort are separate and distinct it can be difficult in a particular case to say whether it is the direct or the indirect form of the tort which has been committed. Thus in *Thomson* it was also argued that the defendants had committed the direct form of the tort. This claim failed because there was no evidence that the defendants had sought to induce Bowaters not to perform their contract with the plaintiffs; the inducement had been an indirect one via the employees of Bowaters. The difficulty of distinguishing between the different forms of the tort can also be seen in the judgments of the House of Lords in *JT Stratford & Sons Ltd* v *Lindley* [1965] AC 269. The plaintiffs (P) hired out barges to a third party (C). The defendant trade union officials wished to exert pressure on P to settle a dispute and they instructed employees of C not to handle any of the barges belonging to P. This action soon had a serious effect on P's business and so they sought an injunction against the defendants to restrain the industrial action. The House of Lords held that the defendants had committed the tort of inducing breach of contract and granted the injunctions. It was not entirely clear, however, which form of the tort had been committed. The majority treated it as a case of indirect procurement because they thought that the defendants had persuaded the employees of C to break their contracts, whereas the minority treated it as a case of direct procurement because they thought that the defendants had persuaded C not to perform their contract with P. Although in *Stratford* it did not really matter which form of the tort had been committed, it may be important to know which was committed in some cases because unlawful means is essential to the indirect form of the tort but, in the case of the direct form of the tort, it need only be shown that the defendant persuaded a contracting party to break his contract with the plaintiff.

Knowledge and intention

Once it is established which form of the tort was committed, it must be shown that the defendant acted with the requisite knowledge and intention. This tort is a tort of intention and so does not encompass the negligent invasion of contractual rights. The defendant must be shown to have knowledge of the contract which has been broken and must have acted with the intention of bringing about a breach of that contract.

Although it must be shown that the defendant knew of the contract which was broken, it need not be shown that the defendant knew the exact term of the contract which was broken. In many cases it will be inferred that the defendant knew that the industrial action was likely to lead to a breach of contract. In *Merkur Island Shipping Corp* v *Laughton* [1983] 2 AC 570 both the Court of Appeal and the House of Lords were prepared to hold that the defendant trade union officials, by virtue of their work in the trade, must be deemed to know that the industrial action would lead to a breach of contract.

While it must be shown that the defendant intended to procure a breach of contract, this requirement can be satisfied by demonstrating that the defendant was reckless as to whether a contract was breached or not. In *Emerald Construction Co Ltd* v *Lowthian* [1966] 1 WLR 691 Lord Denning said that:

> 'Even if [the defendants] did not know of the actual contract, but had the means of knowledge – which they deliberately disregarded – that would be enough. Like the man who turns a blind eye. So here, if the officers deliberately sought to get this contract terminated, heedless of its terms, regardless whether it was terminated by breach or not, they would do wrong. For it is unlawful for a third party to procure a breach of contract knowingly, or recklessly, indifferent whether it is a breach or not.'

Breach

As the tort is entitled inducing breach of contract it would be reasonable to assume that the plaintiff must show that the defendant induced a breach of contract. But this is not necessarily so. At first instance Hoffmann J in *Law Debenture Trust Corporation* v *Ural Caspian Oil Corporation Ltd* [1993] 1 WLR 138, 151 stated that it was sufficient that 'the right which has been violated is a *secondary* right to a remedy arising out of the tortious inducement of a breach by a third party of its primary obligation under a contract.' Thus where the defendant induces a third party to break his contract with the plaintiff with the result that the plaintiff is deprived of a remedy which he would otherwise have had against the third party, the conduct of the defendant may be tortious. This view, however, was rejected by the Court of Appeal ((1994) The Independent 10 March) which held that the defendant had acted legally and hence was not liable to the plaintiff.

However, it may be sufficient to show that the performance of the contract was interfered with. The origins of this development can be traced back to the case of *Torquay Hotels Co Ltd* v *Cousins* [1969] 2 Ch 106. The defendants, during the course of an industrial dispute, persuaded various petrol companies not to deliver oil to the plaintiffs' hotel. Esso, the plaintiffs' principal suppliers, did not deliver any oil because their drivers were members of the defendant union and so would not cross the picket line. The plaintiffs managed to procure some alternative supplies for a short period of time but the alternative suppliers were soon warned off by the defendant union. The plaintiffs brought an action against the defendants seeking an injunction restraining them from inducing a breach of contract between Esso and themselves. The difficulty was that their contract with Esso contained an exclusion clause or a force majeure clause which absolved Esso from the obligation to deliver oil when their failure to deliver was caused by events outside their control, including industrial action. So it appeared that there was, in fact, no breach of contract. Nevertheless the defendants were held to have committed a tort and the plaintiffs were granted their injunctions. There are two ways in which this finding that the defendants were liable can be analysed.

The first way is to adopt the narrower approach based upon the reasoning of the majority in *Torquay Hotels*. This approach focused upon the existence of the exclusion clause. The majority perceived the exclusion clause in defensive rather than definitional terms; that is, they saw the exclusion clause as providing a defence to a breach of contract. On this view of the nature of the exclusion clause there was a breach of contract and, while the exclusion clause provided Esso with a defence to any action brought on the contract against them by the plaintiffs, it could not be relied upon by the defendants who were not party to the contract. This interpretation does not conflict with the requirement that there must be a breach of contract because it holds that there was, in fact, a breach of contract and that the reason the defendants were held to be liable was that they could not rely on an exclusion clause which had been drafted for the benefit of someone else. The difficulty with this view is that it misrepresents the true nature of an exclusion clause, which is to define the obligations which the parties have accepted and not to act as a defence to a breach of an obligation (see Yates *Exclusion Clauses in Contracts* (2nd ed) chapter 1 and the judgment of Lord Diplock in *Photo Production Ltd* v

Securicor Transport Ltd [1980] AC 827). The perception of the exclusion clause in definitional terms would have required the majority to give a direct answer to the question whether a breach of contract was a necessary ingredient of the tort.

The second way of analysing the case is to adopt the wider principle laid down by Lord Denning in the following terms:

> 'Interference is not confined to the procurement of a breach of contract. It extends to a case where a third person prevents or hinders one party from performing his contract, even though it be not a breach.'

This statement appears to be a much broader statement of principle than that adopted by the majority. However it is unclear whether Lord Denning was referring to the direct form of the tort or the indirect form. The better view is that he was referring to the direct form of the tort (see *Clerk and Lindsell on Torts* (16th ed) para. 15–05). If this view is correct it creates a tort of rather uncertain limits. Presumably it would not apply to the case where a defendant induced a contracting party to exercise an option to terminate a contract because in terminating the contract no unlawful act was committed. The difficulty is that, where there is interference with performance short of a breach, no unlawful act is committed by the defendant and it is virtually impossible to mark out the limits of liability with any degree of certainty.

However, in *Merkur Island Shipping Corp* v *Laughton* (above) Lord Diplock interpreted Lord Denning's judgment as relating to the indirect form of the tort (for criticism see Wedderburn (1983) 46 MLR 632). In *Merkur* the House of Lords held that there was a tort of interfering with contractual rights by unlawful means. Lord Diplock held that the four-stage approach to the tort of indirectly inducing a breach of contract adopted by Jenkins LJ in *Thomson* v *Deakin* (above) was not confined to cases of breach of contract but that it also extended to cases where there was interference with the performance of the contract short of breach. The same four-stage approach is to be adopted in cases of interference with performance by unlawful means except that at stages one and four the reference is to interference with performance rather than breach. So it is now clear that in the case of the indirect form of the tort it is not necessary to show that there has been a breach of contract but the position is wholly unclear in relation to the direct form of the tort. Much depends on the interpretation placed upon Lord Denning's judgment in *Torquay Hotels* (see too the decision of the House of Lords in *Dimbleby and Sons Ltd* v *National Union of Journalists* [1984] 1 WLR 427, noted by Carty (1984) 100 LQR 342).

The Court of Appeal has, however, recently stated that it is most important not to extend the principle of *Lumley* v *Gye* outside its proper limits. In *Middlebrook Mushrooms Ltd* v *Transport and General Workers Union* (1993) The Times 18 January a trade union's campaign of distributing leaflets outside supermarkets urging members of the public to support dismissal of employees of a mushroom producer by refusing to buy the producer's mushrooms was not tortious. If the case was to fall within the *Lumley* v *Gye* category the persuasion had to be directed to one of the parties to the contract; the union's leaflet was directed to the customer, not the management of the supermarkets who were neither encouraged nor discouraged to take any action. Where direct pressure was brought to bear on strangers to the contract and the effect on the contracting party was indirect it was necessary to show that some unlawful means had been used if the conduct was to be actionable.

Damage

Damage is the very gist of this tort but the courts are willing to infer that the defendant's inducement of the breach of contract has caused loss to the plaintiff.

Justification

The scope of the defence of justification as a defence to the tort of inducing breach of contract was helpfully discussed by the Court of Appeal in *Edwin Hill & Partners* v *First National Finance Corporation* [1989] 1 WLR 225. Stuart-Smith LJ identified two circumstances where the defence has succeeded. The first was 'where the contract interfered with is inconsistent with a previous contract with the interferer' (*Smithies* v *National Association of Operative Plasterers* [1909] 1 KB 310). The second was where there was a 'moral duty to intervene'. Such was the case in *Brimelow* v *Casson* [1924] 1 Ch 302. The defendant trade union official induced actresses working for the plaintiff theatre manager to break their contracts of employment. His justification for inducing them to break their contracts was that their wages were so low that they were compelled to resort to prostitution to supplement their wages. It was held that this was sufficient to justify the defendant's actions. On the other hand, Stuart-Smith LJ noted that the following factors have been held not to constitute justification: 'absence of malice or illwill or intention to injure the person whose contract is broken' (*South Wales Miners' Federation* v *Glamorgan Coal Co* [1905] AC 239), 'the commercial or other best interests of the interferer or the contract breaker' (*South Wales Miners' Federation* v *Glamorgan Coal Co* (above)) and the 'fact that A has broken his contract with X does not of itself justify X in revenge procuring a breach of an independent contract between A and B' (*Smithies* v *National Association of Operative Plasterers* (above)).

29.5 Intimidation

The tort of intimidation was resurrected from obscurity by the House of Lords in the important case of *Rookes* v *Barnard* [1964] AC 1129 The plaintiff was an employee of BOAC. The three defendants were trade unions officials, two of whom were employed by BOAC. Despite an informal agreement between the union and BOAC that all employees at the plaintiff's place of work would be union members, the plaintiff resigned from the union. The defendants then notified BOAC that there would be a strike unless the plaintiff was dismissed. BOAC gave in to this threat and lawfully determined the plaintiff's contract. The plaintiff, having no cause of action against BOAC, brought an action for damages against the defendants. It was held that the defendants had committed the tort of intimidation and that there was no statutory immunity for this tort and so the plaintiff was entitled to succeed. There are five basic ingredients of this tort. The tort consists of a threat by the defendant against a third party that the defendant will use some unlawful means against the third party unless the third party does or refrains from doing some act which he is entitled to do and as a result the plaintiff suffers loss. The five ingredients of the tort are as follows.

Threat

The defendant must threaten the third party or put pressure upon him to adopt a particular course of action. This was satisfied in *Rookes* by the defendants' threat that there would be a strike unless the plaintiff was dismissed. The courts formally distinguish between a threat and a warning, the latter being insufficient to ground an action in the tort of intimidation. A threat must be of the 'or else' kind, although there is no requirement that the warning be express rather than implied.

Unlawful act or means

The defendant's threat to the third party must be a threat of some unlawful act. If the defendant simply threatens to do that which he has a legal right to do the tort is not committed. The difficulty here concerns what constitutes unlawful means. It is clear that it encompasses threats of a criminal nature or threats to commit a tort. The important point which *Rookes* established was that, for this purpose, a breach of contract counts as unlawful means. Lord Devlin said that there was nothing to distinguish a threat to breach a contract from a threat of violence; the one could be as coercive as the other (for full consideration of *Rookes* and the finding that a breach of contract can constitute unlawful means see Wedderburn (1964) 27 MLR 257 and Hoffman (1965) 81 LQR 116).

Submission to the threat

Thirdly the third party must submit to the threat of the defendant. This was satisfied in *Rookes* because BOAC gave in to the threat and dismissed the plaintiff. This requirement is, in many ways, an obvious one because it is only through the third party submitting to the threat that damage is caused to the plaintiff. Had BOAC in *Rookes* not submitted to the threat, the plaintiff would not have lost his job and he would not have suffered any damage.

Damage

The fourth element of the tort is that the plaintiff must suffer damage as a result of the third party submitting to the defendant's threat. Once again damage is the very essence of the tort.

Justification

It is unclear whether or not there is a defence of justification to the tort of intimidation. A good argument can be made out that there should be no such defence because the tort is only committed where there has been the use of some unlawful means and a defendant should not be able to justify an unlawful act. In *Rookes* Lord Devlin expressly left the point open as it did not arise for consideration on the facts of the case. However, in the case of *Morgan* v *Fry* [1968] 2 QB 710 Lord Denning suggested that the defence may be available to trade union officials who commit the tort when intimidating an employer to dismiss people who are 'really troublemakers' (see to similar effect his judgment in *Cory Lighterage Ltd* v *TGWU* [1973] ICR 339). The exact status of these dicta remains uncertain.

So far we have been considering three-party intimidation, where the threat is made against a third party with the intention that damage be done to the plaintiff. But does the tort exist in the two-party form? This could arise where A threatens B with an unlawful act unless B does or refrains from doing some act which he is entitled to do and thereby loss is intentionally caused to B. There is a dearth of authority on this particular point. In *Rookes* v *Barnard* Lord Evershed was of the opinion that the tort could be committed in the two-party form, as were Lord Denning and Lord Pearce in *Stratford* v *Lindley* (above). However, in *Stratford* Lord Reid said that he was not convinced that two- and three-party intimidation were truly comparable. The main difference is that, in the case of two-party intimidation, the plaintiff has an alternative remedy open to him (for example, if he is threatened with a breach of contract he has a remedy in contract) whereas, in the case of three-party intimidation, the only possible remedy available to the plaintiff is in tort. A strong argument can be made that the plaintiff should be confined to his remedy in contract, especially since the development of the doctrine of economic duress in contract, but the balance of the authorities suggests that the plaintiff will also have an action in the tort of intimidation.

29.6 Economic duress?

In *Universe Tankships of Monrovia* v *International Transport Workers Federation* [1983] 1 AC 366 Lord Scarman suggested that there was a tort of economic duress. He said that it was established law that:

> 'Duress, if proved, not only renders voidable a transaction into which a person has entered under its compulsion but is actionable as a tort, if it causes damage or loss.'

Lord Scarman cited two authorities in support of this proposition, *Barton* v *Armstrong* [1976] AC 104 and *Pau On* v *Lau Yiu Long* [1980] AC 614, but neither of them make any mention of there being such a tort. The recognition of such a tort would have serious implications for the general rule that liability in the economic torts rests upon the unlawfulness of the defendant's acts. The reason for this is that the boundary of economic duress lies in the distinction between legitimate and illegitimate pressure and not between lawful and unlawful pressure. So, if Lord Scarman's view was to be accepted, it would mean that liability could exist in the absence of unlawful means, something which is not countenanced by *Allen* v *Flood*. It is therefore submitted that Lord Scarman is wrong and there is no tort of economic duress (see too Carty and Evans [1983] JBL 218).

29.7 Interference with trade by unlawful means

We have already noted that unlawful means is an essential ingredient in three of the nominate torts which we have discussed so far. It is an essential element in conspiracy to injure by unlawful means, the indirect form of the tort of inducing breach of contract and in intimidation. Unlawful means is also an essential component in the tort of interference with contractual rights which was recognised by the House of Lords in *Merkur Island Shipping Corpn* v *Laughton* (above). This leaves out the anomalous tort of conspiracy to injure by lawful means and it also does not take account of the direct form of the tort of inducing breach of contract. It could be argued that in the latter form of the tort there is a breach of contract which is induced and that that could be called unlawful means. However, it is submitted that this is the wrong way of looking at the direct form of the tort because it is really concerned with the protection of contractual rights rather than the prohibition of the use of unlawful means. Thus the direct form of the tort really lies in a separate category from the other economic torts because of its purpose of protecting contractual rights.

Nevertheless, direct inducement of a breach of contract apart, unlawful means plays a crucial role within the economic torts and there have been suggestions that the nominate torts be drawn together into one innominate tort entitled interference with trade or business by unlawful means (see generally Carty 'Intentional Violations of Economic Interests: The Limits of Common Law Liability' (1988) 104 LQR 250).

There has also been some judicial recognition of the existence of such a tort. Lord Reid said in *Stratford* v *Lindley* (above) that the defendants' industrial action made it 'practically impossible' for the plaintiffs to continue with their business and that 'it was not disputed that such interference with business is tortious if any unlawful means are used'. The leading proponent of this tort has, however, been Lord Denning. He referred to the existence of the tort in *Daily Mirror Newspapers Ltd* v *Gardiner* [1968] 2 QB 762, *Acrow* v *Rex Chainbelt* [1971] 1 WLR 1676 and, in *Torquay Hotels* v *Cousins*, he said:

> 'I have always understood that if one person deliberately interferes with the trade or business of another, and does so by unlawful means, that is, by an act which he is not at liberty to commit, then he is acting unlawfully, even though he does not procure or induce any actual breach of contract.'

The existence of the tort was also recognised by the House of Lords in *Merkur Island Shipping*, although there Lord Diplock talked mainly about the tort of interference with the performance of a contract by unlawful means and only gave passing approval to the wider tort of interference with trade by unlawful means. The tort was also recognised by the Court of Appeal and the House of Lords in *Hadmor Productions* v *Hamilton* [1982] 2 WLR 322 and by the Court of Appeal in *Lonrho plc* v *Fayed* [1990] 2 QB 479) and in *Department of Transport* v *Williams* (1993) The Times 7 December where it was held that the criminal offence established by s303 of the Highways Act 1980 of wilfully obstructing any person carrying out his duties under the Act also constituted the tort of wrongful interference with business..

Given that there is now a substantial body of authority which recognises the existence of this tort, the vital question now becomes: what are its limits? In *Lonrho plc* v *Fayed* (above) the Court of Appeal held that it was not necessary to establish that it was the predominant purpose of the defendant to injure the plaintiff. On the other hand, it was held that the plaintiff must prove that the unlawful act of the defendant was directed against the plaintiff or was intended to harm the plaintiff. The crucial question, however, is: what constitutes unlawful means? It is reasonably clear that a crime, a tort and a breach of contract may constitute unlawful means. But it is not yet clear that English law has reached the stage where it is ready to recognise that a wide range of wrongs may constitute unlawful means. For example, in *Lonrho* v *Shell Petroleum* (above) the defendants did breach a penal statute and that breach did interfere with the plaintiffs' business, but the plaintiffs were unable to recover from the defendants in tort. It may be that this was because the action was held not to be aimed at the plaintiffs or it may be that it was because there are certain types of breaches of penal statutes which do not count as unlawful means. On the other hand, the Court of Appeal in *Associated British Ports* v *Transport and General Workers' Union* [1989] 1 WLR 939 envisaged a much wider role for unlawful means, holding that a non-actionable contravention of a statute could count as unlawful means provided that there was a sufficient intention to injure the plaintiff. Although the decision of the Court of Appeal was subsequently reversed by the House of Lords on the construction of the particular regulations which were the subject-matter of the dispute, the House of Lords did not comment upon the wider dicta of the Court of Appeal and it remains to be seen how far, if at all, the reasoning of the Court of Appeal remains authoritative.

This doubt about the generality of unlawful means can also be seen in the case of *Chapman* v *Honig* [1963] 2 QB 502. The defendant landlord gave the plaintiff notice to quit because the tenant had given evidence in an action brought by other tenants against the landlord. In taking this action against the plaintiff the defendant was guilty of a criminal contempt of court. Yet the majority of the Court of Appeal held that the commission of this criminal offence did not give the plaintiff a cause of action in tort. On the other hand in *Acrow* v *Rex Chainbelt Inc* (above) a different result was reached. This time the defendants inflicted loss upon the plaintiff's business through ignoring a High Court injunction, thereby committing a contempt of court. It was held that unlawful means included a contempt of court and that, provided the defendants' actions were done with the intention of harming the plaintiffs' business, that was sufficient to establish liability in tort. However the *Chapman* case was not discussed and so it is difficult to know how to attempt to reconcile the two cases (see too the conflict between the two 'bootlegging' cases *Ex p Island Records* [1978] Ch 122 and *RCA* v *Pollard* [1982] 3 WLR 1007).

So, although it is possible to argue that English law does recognise the existence of a tort of interference with trade by unlawful means, the tort is still at a very early stage in its development. Thus conflicts arise as to what constitutes unlawful means and the courts appear to give inconsistent answers to this particular question. It is only as the courts build up a body of case law that principles will begin to emerge which will help us to understand exactly what constitutes unlawful means for the purpose of this tort.

29.8 The statutory immunities

Many of the cases which we have discussed are cases concerned with industrial action. It is important to note that many of these cases were decided against the backdrop of a statute which provided persons engaged in industrial action with certain immunities from suit in tort provided that they were acting in 'contemplation or furtherance of a trade dispute'. This is not the place for an in-depth analysis of the trade dispute immunities. All that will be done is to provide a brief summary of the principal immunities contained in the legislation.

Section 13(4) of the Trade Union and Labour Relations Act 1974 (TULRA) provides an immunity for the tort of conspiracy to injure by lawful means. Partial immunity is also provided for the tort of conspiracy to injure by unlawful means because the immunity is only withdrawn in respect of acts which would be actionable in tort if done by one person. Section 13(1) of TULRA also provides an immunity in respect of the tort of intimidation and in respect of all three forms of the tort of inducing breach of contract. These immunities are fairly water-tight and there has been relatively little discussion of these torts in recent cases. Instead employers have, in recent years, chosen to argue either that the defendant is not entitled to the immunity because the tort was not committed 'in contemplation or furtherance of a trade dispute' or that the defendant is not entitled to the immunity because it has been withdrawn, for example because the tort was committed in the course of unprotected secondary action (see s17 of the Employment Act 1980) or in the course of industrial action embarked upon without the support of a ballot (see the Trade Union Act 1984).

Nevertheless there have been some cases in which it has been argued that the defendants have committed a tort for which no immunity has been provided. For example there is no specific immunity for the tort of interference with trade or business by unlawful means, although, as we have noted, there are immunities for the various nominate torts which are components of the innominate tort. However if the plaintiff can find unlawful means which are not rendered immune by s13 then he can argue that the defendant has committed a tort for which there is no immunity. Such was the case in *Barretts & Baird (Wholesale) Ltd* v *Institution of Professional Civil Servants* [1987] IRLR 3 (noted by Fredman (1987) 103 LQR 176). The plaintiffs argued that the defendants had committed the tort of interference with trade or business by unlawful means. The unlawful means were alleged to be the breach of statutory duty committed by the employees in going out on strike and the breach by the striking employees of their contracts of employment. Neither of these alleged unlawful means are given immunity in s13 of TULRA. It was held that the defendants' predominant purpose was not to injure the plaintiffs but to achieve a better pay deal and so, applying the test laid down in *Lonrho* v *Shell Petroleum* (above), the defendants were not liable. Henry J did, however, consider the alleged unlawful means. He held that breach of statutory duty could, in an appropriate case, constitute unlawful means but that, on the facts, there was no evidence that a series of one day strikes would lead to such a total breakdown of the statutory system as to give rise to an action in tort. On the other hand he held that there was an arguable case that a striker's breach of his own contract of employment could constitute unlawful means. It had been provided in s13(3)(b) of TULRA that, 'for the avoidance of doubt', a striker's breach of contract was not to be regarded as unlawful means for the purposes of an action in tort. That provision was, however, repealed by the Employment Act 1980 and Henry J held that there was now an arguable case that a breach of contract could constitute unlawful means.

This type of argument is one that is likely to feature heavily in the courts as employers seek to find some 'unlawful means' which is not rendered immune under s13 of TULRA. This is one of the reasons why it is important to consider whether or not there is a tort of economic duress (see 29.6) because, if there is, there appears to be no immunity provided for it in s13 and so employers would gain a cause of action against the unions. So we are likely to see further arguments about breach of statutory duty as unlawful means and breach of contract as unlawful means as employers seek to outflank the immunities.

29.9 Conclusion

English law recognises that there are distinct nominate economic torts, but the major issue for the courts today concerns the existence of the innominate tort of interference with trade by unlawful means. This issue is likely to arise in trade dispute cases in the future. It is less likely to arise in the context of alleged unlawful competition because the legal regulation of competition is now heavily dominated by statute and the common law has little role to play. The difficulty with the heavy influence of trade dispute cases on the development of the economic torts is that most of these cases are heard on interlocutory proceedings where the discussion of the case law and of legal principles is, of necessity, very brief. This is not the best way for the development of the law to occur and it may take some years for the courts to put this area of law on a coherent basis and to decide what exactly constitutes unlawful means.

30

Remedies

30.1 Introduction

30.2 Types of damages

30.3 The protection of the reliance interest

30.4 Pecuniary loss

30.5 Loss of earnings: actual and prospective

30.6 The lost years

30.7 Loss of earning capacity

30.8 Loss of pension rights

30.9 Loss of housekeeping capacity

30.10 Medical expenses

30.11 Deductions

30.12 Other pecuniary losses

30.13 Non-pecuniary loss

30.14 Pain and suffering

30.15 Loss of amenity

30.16 Loss of expectation of life

30.17 The injury itself

30.18 Interest

30.19 Death in relation to tort

30.20 Damage to property

30.21 The commitment to the protection of the reliance interest

30.22 Tort and the expectation interest

30.23 Injunctions

30.24 Self-help

30.1 Introduction

The remedies available to a litigant in a tort action tell us a great deal about the interests which the law of tort seeks to protect. For example, one of the issues which was discussed in chapter 1 was whether the aim of tort law is to compensate the victims of torts or whether it is to punish those who commit torts. It is in the area of remedies that we are able to find an answer to that question.

The principal remedies which may be available to a plaintiff in a tort action are damages, an injunction and self-help. In this chapter we shall confine ourselves to a discussion of the general principles which are applicable to the granting of a remedy in tort. Where there are particular rules applicable to particular torts these have been discussed when dealing with the substantive law of that tort.

As damages is the most important remedy in tort law we shall concentrate upon the general principles applicable to the grant of an award of damages.

30.2 Types of damages

The general principle which lies behind the award of damages in a tort action is that damages are awarded to put the plaintiff in the position which he would have been in had the tort not been committed, in so far as this can be done by an award of damages. Tort law therefore aims to protect the reliance interest rather than the expectation interest (see further the discussion at 1.4). Since the aim of tort law is to protect the reliance interest of the plaintiff it is clear that the primary aim of damages is compensatory, rather than punitive (see *Cassell* v *Broome* [1972] AC 1027 and the discussion of this issue at 1.2). Although this is the general purpose behind a damages award there are, in fact, a number of different types of damages which may be awarded in a tort action. The principal ones are as follows.

Nominal and contemptuous damages

Nominal damages are awarded where some right of the plaintiff's has been infringed but the plaintiff has suffered no loss. The plaintiff receives a very small sum of money by way of damages, which has the effect of vindicating the right that has been infringed. Such was the case in *Constantine* v *Imperial Hotels Ltd* [1944] KB 693 where the plaintiff, who was a famous West Indian cricketer, was refused accommodation in one of the defendants' hotels but was given accommodation elsewhere. It was held that the defendants were in breach of their duty as common innkeepers because their refusal to give the plaintiff accommodation was unjustified. The plaintiff was therefore awarded five guineas damages.

Contemptuous damages are awarded where the court awards a derisory sum, which is the smallest coin of the realm, and which indicates that, while the plaintiff's action was technically justified, it was without any merit and should not have been brought. Such awards are most commonly made in libel actions. Where the court awards contemptuous damages the plaintiff also runs a considerable risk that the court will also express its disapproval of him having brought his action by refusing him costs or even ordering him to pay the defendant's costs.

General and special damages

General damage need not be specifically pleaded because it is the damage which is presumed to be caused by torts, such as libel, which are actionable per se. Special damage, on the other hand, must be specifically pleaded because, as in the tort of negligence, damage is part of the cause of action and so must be proved to have been suffered.

The terms general and special damages may, however, be used in another sense. In personal injuries cases losses which are capable of reasonably precise calculation, such as loss of earnings to the date of trial, are known as special damages and must be specifically pleaded. General damages are damages which are not capable of reasonably precise calculation, such as future loss of earnings and loss of amenity.

Aggravated and exemplary damages

Aggravated damages are said to be a species of compensatory damages in the sense that they are awarded to compensate the plaintiff rather than to punish the defendant. Aggravated damages may be awarded where the conduct of the defendant in committing the tort was such as to cause injury to the feelings or pride of the plaintiff. Where aggravated damages are awarded they should be 'moderate' (see *Archer* v *Brown* [1985] QB 401 and *W* v *Meah* and *D* v *Meah* [1986] 1 All ER 935). However the court may be reluctant to award aggravated damages in a negligence action. This can be seen in the case of *Kralj* v *McGrath* [1986] 1 All ER 54. The plaintiff suffered excruciating pain as a result of the negligence of the defendant obstetrician in delivering her twins. The defendant's negligence caused one of the twins to be born with severe disabilities and it died shortly after it was born. Woolf J stated that the conduct of the defendant was 'wholly unacceptable' and that he had put the plaintiff through the most dreadful agony. However, he held that medical negligence cases were not appropriate for the grant of aggravated damages because of the conflict with the general principle that damages in a negligence action were to be compensatory. Instead the proper approach was to increase the compensatory element of the damages recoverable to take account of the fact that the defendant's conduct had made it more difficult for the plaintiff to recover.

The effect of *Kralj* may be to make it more difficult to distinguish between cases where the appropriate course of action is to award aggravated damages and cases where the proper course is simply to increase the compensatory damages recoverable. At the other end of the scale it can also be difficult to distinguish between aggravated damages and exemplary damages (on which see Lord Wilberforce in *Cassell* v *Broome* (above)). The difference between the two is that the function of exemplary damages is to punish the defendant, whereas the function of aggravated damages is to compensate the plaintiff but, as Lord Wilberforce pointed out in *Cassell*, in practice it can be very difficult to say where compensation ends and punishment begins.

In *Rookes* v *Barnard* [1964] AC 1129 Lord Devlin set out the circumstances in which exemplary damages can be recovered in English tort law and this approach was applied by the House of Lords in the later case of *Cassell* v *Broome* (above). Exemplary damages are an exceptional remedy in English tort law because they are not consistent with the compensatory function of tort law. In *Rookes* v *Barnard* Lord Devlin held that, apart from the case where the grant of exemplary damages is authorised by statute, there are only two cases in which exemplary damages are available in English tort law. In *Cassell* it was held that exemplary damages are not available in any other case, no matter how illogical the present state of the law is, on the ground that exemplary damages are an anomaly and that their availability is not to be extended beyond these two cases.

Before considering the two cases in which exemplary damages can be recovered in tort, it is necessary to state a further qualification which has recently been reasserted by the Court of Appeal in *AB* v *South West Water Services Ltd* [1993] 2 WLR 507. There the plaintiffs alleged that they had suffered injury as a result of drinking water which had been contaminated at the defendants' water treatment plant at Camelford in Cornwall when 20 tons of aluminium sulphate were accidentally discharged into the water system. Their claim was made on a number of different grounds, one of which was public nuisance, and the issue which arose before the Court of Appeal on a preliminary hearing was whether or not the plaintiffs could make a claim for exemplary damages in public nuisance. The Court of Appeal held that they could not, even on the assumption that the defendants had acted in an arrogant and high-handed manner in ignoring the plaintiffs' complaints and in sending out a misleading letter which stated that the water was safe to drink. It was held that exemplary damages could only be awarded in respect of a tort for which exemplary damages had been awarded prior to the decision of the House of Lords in *Rookes* v *Barnard*. As the plaintiffs were unable to find a case in which exemplary damages had been awarded in a public nuisance case pre-1964 their claim for exemplary damages failed. It was suggested that this conclusion is unfortunate because it focusses attention upon the cause of action which had been pleaded rather than upon the quality of the defendants' conduct and it enables defendants to escape the imposition of exemplary damages if they have the good fortune to be able to show that such a claim had not been made pre-1964. The class of torts for which exemplary damages may be claimed has therefore been frozen.

The first case where exemplary damages are available is the case of oppressive, arbitrary or unconstitutional action by a servant of the government. 'Servants of the government' is not confined to central government but includes servants of local government and the police. In *Cassell* Lord Reid said that this category did not extend to oppressive action by a private corporation, however illogical such a distinction may be. In *AB* v *South West* Water *Services Ltd* the Court of Appeal stated, on the assumption that they were wrong on the jurisdiction point, that the plaintiffs' claim did not fall within this category because, even assuming that governmental functions could be delegated to a nationalised industry, the defendants were not acting in the exercise of executive power derived from government. In *Holden* v *Chief Constable of Lancashire* [1987] QB 380 it was held by the Court of Appeal that exemplary damages could be awarded in cases of unlawful arrest irrespective of the lack of oppressive behaviour by the arresting officer. This was because the requirement was that there be 'oppressive, arbitrary *or* unconstitutional action' by a servant of the government and not that there be 'oppressive, arbitrary *and* unconstitutional' action. This seems a rather literal approach to the interpretation of the judgment of Lord Devlin and it fails to follow the tenor of his judgment which was that exemplary damages are an exceptional remedy and not to be widely awarded. However, it was held that, although the issue of whether or not to grant exemplary damages should not have been withdrawn from the jury, the jury should have been directed to take account of the lack of aggravating circumstances in making their award of exemplary damages.

The second case in which exemplary damages may be available is where the defendant has calculated that he will make a profit for himself by committing the tort, even after paying compensatory damages. *Cassell* itself came into this category. The defendants published a book which made defamatory statements about the plaintiff. The book was published in the face of threats by the plaintiff that he would bring a libel action against the defendants. The jury awarded the plaintiff £15,000 compensatory damages and £25,000 exemplary damages. The defendants appealed on the ground that the damages which the jury had awarded were excessive. It was held that this was a case in which the jury was entitled to award exemplary damages because the defendants had calculated that it was worth running the risk of the book being held to be libellous because of the profits which they thought they would make from the sales of the book. It should be noted that the mere fact that a publication is published with the intention of making a profit is not sufficient, of itself, to bring the case within this category; there must be some evidence that the defendant decided that there was a profit to be made out of his wrongdoing. In other words the courts are saying to potential tortfeasors that tort does not pay. But this category was the subject of a narrow construction by Stuart-Smith LJ in *AB* v *South West Water Services Ltd* (above). He stated that the case did not fall within this category because the defendants had not calculated that they would make a profit from the tort. It was true that they might have been seeking to limit the damages payable to the victims of their wrongdoing but he argued that that was not the same as conduct calculated to make a profit from the commission of a tort.

30.3 The protection of the reliance interest

So the general principle is that the object of damages in tort is to restore the plaintiff to the position which he was in before the tort was committed, as far as this can be done by an award of damages. The law of tort is therefore, in theory, fully committed to the protection of the reliance interest. We shall examine the principles which the courts have applied in personal injury cases and in cases of damage to property and then consider the commitment of the law of tort to the principle of full compensation and to the protection of the reliance interest (see 30.21).

We shall start our analysis by considering the general principles applicable in personal injury cases (30.4 – 30.18) and then consider the principles applicable to damage to property (30.20). In seeking to compensate the plaintiff in a personal injuries case the damages which may be awarded by the courts can be divided into two categories: pecuniary loss (see 30.4 – 30.12) and non-pecuniary loss (see 30.13 – 30.17). We shall now consider the approach which the courts adopt in awarding damages in each of these two categories.

30.4 Pecuniary loss

Where the plaintiff suffers serious injury as a result of the defendant's negligence then pecuniary loss is likely to constitute the major element of the plaintiff's claim. Loss of earnings is likely to constitute the principal component of a claim for pecuniary loss, although it may include a wide variety of other losses such as the cost of medical treatment or the loss of pension rights.

30.5 Loss of earnings: actual and prospective

The plaintiff can recover for his loss of earnings to the date of trial. This is so no matter what the plaintiff was earning; he is entitled to have his earnings maintained by the tortfeasor. This is consistent with the aim of a damages award in returning the plaintiff to his pre-accident position. The effect of this principle is that it is cheaper negligently to run over a tramp than it is negligently to run over a millionaire. This complete protection of the plaintiff's pre-accident earnings has come under considerable criticism. Professor Atiyah has argued (*Accidents, Compensation and the Law* (4th ed) pp169–75) that there is no justification for preserving wage differentials when people are no longer at work and that people whose earning power is greater do not pay more for their insurance than do people who are less well off and so there is no reason why people with greater earning power should get more out of the system when they are injured. Professor Fleming has also noted (*The Law of Torts* (7th ed) p185) that the maintenance of wage differentials is 'starkly individualistic' and that it:

'... sharply contrasts with the pattern of social security systems which tend to limit disability benefits to average earnings or at least to impose an absolute ceiling, with the corollary that persons of exceptionally high earnings must make their own arrangements for any excess rather than burden and distort the compensation fund.'

Despite these criticisms the courts have remained committed to the goal of protecting the income levels of tort victims (see *Lim Poh Choo* v *Camden and Islington AHA* [1980] AC 174).

The greatest problems arise, however, with loss of future earnings because the courts have to engage in what is no more than educated guesswork. It requires the court to consider such imponderables as how long the plaintiff would have lived, how long he would have continued to work, what his prospects of promotion were and the rate of inflation in the future. The courts have consistently refused to award damages on the basis of actuarial tables (see, for example, *Taylor* v *O'Connor* [1971] AC 115) and have chosen to use a system which, as they see it, achieves a rough and ready form of justice.

Basically what the courts do is to calculate the plaintiff's net annual loss (which the courts call the multiplicand) and then multiply that loss by a figure based upon the number of years for which the disability is likely to last (which the courts call the multiplier). We shall consider separately how the courts calculate the multiplicand and the multiplier.

In assessing the plaintiff's net annual loss the courts start by calculating the plaintiff's gross earnings which he would have earned but for the accident. The starting point for this calculation is the plaintiff's earnings at the date of the accident but allowance is then made for the possibility of an increase in pay or for promotion (see *Ratnasingam* v *Kow Ah Dek* [1983] 1 WLR 1235). Once this sum is calculated then a deduction must be made for the tax which the plaintiff would have paid on his earnings (*British Transport Commission* v *Gourley* [1956] AC 185) and for social security contributions which he would have paid.

Once the net annual loss is calculated then an appropriate multiplier must be selected. However it is not simply the case that a calculation is made of the likely duration of the disability. In practice the multiplier tends to be lower than that, with the maximum multiplier being in the range of 16–18. There are two main reasons behind the courts' refusal to award the full number of years purchase. The first is that the courts discount for what is known as the 'general vicissitudes of life'. For example, in *Jobling* v *Associated Dairies* [1982] AC 794 Lord Bridge said that the vicissitudes principle flowed from the fundamental principle that the object of an award of damages is to put the plaintiff, so far as this can be done, in the position which he would have been in had it not been for the defendant's wrong. The assumption that the plaintiff would, in every case, continue to work for the rest of his life would result in the over-compensation of plaintiffs. So the courts discount at a rate of approximately 10 per cent for the vicissitudes of life (see Atiyah *Accidents, Compensation and the Law* (4th ed) p176).

The second reason why the courts do not award the full number of years purchase is that the plaintiff has received the money in a lump sum and so discount must be made for his accelerated receipt of the money. The sum is calculated on the basis that the lump sum paid will be exhausted at the end of the period of disability and that the lump sum, plus the interest which that sum has earned, will be sufficient to maintain the plaintiff at his pre-accident position. The difficulty with this method of calculation is that there is a danger that high levels of inflation will erode the value of the plaintiff's award. This was especially so in the 1960s and the 1970s. Professor Atiyah cites (*Accidents, Compensation and the Law* (4th ed) pp178–9) the example of *Thurston* v *Todd* [1965] NSWLR 1158 where a damages award made in 1965 to cover the cost of future nursing and medical costs was insufficient, by 1973, to pay for the nursing services which the plaintiff needed, despite the fact that her mother provided unpaid services for her each day. Despite this, the courts have consistently refused to make special provision for the impact of inflation and have assumed that, even in inflationary times, it is possible to obtain a real rate of return and so they have discounted at a rate of 4–5 per cent (see *Cookson* v *Knowles* [1979] AC 556 and *Taylor* v *O'Connor* [1971] AC 115). This assumption was demonstrably false during the 1970s when inflation raced ahead of the rate of interest, but it is closer to reality today. However, even today the plaintiff may be unable to make the right investment choice which will enable him to protect his damages award from the ravages of inflation. In many cases the plaintiff will be unable to obtain the best rate of return on his money (which can usually only be obtained by locking the money away for a period of time) because he has to rely upon the lump sum for his day to day maintenance and so the money must be in a place where he can have ready access to it.

The courts have also refused to increase the multiplier to take account of the fact that the income likely to be produced by the award may attract tax at the higher rates (*Hodgson* v *Trapp* [1989] AC 807). The incidence of taxation may be a factor to be taken into account in selecting a multiplier towards the top of the conventional scale but, once having selected a multiplier on the conventional basis, extra years should not be added on to take account of possible higher rates of taxation.

In many ways this problem raises the question of what we mean by the word 'compensation'. The effect of protecting all tort victims from the effects of inflation may be to put the plaintiff in a better position than the rest of society, who all suffer the effects of inflation (see to that effect the judgment of Lord Scarman in *Lim Poh Choo* v *Camden and Islington AHA* (above)). A solution which has much to commend it is to compensate the plaintiff for his loss of use of money by awarding a real rate of interest and compensating him for the loss of value by reference to annual changes in the consumer prices index (see Hammond (1983) 99 LQR 68). The advantage of using such an index is that the plaintiff is treated in the same way as the rest of society.

The other way of overcoming the problem would be to award damages in the form of periodical payments rather than a lump sum. Such a solution would not only help with the problem of inflation, but also with the many other situations in which the courts have to guess at what is likely to happen to the plaintiff in the future.

However no attempt has been made to introduce such a system in England. The general principle is that the plaintiff can only bring one action in respect of the defendant's wrong and that he can recover damages only once (*Fetter* v *Beale* (1701) 1 Ld Raym 339, 692). This rule does admit of certain exceptions, for example where two distinct rights of the plaintiff are violated (*Brunsden* v *Humphrey* (1884) 14 QBD 141) and where the damage is of a continuing nature (*Darley Main Colliery Co* v *Mitchell* (1886) 11 App Cas 127), but these exceptions do not constitute a major inroad into the general principle.

A token step was made in the direction of periodical payments in s32A of the Supreme Court Act 1981 (inserted by s6 of the Administration of Justice Act 1982) which applies to personal injuries cases in which there is:

> '... proved or admitted to be a chance that at some definite time in the future the injured person will, as a result of the act or omission which gave rise to the cause of action, develop some serious disease or suffer some serious deterioration in his physical or mental condition'.

In such a case the court has power to make a provisional award, in which damages will be awarded on the basis that the disease will not materialise but where, if it does, the plaintiff can come back to court for a further award of damages in respect of the disease. The meaning and likely impact of s32A was considered by Scott Baker J in *Willson* v *Ministry of Defence* [1991] 1 All ER 638. The plaintiff applied for an award of provisional damages after he slipped on a polished floor at work and broke his ankle. Scott Baker J held that there were three stages to be applied in considering the plaintiff's claim. At the first stage there must be shown to be a 'chance', at the second stage there must be a 'serious deterioration' and thirdly the court must decide, in the exercise of its discretion, whether or not to award provisional damages. Scott Baker J held that to 'qualify as a chance it must be measurable rather than fanciful'. On the facts the plaintiff did have a chance of osteoarthritis developing. He also held that a 'serious deterioration' was 'something beyond ordinary deterioration' but the difficulty for the plaintiff was that osteoarthritis was a 'progressive condition' and so could not be said to be something beyond ordinary deterioration; the plaintiff was therefore, on this ground, not entitled to an award of provisional damages. But Scott Baker J also proceeded to consider the approach to be adopted in exercising his discretion whether or not to award provisional damages. It is important to note that he affirmed that the general rule remained that damages are assessed on a once-and-for-all basis and that s32A was therefore merely a 'valuable statutory exception'. The court must therefore weigh up the 'possibility of doing justice by a once-and-for-all assessment against the possibility of doing better justice by reserving the plaintiff's right to return'. This suggests that the courts will tend to favour the assessment of damages on a once-and-for-all basis. In conclusion it must be aid that s32A is only a piecemeal attempt at resolving the problem (see James (1986) 136 NLJ 231) and there appears to be no particular policy reason for confining the section to changes in the plaintiff's medical condition. A number of arguments can be adduced in favour of introducing a system of periodical payments on a much wider scale.

The first is that it would reduce the element of speculation in a damages award because the periodical payment could be adjusted as the plaintiff's position changed. This ability to adjust the periodical payment makes it more likely that the purpose of a damages award will be secured in putting the plaintiff in the position which he would have been in but for the defendant's negligence. The second is that it can provide the plaintiff with long term security where the damages award is his main source of income and it can help avoid cases such as *Thurston* v *Todd* (above) where inflation eroded the value of the plaintiff's award. The third argument is that periodical payments would be easier to integrate into the tax and social security system (see 30.11).

However, there are a number of arguments against the introduction of a system of periodical payments. The first is that it does not promote finality in litigation and, to that extent, may be said to be contrary to public policy. The second is that periodical payments are more expensive to administer, especially where inflation is high and continuous adjustments need to be made. Thus they are likely to be unpopular with insurance companies. The third argument is that the system would be impracticable in small cases (for example below £5,000) and these cases would constitute the majority of cases. The fourth argument is that there is no evidence that plaintiffs want periodical payments. The fifth is that it is unclear what would happen to out-of-court settlements: would they be expected to follow suit or would they continue to be resolved on the basis of a lump sum payment? Finally difficulties would emerge where the plaintiff died shortly after the payments started. Would the payments cease or would they enure for the benefit of his dependants?

Despite these objections the majority of the Pearson Commission recommended (in chapter 16 of their report) that a system of periodical payments be introduced for serious and fatal cases. However, no steps have been taken to implement this proposal. It has been judicially noted that the present system is in need of reform (see the judgment of Lord Scarman in *Lim Poh Choo* v *Camden and Islington AHA* (above)) but Lord Scarman stated that such a reform 'calls for social, financial, economic and administrative decisions which only the legislature can take'. So it is only Parliament which can bring about such a drastic change in the law and so far Parliament has not shown the slightest interest in bringing about such a radical change in the method of paying tort damages (although it should be noted that the Law Commission has recently issued a Consultation Paper (No 126) which advocates a number of important changes to the present system for the payment of damages. The most significant feature of the consultation paper is the encouragement which it gives to structured settlements as a means of paying damages rather than the usual lump sum method. The Law Commission has also recommended that the courts should make greater use of actuarial evidence and that they should pay greater regard to information from the financial markets in deciding the extent to which it is appropriate to discount the multiplier to take account of the interest which the lump sum will yield).

30.6 The lost years

The plaintiff may, as a result of the tort of the defendant, have a reduced expectation of life. The effect of this is that the plaintiff suffers a loss of earnings in the period in which he would have worked had it not been for the tort of the defendant. It had been held by the Court of Appeal in *Oliver* v *Ashman* [1962] 2 QB 210 that the plaintiff could not recover for such a loss. The Court of Appeal interpreted the decision of the House of Lords in *Benham* v *Gambling* [1941] AC 157 as denying the existence of such a claim.

However, a different approach was adopted by the House of Lords in *Pickett* v *British Railways Engineering Ltd* [1980] AC 136. As a result of the negligence of the defendants, the plaintiff, who was 52, only had an expectation of life of one year. He claimed for the loss of earnings in respect of the years which he would have worked had it not been for the negligence of the defendants. The House held that he was entitled to recover for his earnings in the lost years and so overruled *Oliver*.

The defendants had argued that the true loss was not the loss of the plaintiff but the loss of his dependants and that the correct way of proceeding was to change the law so as to enable them to sue for such losses (they were unable to sue because a claim could not be brought under the Fatal Accidents Act 1976 where the deceased, while he was still alive, had sued the tortfeasor to judgment or had settled the claim). Lord Wilberforce saw the force of this argument but he held that it did not correspond with the expectations of the victim because his future earnings were of value to him. So he held that a rule which entitled the victim to recover in respect of his earnings in the lost years came closest to the expectations of the ordinary man.

The defendants also argued that the assessment of damages was too speculative and so the courts should not award damages in respect of the lost years. This argument was dismissed on the ground that chances and hypotheses are part of the system of personal injury litigation and that the judges were capable of dealing with this. However, the courts have had some difficulty in identifying the expenses which are to be deducted from the plaintiff's prospective earnings. The issue was finally resolved in *Harris* v *Empress Motors Ltd* [1983] 3 All ER 561 when it was held that the sums to be deducted were those which the plaintiff would have spent exclusively upon himself and not those he would have spent on his dependants. Where the plaintiff would have spent money on heating and lighting which would have been of benefit both to himself and to his dependants, the proportion to be deducted is the plaintiff's share of that cost, but not the dependants' share. In cases of very young plaintiffs the court is extremely unlikely to award the plaintiff damages in respect of the lost years because the process is so speculative (*Croke* v *Wiseman* [1981] 3 All ER 852). However, where the plaintiff is a five-year-old superstar he or she may be able to recover something for the lost years because the process then ceases to be entirely speculative (see *Gammell* v *Wilson* [1982] AC 27, 78).

30.7 Loss of earning capacity

The plaintiff may, in cases of continuing disability, remain in his pre-accident employment but subject to the risk that, should he lose that job, he will be placed at a disadvantage in the labour market. Such was the case in *Moeliker* v *A Reyrolle Ltd* [1977] 1 All ER 9. The plaintiff lost part of his thumb at work due to the negligence of the defendants. He was able to continue in his pre-accident job but he claimed that he would be at a disadvantage were he to lose that job and be thrown into the open labour market because his disability made it more difficult for him to do his job. It was held that an award of damages in respect of loss of earnings capacity should only be made where there is a real or substantial risk that the plaintiff will lose his job before the end of his working life. Where there is such a risk then damages should be awarded. Where the risk of him losing his job is low then an award measured in hundreds of pounds should be given, but where the risk is serious then the damages should be measured in thousands of pounds. On the facts the risk was low and the plaintiff was awarded £750.

However in the case of *Foster* v *Tyne and Wear CC* [1986] 1 All ER 567 Lloyd LJ doubted whether there was a separate head of damages called loss of earning capacity, which was separate from loss of future earnings. He noted the decision of the Court of Appeal in *Moeliker* but said that, while it was not necessary to decide the point, he preferred the view of the Pearson Commission and the Law Commission that there was no difference between the two except the degree of precision with which it was possible to quantify the loss.

30.8 Loss of pension rights

Where the plaintiff suffers a loss of future earnings he may also suffer a loss of pension rights. He is entitled to be compensated for such a loss, although the calculation of his pension had he continued to work may give rise to considerable practical difficulties (see *Auty* v *National Coal Board* [1985] 1 All ER 930).

It should also be noted in this context that in *Dews* v *National Coal Board* [1988] AC 1 the House of Lords held that the plaintiff could not recover, as part of his loss of earnings, the contributions which would have been made to a compulsory pension scheme had he not been absent from work when he was injured by the negligence of the defendants. It was held that the plaintiff was not entitled to recover these unpaid contributions because the failure to pay these contributions did not result in any loss of pension rights and so he had not suffered any loss.

30.9 Loss of housekeeping capacity

It may be that the plaintiff does not work in paid employment but that he or she plays an important part in the running of the household. In *Daly* v *General Steam*

Navigation Co Ltd [1980] 3 All ER 696 the plaintiff was injured as a result of the negligence of the defendants and suffered a partial disability to perform her housekeeping duties. It was held that the losses caused by this disability pre-trial were recoverable as part of the damages for pain and suffering (contrast *Roberts* v *Johnstone* [1989] QB 878) but that the plaintiff could recover for future loss of housekeeping ability and that the proper measure of damages was the cost of employing domestic help for eight hours per week. The plaintiff was not, however, under any obligation to employ a domestic help. It was up to her how she wished to spend the damages awarded and if she wished to struggle through the housekeeping on her own and spend the damages on something else then she was perfectly free and entitled to do so.

30.10 Medical expenses

The plaintiff may incur substantial expense in obtaining medical treatment and the general principle is that the plaintiff is entitled to the cost of medical expenses which he reasonably incurs as a result of his injury (*Cunningham* v *Harrison* [1973] QB 942). Section 2(4) of the Law Reform (Personal Injuries) Act 1948 provides that in determining the reasonableness of any expenses the possibility of obtaining them on the National Health Service is to be ignored. Given that we have had a National Health Service for 40 years, the wisdom of such a provision is far from obvious (see Atiyah *Accidents, Compensation and the Law* (4th ed) pp181–3). Even the Pearson Commission recommended that the cost of private medical care should only be recoverable where it was reasonable on medical grounds for the plaintiff to obtain private medical care.

Damages under this head include the cost of transport to and from hospital and the cost of going on a special diet. But s5 of the Administration of Justice Act 1982 provides that 'any saving to the injured person which is attributable to his maintenance wholly or partly at public expense in a hospital, nursing home or other institution shall be set off against any income lost by him as a result of his injuries'.

One other interesting problem which arises under this head concerns the case where the injured party is cared for by a member of the family. Can the defendant be required to pay for the cost of this care? Two possibilities arise. The first is that the volunteer could proceed directly against the tortfeasor. The difficulty here is that the volunteer has no action in tort against the tortfeasor nor does he have a contract with him. So the only possibility is a restitutionary action against the tortfeasor on the ground that the tortfeasor has been unjustly enriched at the expense of the volunteer. However the courts have preferred to hold that the loss is truly the loss of the injured party because, as the result of the negligence of the defendant, he has a need of medical care and should be compensated for that need. In *Housecroft* v *Burnett* [1986] 1 All ER 332 it was affirmed that the loss was truly that of the injured person and that the purpose of the award was to provide for the reasonable and proper cost of the care (see also *Roberts* v *Johnstone* [1987] QB 878). It was held that where a relative (or even the defendant: *Hunt* v *Severs* [1993] 3 WLR 558) gives up work to look after the plaintiff the court will award a reasonable recompense to the plaintiff, but that the ceiling on such an award is the commercial rate for providing such care (see too *Donnelly* v *Joyce* [1974] QB 454). This solution works well unless the plaintiff refuses to hand over any money to the volunteer. In *Cunningham* v *Harrison* (above) Lord Denning said that the damages recovered were held on trust by the plaintiff for the volunteer, but such a solution was disapproved by the Court of Appeal in *Housecroft*. The only possible basis for recovery would appear to be a contractual action by the volunteer against the plaintiff, but where they are members of the same family it may be difficult to overcome the presumption that there was no intention to create legal relations and so it may not be possible to show that there was a contract to provide such care.

30.11 Deductions

In an effort to ensure that a plaintiff is not over-compensated as the result of an award of damages, deductions may be made from the award to reflect benefits which the plaintiff has received as a result of his injuries. The theme which has been clear in recent developments is this desire to ensure that plaintiffs are not over-compensated as a result of an award of damages; therefore deductions are now made in a greater range of circumstances than has been the case hitherto and the risk of plaintiff under-compensation has emerged.

Section 82 of the Social Security Administration Act 1992 (first enacted in s22 of the Social Security Act 1989) enacts major changes relating to the recovery of social security benefits paid to plaintiffs. There are two principal philosophies behind the Act; the first is that the state should not subsidise tortfeasors and the second is that accident victims should not receive a windfall in the form of double recovery. The clear aim of avoiding double compensation should be contrasted with the political compromise which prevailed prior to 1989 under which half the value of certain benefits receivable by the plaintiff in the five years following the accident were deducted from the damages received for loss of earnings (s2 of the Law Reform (Personal Injuries) Act 1948).

The 1992 Act applies to any compensation payment made on or after 3 September 1990 in respect of an accident, injury or disease occurring on or after 1st January 1989 and provision is made for full deduction of all prescribed benefits. Section 82(1) states that a person who pays compensation (described in the Act as 'the compensator') shall not make a payment until the Secretary of State has furnished him with a 'certificate of total benefit'. The obligations of the compensator are essentially threefold. First he must not make a payment until he has been notified by the Secretary of State of the amount of benefit to be deducted. Second he must deduct the stated sum and pay it to the Secretary of State. Thirdly, he must notify the victim of the amount which has been so deducted.

So the compensator must deduct from the payment (which includes both an award made under a court order and an out-of-court settlement, in the latter case whether or not liability has been admitted) a sum equal to the gross amount of any 'relevant benefits' paid or likely to be paid to or for the victim during the relevant period (being five years from the date of the accident, injury or disease) in respect of that injury, accident or disease. The amount of any relevant benefits must be deducted from the entire sum, including for this purpose compensation for pain and suffering. The Secretary of State has power to make regulations providing that any prescribed payment shall be an exempt payment for the purposes of s82 (see s81(3) and (4) which list a number of payments which are to be 'exempt payments', including any 'small payment' (s81(3)(a)), as defined in s85 and regulations made thereunder (but it should be noted that Schedule 4 paragraph 22 of the Social Security Act 1989 provides that such payments will 'still be subject to the 50 per cent offset under s2 of the Law Reform (Personal Injuries) Act 1948', as amended), payments under s35 of the Powers of Criminal Courts Act 1973 (s81(3)(b)), damages awarded under the Fatal Accidents Act 1976 (s81(3)(c)), awards of criminal injuries compensation (s81(3)(f)), payments under accident insurance policies entered into by the victim before the accident (s81(3)(h)) and 'any redundancy payment falling to be taken into account in the assessment of damages in respect of an accident injury or disease' (s81(3)(j)).

As far as other benefits and other sources of income are concerned resort must be had to the common law. In *Parry* v *Cleaver* [1970] AC 1 the general principle was stated that a benefit was only to be deducted where the benefit truly reduced the loss which the plaintiff had suffered. Thus wages or sick pay paid by the employer as a matter of contractual obligation are deductible in full because they reduce the plaintiff's loss but it appears to be the case that ex gratia payments made by employers are not deductible (see *Dennis* v *London Passenger Transport Board* [1949] 1 All ER 779). Money received under a disablement pension scheme is not deductible, even where the tortfeasor is the plaintiff's employer and therefore the 'provider' of the pension scheme, because the pension is the fruit of the employee's work and is attributable to his work in the past; it is not a replacement for his loss of earnings (*Smoker* v *London Fire and Civil Defence Authority* [1991] 2 AC 502). Unemployment benefit received before the trial is deductible in full (*Nabi* v *British Leyland (UK) Ltd* [1980] 1 All ER 667), as is supplementary benefit received before the trial (*Lincoln* v *Hayman* [1982] 1 WLR 488). However the proceeds of an insurance policy are not deductible (*Bradburn* v *Great Western Railway* (1874) LR 10 Ex 1), nor are charitable donations (unless, perhaps, the charitable donation is provided by the tortfeasor, see *Hussain* v *New Taplow Paper Mills Ltd* [1988] 2 WLR 266). Lord Reid said in *Cleaver* that in the case of charitable donations it would be unjust if the only person who benefited from the receipt of charitable donations was the tortfeasor because his obligation to the plaintiff would thereby be reduced.

In *Hussain* v *New Taplow Paper Mills Ltd* [1988] AC 514 the defendant employers took out insurance against their contractual obligation to their employees to maintain them at a rate of 50 per cent of their pre-accident earnings under a long-term sickness benefit scheme, which was payable where the employee had been incapacitated for work as the result of an accident in the course of his employment and after the employee had been off work for 13 weeks (during which period he received his full pay). The insurance scheme was funded entirely by the employers and there was no evidence that the plaintiff's wages would have been higher if the defendants had not operated such a scheme. The defendants argued that the proceeds of this long term sickness benefit scheme were deductible because they were in the nature of earnings. The plaintiff argued that they were not deductible because they were in the nature of payments from an insurance policy and so were not deductible under the principle laid down in *Parry* v *Cleaver* (above). It was held that the sums were deductible because they were in the nature of earnings as the scheme was stated to be a continuation of salary and there was no policy reason why these payments should be left out of account because they went directly to reduce the plaintiff's loss. Lord Bridge stated that to hold that the plaintiff, who had paid no insurance premiums, should receive his full wages from two different sources (the employer and the tortfeasor) positively offended his sense of justice, and this sense of injustice was even more acute where, as here, the employer and the tortfeasor were one and the same person. It should be noted, however, that the House of Lords did not consider the situation where the plaintiff is able to show that the payments are part of his wage structure in the sense that his wages would be higher if the insurance scheme were not in operation (although in the Court of Appeal, [1987] 1 All ER 417, Kerr LJ stated that in such a case the conclusion may be that the sums are not deductible).

In *Colledge* v *Bass Mitchells & Butlers Ltd* [1988] 1 All ER 536 the Court of Appeal held that a redundancy payment which had been paid by the defendants should be deducted from the damages payable to the plaintiff. The plaintiff, who was an employee of the defendants, was injured at work due to the negligence of the defendants. Before the action was heard the plaintiff was offered voluntary redundancy by the defendants. The plaintiff accepted this offer and was given a redundancy payment of £9,000. The defendants argued that the redundancy payment should be deducted from the damages award. However, the trial judge held that the redundancy payment was not to be deducted because it was a reflection of past service and was not attributable to the accident. On appeal the Court of Appeal held that, as it was unlikely that the plaintiff would have been made redundant apart from the injury, the money fell to be deducted. In the words of Lord Reid in *Parry* v *Cleaver* (above), the redundancy payment had been received as a result of the accident and therefore it fell to be deducted.

Reference must also be made to the judgment of Lord Bridge in *Hodgson* v *Trapp* (above). More important than the narrow point of law at stake in this case (whether attendance and mobility allowances were deductible) was the *manner* in which Lord Bridge dismissed the plaintiff's argument. He rejected the argument that such state benefits were analagous to charitable payments, stating that he found the concept of public benevolence a 'difficult one to comprehend'. Significantly, he added that to refuse to make a deduction would only:

'... add to the enormous disparity, to which the advocates of a 'no-fault' system of compensation constantly draw attention, between the position of those who are able to establish a third party's fault as the cause of their injury and the position of those who are not.'

It is clear that the courts wish, as far as possible, to avoid the conclusion that a plaintiff can be compensated twice for the same loss. The point can be neatly illustrated by reference to the case of *Berriello* v *Felixstowe Dock & Railway Co* [1989] 1 WLR 695. The plaintiff, who was an Italian seaman, was injured as a result of the negligence of the defendants. The Cassa Marrittima Meridionale (administered by the Italian State) paid him a sum of money on account of his injuries and notified him that a further sum would be paid. Crucially, the money was recoverable by the CMM if the plaintiff recovered damages in respect of the loss for which the payments had been made. The Court of Appeal held that the payments made by CMM were not deductible because here, unlike *Hussain* and *Hodgson*, there was no fear of double compensation; the plaintiff was required to repay the money received to CMM. Dillon LJ stated that, if an English statute were to provide that a welfare benefit was to be recoverable from the recipient if he recovered damages from a third party in respect of the loss in relation to which the welfare benefit had been paid, then he could not 'conceive that the English courts would require the welfare benefits to be deducted in the assessment of the amount of damages payable to the injured person'.

Finally, it should be noted that one recent case sits rather uneasily with the policy of prevention of double compensation. That case is *McCamley* v *Cammell–Laird Shipbuilders Ltd* [1990] 1 All ER 854. The plaintiff suffered serious injury in an accident caused by the negligence of the defendants, his employers. The defendants' holding company had taken out a policy of insurance under which the defendants were described as the insured and the employees as insured persons. Payments were made independently of fault and were calculated by a multiplication of the plaintiff's earnings and were paid in the form of a lump sum. The plaintiff was unaware of the existence of this policy until after his accident when he received the sum of £45,000 which had been paid to the defendants under the policy. The Court of Appeal, distinguishing *Hussain*, held that the £45,000 was not to be deducted because it was an act of benevolence. The critical features of *McCamley* appear to be that the money was paid in the form of a lump sum (and not in the form of a replacement for wages), the money was payable regardless of fault and the money was not attributable to any particular recognised head of damage.

30.12 Other pecuniary losses

The plaintiff may suffer other types of pecuniary loss, such as the loss of ability to carry out a profitable hobby. Another example was provided by the Court of Appeal in *Jones* v *Jones* [1985] QB 704 where the plaintiff's injuries resulted in the breakdown of his marriage. It was held that he was entitled to recover from the defendant the cost of maintaining two homes, instead of one (see too *Meah* v *McCreamer* [1985] 1 All ER 367). However, in *Pritchard* v *J H Cobden Ltd* [1988] Fam 22 a differently constituted Court of Appeal held that the financial consequences of a divorce were not recoverable on the grounds that divorce was not a loss but was a redistribution of the parties' assets; it was too remote and as a matter of policy it was not recoverable. So the Court of Appeal refused to follow *Jones* v *Jones* and it is unclear which decision will now be followed.

30.13 Non-pecuniary loss

The difficulties in assessing damages become even more acute when we consider non-pecuniary losses. Professor Atiyah has argued (*Accidents, Compensation and the Law* (4th ed) p183) that 'such damage awards could be multiplied or divided by two overnight and they would be just as defensible or indefensible as they are today'. Non-pecuniary losses can be divided into four categories, which we shall now discuss.

30.14 Pain and suffering

The plaintiff is entitled to recover for the pain and suffering which he has endured and which he will endure as a result of the negligence of the defendant. Where the plaintiff is unaware that he has suffered any pain and suffering because, for example, he has remained unconscious throughout, then he cannot recover any damages under this head (*Wise* v *Kaye* [1962] 1 QB 638). A plaintiff cannot recover for pain and suffering which takes the form of sorrow and grief; it must be shown that the plaintiff has suffered recognised nervous shock (*Kralj* v *McGrath* [1986] 1 All ER 54). In *Hicks* v *Chief Constable of the South Yorkshire Police* [1992] 2 All ER 65 the plaintiffs died of traumatic asphyxia at the Hillsborough tragedy. The medical evidence established that, once asphyxia had set in, unconsciousness would have followed within a few seconds and death would have occurred shortly afterwards. It was held that damages were only recoverable for the pain and suffering, including the knowledge of impending death, which the plaintiffs had suffered in the few seconds between the onset of asphyxia and the ensuing unconsciousness and death. On the facts it was held that no damages were recoverable at all because these last few seconds were, in reality, part of death itself and 'fear of impending death felt by the victim of a fatal injury before that injury is inflicted cannot by itself give rise to a cause of action which survives for the benefit of the victim's estate' (per Lord Bridge, for criticism see Unger (1992) 142 NLJ 394).

Where the plaintiff has suffered a loss of expectation of life as a result of the negligence of the defendant, the court is required under s1(1)(b) of the Administration of Justice Act 1982 to take into account in assessing damages for the plaintiff's pain and suffering 'any suffering caused or likely to be caused to him by awareness that his expectation of life has been so reduced'.

30.15 Loss of amenity

The plaintiff is entitled to be compensated for his loss of capacity to engage in activities which he enjoyed before his injury. The difficulty which has arisen here is whether the plaintiff must be aware of his loss of enjoyment. The issue was considered by the House of Lords in *H West and Son Ltd* v *Shepherd* [1964] AC 326. The plaintiff was a 41-year-old married woman who suffered severe head injuries in an accident which resulted in cerebral atrophy and paralysis of all four limbs. There was some evidence that she might be aware to some extent of the condition which she was in. The majority of the House of Lords upheld an award of £17,500 to the plaintiff for loss of amenities. There was a strong dissent from Lords Reid and Morris. They argued that one can no more compensate an unconscious person than one can compensate a dead person and that the purpose of an award of damages under this head was to compensate the plaintiff for his loss of happiness and that nothing could therefore be awarded where the plaintiff was unaware of his loss of happiness. The majority replied that a living person should not be treated as though he were dead and that a person who is alive is entitled to recover damages in his own right.

The minority also argued that the approach of the majority would give rise to serious anomalies because the plaintiff who was unconscious but who survived until after the trial would recover damages under this head whereas the person who died shortly before the action would not be able to recover damages. The majority countered this reasoning by pointing out that the only logical stopping point for the minority was to say that the recoverability of damages depended upon the plaintiff's awareness of his loss of amenity and the unhappiness which that loss caused him. Lord Pearce said that it would be 'lamentable' if the recoverability of damages were to depend on protestations of misery by the plaintiff.

In *Lim Poh Choo* v *Camden and Islington AHA* (above) Lord Scarman said that he did not underestimate the 'formidable logic and good sense' of the minority opinions in *West*, but he said that the case had stood as an authority since 1963 and that its reversal would cause widespread injustice unless it was part of a widespread legislative reform of the law. So it is highly unlikely that *West* will ever be overruled. The only point which suggests that the minority approach in *West* has found some favour is that the damages which were awarded in *West* amounted to £17,500, whereas only £20,000 was awarded in 1977 in *Lim Poh Choo*, which, when inflation is taken into account, constitutes a considerably smaller sum than that awarded in *West*. So the only prospect for change is that the damages awarded under this head may decline rather than disappear altogether.

30.16 Loss of expectation of life

In *Flint* v *Lovell* [1935] 1 KB 354 it was held that there was an independent head of damages called loss of expectation of life. However in *Benham* v *Gambling* [1941] AC 157 it was held that damages awarded under this head should be a modest conventional figure, which was fixed at £200. This action was, however, abolished by s1(1)(a) of the Administration of Justice Act 1982 and has been replaced by a claim for bereavement, which is a fixed sum which may be awarded to a spouse for the loss of a spouse and to parents for the loss of a child who at the time of death (not the time of the accident, see *Doleman* v *Deakin* (1990) The Times 30 January) had not attained the age of 18. The level of bereavement damages was raised from £3,500 to £7,500 with effect from 1 April 1991.

30.17 The injury itself

Where the plaintiff loses an arm or a hand as a result of the defendant's negligence then damages may be claimed in respect of that injury. In many cases it will not be easy to distinguish between the injury and the consequences of the injury and the court will award a sum which covers both losses. But in respect of the injury itself the judges set a tariff for the loss of various limbs or faculties. The value placed upon such losses is, to some extent, arbitrary, as there is no market for the replacement of limbs (regard should be had to Kemp and Kemp *The Quantum of Damages*, or to current law, to see the sums currently awarded by the courts for the loss of limbs or faculties). But at least the effect of the operation of the tariff system is to ensure a measure of consistency in the awarding of damages.

30.18 Interest

In times of inflation it is obvious that interest must be claimed on damages because there will usually be a considerable lapse of time between the date of the accident and the date of the trial. In cases of damages for personal injuries or death exceeding £200 the court must, under s35A of the Supreme Court Act 1981, award interest unless there are special reasons for not doing so. Interest can only be claimed on losses to the date of the trial because in respect of future pecuniary losses no loss has been sustained at the date of trial and so no interest can be awarded for such losses.

Pecuniary loss carries interest at the rate of half of the short term interest rate from the date of the accident to the date of the trial (*Jefford* v *Gee* [1970] 2 QB 130 and *Cookson* v *Knowles* [1979] AC 556). Interest on non-pecuniary loss is only at the rate of interest of 2 per cent from the date of the service of the writ to the date of trial because such loss is assessed at the date of the trial and so the plaintiff is not affected by the loss of value of the money and need only be compensated for his loss of use of the money (*Wright* v *British Railways Board* [1983] 2 AC 773).

30.19 Death in relation to tort

Where the negligence of the defendant results in the death of another then special rules have been evolved to deal with this issue. At common law the rule was that death extinguished a cause of action which the deceased may have had against the defendant. At the same time no cause of action accrued for the benefit of the dependants of the deceased. Both these rules have now been abolished so that now two actions are normally available arising out of the death of the deceased.

The first is that under s1(1) of the Law Reform (Miscellaneous Provisions) Act 1934 all causes of action 'subsisting against or vested in [the deceased] shall survive against, or, as the case may be, for the benefit of, his estate'. Thus the effect of this section is to enable the plaintiff's estate to bring an action where the plaintiff was killed by the negligence of the defendant. The principles applicable in assessing damages are generally the same as in a personal injuries case, except that exemplary damages are not recoverable, a claim for bereavement does not survive for the benefit of the deceased's estate and a claim for loss of earnings in the lost years can only be brought by a living plaintiff (s4(2) of the Administration of Justice Act 1982, for criticism see Cane and Harris (1983) 46 MLR 478).

The second action which may be brought is that under the Fatal Accidents Act 1976 the dependants of a deceased person who was wrongfully killed may bring an action in damages under the provisions of that Act. The dependants may only bring an action under the Act if the deceased person would have been able to bring an action against the defendant (s1(1) of the Fatal Accidents Act 1976). Thus any defence which the defendant would have been able to rely on against the deceased is also available against the dependants.

'Dependants' are defined in ss1(2) and 1(4) of the 1976 Act as the deceased's spouse, former spouse or cohabitee, parents, children, grandparents and grandchildren and any brother, sister, uncle or aunt, or their issue. A relationship by affinity (that is, by marriage) is treated as if it were a relationship of consanguinity (blood) and a relationship of half blood is treated as if it were a relationship of the whole blood.

The dependants can maintain an action for damages for bereavement (see 30.16), any funeral expenses which have been incurred and claims for actual and future pecuniary loss. The main problem here lies in assessing damages for pecuniary loss. The purpose behind the award of damages here is to maintain the dependants in the position which they would have been in had the deceased still been alive. The courts start by calculating the deceased's earnings and then deduct a sum to represent the deceased's personal and living expenses. Where the deceased is the mother of a small child who is not in paid employment then the damages are assessed on the basis of the wages which would be payable to a notional nanny and not on the cost of fostering the child (although for criticism of the 'notional nanny' approach see the judgment of Sir David Croom-Johnson in *Hayden* v *Hayden* [1992] 4 All ER 681, 693). In assessing the wages which would be payable to a notional nanny discount must be made for the fact that the extent of the services required by a child decreases as the child gets older (see *Spittle* v *Bunney* [1988] 3 All ER 1031). In *Cresswell* v *Eaton* [1991] 1 All ER 484 the plaintiffs' mother was killed in an accident caused by the negligence of the defendant. For a short while the plaintiffs lived with their grandmother but she died some two years later. In the circumstances the plaintiffs' aunt gave up her job as a traffic warden to look after and care for the plaintiffs. Simon Brown J held that the plaintiffs' losses were of two types. The first was what he called the 'disbursement dependency', by which he meant the plaintiffs' loss of their mother's financial support. The second loss was the 'services dependency', by which he meant the loss of their mother's care. The difficulty here was that their mother had been in employment prior to her death and so was a 'part-time carer', whereas the aunt gave up her employment to become a 'full-time carer'. Simon Brown J held that:

> 'Where a claim is based in large part on a relative's actual loss of earnings reasonably incurred, modest discount only should be made to reflect the part-time nature of the deceased mother's care. And that is so even if it is as much the emotional as the physical needs of the children which make it reasonable for the relative to give up work.'

But he held that there is 'room for a somewhat larger discount' in relation to relatives who do not actually lose any earnings as a result of providing the care. On the facts Simon Brown J made a deduction of 15 per cent for the aunt's care but 30 per cent for the grandmother's care (she did not suffer any loss of earnings).

Once this has been done then the court will calculate the likely duration of the dependants' dependency, which is a process similar to that adopted in calculating the multiplier in a personal injuries action. In assessing damages and the length of dependency the prospects that the deceased's widow will remarry are to be ignored (s3(3) of the 1976 Act), but not the possibility that the parties would have divorced where the evidence reveals that possibility: *Martin* v *Owen* (1992) The Times 21 May.

Any benefits which have accrued or will accrue or may accrue to the dependants from the estate of the deceased or otherwise as a result of the death of the deceased are to be disregarded (s4 of the 1976 Act). Thus in *Wood* v *Bentall Simplex Ltd* (1992) The Times 3 March the Court of Appeal held that in assessing damages it is irrelevant that a loss from one source might be balanced by a benefit since s4 required benefits to be disregarded. This section produces an odd contrast with the rules relating to deductions in a claim brought by an injured plaintiff because s4 clearly sanctions double compensation. The courts have, however, experienced great difficulty in interpreting s4, as can be seen in the following three cases. The first case is *Pidduck* v *Eastern Scottish Omnibuses Ltd* [1990] 2 All ER 69. The deceased was killed as a result of the negligence of the defendants. At the time of his death the deceased was in receipt of a non-contributory pension from his employers and, after his death, his widow continued to receive an allowance based upon her husband's pension entitlement. The defendants argued that the sums paid to the widow under the pension scheme were to be taken into account in quantifying the damages payable to the widow. But it was held that the allowance was a 'benefit' which accrued to the widow 'as a result of' her husband's death and it was therefore to be disregarded under s4. Purchas LJ held that the purpose behind s4 was:

> '... to produce an exception to the common law rules for calculating quantum of damages, namely to prevent the deduction of a benefit which would otherwise have to be deducted in order to arrive at the true loss on a common law basis.'

The second case is *Stanley* v *Saddique* [1992] 1 QB 1. The plaintiff's mother was killed in a road accident caused by the negligence of the defendant. After her death the plaintiff's father met another woman who subsequently became the plaintiff's stepmother and the 'motherly services' which the stepmother provided were of a 'higher quality than could foreseeably be expected to have been provided by the [plaintiff's] mother'. The defendant argued that account should be taken of this benefit to the plaintiff and that s4 only excluded from consideration direct pecuniary benefits. But the Court of Appeal held, after a careful examination of the legislative history of what is now s4, that they were required by the Act to disregard this benefit in calculating the damages payable.

The third and most difficult case is the decision in the Court of Appeal in *Hayden* v *Hayden* [1992] 4 All ER 681 (criticised by Kemp (1993) 109 LQR 173). The plaintiff brought a claim against the defendant, her father, whose negligence had resulted in the death of her mother. The plaintiff was four at the date of the accident. After the accident the defendant gave up work and provided significant services for the plaintiff in caring for her in place of her mother (although there was some controversy as to the quality of the care so provided). The trial judge found that the mother had been an excellent mother and probably would have bestowed on her daughter more attention than her father had been able to do. One of the issues which arose before the Court of Appeal was whether the care provided by the father fell to be disregarded under s4. By a majority, the Court of Appeal held that it was not to be disregarded. McCowan LJ dissented. He relied on *Stanley* v *Saddique* (above) for the proposition that there is to be no reduction in the damages payable to take account of the care voluntarily provided in substitution for the mother's services and that, for this purpose, it was irrelevant that the care had been provided by the tortfeasor himself. The majority disagreed. Parker LJ chose to follow the reasoning of the Court of Appeal in *Hay* v *Hughes* [1975] QB 790 rather than *Stanley*. He and Sir David Croom-Johnson stated that the father was simply discharging his parental duties and it could not be said that the services were provided 'as a result of' the mother's death. Although Sir David Croom-Johnson emphasised that the question of what is a 'benefit' must be regarded as a question of fact, there is clearly a division of opinion as to the proper interpretation of s4 and the matter is in need of urgent consideration by the House of Lords so that the inconsistencies which have arisen can be removed.

Finally, in *Watson v Wilmott* [1991] 1 QB 140 the court considered the impact of adoption on the plaintiff's claim for damages. The plaintiff's mother was killed in an accident caused by the negligence of the defendant and, some months later, his father committed suicide as a result of the depression caused by the death of his wife. The plaintiff was looked after by his aunt and uncle who later adopted him. Garland J held that the adoption had to be taken into account in the quantification of the dependency. In the case of the loss of the plaintiff's father, the loss of dependency was to be calculated by comparing the plaintiff in the position he would have been in had his father lived with his position with his adoptive father; therefore the sum to be awarded was the plaintiff's loss of dependency on his father less his dependency on his adoptive father. But, in so far as his dependency on his mother was concerned, Garland J held that the adoption replaced his non-pecuniary dependency on his deceased mother and that therefore the non-pecuniary dependency on his mother was to be assessed only up to the date of his adoption.

30.20 Damage to property

Where it is the plaintiff's property rather than his person which suffers damage the same principle is applicable, which is that the plaintiff must be returned to the position which he was in before the damage was done. If the property is completely damaged then the proper measure of damages is the market value of the goods at the date they were destroyed (*Liesbosch Dredger v SS Edison* [1933] AC 449). If the goods were used for a profit-making purpose then the plaintiff may recover for the profit which he has lost or he may recover the cost of hiring a substitute if it was reasonable to do so (*Martindale v Duncan* [1973] 1 WLR 574).

Where the goods are damaged rather than completely destroyed the measure of recovery is generally the diminution in value of the goods (*The London Corporation* [1935] P 70). In many cases this will be equivalent to the cost of repair but where the cost of repair exceeds the diminution in value the plaintiff will be confined to the latter sum unless the property is unique (*O'Grady v Westminster Scaffolding* [1962] 2 Lloyds Rep 238) or, perhaps, where it is the plaintiff's land which has been damaged (*Dodd Properties Ltd v Canterbury City Council* [1980] 1 WLR 433).

30.21 The commitment to the protection of the reliance interest

The law of tort is theoretically committed to the principle of full compensation and to the complete protection of the reliance interest. In practice it comes close to the complete protection of the reliance interest. There are, however, certain limitations on the recoverability of compensation. For example a loss which is too remote cannot be recovered (see chapter 11) and discount is made for contingencies and vicissitudes. We have also noted that there is a risk that inflation will erode the value of the plaintiff's award. The plaintiff is also under a duty to mitigate his loss. Thus he cannot recover in respect of any part of his loss which he could have avoided by the taking of reasonable steps (*Darbishire* v *Warran* [1963] 1 WLR 1067). This doctrine is based on the need to avoid the waste of resources in society. The plaintiff need only take reasonable steps to mitigate his loss and what is reasonable depends on all the facts and circumstances of the case. All that can be said is that the standard of reasonableness is not high because a tortfeasor is not entitled to require that his victim take great steps to mitigate his loss. For example in *Selvanayagam* v *University of the West Indies* [1983] 1 All ER 824 it was held that, in the case of personal injuries requiring surgery, the test to apply is whether 'in all the circumstances including particularly the medical advice received, the plaintiff acted reasonably in refusing surgery?' Thus where the surgery involves considerable risk to the plaintiff or its outcome is uncertain it will not generally be unreasonable for the plaintiff to refuse to undergo surgery.

This commitment to the complete protection of the reliance interest puts the victims of torts in a very privileged position when compared with the lot of other victims of misfortune in society. This raises once again the question of why it should be that tort victims are in this privileged position and, as was noted at 1.2, the answer to that question is far from clear.

30.22 Tort and the expectation interest

Although tort is committed to the protection of the reliance interest we have also noted cases in which tort law has intervened to protect the expectation interest, that is the damages award has had the effect of enforcing a promise by putting the plaintiff in the position which he would have been in had the promise been carried out according to its terms and not in the position which he was in before the promise was made. Cases in which the expectation interest has been protected include *Junior Books Ltd* v *The Veitchi Co Ltd* [1983] 1 AC 520 and *Ross* v *Caunters* [1980] Ch 297. These cases have already been discussed (see 1.4, 7.7 and 7.9) and the same ground will not be traversed again; suffice it to emphasise the point that these cases create difficulties in ascertaining the relationship between tort and contract.

30.23 Injunctions

An injunction is an equitable remedy which is available in the discretion of the court. The general principle which guides the court in considering whether or not to grant an injunction is stated in s37 of the Supreme Court Act 1981 to be that it must appear to the court to be 'just and convenient' to make such an order. Injunctions are particularly significant as a remedy in certain torts and of little or no relevance in other torts. For example they are of little or no interest in negligence, but are of great significance in nuisance, trespass and the economic torts. Once again we will confine ourselves to a consideration of the general principles governing the granting of injunctions. Where there are special rules applicable to a particular tort these have been discussed when dealing with the substantive law of that tort. Injunctions can come in different shapes and sizes and there are, in fact, a number of different types of injunctions. The principal types are as follows.

Prohibitory injunction

A prohibitory injunction is an injunction which orders the defendant to refrain from continuing with his tortious activity. This is the form of injunction which is most commonly sought (for example in nuisance cases or cases involving the economic torts). The general principle which the courts apply in considering whether to exercise their discretion and grant an injunction is whether damages would be an appropriate remedy. Where damages are appropriate an injunction will generally not be issued. In many cases of a continuing tort damages will not be an adequate remedy and so this hurdle will be relatively easy to overcome. The court will also have regard to the conduct of the parties who are seeking the injunction, any delay in seeking the remedy and the effect of the grant of an injunction on innocent third parties.

Mandatory injunction

A mandatory injunction is of considerably less significance than a prohibitory injunction. A mandatory injunction is an injunction which requires the defendant to take some positive step, for example to remove something which constitutes a trespass on the plaintiff's land. Such an injunction will not be granted where damages would be an appropriate remedy, but there are other restrictions upon the availability of this type of injunction. In *Morris* v *Redland Bricks Ltd* [1970] AC 652 the House of Lords held that a mandatory injunction will only be granted where the plaintiff shows that there is a very strong probability that grave danger will accrue to him in the future if the injunction is not granted and the injunction must be sufficiently specific for the defendant to be able to know exactly what he has to do to comply with the terms of the injunction.

Quia timet injunction

Where the tort has not yet been committed, but the plaintiff apprehends that he will suffer imminent substantial damage from the commission of the tort, the court has jurisdiction to grant a quia timet injunction which has the effect of restraining the defendant from committing the tort. To obtain such an injunction the plaintiff must show that damage is almost certain to occur and that the damage is imminent.

Interlocutory injunction

The plaintiff may not wish to wait for the full trial of his action to obtain his injunction. So he may attempt to obtain an interlocutory injunction. Such an injunction is granted quickly pending the full trial of the action. This type of injunction is particularly important in trade dispute cases. In considering whether or not to grant such an injunction the court does not inquire into the substantive merits of the case; instead the plaintiff must show that there is a serious issue to be tried and that the balance of convenience lies in his favour (see *American Cyanamid Co* v *Ethicon Ltd* [1975] AC 396 and Gray (1981) 40 CLJ 307). Where the court does grant an injunction it is likely that the court will require an undertaking from the plaintiff that he will compensate the defendant for the damage that the interlocutory injunction has caused him if the defendant succeeds at the full trial of the action.

Damages in lieu of an injunction

The court has a discretion to grant an award of damages in lieu of an injunction. The courts are, however, extremely reluctant to exercise their discretion and award damages in lieu of an injunction (for consideration of the rules applied by the courts see 18.13 and Jolowicz [1975] CLJ 224).

30.24 Self-help

Lastly, the plaintiff may be able to take steps himself to alleviate his position without having resort to the courts. However, the courts are extremely reluctant to allow a plaintiff to take the law into his own hands in this way; see, for example, the restrictions placed on the self-help remedy in *Burton* v *Winters* [1993] 1 WLR 1077 for trespass to land as discussed on 25.6 above. But we have noted that there are certain cases where the plaintiff can take steps to protect himself. For example steps can be taken to abate a nuisance, distress damage feasant may be relied upon, a person who is falsely imprisoned may escape, a person who is being attacked can use self defence and a trespasser may be ejected provided that only reasonable force is used. These remedies are all exceptional and can only be exercised within rigid confines and are unlikely to be extended.

31

Miscellaneous Defences and Limitation

31.1 Introduction

31.2 Mistake

31.3 Illegality

31.4 Necessity

31.5 Limitation

31.1 Introduction

In this chapter we shall be concerned with various defences which may be invoked by a defendant in a tort action. Two of the principal defences, contributory negligence and volenti, have already been dealt with (see chapters 12 and 13) and so will not be dealt with in this chapter. Similarly where a defence is peculiar to a tort then it has been discussed in relation to that tort (as is the case with defences such as justification and fair comment in defamation) and will not be discussed further here. Attention in this chapter will therefore be confined to a miscellany of general defences such as mistake, ex turpi causa, necessity and limitation.

31.2 Mistake

Mistake is not a general defence in a tort action. For example a defendant cannot plead that it was a mistake that he ran the plaintiff down, although if the mistake was such that a reasonable man could have made it then it may indicate that the defendant was not negligent. Similarly, mistake is not a defence to a defamation action. However, there are cases where mistake can operate as a defence. For example an honest but mistaken belief in the truth of a statement will negative liability in deceit.

31.3 Illegality

On grounds of public policy a cause of action may be denied to a plaintiff who suffers damage as a result of the tort of the defendant while participating in criminal activity. This defence is sometimes described in the maxim ex turpi causa non oritur actio. Thus in *National Coal Board* v *England* [1954] AC 403 Lord Asquith stated:

> 'If two burglars, A and B, agree to open a safe by means of explosives, and A so negligently handles the explosive charge as to injure B, B might find some difficulty in maintaining an action for negligence against A.'

The operation of this defence was classically illustrated in the case of *Ashton* v *Turner* [1981] QB 137. The plaintiff suffered injury due to the negligence of the defendant in driving a getaway car from the scene of burglary in which they had both participated. Ewbank J held that, on grounds of public policy, the defendant did not owe to the plaintiff a duty of care (see also *Smith* v *Jenkins* (1970) 119 CLR 397).

There must be a causal connection between the damage which the plaintiff suffered and the crime in which he was participating. This is clearly satisfied in the example given by Lord Asquith in *National Coal Board* v *England* (above). However, another example given by Lord Asquith illustrates the limits of the defence: he said that if B stole A's watch while they were on their way to carry out the burglary then A could bring an action in tort against B because the theft was totally unconnected with the burglary.

The scope of the defence is difficult to define. It has been held that the defence is not confined to cases in which the plaintiff is engaged in criminal conduct (*Kirkham* v *Chief Constable of Greater Manchester Police* [1990] 2 QB 283). In *Euro-Diam Ltd* v *Bathurst* [1990] 1 QB 1 Kerr LJ stated that the ex turpi causa defence rests ultimately:

> '... on a principle of public policy that the courts will not assist a plaintiff who has been guilty of illegal (or immoral) conduct of which the courts should take notice. It applies if in all the circumstances it would be an affront to the public conscience to grant the plaintiff the relief which he seeks because the court would thereby appear to assist or encourage the plaintiff in his illegal conduct or to encourage others in similar acts.'

A similar approach was taken in *Thackwell* v *Barclays Bank plc* [1986] 1 All ER 676, 687, *Saunders* v *Edwards* [1987] 1 WLR 1186. This 'affront to public conscience test' was also adopted by Beldam LJ in *Pitts* v *Hunt* [1991] 1 QB 24 (discussed in more detail at 13.5). There the plaintiff was a pillion passenger who encouraged the first defendant, whom he knew was drunk, had no licence and was uninsured, to drive in a reckless and foolhardy manner which resulted in the death of the first defendant and serious injury to the plaintiff. Beldam LJ held that, if someone had been killed as a result of the activities of the plaintiff and the first defendant, the death would have amounted to manslaughter. He therefore held that it would be an 'affront to public conscience' to permit the plaintiff to bring a claim for damages for the injury which he suffered as a result of his participation in such criminal activity. Dillon LJ, on the other hand said that he found the 'affront to public conscience test very difficult to apply' because 'the public conscience may well be affected by factors of an emotional nature'. He held that the plaintiff's claim was barred because his claim was based directly upon the illegality. This was not a case in which the plaintiff had 'suffered a genuine wrong' to which the allegedly unlawful conduct was 'incidental'. Balcombe LJ adopted an approach similar to that adopted by Dillon LJ. He held that the plaintiff's claim must fail because the joint illegality in which he and the first defendant were engaged was such that the court could not determine the standard of care to be observed.

The defence was considered in some detail by the House of Lords in *Tinsley* v *Milligan* [1993] 3 WLR 126 where it was held that it did not apply to an arrangement which was undertaken to assist in the perpetration of fraud on the Department of Social Security over a number of years. The defendant succeeded on the grounds that her claim was based on an equitable title to property and she was not forced to plead or rely on an illegality, even though the title was acquired in the course of an illegal transaction.

After a full review of the authorities, Lord Goff rejected the public conscience test as constituting a 'revolution' in the law and this view, although expressed in a dissenting judgment, was agreed with by a majority of the Court (Lords Goff, Keith and Browne-Wilkinson). The defendant succeeded on the narrow ground that she was merely seeking to enforce a resulting trust, and the test applied by the House seems to require some reliance on the illegality, at least in contractual situations.

31.4 Necessity

Necessity can operate as a complete defence to negative liability in tort. In such a case the defendant argues that his course of action was the lesser of two evils and that he has intervened to prevent greater damage being occasioned. To be able to rely on the defence the defendant must show that he has acted as a reasonable man would have done. However, the courts are extremely reluctant to rely upon this defence. This can be seen in the case of *Southwark LBC* v *Williams* [1971] Ch 734 where squatters sought to invoke the defence of necessity as a defence to the plaintiff's action. Lord Denning stated that the plea of necessity:

> '... would be an excuse for all sorts of wrongdoing. So the courts must, for the sake of law and order, take a firm stand. They must refuse to admit the plea of necessity to the hungry and the homeless; and trust that their distress will be relieved by the charitable and the good.'

A similar approach was adopted by the House of Lords in *Burmah Oil Co* v *Lord Advocate* [1965] AC 75 when Lord Upjohn stated:

> 'No man now, without risking an action against him in the courts, could pull down his neighbour's house to prevent the fire spreading to his own; he would be told that he ought to have dialled 999 and summoned the local fire brigade.'

But the defence can operate in certain cases; for example the defence may be invoked by a surgeon who operates in an emergency without obtaining the plaintiff's consent.

31.5 Limitation

Statute has intervened to impose time limits within which an action in tort must be brought against a defendant. The general rule contained in s2 of the Limitation Act 1980 (referred to as the 1980 Act) is that an action in tort cannot be brought more than six years from the date on which the plaintiff's cause of action accrued. The crucial issue is to identify when the cause of action accrues because it is from that date that time begins to run. In the case of torts which are actionable per se time begins to run from the date of the defendant's act which constituted the tort. But in the case of torts which are dependent upon proof of damage time begins to run from the date of damage.

However, this general rule is the subject of a number of exceptions. The first arises in the case of actions for damages for negligence, nuisance or breach of duty (whether the duty exists by virtue of a contract or of provision made by or under a statute or independently of any contract or any such provision) where the damages claimed by the plaintiff consist of or include damages in respect of personal injuries to the plaintiff or to any other person (Limitation Act 1980, s11(1) and note that, for this purpose, 'breach of duty' does not encompass intentional trespass to the person, *Stubbings* v *Webb* [1993] 2 WLR 120, discussed by Rogers [1993] NLJ 258). In such a case s11(4) of the 1980 Act states that the limitation period is three years from the date on which the cause of action accrued. The cause of action accrues when the plaintiff suffers actionable damage. This causes unfairness to the plaintiff in a case such as *Cartledge* v *E Jopling & Sons Ltd* [1963] AC 758, where the plaintiff was unaware of the fact that he had suffered damage for more than three years. To remedy this s11(4) provides the alternative that time begins to run from the date of the plaintiff's knowledge of the damage (see further the complex provisions which have been enacted dealing with the issue of the knowledge of the plaintiff in s14 of the 1980 Act). The court has a discretion to allow the action to proceed even if it is commenced outside the three-year period, but the discretion must be exercised in the light of the guidelines contained in s33 of the 1980 Act.

The second exception arises where the plaintiff dies as a result of the tort of the defendant. In such a case, where the death occurs within three years of the accrual of the cause of action, then a fresh three-year period commences in favour of the personal representative or the dependants, running from the date of death or the date of knowledge of the death (s11(5) of the 1980 Act).

The third exception relates to a tortious act which causes latent damage to property. Here the position is governed by the Latent Damage Act 1986. Before considering this Act it is necessary to have regard to the law as it existed prior to the Act. The law prior to the Act was discussed in the case of *Pirelli General Cable*

Works Ltd v *Oscar Faber & Partners* [1983] 2 AC 1. The House of Lords held that in the case of damage to property time begins to run from the date when damage occurs to the property, whether or not that damage is reasonably discoverable (for the present standing of *Pirelli* see McKendrick in *Pirelli* Re-examined (1991) 11 Legal Studies 326). This ruling had serious implications, particularly for purchasers of buildings, because the six-year limitation period could have elapsed before the damage was actually discovered or was even discoverable (although the problem was not confined to building cases; see, for example, *D W Moore & Co* v *Ferrier* [1988] 1 All ER 400, where it related to the negligent drafting of a restraint of trade clause by a solicitor). The Latent Damage Act 1986 essentially provides that in the case of latent damage (other than in the case of personal injury) the normal six-year period operates, with the addition of a three year period which begins to run from the date on which the plaintiff discovered, or ought to have discovered the damage, subject to a longstop which has the effect of barring all claims brought more than fifteen years from the date of the defendant's negligence (see further on this complex piece of legislation Stanton (1986) PN 75).

32

Torts to Chattels

32.1 Introduction

32.2 Common law ingredients of the chattel torts

32.3 Trespass

32.4 Conversion

32.5 Detinue

32.6 The reversionary action

32.7 Redistribution of tort liability by statute

32.8 Title to sue

32.9 Pleading jus tertii

32.10 Double liability

32.11 Improvement to goods

32.12 Forms of judgment

32.13 Effect of judgment on title to goods

32.14 Title to lost goods

32.1 Introduction

In this chapter we shall discuss certain specific torts which exist to protect an owner of goods, or some other person having an interest in goods, from unlawful interferences with those goods. It must be remembered that, quite apart from these specific torts, a wrongful act towards goods can produce liability under one of the more general torts, such as negligence or nuisance. In what follows, however, only those torts which are peculiar to goods will be examined.

All of these specific torts have a long history, and by the mid-twentieth century it had become clear that they stood in urgent need of reform. In 1971 the Law Reform Committee (*Conversion and Detinue*, Cmnd 4774) reported, recommending radical modernisation and clarification of the law. But the legislation which followed – the Torts (Interference with Goods) Act 1977 – fell short of the Committee's proposals and has some unsatisfactory aspects. The result is a continuing state of doubt in several areas.

Despite their antiquity, the chattel torts have proved readily adaptable to modern circumstances. In recent case law, they have been invoked (with varying success) as a means of recovering commercial commodities detained by industrial action (*Howard E Perry Ltd* v *British Railways Board* [1980] 1 WLR 1375; *Harold Stephen Ltd* v *Post Office* [1977] 1 WLR 1172) or pornographic literature from the police (*Roandale* v *Metropolitan Police Commissioner* [1979] Crim LR 254 CA. The remedies provided by the 1977 Act were even invoked by the Secretary of State for Defence in his action against the *Guardian* newspaper to recover photocopied documents 'leaked' by Sarah Tisdall (*Secretary of State for Defence* v *Guardian Newspapers* [1985] AC 339, affirming [1984] Ch 156).

32.2 Common law ingredients of the chattel torts

Until 1978, the law recognised four main torts which could be committed against the personal property of another. These were:

1. Trespass to goods
2. Conversion
3. Detinue
4. The special action on the case for damage to a reversionary interest.

Each tort had its individual sphere of operation, although in practice categories (1) to (3) would substantially overlap. With the exception of detinue – which, as we shall see, was abolished by the 1977 Act – all of these torts survive unaltered today.

32.3 Trespass

Trespass to goods consists of any unauthorised interference with the personal property of another, provided that the act constituting the interference is immediate and direct. Thus, to deliberately damage or destroy a chattel (for example by setting fire to it, or hitting it with a hammer) would be a trespass. The classic illustration is given in *Fouldes* v *Willoughby* (1841) 8 M & W 540 where it was held that scratching the panel of a coach would be a trespass. Trespass does not lie for indirectly caused damage, such as the laying of bait for animals (*Hutchins* v *Maughan* [1947] VLR 131) and for this reason it has occasionally been doubted whether there can be vicarious liability for trespass, although on balance it seems likely that there may.

To use goods without the owner's permission, even without harming them, seems to constitute a trespass (*Penfolds Wines Pty Ltd* v *Elliott* (1946) 74 CLR 204); so does any unauthorised removal of goods, again whether this produces any harm or permanent deprivation or not (*Kirk* v *Gregory* (1876) 1 Ex D 55). If the taking is deliberate, it is no defence to show that the taker honestly believed the goods to be his (*Wilson* v *Lombank Ltd* [1963] 1 WLR 1294), nor is it a defence to show that one removed the goods for their own safety, unless this was actually reasonably necessary for their protection (*Kirk* v *Gregory* (above)). There is, nevertheless, some doubt as to whether all trespass is actionable per se, or whether certain types of trespass to goods, at least, require proof of special damage. It seems clear that a deliberate taking, touching or misuse can give rise to an action in trespass without proof of damage (see *Penfolds Wines Pty Ltd* v *Elliott* (above); *Kirk* v *Gregory* (above) and *Leitch & Co* v *Leydon* 1931 SC (HL) 1). On the other hand, New Zealand authority suggests that, if the trespass is merely inadvertent, actual damage must be proved (*Everitt* v *Martin* [1953] NZLR 298). In England, the question may no longer be significant because after *Letang* v *Cooper* [1965] 1 QB 232 it is possible that trespass to goods, like trespass to the person, is confined to deliberate, intentional interference. *Wilson* v *Pringle* [1987] QB 237, in indicating that, while there need be no actual intent to harm the victim, the touching must be intentional and 'hostile' could have been understood as suggesting that actual harm is not necessary to an action for trespass to the person (and, if so, the same rule may apply to trespass to goods) but *Wilson* must now be seen in the light of the doubt cast upon its correctness by Lord Goff in *re F (mental patient: sterilisation)* [1990] 2 AC 1, 73 (see 24.2).

Certainly a defendant who acts neither deliberately nor negligently cannot be sued for trespass to goods (*National Coal Board* v *Evans* [1951] 2 KB 861). Contributory negligence is no defence in proceedings founded on intentional trespass to goods (s11(1) Torts (Interference with Goods) Act 1977). The use of the word 'intentional' in this section suggests that the law may still recognise other forms of trespass to goods, such as inadvertent trespass.

Generally speaking, co-ownership is no defence to any action founded on trespass to goods (s10 Torts (Interference with Goods) Act 1977).

32.4 Conversion

Conversion was defined by Atkin J in *Lancashire & Yorkshire Ry* v *MacNicoll* (1919) 88 LJKB 601 as:

> '... dealing with goods in a manner inconsistent with the rights of the true owner ... provided ... there is an intention on the part of the defendant in so doing to deny the owner's right or to assert a right which is inconsistent with the owner's right.'

A more modern, but similar, definition was given by Lord Templeman in the Privy Council case of *Maynegrain Pty Ltd* v *Campafina Bank* [1984] 1 NSWLR 258, when he said that '... conversion is committed whenever one person performs a positive wrongful act of dealing with goods in a manner inconsistent with the rights of the owner'.

In one sense, conversion is a tort of strict liability: provided the defendant actually intends to deal with the goods in a manner which in fact interferes with (or is inconsistent with) the owner's rights, the mere fact that the defendant does not intend to violate these rights is no defence. Indeed, the defendant may be totally and blamelessly ignorant of the owner's interest in the goods, or even of his existence, and still be liable for conversion. Thus the innocent purchaser of goods from a thief, who has stolen them from the owner without the purchaser's knowledge, commits a conversion against the true owner by taking delivery of it (*Jerome* v *Bentley* [1952] 2 All ER 114; *Moorgate Mercantile Co* v *Twitchings* [1977] AC 890). Other examples of conversion include deliberate destruction (but probably not mere deliberate damage); the wrongful taking of goods if accompanied by an exercise of the rights of ownership; wrongful detention of goods, likewise if contradicting the rights of the owner (see *Howard E Perry Ltd* v *British Railways Board* (above)); misuse of goods if severe enough to amount to a denial or violation of the owner's title; and the unauthorised sale of another's goods, as in *Willis* v *British Car Auctions* [1978] 1 WLR 438 (where an auctioneer who sold a car at the request of a person whom he honestly believed to be the owner was held liable in conversion to the real owner). The receipt of goods under an unauthorised pledge is also a conversion (s11(2) Torts (Interference with Goods) Act 1977) but by s11(3) of the 1977 Act the mere verbal denial of an owner's title, unaccompanied by some positive conduct actually interfering with that title, is not (cf the position before the Act, as discussed in *Oakley* v *Lyster* [1931] 1 KB 148).

Conversion may even be committed by a defendant who is acting honestly in what he conceives to be the owner's best interests. In *Hiort* v *Bott* (1874) LR 9 Ex 86 the defendant (to whom the plaintiff's goods had been mistakenly delivered) indorsed the delivery order over to X (the plaintiff's supposed agent), who used it to misappropriate the goods to his advantage. It was held that, although the defendant acted solely in order to facilitate the return of the goods to the plaintiff, he was guilty of conversion. The result might have been otherwise, however, if the defendant had actually been put in possession of the goods against his will as an involuntary bailee: in such a case, the mere handing of them over to a third party whom the defendant believes to be the owner's agent will not be conversion unless, in delivering the goods, the defendant has acted without reasonable care (*Elvin and Powell Ltd* v *Plummer Roddis Ltd* (1933) 50 TLR 158).

Conversion can also be committed by the deliberate exposure of the goods to the risk of loss or destruction. In *Moorgate Mercantile Co* v *Finch* [1962] 1 QB 701 the use of a hired car for smuggling led to the confiscation of the car by the customs authorities. It was held that the smugglers were guilty of conversion. In *Garnham, Harris & Elton* v *Ellis* [1967] 2 All ER 940 a haulage company engaged to carry a load of copper wire wrongfully subcontracted the job to a second firm without checking their credentials, and the wire was stolen. It was held that the first carriers were guilty of conversion. Conversion can also be committed by a defendant who candidly acknowledges the true owner's title but refuses to surrender up his goods on the ground that he fears undesirable industrial or other consequences if he does so *(Howard E Perry Ltd* v *British Railways Board* (above) and see *Redler Grain Silos Ltd* v *BICC Ltd* [1982] 1 Lloyds Rep 435). Conversion may also be committed, in appropriate circumstances, by a defendant who was not in possession of the goods at the material time *(Bryanston Leasings* v *Principality Finance* [1977] RTR 45).

As with trespass to goods, contributory negligence is no defence to proceedings founded on conversion (s11(1) Torts (Interference with Goods) Act 1977). No action for conversion will lie, however, where the plaintiff or his agent actually consented to the performance of the acts in question *(Maynegrain Pty Ltd* v *Campafina Bank* (above)).

Generally speaking, co-ownership is no defence to an action founded on conversion (s10 Torts (Interference with Goods) Act 1977).

32.5 Detinue

Detinue could be committed in two ways. First, by wrongfully refusing to deliver goods to the person entitled to them *(Alicia Hosiery Ltd* v *Brown Shipley & Co Ltd* [1970] 1 QB 195). Secondly, detinue could be committed by a bailee's negligently losing the goods in breach of his duty of care under the bailment *(Goodman* v *Boycott* (1862) 2 B & S 1; *Houghland* v *R R Low (Luxury Coaches) Ltd* [1962] 1 QB 694). In the second case, once the goods were shown to have been lost, the burden of proving that he had taken reasonable care rested on the bailee *(Houghland* v *R R Low (Luxury Coaches) Ltd* (above)). The tort of detinue is now abolished in England (see further 32.7).

32.6 The reversionary action

As will be seen later (see 32.8), none of the foregoing actions will lie if the plaintiff had, at the time of the wrongful interference, neither possession of the goods nor the immediate right to their possession. Such a right would be lacking, for example, if A had bailed goods to B for a finite period during which a third party – C – wrongfully damaged, destroyed or misappropriated those goods. To repair this deficiency and to allow the owner with merely a postponed right of possession to sue, the courts devised a special action on the case. The leading authority is *Mears* v *LSW Ry* (1862) 11 CB (NS) 850, where the lessor of a barge which was damaged by a third party during the term of the hirer's possession was held entitled to recover damages from that third party, even though his own right of possession was deferred, and not immediate, at the time of the damage. In order to invoke this special action, however, the plaintiff must prove some lasting impairment of his reversionary interest: either enduring damage or, in the case of loss of the goods, the absence of any reasonable prospect of their being recovered (*Moukataff* v *BOAC* [1967] 1 Lloyd's Rep 396). Further, the plaintiff's loss must be suffered in his capacity as reversionary owner and not in some other capacity *(Candlewood Shipping* v *Mitsui OSK Lines, The Mineral Transporter* [1986] AC 1).

32.7 Redistribution of tort liability by statute

The Torts (Interference with Goods) Act 1977 made certain radical changes to the substantive content of the chattel torts. The most important was the abolition of detinue (s2(1)). In order to preserve that aspect of detinue which arose from the negligent loss of a bailor's goods, s2(2) of the 1977 Act now provides that an action in *conversion* lies against a bailee for the loss or destruction of goods which the bailee had allowed to happen in breach of his duty to his bailor. Conversion is therefore expanded to include a form of wrong which it did not include at common law. No statutory provision is made to accommodate within the tort of conversion the other species of detinue discussed above, concerning the wrongful withholding or detention of goods. In *Howard E Perry* v *British Railways Board* (above) Megarry VC held, however, that all cases of detinue were in any event also cases of conversion at common law; and therefore that the abolition of detinue has not reduced the area of wrongful conduct to goods because such detention, formerly actionable in detinue, always gives rise to an action in conversion. Some authors (see Palmer (1981) 44 MLR 87) regard this equation as questionable, however, and point to the statement of Mansfield CJ in *Morris* v *Pugh* (1761) 4 Burr 1241, 1243 that a wrongful detention was merely *evidence* of conversion.

Conversion and trespass survive largely unimpaired as independent torts, conversion being (as we have seen) substantially expanded by s2(1) of the 1977 Act. These torts are, nevertheless, affected by the 1977 Act in three main ways, as follows.

General collective notion of 'wrongful interference with goods'

The first impact of the Act is that conversion and trespass are grouped, along with all the other torts to chattels, within the general, collective concept of 'wrongful interference' or 'wrongful interference with goods'. In creating this new collective concept, the Act does not create a new substantive tort, nor – apart from detinue – does it abolish the old torts. Rather, the Act merely creates a 'hold-all' phrase in order to group the pre-existing torts together for the purpose of certain general, mainly procedural, reforms. These include the statutory definition of the remedies which a court can order in cases of wrongful interference (ss3,4), the principles whereby a claimant's title to goods may be extinguished upon his/her being awarded damages in a wrongful interference action based on the goods' full value (s5), the rules against double liability (s7), the statutory reversal of the old principle which prevented certain defendants in wrongful interference actions from pleading a superior title in a third party (s8) and special rules for concurrent actions (s9) (most of these procedural reforms will be discussed later in the chapter). By sl of the 1977 Act 'wrongful interference' as used elsewhere in the Act means conversion, trespass, negligence so far as it results in damage to goods or to an interest in goods, and any other tort (except for detinue, which is abolished) so far as it results in such damage. This definition would include the special action on the case for damage to a reversionary interest (see 32.6).

Specific rules affecting individual chattel torts

Certain individual torts are also made subject to specialised substantive reforms by the Act. Examples are the ban on contributory negligence as a defence in conversion or intentional trespass actions (s11(1)), the special provisions whereby an improver of goods might be awarded an allowance based on the extent of his improvement (s6) and the new section which deals with actions as between co-owners of goods (s10).

New rules on disposal of uncollected goods

Finally, the Act introduces new rules as to the disposal of uncollected goods (ss12, 13 and Schedule 1). These will not be separately discussed.

32.8 Title to sue

Before proceeding to a detailed examination of the 1977 Act, however, we shall look at the qualification which a plaintiff must demonstrate, in his relationship with the goods, in order to sue for trespass or conversion. What precise type of interest entitles an aggrieved party to bring these actions?

Trespass

Anyone who was in possession of the goods at the time when the tort was committed can sue in trespass, whether or not he is the owner and even though he may have come by his possession illegally: the law appears to consider it best to protect all possession, however obtained, from the incursions of unauthorised intruders (*Parker* v *British Airways Board* [1982] 1 QB 1004, per Donaldson MR, but cf *Thackwell* v *Barclays Bank plc* [1986] 3 All ER 676, 689, per Hutchinson J).

A person may also sue in trespass if he lacks possession but has an immediate right of possession to the goods at the time of the wrong, provided in this case that the act complained of is also a trespass against the party actually in possession, and thus occurs without that party's consent *(Penfolds Wines Pty Ltd v Elliott* (above)). Occasionally, the latter rule is artificially avoided by holding that a plaintiff who is not in actual custody of the goods nevertheless has legal possession of them for the purpose of enabling him to sustain an action in trespass against a third party who unjustifiably seizes the goods without his consent (see, for example, *Wilson v Lombank Ltd* (above)).

A person who lacks both possession and an immediate right of possession cannot sue in trespass. Thus even an owner of goods may be debarred from suing in trespass if he lacks any immediate possessory entitlement to the goods.

Conversion

As with trespass, the mere fact of ownership of goods will not necessarily qualify their owner to sue in conversion. The plaintiff must show either that he had possession of the goods at the material time, or that he had an immediate right of possession *(Marquis of Bute v Barclays Bank* [1955] 1 QB 202).

Possession
The concept of possession is largely self-explanatory. Possession of the goods is the interest most commonly relied upon by finders of lost property, who wish to enforce their right to retain it against some other person who is not the real owner (see, for example, *Parker v British Airways Board* [1982] QB 1004, discussed at 32.14). It should be noted, however, that in cases where the defendant in a wrongful interference action can actually identify a specific third party as having a better right to the goods than the claimant who is relying on his mere possession, that defendant is entitled to have the third party joined as a party to the proceedings (see s8 of the 1977 Act, discussed at 32.9).

The immediate right to possession
Even if he is the owner, a plaintiff whose right to possession of the goods is suspended at the time of the alleged wrong cannot sue in conversion. This has been recognised since *Gordon v Harper* (1796) 7 Term Rep 9, where a landlord of premises was held unable to sue a third party in conversion for the third party's wrongful seizure of the furniture during the lease, because it was the tenant, not the landlord, who was in possession and had the continuing right to possession at the material time: the landlord's right to assume possession was merely deferred or suspended, and thus the tenant was the proper plaintiff in this case.

It does not necessarily follow, however, that a bailor of goods can never sue in conversion. First, the bailment may be 'at will', entitling the bailor to repossess the goods from the bailee whenever he wishes. In such a case, the bailor clearly enjoys an immediate right to possession, and thus has the necessary qualification to sue in conversion (see, for example, *Manders v Williams* (1849) 4 Ex 339). Secondly, a bailee with an initially secure period of possession (such as a hirer for a 12-month term) may break the terms of the bailment in some particularly fundamental manner (called a 'deviation'). By so doing, the bailee will forfeit his continued right of possession of the goods and will cause the bailor's immediate right of possession to revive, thereby entitling the bailor to bring conversion proceedings not only against the bailee himself but against any third party who thereafter converts the goods. Further, the mere fact that the terms of the bailment set out certain specific events upon which the bailor's right of possession is to revive does not mean that that statement of events is necessarily exhaustive: there may still be other, unspecified forms of fundamental breach which can resurrect the bailor's immediate right to possession (*Union Transport Finance* v *British Car Auctions Ltd* [1978] 2 All ER 385).

According to a majority of the Court of Appeal in *International Factors* v *Rodriguez* [1979] 1 QB 351, a plaintiff whose action in conversion is based on a mere immediate right to possession must show that this springs from some *proprietary* right in the goods: a purely *contractual* right of possession would be insufficient. Whereas this was undoubtedly the rule for actions in detinue (*Jarvis* v *Williams* [1955] 1 WLR 71), however, there is some doubt as to whether it is an accurate expression of the law in relation to conversion (cf *Winkworth* v *Christie, Manson & Woods* [1980] Ch 496, 499, per Slade J and the New Zealand case of *Harris* v *Lombard (New Zealand) Ltd* [1974] 2 NZLR 161).

More recently, Lord Brandon has stated that a purely equitable interest in goods would not be sufficient to ground an action in negligence for loss of or damage to those goods (*The Aliakmon* [1986] AC 785, 812). In his Lordship's view, the equitable owner would have to join the legal owner as a party to the action in order to be able to sue. If that is the rule for actions in negligence, it is likely that a similar principle would be held to apply to an action for conversion. This may, in turn, suggest that a purely equitable interest would not qualify as the necessary 'proprietary right' for the purposes of the principle stated in *International Factors Ltd* v *Rodriguez* (above). However, it should be noted that *International Factors Ltd* v *Rodriguez* itself was a case where the plaintiff had an equitable interest grounding an immediate right to possession and there the claim was successful; moreover, the Privy Council appeared willing to countenance an action in conversion in *Maynegrain Pty Ltd* v *Campafina Bank* (above), where the claimant's interest in the relevant goods was solely that of an equitable pledgee. From these decisions it seems relatively clear that, if it *is* necessary for a plaintiff's immediate right of possession to arise from some proprietary right in the goods before he/she can sue in conversion, a purely equitable right would suffice. A statement by Lord Brandon elsewhere in his judgment in *The Aliakmon* (above) appears to support this view and to indicate that when Lord Brandon spoke earlier of the insufficiency of a mere equitable property interest he was assuming a case where the plaintiff had no current possessory right to the goods. Lord Brandon said that:

> 'There may be cases where a person who is the equitable owner of certain goods has also a possessory title to them. In such a case he is entitled, by virtue of his possessory title rather than his equitable ownership, to sue in tort for negligence ...'

32.9 Pleading jus tertii

At common law there were certain situations where a defendant in an action for wrongful interference with goods was precluded by law from asserting that someone other than the plaintiff had a better right to the goods. This meant in turn that the plaintiff was able to recover the full value of the goods – or the full cost of repairing the damage to them – even though he/she was not the owner.

The first such situation arose when a bailor was suing his/her bailee; the original delivery of possession to the bailee was deemed to give rise to an implied undertaking on the bailee's part not to deny the bailor's title. This obligation was sometimes described as an estoppel on the bailee's part, precluding him/her from pleading 'jus tertii' (the right of a third party *Biddle* v *Bond* (1865) 6 B & S 225). It did not apply when the bailee had been authorised by the real owner to defend the action on his behalf or where the real owner had actually demanded the return of the goods; moreover, in difficult cases the bailee could invoke the interpleader process and drop out of the dispute, but only when an actual demand by a third party had been made on him. If the bailor was not in fact the owner and recovered the full value of the goods from the bailee under this principle, he/she held the residue of that value on trust for the true owner after deduction of the value of the bailor's own interest.

The second situation arose when goods were damaged, destroyed or misappropriated, while in the possession of a bailee or other possessor, as a result of the wrongdoing of a third party. The classic case was *The Winkfield* [1902] P 42, where the Postmaster-General of Natal was held entitled to recover the full value of letters and mail packets destroyed through the negligent sinking of one of his vessels, even though he did not own those letters and packets and suffered no financial loss by virtue of their destruction. The view adopted by the Court of Appeal was that, in the absence of the true owners, possession counted as title. Of course, the possessor in a case like *The Winkfield* held the residue of the proceeds on trust for the real owner after deduction of his/her own limited interest.

These common law examples of 'extra-compensatory' damages proved unsatisfactory and s8 of the 1977 Act appears to have been designed to abolish them. Section 8(1) now provides that a defendant in proceedings for wrongful interference *shall*, contrary to the former position, be entitled to show that someone other than the claimant has a better right to the goods than the claimant, and that the old 'jus tertii' rule is therefore abolished. The remainder of s8 is directed towards enabling the defendant in such a case to have the real owner (or other third party enjoying a superior interest in the goods) involved in the proceedings, so that the court can share out all the respective interests in one single piece of litigation. It has recently been held in *De Franco* v *Commissioner of Police of the Metropolis* (1987) The Times 8 May that s8(1) entitles the defendant to have joined in the proceedings a third party who did have an interest in the goods at the time of the wrongful interference with the goods, but has ceased to enjoy any such interest by the time of the litigation.

32.10 Double liability

Section 8 (above) is designed to operate in conjunction with s7 of the 1977 Act. By this, the court is obliged to give such relief as will avoid double liability on the part of the wrongdoer in any proceedings to which two or more claimants are parties (s7(2)). The court will achieve this result by apportioning the overall value of the goods (or the cost of their repair in a case of damage) among the various claimants according to their respective interests. 'Double liability' is defined for this purpose in s7(1). Special provision is needed, however, when only *one* claimant has appeared in the original proceedings. An example would be the case of a defendant who has paid full damages in conversion to the current possessor of the goods, having been unable at the time of those proceedings to identify any third party as being the true proprietor thereof. In certain circumstances, the true owner might subsequently appear and recover a second set of full damages from the defendant, who would then be doubly liable. Sections 7(3) and (4) attempt to deal with such situations. By s7(3), upon satisfaction, in whole or in part, of any claim for an amount exceeding that which would be recoverable if the rule against double liability applied, the claimant is liable to account over to the other person who has a right to claim, to such an extent as will avoid double liability. By s7(4) where, as the result of enforcement of a double liability, any claimant is unjustly enriched to any extent, he shall be liable to reimburse the wrongdoer to that extent. An illustration of the interaction of those provisions is provided by the special statutory example attached to s7(4):

> 'For example, if a converter of goods pays damages first to a finder of the goods, and then to the true owner, the finder is unjustly enriched unless he accounts over to the true owner under subsection (3); and then the true owner is unjustly enriched and becomes liable to reimburse the converter of the goods.'

32.11 Improvement to goods

Although it is now well established that the plaintiff in an action for trespass or conversion can normally recover as damages no more than his actual loss (*Bryanston Leasings Ltd* v *Principality Finance* [1977] RTR 45; *Butler* v *The Egg Board* (1966) 114 CLR 185), in cases of conversion this measure would often be equivalent to the full value of the goods. Assessment of their value could, however, give rise to difficulty if the defendant had expended money in improving the goods before the action for conversion was commenced against him. The difficulty could be avoided if the act of improvement occurred after the defendant had converted the goods because normally the value for the purposes of liability in conversion was the value at the date of conversion. Even when the improvement preceded the conversion, however, the courts began to allow the defendant to deduct from the value of the goods at the date of conversion an allowance to represent the extent to which he had improved them. The classic illustration of this common law development is *Munro* v *Willmott* [1949] 1 KB 295). The plaintiff was given a temporary licence by the defendant to leave her car in his yard. The plaintiff then disappeared and, some years later, the defendant decided that he wished to convert his yard into a garage. Being unable to get in touch with the plaintiff, he decided that the best thing to do was to do the car up and sell it. This is what he did and he spent £85 doing the car up. Before the defendant did the car up it was worth £20, but he sold it for £100. The plaintiff eventually turned up and sued the defendant for conversion of her car. The defendant was held liable. The car was worth £120 at the date of judgment, but Lynskey J only awarded the plaintiff damages of £35, because he granted the defendant an allowance of £85 for the cost of the improvements which he had made to the car (see too *Greenwood* v *Bennett* [1973] QB 195).

An attempt to clarify the common law position has now been made by statute. Unfortunately, the statute is confined to those improvers who have improved the goods 'in the mistaken but honest belief' that the goods belonged to them, which would exclude a defendant in a position like that of the improver in *Munro* v *Willmott*. According to s6(1) of the 1977 Act, if proceedings for wrongful interference are brought against an innocent improver as described above, an allowance shall be made in the resultant award of damages 'for the extent to which, at the time as at which the goods fall to be valued in assessing damages, the value of the goods is attributable to the improvement'. Similar provisions exist to deal with the consequential problems which can arise when a defendant has bought improved goods in good faith from an innocent improver, or as part of a chain of purchasers which includes an innocent improver (ss6(2)–(4)).

Academic opinion is divided as to whether s6 of the 1977 Act abolishes the somewhat wider common law power to award an allowance to an improver, as acknowledged in cases like *Munro* v *Willmott* (above). A recent decision has now indicated that the old common law allowance (which was not limited to 'innocent' improvers) has survived s6 and now co-exists alongside the narrower statutory allowance (*Highland Leasing* v *Paul Field* [1985] CLY 3224).

32.12 Forms of judgment

Section 3(2) of the 1977 Act sets out the various forms of relief which a court may award, in proceedings for wrongful interference with goods, against a person who is in possession or control of those goods. These categories are an order for delivery of the goods and for payment of any consequential damages; or an order for delivery of the goods but giving the defendant the alternative of paying damages by reference to the value of the goods, together, in either alternative, with payment of any consequential damages; or damages.

A court may award damages under the last of these provisions even though the defendant has returned the goods to the plaintiff or disposed of them to a third party at the time of the judgment, so long as the defendant had actually been in possession or control of the goods at the time when the proceedings were commenced *(Hillesden Securities v Ryjack* [1983] 1 WLR 959). Relief can, however, be given only under one of the three foregoing categories of relief. Relief under the first category is at the discretion of the court (s3(3)(b)), whereas it is a matter for the claimant to choose between the second and third categories (s3(3)(b)). Consequential provisions are contained in s3(4) to 3(8) of the 1977 Act, and s4 of the Act makes broadly equivalent provision as to the forms of relief available in interlocutory proceedings for wrongful interference.

32.13 Effect of judgment on title to goods

In any case of wrongful interference in which the damages awarded to the claimant are (or would fall to be) assessed according to the whole of his interest in the goods, once the defendant pays those damages or settles the claim (as defined by s5(2)) the claimant's title to these goods is extinguished (s5(1)). In other words, the payment of damages based on the value of the goods makes the defendant the owner and expunges the claimant's ownership. A relatively unimportant exception to this principle is created by s5(3), while s5(4) extends broadly the same general rule to cases where a claimant accounts over to a third party under s7(3) of the Act (see 32.10). The extinction of the claimant's title on payment of full damages can be displaced by any agreement between the parties, and must take effect subject to any relevant court order (s5(5)).

32.14 Title to lost goods

An owner of goods who loses them remains, of course, their owner and can always (subject to the Limitation Act) recover them from a finder or an occupier on whose land the goods were lost *(Moffatt v Kazana* [1969] 2 WLR 71). In cases where the true owner does not reappear to claim his property, however, the normal principle is that a finder who has reduced the goods into his possession has a right to them against the whole world except the real owner. Thus in *Armory* v *Delamirie* (1721) 1 Stra 505 a chimney sweep's boy who had found a jewel was held entitled to recover it (or damages for its value) from a jeweller to whom he handed it for valuation, and who had refused to return it to him.

This principle is, however, based upon the assumption that the finder has been the first person to reduce the goods into his possession. If that is so, the old rule enunciated in *The Winkfield* (above) – that possession counts as title – operates in his favour, allowing him to defend his possession against any third party interloper. Nor will the interloper be entitled to avail himself/herself of s8 of the

1977 Act (see 32.9) in this situation because we are assuming that the real owner remains unidentified.

In certain cases, however, someone other than the finder will already have obtained an earlier or 'supervening' possession of the goods when the finder assumes control of them. In such a case, it is that other party, and not the finder, who has the right to retain the goods against everyone but the true owner.

There are two main situations in which supervening possession of this type can arise. The first is where an employee finds goods in the course of his employment, that is where his employment is the cause and not merely the occasion of his finding of the goods. In such a case, the finder's possession is deemed to be that of his employer and the finder gets no possessory right to the goods against his employer (see *Parker* v *British Airways Board* (above) per Donaldson MR and cf *Byrne* v *Hoare* [1965] Qd R 135 (FC), where a policeman on point duty who found a gold ingot on land adjoining the road was held entitled to keep it as against his employer authority).

The second situation arises when goods are found upon land which is occupied by someone other than the finder (or, of course, the goods' owner). In certain circumstances, the occupier's occupation of the land or premises will have conferred upon him an earlier possession over lost goods situated thereon than that of the finder who eventually comes on to the land and picks the goods up. Such prior possession can exist even though the occupier was unaware of the presence of the goods on his land. Certainly the occupier will have acquired such earlier possession when the goods are buried on the land, or attached to it in a manner which suggests that he is asserting exclusive control over the place in question (see, for example, *South Staffordshire Water Co* v *Sharman* [1896] 2 QB 44, where workmen who found gold rings as a result of carrying out instructions to clean out a pool on the water company's land were held not entitled to retain the rings as against the water company, their employer). The question is less clear-cut when the goods have been found merely lying on the premises, and the premises are of a kind to which the public are permitted access. In such a case, the occupier does not obtain a superior possessory right by virtue of the fact of his occupation alone unless he has 'manifested an intention to exercise control over the building and the things which may be in or on it' (*Parker* v *British Airways Board* (above) per Donaldson MR). Such an intention may be difficult to establish, as the *Parker* case itself demonstrates. There a traveller who found a gold bracelet on the floor of an executive lounge at Heathrow Airport was held entitled to retain it as against the defendants, who were the occupiers of the lounge. The nature of the premises, the degree of public access and the quality of the control over the area exerted by the occupiers were such that the Court of Appeal felt unable to conclude that the occupiers had asserted any superior possession over the lost article, prior in time to that of the finder himself. In so holding, the court followed the decision in *Bridges* v *Hawkesworth* (1851) 21 LJQB 75 (see also the Canadian case of *Kowal* v *Ellis* (1977) 76 DLR (3d) 546).

Of course, if the owner of the relevant premises has never occupied them personally before the finder discovers lost goods on or in these premises, the landowner cannot be said to have acquired a superior possession of the article (*Hannah* v *Peel* [1945] KB 509). It has also been stated obiter that a finder who was trespassing on the premises at the time of the find does not acquire any enforceable possessory right against the occupier (*Parker* v *British Airways Board* (above)).

33

Malicious Prosecution

33.1 Introduction

33.2 Prosecution

33.3 Prosecution ended in the plaintiff's favour

33.4 Without reasonable and probable cause

33.5 Malice

33.6 Damage

33.1 Introduction

The tort of malicious prosecution is the commonest form of the group of torts concerned with the abuse of legal procedure. It is a tort of considerable antiquity. It dates back to the reign of Edward I. As such, the tort was developed at a time when there was no police force so it was important that the courts did not develop rules of tort law which would have the effect of discouraging people from bringing prosecutions. On the other hand the courts had to try to ensure that people were not unjustly accused of something which they had not done and then left without means of redress. The courts have tended to give greater weight to the first of these policies rather than to the second. The consequence has been that there have been very few successful actions brought in respect of alleged malicious prosecutions. Winfield and Jolowicz (*Winfield and Jolowicz on Tort* (13th ed) pp543–4) question whether this restrictive approach is still justified today. They point out that prosecutions are brought today by the police and so there is little likelihood of the police being put in fear of bringing such prosecutions by civil actions for alleged malicious prosecutions.

It should be noted that there is a strong connection between this tort and the tort of false imprisonment (on which see 24.4). Where X arrests Y on a false accusation X may be liable for the tort of false imprisonment, but when Y is taken into police custody X ceases to be liable for the tort of false imprisonment. However he may be liable for the tort of malicious prosecution.

There are a number of elements to the tort of malicious prosecution and we shall now give consideration to these separate elements.

417

33.2 Prosecution

The plaintiff must show that he was prosecuted by the defendant. It is not necessary that the defendant conduct the prosecution in person, although it must be shown that the defendant took some steps to initiate the prosecution. A person who simply gives false information to the police, which persuades the police to bring a prosecution, does not commit the tort of malicious prosecution because he does not take the decision to prosecute (*Browne* v *Stradling* (1836) 5 LJPC 295) even where the informant knows that the plaintiff has not committed the offence: *Martin* v *Watson* [1994] 2 WLR 500.

Similarly an expert who prepares a report for the police, on the basis of which the police decide to prosecute, does not commit the tort (see *Evans* v *London Hospital Medical College* [1981] 1 WLR 184). On the other hand, if the defendant actually signs the charge sheet and states that he is prepared to give evidence, that has been held to be sufficient to constitute the initiation of a prosecution (*Malz* v *Rosen* [1966] 1 WLR 1008). The courts draw a distinction between the giving of information and the making of a charge. Where the defendant gives false information at a prosecution brought by another person, the defendant has not brought the prosecution so he has not committed the tort of malicious prosecution.

33.3 Prosecution ended in the plaintiff's favour

It is essential that the plaintiff show that the prosecution brought against him by the defendant was unsuccessful. The courts do not permit this tort to be used as a means of retrying the criminal action. Even if the conviction is obtained by fraud and there is no appeal against that conviction the plaintiff cannot bring an action for malicious prosecution (*Basebe* v *Matthews* (1867) LR 2 CP 684). The reason for this is that the courts are afraid that the plaintiff will use the civil action to retry the criminal action on the merits. In *Reynolds* v *Kennedy* (1784) 1 Wils 232 it was held that the plaintiff was not entitled to bring an action for malicious prosecution where he was convicted but the conviction was reversed on appeal. However, it is unlikely that this case would be followed today.

The plaintiff need not show that he was acquitted; all that need be shown is that the prosecution was not successful. This can be done by showing that the prosecution was discontinued with the leave of the court (*Watkins* v *Lee* (1830) 5 M & W 270), that the prosecution was non-suited (*Goddard* v *Smith* (1704) 1 Salk 21) or that the indictment was quashed because of a defect (*Jones* v *Gwyn* (1712) 10 Mod 148). It is unclear what is the effect of a nolle prosequi (which is the staying by the Attorney-General of proceedings on an indictment). In *Goddard* v *Smith* (above) it was held that the plaintiff could not bring such an action after a nolle prosequi, but it is unclear whether that decision will be followed today.

33.4 Without reasonable and probable cause

The plaintiff must show that the defendant had no reasonable and probable cause for bringing the prosecution. This is difficult for the plaintiff to do because the burden of proof is on him and he is required to prove a negative. There is no distinction between what is reasonable and what is probable (*Herniman* v *Smith* [1938] AC 305). In *Glinski* v *McIver* [1962] AC 726 Lord Devlin stated that it need not be shown that the defendant thought that it was probable that the plaintiff would be convicted; instead it must be shown that the defendant did not have reasonable grounds for thinking that there was a case to be tried.

The requirement that there was no reasonable and probable cause for the prosecution involves the consideration of two distinct questions. The first is: did the defendant actually believe that there was a case for the initiation of a prosecution? This is a subjective test and is a question to be answered by the jury on the basis of the facts known to the defendant at the time which he initiated the prosecution. The burden of proving lack of honest belief is on the plaintiff. The second question is: did the defendant reasonably believe that there were grounds for a prosecution? This time the test is an objective one and it is a question to be answered by the judge. Where the defendant has received legal advice as to whether or not to prosecute and has acted on that advice it will be very difficult for the plaintiff to show that the defendant did not have reasonable and probable cause (see *Abbott* v *Refuge Assurance Co Ltd* [1962] 1 QB 432).

33.5 Malice

The plaintiff must prove that the defendant brought the unsuccessful prosecution maliciously. This is a question of fact for the jury to decide and it is for the plaintiff to show that the defendant was motivated by malice. In *Glinski* v *McIver* (above) Lord Devlin said that malice 'covers not only spite and ill-will but also any motive other than a desire to bring a criminal to justice'. The fact that the defendant had no honest belief in the guilt of the plaintiff is evidence, but not conclusive evidence, that the defendant was actuated by malice. The issue of malice must be kept separate from the issue whether the defendant had reasonable and probable cause. The defendant may be motivated by malice yet have reasonable and probable cause.

33.6 Damage

The plaintiff must show that he has suffered damage as the result of the malicious prosecution brought by the defendant. In *Savile* v *Roberts* (1698) 1 Ld Raym 374 Holt CJ identified the following three types of damage which are recoverable under this tort.

Damage to reputation

Here the plaintiff must prove that the defendant's accusation was defamatory of him. Where the accusation is not defamatory, such as where the plaintiff was falsely accused of pulling the communication cord on a train (*Berry* v *British Transport Commission* [1961] 1 QB 149), the plaintiff cannot recover damages for malicious prosecution.

Damage in respect of the personal security of the plaintiff

Such damage could consist of, for example, detention of the plaintiff.

Pecuniary loss

Such loss could consist of pecuniary loss such as the cost of defending the prosecution (*Berry* v *British Transport Commission* (above)).

Finally, it should be noted that where a plaintiff in a case of malicious prosecution seeks exemplary damages the jury is entitled to take into account the conduct of the plaintiff, so that, where the plaintiff has provoked the defendant or otherwise acted in a manner which is not acceptable, that conduct can be taken into account in the assessment of damages (*Bishop* v *Commissioner of Police of the Metropolis* (1989) The Times 30 November).

Index

Act of State, *14*
Animals, *276*
    common law liability, *276–277*
    dangerous, *277–279*
    defences, *281–282*
    non-dangerous, *279–281*
    protection of livestock against dogs, *284*
    straying livestock, *282–284*
    straying on to highway, *284*
Assault, *317–318*

Barristers, duty of care, *105–109*
Battery, *311–317*
    contact with plaintiff, *314–315*
    defences, *315–317*
    direct act, *312*
    hostility, *314*
    intentional act, *312–314*
Breach of duty, *117–132*
    children, *125*
    common practice, *123–125*
    emergencies, *126*
    foreseeability, *120*
    magnitude of risk, *120–122*
    practicality of precautions, *122–123*
    professionals, *127–129*
    proof of, *129–130*
    reasonable man, *118–120*
    res ipsa loquitur, *130–132*
    sport, *125–126*
    utility of defendant's activity, *122*
Breach of statutory duty, *179–186*
    ambit of statute, *185–186*
    conferring action in tort, whether, *180–181*

Breach of statutory duty (*contd.*)
    defences, *186*
    public right, *184–185*
    remedy provided in Act, *181–183*
    special damage, *184–185*
    statutes for benefit of class, *183–184*

Causation, negligence. *See* Negligence
Chattels, torts to, *402–416*
    common law ingredients, *403*
    double liability, *412*
    effect of judgment on title to goods, *414*
    forms of judgment, *413–414*
    improvement to goods, *412–413*
    pleading jus tertii, *411*
    redistribution of tort liability by statute, *407–408*
    title to lost goods, *414–416*
    title to sue, *408–410*
        conversion, *409*
        trespass, *408–409*
Children, contributory negligence, *163–165*
Conspiracy, *354–357*
    to injure by lawful means, *356–357*
    unlawful means, *355–356*
Contract, tort, and, *8–9*
Contributory negligence, *159–169*
    Act of 1945, *161–162*
    apportionment, *168–169*
    causation, *167–168*
    children, *163–165*
    common law, *159–161*

Contributory negligence (*contd.*)
    emergencies,   *166*
    fault,   *162–163*
    rescuers,   *166*
    standard of care,   *163*
    workmen,   *165–166*
Conversion,   *404–406, 409–410*
Corporations,   *11–12*
Crime, tort, and,   *8*
Crown,   *11*

Damage, remoteness. *See* Remoteness
    of damage
Damages,   *371–394*
    aggravated,   *372–374*
    commitment to protection of
        reliance interest,   *393–394*
    contemptuous,   *371–372*
    damage to property,   *393*
    death,   *390–393*
    deductions,   *383–386*
    exemplary,   *372–374*
    expectation interest,   *394*
    general,   *372*
    injury,   *389*
    interest,   *389–390*
    loss of amenity,   *388*
    loss of earning capacity,   *381*
    loss of earnings,   *375–379*
    loss of expectation of life,   *389*
    loss of housekeeping capacity,
        381–382
    loss of pension rights,   *381*
    lost years,   *380*
    medical expenses,   *382–383*
    nominal,   *371–372*
    non-pecuniary loss,   *387*
    pain and suffering,   *387–388*
    pecuniary loss,   *375, 386–387*
    private nuisance, and,   *252–254*
    protection of reliance interest,   *375*
    special,   *372*
    types,   *371–374*

Death,   *390–393*
Deceit,   *334–340*
    damage to plaintiff,   *340*
    false representation,   *334–335*
    false statement of fact,   *334–337*
    intention that statement be acted
        upon,   *338–339*
    knowledge of falsity of statement,
        337–338
    plaintiff must act on statement,
        339–340
    representation of existing fact,
        336–337
Defamation,   *285–310. See also*
    Libel; Slander
    absolute privilege,   *298–300*
    amends,   *306*
    apology,   *306*
    consent,   *296*
    damages,   *306–307*
    defences,   *296*
    fair comment,   *303–306*
        absence of malice,   *306*
        fairness,   *305*
        public interest,   *303*
        statement of opinion,
            303–305
    judicial proceedings,   *299*
    justification,   *296–298*
    official communications,   *299–300*
    publication,   *294–296*
    qualified privilege,   *300–302*
        common interest,   *302*
        privileged reports,   *300–301*
        statements made in furtherance
            of duty,   *302*
    reference,   *292–294*
    remedies,   *306–308*
    statements in Parliament,   *298*
    truth,   *296–298*
    what is defamatory,   *289–292*
    who may be defamed,   *289*
Defective product, economic loss,
    84–89

Detinue, *406*

Dogs. *See* Animals

Duty of care, *43 et seq.*
alternative remedy, availability of, *61–63*
barristers, *105–109*
breach. *See* Breach of duty
character of plaintiff, *103–105*
development of general principle, *46–47*
economic loss. *See* Economic loss
emergence of general principle, *44–46*
established principles of common law or equity, and, *63–64*
factors inhibiting imposition of, *54*
general principle or reasoning by analogy, whether, *49–50*
incremental approach, *50–53*
insurance
availability, *66–67*
cost, *66–67*
judges, *105–109*
legal representatives, *105–109*
misfeasance, *54–60*
negligence in exercise of statutory power, *112–116*
nervous shock, *94–102*
none recognised before, *64–66*
non-feasance, *54–60*
Parliament, and, *60–61*
police, *109–112*
protected interests, and, *69–102*
'protected parties', and, *103–116*
psychiatric injury, *94–102*
resiling from general principle, *47–49*
solicitors, *105–109*

Economic duress, *364–365*

Economic loss
consequential, *75*

Economic loss *(contd.)*
defective product, *84–89*
Hedley Byrne re-examined, *89–90*
meaning, *70–72*
Ministry of Housing and Local Government v *Sharp*, *93*
Morrison Steamship Co Ltd v *Greystoke Castle (Cargo Owners)*, *93–94*
negligent misstatement, *75–83*
problem, *72–74*
Ross v *Caunters*, *91–93*

Economic torts, *350–369*
ground rules, *351–353*
statutory immunities, *367–368*

Employers' liability, *187–195*
competent staff, *189*
defences, *194–195*
economic welfare of employees, *194*
proper plant and equipment, *189–190*
safe place of work, *191*
safe system of work, *191–194*

False imprisonment, *318–322*

Fatal Accidents Act, *390–393*

Fire, *272–275*
common law defences, *273–274*
common law liability, *272–273*
Fires Prevention (Metropolis) Act 1774, *274–275*
railway statutes, *275*

Foreseeability, breach of duty, and, *120*

Illegality, *398–399*

Immunity, *14–15*
judicial, *14*
statutory. *See* Statutory immunities
statutory authority, *14*
trade unions, *15*

Independent contractors,   *39 – 42*
    exceptions to general rule,   *40 – 42*
Inducing breach of contract,
        357 – 362
    breach,   *359 – 362*
    damage,   *362*
    forms of tort,   *357 – 359*
    intention,   *359*
    justification,   *362*
    knowledge,   *359*
Injunctions,   *394 – 396*
    damages in lieu of,   *396*
    interlocutory,   *396*
    mandatory,   *395*
    private nuisance, and,   *249 – 252*
    prohibitory,   *395*
    quia timet,   *395 – 396*
Insanity,   *13*
Interference with trade by unlawful
        means,   *365 – 367*
Intimidation,   *362 – 364*
    damage,   *364*
    justification,   *364*
    submission to threat,   *363*
    threat,   *363*
    unlawful act or means,   *363*

Joint and several tortfeasors,   *16 – 21*
    contribution,   *18 – 21*
        apportionment,   *20 – 21*
        entitlement,   *18 – 20*
    independent liability,   *16*
    joint liability,   *17 – 18*
    several liability,   *17*

Libel. *See also* Defamation
    slander distinguished,   *286 – 289*
Limitation,   *400 – 401*

Malicious falsehood,   *341 – 344*
    damage,   *344*
    falsehood,   *342 – 343*
    malice,   *343 – 344*

Malicious prosecution,   *417 – 420*
    damage,   *419 – 420*
        personal security of plaintiff,
            420
        reputation, to,   *420*
    malice,   *419*
    pecuniary loss,   *420*
    prosecution,   *418*
        ended in plaintiff's favour,
            418
    without reasonable and probable
        cause,   *419*
Minors,   *13*
Mistake,   *397*

Necessity,   *399 – 400*
Negligence
    breach of duty. *See* Breach of duty
    causation,   *133 – 142*
        but for test,   *133 – 134*
        multiple causes,   *135 – 136*
        omissions,   *135*
        pre-existing condition,
            134 – 135
        proof of,   *136 – 140*
        successive causes,   *140 – 142*
    contributory. *See* Contributory
        negligence
    duty of care. *See* Duty of care
    remoteness of damage. *See*
        Remoteness of damage
Negligent misstatement, economic loss,
        75 – 83
Nervous shock, duty of care, and,
        94 – 102
Novus actus interveniens,   *153 – 158*
    intervening act of nature,
        154 – 155
    intervening act of plaintiff,
        153 – 154
    intervening act of third party,
        155 – 158
Nuisance, private. *See* Private nuisance

Nuisance, public. *See* Public nuisance

Occupiers' liability, *205–231*
 builders, *229–231*
 business, meaning, *226*
 children, *215*
 common calling, *216*
 common duty of care, *213–214*
 contractors, *220*
 contributory negligence, *219–220*
 damage to property, *221*
 exclusion of occupier's duty,
  225–227
 independent contractors, *217–219*
 independent contractors who are
  not occupiers, *227*
 lessors, *227–229*
 occupier, *207–209*
 premises, *213*
 scope of 1957 Act, *206–207*
 trespassers, *221–225*
  knowledge, *222*
 vendors, *227–229*
 visitors, *209–212*
  express permission, *209*
  implied permission, *209–210*
  lawful authority, *211*
  limitations on permission,
   211–212
  multiple occupiers, *212*
  rights of way, *210–211*
 volenti, *219*
 warning of danger, *216–217*

Parliament
 duty of care, and, *60–61*
Parties to action in tort, *10–15*
 immunity, *14–15*. *See also*
  Immunity
 liability, *11–13*
Partnership, vicarious liability, and,
 37

Passing off, *345–349*
 made by trader in course of trade,
  349
 methods, *346–349*
 remedies, *349*
Police, duty of care, *109–112*
Private nuisance, *232–254*
 abatement, *252*
 abnormal sensitivity, *237*
 character of neighbourhood,
  237–238
 coming to, *248*
 conduct amounting to, *235–236*
 damages, *252–254*
 defences, *246–249*
 duration, *236–237*
 fault, *239–240*
 future of action, *254*
 injunctions, *249–252*
 interests protected, *233–235*
 malice, *238–239*
 many people, due to, *249*
 prescription, *246*
 remedies, *249–254*
 statutory authority, *246–247*
 types of harm, *245–246*
  acts interfering with neighbour's
   enjoyment of property,
   245–246
  physical damage to plaintiff's
   land, *245*
 usefulness, *249*
 utility of defendant's conduct,
  238
 who can be sued, *240–245*
  creator of nuisance, *240*
  landlords, *244–245*
  occupier of land, *241–244*
Product liability, *196–204*
 Consumer Protection Act 1987,
  200–204
  defences, *202*
  'product', *201*

Product liability (*contd.*)
    defects in common law,   *199–200*
    historical development,   *196–199*
    'products',   *197*
Psychiatric injury, duty of care, and,
    94–102
Public nuisance,   *255–260*
    elements,   *256–257*
    highway, and,   *258–260*
        condition of,   *260*
        dangers close to,   *259–260*
        dangers on,   *259*
        obstruction,   *258–259*

Reasonable man, breach of duty,
    118–120
Remedies,   *370–396*
Remoteness of damage,   *143–158*
    cases where reasonable foresight test
        does not apply,   *153*
    damage to person,   *146–149*
    damage to property,   *150–152*
    directness test,   *144–145*
    foreseeability,   *145–146*
    intervening acts. *See* Novus actus
        interveniens
    Polemis and *Wagon Mound*
        contrasted,   *152–153*
    Re Polemis,   *144–145*
    Wagon Mound,   *145–146*
Res ipsa loquitur,   *130–132*
Reversionary action,   *406–407*
Rylands v *Fletcher*, rule in,   *261–271*
    accumulation,   *263*
    Act of God,   *269–270*
    common benefit,   *270*
    consent of plaintiff,   *270*
    dangerous things,   *265*
    default of plaintiff,   *270*
    defences,   *269–271*
    escape,   *265–266*
    foreseeability of damage,   *267*
    his own purposes,   *266–267*

Rylands v *Fletcher*, rule in (*contd.*)
    independent act of third party,
        270–271
    non-natural user,   *263–265*
    occupation,   *266*
    protected interests,   *267–269*
        economic loss,   *269*
        owner of land suffering property
            damage on land,   *267*
        owner of land suffers property
            damage but at time of damage
            property not on land,   *268*
        personal injury suffered by
            owner of land,   *268*
        personal injury suffered by
            persons who are not owners,
            268–269
    rule,   *262–263*
    statutory authority,   *271*

Self-help,   *396*
Slander
    imputation of crime,   *288*
    imputation of disease,   *288*
    imputation of unchastity in women,
        288
    imputation of unfitness to trade or
        calling,   *288*
    libel distinguished,   *286–289*
Solicitors, duty of care,   *105–109*
Statutory immunities,   *367–368*
Statutory power, negligence in exercise
    of,   *112–116*

Tort
    contract, and,   *8–9*
    crime, and,   *8*
    current difficulties,   *1–6*
    interests protected,   *6–7*
Trade unions,   *13*
    immunity,   *15*
Trespass to goods,   *403–404*
Trespass to land,   *324–333*
    ab initio,   *328–329*

Trespass to land *(contd.)*
    airspace, to, *327–328*
    damages, *331*
    defences, *329–331*
    distress damage feasant, *333*
    ejection, *332*
    highway, on, *326*
    injunction, *331–332*
    lawful authority, *330*
    licence, *330*
    mesne profits, *332*
    nature of interference, *329*
    necessity, *331*
    possession, *324–325*
        interference with, *325–326*
    re-entry, *332*
    remedies, *331–333*
    subsoil, to, *327*
Trespass to the person, *311–323*
    overlap with criminal law, *322–323*

Unincorporated associations, *12*

Vicarious liability, *22–38*
    assault, *35*
    careless acts, *29*

Vicarious liability, *(contd.)*
    course of employment, *28*
    employee must commit tort, *28*
    express prohibition, *29–32*
    fraud, *36*
    'frolics and detours', *32–34*
    intentional wrongful acts, *34–35*
    master's indemnity, *36–37*
    negligent acts, *29*
    partnership, *37*
    principal and agent, *37*
    rationale, *23–24*
    theft, *35*
    who is employee, *24–28*
Volenti non fit injuria, *170–178*
    agreement, *173–176*
    exclusion clauses, and, *177–178*
    intentional infliction of harm, *171*
    knowledge, *177*
    negligent infliction of harm, *171*
    standard of care, and, *178*
    voluntariness, *171–173*

Wilkinson v *Downton*, rule in, *322*
Wrongful interference with goods, *407–408*